THE JUDAEAN SCROLLS

THE
JUDAEAN SCROLLS

THE PROBLEM AND A SOLUTION

G. R. DRIVER

Honorary Fellow of Magdalen College,
University of Oxford

SCHOCKEN BOOKS—NEW YORK

Published in U.S.A. by
Schocken Books Inc.
67 Park Avenue
New York, NY 10016

CONTENTS

PREFACE

The discovery of the Scrolls was announced in 1947, and they were soon assigned to widely varying dates ranging from the Exile to the Crusades.

In 1950 I expressed distrust of any pre-Christian date, although I went too far in suggesting one long after A.D. 200; but enough was not yet known to control speculation, and trial and error is an inevitable part of research. In 1951, however, Mr. H. E. Del Medico and (apparently independently but simultaneously) Dr. G. Vermès identified the principal scene to which the *Commentary on Habakkuk* referred with an episode known to have occurred in A.D. 66; and in 1953 I showed that the same document alluded to an event which took place in A.D. 70. Both suggestions, if they could be proved correct, would have been fatal to the prevailing opinion that the Scrolls belonged to the 2nd or 1st century B.C.; they were, therefore, dismissed without discussion as untenable or totally disregarded by almost all writers on the subject.

I had at the time overlooked the suggestion of Mr. Del Medico and Dr. Vermès and therefore did not see that mine was complementary to theirs and that, taken together, they might provide the much desired solution to the problem of the Scrolls. When therefore early in 1957 my colleague Dr. C. Roth, who knew my views, drew my attention to the same solution, I saw at once that a fresh investigation would be required, and I invited him to join me in carrying it out; our plan was that he should examine the problem from the historical point of view, while I would try to prove the solution which we were putting forward. Accordingly the original draft of the present work was written; and it was actually in proof when Dr. Roth, unwilling to await the completion of my part of the work (for many other commitments made me a slow partner and seemed likely unduly to delay publication), had a Hebrew translation of his part of the work published in Israel. Meanwhile, I had received an invitation to deliver the Cadbury Lectures at the University of Birmingham on the same subject, and I gladly availed myself of the chance to go over the whole problem again and to enlarge an essay devoted merely to the proof of the solution to a complete study of the whole problem. This, the last draft, is an expanded form of these lectures.

I owe and am here glad to express my gratitude to all who have in various ways advanced the study of the Scrolls and from whom I have drawn much, as the citations in the notes will show, to those who have offered suggestions for the solution of individual problems in them or have supplied references to the relevant literature and to those who have helped me in other ways; for if the ancient Rabbis said

אי זה הוא חכם הלומד מכל אדם

they said also

הלומד מחבירו...אפילו אות אחת צריך לנהג בו כבוד

(*Sayings of the Fathers* iv 1, vi 3). Chief amongst these are Dr. E. Bammel, Dr. M. Gertner, the Rev. Dr. J. N. D. Kelly, Dr. O. H. M. Lehmann, Mr. D. Patterson, Dr. C. Rabin, Mr. C. E. Stevens, Dr. J. L. Teicher, Dr. E. Wiesenberg, and especially the Rev. R. de Vaux (for permission to reproduce the plans, somewhat modified and reduced in scale, of the ruins at Qumrân and 'Ain Fäšḥah) and Prof. Y. Yadin (for allowing the use of two plans, here slightly modified, of the battle-formations described in one of the Scrolls). I also owe much to my former colleague Dr. C. Roth, whose discussions on the Scrolls inspired the original work, as also to the Rev. Prof. G. Lampe and the Cadbury Trustees, who not only gave me the opportunity of examining the whole problem anew and working out the solution here presented in all its details but also provided a platform from which I might publicly try it out.

Lastly, I am especially grateful to the University Grants Committee for a considerable subvention towards the cost of a necessarily expensive publication and to the Publishers for their extraordinary courtesy and generosity in publishing a work whose production was beset by unusual difficulties, and which without their understanding and patience might well have been stillborn.

G. R. Driver.

Oriental Institute,
University of Oxford.
December 8th, 1960
and
April 1st, 1965.

THE DEAD SEA AND ADJACENT AREA

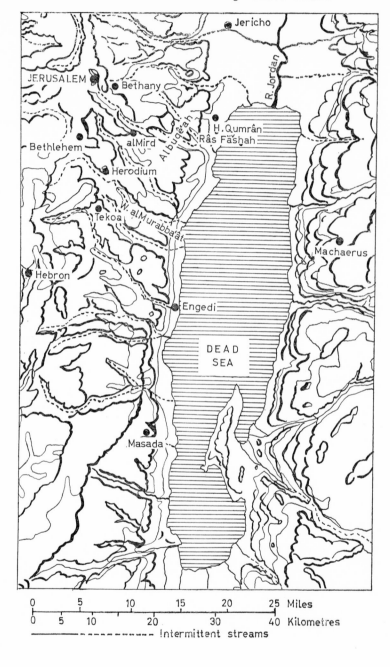

Jericho

JERUSALEM
Bethany
R. Jordan

Bethlehem
alMird
Albuqeah
H. Qumrân
Râs Fâshah

Herodium

Tekoa
W. alMurabba'ât

Machaerus

Hebron

Engedi

DEAD
SEA

Masada

| 0 | 5 | 10 | 15 | 20 | 25 | Miles |
| 0 | 5 | 10 | 20 | 30 | 40 | Kilometres |

———— – – – – – – – – – Intermittent streams

PROLOGUE

The Scrolls found in the caves round Qumrân, which lies on a spur at the north-western end of the Dead Sea, are one of the outstanding archaeological discoveries of the present century. They have posed and still pose many problems, of which the most important is their exact place in history; until this is firmly and accurately determined, they cannot be properly used for historical purposes. They can be assigned without much risk of straying far from the truth to a date between approximately 200 B.C. and A.D. 135, but these margins are far too wide; and the exact dates of the individual documents are equally difficult to determine. The reason is obvious: during all this period literature with political aims was necessarily highly allusive, since clear references to persons or events might be fraught with grave risks to the writer or to the persons named. Whenever the Scrolls may be dated within this period by the identification of persons or events, however, they will yield welcome information about a period of Jewish history for which hardly any documents in the Hebrew language are preserved. Other apocalyptic and apocryphal literature, which has survived only in translation, has little value for historical purposes; and the authors of *I* and *II Maccabees* and the Jewish historian Josephus (whose bias is unfortunately not always above suspicion but can generally be discounted without much difficulty) alone provide a wealth of information in the Greek language, which can be supplemented here and there from the writings of Greek and Latin authors. The lack of information from Hebrew sources is particularly regrettable; for the period, and especially the 1st century A.D., is one of the most momentous in human history.

The importance of the Scrolls, on which the articles, pamphlets and books published since their discovery already are several thousand in number, is very considerable not only for the history of the Second Commonwealth or Temple (to which the majority of those who have worked on them now assign them) but also for the origins of Christianity.

Many, therefore, journalists and scholars alike, conveniently assuming but neglecting to prove a pre-Christian date for the Scrolls, have used them to disprove the originality of Christian doctrine. For

I

example, a Jewish journalist who learned Hebrew 'rather late in life' easily discovered that *les chrétiens sont dérangés, les juifs sont dérangés; moi, je ne suis pas dérangé* and roundly announced that 'the theological structure of the Sect [*sc.* of the Covenanters of Qumrân] was taken apart and the stones re-used by early Christian thinkers to build a new and different house' and that Christianity contributed nothing that was new beyond its peculiar Christology; another asked whether 'the placing him and visualizing him [*sc.* Jesus Christ] in a definite historical setting [will] inevitably have the effect of weakening the claims of divinity that have been made for him by the Church'; and yet another finds that 'the Christian church in its organization, its sacraments, its teaching and its literature, is related [to]—and in its early stages may have been identical with . . . the New Covenanters who were known as Essenes' and 'does not hide for a moment his own wish that the liberal view might be restored', apparently holding everything else lost with the publication of the Scrolls. So, too, a French professor, speaking of the Rightful Teacher, announced that *sans doute était-il un être divin, qui s'incarna pour vivre et mourir comme un homme*; and a French journalist inferred therefore that *désormais, grâce à la trouvaille d'un berger . . . nous savons que le Messie de Galilée n'a rien apporté, absolument rien, qui ne fût depuis longtemps familier aux croyants de la Nouvelle Alliance. Le premier Christ, celui qui périt sous Aristobule II, le second Christ n'a fait que le copier* and again *ce fou* [namely, *le second Christ*], *cet amant de Dieu, eut la sagesse de copier les idées, les valeurs morales, la théologie, la discipline de son prédécesseur, le premier Christ de notre histoire.* Lastly, an English lecturer proclaimed that 'the Scrolls have proved that Christ was not divine'—to the satisfaction of some American schoolboys!

In these attempts to use the Scrolls to throw doubt or discredit on the originality of Christianity, one party finds the doctrines of the Covenanters in the New Testament, the other those of the New Testament in the Scrolls; and so, all unwitting, they contradict one another! The Scrolls, however, contain no reference or allusion to any Christian doctrine except such as can be traced to the Old Testament or can be found in Jewish thought between it and the New Testament, and no hint that the Rightful Teacher may have been regarded as in any sense divine.

All the writers who use the Scrolls for this purpose suffer also from a strange delusion, which colours and vitiates their arguments: it is that agnosticism *per se* confers a lack of bias, an absolute impartiality unattainable by other men, and that 'only an independent scholar, not committed to any religion' can be trusted to give an unbiased and independent opinion where questions of religion are involved. Accordingly, the opinions of all Jewish and Christian students of the Scrolls, however great their knowledge of the Hebrew language and literature

may be, can be dismissed out of hand as resting on religious prejudice, while simultaneously and inconsistently all professional students of the New Testament can be charged with deliberately shirking the study of the Scrolls 'as a menace to a variety of rooted assumptions, from matters of tradition and dogma, to hypotheses that are exploits of scholarship'. Those who hold such views are apparently unaware that unbelief is as much a *praejudicium* as belief, that suspended judgement may be due to nothing else than sloth, and that the *tabula rasa* of a mind which they admire as a guarantee of disinterested scholarship can hardly exist in a normal man, if only because 'he that is not for me is against me'!

Not a few of the works in this class have been premature, hurriedly rushed through the press before the publication of all the relevant texts and without allowing time for any adequate study of the external evidence, both Greek and Jewish; they have been written to prove a point, not to discover and establish the truth. They have brought quick but short-lived reputations to their authors and may now be left to sink into oblivion.

The arguments to establish the pre-Christian date of the Scrolls are fundamentally unsound. Apparently such a date was originally determined after a cursory examination of a photograph of the scroll of *Isaiah A*; the sole reasons were palaeographical, and these cannot stand alone. Indeed, the palaeographical argument in this case is very nearly an *argumentum in circulo*, so little is known of the development of the Hebrew script during the Second Commonwealth; and this argument in the case of a copy of a Biblical text cannot be reinforced by any internal evidence. The date of *Isaiah A*, then, is but a 'conjecture' (as it must be and must remain in default of proof). This 'conjecture', however useful as an 'hypothesis', unfortunately soon became a 'fact' in subsequent discussions and was then invoked as 'evidence' providing a 'proof' of the early date of the other Scrolls. Their contents were then read into the 2nd or 1st century B.C. and regarded as confirming some such date, although the variety of theories should have given warning that something was amiss; for half a dozen identifications of the principal persons and of the scene in which they appeared were proposed in these two centuries. Even so, only some of the characters were identified and those which could not be identified were quietly left out of the picture, a tacit confession of failure.

The method, necessary before the publication of all the Scrolls but now unfortunately still often adopted, has been to isolate one Scroll, then to isolate one episode described in it and then to isolate one person or thing in the scene and identify him or it; the person usually selected has been the Wicked Priest for the obvious reason that wicked priests abound within the permissible period, while the Rightful

Teacher (the most important character in the Scrolls) is either identified with some secondary personage of no importance or left unidentified. Thus, while every writer had his favourite candidate for the Wicked Priest, only some tried to find a suitable person to sustain the part of the Rightful Teacher; and, while everyone proposed a different person for the 'house of Absalom', no one put the 'house of Judah' in the picture. The secondary characters, the 'Young Lion of Wrath' and the 'Man of Falsehood', were almost totally disregarded. A partial solution of a problem, however, is no solution; and multiple solutions, such as the alternative identifications of the 'Kittians' and the 'Wicked Priest', only emphasize the hopelessness of the attempt to find the key to the Scrolls in the 2nd or 1st century B.C. Further, such identifications as have been made in these times can be maintained only by completely overlooking the circumstances in which the characters described in the Scrolls played their parts: for example, the cryptic allusions in the *Thanksgiving Hymns* throw out hints reflecting the background of the period in which they were composed, and the military details so carefully described in the *War of the Sons of Light with the Sons of Darkness* yield positive evidence which cannot be tacitly left out of account.

If the outrage described in the *Commentary on Habakkuk* is considered alone without regard to the occasion and if the evidence of the other Scrolls is entirely disregarded, all means of controlling speculation are gone, and one solution of the problem is as good as another; and thus taken *in vacuo* Alexander VI and Savonarola are nearly as likely to be respectively the Wicked Priest and the Rightful Teacher as any other persons who have been cast for these parts! Any solution of the problem of the Scrolls which rests on a mere selection of the evidence is unsound in method and may be discarded out of hand; that alone can be considered which is based on all the evidence afforded by every one of the Scrolls and by contemporary historical sources.

The variety of solutions put forward suggests that many rest on mere conjecture and dispense with evidence and proof; it shows up not merely the lack of scientific method but also the grave lack of logical cogency exhibited in many of the works which have appeared on the Scrolls. The most frequently used argument is the *argumentum e silentio*, which only too easily passes into the *argumentum per fictionem*, whereby the most surprising results are achieved, including a resurrection otherwise unmentioned in extant records! The history of events which happened nearly 2,000 years ago must necessarily be imperfect and full of gaps, and the historian may legitimately fill these by imaginative reconstruction; but the conjectures put forward to fill in the picture must not themselves be used to prove other conjectures. Some of the fallacies, too, are so obvious and glaring that they can easily be subsumed under logical categories and named; and in several cases

the proof of a solution is unwittingly but fortunately accompanied by its own disproof!

Another common fallacy is to suppose that a word otherwise attested only in a work of such and such a date or a coin dated in such and such a year proves the book or the place, as the case may be, where they are found to be of the same date. Allowance however must be made for accidents of transmission, that a word may have a long history behind it before its first appearance in literature or a coin may have been long in or even out of circulation before being dropped where it has chanced to be found.

One of the worst fallacies committed in the study of the Scrolls has been the attempt to fix their date by the test of radio-activity. This requires the combustion of a considerable quantity of matter in an absolutely pure state; and a test requiring the destruction of any such portion of the Scrolls cannot be applied to them. It has therefore been applied not to them but to the linen in which they are said to have been found. This cannot in the circumstances be chemically pure, and the test as applied to it gives only a remotely approximate date for the pulling of the flax of which the linen is made; and this date has no compelling connection with the date of the Scrolls.

An argument to be valid must be logically sound. Illogical arguments are permissible only when unravelling illogical conclusions. For example, if a Rabbi can believe that a verse of Scripture may have seventy 'faces' i.e. shades of meaning, an interpreter of the Scrolls must be prepared to apply similar methods, though reversed, to recover their often cryptic meaning.[1] Or, if ancient Jewish writers support their arguments by figures based on incorrect chronology, what they mean can be discovered only by using the same incorrect chronology; if a modern corrected chronology is used, the conclusions drawn from it will be wrong. Or again, arguments based on the initial letters of a word or on the numerical value of the letters of the alphabet are logically valueless; but the same principles must be used to unravel what information the ancient writer is trying thereby to convey.

Finally, too many loose and inexact references to literary sources are rife in studies of the Scrolls. For instance, the apocalyptic war of the Covenanters is called a 'time of affliction' or 'trouble', and this expression has been seized as proof that this war must have been the Revolt of A.D. 66–73 because the same expression is so applied in Rabbinic literature; but extensive research has failed to find the usage there, and the only revolt outside the Bible[2] to which it is applied is that of the Jews against the British Mandate in A.D. 1937–9! All quotations ought to be accompanied by exact references to the sources in the

[1] Midrash, R. *Numbers* xiii. 15; cp. P. Talmud *Sanhedrin* iv 2 and Tanhuma *Huqqath* 4.
[2] Dan. xii. 1.

B

footnotes; the reader will then be able to check them and assess their value by his own independent investigation. Especially deplorable is the habit of citing Rabbinic literature, which is to a large extent an uncharted wilderness, by memory; for the human memory is apt to be fallible just on those petty details which may be relevant to the argument.

The present study of the Scrolls has arisen from the conviction that something must be wrong when they can still be seriously assigned to various dates between the Babylonian captivity and the Crusades; it is not concerned with the use or abuse which has or may be made of them but solely with the attempt, by an examination of all the available evidence, both internal and external, to determine their place in history and their relation to contemporary thought. The inability to solve the problem has been due to the three above-mentioned causes, preconceived opinions based on incorrect premises, the failure to apply logically sound methods to resolving the problems involved, and the mistranslation of certain crucial passages; if these errors of method are eliminated, the problem of the Scrolls can and will be solved.

The story has been set out and the problems have been discussed at considerable, possibly even excessive, length in the present work. The reason is that so many divergent and inconsistent opinions have been expressed without any adequate presentation of the facts that the ordinary reader has been confused and even compelled to regard the solution of the problem as a hopeless task; the wisest course has seemed therefore to be to give as full an account of the facts as possible and to examine the principal theories, whether plausible or implausible, which have been based on them, so that the reader may be in a position to reach a judgement on them. Since however such an investigation shows that none satisfies all the conditions implied in all the texts, a fresh attempt is then made to offer a solution of the problem and at the same time to prove it.

Briefly, the explanation of the facts contained in the Scrolls, as here put forward, is that, when all the evidence has been sifted, the Scrolls will be seen to be closely related to the Jewish Revolt against Rome in A.D. 66–73 and that they are therefore more or less contemporary with the New Testament. Consequently they are documents of prime importance for the understanding of the New Testament and present a challenge which Christian scholars will neglect at their peril.

I
ANCIENT AND MODERN DISCOVERIES

1. Previous Discoveries of Manuscripts

The progress of Hebrew studies during the last hundred years has exceeded that in any preceding period of history, that of the Reformation not excepted, and nothing perhaps has been of such importance as the recovery of ancient texts; for this has shown that, however far back the evidence for the text of both the Old and the New Testament is pushed, the fundamental accuracy of its transmission is unimpaired. The essential point has always been and still is the relative unimportance of the variant readings which have come to light; whether few or many, no vital doctrine has been affected.

The discovery of lost manuscripts, however, has been no monopoly of modern times; the difference has lain in the care taken of them and the methods followed in studying them. Two such discoveries, made long ago, call for mention here.

The great Christian scholar Origen, who compiled the famous Hexaplar edition of the Old Testament (containing the Hebrew text in Hebrew and in Greek letters and a number of Greek translations of it) in the early years of the 2nd century A.D., according to a note which he left, says that the *Sexta* (that is, the second of the three anonymous Greek translations which he incorporated in his work) was found 'together with other Hebrew and Greek books in a jar near Jericho';[1] and Eusebius, describing Origen's work, tells[2] of 'certain others (*sc.* other manuscripts of the Scriptures) which had been concealed from remote times, in what out of the way corners I know not'. Neither he nor any other writer, however, introduces a cave into the story. Origen is known to have been in Palestine in A.D. 217, which connects this discovery with that year. How long these manuscripts may have been hidden is not known; for, although Eusebius speaks of 'remote times', the phrase is so vague that no definite sense can be attached to it. Nothing explicit, too, connects these manuscripts with the Scrolls found in caves in the hills at the north-western end of the Dead Sea, and no remnants of any other Greek version of the Old Testament than that of the Septuagint have been recovered there.

---

[1] Mercati *Studi e Testi* V 28–46; cp. Kahle *Geniza* 242–4.
[2] In *Ecclesiastical History* VI xvi 1 (s. McGiffert in *Nicene and Post-Nicene Fathers*, NS I 262).

The next story, to which Prof. Eissfeldt has drawn attention,[1] of a discovery of ancient Hebrew manuscripts is preserved in a Syriac manuscript letter edited by Braun in 1901,[2] which may be dated c. A.D. 800. The writer, Timotheus I patriarch of Seleucia (A.D. 726–819), in a letter to his friend Sergius metropolitan of Elam (who died c. A.D. 805), describes the discovery in the following terms:

'We have learnt from trustworthy Jews, then being instructed as catechumens in the Christian religion, that some books were found ten years ago in a rock-dwelling near Jericho. The story was that a dog belonging to an Arab out hunting, while following game, went into a cave and did not come out again;[3] its owner went in after it and found a chamber in the rock containing many books. The hunter went off to Jerusalem and told his story to the Jews, who came out in great numbers and found books of the Old Testament and others in the Hebrew script; and, since there was a scholar well read in literature among them, I asked him about many passages quoted in our New Testament (as coming) from the Old Testament but found nowhere in it, neither in copies amongst the Jews nor in those amongst Christians. He said: they are there and can be found in the books discovered there.'

Clearly Timotheus distrusted his informant, even though he interrogated other persons when he was not present, and heard the same story without variation. He had written about it also to Gabriel, an eminent Christian physician (who died in A.D. 828) at the court of the caliph Harûn-alRashîd (A.D. 786–809) in Baghdad; he had written, too, to Shûbhalmāran, metropolitan of Damascus, asking him to make enquiries and let him know if a number of such passages, for example 'He shall be called a Nazarene', were in fact found in any of these manuscripts. He seems to have suspected that the catechumen had merely assumed that the disputed passages would be in one or other of the newly found manuscripts; for this man had told him: 'We have found more than two hundred Psalms of David among our books'.[4] Timotheus then goes on in his letter to Sergius: 'I wrote to him about this, thinking that these books had been deposited (sc. in the cave) by the prophet Jeremiah or some one else of those who had heard the word of God and been moved by it; when the prophet learnt by divine revelation of the conquest, plundering and burning, that was to come upon the people for their sins, they then hid and secreted the Scriptures (in holes) in the rocks and in caves, being firmly convinced that no word of God falls to the ground, in order that they might not be burnt by fire or carried off by plunderers. Those however who hid them died in the course of seventy years or before that and, when the people

---

[1] In T. Lz. LXXIV 597–8.   [2] In Or. Chr. I [1901] 304–9.
[3] Cp. p. 18.   [4] Pp. 16, 19, 21.

came back from Babylon, none of those who had deposited the books (*sc.* in the cave) survived . . . If these passages occur in the books named, these (copies) are clearly more trustworthy than those (in use) amongst the Hebrews and amongst us. I have received, however, no answer to my letter from them on these points, and I have no suitable person whom I can send (to enquire of them). This is as fire in my heart, burning and blazing in my bones.'

Unfortunately, the answer to this letter has not been preserved or at any rate has not yet been discovered, and the correspondence ceases as abruptly as it began.

Something further is learned of the discovery of Hebrew manuscripts from both Jewish and Arab sources.[1]

Writers of both races living in 10th and 11th centuries A.D. knew of a Jewish group who had books of Scripture reputed to have been found in a cave; but none apparently knew its locality. The original authorities for the story were 'Abû 'Isă-'lWarrâq, who died in A.D. 909, and David ibn Marwân, who lived in the 9th-10th centuries A.D.; unfortunately the works of both these writers have disappeared and are therefore known only at second hand.

First, a Jewish writer of the Qara'ite sect, Jacob alQirqîsânî (*i.e.* the Circassian), writing in A.D. 937 and citing alWarrâq, in his account of Jewish parties and sects[2] puts some whom he calls the 'cave-men' (*maġârîyah*) between the Sadducees and the Christians and gives as the reason for this name that their doctrines were based on books found in a 'cave' (*maġâr*); and he remarks that both 'Sadducees' and 'cave-men' had ceased to exist by his time. He then goes on to praise two of their principal writers, expressing the opinion that no other writings of this group had any value. He also describes their peculiar doctrines: some of them held laughter an indulgence which ought to be prohibited; they misunderstood various passages of the Scriptures (*i.e.* the Old Testament); unlike the 'Sadducees', they rejected the anthropomorphisms of the Old Testament, explaining them away as applying not to God but to the angel who had created the world; they believed that God had created Adam and Eve and all living creatures as well as sun and moon and stars, complete and perfect from the moment of creation; that the moon reached its median point (*i.e.* became full) on the fourth day of creation when the luminaries were created and that Wednesday therefore became the first day of the month. Second, Ben Ṭâhir alMaqdisî, who was born in Jerusalem in A.D. 946, speaking of a sect whom he calls the 'westerners' (*maġrabîyah*), which is almost

---

[1] Poznańsky in *RÉJ* L 13–23, De Vaux in *RB*, NS LVII 420–4, and Bammel in *ZNtW* XLIX 77–88.
[2] Nemoy *Kitâb al-Anwâr wal-Marâqib* I 11–12 (I ii 8), 41–2 (I vii 1), 59 (I xviii 2) = Nemoy in *HUCA* VII 326–7, 363–4, 391.

certainly a slip on his part or on the part of the copyist for 'cave-men' (*maġârîyah*), says[1] that they allowed travelling and boiling a pot on the Sabbath. Third, 'Abû Rayḥân alBîrûnî (A.D. 973–1048), citing alWarrâq, describes[2] some people whom he too calls 'westerners' (*maġâribah*) or 'middling men' (*muqâribah*), which are equally obvious slips on his part or on that of his coypists for 'cave-men' (*maġârîyah*). According to him these people held that the year began on the day when the full moon appeared in Palestine at sunset on the evening of the fourth day of the week (Wednesday), that the days and months and the annual cycle of feasts ought to be calculated from such a day, and that feasts were legal only when held on it, assigning as their reason that God had created the great luminaries on the fourth day of creation; consequently, they allowed the celebration of the Passover only on a fourth day (Wednesday),[3] adding however that the observance of the rules and rites for this feast was incumbent only on Jews residing in Palestine. These rules, as alBîrûnî says, were unorthodox. Fourth, Muḥammad alShahrastânî (as he was called from his place of origin, the city of Shahrastân in Khorâsân), also a Moslem (A.D. 1071–1153), following Benjamin alNahâwandî and speaking of a people whom he too calls 'middling men' (*muqâribah*) instead of 'cave-men' (*maġârîyah*), says[4] that they held that God spoke to the prophets through an angel whom He had set at the head of all creatures and that everything in the Law and the rest of the Scriptures describing God in anthropomorphic manner referred to this angel, as it was inadmissible to suppose that the Creator should be described in any way; and he adds that the heresiarch Arius (A.D. 256–336), who taught that the Messiah (Christ) was an angel of God and the elect one of the created world, lived four hundred years after the sect of the 'cave-men' and that he derived his doctrine from them.

These four writers, in spite of differences in the name given to the group (for which the obscurities of the Arabic script easily account), are obviously referring to the same people as Timotheus; but, while he was interested only in Biblical manuscripts, especially such as might throw light on the New Testament, they were concerned with texts of the Old Testament and with such others as describe the vagaries of a purely Jewish sect. Harkavy, indeed, long ago took these 'cave-men' for the Essenes and went on to suggest that they and the Therapeuts in Egypt were also connected.[5] Chronologically, the identification fits

---

[1] Huart *Ben Ṭahir elMaqdisî: Le Livre de la Création* IV 34–6 = 32–4.
[2] Sachau *Chronologie orientalischer Völker* (*Kitâbu-l'âtâri-'lbâqiyati 'an ilqurûni-'lḫâliyati*) 284 = *Chronology of ancient Nations* 278.
[3] Pp. 230, 320–1.
[4] Cureton *Kitâb alMilal wan-Niḥal* 169–71 = Haarbrücker *Religionsparteien und Philosophen-Schulen* I 255–6.
[5] Bacher in *JQR* VII 703 and Poznansky in *RÉJ* L 20–22.

the facts; for alQirqîsânî put them between 'Sadducees' or 'Sadduceans'[1] and Christians in his treatment of Jewish parties, while the Essenes took their origin c. 150 B.C.[2] and existed till the destruction of Jerusalem in A.D. 70; and since Arius was put by alShahrastânî four hundred years after the originators of the sect of the 'cave-men', they could well be assigned to a date c. 100 B.C. and so be contemporary, even if not identical, with the Essenes. This identification, however, can hardly be maintained; for not all the doctrines ascribed to the 'cave-men' are Essene. Their dislike of laughter tallies with the sober, even solemn, attitude of the Essenes to life, as it does with that of the so-called Covenanters of Qumrân, and the interest in angels is common to both groups.[3] Otherwise, the doctrines of the 'cave-men' agree rather with those of the Covenanters and others akin to them, for example, their theory of the calendar.[4] At the same time, the Covenanters shared this interest with another contemporary party, the Sadduceans (who are totally distinct from the Sadducees of the New Testament),[5] as they shared other interests with this party, for example the dislike of marriage with a niece and the taking of a second wife while the first was still living and perhaps also of divorce.[6]

That alQirqîsânî,[7] who may even have had a copy of the *Zadokite Documents* in some form or other before him, to some extent distinguishes between the 'Sadducees' or 'Sadduceans' (whichever he here means) and the 'cave-men' does not signify much, and it certainly does not imply that they may not be identified; for, as Prof. Rowley has remarked,[8] he distinguishes the 'Ananites and the Qara'ites, although 'Anan was the founder of Qara'ism. So too he mentions only those points in the doctrines of the 'cave-men' which the Qara'ites did not share with them; the reason may be that other elements of their teaching had been adopted by the Qara'ites by his time and would therefore not be mentioned by him as peculiar to the 'cave-men'. No reason can therefore be derived from alQirqîsânî's remarks for dissociating the 'cave-men' from the Sadduceans, whose leader was executed by the Romans in A.D. 6 and who became prominent in the 1st century A.D.;[9] for he does not necessarily put the 'cave-men' before the Christian era, as Fr. de Vaux argues,[10] in describing them between the Sadduceans and the Christians in his study of the contemporary Jewish political and religious groups.

Not much reliance however can be placed on the details of the

[1] P. 9.
[2] Josephus *Antiquities* XIII v 9 § 171, xi 2 § 311 and *War* I iii 5 § 78.
[3] Pp. 52–3, 66, 101, 108–9.   [4] Pp. 316–35.
[5] Pp. 259–65.   [6] Pp. 86–8, 91, 150, 260–1.
[7] Schechter *Documents* I xx; cp. Ginzberg *Sekte* I 185–91.
[8] In *Zadokite Fragments* 25[3].   [9] Pp. 237–66.
[10] De Vaux in *RB*, NS LVII 423.

information provided by writers living nearly a thousand years after the events which they are describing; and that no orthodox Jewish writer has anything to say about these sects, as Dr. Kahle has noted,[1] and that much of the available information comes from Moslem writers, makes the checking of anything recorded by Qara'ite writers about themselves virtually impossible.

A Jewish writer to whom attention has recently been drawn[2] in this connection is Ḥasdai ibn Shafruth (A.D. 915–90), for some time a diplomatic envoy at the court of the Spanish caliph 'Abd-alRaḥmân III (A.D. 912–61); for in a letter to the king of the Khazars, written probably after the caliph's death, he seems to be referring to these same people. In it he tells the following story: when God sent the Chaldaeans against the Jews to punish them for their faithlessness, they hid their scrolls of the Law in a cave to which they resorted for public prayer; but even so in time they forgot about the scrolls, until a Jew came long afterwards, found them and brought them out of the cave; from that moment they devoted themselves assiduously to the study of the Law and handed down the story of its recovery from generation to generation. This story, he adds, was already old in his own days. According to Ḥasdai the cave was in Mt. Seir, a name which was used in the Old Testament for the land of Edom; this might conceivably here be extended to include the western shore of the Dead Sea, if the story was related to that of the recently found Judaean Scrolls. Even if this difficulty is thus met or evaded, other objections to identifying these events remain. The writer implies that the cave was so easy of access and large that a considerable number of Jews could resort to it for prayer and even remain unaware of the scrolls put away in it; but both the situation and the size of the caves at Qumrân make them unsuitable for such a purpose. Further, he implies that a considerable body of Jews, marrying and giving in marriage, had been settled for many generations in the neighbourhood; but married life could hardly have continued at Qumrân on any large scale for an indefinite period of time.[3] This cave, too, was well known; yet the scrolls of the Law could remain safely hidden in it for a very long time. Finally, that the Chaldaeans were the enemy may be a priori improbable; but there is no certainty that the name is a pseudonym, like that of the Chittians, for the Seleucid Greeks or the Romans, although it may be such. Ḥasdai too, however, lived nearly a thousand years after the people who had hidden the Scrolls in the caves round Qumrân, and his story may represent a garbled recollection of the discovery of which Timotheus writes and so of events at Qumrân. This is all that can be said; the identification of the caves can be neither proved nor disproved.

[1] In VT I 44–5.   [2] Segert in Arch. Or. XXI [1935] 263–9.   [3] Pp. 45–6.

Further, the Qara'ite writers, Sahl ben Maṣlîaḥ (A.D. 900–50) and Ḥasan ben Māshîaḥ (c. A.D. 930), show a knowledge of Zadokite literature in the 10th century A.D.,[1] and the famous Qara'ite author Judah Hadassî (A.D. 1075–1160), who left Jerusalem as a young man when it was stormed by the Crusaders in A.D. 1099 and wandered to Constantinople, where he devoted himself to Hebrew philology and Greek literature and to science, refers[2] to 'three men of the cave' but adds little or nothing to the accounts which his predecessors have given. Lastly, R. Mōsheh ben Ḥasdai, a Qara'ite writer of the 13th century A.D., reported having heard a story that 'the heretic 'Anan and his friends used to compose heresies and falsehoods and bury them in the ground; then they would retrieve them and say: This is what we have found in ancient books'.[3]

These stories, in spite of the difficulty of extracting any certain historical information from them, indubitably bear witness to the persistence of a tradition regarding a Jewish group or sect, possibly called 'Sadduceans', which was formed towards the end of the 1st century B.C. and presumably lasted well into the 1st century A.D. and whose sacred and other books had at some unknown time been hidden in a cave till c. A.D. 750–800; then re-discovered, they gave the impulse to a new Jewish movement, which based itself on meticulous attention to the study of the Scriptures, during the 8th and 9th centuries A.D.[4] This was called 'Qara'ism', a word derived from the Hebrew qarrâ 'reader (of Scripture)' and miqrâ 'Scripture'; and its founder was one 'Anan, copies of whose work entitled the *Book of the Commandments* was found beside the *Zadokite Documents* in the Qara'ite synagogue at Fusṭâṭ (Old Cairo).[5] The stories further are witness to the interdependence of the Covenanters of Qumrân, the 'cavemen' of Arab and Jewish writers and the mediaeval Qara'ites;[6] for all these had books stored in or derived from a cave or caves and shared a common interest in a peculiar calendar.[7] The cave, too, from which the 'cavemen' took their name may be the same as that of which Timotheus and alQirqîsânî speak, as Fr. de Vaux claims;[8] and both may be identified with one or other of those round Qumrân in which the Judaean Scrolls have recently been found. This identification too can be neither proved nor disproved; for neither Timotheus nor any of these writers have left anything on record indicating the exact position of the cave or caves of which they had heard.

---

[1] Teicher in *JJS* II 87–91.
[2] Efendipulo *Judah Hadassi: Sêfer Eshkōl hakkōfer* [1836] 41b–42a §§ 97–8 (where the meaningless *meğâḍîyāh* is an error for *meğârîyāh* 'cave-men').
[3] Blumenfeld *Ozar Nehmad* III p. 62 ll. 7–10 (cp. p. 54 no. 6 ll. 15–18).
[4] Schechter *Documents* II 3–36.   [5] Cp. Kahle in *TLz.* LXXXII 647.
[6] Cp. Van der Ploeg in *Rech. Bibl.* IV 61–2.
[7] Pp. 316–35.   [8] In *RB*, NS LVII 420–4.

Then suddenly, after the lapse of a thousand years, the problem of newly discovered manuscripts was re-opened when one Shapira in 1883 appeared in London with a manuscript written on leather (or rather strips of leather) and containing what purported to be the speeches of Moses in the archaic (pre-exilic) Hebrew script.[1] This was proved beyond any reasonable doubt by Clermont-Ganneau and Ginsburg not to be a manuscript of the Mosaic age or even of the 9th century B.C.[2] Their claim however to have shown it to be a purely modern forgery has recently been contested, and the opinion has been expressed that it may perhaps have been an ancient manuscript of approximately the same period as the Scrolls in view of resemblances to them which it displays in the matter of the leather, the lines ruled to guide the copyist and the archaic script, analogous to that which some fragmentary scrolls of the Pentateuch exhibit.[3] The proof of forgery, however, cannot be reasonably doubted even if it cannot be confirmed, since the manuscript has disappeared; it remains but a literary curiosity which does not affect the present enquiry.

Finally, in 1896 the late Solomon Schechter, when examining the contents of the genîzāh (a hidden or secret chamber attached to a synagogue, in which worn and discarded manuscripts could be put away until a ritually proper means of disposing of them could be found)[4] attached to the Qara'ite synagogue in Fusṭāṭ (Old Cairo), founded in A.D. 896, came upon a work in which a people called the 'Sons of Zadok' were mentioned; when he published the text in 1910, therefore, he called it the Ẓadokite Work.[5] The text was preserved on two incomplete manuscripts, which overlapped one another, one perhaps of the 10th and the other of the 11th or 12th century A.D.; it was, however, even so not complete. Now that a much older fragment of this work has been found in one of the caves at Qumrân[6] (where as at Fusṭāṭ fragments also of Aramaic texts of Jubilees and the Testament of Levi have been found),[7] a connection between the group at Qumrân and the Qara'ites, which had already been suspected from certain similarities in the contents, is confirmed; and the hope may be entertained that the complete work, or at any rate enough fragments to make good the gaps in the Cairene edition, may yet be found. Finally, I. Lévi in 1913 published[8] a very small fragment of a Hebrew text which Shapira had obtained from the same source. Only a few words have survived from the beginning of each of nine lines, one of them (l. 4)

[1] Bardtke Handschriftenfunde I 50–8.
[2] Clermont-Ganneau Fraudes Archéologiques 187–266.
[3] Mansoor in Jewish Chronicle 28 xii 1956, 13 and Teicher in Lit. Suppl. LVI [22 iii 1957] 184; cp. Rabinowitz in JQR, NS XLVII 170–82 and Gottstein in JJS VII 187–93.
[4] Pp. 386–91.   [5] In Documents I 1–20.   [6] P. 18.
[7] Charles Greek Versions of the Testaments of the Twelve Patriarchs liii–lvii 245–56.
[8] In RÉJ LXV 24–31.

having 'concerning the law of things impure and clean' and the other (l. 3) mentioning 'the congregation of the Sons of Zadok', both without context; but these words suffice to identify the piece as coming from a Zadokite work, *i.e.* from one derived from the Covenanters of Qumrân. In 1939 Kenyon, the leading textual scholar of his day, wrote:[1] 'There is, indeed, no probability that we shall ever find manuscripts of the Hebrew text going back to a period before the formation of the text which we know as Massoretic'. Yet, if the old stories of the discovery of Hebrew manuscripts in a cave *c.* A.D. 750–800 had been remembered, no one would have ventured to utter so rash a prophecy; happily its author lived long enough to learn of and rejoice at its disproof.

2. DOCUMENTS FROM THE WILDERNESS OF JUDAH

In the spring of 1947 the learned world was astonished to read of a 'sensational new discovery of Hebrew manuscripts in Palestine', in a cave situated high up in a cliff at the north-western end of the Dead Sea.[2] The accounts are full of discrepancies, of which much has been made; but, briefly summarized, the story is this. An Arab shepherd of the tribe of the Ṭa'âmirah named Muḥammad alD̲îb, whose own story (or what purports to be that) has now been published,[3] was searching for a goat which had strayed out of sight among the rocks;[4] sheltering from a thunderstorm or perhaps merely tired, he sat down in a hollow and began idly throwing stones into a hole in the cliff facing him. Suddenly, a sound of something being broken was carried back to him and he entered the cave, a narrow tunnel of which the entrance was largely blocked; there he found ten earthen jars, all covered with lids, of which he broke nine with his staff but left the tenth intact. All were empty but one, from which he took away some rolled leather covered with writing to use for straps for sandals. On the next day he returned with a friend and removed what he had left, and together they carried it to a dealer in antiquities at Bethlehem. He, thinking that the script was Syriac, sent them to the Syrian monastery of St. Mark, where the Archbishop, Mar Athanasius Yeshu'o Samuel, was equally at a loss to identify the mysterious documents.

Meanwhile the Bedouin, hearing of this discovery, began to carry out a clandestine exploration of the cave, doing much damage as they went on with the work; eventually, they extracted from the debris other Scrolls, more or less injured, and several handfuls of fragments.

---

[1] In *Our Bible and the Ancient Manuscripts* [1939] 48.
[2] Harding in *The Times* 51455 [9 viii 1949] 5; s. Barthélemy & Milik *Discoveries* I 5–7.
[3] Brownlee in *JNES* XVI 236–9; s. de Vaux in *RB*, NS LXVI 88–9.
[4] Cp. p. 8.

In the summer of 1947 Arabs and antiquaries were hawking their Scrolls and fragments of Scrolls round the various scientific institutions in Jerusalem, offering them at very moderate prices. In June the Syrian Archbishop bought three (or rather four; for one of those offered to him actually consisted of two Scrolls) for £24 and showed them in July of the same year to Fr. Van der Ploeg, who identified one of them as a copy of the book of *Isaiah*,[1] who with Mr. Trever was the first to do so[2]; and in December Prof. E. L. Sukenik, who had at once realized the antiquity of the documents, bought three of them for the Hebrew University. The Archbishop in the following February showed his Scrolls to the authorities at the American School of Oriental Research, where they were photographed.

The political situation, following the termination of the British Mandate, now grew steadily worse, and the Archbishop departed to the United States, taking the Scrolls with him. His attempts to sell them there remained for some years unsuccessful; for prospective buyers not unnaturally doubted his title to sell property which was known to have been smuggled out of the country.[3] Eventually Mr. D. S. Gottesmann acquired them for $250,000[4] and gave them to the State of Israel. Thus Prof. Sukenik's lot (*Isaiah B*, the *War of the Sons of Light and The Sons of Darkness*, and the *Thanksgiving Hymns*) and the Archbishop's lot (*Isaiah A*, the *Commentary on Habakkuk*, the *Manual of Discipline* and the *Genesis Apocryphon*) have all come together and will in due time be exhibited in a special chamber constructed for them in the Jewish National Library.[5]

In July 1948 a truce put an end to the Jewish-Arab war, and archaeologists were once more able to scour the region of Qumrân, now a part of Jordan, and very many caves have since then been sounded. Early in 1949, the Department of Antiquities in Jordan and the Dominican *Ecole Biblique et Archéologique Française* with the Rockefeller Archaeological Museum in Jerusalem, helped by the American Schools of Oriental Research, started a systematic examination of the cave, now known as Cave I, directed by Mr. L. Harding and assisted by the Arab Legion. These operations added a considerable quantity to that already known, of which the importance will be discussed hereafter,[6] and some 600 fragments of Scrolls, all unfortunately very small and badly damaged; the original number of separate works has therefore been very variously estimated, ranging from 400 to 75 Scrolls.[7]

[1] Van der Ploeg *Qumran* 9–11.   [2] P. 25.
[3] Cp. Driver *Scrolls* 12[1].   [4] Zeitlin in *JQR*, NS XLVI 149–50.
[5] Yadin *Message* 39–52.   [6] Pp. 17–22.
[7] Cross in *BASOR* CXLI 9–13 (400), Harding in *The Times* 51455 [9 viii 1949] 5 (300–400), Lambert in *Etudes Classiques* XIX 218–19 (200–300), Albright in *Studies in honour of C. H. Dodd* 163[2] (300) and *BASOR* CXV 13 (200), De Vaux in *RB*, NS LVI 593 (150–200), Harding *ap.* Milik & Barthelemy *Discoveries* I 3 (75).

Texts from Cave I,[1] which are additional to the principal Scrolls already named, include a few fragments of the main non-Biblical works (*Genesis Apocryphon, Discipline, War*) and of many Biblical and other books, of which some are new and unknown. Such are fragments of ten books of the Old Testament (*Genesis, Exodus, Leviticus* in the archaic script, *Deuteronomy, Judges, Samuel, Isaiah, Ezekiel, Daniel, Psalms*) and of commentaries on the canonical books (*Micah, Zephaniah, Psalms*). The extra-Biblical pieces include fragments of a Hebrew *Jubilees* and an Aramaic *Testament of Levi*, of a Hebrew *Book of Noah* and some *Words of Moses* and of an Aramaic *Vision of the New Jerusalem*, with other sapiential, apocryphal or eschatological pieces in either language, amongst which a Hebrew *Book of Mysteries* may be mentioned; the liturgical texts include a liturgy of the *Three Tongues of Fire*, a collection of blessings and prayers, notably for the Day of Atonement, and psalms or hymns, all in this group equally fragmentary; further, pieces of work called the *Order of the Community* which has been thought to be connected with *Discipline*,[2] and a phylactery, have been recovered.[3] Many other fragments cannot yet be properly identified.

In February 1952, Arabs of the Ṭaʿâmirah tribe reappeared in the district of Qumrân and opened up another cave, numbered Cave II, situated a short distance from Cave I; and, following them, the *École Biblique* with the American School of Oriental Research and the Rockefeller Museum immediately searched all the crevices and caves in the same cliff over a front of eight kilometres. Some twenty or more caves yielded potsherds of the same type as those found at Hirbat Qumrân. Cave II[4] yielded nearly two hundred fragments of nine Biblical books, in some cases obviously coming from different manuscripts of the same book (*Genesis, Exodus, Leviticus* in the archaic script, *Numbers, Deuteronomy, Ruth, Jeremiah* in a recension virtually identical with the Massoretic text except for variations in orthography and copyist's mistakes, *Job, Psalms*), of one or two non-canonical books (*Ecclesiasticus, Jubilees*), of *testimonia*, of several unknown Hebrew works, including another piece of the *New Jerusalem*, and also of unknown Aramaic apocryphal works, and of a number of miscellaneous Hebrew and Aramaic works, three of them written in cipher. Cave III[5] yielded nearly a hundred manuscript fragments with a legible text, though all damaged by moisture and gnawed by rats almost beyond hope of restoration. These included fragments of six Biblical books (*Genesis,*

---

[1] De Vaux in *RB*, NS LVI 586–609 and LX 88; s. Bardtke *Handschriftenfunde* II 85–175.
[2] De Vaux in *RB*, NS LVII [1950] 426–7; s. Barthélemy & Milik *Discoveries* I 107–8.
[3] Barthélemy & Milik *op. cit.* I 1–155.
[4] De Vaux in *RB*, NS LX 84–5, 553–5.
[5] *Ibid.*, NS LX 84–5, 555–8 and Baillet *ibid.* LXIII 54–5.

Psalms, Lamentations), and one apocryphal book (*Ecclesiasticus*), of a Scroll of the Law and of one Biblical commentary (*Isaiah*), of various Hebrew and Aramaic apocalypses, of a sectarian work and of some other unidentified works. The disappointment caused by these meagre remnants, however, was amply compensated by the discovery of a unique object. This was what looked like two scrolls of copper, which were ultimately found to be pieces of one and the same Scroll, on which writing in square Hebrew characters reversed and in relief could be seen; when unrolled and put together, the pieces formed a scroll 30 cm. wide and 80 cm. long, containing a description of buried treasure.[1]

One evening in September 1952 an old Arab of the Ṭa'âmirah told the young men of the tribe how as a boy he had once followed a wounded partridge into a crevice in the cliffs near Qumrân and had found an ancient lamp and some pieces of pottery;[2] and he described the site of the cave to them. Provided with the necessary means, they proceeded to the place, found the cave, now numbered Cave IV, and let themselves down into it by ropes. They then turned over the earth for a few yards and suddenly came upon thousands of manuscript fragments from perhaps some four hundred manuscripts.[3] Coming to Jerusalem to sell their treasure, they gave a false account of the site where they had found it to put others off the trail; but jealousy caused their secret to be betrayed. The police went out from Jericho, found the Arabs engaged in illicit digging and drove them off. Fr. de Vaux and Fr. Milik soon arrived on the scene and found another hundred or so fragments, pieces of twelve separate manuscripts. They also made a new opening in the plateau close at hand, where they found Cave V, which yielded a few badly mutilated fragments. The Bedouin then entered yet another hole in the cliff near the head of the ravine, where they discovered Cave VI; the manuscript fragments here were few and all of slight importance except one piece containing a portion of the *Zadokite Documents*, which was thus proved to be connected with Qumrân.

The next lot of caves, Caves IV–X, seem to be largely the work of human hands or at any rate to have been improved by human hands in ancient times,[4] having perhaps been originally intended as tombs, which are often cut in the rock in Palestine;[5] this work is dated in the 9th-6th centuries B.C.[6]

The collection of fragments found in Cave IV[7] runs into many

---

[1] P. 30–36.   [2] Pp. 38, 40–1, 402–3   [3] Cross *Library* 18.   [4] Pp. 48–50.
[5] Cp. Isa. xxii. 16, Matt. xxvii. 60, Mk. xvi. 46, Lk. xxiii 53.
[6] Cross *Library* 19[30].
[7] Cross in *RB*, NS LXIII 56–8, Skehan *ibid.* 58–60, Milik *ibid.* 60–2, Allegro *ibid.* 62–4, Strugnell *ibid.* 64–6, Starcky *ibid.* 66–7, and Hunzinger *ibid.* 67.

thousands, possibly representing as many as four hundred separate works;[1] it thus far exceeds that yielded by any other cave if not by all the caves together. The Hebrew texts include pieces of twenty-nine books of the Old Testament (*Genesis, Exodus, Leviticus, Numbers, Deuteronomy, Joshua, Judges, Ruth, Samuel, Chronicles, Ezra, Nehemiah, Isaiah, Jeremiah, Lamentations, Ezekiel, Daniel, Joel, Hosea, Amos, Jonah, Zephaniah, Zechariah, Malachi, Job, Psalms, Proverbs, Canticles, Ecclesiastes*); and most of these are represented in several different manuscripts, as the handwritings show, for example *Deuteronomy* in as many as fourteen distinct manuscripts. Three pieces (*Genesis, Exodus, Job*) are in the archaic script[2], an *Exodus* and a *Samuel* agree with the Greek Septuagint, and one *Exodus* and one *Numbers* agree with the Hebrew-Samaritan Pentateuch rather than with the Massoretic (traditional) Hebrew text. There are also fragments of commentaries on several books of the Old Testament (*Genesis, Isaiah, Hosea, Nahum, Psalms*) and paraphrases of some books (*Genesis, Exodus*); several phylacteries, some *florilegia* of Biblical excerpts (*Exodus, II Samuel, Isaiah, Amos, Psalms, Daniel*) and *testimonia* relating to the Messiah based on the Old Testament, a large section of the Pentateuch which is neither a *florilegium* nor a paraphrase dealing with the Creation and the Deluge, pieces of a non-canonical psalter and of hymns (some containing 'Amen, Amen' at the appropriate places), of a lamentation over Jerusalem and of imprecations uttered by rebellious members against the community. There are fragments, too, of *Tobit* and *Jubilees* and of an unidentified work resembling *Jubilees* or the *Testaments of the Twelve Patriarchs*, of a similar work promising blessings for those who obey the Law and threatening those who disobey it with torments, and of pseudepigraphical stories. One of the strangest texts is a fragmentary planetary *melothesia* in the archaic Hebrew script. There are, too, many pieces of the sectarian works (*Discipline* and the *Rule of the Community; War*, in which some gaps in the published text are filled in, even while the new text shows some divergencies from the old; *Thanksgiving Hymns* and *Zadokite Documents*, both of which are represented by pieces from eleven distinct manuscripts), of the *Book of Mysteries* (of which four pieces from different manuscripts may be identified), of an unknown Hebrew Messianic work resembling the Aramaic *New Jerusalem*, of an *Angelic Liturgy*[3], and of rules for the rotation of the priestly offices.[4] One fragment of leather contains bits of personal names on both sides, and another has the alphabet copied out on both sides in an archaic Nabataean (Aramaic) script. Most remarkable of all the documents from this cave are four Hebrew cryptographic texts. These reveal two types of cipher, of which one (B) has not yet been made out. Texts

[1] De Vaux *Archéologie* 82.   [2] Pp. 447–8.
[3] Strugnell in *VT, Suppl.* VII 318–45.   [4] Pp. 324–5.

in the other (A) are fragments of an astronomical work, another beginning *Word of a Wise Man to the Sons of Dawn*,[1] and a third is called a *Midrash on the Book of Moses*; the last, in which the letters in the individual words run from left to right while the cipher is written from right to left (as in ordinary Hebrew texts), assigns men at birth in various classes to the influence of one or other of the zodiacal signs.[2] Some *papyri*, equally fragmentary, contain two sectarian pieces (*Discipline*, the *Rule of the Community*, the *Thanksgiving Hymns*) and a liturgical text with forms for morning and evening prayers on the front and directions and prayers for a rite of purification on the back. Fragments also of a small number of Aramaic texts were found in this cave. Those on leather include pieces of known apocryphal and pseudepigraphical works (*Tobit*; *Enoch* and *Testament of Levi*, represented by three separate manuscripts), and of others from the Noachic literature, of similar works relating to Esther and Daniel, several pieces of the *New Jerusalem*, and of various cosmological, eschatological and apocalyptic works, including one entitled *Words of the Book which Michael addressed to the Angels*, a remarkable prayer attributed to the Babylonian king Nabû-na'id on his recovery from a seven years' sickness in Têmâ (where he is known to have spent several years of his reign), and various pieces containing *tablettes célestes* and the measurements of the new Jerusalem; and one *papyrus* contains *Genealogies* from the beginning to the end of the period of the Judges with a chronology which lacks the date of the Creation. Lastly, some fragments of a Greek (possibly non-Septuagintal and pre-Christian) translation of the Old Testament were found in this cave.[3] All told, some 330 different works are said to have been identified from this cave.[4]

Two other caves were explored at the same time as Cave IV. The fragments of Scrolls in Cave V[5] were almost entirely decomposed; pieces of only three books of the Old Testament (*Deuteronomy*, *I Kings*, *Jeremiah*) and of the Aramaic *New Jerusalem* could be identified. Those in Cave VI[6] were considerable in bulk, skin 57 pieces and *papyrus* 718 pieces. The Hebrew texts on leather are all fragments: Biblical texts (*Genesis*, *Leviticus* in the archaic script, *Canticles*) and commentaries (*Isaiah*, *Hosea*, *Nahum*), apocalypses related to *Enoch* and an apocryphal prophecy, an unidentified piece of Hebrew poetry, sectarian works (*Discipline* and *Zadokite Documents* or a similar composition) and a genealogical list of priests.[7] Some *papyri*, too, are Biblical (*Kings* and

---

[1] Cp. Isa. xiv. 12.　　　　　　　　[2] Bardtke *Handschriftenfunde* II 174–5.
[3] Kahle in *St. Ev.* LXXXIII 613–21.　　[4] Cross in *BASOR* CXLI 10.
[5] Milik in *RB*, NS LXIII 55–6.　　　[6] Baillet *ibid.* 55.
[7] Pp. 66, 325; cp. Josephus *Life* i § 6 and B. Talmud *Berakoth* 62b and *Kiddushin* 76b.

Daniel in a semi-cursive script), others are historical and administrative. The Aramaic fragments include an apocryphal work akin to the Table of Nations,[1] a number of pieces in a semi-cursive script apparently connected with an apocalypse of Noah, and an undefined work.

In the spring of 1955 four new caves, numbered Caves VII–X,[2] were found, but they yielded little of any interest or value. In Cave VII some pottery, including a piece having *Rômâ* (Rome) painted on it twice in Hebrew letters in black ink, and some few *papyri*, all fragmentary but containing Biblical and apocryphal Greek texts (*Exodus; Epistle of Jeremy*), were discovered. Cave VIII[3] had some broken pieces of a lamp of the 1st century A.D., one sherd inscribed with a single Hebrew letter, two cases with four compartments and one with one for phylacteries, similar to those found in Cave I,[4] a fragment of a phylactery and some pieces of documents inscribed with very fine writing and rolled up. In Cave IX only a single fragmentary *papyrus* with some Hebrew letters written on it and in Cave X some few sherds, one having some Hebrew letters on it, and fragments of a mat, were recovered.

In 1956 Cave XI,[5] which was reported to have been entered by Arabs, was examined. It had been previously occupied in the chalcolithic and Israelite periods, as various objects of iron (small pick, chisel or file, and knife), which were found in it, proved; and a certain amount of other debris was present, together with fragments of leather bearing Hebrew letters in the archaic script. Most important of all were three Hebrew Scrolls (*Leviticus* in late archaic script, a *Psalter*, and *Ezekiel* in very precarious condition, all three incomplete), a fragment containing the *New Jerusalem* and an Aramaic translation or *Targûm on Job*, hitherto unknown;[6] all these are now safely preserved in the Rockefeller Museum in Jerusalem. The *Psalter* just mentioned is of exceptional importance, as the Hebrew text of *Psalm cli* is preserved in it[7]; this has not been found in any Palestinian recension and has been known only in the Greek translation of the Septuagint, so that it throws a welcome light on the possible connection of the Covenanters with Egypt.[8]

The mass of these manuscript fragments from the caves round Qumrân on a superficial view looks immense; but a careful consideration of them in the light of certain relevant facts suggests that the total number of works once deposited in the caves may easily be exaggerated. Many of the Scrolls, especially those containing copies of books of the Old Testament, may either have been very small or may have com-

[1] Gen. x. 1–32.   [2] De Vaux in *RB*, NS LXIII 572–3.
[3] De Vaux *ibid*. LX 544.   [4] Harding *ap*. Barthélemy & Milik *Discoveries* I 7.
[5] De Vaux in *RB*, NS LXIII 573–4.   [6] Cross *Library* 25–6.
[7] Announced in *The Times* 8 ii 1962 (p. 12 col. vi).   [8] S. p. 226.

C

prised several works, *e.g.* the Minor Prophets. Even the Scrolls which have been preserved more or less intact are not very long; so the five principal works (Is. A, D, H, T, W) as reproduced in facsimile scarcely take up a hundred quarto-pages. Alternatively, if they had been broken up like most others, they would have yielded thousands of fragments. The entire collection, therefore, even when allowance is made for the cumbrous nature of ancient books, may not have been so large as it has sometimes thought to be.

Three points must here be noticed. First, some if not many of the identifications of fragments of Scrolls as here given can only be regarded as provisional. Fragments may have come from totally unknown works, or they may be wrongly grouped together by those working on them and so be treated as pieces of works to which in fact they do not belong; and the comparison of a phrase or sentence, possibly incompletely preserved, with something similar in a work which has survived only in translation in a different language is necessarily hazardous and uncertain. Second, Dr. Zeitlin has attacked the authenticity of the Scrolls[1] on the ground, amongst others, that no competent archaeologist was present when they were found. Five indeed of the caves (I, II, IV, VI, XI) were discovered and ransacked by nomad Arabs before archaeological examination; but archaeologists opened the six other caves (III, V, VII, VIII, IX, X), which they found intact. Although then the authenticity of the Scrolls, all of them fragmentary, from the former group (especially that of the Scrolls found in Cave I) may in theory be and has in fact been doubted for this reason, that of the Scrolls from the latter cannot be disputed; and, as the documents in both groups are largely of the same type, the genuineness of the former virtually guarantees that of the latter.[2] Archaeologists also saw a fragment of a Scroll wrapped in a piece of linen and still adhering to a broken jar in Cave I.[3] The Scrolls, therefore, may be accepted as genuine, neither forgeries nor a hoax, whether expert archaeologists have supervised their discoveries and whether every piece can be identified or not. Third, the Scrolls themselves refer to other writings such as the *Book of Study*[4] (Z xi 2, xv 5) and the *Book of the Order of its Time* (W xv 5); no such independent works have been found or, if fragments of them have come to light, they have not yet been identified.

The Scrolls or fragments of Scrolls found in the caves round the ruins of Qumrân at the north-western end of the Dead Sea were not the only documents recovered from the Wilderness of Judah during the last fifteen years. Others were retrieved from caves at spots (which the

---

[1] In *JQR*, NS XL 373–8 XLI 1–17 XLII 145–50 XLVI 231–4, 246–255 XLVIII 246–251, 277–8.
[2] De Vaux *Archéologie* 74–5.   [3] *Ibid.* 78–9.   [4] Pp. 70–1.

Arab finders refused to reveal) in the *Wâdī Murabba'ât*, difficult of access and remote from human settlement, farther to the south in the same region; and yet others were rescued from a subterranean chamber of the ruined Byzantine monastery known as Ḥirbat alMird (called also Marda and Castellion), which replaced the Hasmonaean fortress called Hyrcanion not far to the south-east of Jerusalem. Only the documents in the first group, which belong to the 1st century B.C. and to the 1st or 2nd centuries A.D., are the concern of the present study. Those in the second group range generally from the 8th to the 10th or 11th centuries A.D.; but the most important of them, apart from some Biblical texts, are a group of texts throwing light on the circumstances of the Second Revolt of the Jews against Rome (A.D. 132–5).[1] Those in the third group are chiefly uncial Greek codices of the 5th-8th centuries A.D. containing Biblical and extra-canonical books, Biblical texts in the Syro-Palestinian dialect, and many Arabic *papyri*, mostly private letters, of the 8th-10th centuries A.D.[2] None of the documents in these last two groups is of any use in seeking a solution of the problems raised by the buildings at Qumrân and the texts from the surrounding caves and are not further discussed.

3. Description of the Sectarian Scrolls

The principal manuscripts are in the form of scrolls, written on skins of sheep and goats, prepared as prescribed long afterwards in the Talmud.[3] They are written on the hairy side, which has been cleaned, in accordance with the rule that 'in writing on coarse skins, the hairy side is used',[4] so that they are technically parchments;[5] and they are ruled in accordance with a supposed Mosaic tradition that 'they (*sc.* the Scriptures) must be written in ink on skins ruled with a reed'.[6] The reason why manuscripts only in the form of scrolls have been recovered in the neighbourhood is that the *codex*, that is the book, had only recently been invented;[7] it was perhaps already in use in the 1st century B.C. for transcripts of public documents, legal text-books and school-books, but it was first popularized by the Christian church, which wanted the text of the New Testament in a form convenient for reference.[8] The great drawback to the scroll was the difficulty of finding the place in works of any length. The text on a Hebrew scroll was a series of columns of writing recurring from right to left. The

---

[1] Benoit Milik & de Vaux *Discoveries* II 65–290.
[2] De Langhe in *Onze Alma Mater* VII iv 14–19 and VIII i 3–5.
[3] Sukenik *Scrolls* 25.
[4] Cp. Blau *Studien zum althebräischen Buchwesen* 22–6, 142–50.
[5] Burton & Poole & Reed in *Nature* CLXXXIV 534 and Poole & Reed in *Technology and Culture* III 1–26.
[6] P. Talmud *Megillah* 71d (i 9).   [7] P. 381.
[8] Kenyon *Bible and Archaeology* 212–14.

reader held it in both hands, exposing two or three columns at a time; as he proceeded, he rolled up the finished portion with his right hand and unrolled another column or two with his left hand. Thus, when he had read the whole text, the beginning was inside and the end was outside; for the convenience, therefore, of the next reader, the scroll had to be re-rolled in the opposite direction to bring the beginning back to the outside. This part of a scroll, therefore, often became worn and frayed, and the text might even be lost. The principal Scroll of *Isaiah* is thus much rubbed at the beginning, but the text is not seriously damaged; such rubbing does not necessarily mean that this Scroll is any older than others of which the beginning is not so much worn, but only that it has been subjected to greater use, which is *a priori* likely in the case of the most important of the prophets.

The restoration of the Scrolls and of the manuscript fragments found in the various caves is a long and tedious task, requiring much technical skill in the handling and identifying of fragments of skin which are often minute, badly broken and frayed or stuck together, and on which the writing may be nearly illegible through the fading of the ink or discoloration of the leather or through wrinkles and cracks in it.[1] When they have been repaired, the texts must be photographed and then identified. Biblical documents are easily identified; the texts are well known, and complete concordances containing every word in the Bible are available, so that even a sentence of two or three words can usually be tracked down with tolerable certainty. Portions or even mere fragments of non-canonical, apocryphal or pseudepigraphical texts can also be for the most part identified without undue difficulty; for, although these works are chiefly known only in translation, their contents, characteristic phraseology and key-words are more or less familiar. Finally, a concordance of all the works found at Qumrân has been prepared, so that fragments can be easily placed, for the workers' use; and concordances have already been published.[2] Extracts of unknown works must wait until enough fragments can be brought together to give the reader some notion of the subject matter.

Unfortunately, the collections from the various caves have fallen into two separate lots, the one in the possession of the Hebrew University in Jerusalem (now in the State of Israel) and the other in the Rockefeller Museum in Jerusalem (now in the Arab Kingdom of Jordan); and no comparison of the original text of those in the one place is possible with that of those in the other, so long as the frontier between the two states is closed.

The principal works, which are now all the property of the Hebrew University in Jerusalem, have now all been edited.

[1] Cross in *BA* XVII 15–16.
[2] H. Janssens *Vocabulaire du Manuel de Discipline* (Brussels, 1952) and K. G. Kuhn *Konkordanz zu den Qumrantexten* (Göttingen, 1960).

The first group, which consists of the Scrolls taken by the Syrian Archbishop to the United States, has been edited by American scholars. The complete Isaiah (commonly known as *Isaiah A*)[1], which had been identified by Fr. Van der Ploeg[2] and Mr. J. C. Trever,[3], was published by Prof. M. Burrows with the assistance of Prof. W. H. Brownlee and Mr. J. C. Trever, whose photographs were used for the text; these are reproduced on one page with a transcription into square (printed) Hebrew characters on the opposite page. The Scroll contains fifty-four columns of well preserved Hebrew script, complete but for some small cracks and minute holes affecting very few letters which can be easily restored; parts of the Scroll, however, are badly rubbed or worn, and some of the letters at the ends of the lines seem to have been re-inked at some time. It consists of seventeen skins of somewhat coarse parchment, sewn together with thread; two seem also to have been glued together. These skins vary very much in length, the shortest carrying two and the longest four columns of text; the average of the length is .262 metre, making that of the whole Scroll 7.34 metres in its present state. The height varies from .245 to .27 metres. The manuscript has been badly damaged while still in use, and seven rents of the parchment have been skilfully repaired in antiquity; and the parchment here and there has been reinforced with patches glued on it. The writing is for the most part well preserved, though here and there faded and indistinct; and the ink varies considerably in the different columns, apparently where the pen has been changed. Finally, the text is taken from two manuscripts; for, although it is copied by the same hand, the orthography of the first part (Is. i—xxxix) differs from that of the second part (Is. xl–lxvi).[4]

Many but not all of the sheets are ruled with vertical lines to mark off the columns and with horizontal lines, from which the writing depends in accordance with old Jewish custom, to keep it straight. There are also a number of curious marks, crosses and such-like, in the margins; their purpose is disputed. They have nothing to do with the division of the text into paragraphs, which represent an early form of breaking up the text into sections, but seem to be intended to draw attention to important passages.[5] The copyist has made a number of mistakes, errors both of commission and of omission; some have been at once noticed and corrected by him, others have been left to a reviser or subsequent reader, as the difference of scripts shows, for correction. The corrections are made by erasing what is wrong, which may be further marked with points, and writing the right word above the line; omissions are similarly made good by insertions above the

---

[1] P. 16.   [2] Van der Ploeg *Excavations* 10–11.
[3] Wright in *BA* XI 21–22; cp. Trever *ibid.* 49.
[4] Kahle *Handschriften* 72–7.   [5] Pp. 527–30.

line or occasionally in the margin where, if long, they are written downwards from top to bottom.

The *Commentary of Habakkuk*[1] (published in the same volume as *Isaiah A*), which Fr. Van der Ploeg[2] and Prof. Brownlee identified,[3] is written on a scroll of two strips of soft leather sewn together with thread; all the columns and lines are clearly ruled with a sharp instrument, leaving a fine depression which can be both seen and felt, in accordance with Talmudic rules.[4] The script is bold and clear; it is the best formed of any and has the appearance of being the most developed and therefore one of the latest in the whole collection. In spite of its lateness, the *tetragrammaton* or divine name is regularly written in the archaic script.[5] The Scroll is unfortunately badly mutilated, especially at the beginning; and the bottom of every column except the last is lost. Apart from the severed portion at the beginning, it measures 141.9 centimetres in length; and the preserved portion reaches 13.7 centimetres at the highest point. The Scroll contains thirteen columns, in which the text of the prophet is set out and then followed by the comments of the author; only the first two chapters of Habakkuk are thus subjected to comment, presumably because the third chapter was not relevant to his purpose.[6] The value of this work is very great; for, since its author was applying the prophecies of Habakkuk to the events of his own time, it is the main source for reconstructing the history of the community at Qumrân.[7] It is also valuable as the prototype of the fragmentary commentaries in the Mishnah[8], which was codified in the 2nd century A.D.

The *Manual of Discipline* is the last volume edited by the above-named American scholars. The Scroll, when brought to the American School in Jerusalem, was in two pieces; and who can have sewn them together is not known. When they were put together, it was seen to consist of five skins or sheets sewn together in the same way as those just described. It is almost complete, except for the loss of the opening lines; and the fragment once thought to supply these lines is now generally regarded as a piece of a distinct work. In its present state its total length is a little over 6 feet and its height is about 9 inches. The leather is in very good condition and shows but few signs of handling. The handwriting is similar to but not identical with that of *Isaiah A*. The text deals with the beliefs of the community and the rules governing their lives;[9] it, therefore, with the *Zadokite Documents* is of prime importance for identifying the Jewish group or sect to which the community belonged.

In addition to these Scrolls, which are those bought (as said above)

---

[1] Pp. 126–9. [2] Trever in *BA* XI 52. [3] Van der Ploeg *op. cit.* 11. [4] P. 419.
[5] Pp. 413–4, 447–8. [6] Lambert in *NRT* LXXI 294. [7] Pp. 129–30.
[8] Danby Mishnah xxiv–v (s. pp. 127–30). [9] Wernberg-Møller in *JSS* II 411–12.

from the Syrian Archbishop by Mr. D. S. Gottesmann,[1] the Hebrew University now has four others, which the late Dr. E. L. Sukenik obtained and his son Major-General (Prof.) Y. Yadin has edited.

The text of *Isaiah B* is very imperfect; the leather, except that of the penultimate sheet, is much decomposed and twenty-five chapters are completely lost. Only portions survive of the remaining chapters, of which the text is very close to that of the ordinary Hebrew Bible.

The two most important texts in this lot are the *War of the Sons of Light with the Sons of Darkness* and the *Thanksgiving Hymns*. The former (called briefly the *War*) is over 2.9 metres in length; it now has eighteen columns on four sheets and part of one column on the fifth sheet, *i.e.* nineteen columns of writing, each containing seventeen or eighteen lines, ranging from 10.5 to 16 cms. in length.[2] Unfortunately, the bottom of every column is mutilated and worn away if not entirely lost, so that the number of lines cannot be exactly determined, and gaps caused by the decomposition of the leather appear on most sheets. The text is carefully copied and such few errors as the copyist has made are methodically corrected. The subject is a pseudo-apocalyptic war in which the 'Sons of Light', *i.e.* members of the community at Qumrân, will engage the 'Sons of Darkness', *i.e.* their enemies in the world, and from which they will eventually emerge victorious.[3] The latter is the collection of poems which its editor calls *Thanksgiving Hymns* or, as in the texts, *Thanksgivings* (D x 23 T xi 4, 33 W xv 5). It reached Dr. Sukenik badly mutilated, in two parts; the first consisted of three leaves each with four columns of writing, the second was a badly crumpled package consisting of some seventy detached pieces of leather of various sizes. Large parts of the leather were dry and extremely fragile, others crumbling or completely rotted and frequently covered by a thin layer of decomposed leather; much of the text therefore could be read only with the help of infra-red rays. The columns of writing are 32 centimetres high but the tops of ll and the bottoms of most are lost, so that the original height cannot be determined; the number of lines varies from 35 to 41 in a column. Two scribes were engaged in copying it. The one was reasonably skilful, though inferior to the scribe who wrote the *War*, and he occasionally affected the archaism of writing the Hebrew word for 'God' in the pre-exilic script; the other scribe, who began work towards the end of a column (col. xi l. 27), was crude and careless. The work seems once to have consisted of some thirty-five hymns; but the difficulty of placing all the fragments in their proper positions and of estimating how much text has been lost makes the task of determining the actual number very precarious. These *Hymns* quote so extensively from the Old

[1] P. 16.   [2] Cp. Sukenik *Megilloth Genuzoth* I 18.   [3] Pp. 168–79.

Testament, which at times their author or authors misunderstand, that much of them becomes patch-work; where they are original, the thought is often as poor as it is obscure. This extreme use of the Old Testament prompts the question whether they may not be the 'two hundred Psalms of David' of which Timotheus speaks in the letter quoted above.[1] Their theme is the deliverance of their author or authors from some great disaster, possibly the defeat of the party or of the nation by a powerful external enemy.[2]

The Scroll which has been published last is the so-called *Genesis Apocryphon*, edited by Dr. N. Avigad and Major-General Y. Yadin. This long defied all efforts to unroll it, and so bad is its condition even now that the editors have ventured to publish only five columns, all imperfect (cols. ii, xix–xxii); the reason for this is that, though found in Cave I, it was probably not one of those which were originally stored in jars or were in still unbroken jars when the Bedouin stumbled on them. Both beginning and end are missing, and the lower part had probably been exposed to dampness and so was very seriously impaired. Further, its condition probably deteriorated through its being hawked from place to place by the Arab finders. The Scroll in its original form consisted of four sheets sewn together with a tendon, and the sheets were ruled with horizontal lines to guide the writing and with perpendicular lines marking out the columns; the lines were made with a sharp instrument, apparently shaped out of bone, and they ran between points punched in the leather to give the alinement. The length of the Scroll as preserved is 2.82 metres and its height is 31 cm.; there are 22 columns of text having 34 to 37 lines each.[3] When the first attempts to deal with this unpromising Scroll were made, the name of Lamech[4] was read, and it was therefore thought to be an *Apocalypse of Lamech*,[5] but enough has now been unravelled to show that its subject is a paraphrase of the stories of the patriarchs,[6] filled out with much stylistic elaboration and fanciful matter.[7]

That the Scrolls and fragments of Scrolls, or the majority of them, found in the eleven caves round Qumrân emanated from the same group of people and reflect the same background is beyond reasonable doubt. Their inter-connection is especially important in attempting to discover what that background is; for none of them gives anything like a complete picture of it. The Scrolls which alone can be used for this purpose are those which are not copies of ancient (*e.g.* Biblical and apocalyptic) works but any which give an account of the institutions and practices, beliefs and thoughts, of the society settled at Qumrân

[1] Pp. 8–10.   [2] Pp. 197–216.
[3] Avigad & Yadin *Genesis Apocryphon* 12–15.   [4] Gen. iv. 18–24.
[5] Trevor in *BASOR* CXV 8–10.   [6] Gen. iv–xv (as so far published); s. pp. 560–1.
[7] Avigad & Yadin *op. cit.* 16–39 (s. pp. 460–1).

round which they have been found. These are, first, the original and independent works, namely the *Manual of Discipline*, the *Thanksgiving Hymns* and the *War*, together with the *Zadokite Works* found in a synagogue at Cairo. Second, the commentaries whose authors interpret the Scriptures in the light of the events of their own days; the *Commentary on Habakkuk* stands pre-eminent in this class. Accordingly, when Mrs. Atkinson says[1] 'a sound historical approach requires rather at this stage in our knowledge (or rather, lack of knowledge) that we should assume that the Scrolls may have been composed at various and even widely-separated dates and so should carefully avoid arguing from one to the other, unless in special direct cases direct and close connection can be demonstrated', she is saying what appears scientific but is in fact unscientific. For, if anything is indisputable, it is that these five works are indissolubly inter-related and must be taken together, although their composition may be spread over a considerable number of years (*c.* A.D. 45–115 or even 135).[2] That that containing the *Zadokite Documents* is a late copy from Egypt proves nothing, if only because fragments of it have been found in one of the caves[3] and because the work itself has many points of contact with *Discipline*, of which the subject is similar;[4] that four come from the same cave, all having perhaps been stored in the same jar, may be accidental and is anyhow immaterial, since the external evidence is nothing compared with the internal evidence of the texts themselves.

The various Scrolls reveal a common terminology and a common ideology which cannot be disregarded. For example, the society is called in the several Scrolls a 'holy congregation' (D, Z) and its members are described as 'those who enter the covenant' (D, Z), which is the 'covenant of God' (D, Z) and which in due course gives place to a 'new covenant' (H, Z),[5] and as 'Sons of Zadok' (D, Z) and 'sons of light', while their opponents are dubbed 'sons of corruption' (D, Z) and 'sons of darkness' (D, W); these include a 'Man of Falsehood' (H, Z), and some of them are described as seeking after 'smooth things' (T, Z). Further, their external enemies are the 'Kittians (Caittians)' (H, W). The mass of ordinary members are 'the Many' (D, Z), who are 'living as a unity' (D, Z) in the 'last generation' (H, Z), they are under an 'inspector' or 'censor' (D, Z), and they have a 'prince of the whole congregation' (W v 1, Z ix 9) and a 'Teacher of Righteousness' or 'Rightful Teacher' at their head (H, Z); they look for a Messiah or perhaps Messiahs from Aaron and Israel, *i.e.* a priestly and a lay Messiah (D, Z); they call the angels 'holy ones' (D, T, W) and owe allegiance to the 'prince of lights' against the 'angels of destruction', and they hope for 'eternal' or 'victorious life' as their final reward

[1] In *BJRL* XL 274.   [2] Pp. 359–73.   [3] Pp. 18.
[4] Cp. Burrows in *Oudt. St.* VIII 180–4.   [5] Pp. 305–10.

(D, Z). They have their own terminology, which includes special terms for such conceptions as the 'community' (D, Z) and the common 'council' (D, Z), for 'convention, prescribed ordinance' (D, T, W), for a 'lot, party' of people (D, W) and for communal and military 'organization' (D, W), for 'order, rank' (D, H, W), for the 'crucible' in which men are tested (D, W, T), for the 'sabbath of rest' (H, W)[1] and also for a defined 'period of time' (D, H, T, W, Z); and they observe their own peculiar calendar (D, W, Z). Further, two of the Scrolls have a unique word, otherwise unknown in Hebrew literature, for 'body, limb' or the like (D iv 20, T xvii 25 and fr. xlvii 5). Lastly, the Wicked Priest who pursued the Rightful Teacher on the Day of Atonement sought 'to swallow him up' (H xi 5), and one of the survivors long afterwards, giving thanks for his escape, possibly echoed that event when he exclaimed in similar language 'I will answer them that would swallow me up' (T ix 8), if the expression is there rightly explained.[2] Many ideas and concepts also overlap in several Scrolls (D, Z);[3] and a noticeable feature running through a number of them (D, H, T, W, Z) is the development of the doctrine of the last things which shows that 'all the documents of this sequence belong to a single cycle of waning and waxing eschatological hope'[4] These overlapping contacts can hardly be accidental; the various Scrolls, therefore, are inextricably bound up with one another and cannot be treated in isolation.[5]

4. SCROLL OF COPPER

A unique object, already mentioned,[6] in the possession of the Kingdom of Jordan is the Scroll of copper, found in Cave III. This cave yielded very few manuscript scraps, although fragments of forty jars and twenty-six lids showed that it had once held a collection of books. The disappointment of the excavators, however, was offset by the discovery of a rolled-up strip of copper lying against the wall of the cave, near to its entrance. This strip was broken across at an inner riveting into two separate 'scrolls'; these had once formed a single plate of metal measuring about 8 feet in length and 12 inches in width. Traces of other riveting in the centre of the larger scroll showed that there had once been three sheets. The metal was heavily oxidized, but Hebrew or Aramaic letters indented in reverse could be seen on the outside. The pieces were therefore taken to the College of Technology at Manchester, where they were successfully unrolled,[7] where-

---

[1] G. Mishnah *Tamid* viii 4.   [2] Pp. 128–30, 269–71.
[3] Brownlee in *BA* XIII 50–6.
[4] Rabinowitz in *VT* III 180.   [5] Pp. 371–3.
[6] Pp. 18.   [7] Baker Wright in *BJRL* XXXIX 45–56.

upon the Scroll was found to carry twelve columns of script. The subject of the text, surprisingly enough, as Dr. Kuhn had already divined,[1] was a list of treasure with the places where it was hidden. The hiding places, some sixty in number, are mostly in or near Jerusalem; but a few may have been as far away as Bethshean (if this name is rightly read) and Mt. Gerizim (if the Samaritan hill of this name and not another of the same name near Jericho is meant)[2] in the north and Hebron in the south.[3]

Two accounts of this Scroll have been published, one by Fr. Milik giving only a translation of the Hebrew text before publication[4] and another by Mr. Allegro giving both a transcript of the text and a translation;[5] the two renderings differ to a considerable extent in matters of detail, but the discrepancies cannot be reconciled or removed until a photograph of the original text is published.

The details of the treasure as given respectively by Fr. Milik (marked M) and Mr. Allegro (marked A) are the following:

gold	324 (M) or 1927 (A) talents
silver	2209 (M) or 675 (A) talents
gold and silver mixed . .	1928½ (M) or 1928 (?)+x(A) talents
gold in bars, numbering .	165 (M) or 65 (A)
silver in bars, numbering .	600 (M)
bars of unspecified metal, worth	4 double minas (M) or staters (A)
vessels of gold and silver, worth	71 talents and 20 minas (M, A)
vessels of gold and silver with their contents, worth	600 talents of silver (M, A)
vessels of gold and silver (A) or vessels with such contents (M), numbering . .	609 (M, A)
pots of silver (M) or pots filled with silver (A), numbering . . .	2 (A)
pitchers of silver, numbering	6 (A)

The list further includes a considerable amount of miscellaneous stuff, namely 'much silver' (M), many vessels full of aromatic spices (M) or tithe-offerings (A) of various sorts (dema', probably incense[6] rather than offerings of tithe[7]), stuff dedicated to the use of the Temple and the priesthood (ḥērem), and quantities of coin ('aslām, if the word is rightly so translated (A)), of garments and of books (sᵉfārîm);[8] it includes also a chest with its contents, which are not specified, and twenty jars 'smeared with pitch' (M) which, if the word is rightly trans-

---

[1] In *RB*, NS LXI 193–205 and *TLz.* LXXXI 541–6.
[2] Cp. Allegro *Treasure* 75–8. [3] Pp. 374–5. [4] In *RB*, NS LXVI 323–8.
[5] In *Treasure* 32–55. [6] Cp. Driver in *JSS* VI 276.
[7] Cp. Lauterbach *Mekilta* III (*Kaspa* 1) p. 153 ll. 88–90. [8] P. 377.

lated, are interesting in view of the care with which the jars containing the Scrolls seem to have been sealed.[1]

The uncertainties in the interpretation of this document are due not only to the difficulty of reading the text and the use of words which are unknown or if known may have unusual meanings, but also to the scribe's frequent failure to say whether gold or silver or what unit of weight is meant; and this is unfortunately a common omission in Jewish historical works.[2] Even so, the quantities at the outside (namely $6105 + x$ talents of gold and silver, with 765 bars and 617 vessels of these metals) do not mount up to an impossibly large sum.

There is indeed nothing absurd or improbable in connection with this Scroll of copper, and its authenticity cannot be doubted.[3]

Inscribed tablets of metal must have been well known to many Jews. Seleucus I Nicator (312–280 B.C.), conferring various privileges on the Jewish community in Antioch, had them engraved on plaques or tablets of copper, which Mucianus and Titus refused to remove;[4] the treaty which Judas the Maccabee made with the Romans c. 162–161 B.C.[5] and the decree recording the services of Simon the Maccabee to the Jewish nation and conferring on him the office of high-priest in 140 B.C. were also engraved on tablets of bronze;[6] and Caesar's decree in 44 B.C. making certain awards and concessions to the Jews was similarly published.[7]

The amount of buried treasure listed on the Scroll, too, does not seem to be beyond all reason in comparison with the wealth known to have belonged to or to have been stored in the Temple; for this is said to have served, like other temples in antiquity, also as a bank.[8] Early in the 2nd century B.C. Heliodorus was informed that wealth in the treasury of Jerusalem was 200 talents of gold and 400 talents of silver,[9] including 'many myriads' of private money deposited there because of the sanctity of the Temple;[10] Antiochus IV Epiphanes c. 170 B.C. took 1800 talents of unspecified treasures;[11] the high-priest Aristobulus II c. 65–63 B.C. was lavish with bribes (derived, presumably whether directly or indirectly, from public funds), of which Gabinius got 300 talents and Scaurus 300 or 400 (for the figure varies in the accounts)[12] of unspecified metal, while Pompey received a vine of gold worth 500 talents;[13] Pompey in 63 B.C. found stored in it 2000 talents of 'sacred money', vessels of solid gold and an accumulation of spices,

---

[1] Cp Mishnah *Sanhedrin* X 6.   [2] Cp. p. 33.
[3] Cp. Rabin in *Jew. Chron.* 15 vi [1956], 19 and Kuhn in *TLz.* LXXXI 544-5.
[4] Josephus *Antiquities* XII iii 1 §§ 119–21 and *War* VII v 2 §§ 108–11.
[5] I Macc. viii. 22.   [6] I Macc. xiv. 27, 48–9.
[7] Josephus *Antiquities* XIV x 3 § 197.
[8] II Macc. iii. 6; Josephus *War* VI v 2 § 282.   [9] II Macc. iii. 11.
[10] IV Macc. iv. 3.   [11] II Macc. v. 21.
[12] Josephus *Antiquities* XIV ii 3 §§ 30–2, iii 2 § 37 and *War* I vi 2 § 128.
[13] *Ibid.*, XIV iii 1 §§ 34–6.

all of which he spared, and the Romans in a short space of time collected 10,000 talents from the state;[1] Crassus in 54 B.C. found the 2000 talents in cash which Pompey had left in the treasury and stripped the sanctuary of all its gold amounting to 8000 talents (apparently gold worth 8000 talents of silver) besides other objects of value;[2] Sabinus in 4 B.C. collected some 400 talents;[3] and Florus in A.D. 66 extracted 17 talents as a fine from the Temple.[4] Unfortunately, the historian again does not specify gold or silver in several of these cases.[5] The treasure, however, whatever its amount in either or both metals, would probably have increased considerably between the time of Pompey and the First Revolt, which was a period of general prosperity in the Roman Empire; but common prudence would have dictated that as much as possible should be stowed away in hiding places, which would have been kept closely guarded secrets, before the outbreak of hostilities in A.D. 66.

Gold and silver, too, seem to have been concealed in other places in Jerusalem besides the Temple. So, for example, Hyrcanus I, who had already in 134–5 B.C. been able to pay 500 talents of silver (taken presumably from the treasury or the Temple) to Antiochus Sidetes as his price for raising the siege of Jerusalem and withdrawing the Syrian army,[6] was driven *c.* 127–126 B.C. to ransack David's tomb, from which he took 3000 talents of silver to levy a mercenary force.[7] Long afterwards, Herod the Great raided the same tomb, in which he found no coin but vessels of gold and other valuable objects, which he took away.[8] Stories, too, of hidden treasure were current in the 1st century A.D.[9] and the search for them occasionally ended in riots;[10] and these might well have some foundation in fact, however unhistorical they might be in form.

The only real difficulties lie in such small points as the large quantity of treasure stored in some of the receptacles, *e.g.* 80 talents of gold in 2 pitchers (SC vii 16) and the trifling value of odd deposits, *e.g.* 4 staters of gold hidden in the lining of a gutter (SC ix 1–3)[11]. These may be due to errors in the figures, which are common enough in ancient calculations; or they would perhaps disappear if the value of the weights and coins and the size of the vessels were accurately known.

Enough has been said to show that the contents of this Scroll fall well within the bounds of historical probability; but in spite of this the

[1] Josephus *Antiquities* XIV iv 4 § 72 and § 78 and *War* I vii 6 §§ 152–3.
[2] *Ibid.*, XIV vii 1 §§ 105–9 (s. Reinach *ap.* Marcus *Josephus* [Loeb] and *War* I viii 8 § 179.
[3] *Ibid.*, XVIII xvii 102 and *War* II iii 3 § 50.
[4] Josephus *War* II xiv 6 § 293.
[5] Pp. 32–3.
[6] Josephus *Antiquities* XIII vii 3 § 247.
[7] *Ibid.* 4 § 249.
[8] *Ibid.* XVI vii 1 §§ 179–80.
[9] II Baruch vi. 6–10.
[10] Josephus *op. cit.* XVIII iv 1 §§ 85–7.
[11] Allegro *op. cit.* 58–60.

authenticity of the record has been called in question, and various attempts have been made to explain it away.

The prevailing view is that the list is a record not of some actual treasure but legend or folk-lore,[1] *e.g.* of that which the patriarch Joseph was supposed to have amassed and which Moses was said to have hidden on Mt. Gerizim,[2] or of king Solomon's wealth,[3] or of that which the prophet Jeremiah was thought to have salved from the Temple and hidden;[4] and that, whichever it was, this was engraved on copper at some time between the First and the Second Revolt (A.D. 73–132). Indeed, not a few stories of hidden treasure were current.[5] Another theory[6] is that, since the list seems to include vast quantities of incense, of which the use was forbidden under pain of death except in the service of the Temple,[7] the treasure must have belonged not to the Covenanters, who in any case would not be likely to have possessed such immense wealth, but to the Temple, and that it was what had been salved when Nebuchadrezzar sacked it in 586 B.C.; and several copies, both on bronze and on marble, of a fictitious medieval account of the concealment of this treasure on Mt. Carmel are still extant.[8] The Scroll then would offer nothing but an imaginary list of treasures supposed to have been spirited away and hidden on that occasion; for a legend long persisted that the wealth of the First Temple would remain concealed only 'until God gather the people again together and mercy come', when it would reappear.[9] Both explanations are equally improbable; for why should a mere piece of folk-lore or a phantasy of the imagination be laboriously inscribed on costly sheets of copper which were then concealed in a remote cave? And this must have been done twice; for a second copy of the text with 'its interpretation' is said to have been made (cp. SC xii 10–13)[10] and found,[11] although this has been denied.[12] The detailed specifications, too, in the list are unlike folk-lore and give the impression of a genuine record, even if the figures are inaccurate or exaggerated, as they often are in ancient documents. Yet another suggestion, that the list must have been an 'ostentatious, fictitious inventory' of the treasures of the Temple used in Zadokite 'lodges' for the administration of oaths[13] seems far-fetched, even though Jesus, saying that 'whosoever shall swear by the temple, it is nothing; but whosoever shall swear by the gold of the temple, he is a debtor''[14] may

---

[1] Milik in *BA* XIX 63 and *RB*, NS LXVI 322–3; Cross *Library* 17–18.
[2] Josephus *Antiquities* XVIII iv 1 § 85; cp. II Baruch vi. 5–10.
[3] Midrash R. *Numbers* xv § 10.   [4] II Macc. ii. 4–8.
[5] Cp. Ginzberg *Legends of the Year* IV 320–21, 350.
[6] Mowinckel in *JBL* LXXVI 261–5.
[7] Exod. xxx. 37–8; cp. Lev. x. 1–2, Num. xvi. 1–40, 2 Chron. xxvi. 16.
[8] Milik in *RB*, NS LXVI 567–75.   [9] 2 Macc. ii. 4–8.
[10] Pp. 376–7.   [11] Rowley *Scrolls* 21.   [12] Milik in *RB* NS LXVI 321.
[13] Del Medico *Énigme* 255–61.   [14] Matt. xxiii. 16.

seem to lend colour to it; for nothing is actually known of such a practice amongst the Zadokites.

That the Scroll contains a list of real treasure hidden in or around Jerusalem is suggested by the repeated discovery of deposits of treasure by the Romans after the collapse of the First Revolt.[1] Another factor giving reality to this Scroll is the statement in it that some of the treasure was concealed 'in Zadok's tomb' (SC xi 2–7), since tombs were natural hiding places for treasure in antiquity in consequence of the sanctity attaching to them; so, for example, David's tomb was used for this very purpose.[2] There is, too, a tomb bearing the name of Zadok (whether rightly or wrongly and what Zadok is meant, are unknown), which may well have been one of the chosen hiding places; but the choice of this place, amongst others, will have had no necessary connection with the 'Sons of Zadok', *i.e.* the Zadokites or Sadducaeans of the Scrolls; for these people are very unlikely to have soiled their hands with the treasures of the Temple, the fruits of shameless plunder in their opinion (H ix 4–7).[3] However this might be, a tradition long survived[4] that the treasure of the Temple (fancifully said to have been collected by the patriarch Joseph) was reserved for 'the righteous (*saddîqîm*)', which is perhaps an error for 'Sadducaeans' or 'Zadokites (*Saddûqîm*)', as Mr. del Medico suggests;[5] and this would incidentally imply that the treasure of the Temple, or much of it, was successfully put away and survived the destruction of the Temple in A.D. 70 and so support the authenticity of this account of the places where it was hidden. The coincidence of names, however, may be purely fortuitous, and no weight can be attached to them.

As the Scroll shows, the hiding places fall into two main groups: those in and around Jerusalem and those in the country to the south-east of the city, towards the Dead Sea. If then it relates to the period of the First Revolt (A.D. 66–73), as argued below,[6] this division of the hiding places is easily explained: part of the treasure was kept, though concealed, close at hand where it would be readily accessible for the current expenses of the administration of the city and the Temple and of the conduct of the war, while the rest was stored away outside against the worst eventuality, the capture of the city. That much was still kept there would explain how the two priests, Jesus son of Thebouti and Phineas the treasurer of the Temple, could seek to save their own lives by surrendering sacred vessels of solid gold and precious stones, vestments and spices, to the Romans.[7] Josephus, too, would not be far from the truth in claiming[8] that the Temple, when burnt and razed

---

[1] Pp. 374–5.   [2] P. 33.   [3] Dupont-Sommer *Écrits Esséniens* 400.
[4] B. Talmud *Pesachim* 119a and *Sanhedrim* 110a; cp. Prov. xiii. 22.
[5] In *Énigme* 259–60.   [6] Pp. 374–5.
[7] Josephus *War* VI viii 3 §§ 387–91.   [8] *Ibid.* VI v 1 § 282 and ix 3 § 432.

to the ground by the Romans, contained 'vast sums of money, vast piles of raiment, and other valuables', and that 'many precious objects were found in these passages (*sc.* those under the city and the Temple)'. As much might have been found there and removed by the Romans as had been conveyed by the Jews to places of safety in the country.

A final point to which attention may be drawn is this: the Hebrew statement of the amount of each commodity is accompanied in several places by Greek or Latin letters used as numbers to give the same information.[1] Such notices could only have served any useful purpose in an age when the Greek and Latin languages were both as familiar to Jews as Hebrew; and such a device would hardly have been introduced by a mere story-teller. The most probable period for these additions would be the 1st century A.D., when most Jews had some acquaintance with all three languages.[2]

These problems cannot be definitely solved until the position of all the Scrolls in history has been decided and must therefore be held over for final discussion until the general problem has been settled.[3]

5. EXCAVATIONS AT QUMRÂN AND 'AIN FĂŠHAH

The caves, now famous for the Scrolls found in them, are situated on the cliffs to the N.W. and S.W. of the ruins of Qumrân, which are significantly called also the 'Jews' Ruin' (*Hirbät Yahûd*);[4] these lie on a spur of the steep range of hills overlooking the Dead Sea, on its western side, at a point approximately one mile inland and ten miles from the mouth of the Jordan. The site was visited by de Saulcy in 1851, who concluded[5] that it was the ancient Gomorrah; but, as Clermont-Ganneau at once pointed out,[6] this identification had neither philological nor other evidence to support it. The origin of the name, too, is still disputed. It has been derived from the Arabic *qamr* 'moon' and interpreted therefore as meaning 'lunar'; this, Fr. North suggests,[7] might connect it with Jericho, of which the name has (though with great improbability) been connected with the Hebrew *yeraḥ* 'moon' and so been thought to suggest that the place was a centre of moon-worship. The most likely suggestion, perhaps, is that of Fr. Milik,[8] who identifies it with *Calamon*, the name given by monastic writers to the coastal plain where the Jordan enters the Dead Sea; here the pilgrim Chariton lived *c.* A.D. 320 with his followers in caves overlooking the

---

[1] Ullendorff in *VT* XI 227–8.   [2] Cp. Lk. xxiii. 38 and Jn. xix. 19–20.
[3] Pp. 374–7.   [4] Masterman in *PQS* XXXIV 161.
[5] In *Voyage autour de la Mer Morte* II 165–7.
[6] In *Archaeological Researches in Palestine* II 14–16.   [7] In *CBQ* XVI 427.
[8] In *RB*, NS LX 538[8]; cp. Milik & Cross *ibid.* LXIII 75.

sea.[1] That it is the City[2] of Salt mentioned in the division of the land amongst the tribes after the conquest of Canaan[3] is uncertain but possible.[4]

Clermont-Ganneau explored the site in 1873-4 and described[5] the ruins as insignificant. He found some low stone-walls, much broken down, with a small pool entered by some steps; and he also reported that the whole site was strewn with potsherds of all descriptions and that, if there ever had been a town there, it must have been very small. The main plateau and the neighbouring mounds were covered by a large number of tombs. Dalman, who also had visited the site, described it in two articles in 1914 and 1920.[6] He said that no traces of any ancient buildings were visible and that the ruins could not represent a Christian monastery, since no tradition of a church in this neighbourhood existed; a fragment of the base of a pillar which he saw suggested a Roman or Byzantine edifice. He concluded that the ruins were those of a military outpost of the Roman period,[7] which is not in some respects far from the truth.[8]

In 1949 Mr. Harding and Fr. de Vaux carried out a preliminary sounding of the ruins but found no evidence connecting them with the contents of the cave.[9] When they resumed work in 1951, however, they thought, arguing chiefly from the pottery, that the site had been used at the same time and by the same people as the caves, and that the cemetery could be assigned to the same period.[10] The excavation of the site was completed in the course of campaigns conducted in 1953 and 1954.[11]

The ruins show four levels of buildings. The lowest reveals only scanty traces of a fort which can be assigned on the evidence of the script on an inscribed stamp and a potsherd to the Israelite period (8th-7th centuries B.C.); and they have accordingly, even though somewhat speculatively, been connected[12] with king Jehoshaphat (c. 870-848 B.C.) who 'built castles and cities of stone in Judah'[13] or with king Uzziah (c. 767-739 B.C.) who 'built towers in the wilderness and hewed out many cisterns'.[14] This building afterwards lay in ruins for several centuries, when a modest structure was erected on the same site (Level I A), possibly in the times of the high-priests Jonathan

---

[1] Migne *Patrol. Gr.* CXV 909-12 § 10; cp. §§ 8, 11-12.
[2] Or perhaps 'Depression' (Heb. *'îr* = Arab. *ġuwair* 'little depression').
[3] Joshua xv. 61-2.
[4] Noth in *ZDP-V* LXXI 111-23; s. Gasov-Ginzberg in *Palestinskiy Sbornik* IV [LXVII] 12-16 and de Vaux *Archéologie* 71-2.
[5] In *op. cit.* II 14-15.   [6] In *P.-Jb.* X 9-11 and XVI 40-1.
[7] Cp. Masterman in *PQS* XXXV 264-7.   [8] Pp. 46-50.
[9] De Vaux in *RB*, NS LVI 586[2].   [10] De Vaux *ibid.* LX 83-106.
[11] De Vaux *ibid.* LXI 206-36 and LXIII 533-77.   [12] Cp. Milik *Dix Ans* 41-4.
[13] 2 Chron. xvii. 2, 12-13 (s. Du Buit *Géographie de la Terre Sainte* 161).
[14] 2 Chron. xxvii. 10.

D

(160–143 B.C.) or Simon (143–134 B.C.); this followed the main lines
of the fort but was improved with channels and a cistern for water and
several separate chambers. The buildings of the next period were
greatly elaborated (Level I b) and indeed laid down the lines which
those of the next would follow; they were apparently, according to the
evidence of the coins found in them, put up just before or about the
time when John Hyrcanus I became high-priest (135–104 B.C.) and
were continuously occupied till the time of the high-priest Mattathias
(40–37 B.C.) and perhaps till the great earthquake of 31 B.C.,[1] which
left its mark in several great cracks across them. These buildings then
lay in ruins for most of the reign of Herod the Great (37–4 B.C.), were
restored and reoccupied (Level II) early in the reign of Archelaus
(4 B.C.–A.D. 6) and were continuously occupied till the First Revolt of
the Jews against Rome (A.D. 66–73). They were then completely
destroyed; but a small fort of crude Roman work was constructed out
of the ruins (Level III), which were intermittently occupied till the
Second Revolt (A.D. 132–5), when Jewish rebels again used them.[1]
This approximate chronology, based on the evidence of pottery and
coins, agrees also with that of the palm-wood found in the 'monastery',
for which the test of radioactive carbon gives a mean date of c. 7 B.C.–
A.D. 18, each with a deviation of 80 years.[2] Thus the main period in
the history of the site was the Graeco-Roman, which was also that of
the Scrolls. Finally, a few Byzantine and Arab coins afford evidence
that it may have been sporadically occupied or visited during those
epochs.[3]

   The area covered by the ruins of Level II is rectangular, measuring
approximately 30 by 40 yards; and these must be described in some
detail in view of their importance for the study of the Scrolls.

   An aqueduct, bringing water from the neighbouring ravine, called
Wâdī Qumrân, entered this enclosure at the north-western corner, from
which it was distributed amongst numerous cisterns in both blocks of
buildings. The rooms to the south of the point at which the aqueduct
came in, covering the whole western side of the enclosure, were non-
residential, being used as workshops or store-rooms; several cisterns
lay on either side of a channel running from the aqueduct southwards
and discharging its water into a large cistern.

   At the north-western end of the main block of buildings, which
measured 30 metres by 37 metres, the excavators found the remains of
a massive tower, two stages high, of which the walls were more than
3 feet thick. It had several rooms which had no windows, except for
two slits in one wall, but which communicated directly with one
another; it had no door on the outside and was separated by two un-

---

[1] Josephus *Antiquities* XV v 2 § 121 and *War* I xix 3 §§ 370–1.
[2] Burton *ap.* Sutcliffe *Monks* 38–9.   [3] De Vaux *Archéologie* 1–39, 91.

roofed passages on the east and the south from the rest of the building. Its base was strengthened on all sides by embankments of stone, possibly raised after the earthquake which greatly damaged the buildings in 31 B.C. This tower was clearly no merely ornamental feature but was intended to serve as a defensive work and goes far to show that the whole complex of buildings was no ordinary monastery; it had served also a military purpose.

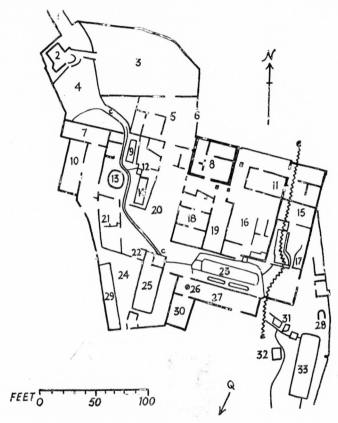

Plan of building before the earthquake at Qumrân (Level II)[1]

KEY TO PLAN (reproduced by kind permission of Fr. R. de Vaux):

    1, Aqueduct; 2, 31, baths; 3, 5, 16, 20, 24, courtyards; 4, reservoir; 6, main entrance; 7, 10, store-rooms; 8, tower; 9, 12, 13, 14, 23, 25, 33, cisterns; 11, kitchen; 15, 17, latrines; 18, library; 19, *scriptorium*; 21, oven; 22, mill; 26, *podium*; 27, hall of assembly; 28, potter's kiln; 29, stables; 30, pantry; 31, potter's pool.

    Q way to Qumrân; c conduit; e . . . e rift caused by earthquake.

[1] De Vaux in *R.B.*, *N.S. LXI* 206–36 (plans v and vi) and LXIII 545–47 (plan).

To the east of the tower was a room with several fireplaces, which was perhaps the kitchen; adjoining this room to the south were perhaps the laundry and the latrines. To the south of the tower were several large rooms, which would probably be those in which the community transacted its ordinary business and worked; for the middle room, which was thought to be the library, had a long low bench of plaster running along the walls. To the east of these rooms ran a long narrow chamber, measuring 40 feet by 13 feet;[1] it contained a number of curiously shaped fragments of plaster which, when put together, formed long narrow tables[2], one of them 16 feet long, a bench and a low platform with two shallow depressions hollowed out on the top.[3] The purpose of these objects seemed obvious when three ink-wells,[4] one of bronze and two of earthenware, both work of the Roman period, were discovered; one of them still held some dried ink. The room might have been the *scriptorium* or office of the community or perhaps the office of members of the Jewish resistance or of a Roman garrison;[5] the shallow depression, then, might have contained water for the use of the scribes employed in it.

Another large chamber, whether assembly-hall or refectory, capable of seating some two hundred people, was uncovered to the south of the main block of buildings. This chamber measures 22 metres by $4\frac{1}{2}$ metres; and it has a slightly raised circular podium, of which the purpose is unknown. The only suggestion offered so far is that it might have been a dais from which one of the members of the community read an edifying work aloud during meals,[6] as in modern monasteries; but nothing is known of such a practice amongst Jews. The discovery of some thousand bowls stacked in an adjoining room supports the suspicion that this chamber or hall may have been the community's refectory; but it is an objection to this conjecture that the supposed kitchen does not adjoin the hall. That, however, is often the case in colleges at Oxford and Cambridge. Contrariwise, if it was the assembly hall, what was the reason for stacking an immense number of bowls in the adjoining room?

One of the most interesting discoveries was made at the south-eastern quarter: this was a kiln for pottery, the best-preserved factory so far uncovered in Palestine, constructed apparently before the earthquake of 31 B.C.[7] Here the community perhaps made their domestic vessels, such as the bowls found in the pantry and probably also those in which the Scrolls were packed. These are of an unsual though not unique type, since similar jars have been found in Egypt;[8] and they

[1] Muilenberg in *BASOR* CXXXV 28.   [2] S. pp. 403–4.
[3] Van der Ploeg *Qumran* 78–9.   [4] De Vaux in *RB*, NS LXI 211–12.
[5] Del Medico *Énigme* 99–101.   [6] Del Medico & Garner *Riddle* 89.
[7] Zeuner in *PQS* XCII 30–3.   [8] Milik *ap.* Molin *Söhne* 198.

can hardly have been designed to hold the Scrolls, as they seem to have been used also for domestic purposes. They are cylindrical, some as much as 2 feet high and 10 inches in diameter, and they had inverted bowls which served as lids. The texture of the pottery was that of the Roman period, which would agree well with the date suggested by coins and other evidence for the occupation of the site[1]. Other rooms were used for flour-mills and storage-bins and as workshops, in which tools of metal were discovered. Thus the 'monastery' would be a self-contained unit. Further, a containing wall joined it to the buildings at ʿAin Fäšhah together with the adjacent farm-land, making a single estate.

No manuscripts have come to light in the ruins; but some potsherds bearing proper names and a copy of the Hebrew alphabet, dating from an early phase of the occupation and intended apparently for the use of a learner or learners or for the guidance of masons (who indicated the order in which stones were to be laid by scratching letters on them),[2] have been found. The Scrolls therefore, or at any rate such as were composed before the destruction of the place, might have been written here; but nothing has been found either to prove or to disprove this generally accepted conjecture.[3]

In the same quarter two large cisterns were uncovered, several large sinks and a latrine. These cisterns were lined with plaster, and the deepest were entered by a flight of fourteen steps; the upper steps were railed off into four passages. The water was brought into them by a channel from another large cistern just outside the southern wall. The water for all these was conveyed across the plateau from the natural reservoirs at the base of the cliffs by an aqueduct of stone, running partly through a tunnel, of which traces still remain. Seven other large cisterns and six small pools, basins or baths have also been uncovered and cleared.

The total number of plastered cisterns and artificial pools, which would hold enough water for the community living in the buildings for the nine or ten months of the year when the cascades which fed them were dry, is estimated to be about forty;[4] the two largest cisterns measured respectively about 18 yards by 5 yards and 15 yards by 4 yards. Their purpose has been much debated and has become the subject of many guesses. The huge open cisterns were entered by steps running down into them, the large ones by steps as wide as themselves and the small ones by narrow steps down one side; in the large cistern constructed inside the southern wall the steps are divided into small groups of three or four with a wide step separating each group from the next, and in that at the south-eastern corner just outside the main

---

[1] Pp. 49, 460–7.   [2] Cp. Driver *Semitic Writing*[2] 115–17.
[3] Pp. 46–7.   [4] Cross *Library* 49.

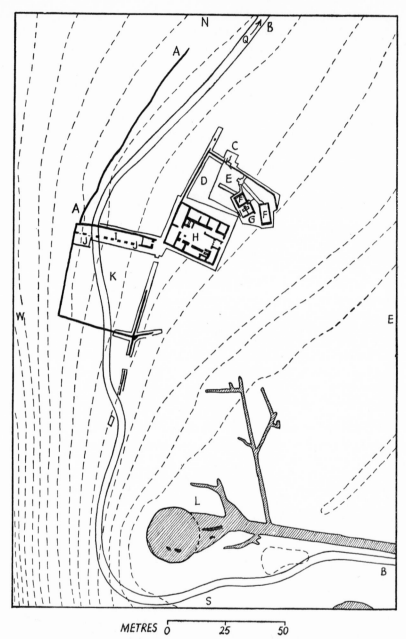

Plan of buildings at 'Ain Fäšḥah (De Vaux in *R.B.*, *N.S. LXVI* 225-55 (plan i).)

A, wall joining farm at 'Ain Fäšḥah with monastery at Qumrân; B, modern track;
C, conduit; D, small courtyard; E, vat; F, cisterns; G, tannery or fish-breeding
installation (?); H, courtyard surrounded by living rooms, offices and store-
chambers; I, rooms for drying dates; J, shelters; K, large courtyard; L, spring
('Ain Fäšḥah). Q way to Qumrân.

building the uppermost of the fourteen steps are railed off into three gangways as though to guide people into the water. These steps, too, have inspired various suggestions. On the one hand, the prevalent idea is that the cisterns and tanks were constructed for baptismal or other lustral rites[1] demanding total immersion, for which steps would be a convenience if not a necessity. No archaeological evidence for such a use of the cisterns has been produced, while the archaeologist's inclination to take every pool for a sacred spring and every cistern for a font and the danger of exaggerating the argument from their existence must not be overlooked. That the Covenanters required baptism as a condition of admission to their society is by no means clear or certain;[2] and, even if they had required it, such extensive installations could not have been needed for occasional celebrations of the rite. The number of cisterns, too, would be excessive for lustration from impurity incurred by contact with the world, since the members living at Qumrân had little to do with it. Further, how far water, which might often have been long-standing and stagnant, would satisfy the Rabbinical regulations governing ritual bathing might often have been open to doubt.[3] At Qumrân the water of the spring called 'Ain Fäšhah, though slightly saline,[4] or that of the Jordan, which was hardly too far away, would surely have been preferred for baptisms.[5] On the other hand, the Roman bath-house was well known in Palestine in the Rabbinic period and would readily have suggested the desirability of, and afforded a means of, bathing for a large community of men working out of doors in a hot climate;[6] and stepped reservoirs have been found elsewhere, both at Gezer[7] and in Jerusalem.[8] The obvious conclusion, which Dr. Cross draws,[9] is that the cisterns at Qumrân are typical examples of reservoirs well known from other sites and that the small pools, including the shallow pool at the entrance to the settlement, will have been baths; no one is likely to have bathed in the cisterns, which must have contained water for drinking as well as for other purposes. The quantity of water required by a community possibly numbering some two hundred persons,[10] for ordinary mundane purposes as well as for the fulfilment of such ritual needs as the Covenanters recognized, must have been enormous. The intense heat of the valley of the Dead Sea, which is the deepest rift below sea-level in the whole world, will have induced excessive perspiration, making drinking water and baths an ever-present

---

[1] Dupont-Sommer & Barnett *Jewish Sect of Qumran* 167–8.
[2] Pp. 496–505.   [3] Cp. Schürer *Geschichte*[3] II 481–3.
[4] Masterman in *PQS* XXXV 267 and De Vaux in *RB*, NS LXVI 230.
[5] Nielsen *Håndskrift fundene i Juda Orken* 81; cp. Wernberg-Møller in *JSS* II 410.
[6] Jacobs in *JSS* II 357–8.   [7] Macalister *Excavation of Gezer* I 274–6.
[8] Macalister *Excavations in Palestine* 21.   [9] In *Library* 49–50.
[10] Cp. De Vaux *Archéologie* 69–70.

need; the cisterns will have required constant cleansing to keep the water sweet and wholesome, so that the steps can easily be explained as intended for the convenience of the cleaners; and the rapid evaporation of the water in the heat in a place where the rainfall is only 4–8 inches in the year,[1] as well as the number of people using it and the varied purposes to which it may have been put, will account for the large number and great size of these reservoirs.[2]

A wall ran from the west of these buildings to the north-western corner of the farmstead at 'Ain Fäšḫah; it was perhaps once the boundary of the whole 'monastic estate', comprising the settlements at both places.[3] The buildings here have the usual rooms and court-yards characteristic of a farm; but the most remarkable features are apparently a place for drying dates and two chambers with basins far from the various springs, used perhaps for preparing parchment from skins or tanning hides (although nothing definitely indicating a tannery has been found in them[4]; they are however at the N.E. end of the buildings, approximately in accordance with Rabbinic law requiring a tannery to be situated on the E. side of a town[5]) or for breeding fish, which may once have been possible on a considerable scale, for the water-level seems to have fallen since Roman times.[6]

The difficulty of maintaining life at Qumrân seems to have been exaggerated;[7] for the farm at 'Ain Fäšḫah and the neighbourhood will have provided almost everything necessary for a modest subsistence,[8] as Dr. Masterman's reports[9] of several visits in the early years of the present century show[10]. The Bedouin come every year in January and February with flocks of camels, goats and sheep; they live in the caves round Qumrân (which may explain why the contents of so many of them have been found disturbed and damaged), while their beasts find pasture in the neighbourhood. The climate at 'Ain Fäšḫah is fresher and healthier than in the main coastal plain; it catches the breezes and is well watered. A number of springs discharge themselves into a pool near the farm; this measures some 60 feet across and is also fed by several springs from underneath, and fish are found at one end of it. Many small springs also irrigate the slopes running down to the shore, and their water, though brackish in places, is generally drinkable. Fish, too, can be found even in the Dead Sea where the fresh water from these springs is poured into it. The occupants of

---

[1] Wright in *BA* XXII 99.   [2] Cp. De Vaux *op. cit.* 98–9.
[3] Cp. Bardtke in *TLz.* LXXXV 265–b.
[4] De Vaux in *RB*, NS LXVI 232–6, 255 and *Archéologie* 59, 62–6; cp. Poole & Reed in *PQS* XCIII 114–23.
[5] Mishnah *Baba Bathra* ii 9.   [6] Zeuner in *PQS* XLII 33–6.
[7] *E.g.* Del Medico *Énigme* 107.
[8] De Vaux *ibid.* 96–8; cp. Bardtke *Handschriftenfunde* II 12–17, 185–6.
[9] In *PQS* XXXIV 160–7 XXXVI 167–8 XL 160–1, 197.
[10] Cp. Farmer in *Th. Zeitschr.* XI 298–304.

Qumrân may also have grown their vegetables in the vicinity, if Fr. de Vaux is right in supposing[1] that Johannes Moschus of Jerusalem, who visited the neighbourhood towards the end of the 6th century A.D. and died *c*. A.D. 619 at Rome, refers[2] to this place when he speaks of a vegetable garden cultivated by anchorites 'at the sixth mile-stone' from a place called Μαρες, which may be alMird;[3] for this lies about 9 km. from ʿAin Fäšḥah. The desert-olive[4] and the palm may also have grown here[5] but it cannot be proved; for the beams of palm-wood and the kernels of dates found in the various caves and buildings are no proof *que le palmier était autrefois cultivé aux environs*,[6] since they may have been imported from elsewhere (*e.g.* Jericho or Engedi). Lastly, both game (conies, gazelles, ibex, jackals, wild boar) and fowl (pigeons, grouse, partridges, wild duck and geese) are plentiful in the whole district.[7] Whether however the natural resources of the region can have sufficed for the continuous maintenance of so large a community as that at Qumrân is supposed to have been during several centuries must remain an open question; poor soil may quickly become exhausted and wild life is easily driven away or extinguished.

Extending to the east of the buildings at Qumrân is a vast cemetery[8] containing some 1200 graves, laid out in parallel rows. The bodies lay on their backs in a small mortuary chamber at the bottom of a trench, closed in by a little wall of unbaked brick and a slab of stone; and each grave was marked by two upright stones with a row of pebbles between them. The heads were towards the south and the feet to the north in accordance with a custom still followed by Qara'ite Jews.[9] No objects of value had been buried with the bodies; but a few potsherds found in the filling of the graves were of the same ware as those found in the monastery, so that the bodies were in all probability those of members of the community. Only men (none apparently over forty years of age) were buried in the main cemetery, except for one woman whose grave was out of alignment with the rest; but skeletons of four women and one child were found in an annex at its eastern end and those of one man and one woman in another annex[10]. The presence of these few skeletons might prove that the community was one which to some extent admitted married members;[11] but the preferable view, however, would seem to be that these women, who were very few, were buried apart from the men because they were not members of the community.[12]

[1] In *RB*, NS LXVI 265–6.
[2] Migne *Patrol. Gr.* LXXXVII iii (*Pratum Spirituale*) 3025 (§ 158).
[3] Cp. pp. 23, 109–110.   [4] Cp. 2 Sam. xv. 18 (Septuagint).
[5] Bardtke in *T. Lz.* LXXXV 265–6.   [6] De Vaux in *RB*, NS LXVI 229–30.
[7] Cp. de Vaux *Archéologie* 68–9.
[8] De Vaux & Steve in *RB*, NS LVI 102–38 and de Vaux *ibid.* LXIII 569–72; cp. Masterman in *PQS* XXXV 267.
[9] Dupont-Sommer *Nouveaux Aperçus* 107.   [10] De Vaux *Archéologie* 38, 46–7.
[11] De Vaux & Steve *ibid.* LVI 103.   [12] Cp. de Vaux *op. cit.* 96–7.

This conclusion agrees with the fact that women members seem to have been recognized in the ' camps ', *i.e.* in the groups living in the world, while they may not have been normally permitted in the 'monastery', *i.e.* at the headquarters of the community at Qumrân.[1]

The arguments and deductions of the archaeologists regarding the occupation of Qumrân and the neighbourhood raise several problems.

When did the Covenanters, if ever, occupy these buildings? The generally accepted opinion is that these people were the Essenes, who arose in the 2nd century B.C. and lived at Qumrân from their earliest beginnings or very soon afterwards but abandoned it after the earthquake in 31 B.C. and did not go back to it till after the death of Herod the Great in 4 B.C. The argument on this point is to the following effect. Herod can have had little liking for a religious group with moral principles totally at variance with his own way of life; he was, too, a lover of Greek culture and was especially hated by the Pharisees on account of his contempt for Jewish customs, even though he never actually broke with them; and he would not be likely to have tolerated one of the strictest of all the Jewish groups, possibly an offshoot of the Pharisaic party,[2] so near to his own palace at Jericho. Further, the Messianic hopes of the community and their impatience of any other ruler than God might have been regarded by him as a threat to his own dynasty and might easily have prompted him to drive the party out of his kingdom; for what he is said to have done when he heard about Him 'that is born king of the Jews'[3] and his threat shortly before his death to have the elders of Jerusalem executed[4] shows how he was ever ready to act against a potential or actual enemy. Finally, his dislike, even his fear, of the group would be augmented by the military nature of the 'monastery', which was at the same time a fortress, in which they lived; it could easily, too easily, become the resort of every person or group, criminal or political, opposed to his government. This final argument, however, excludes the possibility of identifying the Covenanters with the Essenes, with whom they are commonly confused;[5] for from early life 'he (*sc.* Herod) continued to have all the Essenes in honour'.[6]

A somewhat different sketch of the history of the site may therefore be attempted. That the original occupation goes back to the Israelite, *i.e.* pre-exilic, age may be accepted on archaeological grounds. Archaeology, however, can throw no light on the identity of these original occupants or of their successors; but written history may enable an outline of the occupation to be hazarded. The original buildings had possibly been built for political purposes; after the exile they perhaps

---

[1] P. 63.
[2] Pp. 94–5.
[3] Matt. ii. 1–18.
[4] Josephus *Antiquities* XVII vi 5 §§ 174–8.
[5] Pp. 100–21.
[6] Josephus, *op. cit.* XV x 5 § 378.

came to be used as a refuge from persecution or oppression, from injustice or even from justice. Early in the 2nd century B.C. Maccabaean or Hasidaean refugees might perhaps have taken possession of them and have even made them into a permanent settlement, as the Essenes established themselves further south at Engedi for similar reasons; there they would have remained, more or less unmolested, until the buildings were destroyed by an earthquake in 31 B.C. These were then abandoned till c. A.D. 4–6, when they were rebuilt. The new occupants, whom nothing connects with their predecessors, would be the followers of Judah and Saddok, dispersed after the abortive rising in A.D. 6, when Judah fell into the hands of the Romans. Such an adaptation of an old building to a new purpose would be nothing strange. So, for example, St. Athanasius in his account of St. Anthony's flight into the Egyptian wilderness, says[1] that 'he hurried to the mountains; and, having found a fort, so long deserted that it was full of creeping things, on the other side of the river (sc. the Nile), he crossed over and dwelt there', occupying it for twenty years, until 'it happened in the end that cells arose in the mountains, and another wilderness was colonized by monks'. Somewhat similarly the fort called Hyrcania or Hyrcanion, after being reduced to or falling into ruins, was rebuilt as a monastery and renamed Castellion or Marda (alMird) by Byzantine monks.[2] In fact, the conversion of ruins to some purpose quite alien to the intentions of the original builders is a commonplace of archaeology and history.

These last occupants of the buildings, which they had reconstructed ex hypothesi for their own purposes, were closely connected if not identical with the Covenanters and the Zealots, as argued below[3]. When then these parties came to an end with the suppression of the First Revolt of the Romans (A.D. 66–73), the buildings were destroyed or fell into ruin once again. The series of coins found in the ruins runs to A.D. 68–9; but this year must not be taken as the indisputable date of the destruction of the buildings, since the deposit of odd coins in a place is largely a matter of chance and cannot be accepted as fixing an absolute date in default of supporting evidence.[4] Yet, however the evidence afforded by them is evaluated, the general picture may be accepted as substantially correct; for the buildings, if not destroyed in A.D. 68–9, would hardly have been spared in A.D. 73, when the Revolt finally ended.[5]

Mr. Del Medico has argued[6] that the proximity of an extensive cemetery makes the site at Qumrân an unnatural place for a settlement of an ultra-orthodox Jewish community. An ordinary Jew became

---

[1] In *Life of St. Antony* (Robertson *Nicene and Post-Nicene Library* IV 199–200) §§ 12–14.
[2] Pp. 23, 45, 109–10.   [3] Pp. 237–51.   [4] Pp. 394–6.
[5] Pp. 395–6.   [6] In *Énigme* 109–11.

unclean by contact not only with a corpse but even with a grave[1] and would not touch mould rendered unclean by contact with a dead body;[2] and a Covenanter considered himself defiled by wood or stone or even dust which had been in contact with a corpse (Z xiv 15). These graves, too, were apparently not those of previous occupants of the site but of members of the society, so that the difficulty would only be increased; for Jews as strict as the Covenanters would not be likely to have buried the bodies of deceased members, as it were, at their front door, especially if it had been from the beginning a religious establishment. The distance, however, between the buildings and the nearest graves is some 40–50 metres, which is twice that required by Rabbinic law between a cemetery and a city, namely 50 cubits[3]; the argument therefore has no force.

Yet another difficulty is that, since the graves are as many as 1200 or thereabouts in the main cemetery and this number will be considerably exceeded when the neighbouring cemeteries have been examined, whereas the society's number is put at 150–200 members[4], they presuppose an abnormally high rate of mortality for a body of that size over some 100 years, c. 25 B.C.–A.D. 75[5]; this seems indeed to exceed that of any English monastery in the Middle Ages except during the 'Black Death'. This objection might perhaps be met by supposing that the bodies of deceased members living elsewhere were conveyed there for interment as in holy ground, as other religious groups bring those of their adherents to be buried beside the shrines of their saints; but no hint of such a practice can be found in the Scrolls themselves. Possibly, then, the neighbourhood, including the caves, harboured a number of people in addition to those resident in the buildings themselves.

Nothing that could be taken for a dormitory was found in the buildings. Did the Covenanters then sleep in the caves, some of which were found by the archaeologists to have been inhabited, although others were clearly uninhabitable?[6] A hatchet has indeed been found in Cave XI;[7] but nothing proves that it can or must have been put to the same natural purpose as the Essenes are said to have put the similar tool given to them at their initiation,[8] and it seems to have been quite unsuitable on the score of both shape and size for any such purpose. Its use therefore must have been quite different. Certainly, it can establish no connection between the Essenes and this cave; for the Essenes cannot be identified with the Covenanters,[9] and a hatchet must have been one of the commonest tools in the country.

[1] Num. xix. 11–16.   [2] Mishnah *Nazir* vii 2.
[3] Mishnah *Baba Bathra* ii 9.   [4] Strugnell & Milik *Discovery* 97.
[5] Cp. De Vaux *op. cit.* 45.   [6] De Vaux *Archéologie* 45–6.
[7] De Vaux *ibid.* 99–100, 104–5; s. *VT* IX 399–405.
[8] P. 101.   [9] Pp. 109–21.

The same point may be made of the pottery; for even though that in the 'monastery' and that in the caves, and especially the unique jars for the safekeeping of the Scrolls, are of the same type,[1] the people using it are not necessarily, even though they may well have been, identical. For example, the inhabitants of the 'monastery' might have

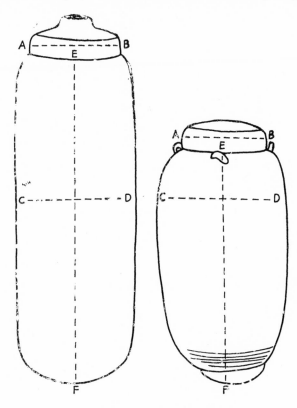

Jars from Cave I at Qumrân

$$I\begin{cases} \text{A—B: } 18\cdot6 \text{ cm.} \\ \text{C—D: } 25\cdot0 \text{ cm.} \\ \text{E—F: } 65\cdot7 \text{ cm.} \end{cases} \qquad II\begin{cases} \text{A—B: } 7\cdot5 \text{ cm.} \\ \text{C—D: } 26\cdot5 \text{ cm.} \\ \text{E—F: } 47\cdot5 \text{ cm.} \end{cases}$$

been one type of community, while the people living in the caves might have been totally different. That the community as a whole normally lived in the caves is beyond belief; these, even those improved by human hands,[2] were almost uninhabitable[3] (for even the Arab searchers and the archaeologists were able to stay in them for only very brief

---

[1] Pp. 406–7.   [2] De Vaux *Archéologie* 42–3, 45–6.   [3] S. p. 18.

periods of exploration on account of the intense heat), and their inaccessible positions would make all or at any rate many of them difficult to keep supplied from a farm several miles distant.[1] Nothing, too, in the texts suggests that the Covenanters lived like hermits in caves; but they might have concealed themselves in them with other refugees in times of persecution.

These objections are not intended to prove either that the Covenanters never lived in the caves or to exclude the possibility that a religious community occupied the buildings in the 1st century B.C. and the 1st century A.D.; the two suppositions are not mutually exclusive. At the same time the strength of the structures at Qumrân seems to indicate that they served not only a religious but also a military purpose, harbouring not only 'monks' but also other, *e.g.* political or revolutionary or military, groups. The problem, then, is to discover how such diverse groups can have been related to one another and what connection any of them may have with the Scrolls found in the caves; and the solution of this problem must be sought not on the archaeological but on the historical plane.

[1] De Vaux in *RB*, NS LXIII 576–7 and *Listener* LIX 1007–8.

II

PARTIES IN JUDAISM

1. COVENANTERS OF QUMRÂN

The doctrine and rule of life of the community at Qumrân are described in the *Manual of Discipline*[1] or *Rule of the Community*,[2] and in the *Zadokite Documents*. The former, which may be described as the *regula* of the order, sets out the doctrine of the community, the manner and terms of admission into it, and the rules governing the common life of those of its members who lived out of the world; the latter set out what is required of those who wish to join the community and then gives a number of rules regulating the life and conduct of its members living 'in the world', *i.e.* in or beside towns and villages. These would have been places where members had settled after escaping persecution, when wanted by the authorities or pressed by enemies in Palestine itself (Z xv 1); others went north, where the principal place would be Damascus itself (Z ix 8) or the surrounding territory (Z viii 6, 15; ix 8, 37).

Neither document is a unity; both are compilations, both perhaps based on or containing old matter. Indeed, a community has no need of written laws when it is young, its members few and its ardour unimpaired; these become necessary only when the zeal of the original members grows cool or is diluted by unworthy recruits or when through disaster or dispersion the rule is in danger of being corrupted or forgotten. Then compilers collect what information they can from traditions handed down from members long since dead and from the memories of old members still living and set it down in books which at once betray their composite origin; such works come not at the beginning but at the end of a long process of growth and development. The composite nature of *Discipline* has indeed been much exaggerated, principally by Mr. Del Medico,[4] but is tolerably clear; for example, the long section on the two instincts of man (D iii 13–iv 26) comes in strangely between sections on the classes of people who are to be admitted to or excluded from the community and on the social relations of its members; and the concluding section on the seasons observed and taught by wise men together with the closing poem (D ix 12–xi 22)

---

[1] Burrows in *Oudt. St.* VIII 156–7.
[2] Cp. Van der Ploeg *Excavations* 131, 170.   [3] Pp. 303–10.
[4] In *Deux Manuscrits* 27–30 and *Énigme* 155–62.

give the impression of having been awkwardly added after that dealing with the discipline of the community. The disunity of the *Zadokite Document(s)* is beyond doubt; it falls easily into two parts, which Dr. Rabin has named respectively the 'Admonition' (Z i 1–ix 28) and the 'Laws' (Z x 1–xx 12).[1]

The *Zadokite Documents*, as just said, begin the 'Admonition' with a historical introduction, which gives the reasons for and the occasion of the foundation of the society.

In the 390th year of the Captivity[2] God visited His people and caused a shoot to grow out of Israel and Aaron, although for twenty years the people remained as blind men groping after the way; He then considered that they sought Him in sincerity and raised up a Teacher of Righteousness or Rightful Teacher to make known what He would do to the last faithless generation which rejected Him (Z i 1–8). God's judgements on the wicked, whom He has always known and whose end has always been determined, are then described; and the wicked are listed from Noah down to the kings who, having entered into God's covenant, abandoned it. Yet God made an everlasting covenant with the righteous remnant, revealing to them the hidden things, notably the holy sabbaths and glorious feasts, in regard to which Israel had gone astray, His righteous laws, His true ways and the purpose of His will; all the glory of Adam[3] belongs to those that hold fast to them, and they are destined for eternal life. Meanwhile Belial (that is, wickedness personified) will be let loose in Israel, laying three snares—fornication, lucre, desecration—which will be made to resemble righteousness; he who escapes one will be caught by another. Fornication is then defined as taking two wives at the same time, in clear allusion to contemporary practice; this definition may be found helpful when the time comes to attempt the identification of the group.[4] Few escaped the general condemnation (Z i 9–viii 2). Nevertheless, God remembered the covenant which He had made with their forefathers and 'He raised men of understanding from Aaron and men of wisdom from Israel', *i.e.* both priests and laymen, and made the remnant listen to them; and 'these digged a well', which is the Law[5]. These are those who repented and, leaving the land of Judah, dwelt 'in the land of Damascus' (Z viii 3–6). This is no figure of speech but denotes the actual Damascus, in which a colony of the party had apparently long been settled.[6] These are they 'who have been brought into the covenant' (Z viii 11) or 'who enter the new covenant' (Z viii 15)[7], *i.e.* the members of the original covenant and those of the new covenant into which they have entered in exile

---

[1] In *Zadokite Documents*[2] x–xi (2–43 and 44–77).   [2] S. pp. 313–6.
[3] S. pp. 448–9.   [4] Pp. 86–8, 91, 260–1.   [5] S. p. 518.
[6] Pp. 303–7.   [7] Pp. 73–4, 305–10; cp. p. 454.

(Z viii 3–11);[1] the members of the community or society have therefore
been aptly named the 'Judaean covenanters'.[2] The covenant requires
them

to obey the law exactly;
to shun the 'sons of perdition';
to abstain from ill-gotten wealth;
not to lay hands on anything appropriated to the sanctuary;
not to rob the poor or widows or to procure the death of the orphan;
to distinguish clean from unclean, profane from holy;
to observe the Sabbath, all feast-days and fast-days;
to pay all their dues as required;
to love their neighbours as themselves;
to help the poor and needy and the stranger;
to seek one another's welfare;
not to commit any sin against their own kin;
to refrain from fornication;
not to bring a charge against anyone except by process of law;
not to cherish a grudge from one day to another;
to avoid all unclean things as properly prescribed;
not to defile the spirit of holiness within them (Z viii 12–20).

God's covenant will then be made good to all who faithfully
observe all these rules (Z viii 21).

All who reject God's offer of the covenant, like apostates in olden
times, will be delivered to the sword 'when the Messiah of Aaron and
of Israel appears' (Z ix 10);[3] all who enter into this covenant in the
land of Damascus but subsequently relapse shall not be reckoned
members of the community nor inscribed in the roster 'from the Day
of the ingathering of the "Unique Teacher" or the "Teacher of the
Community" (*sc.* to his forefathers) until a Messiah shall appear from
Aaron and from Israel' (Z ix 29); and those who, having entered it,
show themselves reluctant to fulfil its obligations will be expelled
from the community. This rule shall be applied also to all who join
the ranks of the scoffers; neither they nor their families have any share
in the Law (Z ix 2–38).

Then the author says 'from the day that he who used to teach the
Community' or 'the Unique Teacher is gathered in until all the men of
war who went aside with the Man of Falsehood' or 'Lies will be forty
years; and in that period the wrath of God will be kindled against
Israel, as He has said: there will be no king and no officer and no
judge and none to reprove in righteousness' (Z ix 39–40). The allusion
here refers to the time when country or party is without a ruler, but

---

[1] S. p. 73.   [2] Burrow in *Oudt. St.* VIII 157.
[3] Pp. 468–73.

E

what period is meant is much disputed and will be discussed hereafter.[1]

According to *Discipline* all the members of the community, who are described as 'passing' or 'entering into the covenant' (D i 20, 24 ii 10, 18),[2] bound themselves by a solemn oath in the presence of the Community to return whole-heartedly to the law of Moses as revealed to the Sons of Zadok, defined as the priests who shall keep the covenant and do God's will. No member 'might enter into water to attain the purity of holiness',[3] since men are purified not by baptism but by repentance (D v 13–14). God regards all who transgress His word as impure, and no member may associate with such persons in doctrine or law or in food. Members were forbidden especially to discuss religious questions with the 'men of perdition' but were urged to discuss 'knowledge of truth and right judgement with those who choose the right way, that their minds might be thus guided to understand God's ways and whatever was happening and to walk blamelessly in all that had been revealed in harmony with their fellows' (D v 7–13).

Members must shun the company of the perverse but adhere to the Community both in respect to doctrine and to property; they must abide by the decisions of the 'Sons of Zadok', *i.e.* the priests who are loyal to the covenant, and of the majority of the Community who follow them. They must together practise truth, humility, righteousness, justice, charity, decency; they must rid themselves of all 'uncircumcision of desire' and 'stiffness of neck'. They must lay a foundation of truth for Israel and be united in an indissoluble bond, making propitiation for priests and laymen who have dedicated themselves to a life of holiness, make common cause in suit and judgement and seek to convict all who transgress the law. Put briefly, the member must live in sanctity, loving the good and hating the evil, if he wished to understand the times. He must leave the pursuit of wealth to men of ill repute while himself acting in a manner acceptable to God in all that he undertakes, zealously and punctiliously fulfilling every precept of the Law 'against the day of vengeance'; he must make all his own actions well-pleasing to God, eschew all that He has not commanded and bless Him in all the vicissitudes of life (D v 3–20, ix 12–24).

Such were the general principles on which the constitution of the Covenanters was based and the circumstances in which it was founded and renewed.

The members of this society, like those of all religious groups, regarded themselves as 'the majority[4] of Israel who offered themselves for turning round to join His (*sc.* God's) covenant' (D v 22), in other words as the only true people of God; accordingly, the organization of their society was essentially theocratic.

When a man applied to be admitted a member of the community,

---

[1] Pp. 368–9.   [2] Pp. 72–3.   [3] P. 101.   [4] Pp. 59–60.

the 'officer (*paqîd*)[1] at the head of the Many'[2] examined his intelligence and his conduct; if he found him satisfactory, he admitted him to the covenant and instructed him in the rules. Until a period of probation had elapsed and his spiritual aptitude and conduct been tested, the candidate had nothing to do with the common funds and 'he must not touch the purity of the Many'. When he presented himself for admission to full membership, every member of the society was asked for his opinion about him, and he was then admitted or rejected by the votes of the majority. After spending a whole year with the community, the members reviewed his case; if he was approved by both the priests and the 'men of their covenant', *i.e.* fellow members in the society, his property and 'his work', *i.e.* anything that he had earned by his work, was handed over to the censor who had charge of the community's property; he entered them in the books but did not use them for the benefit of the community. After another year 'he (*sc.* the postulant) may touch the drink of the Many'; if after a final examination by the Many at the end of the year he was accepted as fit for membership, he was registered in the position which he was to occupy on all official occasions; he might then express his opinion and cast his vote on all matters submitted to the members of the community in session (D v 20–5, vi 13–23).[3]

These rules for the admission of a postulant to the society raise two questions of interpretation in the statements that on entering the probationary period of two years 'he may not touch the purity of the Many until they investigate his spirit and his conduct, until he has completed a full year' (D vi 16–17), and 'he shall not touch the drink of the Many until he has completed a second full year among the men of the community' (D iv 20–21). This rule is then repeated in negative form in respect to a lapsed member who, if he repents and returns to the society, shall be penalized (*i.e.* discommonsed) for two years: 'in the first he shall not touch the purity of the Many and in the second he shall not touch the drink of the Many, and he shall take his seat after all the men of the community' (D vii 19–20).

The problem is to decide what 'touching the purity' and 'touching the drink' of the Many exactly connote. First, the prevalent view has been that 'purity' denotes the general state of purity of the 'holy company', as the society is sometimes called (D v 20), while 'drink' is then taken as standing for the common meal (since the Hebrew term can have also this extended sense) of the members.[4] Alternatively, Dr. Liebermann has forcibly argued[5] that 'purity' must here connote solids while 'drink' denotes liquids, and this interpretation is almost certainly correct; for 'purity' was commonly used by the Rabbis as a

[1] S. p. 62.　　　　[2] S. pp. 58–60.　　　　[3] Pp. 114–6.
[4] Gaster *Scriptures* 60–1, 107 (58, 60).
[5] In *JBL* LXXI 203; cp. Rabin in *Scr. Jud.* II 79.

technical term for ritually pure articles, including solid food, while anything liquid was regarded as exceptionally liable to contract or spread ceremonial impurity because it ran. This explanation further agrees with the use of 'purity' in a concrete sense (D vii 25, where it is parallel with wealth), and with the reverse rule that no member of the society may eat or drink with anyone who refuses to join it (D v 16–17). It explains also why drink stands in the second position; for liquids called for special precautions to prevent contamination, and the candidate had therefore to be further advanced in his probation before touching it. Also, food and drink go well together as a natural pair; and admission to full membership, marked by eating and drinking together, is thus attained by stages. Second, the Hebrew verb translated 'touched (*nāgaʻ*)' nowhere connotes eating or drinking, as Fr. Sutcliffe points out,[1] so far as the dictionaries show; and the author or compiler of *Discipline* elsewhere proves himself capable of saying 'ate (*'āḵal*)' and 'drank (*šāṭāh*)' when he wishes (D v 16, vi 4–6). In the same way the corresponding Greek verb for 'to touch (ἅπτεσθαι)' is so used only negatively or metaphorically (where eating is not necessarily meant) or in reference to abnormal foods. Josephus too clearly distinguishes[2] between 'touching (ἅπτεσθαι)' and 'partaking (μεταλαμβάνειν)' of food; he says that Essene novices had to take fearful oaths 'before touching the common food', but that expelled Essenes, not being allowed 'to partake of other men's food', ran the risk of death by starvation. He says[3] too that the Essenes had 'good men and priests, who had to prepare their corn and their food for them'. Further, a rule that the Covenanters would allow their novices to eat with them after one year but drink with them only after two years would be as hard to explain as it would be to enforce; and *Discipline* makes no provision for them to have separate meals. The only possible inference is that 'touching' refers to the preparation of the food and that the society allowed no novices, but only fully qualified members, to prepare its food and drink, lest they should unwittingly infect the whole community with ceremonial uncleanness, but that it admitted them to the common meal.[4] Such a rule was important in view of the ease with which this was conveyed by food and drink; it would not necessarily connect the Covenanters with the Essenes, as the Pharisaic 'associates' were similarly forbidden to prepare their food in the house of a common person[5] and ordinary Jews in pious families liked to employ priests in such tasks as processing oil and other foodstuffs in order to anticipate any risk of pollution.[6]

---

[1] In *HJ* I 62–4; cp. *Monks* 105–6.   [2] In *War* II viii 7 § 139 and 8 § 143.
[3] In *Antiquities* XVIII i 5 § 22.   [4] Cp. pp. 497–8.
[5] Tosefta *Demai* ii 2 and *Aboth dR. Nathan* § 40.
[6] Büchler *Der galiläische ʻAm-hāʼāreṣ des zweiten Jahrhunderts* 156–7.

When postulants made their solemn entry into the order, the priests recited God's wonderful works and His unfailing love for Israel, while the Levites recited the tale of Israel's iniquities. The postulants, having confessed their sins, were blessed by the priests, whereupon the Levites cursed 'all the men of Belial's lot';[1] finally, both priests and Levites called down curses on all who might enter the society without sincerity of heart. Year by year an annual review took place, in which the characters of all members, including those of priests and Levites, were re-examined that all might be apprised of their standing 'in the community of God', none being exalted above and none degraded beneath his rightful place in it (D i 21–iii 12).

If a member after admission abandoned the community and subsequently repented and sought readmission, he was penalized for two years; in the first 'he shall not touch the purity (*i.e.* food) of the Many';[2] in the second 'he shall not touch the drink of the Many' and must take a seat behind the other members. After this period he was re-examined and, if approved, readmitted to full membership. If one who had been a full member for ten years lapsed, he might never be readmitted, and any member who associated with him was expelled from the order (D vii 18–21).

Nothing certain is known about the number of recruits to the society. Both *Discipline* and the *Zadokite Documents* speak of applicants for admission coming forward 'by thousands and hundreds, by fifties and tens' (D ii 21–2, Z xiii 4), but this can only be wishful thinking;[3] for ancient numbers are commonly much exaggerated. The 'four thousand' Essenes who presently become 'countless thousands'[4] and the 'three thousand' or 'five thousand' early Christians who equally easily grow into 'myriads'[5] probably represent similar exaggerations.

The general mass of ordinary members were called 'the Many' (*hā-rabbîm*),[6] as in other contemporary societies.[7] This term was presumably intended as a *double entente* which at one and the same time recalled 'the many' summoned to 'righteousness (*sedeq*)' in the Old Testament[8] and defined their position in the society. That 'the Many' were all of them ordinary full members of the society[9] is shown by certain obligations laid on them, *e.g.* nightly vigils for study and attendance at plenary sessions of the community; for novices were excused these duties. In fact 'the Many' were the community, exclusive of the novices; the common possessions of the whole body were called 'the property of the Many', and their common meals were similarly

---

[1] P. 559.   [2] S. pp. 55–6.   [3] Cp. Burrows *Scrolls* I 231.
[4] Philo *Every Good Man* xii 75 and Eusebius *Preparation for the Gospel* viii 11 (379a).
[5] Acts ii. 41, iv. 4 and xxi. 20.   [6] Cp. Wernberg-Møller in *JSS* I 124–5.
[7] Pp. 101–2, 107, 521, 424.   [8] Isa. liii. 11 and Dan. xii. 3.
[9] Cp. Dan. xi. 33 and xii. 3 (where 'people' and 'the many' are interchangeable terms).

described (D vi 18, 20 vii 20, 25; cp. vii 16). The members dined, took counsel and worshipped together; and everyone obeyed his superior 'in work and wealth' (D vi 2). They met for the transaction of business in public session, as it were 'in chapter', in meetings at which they sat and spoke in order of rank—priests, then elders and then ordinary members. These sessions were governed by rules designed to ensure good order and harmony: for example, every member was entitled to be asked his opinion and might speak when so asked only in his proper turn, he might not interrupt another speaker, and he must confine himself to matters of communal interest and agreeable to the presiding officer; anyone 'not in the position of one asking for the counsel of the community', *i.e.* who was not in the 'chair (*ma'ămāḏ*)', but wished to make a statement, had to ask permission to address the community. Appropriate penalties were laid down for any breach of these rules (D vi 8–13 vii 10–15). At these meetings the members discussed every kind of official business affecting the welfare of the community, such as the admission of new members and the expulsion of unruly members or their readmission if penitent (D vii 16–25), the management of their property and judicial enquiries. A salutary precaution required in such cases that a member should bring an offending fellow member before witnesses for private rebuke before summoning him before 'the Many' (D vi 1; cp. vi 26).[1]

The designation of the corporate body and its members raises a difficulty; for they are apparently designated now not only 'the Many (*ha-rabbîm*)'[2] but also the 'multitude' or 'majority' or 'seniority (*rôḇ*)', as this term may be provisionally translated. The question then is: are the *rôḇ* and the *rabbîm* the same or different groups?

The *rôḇ* is mentioned in three places with the priests: 'the men of the community' separate themselves from 'the congregation of perverse men' to become a community in Law and property, giving *responsa* on legal and moral questions 'at the mouth of the priests . . . and at the mouth of the *rôḇ* of the men of the community' (D v 2–3); all who enter the counsels of the community come into God's covenant in the sight of those who have voluntarily entered the society, and each such person stakes his life on oath to return to the law of Moses according to all his commands 'in respect to everything revealed . . . to the priests . . . and to the *rôḇ* of the men of their covenant who offer themselves freely to (the service of) His (*sc.* God's) truth' (D v 8–10); and, when a novice presents himself after the first year of probation for admission as a full member, the *rabbîm* enquire into his intelligence and

---

[1] Cp. p. 581.

[2] Cp. Dan. xi 33 xii 3 (whence the term is derived) but not Mt. xx 28 = Mk. x 45 and Mt. xxvi 28 = Mk. xiv 24 (where the reference is general, as the absence of the definite article shows).

conduct and, if 'the lot falls for him to approach the society of the community at the mouth of the priests and the *rôḇ* of the men of their covenant', his property is handed over to the appointed officer for administration (D vi 18–20). Here *rôḇ* and *rabbîm* seem to be distinct. Elsewhere only the *rabbîm* are named. The general assembly of the community is called 'the session of the *rabbîm* (D vi 8, 11' vii 10, 13); it deliberates 'on every purpose and affair of the *rabbîm*' (D vi 9), and members address it 'at the mouth (*i.e.* at the bidding, by the leave) of the *rabbîm*' (D v 11–13); the 'inspector over the *rabbîm*' presides at ordinary meetings (D vi 11–12) and the same or a similar officer[1] 'at the head of the *rabbîm*' presides at the examination of postulants for admission to the order (D vi 14); the *rabbîm* are consulted about their knowledge and conduct (D vi 15–18 vii 21), they are examined 'at the mouth of the *rabbîm*' (D vi 21), who also admit novices after probation to membership (D vii 21), and similarly offenders and lapsed members may be readmitted 'at the mouth of the *rabbîm*' (D viii 18–19 ix 2); charges against offending members are brought 'before the *rabbîm*' (D vi 1), and slander of the *rabbîm* entails expulsion from the order (D vii 16); and lastly the ritually pure food and drink of the society are called respectively 'the purity of the *rabbîm*' and 'the drink of the *rabbîm*' (D vi 25 vii 3, 16, 19–20).

Clearly the priests and the *rôḇ* are distinct orders; this term must therefore designate or include the lay members of the society. The problem then is to determine how the *rôḇ* differ from the *rabbîm* who according to current Jewish usage are the full members of the society[2] as distinct from the novices.

Three explanations are possible. The usual rendering of *rôḇ* is 'majority'[3] in accordance with the common meaning of the term;[4] but this, although it may explain why no precedence is assigned to them (D vi 8–9), is impossible when the priests and the *rôḇ* are said to act together, as the totality of the priests and a mere majority of other members (unknown until they have voted) are disparate terms. Or the *rôḇ* may be the mass[5] of lay members, distinct on the one side from the priests (cp. D v 2–3, 9–10) and on the other from the novices; and this sense suits another passage which speaks of 'the *rôḇ* of Israel who offer themselves freely to turn back in the community to His (*sc.* God's) covenant' (D v 22), where the word can mean only the total number (not the majority) of the Israelites who join the society. If this meaning were accepted, the *rôḇ* and the *rabbîm* would be identical, the former the whole body in its corporate capacity and the latter the same body regarded as individual members. The objections to this view, however,

---

[1] P. 62. [2] S. pp. 57–8.
[3] *E.g.* Brownlee *Discipline* 18, 20, 26. [4] Levy *Wörterbuch* (*TM*) IV 410–11.
[5] Bardtke *Handschriftenfunde* I 93, 97 and Nötscher *Vom Alten zum Neuen Testament* 210.

are strong: that the spelling of *rōḇ* in this one passage is different, that the distinction implied is over-fine, and that the *rabbîm* and the *rōḇ* seem to have different functions at the admission of novices to full membership. Or, finally, the *rōḇ* may be a special group of senior members chosen perhaps by rotation or election and charged with special responsibilities (like the 'seniority' or 'thirteen seniors' in times past in some of the colleges at Oxford and Cambridge); and indeed the reference to 'the *rōḇ* of the men of their (*sc.* the society's) covenant' points to a separate group within the general body of the members. That the *rōḇ* receive no precedence is not an argument of any force against this suggestion; for they may have tacitly taken rank with the elders by birth (*zᵉqēnîm*). The only objection to this explanation of *rōḇ* is that it has no such *nuance* elsewhere; but the difficulty can perhaps be met by supposing that the Hebrew term has acquired a restricted connotation partly from the needs of the society and partly under the influence of the corresponding Greek used for 'mass, multitude (πλῆθος)', which is used in the Hellenistic period also for restricted groups *e.g.* of elders[1] or priests.[2] This suggestion may be further supported by the corresponding use to which the Greek term is apparently put in the New Testament. In this case the force of the term is somewhat different in 'the *rōḇ* of Israel who offer themselves freely to turn back . . . to His covenant' (as a scribe has indicated by changing the spelling of the word to show that it is used in a non-technical sense); here, again like the Greek word for 'multitude (πλῆθος)', it refers to the mass or total number of converts to the new society.[3]

The rules required a priest to every ten enrolled members; and, when they sat in his presence or met to take counsel together, they took their places in order of rank. A member as 'interpreting in the Law'[4] had always to be present with every such group, both day and night; and the members were bound to perpetual study of the Law,[5] remaining awake each in turn for a third part of the night throughout the year, engaged in the study of the Law and in communal worship (D vi 2–9). This *quorum* of ten members was a customary requirement for groups of Jews meeting for such study and became the requisite number of male members for worship in a synagogue.[6]

Priests presided at the admission of new members (D i 18–19 vi 18–20), and they were the first to enter the covenant at the annual review or re-dedication of all members, when they were followed by the Levites and 'all the people' (D ii 19–21), *i.e.* the mass of ordinary

---

[1] Ecclus. vii. 7, 14.
[2] Moulton & Milligan *Vocabulary of the Greek Testament* 518.
[3] P. 521.   [4] Cp. pp. 477–80.   [5] Cp. Josh. i 8.
[6] Mishnah *Aboth* iii 6 and *Sanhedrin* i 2; cp. pp. 511–2.

members; at these ceremonies they chanted the blessings while the Levites recited the curses (D i 21–ii 18). They also gave the blessing at all common meals (D vi 5–6), they took the first place in all gatherings, followed by the elders and 'all the people', and were asked to give their opinions first on such occasions (D vi 8–9).

A small body of three priests and twelve laymen was, or was to be, set up 'within the council (*ʿēṣāh*) of the community'.[1] These were appointed to take cognizance of 'every matter which has been hidden from Israel and is found by him who seeks'; for they were expected to be 'perfect in all that is revealed in the whole Law (*i.e.* the law of Moses) through the practice of truth and righteousness and justice and loyalty and walking humbly each with the other in order to maintain good faith in the land with steadfast intent and broken (*i.e.* meek) spirit and to expiate iniquity through the practice of justice and the torment of the refining furnace[2] and to walk with all men by the standard of truth and the proper reckoning of the time';[3] in other words, they were specially recognized members, who by their lives and doctrine should serve as models for ordinary members of the society in the conduct of their own lives and in the due observance of the days of obligation which the community recognized and assist them in their deliberations (D viii 1–4).[4] The members of this body were subject to special penalties derived (if not always by an obvious interpretation of the sacred text) from the Old Testament,[5] if they contravened any of the rules of their order. So 'whoever with a high hand (*i.e.* deliberately) leaves undone any commandment (*sc.* of God) shall not touch the purity of the saints or have any knowledge of their counsel' until he has purged his conduct, when he may be readmitted to it (D viii 16–19); whoever deliberately or deceitfully transgresses any provision of the Mosaic Law[6] shall be expelled for ever from the counsel of the community and have no dealings in any matter with the saints; but, if he has inadvertently done so, he shall be separated 'from the purity and from the counsel' and be debarred from sitting as a judge or being consulted on any matter for two years, after which on proof of satisfactory conduct he may be readmitted to his former position (D viii 21–ix 2). Such a body would be 'like an eternal plantation, a holy house for Israel, a most holy institution for Israel'; at the same time, when such a group could be found or formed, the community itself would be considered to have been established as an 'eternal plantation' (D viii 4–8).[7]

The reason for the number of these officers has been much discussed. It is possibly based on that of the twelve tribes of Israel and the three

---

[1] S. pp. 200, 523.   [2] S. pp. 532–3, 579.   [3] S. pp. 252, 343–4.
[4] Cp. Sutcliffe in *JSS* IV 134–8.   [5] Cp. Wernberg-Møller *Discipline* 132.
[6] Cp. Josh. xi. 15 (where the same expression is used).
[7] Sutcliffe *ibid.* 134–8.

Levitical orders (Gershonites, Kohathites, Merarites)[1], hardly on similar groups such as the three Major and twelve Minor Prophets, although the Covenanters are known to have studied their works, chosen to represent the ideal proportion of priests to laymen.[2] In any case three and twelve are often used as typical numbers.[3]

That these three priests and twelve laymen constitute a distinct group is clear; they may therefore perhaps be tentatively identified with the 'majority (*rôb*)' at Qumrân and be compared with the four priests and six laymen serving as judges in communities of Covenanters elsewhere (Z xi 1–2). That they are to be regarded as an inner council or conclave within the governing council, however, is very dubious;[4] for the existence of this other 'council' depends on the interpretation of the rule regarding novices presenting themselves 'to the council (*'ēṣāh*)' and being admitted 'to the society (*sôd*) of the community' (D vi 14, 19). The use of two terms to describe what is apparently the same body is against taking them as technical terms for a superior 'council', and the context suggests rather an informal body of experienced and highly respected members.

Besides these ecclesiastical and lay officers there were also one or perhaps two special officers, called respectively the 'inquisitor, inspector' or 'censor (*mᵉbaqqēr*)', and the 'officer (*pāqîd*)'.[5] The latter conducted the examination of applicants for admission to the order (D vi 14); the former, described as 'over the labour of the Many', administered the property of the novice when he had been admitted to the second year of probation (D vi 19–20) and presided at general meetings of the society, which no member might address without his leave (D vi 11–12). These two officers perform the same office; for, whereas in *Discipline* the 'officer' is concerned with the admission of new members (D vi 14), in the *Zadokite Documents* this duty falls on the 'censor' (Z xvi 4). Moreover, the 'officer' is described as being 'at the head of the Many' (D vi 14), while the 'censor' is called 'the censor for the Many' (Z xix 8); and titles defined in such similar terms can hardly be kept apart. Consequently that translated 'officer', which means literally 'appointed person', may confidently be taken as a general term subsuming 'censor', who is the principal lay officer of the community.[6]

The 'wise man (*maśkîl*)'[7] has also been included among the officers of the society because he is charged in some passages with teaching his fellow-members about good and evil spirits, the periods of affliction and of well-being, and so on (D iii 13–15) and generally of encouraging

---

[1] Freedman in *JBL* LXXVIII 331–2 and Vermès *Scrolls* 17–8.
[2] Sutcliffe in *JSS* IV 134.   [3] König in Hastings *DB* III 562–3.
[4] Brownlee *Discipline* 31 and Black *Scrolls* 116.   [5] Cp. pp. 521–3.
[6] Cp. Rowley *Zadokite Fragments* 37[1].
[7] Cp. Dan. xi 23, 35 and xii 3, 10 (which may be the source of this term).

them in their vocation (D ix 15–16); that the rules and regulations set out in this Scroll are elsewhere addressed directly to him (D ix 12–15 Z xv 2–3; cp. xvi 10), however, militates against taking him as an officer having any such duties. Alternatively, he has been thought to be a kind of precentor or choral chaplain, because a fragmentary Scroll speaks of 'the words of the blessing for the wise man to bless those who fear God' (IQ *28* B i 1); but the fragment is so imperfectly preserved that it can hardly support the conclusion drawn from it. The term seems, then, not to designate any special officer, whether a 'spiritual director' or a 'precentor', but rather to be describing any full member who in virtue of his moral and other qualities is or may be expected to advise and help other members not so far advanced as himself in the religious life, and even on occasion to pronounce a blessing over priests.[1]

The 'Laws' contained in the *Zadokite Documents*, while adding some details to this account, present a somewhat different picture; for the organization, which was originally designed for a small religious group living in community, had need to be adapted to the circumstances of like-minded persons living in 'camps', *i.e.* special quarters or settlements (somewhat like those of the Qara'ites in Cairo or the 'ghettoes' in medieval Europe)[2] in villages and towns.

In this document the society is said to consist of 'the priests and the Levites and the Sons of Zadok'; the priests were 'the penitents of Israel who have come out from the land of Judah' and the Levites 'those who have joined themselves to them' (where the writer plays on their name; for 'Levi' means 'joined'),[3] while 'the Sons of Zadok' were 'the elect of Israel, those called by name who shall arise in the end of the days' (Z vi 1–2; cp. v 7). Ezekiel, to whom the author is referring, identified the 'sons of Zadok' with 'the priests the Levites';[4] but the author here distinguishes them by inserting a conjunction (which is found in no manuscript or ancient version of the Old Testament) before 'Sons of Zadok'. Consequently 'Sons of Zadok', which elsewhere is an appellation of the priestly members as priests of the line of Zadok (D v 2, 9; cp. I Q *28* A ii 3), David's chief priest who crowned Solomon, here designates the lay members of the society, as distinct from the priests and Levites who also belonged to it (cp. D ix 14). No practical inconvenience would have been caused by this twofold use of the expression, which will be explained hereafter,[5] since it was normally restricted to the priests and was replaced by 'the Many' in the legal part of the work wherever the main or whole body of the members was intended (Z xvi 1 xvii 5 xviii 1 xix 8).

---

[1] Cp. Nötscher *Von Alten zum Neuen Testament* 212–4 and Roberts in *BJRL* XLVI 176–8.   [2] Cp. Del Medico *Énigme* 124.
[3] Cp. Gen. xxix. 34.   [4] Ezek. xliv. 15.   [5] Pp. 253–4.

A priest was appointed to be in charge of the Many, aged between thirty and sixty years and 'skilled in the *Book of Study*[1] and in all the ordinances of the Law' (Z xvii 5). A priest, learned in the same book, was attached to every group of ten members; but, if he was not expert in such matters, a Levite with the necessary knowledge might take his place, and all the members were bound to obey him. If a question of the law of skin-diseases arose,[2] the censor was required publicly to explain its provisions to the priest; and, if he proved to be simple or incapable, the censor might lock him up, 'although the judgement is theirs' (Z xv 1–8). The reason for these provisions was that the priesthood was hereditary and consequently the quality and standards of the priests fluctuated, and in such a case as disease an incorrect diagnosis might have serious results; the censor therefore was empowered, if the need arose, to overrule the priest, although the decision was regarded as theirs, *i.e.* that of the priests. So the Mishnah required a layman to advise the priest in such cases, although the actual declaration of cleanness or uncleanness was left to the priest.[3]

The censor, who had general supervision of all the 'camps', had to be between thirty and fifty years old, a 'master of every secret of mankind' and able to converse with people in their own language (for Jews unable to speak Hebrew or foreign proselytes might enter the order), especially in outlying settlements; he dealt with complaints and disputes (Z xvii 6–8), and he conducted the investigation of capital charges (Z x 10–13). He alone was responsible for examining and admitting everyone applying for admission to the order and for assigning a place to him on admission in the order of the community, also for the readmission (Z xvi 4–5 xvii 7 xix 11–12). He was also responsible for imparting religious knowledge to them (Z xvi 1–3) and for instructing priests in the technicalities of the law (Z xv 7), and also for receiving members' contributions for the relief of those in need (Z xv 7).

There were also ten judges,[4] 'selected'[5] four from the tribe of Aaron and Levi and six 'from Israel', *i.e.* laymen, aged from twenty-five to sixty years; these, too, were required to be 'skilled in the *Book of Study*[1] and the principles of the covenant' (Z xi 1–4). These judges were an innovation,[6] due to the changed circumstances of life in exile—for example, the acquisition of wealth by members of the society in consequence of the growth of trade and commerce amongst them. Only three of their duties are mentioned: they must administer the oath to a member who purges himself of an offence, since the aggrieved

---

[1] S. pp. 70–1.   [2] Lev. xiii. 1—xiv. 57.   [3] Mishnah *Negaim* iii 1; cp. ii 5.
[4] Cp. Mishnah *Sanhedrin* i 3 (s. Gaster *Scriptures* 309).
[5] Cp. *ibid.* iii 1 (where the same verb is applied to the 'selection' of judges in non-capital cases).
[6] S. p. 521.

party might not take the law into his own hands (Z x 6); they must satisfy themselves that the witnesses in a capital case were qualified to give evidence (Z x 15); and they also supervised the distribution of charity (Z xviii 2). They would probably have had also a wide jurisdiction in both civil and certainly in criminal cases.

Lastly, due precedence must be observed in the settlements. Everyone was entered by name in a roster in the order of his class: first priests, second Levites, third 'sons of Israel', *i.e.* lay Israelites, and fourth 'strangers', *i.e.* proselytes.[1] In this order they must be seated and in it they were asked to express their opinions at meetings (Z xvii 1–3).

In addition to such rules as these governing the organization of the society, both *Discipline* and the *Zadokite Documents* (for both alike were without doubt intended to be applicable *mutatis mutandis* to all members)[2] contain a number of precepts and rules regarding the daily conduct of its members; these are the basis of the community's social life, without which no society can maintain a corporate existence.

In *Discipline* the regulations are enforced by a clearly defined scale of punishments, of which the principal is the reduction of the offender's commons by one quarter for a prescribed period of time (D vi 25); he may also suffer an additional penalty which is perhaps segregation or expulsion from the society for a period of time, or he may in cases of extreme gravity be expelled from the society for life. Such expulsion may have had serious consequences if the practice of the Essenes may be taken as a guide; for Josephus, who says nothing of graded penalties, reports[3] that the expelled member often comes to a most miserable end. Such a person, being bound by the oaths and usages of the order, is not free to partake of other men's good and so falls to eating grass and wastes away until he dies of starvation. This has led the order in compassion to receive many back when in the last stages of exhaustion, deeming that torments which have brought them to the verge of death are a sufficient penalty for their misdeeds.

The offences, all committed against God, the society and fellow members, and the appropriate penalties, are the following:

(i) reduced commons for ten days

for interrupting a speaker (D vii 9–10) and 'putting out the left hand' for a purpose variously explained as 'to dig (*lāšûaḥ*)' for relieving nature,[4] when the prohibition must be an intentional alteration of the Rabbinic rule to use the left hand for this purpose,[5] or 'to recline

---

[1] Cp. Mishnah *Horayoth* iii 8. [2] Gaster *Scriptures* 44.
[3] In *War* II viii 8 §§ 143–4.
[4] Marcus in *JNES* XI 209 and Driver in *TICP* IV (*Mélanges Bibliques*) 67.
[5] B. Talmud *Berakhoth* 62a (cp. *Menahoth* 36b–37a) and *Aboth dR. Nathan* § 40.

(*lāśōaḥ*)',[1] namely reclining instead of sitting in company,[2] when the prohibition will be aimed at the customary laxity of allowing either position (D vii 15);[3]

(ii) reduced commons for one month

for immoderate laughter (D vii 14–15);[4]

(iii) reduced commons for three months

for neglect of another's interests or hurling invectives at another (D vii 5–6), failure to make good common property lost through negligence (D vii 8), using obscene language (D vii 9), indecent exposure of the person when 'not compelled (?)',[5] or putting out a hand in such a way as to expose oneself when clothed in rags (D vii 12–14);[6]

(iv) reduced commons for six months

for speaking angrily with priests when unaware that they are 'inscribed in the book', *i.e.* that they have Zadokite (?) ancestry recorded in the official genealogical lists (D vii 3),[7] deliberately lying (D vii 3–4), speaking haughtily or acting with intent to deceive (D vii 5), and murmuring without cause against another member (D vii 17–18);

(v) reduced commons for one year (corrected above the line from six months)

for bearing a grudge without cause or seeking revenge (D vii 8–9);

(vi) reduced commons and 'being separated to oneself', *i.e.* isolated, for one year

for speaking angrily to a priest when aware that he is one of those 'inscribed in the book' (D vii 2–3);

(vii) reduced commons and expulsion from the society for one year

for lying about personal property (D vi 24–5),[8] answering with impatience and refusing to be corrected (D vi 25–7), denigrating another deliberately (?) and without cause (D vii 4–5), and spreading tales about another (D vii 15–16);

(viii) reduced commons for two years and degradation to the rank of a novice

for apostasy after repentance and readmission (D vii 18–21);

---

[1] Cp. Ecclus. xliii 10.   [2] Wernberg-Møller *Discipline* 118.
[3] Mishnah *Berakhoth* vi 6; cp. Ecclus. ix. 9, xxxi. 16, xxxii. 1 (reclining) and xxxiv. 12, 18 (sitting).
[4] S. p. 11; cp. B. Talmud *Berakoth* 31a.
[5] Ginsberg *ap.* Wernberg-Møller *op. cit.* 117–18.   [6] Cp. *ibid.* 118.
[7] Pp. 20, 325.   [8] Cp. pp. 115, 524.

(ix) permanent expulsion from the community

for blaspheming through fear of persecution or for any other cause when reading Scripture or giving a blessing (D vii 1–2), for spreading tales about the Many and murmuring against the principles of the society (D v ii 16–17), and for apostasy after ten years' membership of the society (D vii 22).

Further, a member who loses or destroys property belonging to the society must make it good to the full amount (D vii 6–7).

Penalties are prescribed also for four offences committed by members 'in session', *i.e.* at plenary meetings of the society. These are reduced commons for ten days for leaving a meeting more than three times without good reason, *i.e.* presumably to relieve nature (D vii 10–11), and for one month for falling asleep at a meeting, leaving before the voting (?), and spitting 'into the midst of a meeting'[1] (D vii 10–13).

Unfortunately, the meaning of some of the terms used, both for the offences and for the penalties, cannot be certainly or exactly defined; and several rules have been lost in a damaged passage. Enough however can be made out to show the general sense of the text.

The rules set out in *Discipline*, which are proved to have been enforced by fragments of administrative texts (still unpublished) giving the names of individual offenders with details of their offences,[2] are amplified and modified in the legal sections of the *Zadokite Documents*, where they are followed by a number of Laws, *i.e.* practical regulations prescribed for members of the party living in urban communities away from the mother-house at Qumrân.

The first group of regulations are declared to be 'the order of any settlement in the cities of Israel' (Z xv 1), which may now be briefly summarized.

A member who told tales to a superior or brought a charge against another member in anger or without witnesses to prove it must be counted as one who bore a grudge against a neighbour, whom the Law condemns (Z x 2–5).

If property had been lost and the thief was not known, the owner must make a deposition on oath; lost property which was found but not claimed must be deposited with the priest (Z x 7–9).

If a member saw a capital offence committed and was alone at the time, he must report it to the censor in the presence of the culprit, and this officer must make a record of it; if the culprit repeated the offence again in the presence of only one man and the latter reported it to the censor, the offence was regarded as proved. If there were two witnesses and they were trustworthy and laid information on the day when the offence was committed, the culprit was excluded 'from the

---

[1] Pp. 102, 107, 113.   [2] Bardtke *Handschriftenfunde* II 153–5.

purity', *i.e.* from helping to prepare the common food of the society.[1] Two trustworthy witnesses, who must have completed their period of probation in the order, were required also in charges concerning property (Z x 10–16).

No one might bathe in dirty water or in such as was insufficient to cover a man;[2] and an unclean man who came into contact with so small a quantity of water in a pool defiled it instead of being himself cleansed (Z xii 1–2).[3]

The Sabbath must be strictly observed in regard to every detail of law and custom.[4] Especially no one might lay any but the statutory burnt offering for the Sabbath on the altar on that day,[5] and no one might send an offering to the altar by a person in a state of impurity nor approach a place of worship in such a state himself (Z xiii 1–27). A member who profaned the Sabbath, being possessed by 'spirits of Belial' (*i.e.* demons) and being therefore not responsible, must be kept under guard on a feast-day; if he was cured, he must be kept under observation and might be readmitted to the community only after seven years' observation (Z xiv 5–6).

No member might have any dealings with the heathen (which can have been possible only when living in the world) or eat any unclean food; and members must avoid contagious impurity, such as that contracted by contact with a dead body (Z xiv 7–16).[6]

These rules are followed by a section setting out 'the order of any settlement in camps' occupied 'in the period of wickedness till the appearance of the Messiah of Aaron and Israel' (Z xv 4).

Members had to surrender their wages for two days in every month to the censor, and he passed them on to the judges who distributed the funds thus accumulated for the support of orphans, the poor and needy, the aged and dying, captives, unprotected and unmarried girls, and for use on public works (Z xviii 1–5).

Fraud in matters of money was punished with a penalty of six days; but the text nowhere defines this penalty (Z xviii 9). The analogy of *Discipline* suggests that it may have been a reduction of rations and possibly also segregation from the society of other members.

Oaths must not be sworn by the name of God or by the Law of Moses; a formula of agreement had to be used (Z xix 1–5, Rabin). Whoever entered into the covenant, *i.e.* joined the community, must impose the oath of the covenant on his sons when they reached the age of entering the ranks of the order. Anyone who repented his evil ways in the world might be admitted so soon as he confessed them to the censor, when he had to swear 'to return to the Law of Moses'; but no one should acquaint him with the regulations of the community until he stood in the presence of the censor, lest on examination he showed

[1] Pp. 55–6.   [2] S. p. 501.   [3] Cp. p. 43.   [4] Cp. pp. 90–1.   [5] S. p. 119.   [6] S. pp. 47–8.

himself simple. If he failed to understand points of law intelligible to the normal man, he should be kept in confinement for a year. Anyone who had bound himself by oath to execute any precept of the law should not release himself from it even to save his life (Z xix 6–xx 6). A woman's father or husband must declare her oath void if it involved any violation of the Covenant; he might let it stand, however, if he did not know whether it ought to be made good or be voided (Z xx 7–8).[1]

These last rules are exceptionally important as showing that members married and brought up families. This conclusion is supported by two other rules: first, the *Zadokite Documents* include a rule that a nurse might not carry a baby on the Sabbath (Z xiii 20); and a broken passage suggests that they even apparently included rules for divorce (Z xvi 8). Second, a fragment of the so-called *Rule of the Order*, recently published, lays down the rule that both women and children should be present at the public reading of the Covenant, that every member must be instructed in the *Book of Study* from childhood, and that no young man might have intercourse with a woman until he was twenty years old (I Q *28* A i 4–11)[2]. A hint to the same effect has also been detected in *Discipline*, which speaks of members enjoying the 'fruit of seed' (D iv 7), which therefore is not necessarily a mere figure of speech;[3] and the obvious conclusion which has been drawn from this passage is perhaps supported by the discovery of a few skeletons of women and children in annexes to the main cemetery at Qumrân.[4] These however might be those of women who had lived there before its occupation by the Covenanters or of women members of the order whose bodies had been brought there from elsewhere to be buried in holy ground; but *War* contains the significant regulation that 'no boy or lad or woman shall enter their camps when they leave Jerusalem to go out to war until they come back' (W vii 3–4). Since the 'monastery' at Qumrân was also a fortress,[5] it might be included (possibly only if the military situation demanded it) in this prohibition; in that case women would not normally be resident there. The reason for the distinction in this respect between *Discipline* and the *Zadokite Documents* is that the emphasis is different. The former was dealing with a fairly large but compact community living in a desert stronghold, for much of the time to all intents and purposes an armed garrison, where women and children would not be much wanted nor would want to live, while the latter was concerned with small communities living in or near to towns and villages where questions of marriage would be bound to come up and the presence of women would raise no unusual difficulties. The idea, therefore, that the Covenanters were necessarily and

---

[1] Cp. Num. xxx. 2–8.   [2] Cp. Mishnah R. *Genesis* xiv § 7
[3] Barthélemy *ap.* Wernberg-Møller *Discipline* 79.
[4] Pp. 45–6.   [5] Pp. 38, 46.

F

everywhere a celibate body, though generally held, must be abandoned.

Two other passages in the *Zadokite Documents* are of considerable interest, though for an entirely different reason. One is the statement that capital punishment was carried out 'by the statutes of the Gentiles' (Z x 1); these must be the Romans, who took away the *ius gladii* in A.D. 6 from the Jewish authorities.[1] The other is a prohibition of intercourse with a woman 'in the city of the sanctuary' (Z xiv 4), *i.e.* Jerusalem; for this must refer, as Eisler has seen,[2] to a period when no Jew might set foot in it, *i.e.* A.D. 70–135. The only other possibility, which Dr. Rabin suggests,[3] is that the prohibition refers to pilgrims, as it does in Moslem cities; but the text contains no hint of any such limitation. Both the statement and the rule will evidently have some bearing on the date of the Scrolls and will be discussed hereafter.[4]

A fragmentary *Rule of the Community* from Cave IV adds one noteworthy point: no one ritually unclean or physically defective may attend the society's meetings; for 'holy angels are in their [assembly]' (I Q *28* A ii 3–9 i; cp. A Fl.c. i 3–4). This notion occurs elsewhere only in the first century A.D., when the apostle Paul bids women be veiled in church 'because of the angels'.[5]

The references to the *Book of Study* (*sēfer hehāgû* or *hehāgî*) are puzzling (Z xi 2 xv 5; cp. I Q *28* A i 7), as no such work is known; but the suggestion that it is a figment of the author's imagination has nothing to commend it,[6] inasmuch as it makes nonsense of the passages in which it is mentioned. It cannot be *Discipline*[7] if a fragmentary text in which it is mentioned is rightly supposed to belong to that work,[8] nor the Laws[9] contained in the *Zadokite Documents* (Z x 1–xx 20), as the reference seems to be to some work external to these documents. It can hardly be the Law[10], which is regularly called *tôrāh* in the Scrolls; may it then be a designation of the whole Old Testament?[11] Alternatively, the title has been rendered *Book of Mourning*, since the root (which basically indicates any repetitive sound) is so used;[12] it is then explained in the light of the plaint of the author (of one of) the

---

[1] Josephus *Antiquities* XVIII i 1 § 2 and *War* II viii 1 § 107; cp. Jn. xviii. 13.
[2] In *Occident and Orient* (Gaster Anniversary Volume) 123.
[3] In *Zadokite Documents*[2] 59.   [4] P. 369.
[5] I Cor. xi 10.   [6] Zeitlin in *JQR*, NS XLI 263.
[7] Brownlee in *BA* XIII 54; cp. Dupont-Sonmer *Écrits Esséniens* 85–6.
[8] Barthélemy & Milik *Discoveries* I 109–11 *28*A i 7.
[9] Del Medico *Énigme* 126–7.
[10] Yadin *Message* 125.
[11] Rabinowitz in *JNES* XX 109–114 and Vermès *Scrolls* 19; cp. Josh. i 8, and Ps. i 2, where the cognate verb is applied to the study of the Law, and B. Talm. *Berakoth* 28b, where another noun derived from the same root has been taken to mean Scripture (Rashi; s. Buxtorf & Fischer *Lexicon* [1869] 303b). Further, teachers or students of the law are called *hôgîm* (Midrash R. *Deuteronomy* xi §6 and *Lamentations* Pr. 2).
[12] Cp. Ezk. ii 10 (where *hegeh* means 'mourning').

Thanksgiving Hymns, who speaks of 'mourning with bitter mourning, grief and wailing, until iniquity comes to an end' (T xi 21–2), when the work will have been a book of commandments including one to mourn till that event, from which it may be supposed to have taken its name.[1] Such an explanation of the title, however, seems very far-fetched, especially as nothing is known of a work of this nature. Indeed, the only certain point is that it must have been composed before any work in which it is mentioned;[2] but that throws no light on its contents. The wisest course is to suspend judgement;[3] for so many fragments of unidentified works have been found that it may yet be proved to be one of them or an as yet undiscovered work.

These rules and regulations are basically echoes of the Old Testament: such are the commands to love one's neighbour as oneself,[4] to seek the welfare of others,[5] to refrain from fornication and whoredom,[6] the requirement of two witnesses,[7] and so on. The prohibition not to swear by the names of God or the Law of Moses is not found *totidem verbis* in the Old Testament but is implicit in that of taking the name of the Lord in vain;[8] and many others can be indirectly referred to the Old Testament.

The fundamental theology of the Covenanters is indeed that of the Old Testament and as such does not call for detailed description. It was based on the historic experience of the people of Israel, whom God had punished for their continuing wickedness by the Exile and the misfortunes that followed it; but it is informed by a clearly marked predestination and a dualism,[9] ultimately of Iranian origin, which had crept into it.

According to the teaching of *Discipline*, God has predetermined everything and in doing so has appointed two spirits for man, whom He has created to rule the world: these are the spirits of truth and of perversity, by whose guidance man must walk till the final scrutiny to which all men will come. The origin of truth is in a 'fountain of light' and that of perversity in a 'well-spring of darkness' (D iii 19); those who do right are ruled by the Prince of Light and walk in ways of light, while those who practise perversity are under the dominion of the Angel of Darkness and walk in ways of darkness and will so continue till God's appointed time. All the spirits attendant on the Angel of Darkness are bent on causing the Sons of Light to err, but the God of Israel and His true Angel are there to help them. God created these

---

[1] Gottstein in *VT* VIII 286–8. [2] Rowley *Zadokite Fragments* 76.
[3] Cp. Holm-Nielsen *Hodayoth* 325. [4] Lev. xix. 18.
[5] *E.g.* Lev. xix. 13, xxv. 25–8, 35–55 and Deut. xv. 7–18, xxii. 1–4.
[6] Lev. xix. 29 and Deut. xxiii. 17–18.
[7] Deut. xvii. 6, xix. 15; cp. Num. xxxv. 30.
[8] Exod. xx. 7 and Deut. v. 11.
[9] Nötscher in *BZ*, NF IV 98–109.

spirits, making them the instigators of man's every act; He loves the one but hates all contact with the other to all eternity. The operation of these spirits is thus defined: of the former, humility and patience, compassion, goodness, discrimination, a sense of God's power, knowledge informing every plan, zeal for righteous government, a hallowed mind united to self-control, love of those who follow the truth, purity and modesty, prudence and discretion; of the latter, greed, indolence in doing what is right, wickedness and falsehood, pride, deceitfulness, cruelty and arrogance, shortness of temper and unrestrained folly, lewdness and unchastity, blasphemy, blind eyes and deaf ears, stiffness of neck and hardness of heart. The reward of those who walk in the spirit of truth is health and prosperity, long life and 'fruit of seed', *i.e.* delight in posterity,[1] 'joy through ages in eternity of life and a crown of glory with a robe of honour[2] in the light of the ages' (D iv 6–8); the penalty of those who yield to the spirit of perversity is countless afflictions at the hands of all the 'angels of destruction', perdition throughout the ages in consequence of the wrath of an avenging God, eternal horror and utter disgrace, in a murky fire through all the vicissitudes of the ages, sorrowful mourning and bitter misfortune and dark ruin ending in total extinction (D iii 13–iv 14).

All men are born to one or other of these destinies, each according to his inheritance. God has appointed these two fates to exist in equal measure till the final age and has put eternal enmity between the two groups; but He has appointed a term for the existence of perversity and, when the time of scrutiny comes, He will destroy it. All men will then be purged in the crucible of His truth, sprinkled 'with water (to get rid) of impurity',[3] and Truth will emerge triumphant in all the world (D iv 15–26).

Meanwhile God has offered man a 'covenant', by accepting which he can avoid the dilemma presented by predestination. This covenant is entered by joining the society or community of the Sons of Light; and 'all volunteers to serve His (*sc.* God's) truth must bring all their knowledge and their strength and their wealth into the community' (D i 11–12) and 'all who enter the order of the community must pass under the covenant in the presence of God to act according to all that He has commanded and not to turn away from Him through any fear or terror or trial to which they may be subjected by the dominion of Belial' (D i 16–18). In other words, the community requires the dedication of all a member's intellectual and physical gifts and material possessions to the service of God within its fold with unflinching devotion, even in face of torture and death. No one who persists in following the stubborn dictates of his own will and has shown no firmness in amending his conduct may be admitted to the community; for 'he

[1] Pp. 69, 112.   [2] Cp. pp. 520, 568.   [3] Cp. p. 54.

cannot be cleansed by ceremonies of atonement nor purified by waters (for the removal) of impurity nor sanctified by seas and rivers nor purified by waters of ablution.' Only by submitting himself to all the ordinances of God can a man be cleansed; neither lustration nor baptism is of any avail[1] (D i 16–11 12).

Writers on the Scrolls habitually speak of this covenant, into which members of the community at Qumrân entered to escape from the world, as the 'new covenant'; and this supposed 'new covenant' has been compared with the Christian 'New Covenant' or 'New Testament'. The comparison is superficial[2] and the error due to over-looking the distinction between *Discipline* and the *Zadokite Documents* in language and date; these two works, the earlier and the later, although both speak of the 'covenant of God' (D v 8 x 10; Z vii 12 xvi 12), are here referring to different things in their use of these two expressions. The former nowhere speaks of a 'new covenant' but talks of 'the covenant of the community' (D viii 16); and it describes its members as 'entrants into the covenant' (D ii 18; cp. ii 12 v 20) or 'those who pass into the covenant' (D i 20, ii 10; cp. i 16, 18) and as 'a community of an eternal covenant' (D v 5–6). The latter retains 'entrants into the covenant' for members entering the original community at Qumrân (Z ii 1 ix 12; cp. xix 6), but substitutes 'entrants into the new covenant' when referring to that drawn up at Damascus (Z viii 15; cp. ix 28, 37). The *Commentary on Habakkuk*, too, refers perhaps once to the 'new [covenant]' (H ii 3).

This distinction reflects a dichotomy in the history of the Covenanters; for it apparently refers to a schism which broke out amongst the exiles in Damascus and those who remained faithful to the old order and the traditions of Qumrân and drew up and entered into a new covenant amongst themselves, excluding all members of the schismatic group from it. These two parties, the faithful remnant and those who de-faulted, are clearly described: the former are the 'house of division (*peleg*)'[3] who went forth from the Holy City and leaned upon God in the epoch when Israel was faithless and defiled the sanctuary, turning back to God'; the latter are all who, having entered into the covenant (*sc.* the old covenant at Qumrân), broke out of the bonds of the Law and who 'will be cut off from the midst of the camp together with all evil-doers in Judah at the time of his testing, when the glory of God shall appear unto Israel' (Z ix 46–9). Consequently, the covenant into which members had entered at Qumrân was 'the covenant' *par excellence* and without qualification; and it was modelled on the original covenant between God and His people in the Old Testament. It was the 'covenant' of the Old Testament renewed after the breach caused

---

[1] Pp. 111–2.   [2] Cp. Black *Scrolls* 97–8.   [3] Pp. 296–7.

by national apostasy in a fresh offer made by God to the 'penitents of Israel' (Z viii 6), *i.e.* the community at Qumrân. Contrariwise, the 'new covenant', while verbally recalling that of Jeremiah, was in fact the old covenant of Qumrân, as renewed and modified after the schism to meet the needs of a new situation. In other words, the covenant of Qumrân was the 'covenant of God' as offered to those who joined the society (D v 8 x 10), while the covenant at Damascus was the 'new covenant', a local covenant made after the schism in place of the original covenant; it has nothing whatsoever to do with the 'New Covenant' or 'New Testament' of the Christian Church. This explanation of the two expressions is in harmony with the conclusion reached on other grounds, that *Discipline*, which speaks only of a 'covenant', must be dated before the *Zadokite Documents*, in which a 'new covenant' takes its place.[1]

The Covenanters had or expected an inspired Teacher or succession of Teachers, who apparently held an hereditary office and would lead them out of darkness into light. They also cherished the hope that God would in due time raise up the promised Messiah from their own ranks: this Messiah would be 'a Messiah of Aaron and of Israel'. Sometimes the idea seems to be that these would be two distinct Messiahs, one of priestly and one of lay lineage, at others that there was or would be only one Messiah combining both offices. The most probable view is that the Community began by thinking of two such Messiahs but ultimately came round to the orthodox view of a single Messiah; for there is a suggestion that the last Rightful Teacher, being in some sense a priest but also claiming royal privileges, would himself become both lay and priestly Messiah.[2]

The opinions of the Covenanters on a future life are not altogether clear.

Possibly three passages more or less clearly imply a bodily resurrection; these are the promise that 'all His (*sc.* God's true sons, the members of the Community) shall awake . . . at [the destruction of] wickedness, and all the sons of guilt shall be no more' (T vi 29–30), and 'those who lie in the dust have raised up a standard and dead men's worms have hoisted a banner' (T vi 34), and also 'to raise dead men's worms from the dust for a counsel of . . . ' (T xi 12, where the end of the line is lost). These last two passages, of course, are little but echoes of the Old Testament, notably the well-known prophecy that 'many of them that sleep in the dust shall awake'.[3] Further, in the final war 'the hosts of Thine (*sc.* God's) elect' are found fighting beside the angels (W xii 4), where the elect seem to be the pious dead of previous generations;[4] but the mention of 'those who rise on' or 'from the earth'

---

[1] Pp. 305–10.   [2] Pp. 471–6.   [3] Dan. xii. 2.
[4] Cp. Yadin *War* 219–20.

in the same passage cannot be invoked as evidence of any such doctrine, since the broken context leaves it uncertain whether 'rebels on earth'[1] or 'those who rise from (their graves in) the earth', are meant.[2] At the same time, many passages prove beyond doubt that the righteous, *i.e.* the elect or the members of the Community, looked for 'everlasting peace and perpetual salvation' (T xv 16), expecting to live for ever: for example, 'those who cling to it (*sc.* the sure house in Israel, presumably that of the Rightful Teacher) are for eternal life' (Z iii 6), and 'the covenant of God shall stand fast with them to keep them alive for a thousand generations' (Z viii 21), and again 'those who are in harmony with Thy will shall stand before Thee for ever and those who walk in the way of Thy heart shall be established to eternity' (T iv 21—2), when crowned and robed they will enjoy eternal life (D iv 7–8).[3] The conclusion, then, seems to be that the Covenanters had some vague notions of a physical resurrection and certainly believed in a future angelic existence in eternal bliss in communion with God,[4] if only as a corollary to the eternal damnation of their enemies, but perhaps not in any resurrection of the body.[5]

If, as argued hereafter,[6] the Covenanters may be identified in some sense with the Zealots, the last speech of the Zealot leader Eleazar before committing suicide with all his comrades in arms at Masada in A.D. 73 is not inapposite to the present consideration of the Covenanters' views on an after-life. He says that 'it is death which gives liberty to the soul and permits it to depart to its own pure abode, there to be free from all calamity' and that 'it is not until, freed from the weight that drags it down to earth and clings about it, the soul is restored to its proper sphere, that it enjoys a blessed energy and a power untrammelled on every side, remaining like God Himself invisible to human eyes; unperceived it comes and unseen it again departs, itself of a nature one and incorruptible but a cause of change to the body. For whatever the soul has touched lives and flourishes, whatever it abandons withers and dies; so abundant is its wealth of immortality'; and he goes on to compare death to sleep 'in which the soul, undistracted by the body, while enjoying the most delightful repose in perfect independence, holds converse with God by right of kinship, ranges the universe and foretells many things that will come to be, and ends by urging his hearers not 'to grudge ourselves that which is eternal'.[7] These sentiments go far beyond anything in the Scrolls, but they must not be taken as a true summary of the views of the Covenanters; it is a patchwork of Greek philosophy which Josephus has put

[1] Gaster *Scriptures* 275.   [2] Dupont-Sommer *Écrits Esséniens* 202.
[3] Cp. pp. 520, 568.   [4] Cp. Luke xx. 35–6.
[5] Cp. Black *Scrolls and Christian Origins* 135–42.
[6] Pp. 237–51.   [7] Josephus *War* VII vii 7 §§ 344–50.

into a Jewish hero's mouth. Only a woman and some children who had heard him survived the final destruction of the place by the Romans.

Finally, the Covenanters seem to have developed a great interest in angelology, as a recently discovered *Angelic Liturgy* shows;[1] and the texts already known confirm this interest. They believed the world to be peopled with good and evil spirits warring for the possession of the souls of men,[2] and that God had a 'multitude of holy ones' and 'armies of angels', whose names are recorded in His book, to serve in His wars (W xii 1–7). Four (possibly also others; for the text is incomplete) of these names are inscribed on the bucklers carried by the Sons of Light; these are Michael, Gabriel, Sariel, Raphael (W ix 14–16).[2] In the final apocalyptic struggle, in which both men and 'gods (*'ēlîm)'* will be engaged (W i 9–10), the might of 'the army of the angels' and 'the army of His spirits' will stand beside His servants the Sons of Light (W xii 8–9); and at the critical moment He will summon 'the angels of His dominion' and will show Himself in glory '[with the company of] the Holy Ones' to ensure their victory (W i 15–16).

The question must now be asked: can the Covenanters be identified with any known group or party in Jewry within the limits of the period allowed by archaeology and history, *i.e.* roughly between the end of the Persian age and the Jewish risings against the Romans in the First or perhaps the Second Revolt?[3] The principal political and religious parties of this period, which must be considered in the present connection, are those of the Sadducees and the Pharisees together with the adherents of the 'fourth philosophy', who seem to have been an offshoot of the Pharisees; other groups are the Essenes, the Dositheans and the Mandaeans, and perhaps also the Gnostic sects who may have left some mark on the doctrines of the Covenanters.

2. SADDUCEES

The Sadducees are generally supposed to take their name from Zadok, the head of the priesthood in the days of David and Solomon; for his family had been singled out by Ezekiel, under the title of the 'Sons of Zadok', to be entrusted with supreme authority in the Temple, and members of it formed the hierarchy down to the time of Ben Sirach and afterwards. The 'Sons of Zadok', *i.e.* the priestly aristocracy, yielded to the influence of Hellenism in the Seleucid period and so came to be regarded by their Pharisaic opponents almost as traitors to Jewry. The Sadducees apparently maintained that the kingship was vested in the priestly line, in accordance with the Pentateuch; and

---

[1] Strugnell in *VT, Suppl.* VII 318–45.   [2] Cp. p. 176.
[3] Josephus *Antiquities* XVIII i 6 § 23 and *War* II viii 1 § 118.

the consequent assumption of the priestly and royal dignity in one person by the Hasmonaean princes further excited the hostility of the Pharisees. Thus the Sadducees had come to represent nobility, power and wealth, and were therefore involved in political affairs, by which the spirituality of many if not of all was only too easily debased. At the same time they accepted a secular office like the magistracy with apparent reluctance, when they made a show of adopting Pharisaic opinions in order that they might gain a hearing with the people; for their philhellenism easily gave place in due course to pro-Roman sympathies, which further alienated popular sentiment. Moreover, in character they were thought harsh towards their peers and rude to those outside their own circle.[1]

In doctrine the Sadducees disbelieved in fate and removed God beyond not merely the commission but the very sight of evil, as Josephus[2] says in contrasting them with the Pharisees; they maintained that man has the freedom to choose between good and evil, and the choice whether he follows the one or the other rests entirely with the will of each individual person. They denied the resurrection[3] and the persistence of the soul after death as well as the theory of rewards and punishments in the after-life on the ground that they were incapable of proof from the written Law of the Pentateuch; but that they were said to deny the existence of angels and spirits probably meant only that they rejected the developed angelology of their time for the same reason. They would, too, have nothing of the Messianic doctrine, which could similarly not be proved in their opinion. Indeed, they refused to accept any ordinance unless it was based directly on the written Law as well as any doctrines or practices found in other parts of the Scriptures which conflicted with it.[4]

The influence of the Sadducees was naturally greatest within the precincts of the Temple, while the Pharisees were supreme outside it; but, although there were many Pharisaic priests and the Pharisees had been able for a century before A.D. 70 to make their influence felt in it, they did not secure complete power till c. A.D. 50–60. The Sadducees meanwhile were losing ground, and their power still further declined after the destruction of the Temple in A.D. 70.

Schechter, when editing the *Zadokite Documents*,[5] first hinted at the possible identity of the Covenanters as 'Sons of Zadok'[6] with the Sadducees, but immediately abandoned it; and Leszynsky,[7] who also advocated it, did not improve the case by presenting the Sadducees as a

---

[1] Josephus *War* II viii 14 § 166.
[2] In *Antiquities* XIII v 9 § 173 and *War* II viii 14 §§ 164–5.
[3] Matt. xii. 23.
[4] Josephus *Antiquities* XIII x 6 § 297.   [5] In *Documents* I xxi–xxii.
[6] Cp. North in *CBQ* XVII 44–68.   [7] In *Die Sadduzäer* 142–67.

deeply religious group, in complete disagreement with all that contemporary writers say of them.[1]

The Covenanters or Zadokites differed from the Sadducees in many
essential respects. The Covenanters, so far as the Scrolls show, were
neither a high-priestly nor an aristocratic body, and they had little or
nothing to do with the Temple (*cp.* Z iv 1); they obviously had neither
power nor wealth, at any rate as individuals, and they often spoke of
themselves as 'poor' (H xii 3, 6, 10, W ix 9, 13 xiii 14), whereas the
Sadducees could not possibly be so described.[2] The Covenanters, too,
could not be called harsh or rude in their dealings with their fellow
men, so far as their character was reflected in the rules of their order;
and they were vehemently opposed to foreign domination, as their
bitter opposition to the 'Kittians' (*i.e.* Romans)[3] showed, whereas the
Sadducees were philhellene and tolerated Roman rule.[4] The doctrines
of the Covenanters also distinguished them clearly from the Sadducees:
for example, the Covenanters believed in a kind of predestination and
in a future life with rewards and punishments after death, they
looked for the coming of a Messiah, and they accepted the whole body
of Scripture (for every book of the Old Testament except that of
Esther[5] is represented at Qumrân), whereas the Sadducees rejected
these doctrines. Lastly, the Sadducees were strictly orthodox, whereas
the Covenanters were on many points definitely heterodox. These
differences absolutely preclude the identification of the Covenanters
with the Sadducees, as Josephus and the writers of the Gospels have
depicted them.

On second thoughts Schechter,[6] while saying that 'Zadokites' as a
descriptive term naturally suggested 'Sadducees', admitted that
present knowledge of the teaching and practice of the Sadducees was
not enough to identify them with the Zadokites, *i.e.* the Covenanters;
and he went on to think of the 'Sadducaeans' (as they may be called to
distinguish them from the Sadducees of the New Testament), who are
mentioned by early Qara'ite writers and some Arab historians. Much
can be said in favour of this suggestion, which will be examined in
detail hereafter.[7]

3. Dositheans and Samaritans

Schechter[8] then went on to speak of the Dositheans, of whom only
very confusing accounts had been handed down by ancient writers.

---

[1] Cp. Rabin in *JJS* VII 5 (where Habermann too is said to have sought to identify
the Sadducees with the Zadokites).
[2] Josephus *Antiquities* XIII x 6 § 298.   [3] Pp. 197–216.
[4] Cp. John xix. 15.   [5] S. pp. 385–6.   [6] In *Documents* I xviii–xxi.
[7] Pp. 259–66.   [8] In *Documents* I xxi–xxvi.

Great uncertainty prevails about these people. Their eponymous founder Dôstân or Dositheus appears to be only a mythical figure; and whether the two groups into which they fall according to the ancient authorities, who assign them now to the 3rd–2nd centuries B.C. and now to the 1st–3rd centuries A.D., are indeed distinct can hardly be made out. Whatever the solution of this problem may be, they show clear affinities with the Essenes and with the Covenanters both in doctrine and in practice.[1] They declared their founder, who was supposed to have retreated to a cave in pursuit of wisdom, to be the Messiah, recognizing him as the 'star out of Jacob',[2] regarded him as unique and called him the Only Teacher (cp. Z ix 8, 29); and they expected the speedy resurrection of the dead. They observed a calendar in which every month had thirty days (which they perhaps adjusted in the same way as the Covenanters)[3]; they were strict sabbatarians, celebrating their feasts only on a sabbath and refraining from giving food and drink to their beasts on that day (cp. Z xiii 14), preferring to lay it out for them on the previous day; they were also strict vegetarians, going so far as to refuse to drink water from springs in which living creatures swarmed (cp. Z xiv 12). Like the Essenes, they covered their bodies during ablutions; and like some Essenes and some Covenanters they, or some of them, abstained from marriage. Lastly, all these groups, as well as others (*e.g.* the Church), had each its own peculiar organization.

Ancient writers definitely connect the Sadducees (meaning presumably the Sadducaeans or Zadokites, *i.e.* the Covenanters of Qumrân) with these people. For example, Origen says[4] that a certain Samaritan named Dositheus about the time when John the Baptist and Jesus lived gave himself out to be the Messiah and won many adherents. Hegesippus[5] and Epiphanius[6] call the same person one of the first leaders of the Sadducaean sect, while Jerome[7] declares that he made himself leader of the Samaritans who rejected the prophets and that the *Sadducaei* (here confused with the Sadducees of the New Testament) who denied the resurrection of the body took their origin from him; and Filaster adds[8] that he was the teacher of Zadok. So too the Arab historian Mas'ûdî in the 10th century A.D. regarded the Dositheans as an offshoot of the Samaritans[9], and the Samaritan chronicler 'Abu-'lfath in the 14th century A.D. identi-

---

[1] Cp. Epiphanius *Panarion* XIII i 1–4 and Vilmar *Abulfathi Annales Samaritan* p. 82 l. 3—p. 83 l. 10 and p. 151 l. 11—p. 164 l. 11.
[2] Num. xxiv. 17.   [3] Pp. 325-6.
[4] In *in Matthaeum* 33, in *Lucam* 25, in *Celsum* i 57.
[5] Eusebius *Ecclesiastical History* IV xxii 5.   [6] In *Panarion* XIV ii 1.
[7] In *adversum Luciferianos* 23.
[8] Oehler *Corpus Haeresiologicorum* I i 4 § 5.
[9] Barbier de Meynard & de Cauteille *Maçoudi: les Prairies d'Or* I 114-5.

fied the Dositheans with the 'Sadducaeans' and regarded them as heretical.[1]

That a fragment of the Pentateuch reflecting the Samaritan recension has been found in Cave IV at Qumrân[2] is therefore significant and strengthens the suspicion of a connection between the Samaritans and the Covenanters; further, the Samaritans took much interest, like the Covenanters, in the calendar but, unlike them, made no claims to a Zadokite priesthood.[3] Indeed, what such a connection can have been is not very clear. The two groups cannot be identified out of hand, inasmuch as differences can be detected between them, *e.g.* in the use of the divine names. Possibly at an early date a Samaritan group allied itself with the Covenanters, or perhaps rather the Covenanters (or a party of them) settled amongst the Samaritans and became sooner or later assimilated to them.[4] The most likely time for such an event would be after the destruction of Jerusalem in A.D. 70, when all the religious groups in the country were scattered and found refuge where they could.

The connection of the Dositheans with the Samaritans and the Sadducaeans, then, is obscure but may repay investigation. The Sadducaeans or Zadokites, however, must be kept in mind as possibly, even probably, identical with them, even if the Dositheans cannot be brought into the picture.

4. PHARISEES

The relationship of the Covenanters to the Pharisees, of whom the Sadducaeans seem to have been an offshoot, also calls for examination; for, if the Covenanters can be shown to be in any way connected with the Pharisees, the probability of a connection with the Sadducaeans will be strengthened.

The Pharisees are said to have been so called either as 'separatists', *i.e.* as separated from loyalty to the king, because they disapproved of those Hasmonaean princes who added the title of king to that of high-priest, as 'seceders' from the Sanhedrin or as 'distinguished' from the Sadducees, of whom they disapproved, or else as 'separated', *i.e.* holding themselves aloof, from impure persons or things in order to attain a degree of holiness proper to those who sought communion with God;[5] at the same time the name may have been used as playing on the term for the 'interpretation (*pērūš*)' of Scripture as their principal

---

[1] Villars *op. cit.* p. 160 ll. 10–15 (*Sadûqây*), where the Sadducaeans are treated apart from the Biblical Sadducees, although both are called by the same name, and p. 163 ll. 1–4 (sons of *Yiṣdaq* or *Ṣadûq*).
[2] Skehan in *JBL* LXXIV 182–87 (Exod. vi. 25—xxxvii. 15).
[3] Cp. Rowley *Men of God* 264[2].   [4] Cp. Black *Scrolls* 60–1.
[5] Cp. Schürer *Geschichte* [3]II 396–9.

occupation.[1] Whatever the origin of the name was, Pharisaism as an active movement emerged from the Maccabaean conflict with the neighbouring heathen states, being first mentioned in the middle of the 2nd century B.C.; and it lasted till their destruction of the Jewish national life in the reign of Hadrian, after which it lived on only in Rabbinic memories.

Josephus, after saying how he had studied the teaching and tried the mode of life of the various parties, adds[2] 'when I had accomplished my desires, being now nineteen years old, I came back to the city and began to follow the rules of the party of the Pharisees, which is akin to the sect of the Stoics'; and he proceeds to give a very favourable account of the party, with which his sympathies obviously lay, although he came of a priestly family. He says that the Pharisees lived modestly and despised delicacies in food; they followed the dictates of reason; they showed proper respect for the aged and refrained from contradicting them in any matter. They were the most accurate interpreters of the Law and had become the leading party in his time. They attributed everything to fate and to God, holding that right or wrong action otherwise rests for the most part with man but that fate cooperates in every action. They held that the soul is imperishable, but that, while the soul of the good man alone passes into another body, that of the wicked man suffers eternal punishment. He adds that they were affectionate to one another and lived in harmony with the community. In this respect as in doctrine and political outlook they were in his opinion the opposite of the Sadducees.

The Pharisees carried on the work which the early teachers of the Law, the so-called 'scribes', had begun, that of applying it to the practical needs of daily life. The teaching of the early scribes rested on the plain text of the Law with a certain amount of simple explanation; their activity in this direction ceased when Greek influence was beginning to be severely felt in Jewish national life. New customs and practices arose for which the Law, literally interpreted, made no provision, and there arose a body of lay teachers, as distinct from the old priestly 'scribes', to devote themselves to the exposition of the Law as a matter of private study. Thus there was no authoritative teaching from the disappearance of these 'scribes' c. 270 B.C. to the institution of the Sanhedrin c. 190 B.C., a body of priests and lay teachers able officially to regulate the religious affairs of the nation, onwards. Their task was to harmonize the ancestral Law with the needs of contemporary life; this was to be effected by the issue of special decrees on specific points. In this body the priestly element would wish to maintain the

---

[1] Cp. Gertner in *BSOAS* XXVI 248–57.
[2] In *Life* ii 10–12; cp. *Antiquities* XIII v 9 § 172, XVIII i 3 §§ 12–15 and *War* II viii 14 §§ 162–3, 166.

character of the written Law as sacred and obligatory apart from newly introduced customs, while those who eventually crystallized into the Pharisaic party were willing neither to accept any such extension of priestly authority, holding their own authority as teachers to be equal to that of the priests, nor to find all the necessary rules to be already contained or implied in the written law; their methods resulted in Midrash and Mishnah, the two types of exposition by which they expounded the original Law and adapted it to their own times. Thus the oral law, as Lauterbach contended,[1] was a legal fiction invented by the Pharisees to lend authority to religious customs which had already become established in popular uses; they were therefore not 'the advocates of an old oral tradition but the innovators of a radical reform'.

The Pharisees were a democratic party, mainly drawn from the people, and they safeguarded the privileges of the laity against the claims of an aristocratic and exclusive priesthood. As Josephus says,[2] the Pharisees led the people, compelling even the priestly aristocracy to yield to them; and their influence on the people was correspondingly great. They invested the observance of the sabbath and holy days with special sanctity in the home, introduced the recitation of daily prayers beside the sacrifices in the Temple and instituted the deputations of laymen at the daily sacrifice there; further, they laid stress on the use of phylacteries (*i.e.* amulets containing excerpts from the Scriptures which were worn on the forehead and arm). Especially, in regard to the Day of Atonement, they transferred the atoning power from the high-priest to the day itself, so that atonement might be effected without priest or sacrifice; the one thing which was absolutely indispensable was repentance. They were responsible also for fixing the canon of Scripture, building up the service and liturgy of the synagogue and establishing a system of religious instruction in it and in the schools. Their ruling idea was that religious doctrine could be impressed on the people by carefully formed habits of religious observance; ceremonial observance, as Box has said,[3] was valued mainly because of its educational worth. The three religious duties which were most emphasized by them were penitence and prayer and the practice of charity. Finally, the Pharisaic religion, as Box also remarks, never failed to produce genuine examples of profound piety, although it was undoubtedly marred by the great danger of formalism, externalism and unreality, inherent in a legalistic religion; consequently, the Pharisees multiplied precepts and rules.

The Pharisees had taken over the doctrine of a future life from the earlier apocalyptists; consequently they admitted the apocalyptic

---

[1] In *Rabbinic Essays* 23–48, 54–5.   [2] In *Antiquities* XVIII xii 3 § 12.
[3] In Hastings' *ERE* IX 835.

Daniel into the canon of the Scriptures. Subsequently an anti-apocalyptic bias showed itself, resulting in the rejection of the later apocalyptic literature. Pharisaism indeed was far from other-worldly; its main interest was to bring the sanction of religion into life on earth. This tendency appeared in the Messianic doctrine, which played a prominent part in the liturgy of the synagogue; for the Messiah of Pharisaism was not the heavenly or transcendental figure of the apocalyptists but a human son of David.[1]

Some, *e.g.* Ginzberg,[2] have thought of the Covenanters as the Pharisees; and yet others, *e.g.* Dahl,[3] have suggested that they were an offshoot of the Pharisees. This last view has much truth in it; but, although the Covenanters may show many contacts with the Pharisees, the identification cannot be accepted absolutely and without reserve, inasmuch as they show differences, numerous if often small, even where they most closely resemble one another.

In the spiritual sphere one of the outstanding marks of Pharisaism was the institution of three daily times of prayer, in the evening and in the morning and also at midday;[4] these were based on precepts extracted from the Old Testament.[5] The Covenanters, too, insisted on daily prayers 'at the beginning of the dominion of light and at its turning point (*i.e.* at midday) and at its disappearance' (D ix 25–x 1; cp. T xii 3–5); but at the same time they required also three times of prayer during the night 'at the beginning of the watches of the night . . . and at its turning point (*i.e.* at midnight) . . . and when lights shine forth from the holy and high habitation' (D x 2–3; cp. T xii 5–7). These last three times of prayer at night are in keeping with the rule requiring the division of the night into three separate watches[6] for the study of the Law (D vi 6–8).[7] Thus the Covenanters are distinguished in this as in other matters by intensifying the customary requirements; for, while they required six times of prayer in every twenty-four hours, the Pharisees required only three, and the Essenes were said to offer prayer only once a day, namely at dawn.[8] Both Pharisees and Covenanters said a grace at meals; but while the Pharisees required one before and after meals,[9] the Covenanters like the Essenes[10] said one only before meals;[11] herein the Covenanters showed themselves for once not so exacting as the Pharisees. In connection with the Pharisees, too, the discovery of phylacteries in the caves near Qumrân[12] is also significant; for the phylactery is known as a device especially dear to the

---

[1] Pp. 462–5. [2] In *Sekte* I 373–80. [3] In *Das Volk Gottes* 129–32.
[4] Mishnah *Berakoth* iv 1; s. Moore *Judaism* II 219–20 and Oesterley & Box *Literature of Rabbinical and Mediaeval Judaism* 172.
[5] Ps. lv. 17–18 and Dan. vi. 10. [6] Pp. 329–30.
[7] Cp. Talmon in *RQ* II 475–500. [8] Josephus *War* II viii 5 § 128.
[9] Mishnah *Berakhoth* iii 3–4. [10] Josephus *War* II viii 5 § 131.
[11] P. 107. [12] Pp. 17, 19 i cp. p. 21.

Pharisees.[1] Both parties indeed were insistent on the need for the proper performance of spiritual duties as against the mechanical repetition of religious rites and on the necessity of true repentance, without which these would be valueless; and the spirituality of the Covenanters as reflected in the Scrolls can be seen as a consequence of the Pharisees' application of the sanctions of religion to daily life.

Little emphasis was laid on sacrifice, which was held to be of no avail in comparison with righteousness (D ix 3–5); but this view of sacrifice, being Biblical,[2] was based not so much on a conscious desire to depreciate it by another uniquely spiritual sacrifice as on the realization that in the 'period of Belial' (D ii 19 W xiv 9) it was something more or less impracticable which might be subsequently restored.[3] Accordingly the society, like the priests to whom Malachi refers, is forbidden to offer sacrifice; for 'as for all admitted to the covenant with intent not to kindle the fire on His altar—they become "shutters of the door", as God has said: Oh that there were amongst you that would shut the doors, that ye might not kindle fire on mine altar in vain![4] They must surely be careful to do according to the interpretation of the Law for the period of wickedness and to separate themselves from the sons of perdition'[1] (Z viii 11).

The reason for this abstention from sacrifice by the Covenanters is not clear. Possibly they regarded the official priesthood in Jerusalem as in the strict sense non-Zadokite and therefore unfit to serve in the Temple; and the hierarchy might have discouraged the attendance at public worship of a group whose orthodoxy might seem doubtful to them. Possibly, too, they might have feared contamination on such occasions by contact with persons whom they might regard as insufficiently strict in matters of ceremonial or ritual defilement.[5] Also, the use of a peculiar calendar must have made participation in public worship difficult,[6] since the dates of feasts and fasts would not necessarily coincide; for the Covenanters held that the dates of holy days and Sabbaths were among 'the hidden things concerning which all Israel had gone astray' (Z v 1–2) and that their true dates were known only to themselves.[7] Thus the hierarchy, who had given up the old sacred calendar to which the Covenanters still clung, in favour of the new profane (Hellenistic) calendar, might well be stigmatized as 'sons of perdition'; so the author of *Jubilees* once described those Jews who rejected circumcision.[8] Sacrifice was permitted only in the Temple; but whether the Covenanters actually offered sacrifices at Qumrân is a disputed point; for the presence of animal bones,

---

[1] S. p. 82; cp. Matt. xxiii. 2–7.   [2] Cp. Ps. li. 18–19.

[3] Carmignac in *RB*, NS LXIII 524–32.

[4] Mal. i. 10; cp. Kahle *Opera Minora* 102–3.   [5] Black *Scrolls* 40.

[6] Talmon in *Scr. Hieros.* 164–6.   [7] Pp. 311–30.   [8] Jubilees xc 26.

though meticulously buried, in the ruins[1] proves nothing certain. These might have been the remains of a meal; for the bones of beasts at ordinary secular meals cannot have been left lying about the buildings or thrown out of doors but must have been decently put away. Alternatively, they might be the bones of beasts over which a blessing had been said at any of their ordinary daily meals (for they did not apparently practise abstinence from flesh) and which were afterwards burnt because 'consecrated bones could not be carelessly thrown away'.[2] If so, they were perhaps treated as the bones of substitute sacrifices which for the time being had taken the place of the regular sacrifices at the Temple;[3] for the Covenanters, if they could not offer their sacrifices there in person, could equally not run the risk of defiling their offerings by sending them by persons possibly not ceremonially clean (Z xiv 1), and true sacrifices elsewhere would be inconceivable before and impossible at the Temple after A.D. 70.

The rules then laid down (Z xiii 27–xiv 1) show that after that event (when the *Zadokite Documents* must be dated)[4] the Covenanters regarded the old sacrifices as something which was almost impure (cp. Z viii 11), but which they would like to see purified and restored as part of the ideal state of affairs (cp. Z v 7) and which the author of *War* actually enjoined (W ii 4–6). Thus, just as the references to sacrifice and the Temple would not necessarily imply that this was practised in the period of the Scrolls,[5] so abstention from sacrifice was in either case, both before and after A.D. 70, unavoidable for the Covenanters for the same reason as it had been for the Essenes.

Another point on which the Pharisees and the Covenanters were at variance was the annual contribution of a half-shekel which every adult male Jew made to the upkeep of the Temple[6]; for the Covenanters restricted the payment of this tax to once in a life-time (A Ord. ii 6–7).[7]

Doctrinally the Covenanters and the Pharisees were not far apart. Both held that fate played a large part in man's life on earth; but, while for the Pharisees 'to do right or otherwise rests for the most part with men, while fate also helps towards each',[8] amongst the Covenanters complete predestination applied only to two classes. These were the wicked, 'since God has not chosen them from of old, from eternity; and He knew their work before they were established and abhorred the generations when they arose' (Z ii 6–7), and the righteous, the 'elect of Israel, the men called by name who shall arise at the end of

---

[1] De Vaux *Archéologie* 9–11; cp. Cross *Library* 75–6 and Zeuner in *PQS* XCII 28–30 (oxen, cows, sheep, goats).
[2] Schubert *Community* 52–3; cp. Exod. xii. 5–7 and Deut. xii. 5–7.
[3] De Vaux in *RB*, NS LXIII 549–50; cp. *Archéologie* 10–11, 21.
[4] Pp. 367–9.   [5] Rabinowitz in *VT* III 180–1.
[6] Cp. Matt. xvii. 24–27.   [7] Allegro in *JSS* VI 71–3.
[8] Josephus *War* II viii 14 § 163.

G

the days; the exact statement of their names according to their genealogies, the epoch of their existence, the years of their sojourning and the exact statement of their works [are all known to Him]' (Z vi 2–3). That the Covenanters believed possibly in some form or other of resurrection and certainly in a future life in which the righteous were rewarded for their life on earth with eternal bliss while the wicked were punished for their sins has already been shown[1]; and their standpoint was that of the Pharisees. So in the words of the Mishnah[2] 'he who says that the resurrection of the dead is not to be inferred from the Law has no part in the world to come'; and Josephus adds[3] that the Pharisees held 'that every soul is imperishable' and that 'an immortal strength belongs to souls and that there are beneath the earth punishments and rewards for those who in life devoted themselves to virtue or vileness, and that eternal imprisonment is appointed to the latter but the possibility of returning to life to the former'. The views, then, of the two parties on this subject were not entirely dissimilar, although the one inclined to a bodily resurrection and the other rather to the immortality of the soul.

Accordingly, the two parties differed considerably on the question of the Messiah.[4] On the one hand, when the evangelists describe a Pharisee as one 'who . . . waited for the kingdom of God',[5] they make it plain that such an attitude was regarded as something exceptional; for an active Messianism was no part of the Pharisaic creed. Messianic expectations were limited to the circle of apocalyptists and popular preachers, whom the Pharisees discountenanced, and they did not become a part of their regular teaching till after the fall of Jerusalem in A.D. 70. On the other hand, such speculations formed an integral part of the beliefs of the Covenanters, who even embraced the doctrine of two Messiahs, a priestly and a lay Messiah.[6] The memory of their active Messianism seems to have lasted long after the time when the Covenanters may be supposed to have ceased being an effective body in the state; for R. Jonathan, an anti-Messianist of the middle of the 2nd century A.D., is reputed to have said 'may the life-blood go out of them that calculate the epochs!'[7] This saying is certainly an apt description of and possibly a direct allusion to the Covenanters, whose intense interest in 'epochs' is clearly demonstrable (D ix 26–x 5 W i 6–9 T i 23–5 vi 29 xii 7–9, 22 Z ii 8 vi 3–7).[8]

There were other clear differences between the Covenanters and the Pharisees, of which the most noteworthy are their respective attitudes to marriage with a niece and to taking a second wife during the life of

---

[1] Pp. 74–6.
[2] In *Sanhedrin* x 1.
[3] In *War* II viii 14 § 163 and *Antiquities* XVIII i 3 § 14.
[4] Cp. Schubert *Community* 124–5.
[5] Mk. xiv. 43 and Lk. xxiii. 50.
[6] Pp. 468–74.
[7] B. Talmud *Sanhedrin* 97b.
[8] Cp. Roth *Background* 58.

the first: the Pharisees allowed both practices as not contravening Biblical Law,[1] whereas the Covenanters condemned both.

Marriage with a niece was, so far as the records show, rare during the early period of the Second Temple, only becoming common in the 1st century A.D.[2]; it was, however, an ancient custom which came to be forbidden by certain groups, e.g. Samaritans, Sadducaeans and Qara'ites.[3] The only known early instance seems to be one in the priestly Tobiad family c. 200 B.C.,[4] but between the last half of the 1st century B.C. and the first half of the 2nd century A.D. many cases are known. The family of Herod the Great, including the king himself who had both a brother's and a sister's daughters among his wives, affords six instances,[5] and three are known in that of the patriarch Gamaliel II.[6] Polygamy was common again both in the family of Herod the Great, who himself had ten wives[7] (though not all at the same time), and in the high-priestly families.[8] Implicit Christian teaching[9] and the rules of the Covenanters were apparently the earliest attempts seriously to restrict the custom of polygamy before the Amoraic period c. A.D. 300; they were disputed by the Babylonian Rabba but were accepted by the Qara'ites, and the practice was not finally prohibited till the middle of the 11th century A.D.[10]

The attitude of the Covenanters to divorce is not clear, although a reference to the custom has been found in two passages.[11] The first condemns 'taking two women (in marriage) during their lives' (Z vii 1), which certainly refers not to marrying a second wife after the divorce of the first but to having two wives at the same time;[12] in the second the text is damaged and only 'and likewise for one who divorces [his wife]' can be read (Z xvi 8), which looks as if it is intended to permit divorce in some qualified form or under some restriction.[13] If so, the Covenanters, like Jesus[14], were trying to check what was becoming a serious social abuse in their time; for it was practised in the highest circles of society

---

[1] Mishnah *Nedarim* viii 7 and *Ketuboth* x 1–6; cp. Tosefta *Kiddushin* i 4.
[2] Ginzberg *Sekte* I 182.   [3] Aptowitzer in *HUCA* IV 232–7.
[4] Josephus *Antiquities* XVII i 3 § 19 (Joseph with a daughter of his brother Solymius).
[5] Josephus *War* I xxii 4 § 441 (Herod's uncle Joseph with Salome, Herod's sister); *Antiquities* XVII i 3 § 19 (Herod with a brother's and a sister's daughter), XVIII v 1 §§ 109–118 (Herodias with two uncles in succession) and 4 § 137 (Herod's son Philip with Salome daughter of Herodias), XIX v 1 § 276 (Herod king of Chalcis with his niece Berenice daughter of Herodias).
[6] Goldin *R. Nathan* 84–5 § 16 (Eliezer ben Hyrcanus), B. Talmud *Yebamoth* 15a (Abba), Midrash R. *Genesis* xvii § 3 (R. Jose of Galilee).
[7] Josephus *Antiquities* XVII i 3 §§ 19–23 and *War* I xxviii 4 §§ 562–3.
[8] Tosefta *Yebamoth* i 10 ('Alôbai and Qaifâ)=P. Talmud *Yebamoth* i 4 ('Anôbai and Neqîfai) and B. Talmud *Yebamoth* 15b (Ben 'Akmai and Ben Quppay).
[9] Matt. xix. 4–6 and Mk. x. 5–9; cp. Tit. i. 6 and 1 Tim. iii. 2, 12, v. 9.
[10] Ginzberg *op. cit.* I 183–5.   [11] Cp. Rowley *Zadokite Documents* 36[3].
[12] Charles in *Apocrypha and Pseudepigrapha* II 810.
[13] Segal in *JQR*, NS II 138.
[14] Matt. v. 30–1, xix 3–9; Mk. x. 2–12; Lk. xvi. 18.

from Herod the Great downwards.[1] Such a conclusion would agree
with alQirqîsânî's statement that the Sadducaeans forbade divorce;
and this strengthens the suspicion that the Qara'ites, the Sadducaeans
and the Zadokites or Covenanters must have been in some way
inter-connected.[2]

The strictness of the Covenanters in regard to marriage was not due
to the possession of more lofty principles than the Pharisees, but to
the passion for a more rigorous interpretation of Scripture, as many of
their rules which involved no moral principles clearly showed;[3] and
the driving force compelling them towards this rigorist attitude was as
much political as religious. Their objections, too, to such practices
as those tolerated or adopted by their rivals would not have arisen
from a single isolated instance or a few such instances; it could only
have grown up at a time when they had become notorious. It would
reflect therefore not the Tobiad but the Herodian and late Tannaitic
ages. The attempt therefore to eliminate this divergence between the
practice of the Pharisees and that of the Covenanters by assuming the
rules on marriage (as well as those embodying other divergencies
between the two parties) in the *Zadokite Documents* to be interpolations
made long afterwards in the Qara'ite interest (in so far as the Qara'ites
disapproved of both the practices in question)[4] is as unconvincing a
device as it is needless; the strictness of the Covenanters as against the
laxity of the Pharisees is but part and parcel of a contemporary
movement which finds expression also in the Gospels. The Qara'ites
are as likely to have inherited the objection to these matrimonial
abuses from the Covenanters as to have invented them.

Although, too, other rules in the *Zadokite Documents* are for the most
part in accord with Pharisaic 'law and custom (*hǎlākāh*)', they are
often more but rarely less rigorous than the corresponding rules of the
Pharisees, as several examples show. Such divergencies began with the
schools of Hillel and Shammai in the middle of the 1st century B.C.,
that of Hillel being the more lenient and that of Shammai the stricter in
their interpretation of the Law; and the so-called 'additions of the
Sabbath' were already known by the 3rd century A.D.[5] The Scrolls,
showing the beginnings of these additions, must therefore in all
probability be dated within these limits.

For example, the Rabbis laid down a number of punishments for
the profanation of the Sabbath which were generally not so severe as
those prescribed by the Covenanters. The Rabbis allowed the necessity
of saving life to override the law,[6] but the Covenanters forbade it

---

[1] Josephus *War* I xxii 1 § 432 and xxix 4 § 591 (Doris twice repudiated by Herod).
[2] Pp. 259–66.   [3] Cp. Moore *Judaism* I 201–2.
[4] Wernberg-Møller in *RQ* I 140–3.
[5] Ginzberg *Sekte* I 149–51 and Rabin *Zadokite Documents* 52–9.
[6] Cp. Jubilees ll. 12–13.

(Z xiii 26, if the text is rightly taken);[1] according to the Rabbis the foetus might not be extracted from a female beast but she might be otherwise assisted,[2] and her young if dropped into a cistern or pit might be rescued,[3] but neither action was allowed by the Covenanters (Z xiii 22–3); the Rabbis allowed a man to travel 1000 or 2000 cubits (for the figures vary)[4] and even tolerated evasions of the rule, but the Covenanters restricted him without exception to 1000 cubits (Z xiii 7); according to Rabbinic law a man might not employ a Gentile to do what he might not do himself,[5] although this rule was apparently disapproved by some authorities,[6] but the Covenanters might not drive even a slave of either sex or a hired labourer to work (Z xiii 21); according to the Rabbis the Sabbath was a day of rest for beast as well as for man,[7] while according to the Covenanters a beast might not be struck or even driven out of the house to work it if it was refractory (Z xiii 15); the Rabbis allowed a vessel to be broached to obtain necessary food[8] and drink, but the Covenanters forbade it (Z xiii 7); the Rabbis permitted borrowing and lending under certain conditions,[9] but the Covenanters absolutely forbade it (Z xiii 3); the Rabbis originally prohibited taking things into or out of a house[10] but came to allow the evasion of this rule by certain subterfuges,[11] whereas the Covenanters continued to forbid a thing to be taken into or out of a house or even a booth (Z xiii 16); the Rabbis allowed an adult to be carried on a stretcher or a child to be dragged along by a woman on the Sabbath,[12] but the Covenanters would not even allow a nurse or attendant to go in or out of doors carrying an infant (Z xiii 20); the Rabbis did not prohibit staying in a place in proximity to Gentiles but said that it ought to be avoided,[13] whereas the Covenanters prohibited it (Z xiii 24); the Rabbis forbade men after a seminal effusion or women in menstruation to enter the precincts of the Temple,[14] but the Covenanters refused to allow marital intercourse even in the holy city (Z xiv 4); the Rabbis said that the Paschal lamb might be offered on this day,[15] but the Covenanters only allowed the sacrifices proper to it to be offered then (Z xiii 27); and lastly swearing an oath by the name of God was permitted in certain cases by the Rabbis, it was restricted by the teachers of the Talmudic age, the so-called Amoraim (c. A.D.

[1] *E.g.* Mishnah *Shabbath* xviii 3 and *Yoma* viii 6–7 (s. Schubert *Community* 161–2).
[2] Cp. Rabin *Zadokite Documents* 57.
[3] Mishnah *Shabbath* xviii 3 and B. Talmud *Shabbath* 128b.
[4] Mishnah *Erubin* v 8 and B. Talmud *Erubin* 51a.
[5] Mishnah *Shabbath* i 8 and B. Talmud *Shabbath* 19a; cp. 122a.
[6] Philo *On the Special Laws* ii 66–8.   [7] Mishnah *Yom Tob* v 3.
[8] Mishnah *Shabbath* xx 1, xxii 3.   [9] *Ibid.* xxiii 1.
[10] *Ibid.* i 1; cp. Jubilees ii 30.   [11] Talmud *Shabbath* 5b–6b.
[12] Mishnah *Shabbath* x 5, xviii 2 xxi 1.
[13] B. Talmud *Erubin* 62a; cp. Mishnah *Abodah Zarah* ii 1.
[14] Mishnah *Kelim* i 8 and Josephus *War* V v 6 § 227.
[15] Mishnah *Pesachim* v 8.

200–500), and was finally discontinued in the time of the Geonim (A.D. 589–1034),[1] whereas the Covenanters had already prohibited it (Z xix 9). The excessive severity, if not harshness, of the laws governing the Sabbath, which Jesus sternly denounced,[2] was to some extent mitigated in practice by popular opinion;[3] but only two cases in which the Covenanters relaxed it can be found. The first is their rule which forbids drinking water on the Sabbath unless it is found in the camp (Z xiii 9); for the Rabbis, while allowing it to be drawn only from a well inside a house,[4] forbid it to be taken from any other source even in a courtyard.[5] The second is their reluctance to enforce the extreme penalty for its violation (Z xiv 6), although it had both Biblical[6] and Rabbinic[7] sanction.

The same strictness of interpretation which marks the attitude of the Covenanters to the rules governing the observance of the Sabbath is found, though not so often, in their attitude to the ordinary law.[8] For example, the Rabbis did not allow certain classes to act as witnesses, *e.g.* dice-players and usurers, pigeon-racers and dealers in the produce of the Sabbatical year;[9] contrariwise the Covenanters in ordinary cases did not admit as a witness 'one who has transgressed any of the commandments with a high hand until they (*sic*) are purified by virtue of repentance', and in capital cases refused to admit any witness 'whose days have not been completed that they may be mustered as one who fears (*sic*) God', *i.e.* who have not become fully qualified members of the society (Z x 15–6). Even though these rules seem to refer only to appearing in cases between members of the community, they reflect a protest against the slackness, as the Covenanters will have regarded it, of contemporary Pharisaic or Rabbinical practice. The society also even allowed a wife in one case to give evidence against her husband (IQ 28A i 11); this provision is indeed surprising but ought not therefore to be eliminated by emendation,[10] inasmuch as no Jewish copyist could have inserted it if it were not a fact (*difficilior lectio potior*). Again, the Covenanters' rule that 'no man shall defile himself with any living or creeping thing by eating them from the grubs of bees (in honey) to all living things that teem in water' (Z xiv 12), which was taken over by the Qara'ites,[11] contradicts the sensible Rabbinic rules that water may be drunk from any pit or cavity or cave even though *larvae* may be breeding in it[12] and that insects originating in vinegar or wine may be consumed without risk of ceremonial defilement.[13] Lastly, the Coven-

[1] Rashi on B. Talmud *Shebuoth* 38a.   [2] Lk. xiv. 1–6.
[3] *E.g.* Matt. xii. 11–12.   [4] Mishnah *Erubin* viii 6–8.   [5] Jubilees 1 8.
[6] Num. xv 35.   [7] Jubilees l 12–13; s. Rabin *Scr. Jud.* ii 86.
[8] Cp. Liebermann in *PAAJR* XX 395–404.
[9] Mishnah *Sanhedrin* iii 3; cp. Tosefta *Sanhedrin* v 5, B. Talmud *Sanhedrin* 24b–26a and *Pesachim* 49b (s. Rabin in *Scr. Jud.* II 64–6).
[10] Baumgarten in *JBL* LXXVI 266–9.   [11] Liebermann *ibid.* 402 (55, 56).
[12] B. Talmud *Hullin* 67a.   [13] Tosefta *Berakoth* vii 6 and *Terumoth* vii 11.

anters' rule that they may not eat fish unless split while still alive and drained of blood (Z xiv 13) contradicts the Rabbinic rule that fish and locusts may be eaten without hesitation whether alive or dead.[1]

These extensions of the Law, especially of the laws governing the observance of the Sabbath, though often trifling in themselves and 'hovering in the air', as the saying was,[2] have a twofold importance. First, they prove that the Covenanters were not strictly orthodox Pharisees, inasmuch as they admitted or required a number of deviations from Pharisaic norms, even though they were but modifications of the old law.[3] Second, as already said, no such divergencies were known before the emergence of the rival schools of Hillel and Shammai,[4] from whose debates they derived in the middle of the 1st century A.D.; and their number had risen from the 39 heads under which they were originally subsumed[5] to $(39 \times 39 =)$ 1521 such differences by the 4th century A.D.[6] That the *Zadokite Documents* therefore cannot be assigned to a date before these two schools agrees with the suggestion that the Zadokites did not come back from Egypt to Palestine till after Pompey's capture of Jerusalem in 63 B.C., as argued hereafter;[7] but the divergencies are so few in comparison with the final number (which, though itself obviously artificial, may be taken as indicating a very large number) that the work must have been composed early rather than late in this period.

That the Zadokite deviations from the Pharisaic law have a definite political purpose is clear enough; for they are surely directed against three specific groups within Judaism.

First, the author of the *Zadokite Documents* twice refers to 'the builders of the wall'; in the first he says that 'the builders of the wall who have walked after vanities[8] . . . are caught on two points: on whoredom by taking two wives during their lives . . . ; and they marry each man his brother's daughter and his sister's daughter' (Z vii 1–9); and in the second, after describing the prevalent wickedness and the punishment brought upon the nation by 'the kings of the nations' and 'the chief of the kings of the Greeks'[9] whom God has sent to take vengeance on them, he says that 'those who built the wall and daubed it with spittle[10] did not understand these things, because one coming like the wind and bringing storms and spluttering falsehood spluttered (falsehood) at them, so that God was angry with His whole congregation' (Z ix 21–2). The allusion is as clear as daylight. Josephus[11] says that the Pharisees

---

[1] Tosefta *Terumoth* ix 6.
[2] Tosefta *Hagigah* i 8.
[3] Cp. Jubilees ii 30, l 8, 12–13.
[4] Tosefta *Hagigah* ii 9.
[5] Mishnah *Shabbath* vii 2.
[6] P. Talmud *Shabbath* vii 2.
[7] Pp. 226–37.
[8] Hos. v. 11 (s. Driver in *JBL* LV 105–6).
[9] Pp. 219–21.
[10] Ezek. xiii. 10–16.
[11] In *Antiquities* XIII x 6 § 297.

handed down a great many rules not found in the Mosaic Law and that the Sadducees rejected these additions to it, accepting only what was found in Scripture and refusing to observe what was merely derived from the tradition of their forefathers. Thus R. 'Aqîbâ, who was executed by the Romans *c.* A.D. 132, taught that 'tradition is a fence for the Law'; and the Pharisaic advice given to students of the Law was 'Make a fence for the Law'.[1] This process of hedging in the Mosaic Law with a mass of rules and customs ultimately culminated in the Mishnah, which was the work of a long succession of Pharisaic teachers and Rabbis, codified and put into written form under Rabbî, namely R. Judah I the patriarch, who was born in A.D. 135. Clearly then 'the builders of the wall', to whom the Covenanters were thus vehemently opposed, were those who made 'a fence for the Law' but whose work was shoddy and left many loopholes for evading it, namely the Pharisees and the Rabbis, as Schechter suggested long ago.[2]

Second, the offences with which the Covenanters charged some of their opponents were such as were rampant in the 1st and 2nd centuries A.D. in the Herodian family and especially in that of R. Gamaliel II, patriarch *c.* A.D. 90–110 and father of R. Judah the compiler of the Mishnah. The 'princes of Judah (*śārê yᵉhûḏāh*)' therefore whom the same writer denounces as having become 'like them that remove the landmark (*i.e.* amass vast estates)' and 'over whom the wrath (*sc.* of God) shall be poured . . . inasmuch as they entered a covenant of repentance but defiled themselves in practices of whoredom and wicked wealth, . . . approaching unchastity and acting overbearingly for the sake of wealth and gain' (Z ix 13–15) may well be members of the patriarchal house and other highly placed Pharisees, some perhaps former Covenanters, whose marriages and accumulation of wealth are a growing scandal throughout this whole period; for the authors of the Scrolls pass easily from one age to another, taking the past as a prototype of the present.

In this connection a fragment of a Scroll, hitherto imperfectly understood, gains point. It refers to the disappearance of 'all the wickedness at the end of the completion of the forty years when no wicked man will be found on the earth' and goes on to speak of 'the poor who accept the period of affliction and will be delivered from all the snares . . .' and of 'those who turn aside to' or 'the penitents of the wilderness who will live for a thousand generations' when 'the congregation of His (*sc.* God's) elect will be chiefs and princes (*śārîm*)' and then foretells the doom of 'the princes of wickedness (*śārê hā[riš⁽ā]h*) who have oppressed His holy people, who will perish like the smoke of a flame in the wind' (APs. a i 5–ii 8). The 'poor men' are the

---

[1] Mishnah *Aboth* i 1, iii 20.　　　　　[2] In *Documents* I xxxvi; s. *RÉJ* LXII 191–2.

Covenanters (as the whole tenor of the text proves; for the rest of it deals with the Rightful Teacher), while the 'princes of wickedness' are their oppressors in the world; these (if not the Romans[1]), will be the same 'princes of Judah' or may include many such who have been denounced for amassing wealth at the expense of their neighbours and who will disappear from the face of the earth at the end of forty years, *i.e.* when the Messiah comes to rescue 'those who are waiting for the Lord',[2] here equated with the Covenanters living in the wilderness.

Third, the Scrolls refer also to certain opponents of the Covenanters as 'seekers after divisions' or 'smooth things'. Possibly the phrase conveys a hint of sectarianism, as the Talmudic expression for 'sectarians (*ba'ălê maḥălōqeṭ*)' suggests[3]; but this is not properly its import in the Scrolls. Here it describes the faithless Israelites of past centuries[4] as having incurred God's wrath 'because they have sought smooth things and chosen delusions and looked for breaches (in the Law) and chosen the fair neck[5] and pronounced the wicked righteous and the righteous wicked and caused others to violate the covenant and transgressed the law and lain in wait for the soul of the righteous and abhorred all that live innocent lives and persecuted them with the sword and provoked quarrels among the people' (Z i 13–16); in other words, they are people who have tampered with the Law, interpreting it to their own advantage and stirring up disputes about it. Accordingly, the author of the *Hymns* declares that he has become an object of hatred to 'the seekers after smooth things' and gives thanks to God for his deliverance from them (T ii 15, 32). Another aspect of these same people appears in a fragment of a *Commentary on Nahum*, whose author speaks of Demetrius 'king of Greece who sought to enter Jerusalem by the counsel of the seekers after smooth things' and of their connection with the Young Lion of Wrath 'who used to hang men alive' (ANa. 2–8).[6] Whether Demetrius I or Demetrius III is meant, he must be a foreign king whom the Hasidaeans or their successors the Pharisees invited on some occasion or other to help them against a rival party in the state;[7] and their conduct on the occasion, whenever it may have been, seems to be cited in illustration of similar conduct on some subsequent occasion, *e.g.* that of the admission of Simon bar Giora (if he is rightly identified with the Young Lion of Wrath')[8] into Jerusalem during the siege in the spring of A.D. 67[9]; for, although the high-priest Matthias and other highly placed priests were the prime movers, the invitation was actually put into effect by 'men from Jerusalem' and 'the people',[10] who would

---

[1] Pp. 202–3.   [2] Ps. xxxvii. 4.   [3] Cp. Gertner in *BASOS*. XXV 1–2.
[4] Cp. Dan. xi 32.   [5] Cp. Hos. x. 11.   [6] Pp.288–92.
[7] Pp. 292–3.   [8] Pp. 291–8.   [9] P. 289.
[10] Josephus *War* IV ix 11 § 571 (high-priests) and § 574 (men from Jerusalem), V xiii 1 § 528 (people).

have included Pharisees in their number. In other words, these ancient 'seekers after smooth things' had their modern successors long afterwards in Israel.

These 'seekers after' or 'expounders of smooth things' can only be the heirs of the Hasidaeans, namely the Pharisees. As Josephus says,[1] traditionally 'the Pharisees are lenient in the matter of punishments'; and by the same token the people, whom the Covenanters seem by their rigorous attitude to the Law to be implicitly accusing of laxity in their interpretation of it, must be these same Pharisees. This identification is strengthened if Dr. Brownlee is right, as he surely is, in suggesting[2] that 'smooth things (ḥălāqôt)' is a deliberate alteration of or a play on 'legal customs (ḥălākôt)'; for these were the main preoccupation of the Pharisees, as both the New Testament and Jewish writings attest. At the same time the Covenanters were fanatically opposed to the foreign enemy whom they called the 'Kittians', i.e. the Romans,[3] as a people 'who do not believe in the statutes of God' (H ii 12–iii 1); contrariwise, the Pharisees were notorious for their pro-Roman sympathies before and during the Revolt of A.D. 66–73, and the historian Josephus, who was a Pharisee, after his capture did all that he could to promote the policy and the interests of the Romans.

Thus an unmistakable *double entente* underlies this appellation of the Pharisees: as expounders of the Law they sought those interpretations which were the easiest for themselves and offered them ways of circumventing or evading the full rigour of its provisions and were therefore heterodox in the eyes of the Covenanters; and politically, however much they disliked or disapproved foreign rule, they were appeasers always ready to take the easy way if they could thereby avoid a clash with the Romans.[4] That the Rabbis, who derived from the Pharisaic party, were still remembered as appeasers long after the 1st century A.D.,[5] supports this identification of the Pharisees.

These and similar points suggest, as Dr. Rabin argues,[6] that the Covenanters must be regarded as an ultra-strict group of the Pharisees trying, in accordance with the old law[7], to uphold what they considered genuine Pharisaism against the flexible ideology introduced by the Rabbis in authority[8]; but their deviations from Pharasaic norms were mostly mere heterodoxy, what the Rabbis tolerated as 'another way (derek 'aḥeret)', not what they condemned as 'heresy' (mînût). These variations were such as began in the 1st century B.C. and continued to be debated in the schools in the next few centuries; but unfortunately the unhistorical attitude of Tannaitic (c. A.C. 10–220) and Amoraic (c. A.D. 220–500) writers makes the determination of exact dates in

---

[1] In *Antiquities* XIII x 6 § 294.   [2] Burrows *Scrolls* 249–50.
[3] Pp. 197–216, 225.   [4] Cp. Roth *Background* 40–2.   [5] B. Talmud *Gittin* 56a.
[6] In *Scr. Jud.* II 66–70.   [7] Deut. iv. 2.   [8] S. p. 528.

these periods extremely hazardous; and, if anything is certain, it is that such groups as the Covenanters in both doctrine and practice are likely to reflect not long past but contemporary conditions. Protests are made not against historical but against contemporary crazes or current abuses.

5. GROUPS AMONG THE PHARISEES

An Israelite might be born a Pharisee, as the apostle Paul claimed to be as the son of a Pharisee;[1] or he might become one, as the historian Josephus, the son of a priest, shows when he says[2] that 'being now nineteen years old, I came back to the city (sc. Jerusalem) and began to conduct myself according to the rules of the sect of the Pharisees'. A man had presumably to be of a suitable social standing and sufficiently well educated to be accepted as one of themselves by the Pharisees; for they were outspoken in their contempt for 'the people of the land' i.e. the common people, declaring that even 'the clothes of the people of the land are unclean for those who are separated',[3] i.e. the Pharisees. In the same way the Covenanters were never tired of proclaiming how they were 'distinguished' (cp. D v 1–2, 10–11 viii 13 Z viii 12) from other people, whom they described as 'men of perversity' and 'sons of corruption' or 'the pit' (D v 10 viii 11, 13 ix 5 Z viii 12); accordingly they regarded themselves as the 'elect of Israel' (Z vi 2) and 'united as a holy of holies and a house of community for all Israelites who walk in perfection' (D ix 5–6). Indeed, Geiger long ago identified[4] the two terms used for 'distinguished' (nibdālîm) and 'separated' (p^erûšîm) as found in the Old Testament and Rabbinic literature without knowing anything of the terminology of the Covenanters. As too the Pharisees would have nothing to do with 'the people of the land', so one of the *Hymns* in an address to God contains the significant statement that 'Thou didst impose respect for them (sc. the Covenanters) on Thy people and didst make them a hammer for the common people' (T iv 26; cp. Z ix 17), using the same contemptuous expression as the Pharisees for such persons.

None the less, as Israelites outside the community of the Covenanters could obtain admission to that body by undergoing a novitiate, so a 'common person' could become a member of a Pharisaic 'sodality (ḥăḇûrāh)' by passing through an initiation. The accounts of this process show three groups of persons: the 'common person' who kept neither the law of tithes nor those of Levitical purity but did observe certain others, so that eating in his house was not deemed a sin, although it brought one who did so into danger of eating untithed food; the 'con-

---

[1] Acts xxiii. 6.   [2] In *Life* ii 10.   [3] Mishnah *Hagigah* ii 7; cp. *Demai* ii 3.
[4] In *Urschrift und Uebersetzungen* 103.

firmed (*ne'ĕmān*)', who paid tithes and did not eat with a 'common person' and the 'associate (*ḥāḇĕr*)', who observed all the law of tithes and of Levitical purity in eating, though a layman.

The accounts of the procedure vary somewhat and are not always easy to understand. The Pharisaic novitiate seems, however, so far as the accounts of it can be followed, to have been passed in the four following stages:[1]

(i) the 'common person' accepted the obligation to pay tithes after a declaration to this effect before a *quorum* of three members, whereupon he was regarded as 'confirmed' in his intention;

(ii) after an unspecified period of time he renewed this obligation and further undertook not to take a meal in the house of a 'common person' and to observe certain rules in regard to clothing and other things, and he also underwent instruction for twelve months;

(iii) he was then examined and, if accepted, was 'brought close' to the society and was regarded as 'confirmed' also in respect of pure food (namely as ritually fit to have access to the common meals) during a period of twelve months (or of one month according to a variant account);

(iv) after this period he was accepted also in respect of drink and became an 'associate' of an 'association' of the party of the Pharisees.

The initiation of a novice to the society of the Covenanters, as set out above[2], falls also into four clearly defined stages:

(i) on application he was examined by 'the officer at the head of the Many' as to his intelligence and conduct and, if found capable of instruction, was 'brought into the covenant' and instructed in the statutes of the order;

(ii) after an unspecified period of time he was brought before the Many who voted on the question of his admission and according to the result of the ballot he was either rejected or permitted to come before 'the council of the Many', but might not touch 'the purity of the Many' nor have anything to do with the common property until his character and conduct had been tested for a full year;

(iii) at the end of the year the Many were consulted about his intelligence and his conduct 'in the Law'; he was then presumably (for the account is not free from ambiguity) allowed 'to touch the purity of the Many' and to have to do with their property; his own property and earnings were registered by 'the censor in charge of the labour of the Many' but not used;

(iv) after another year, he was allowed 'to touch the drink of the Many' and was referred to the Many for a final decision; if their votes

---

[1] Liebermann in *JBL* LXXI 199–206 and Rabin *Scr. Jud.* II 11–19; cp. Vermès *Manuscrits* 53–7.
[2] Pp. 54–5; cp. Rabin *Scr. Jud.* II 1–9.

were favourable, he was registered as a member and had his place amongst the brethren assigned to him 'in respect to law and judgement and purity and the administration of his property', and his counsel was available for the benefit of the community (D v 20–25 vi 13–23).

Nothing is said of any oath in these rules; but *Discipline* in a previous passage lays down that 'everyone who comes to the counsel of the community shall enter into God's covenant in the sight of those who freely offer themselves and shall take a binding oath to return to the law of Moses' (D v 7–8); this leaves the time when the oath was sworn uncertain. The *Zadokite Documents* however add that 'on the day that he (*sc.* the postulant) speaks with the censor of the Many they shall put him to the oath of the covenant which Moses made with Israel, namely the covenant to return to the Law of Moses . . .; and let no man teach him the rules until he has appeared before the censor, lest he is found to be simple when he examines him' (Z xv 8–10). A comparison of these passages with that setting out the rules for the admission of members leaves no doubt that the oath was administered immediately after the censor's preliminary examination of the candidate.

As Dr. Rabin has remarked,[1] the resemblances between the procedure of the Covenanters and that of the Pharisees are striking. Both included a declaration or oath at the beginning of the procedure; both implied a pre-novitiate followed by a novitiate proper of three stages. The first stage in the Pharisaic novitiate required no special Pharisaic obligation but only those incumbent on all Israelites, and so amongst the Covenanters it demanded of the novice only 'to return to the law of Moses'. This novitiate was a period of instruction, and it was followed by two distinct stages; the permission to touch pure food came in the second stage, while that of touching the common drink marked full admission.[2] Only two divergencies between the procedure of the Pharisees and that of the Covenanters occur: the declaration in the former case was made before a public body whereas in the latter the oath was taken before the censor; and the Pharisees, unlike the Covenanters, required a second declaration before actual entry upon the novitiate. The two forms of initiation can hardly be identified, if only because that of the Covenanters was something far more elaborate and stable than that of the Pharisaic sodalities.[3] At the same time, they annot be entirely separated; either the one was borrowed from the other or both derived from a common origin, which is not impossible; for at any rate, as Dr. Gaster remarks[4], the four stages of the novitiate may reflect the four stages of 'purity' recognized in Rabbinic law.[5] In either case, they argue a close connection between the Pharisees and the Covenanters.

---

[1] In *Scr. Jud.* II 20–1. [2] Cp. p. 111. [3] Cp. de Vaux *Archéologie* 95–6.
[4] In *Scriptures* 107. [5] B. Talmud *Hagigah* 18b.

Other technical terms and practices of these Pharisaic associations resembled those of the community at Qumrân. When a new member is admitted to the society of the Covenanters, the text speaks of his 'presenting himself (q⁽e⁾rōḇ)' or says that the officer sponsoring him 'has presented (qērēḇ)' him to it (D vi 16, 19, 22 vii 21 viii 18); and this same verb is used of the admission of a new member to one of these associations.[1] The 'associates (ḥăḇērîm)', too, are occasionally called 'the Many (hā-rabbîm)',[2] which immediately recalls the Covenanters, who were similarly described as full members in their corporate capacity.[3] The 'association' or 'sodality (ḥăḇūrāh)', exercised some sort of disciplinary control over its members. It collected tithes from its members, the so-called 'second tithe', which was devoted to the relief of poor members as well as to other deserving objects, and some members were maintained by a central fund; so the Covenanters contributed two days' wages a month for the assistance of needy members and had a common fund in 'the property of the Many'.[4] That the Pharisaic 'associates' had common meals is not certain; but the custom was suspected long before the discovery of the Scrolls.[5] Finally, both the Pharisaic 'associations' and the Covenanters expelled members for various offences; but, while expulsion from the society of the Covenanters might in certain circumstances be permanent (D vii 1–2),[6] the Rabbis disputed whether it might ever be so even when an 'associate' reverted to his former way of life.[7]

When the system of Pharisaic associations was first instituted or grew up is unknown, and their end is obscure. Dr Mendelsohn assigns[8] them to the closing decades of the 2nd century B.C.; but Dr Zeitlin has denied[9] their existence under the Second Commonwealth on the ground of lack of evidence; but the absence of any mention of them during that period is as likely to be due to the lack of the relevant literature as to any other cause. The first mention of a custom, too, is not necessarily synchronous with its institution, and a historian can only describe what already exists. Dr. Rabin may therefore well be right[10] in holding that the institution probably existed already in the time of the Second Commonwealth and came to an end c. A.D. 70, when the whole fabric of Jewish society in Palestine was destroyed, even though echoes of these associations continued to be heard long afterwards. He therefore concludes[11] that, although he is inclined to assign the Covenanters to a date after the destruction of Jerusalem in that year, various points

<hr/>

[1] P. Talmud *Demai* ii 3 (23a); cp. Mishnah *Eduyoth* v 7.
[2] Cp. P. Talmud *Demai* ii 2 (22d) w. B. Talmud *Bekhoroth* 30b; s. Liebermann in *JBL* LXXI 200–3.
[3] Pp. 57–60.
[4] Pp. 114–16.
[5] Geiger *Urschrift und Uebersetzungen* [1857] 121–4.
[6] Pp. 65–7.
[7] B. Talmud *Abodah Zarah* 7a–7b.
[8] In *JE* VI 124.
[9] In *JQR*, NS XLVI 240.   [10] In *Scr. Jud.* II 36.   [11] *Ibid.* 66–7.

are applicable also to a date in the first half of the same century; he has been compelled to rely on evidence from the second half of it only because more is known about it.[1]

The Covenanters refer to themselves also as 'men of holiness' (D v 3 viii 17, 23 ix 8; cp. v 18) and to their society as a 'congregation of holiness' (D v 20; cp. Z ix 48); and Dr. Rabin has drawn attention[2] to the significance of this designation in comparison with that of the 'holy congregation' which is mentioned in the Mishnah and other Rabbinic works. This was a group which was already in being in the earlier years of the 2nd century A.D. and which came to be regarded by later generations as having great importance. Its teachings, curiously enough in the present connection, were handed down not under the names of individual teachers but collectively; the obvious explanation of this fact is that their decisions were collective and formed part of the regulations of the 'holy congregation'. There are indications, too, of some kind of cultural association and also perhaps of communal life; the group even divided the day into three parts, one for study of the Law and one for prayer and one for labour,[3] just as the Covenanters kept vigil in three shifts devoted to study of the Law and to prayer throughout the night (D vi 6–8).[4] Another curious point of contact between the Community of the Covenanters and the 'holy congregation'[5] is the requirement that the censor must be skilled 'in every language according to their families' (Z xvii 6); for the only scholars in the Jewish centre at Yabneh (Yamnia) after the capture of Jerusalem in A.D. 70 who were said to be masters of 'seventy languages' were four members of the 'holy congregation'.[6] The dispersion made a knowledge of foreign languages essential. These facts do not compel the identification of the Covenanters' 'congregation of holiness' with the Pharisaic or Rabbinic 'holy congregation'; but they do suggest that they may be derived from the same stream, even if they are not contemporary; for they seem to have had the same or a similar purpose, *i.e.* the cultivation of certain ascetic mystical and esoteric doctrines which may well have had a common origin. The connection, however, if admitted can but have been extremely tenuous and may well not go beyond the name.[7]

In close connection with the Pharisees Josephus refers[8] to a 'fourth philosophy' current in his time in Judaism.[9] This was the philosophy of a party which Judah the Galilaean or Gaulonite (for Josephus applies both terms to him) and a Pharisee named Zaddok or Zadduk taught. Their doctrines, he says, agreed in all respects with those of the Pharisees except that they had an invincible passion for liberty and would

---

[1] Cp. Bonsirven *Judaïsme Palestinien* I 59–62 and Rubinstein in *JTS*, NS IX 343–4.
[2] In *Scr. Jud.* II 37–52.   [3] Midrash R. *Ecclesiastes* IX ix § 1.
[4] P. 57.   [5] Rabin *op. cit.* 45.
[6] P. Talmud *Sheqalim* v 1.   [7] Cp. Wernberg-Møller in *RQ* I 143–4.
[8] In *Antiquities* XVIII i 6 § 23 and *War* II viii 1 § 118.   [9] Pp. 239–42.

tolerate no ruler but God; they preferred any kind of death for themselves and even for their familes to paying taxes and so admitting any human being as lord and master. Their doctrine as well as their activities were in fact directed against Roman sovereignty, and Josephus does not conceal his feelings regarding them. What they did, he says, was done 'in pretence indeed for the public welfare but in reality for hopes of gain for themselves', and resulted in murder and sedition, famine and violent war; 'for the whole nation became infected with this doctrine to an incredible degree'. The resemblances between Covenanters and Pharisees are remarkable enough, but those between them and the adherents of the 'fourth philosophy', which was an offshoot of Pharisaism, are striking and will call for careful examination; and something will be said of them hereafter in another connection.[1]

6. ESSENES

The Essenes or Essaeans, of whom Philo[2] and Josephus[3] give detailed accounts, are of exceptional importance for the study of the Covenanters, since their manner of life seems from the various accounts to be very similar; this resemblance has caused the two groups to be identified by many writers. Dr. Sukenik seems to have been the first to propose this identification, while Prof. Dupont-Sommer has gone furthest[4] in working it[5] out in detail. Of the two ancient authorities Josephus is especially valuable; for, although he often shows considerable bias, he can in this matter be trusted, since he was in close contact with them for some time in his youth, as he records in his autobiography.[6] Philo, however, whose account tallies very well with, and can therefore be used to a limited extent to check, what Josephus says, had no real knowledge of the Essenes at first hand; he had spent most of his life in Egypt and visited Jerusalem only once, in A.D. 40, when returning home late in life after an embassy to Rome, as he himself reports.[7] Yet these two accounts coincide so closely that they may be put together to make a single story.

The Essenes[8] (᾽Εσσηνοί, ᾽Εσσαῖοι), whose name was very dubiously derived from the Greek word for 'holy' (ὅσιος),[9] were of unknown origin.[10] The abbot Nilus of Ancyra (c. A.D. 400) asserted[11] that they were

---

[1] Pp. 232–4, 239–42.   [2] In *Every Good Man* xii 75–87 and *Apology* xi 1–18.
[3] In *Antiquities* XIII v 9 § 172, XVIII i 2 § 11 and *War* II viii 2 § 119–12 § 159.
[4] In *Megillot Genuzoth* I 16.
[5] In *Aperçus Préliminaires* 105–17 and *Nouveaux Aperçus* 90–104.
[6] In *Life* ii 11.   [7] In *Providence* ii 64.
[8] Cp. Lightfoot *Colossians* 114–28.
[9] Philo *Every Good Man* xii 75; s. Baron *Social History of the Jews*[2] II 347.
[10] Cp. Audet in *RB.* NS. LXVII 373–87, deriving the name from Hazazon Tamar *i.e.* Engedi (II Chron. xx 2).
[11] In *de monastica exercitatione* 3.

descendants of Jonathan son of Rechab, who drank no wine, arguing apparently from the absence of any reference to drinking wine in the ancient account of them; the inference, however, is most precarious. They first became prominent when John Hyrcanus I was high-priest (135–104 B.C.);[1] and by the 1st century A.D. they were known as an ascetic group of some 4000 persons living some at Engedi to the west of the Dead Sea and others in various Judaean villages (shunning cities because of the lawlessness of their inhabitants), where they formed large and populous societies and devoted themselves to the worship of God. They repudiated marriage, regarding women as licentious, selfish and jealous, clever at decoying men and bringing them into subjection by continued cajolery, liable to be puffed up with pride and to make exorbitant demands on their husbands if they bore children. The society's numbers were replenished and maintained by the adoption of other people's sons; for it was based not on human descent but on zeal for virtue and the love of their fellow men. The society, therefore, had no children, scarcely even a lad or a young man with a beard amongst its members; they were all grown men, generally still young enough to be indoctrinated with the tenets of the society but sometimes verging on old age, not liable to be carried away by bodily passions and therefore enjoying genuine liberty.

Anyone desiring to join the community was not immediately admitted. The novice received a small spade for use when emptying the bowels,[2] a girdle and a white robe, and was required to follow the community's way of life for one year, while still remaining an outsider, before admission. After proving his continence for such a period, he was allowed to take part in the society's 'purification by waters' but was still excluded from full fellowship. After another two years of probation, if accepted as worthy, 'before touching the common food'[3] he took certain oaths, binding himself to be pious towards God, to practise justice towards men, to injure no man of his own accord or under compulsion, to hate the wicked and to take the part of the righteous (cp. D i 10–11),[4] to show good faith to all men and especially to those in authority, not to vaunt his own authority if himself in authority nor to outshine his subordinates in dress, to love the truth and denounce falsehood, to refrain from unhallowed gain, theft and brigandage[5] (which was widespread at this time),[6] to keep no secret from his fellow members and to betray none to other people even under threat of death, to preserve the society's sacred books and the names of the angels with proper care and to communicate its principles (sc. to new members) precisely as he had received them.

The order was meticulously careful in the infliction of penalties. No

[1] Josephus Antiquities XIII x 5 § 288–6 § 289.   [2] Cp. p. 48.   [3] Cp. p. 97.
[4] Josephus War II viii 7 § 139.   [5] Ibid. § 142.   [6] P. 116.

H

sentence was passed except by a court of a hundred members, but a decision so reached was irrevocable; and all members made it a point of honour 'to obey the elders and the majority (τοῖς πλείοσιν).' Any member found guilty of heinous sins was expelled from the order, and one who had been expelled often met a wretched death; for by the bond of his oaths and ingrained religious habits he was prevented from receiving food at the hands of ordinary people, so that, being reduced to feeding on herbs, he perished by slow starvation. The order therefore out of compassion often took back an expelled member, considering that his sufferings had been sufficient punishment for his sins.[1]

Next to God members revered the name of their lawgiver (Moses), and any blasphemy of him was punished with death.

The order was divided into four classes according to length of discipline and the seniors were so far above juniors that, if they were touched by one of them, they washed themselves as though they had been defiled by contact with a foreigner. Juniors obeyed their seniors in all things; and all accepted the decisions of the majority. They forbade spitting straight forward or to the right side when present at sessions of the members. They avoided work on the Sabbath more strictly than ordinary Jews; but Hippolytus was surely exaggerating when he said[2] that some Essenes spent the Sabbath in bed to avoid committing any sin on it. Not only did they prepare all food on the previous day to avoid lighting a fire on the Sabbath, but they did not dare even to move a vessel or evacuate their bowels into it; on other days, when thus engaged, they retired somewhere out of sight and covered themselves with a mantle to avoid offending the rays of God, and they washed themselves after the act as if it had defiled them.

All members rose before dawn and indulged in no profane conversation until they had said a prayer facing the sun; this practice led to their being regarded by some observers as sun-worshippers. They were then despatched by the overseer to their respective tasks. They worked till the fifth hour, when they came home, had a cold bath and put on white cloaks. They then entered the dining-room, where each quietly took his place; the baker then put loaves before them all in order and the cook laid a dish before each member. They sat together in messes and were content with a frugal and almost unvarying meal; but they touched no food until the priest had offered a prayer and did not leave their places after the meal until he had done so again. They then laid aside the special garments which they had been wearing and went back to their work till the evening, when they returned home and had supper in the same way. They abstained also from the use of oil on

[1] Josephus *War* II viii 8 §§ 143-4 and 9 § 146; s. p. 65.   [2] In *Refutation* IX xxiv 2.

the body; the reason may have been the same as that for which the Pharisees did not use it on fast-days, that they regarded it as a luxury,[1] or that they feared defilement[2] because it might have been in contact with heathen hands,[3] or that it was connected with the rites of the Temple.[4] Thus they passed their whole time, following a regular routine and making no excuses on the score of the weather; and, thanks to their simple diet and regular habits, they were unusually long-lived and many of them reached their century. They undertook every kind of work or business that might serve the common welfare, different members having different occupations. They tilled the soil, kept flocks and herds, tended bees, or pursued such various arts and crafts as were beneficial to themselves and their neighbours and consonant with peace, rejecting no innocent way of making a living. They therefore included no makers of weapons of war in their society, and no member busied himself in the slightest degree with any military occupation or even such as might in peace be turned to any warlike purpose; but they carried weapons on journeys for the purpose of self-protection. They were totally ignorant of seafaring, trade and commerce, as inducing covetousness, and were scrupulous to acquire neither silver nor gold nor large estates; they remained destitute of money and possessions, regarding to be frugal and contented as great wealth.[5] Further, they owned no slaves; for they considered the position of a master unjust as a breach of equality and impious as violating the law of nature by which all men were born alike.

Members, who had no private property, put all that they had into a common stock, whence it was distributed for use amongst all; and they appointed overseers to take charge of the common property, to manage the business of the society and attend to the needs of members. They also paid any money which they earned into a common pool and might give nothing even to their relations except as the overseer allowed; the only money left to them to use at their own discretion was that which they might set aside for charitable purposes, such as the relief of the poor and needy, the starving and the sick. Their own sick, even though unable to contribute anything to the common pool, received every possible attention and had all their needs relieved. All members had two garments, a thick cloak for winter and a thin tunic for summer, kept in a common store, from which each took what he wanted as the need arose; and neither garments nor shoes were discarded until they were quite worn out. Food and drink were supplied exactly in accordance with each man's needs, and strict sobriety was observed in the

---

[1] Mishnah *Yoma* viii 1; cp. B. Talmud *Yoma* 76b.

[2] Josephus *War* II viii 3 § 123 and Hippolytus *Refutation* IX xix 2.

[3] Cp. Josephus *Life* xiii 74, *Antiquities* XII iii 1 § 120 and *War* II xxi 2 § 591; cp. B Talmud *Shabbat* 17b.

[4] Zeitlin in *JQR*, N.S. XLV 93–4.   [5] Cp. I Tim. vi 6.

use of them. No member had his own house, but all lived together in companies or groups. They carried no provisions with them on their journeys, but on arriving at a place searched for the order's relieving officer, who supplied them with food and clothes according to their needs; and they kept open house for visiting members, who entered the homes of complete strangers and stayed with them as though they were intimate friends. Perfect order was maintained in their houses; there was no brawling and each spoke in turn. The elders were treated with respect and honour and the old were tended with loving care.

The members eschewed pleasures as vicious; they were scrupulous in piety and devoted themselves to those studies best calculated to bring about and encourage a holy frame of mind. The passions were kept in check and oaths not permitted (cp. Z xix 1); for members considered themselves the champions of good faith and peace. They avoided logical studies as mere word-catching and physical science as too lofty for men, the one as unnecessary to the pursuit of virtue and the other as fit only for theorists, except in so far as it included the study of the existence of God and the formation of the universe; but they gave much attention to the study of herbs for their medicinal value, to the management of their property ($o\overset{i}{\iota}\varkappa ovo\mu\acute{\iota}\alpha$) and to the administration of the affairs of their society ($\pi o\lambda\iota\tau\epsilon\acute{\iota}\alpha$). For the rest, they devoted all their energy to moral philosophy under the guidance of their ancestral laws, in which they were instructed on the Sabbath, when all work ceased and they resorted to the synagogue; there they sat in order according to their respective ages and listened attentively to their teachers. One man read aloud passages from the sacred books, and the most experienced member then came forward and expounded what had been read; for the greatest part of their lore was conveyed through symbols or figuratively. Thus they learnt piety and holiness, justice, the knowledge of good, indifferent and bad, to seek the good and to shun the evil. They applied three tests or standards in these studies: the love of God, the love of virtue, and the love of mankind. Thus they afforded numerous examples of the meaning of the love of God by life-long purity, by abstinence from oaths and falsehood, and by regard for God as the cause of all good but of no evil; of the love of virtue by not coveting money or fame or pleasure as well as by self-control, firmness and endurance, contentment, simplicity and good humour, modesty and regard for law; of the love of mankind by giving proof of goodwill, impartiality and an indescribable bond of fellowship. Their spirits enabled them to rise superior to pain, and they endured every conceivable torture at the hands of the Romans rather than blaspheme their lawgiver or eat forbidden food; and they preferred death encountered with glory to a long life. Their firm opinion was that, while the body is corruptible and its substance transient, the soul is permanent and immortal; that the soul emerges from the thinnest air, by a sort of natural spell, to be imprisoned in the body and that, on being released from the bonds of the body, it joyfully soars into freedom. They believed that good souls dwell beyond the ocean in a land untroubled by snow or rain or heat and refreshed by a gentle breeze from the west, but that evil souls depart into a gloomy den full of storms, where they endure unending punishment.

Josephus further says[1] that the Essenes, when sending their offerings to the temple at Jerusalem, did not present the usual sacrifices, since they thought that they had superior means of purification, and that they were therefore excluded from the common court of the Temple as ceremonially defiled;[2] in this statement he more or less agrees with Philo's remark[3] that they refrained from animal sacrifice but studied to keep themselves in a holy frame of mind. Josephus also apparently describes[4] their relieving officers as 'good priests', thus employing this term in an unusually loose sense (if the text may be trusted at this point).

Josephus[5] concludes one of his accounts by saying that there was also 'another order of Essenes' who shared the life, habits and customs of the main body except that they permitted matrimony, arguing that only so would the race not soon cease to exist. They therefore took wives but put them on probation for three years and only married them when they had attested their power to conceive by three menstruations; they married not for pleasure but for the sake of offspring. Lastly the women wore gowns but the men drawers in the bath.

Pliny[6] the elder adds one or two small points to this information. He says, after describing the Dead Sea, that the Essenes dwelt among palm-trees on its western side, avoiding the shore-line, being settled above the town of Engada (Engedi), which was once second only to Jerusalem in fertility and the growing of palm groves but now simply another ash-heap; that their membership was steadily kept up by recruits from the large number of persons 'wearied of life's struggle with the waves of adversity', and that the race had lasted in this strange way for thousands of centuries, although no one was born in the community. The exaggeration in this account is obvious and may be discounted; but the statement about the locality is interesting.[7]

Josephus and Philo may have trimmed their accounts of the Essenes to bring out the points which they wished to emphasize; for example, Philo says nothing of their presence in the cities of Palestine, concentrating his attention on their semi-monastic mode of life. Josephus may have erred in saying that 'another order of Essenes' permitted matri-

---

[1] In *Antiquities* XVIII i 5 § 19.   [2] Cp. Black *Scrolls* 40–1.
[3] In *Every Good Man* xii 75.
[4] In *Antiquities* XVIII i 5 § 22; s. Schürer *Geschichte*[3] II 571(63).
[5] In *War* II viii 13 §§ 160–1.   [6] In *Natural History* V xv 73.
[7] S. pp. 400–1.

mony,[1] which runs counter to everything else which he reports of them; he may perhaps have confused them with the Covenanters.[2] There is no need, however, to say with De Quincey[3] that 'this tale happens also to be a lie; secondly, a fraudulent lie; thirdly, a malicious lie', or with Mr. Del Medico[4] to consider all these accounts of them to be late interpolations in the works in which they are now found, myths *nés de l'imagination d'un Philon, de la crédulité d'un Pline et du manque de probité de copistes partiaux*, which have grown into a legend. Such extreme scepticism makes nonsense of history, if no ancient authorities, consistent or inconsistent as they may be, can be utilized; and the Scrolls put the theoretical possibility of such a society beyond reasonable doubt, even if the Essenes and the Covenanters are not treated as one and the same group.

The Essenes have been described at length, because their obvious resemblances to the Covenanters, which Bonsirven had already noticed[5] in connection with the *Zadokite Documents*, before the discovery of the Scrolls, have now made them the favourite candidates for identification with the Covenanters. This view has been argued by many scholars, most fully and plausibly by Prof. Dupont-Sommers,[6] but the resemblances are mostly superficial or shared with other parties of the period, when they lose much of their value as evidence, while the differences are often fundamental.[7]

Some of the resemblances common to the Essenes and other religious groups are found in the organization of their respective societies. The Essenes were called a 'gathering, group ($\delta\mu\iota\lambda o\varsigma$)'[8] and the Covenanters described themselves as a 'unit, society (*yaḥaḏ*)' (D i 16 and *passim*); but the notion that the use of these two words proves the identity of the two groups[9] has nothing to commend it, as they are not known to be corresponding terms from any other sources. The Essenes had their 'overseers' and 'managers' and also their 'seniors',[10] as the Covenanters had their 'inspector' or 'censor' and 'elders',[11] and perhaps also the 'holy congregation' had its 'elders',[12] who each enjoyed a certain precedence; and the Essene $\dot{\epsilon}\pi\iota\mu\epsilon\lambda\eta\tau\dot{\eta}\varsigma$ was in charge of the work of the members[13] exactly as the Covenanters had an 'inspector over the work of the Many' (D vi 20); but the Christian Church had a similar

---

[1] S. pp. 69–70.   [2] Brownlee *ap.* Burrows in *Oudt. St.* VIII 180.
[3] In *Works* VI [1863] 275.   [4] In *Énigme* 79–95 and *Mythe* 300–8.
[5] In *Judaïsme Palestinien* [1934] I 67–70; cp. Brownlee in *BA* XIII 56–66.
[6] In *Habacuc* 26–9 and *Discipline* 5–30; cp. *Aperçus Préliminaires* 105–17 and *Nouveaux Aperçus* 90–104.
[7] Cp. Burrows in *Oudt. St.* VIII 165–80.
[8] Josephus *War* II viii 7 § 138, Philo *Every Good Man* xiii 91 and *Hypothetica* xi 2.
[9] Mendelsohn in *JBL.* LXXI 207–9.
[10] Josephus *War* II viii 6 § 134 ($\dot{\epsilon}\pi\iota\mu\epsilon\lambda\eta\tau\alpha\grave{\iota}$ and $\dot{\epsilon}\pi\acute{\iota}\tau\rho\sigma\pi\sigma\iota$) and 10 § 150 ($\pi\rho\sigma\gamma\epsilon\nu$-$\acute{\epsilon}\sigma\tau\epsilon\rho\sigma\iota$); cp. Philo *Hypothetica* xi 10 ($\tau\alpha\mu\acute{\iota}\alpha\varsigma$).
[11] Pp. 60, 62, 64, 178.   [12] Rabin *Scr. Jud.* II 49.
[13] Josephus *ibid.* 5 § 129.

hierarchy, which included 'overseers', *i.e.* 'bishops' and elders.[1] The main body of the Essenes was called 'the Most (οἱ πλεῖστοι)' or 'the More (οἱ πλείονες)',[2] as also the main body of the early Church was called;[3] and similarly that of the Covenanters consisted of 'the Many (hā-rabbîm)',[4] exactly as the members of the Jewish 'sodalities' or 'associations (ḥăḇūrôṯ)' were called[5] and as the Jewish community as a public body was designated.[6] Such terms, then, were common form in the 1st and 2nd centuries A.D. and cannot be cited to prove the identity of those who used them; they do however suggest that all such parties were approximately contemporary with one another. Other resemblances arising out of the organization of these communities are the long and strikingly similar novitiates, which are not confined to the Essenes and the Covenanters but can be traced also in the Pharisaic 'sodalities',[7] the grades of membership,[8] the careful observance of precedence amongst members, the common meals preceded by a grace (D vi 5; cp. I Q 28A B iii 17–20)[9] such as also other Jews said before meals,[10] the reading aloud of and instruction in the Scriptures, the intense study of the Law and devotion to ancestral customs.[11] The frequent ablutions or lustrations (D iii 4–5, 9 v 13–14; cp. Z xii 1–2) prescribed in the rules of both orders, too, were not peculiar to them but were practised by other various orthodox Jewish groups;[12] and this fact would militate against the theory that they were intended, like the (supposedly sacred) common meal, as compensation for loss of participation in the official cult of the Temple.[13] Participation in non-sectarian meals was forbidden to both Essenes[14] and Covenanters (D v 16); but other Jews were equally strict,[15] and Christians were warned to eschew meat offered to idols.[16] The prohibition of spitting at the public meetings of their respective societies, which was pre-scribed by both Essenes[17] and Covenanters (D vii 13), though in itself a small matter, has too a certain significance in this connection; for the practice was expressly disapproved also by the Rabbis of the syna-gogue.[18] All such regulations are features common to every type of monastic organization; for life in community cannot continue without

---

[1] Pp. 60, 62, 521–4.
[2] Josephus *Antiquities* XVIII i 5 § 22 (πλεῖστοι) and *War* III viii 9 § 146 (πλείονες); s. Dupont-Sommer in *JSS* II 261–366.
[3] P. 521.   [4] Pp. 57–60.   [5] Pp. 95–6, 98.
[6] *E.g.* Mishnah *Gittin* viii 2 and *Kiddushin* iv 5.   [7] Pp. 95–8.
[8] P. 62, 65, 520–1.   [9] Pp. 506–16.   [10] Josephus *War* II viii 5 § 131.
[11] Aristeas *Letter* §§ 184–5; Mishnah *Berakoth* vi 4–7, Matt. xiv. 19, Mk. vi. 41, Lk. ix. 16, Jn. vi. 11.
[12] Pp. 496–508.   [13] Cp. Black *Scrolls* 41–2.
[14] Josephus *War* II viii 8 § 143.
[15] *E.g.* Mishnah *Demai* ii 3; cp. Lk. vii. 34, xv. 2.
[16] 1 Cor. x 25–31.   [17] Josephus *op. cit.* II viii 9 § 147.
[18] P. Talmud *Berakoth* iii 5 ix 8; cp. Mishnah *Berakoth* ix 8 and B. Talmud *Berakoth* 62b–63a.

rules governing the relations of the members towards one another and enforcing public decency, while at the same time making provision for spiritual and intellectual exercises, *e.g.* by the collecting, copying and studying of sacred and other books as well as for manual occupations. In the same way all religious bodies must keep themselves unspotted from the world. None of these habits or customs, therefore, have any particular significance in the present connection.

Another small point which has been urged for identifying the Essenes and the Covenanters is that the former are said to have sought out remote places for relieving nature, from which further they abstain on the Sabbath,[1] while the latter put 'the place of the hand' *i.e.* the latrines (cp. D vii 15), at a distance of 2000 cubits from the camp (W vii 6–7). The first rule, however, refers to daily life in the community, while the second is a military regulation for life in camp; and 2000 cubits seems to have been chosen as the furthest distance allowed for a Sabbath's journey[2] and therefore as permitting this act to soldiers on that day as on ordinary workdays, whereas civilians may go only 1000 cubits on it (Z xiii 7). Further, the position of latrines outside the camp is a natural sanitary practice found also in the Old Testament[3] and is indeed a necessary safeguard for preserving the health whether of an army or of a civilian community, especially in a hot country. This rule, too, therefore has no value as evidence for or against the identity of these two parties; rather, at any rate in so far as it concerns the Sabbath, it distinguishes them.

In the same way, many of the points of doctrine cited to turn the Covenanters into Essenes are common not only to these two groups but also to other contemporary parties. For example, the recognition of the belief in the sanctity of the Scriptures and in the value of the prophetic writings, the devotion to the study of 'the writings of the ancients',[4] and the use of the allegorical methods of interpretation of Scripture[5] were shared also with Pharisees and with Christians; the reverence for Moses as the national lawgiver, the high regard for the Sabbath (on which the Covenanters increased the already intolerable restrictions)[6] and the other feast-days, were common to all Jews. The prohibition of invoking the divine name in oaths, found also in Christianity, whose Founder bade His followers 'let your communication be yea yea, nay nay',[7] goes back to the Old Testament.[8] The Essenes swore 'to preserve the names of the angels',[9] while the Covenanters had a developed angelology;[10] but both drew their

---

[1] Josephus *op. cit.* II viii 9 §§ 148–9.   [2] Cp. Yadin *War* 68–9.
[3] Deut. xxiii. 13–14.
[4] Josephus *Antiquities* II viii 6 § 136; cp. Philo *Every Good Man* xii 81–2.
[5] Pp. 531–2.   [6] Pp. 88–91, 326–8.   [7] Matt. v 37.
[8] Exod. xx. 7 and Deut. v. 11.   [9] Josephus *op. cit.* II viii 7 § 142.
[10] Pp. 19, 76.

inspiration from the apocryphal literature. The doctrines of the sovereignty of fate and of a resurrection with future rewards and punishments, too, are already implicit in the Old Testament and are explicitly taught in some of the apocryphal books. These and such-like ideas and practices are but part of the marked spirituality of the two groups as they are of all that is best in Judaism and have no evidential value for identifying the Essenes and the Covenanters.

If the resemblances between the two parties are largely immaterial, the same thing cannot be said of the differences; for, even though some of these may be trivial and others unreal, being based on the argument from silence, others are charged with significance and cannot be so lightly dismissed.

These differences begin with the very names of the two groups and the sites of their respective settlements. First, although the name of 'Essenes' seems to have been so well known that not only Jewish but also non-Jewish writers freely use it, the Covenanters nowhere in their published writings apply it to themselves or use it in any connection, although they often call themselves 'men of holiness' (D v 13 viii 17, 23 ix 8)[1] and so on. So too, although the Covenanters describe themselves by various titles, notably as the 'Sons of Zadok', none of these are so much as mentioned by any ancient authority in connection with the Essenes; the confusion is purely modern. Further, although Josephus knows of Saddok or Sadduk as the co-founder of a party within Judaism[2] and also gives a full account of the Essenes, he treats them separately in both his historical works and in no passage does he connect anyone of that name with the Essenes[3]. Again, the two groups were settled in different places though at the same time; the Essenes had permanent headquarters at Engaddi, but the Covenanters had theirs at Qumrân, which lay 20 miles away across the mountains.

This proximity of the Essenes to the Covenanters has however been used as an argument to support their identity on the ground of the supposed impossibility of two different groups maintaining a separate existence when living so close together.[4] Such an objection to distinguishing the two groups, however, comes very near to being an argument in favour of keeping them distinct; for it is a commonplace of history that monastic communities, often of different orders, tend to congregate wherever they can find isolated or inaccessible localities suitable for the solitary life. For example, the Buqê'ah, a small plain in the wilderness of Judah, lying to the south-east of Jerusalem and the north-east of Bethlehem and bounded on the west by desolate moun-

---

[1] Pp. 101–2.　　　　[2] Pp. 252–9.
[3] In *Antiquities* XVIII i 1 §§ 4–10 and 6 § 23 (fourth philosophy), i 5 §§ 18–22, (Essenes), and *War* II viii 1 § 108 (fourth philosophy) and 2 § 119–12 § 159 (Essenes).
[4] Burrows *Scrolls* I 280.

tains and on the east by jagged hills falling away abruptly to the cliffs overlooking the Dead Sea, was chosen by Byzantine monks for a chain of monasteries, of which a few still remain;[1] and the monasteries of St. Sâbâ and alMird (Marda or Castellion) were not as far apart as the establishments at Qumrân and Engaddi were. The Nitrian desert in Egypt and Mt. Athos in Greece afford other instances of the same practice. Proximity does not import identity; and a celibate and a non-celibate society are likely to have avoided undue proximity.

These arguments for distinguishing the Essenes from the Covenanters are slight and superficial and have not much value; contrariwise, the positive arguments for keeping the two groups distinct are extremely strong and practically decisive.

Once again, as Dr. Rabin has observed,[2] the novitiate is as important in comparing the Covenanters with the Essenes as with the Pharisees.

Josephus is known to have had personal knowledge of the Essenes, so that his statements may be taken as substantially accurate; for, even if his memory may have left him uncertain on details, he can have had no reason for misrepresenting the facts on any point. He gives the following account[3] of the stages in the novice's initiation into the order:

(i) applying for membership, he received a small hatchet[4] for use when he went to relieve nature,[5] an apron or girdle and a white garment, and was required to follow the same manner of life as a full member, though excluded from actual membership, for two years;

(ii) having thus given proof that 'he can observe their continence', he was allowed to approach 'nearer to their way of living' and was made 'partaker of the waters of purification' (*i.e.* of the order's ritual baths), though still not permitted to live with the members;

(iii) after this test of his strength of purpose, his character was put to another two years' proof, whereupon he was admitted to full membership; but he had to take 'fearful oaths' before 'touching the common food'.

The similarities are three: both bodies required a pre-novitiate of one year's length, followed by a novitiate proper of two years; both methods required periodical examination of the novice, and the candidate's progress depended as much on ritual as on moral or intellectual qualifications.

The differences, which can only be discounted by assuming that Josephus has erred,[6] are the following: the applicant for admission to the community of the Covenanters received no special gifts like those which were bestowed on the Essene novice[7], although the hatchet at

---

[1] Cross in *BA* XIX 12–13.   [2] In *Scr. Jud.* II 9–11.   [3] In *Life* ii 10–11.
[4] Josephus *War* II viii 7 §§ 137–42.   [5] *Ibid.* § 148.   [6] Cp. Cross *Library* 63.
[7] Cp. de Vaux *Archéologie* 99–100 (who has abandoned the suggestion that the hatchet found in Cave XI represents the ἀξινάριον bestowed on the Essene novice).

any rate was probably required;[1] the Covenanters required the oath
at the beginning, the Essenes at the end, of the novitiate; the Covenanters instructed the novice in all the rules of the order, since he had
already sworn the oath of secrecy, whereas the Essenes must have withheld much of this instruction during the novitiate, since the novice
swore 'never to disclose any of their secrets to others' only at the end
of his period of probation, when they imparted it to him (for he would
hardly have been taught them before being sworn to secrecy); the
stages of the novitiate were differently divided, 'touching the purity of
the Many' coming in the second stage amongst the Covenanters
(D vi 16), and 'touching the common food' coming only in the third
and last Essene stage; finally, 'touching the drink of the Many' marked
full admission to the society of the Covenanters (D vi 20)[2] but was not
a stage in the Essene novitiate; and, lastly, the Essenes allowed the
novice 'to participate in purer waters for lustration',[3] i.e. to take part
in the community's ceremonial ablutions, after one year, whereas the
Covenanters prescribed no such ablutions in keeping with their
attitude to such rites.[4]

Another difference arising out of the novitiate, to which Dr. Gottstein[5] has drawn attention, is that admission to the Essene order was
by a single act of initiation, and a member once admitted was a
member for life; but the Covenanter was subject to an annual ceremony of review or re-dedication (D ii 19; cp. v 23–5). The act of
initiation, however, was certainly not baptism in either case, although
both societies apparently used lustral baths; according to the ancient
authorities it was not prescribed as an act of initiation for the Essenes,
and according to the Scrolls it was perhaps only tolerated and certainly
not required by the Covenanters as a condition of admission to their
society.

Certain points remain uncertain. The Essene pre-novitiate of one
year was designed to discover whether the novice could bear the
rigorous life of the order, whereas that of the Covenanters was essentially a period of study; but both aspects would probably have been kept
in view by each community. The Essene novitiate proper lasted for
two years and was apparently not subdivided as that of the Covenanters was. The Essenes further allowed the novice to use ritual baths
after the first year, whereas the Covenanters apparently had no
precise rule on this point; for *Discipline* merely says that 'these may not
enter water in order to touch the purity of the saints (*sc.* full members);
for they will not be cleansed unless they have turned from their wickedness' (D v 13–14). In other words, they are not qualified by mere

[1] Cp. Deut. xxiii. 13–14.   [2] Pp. 96–7; cp. Rabin in *Scr. Jud.* II 7–9.
[3] Josephus *War* II viii 7 § 138.   [4] Pp. 72–3.
[5] In *VT* IV 146.

ceremonial lustration to engage in the work of preparing the society's meals; for they might, if themselves unclean, thus contaminate the whole body of the members.

As Dr. Rabin says,[1] the differences, of which the position of the oath or declaration is the most important, are much more significant than the similarities, although the latter are certainly evidence of a general mental climate in which there was a recognized pattern of procedure. These differences, then, are but another warning against treating the Essenes and the Covenanters as identical groups, as most writers now do. Contrariwise, the agreement between the procedures of the Covenanters and the Pharisees is far closer than those between those of the Essenes and the Covenanters; thus that of initiation constitutes a strong link between the Pharisaic societies and the Covenanters and argues a common origin for their two forms of the novitiate if not for the two communities employing them.

Not a few other differences between the Essenes and the Covenanters, some small but others significant, may be summarized. The Essenes were greatly respected and on good terms with the ruling authorities, to whom they were loyal and by whom they were left unmolested till the revolt against Rome in A.D. 66–73,[2] whereas the Covenanters were in a state of continuous disagreement and even rebellion.[3] The Essenes were settled in considerable numbers in every town in Palestine;[4] the Covenanters similarly lived in cities (Z xv 1–3) but also occupied 'camps', *i.e.* settlements outside the cities or in the country (Z xv 4–xvii 8), while Damascus had a considerable colony of them (Z ix 8).[5] The Essenes were an ascetic group who neither married wives nor begot children but kept up their numbers by 'adoption'[6] (*sc.* by recruitment) whereas the Covenanters might have wives and children (Z xvi 8 [?] xx 7; cp. D iv 7) whom they were bound to bring into the order (Z xix 6; cp I Q *28*A i 6–11), even if they also recruited new members from outside, and they had no marked leaning towards asceticism; and the threefold classification of the virtues, which is given as a mark of Essene philosophy,[7] is not found in the teaching of the Covenanters. Priests played by no means so notable a part in the Essene order as they did in that of the Covenanters, where they were extremely prominent (cp. D vi 3); and those of the Covenanters were anointed with oil (W ix 7-9, if the words are intended to be taken in the literal sense), which the Essenes regarded as a luxury and even as a defilement. Both the Essenes in Palestine and the Therapeuts in Egypt[8] observed the practice of daily prayer before

---

[1] In *Scr. Jud.* II 21. [2] Josephus *War* II viii 7 § 140 and 10 §§ 152–3.
[3] Pp. 168–225.
[4] Josephus *War* II viii 4 § 124 and Eusebius *Preparation for the Gospel* viii 11 (379a–b).
[5] Pp. 303–7. [6] Josephus *War* II viii 2 § 120.
[7] P. 104. [8] Philo *Contemplative Life* iii 27.

dawn, while no such custom is recorded of the Covenanters; but not too much must be made of another difference, that the Essenes offered such prayers to or facing the sun,[1] although again no such practice is ascribed to the Covenanters, as its explanation is not entirely clear. Like the Hasidaeans, from whom they apparently took their origin[2], the Essenes probably used the lunar calendar, if indeed they diverged from normal practice in this matter;[3] the Covenanters certainly preferred to observe the solar year.[4] The Essenes punished any ir-reverence towards the name of the national lawgiver with death, whereas the severest penalty inflicted by the Covenanters was expulsion from the order;[5] and the particular offence which the Essenes so punished is not so much as mentioned in the Scrolls. The Essenes forbade spitting to the right side (obviously as the side of good omen) and into the midst of a session of even ten members,[6] while the Coven-anters prohibited it absolutely at meetings of the community (D vii 13). Some such rule is a necessity of the meetings of a community, as the orthodox prohibition of spitting in the synagogue shows,[7] and therefore proves nothing. The Essenes were forbidden to possess slaves whereas the Covenanters, or at any rate those of them who lived in the world, owned them (Z xiii 12). The Essenes had nothing to do with trade or commerce,[8] while the Covenanters, or at any rate those in the world, practised it, as the rules prohibiting it on the Sabbath prove (Z xiii 25, xiv 9–10); the Essenes are even said never to have handled coins,[9] whereas many hundreds have been found in the 'monastery' at Qumrân[10] (although these may perhaps be regarded as communal funds).[11] Individually, some of these differences have little weight, but taken together their cumulative effect as evidence is considerable.

A serious misconception has been also the generally accepted view that the Covenanters, like the Essenes, practised community of pro-perty; but Dr. Rabin[12] has recently argued that the Hebrew verb, on which this theory is based, cannot bear the sense put upon it.

As already noticed, both Josephus and Philo are witnesses to the existence of communism amongst the Essenes. Josephus says[13] that 'those who enter surrender their property to the order so that there is... one property for all as brethren, formed by the collection of the pos-

---

[1] Josephus *Antiquities* II viii 5 § 128 (s. Strugnell in *JBL* LXXVII 111–13).
[2] S. p. 144.   [3] Cp. Talmon in *Scr. Hieros.* IV 196–8.
[4] Pp. 321–6.   [5] Josephus *War* II viii 9 § 147.
[6] *Ibid.* II viii 9 § 147.
[7] P. Talmud *Berakhoth* 59b (ix 8), 62b–63a (ix 9).
[8] Philo *Every Good Man* xii 78.
[9] *Ibid.* xii 76, Pliny *Natural History* V xv 73, Josephus *War* II viii3 § 122, Hippo-lytus *Refutation* IX xix 1.
[10] De Vaux *ap.* Barthélemy & Milik *Discoveries* I 9.
[11] De Vaux in *RB*, NS LXVI 104.
[12] In *Scr. Jud.* II 27–31; cp. Black *Scrolls* 32–7.
[13] In *Antiquities* XVIII i 5 §§ 20–22 and *War* II viii 3 §§ 122–3 and 6 § 134.

sessions of individual members'; that 'they neither buy nor sell amongst themselves; but, while one gives what he needs to another, he receives back what is useful to himself, and without anything in return they freely receive whatever they want'; that 'overseers of the common property are chosen, each being selected by all for the administration of the possessions of the community'; and finally that 'they chose suitable persons as receivers of revenues and of the produce of the earth'. Philo[1] fills in this picture, saying that 'none desires to have any property of his own, neither house nor slave nor estate nor anything whatsoever that constitutes wealth; but by pooling everything without distinction they enjoy the common use of all'; that 'they give the wages which they earn by various kinds of work to the elected steward; he receives them and buys what is wanted and dispenses abundant provisions and whatever else human life requires'; that 'they have not only food but also clothing in common; for what one has is regarded as the property of all and what all have as that of every member'; and summarizing, he says that 'there is one purse for all and common expenses, common clothes and common food in common meals; for community of dwelling, of life and of meals, is nowhere so firmly established and so developed as with them . . .' This pooling of property appears to be absolute and represents a genuine communism as practised by the Essenes; equally clearly the Scrolls do not justify anything so far-reaching,[2] even though they show that the members to some extent pooled their resources in a common life, sharing a common home and common meals, so far as they had not left the community for the world. Essenes, however, even in the world, remained so far as possible communistic; for a relieving officer was appointed in every town to provide for the needs of travelling members of the order, as they had no personal means.

The sense of the verb used in connection with the supposed 'pooling' (*hiṯʿārēḇ*) of members' property in *Discipline* is ambiguous. In the Old Testament it everywhere denotes having dealings, mixing or mingling with other people[3] or sharing in a thing;[4] in the Mishnah it is similarly used in both a literal and a metaphorical sense. In *Discipline*, however, something like having dealings with someone or in something must be intended, since this suits all the relevant passages, whereas pooling or sharing is impossible in some of them. Thus, when the novice has passed the first year of probation, his property and the produce of his labour are conveyed to 'the censor over the produce of the Many' who enters it to his credit but may not spend it for the benefit of the com-

---

[1] In *Hypothetica* xi 4, 10–12 and *Every Good Man* xii 86.
[2] Cp. Teicher in *JJS* III 87–8.
[3] 2 Kings xviii. 23 = Isa. xxxvi. 8, Ps. cvi. 5, Ezra ix. 2, Prov. xiv. 10 xx. 19 xxiv. 21.
[4] Rabin *op. cit.* 27–30.

munity; on the conclusion of the second year, the censor is authorized to enrol him 'and to deal *leʿārēḇ* with his property' (D vi 22). So, until he has passed the period of probation, he 'shall not involve himself in dealings (*yitʿārēḇ*) with the property of the Many' (D vi 17); here the idea of the novice 'being pooled' or 'pooling himself with the property of the Many' is preposterous! In the same way an expelled member 'shall not come back and have dealings with the saints in (the matter of) his property' (D viii 24) and 'any member of the community who has dealings with him in (the matter of) his purity and of his property with which he (*sc.* the censor) has dealt in common with the property of the Many' comes under the same condemnation (D vii 24–6). The meaning of the verb is made clear by a parallel passage in the *Zadokite Documents*, which says of an unruly member that 'no one shall have any dealings with him in (the matter of) property and labour' (Z ix 33). Lastly, the Aaronite priests have certain duties and privileges and 'there shall be no dealing in their property as in that of the men of deceit' (D ix 16). In the last passage pooling is not really conceivable as a translation; and as it is improbable or impossible in the others, it must be given up also here. The idea of pooling is finally put out of court by various rules which imply the ownership and free disposition of property on the part of the individual Covenanters. No member may eat or drink anything belonging to a 'son of perdition', *i.e.* a non-member, nor accept anything from such a person 'except for a price' (D v 16–17), and one who through negligence damages the property of the community must make it good, or, if he cannot afford to do so, is condemned to reduced rations for sixty days (D vii 6–8); a member may not lend or press for repayment nor do anything for gain nor engage in buying or selling even the produce of his own threshing floor or wine-press on the Sabbath (Z xiii 3, 25 xiv 10 xix 9–10), and he may not deal with a gentile except for cash and with the censor's permission (Z xvi 8). Lastly, two witnesses are required in disputes about property (Z x 14). The first rule applies to members living in the community and the rest to those in the world, so that both classes in some sense still owned and disposed of their own property. When therefore the law says that 'if a man who lies in the matter of wealth is found among them (*sc.* in the community) having acted wittingly' or 'and he is known (cp. Z xviii 9), they shall exclude him from the purity of the Many for one year and he shall be mulcted of one-fourth of his allowance of food' (D vi 24–5), it is referring to one who hopes by concealing his private means to obtain something to which he is not entitled from the community. Although then the offence is described as 'lying', it is not that which Ananias and Sapphira are said to have committed.[1]

[1] P. 524; cp. Schmitt in *Colloque du Strasbourg* 105.

The difference between the Essenes and the Covenanters, then, in
this respect is perfectly clear. The former, if what Josephus says is
accurate, pooled their possessions and no individual member had any
power of disposition over his own; everything was common. The latter
surrendered their individual property to the appointed officer for
administrative purposes but were still able to use it as they wished,
though subject to certain restrictions; at the same time the community
as a body owned property, derived presumably from the proceeds of
members' labour, from gift or bequest, since there are several references to such corporate property in the Scroll (D vi 17, 20 vii 6). The
various hoards of coins, therefore, which have been found in the
'monastery' at Qumrân may represent the common property of the
community or that of individual members 'banked' with the officer in
charge of its funds.[1]

Another important distinction between the Essenes and the Covenanters lay in their respective attitudes to physical violence.

Essene novices were required to take an oath 'to abstain from
brigandage' ($\dot{\alpha}\varphi\acute{\epsilon}\xi\epsilon\sigma\theta\alpha\iota$ $\tau\tilde{\eta}\varsigma$ $\lambda\eta\sigma\tau\epsilon\acute{\iota}\alpha\varsigma$),[2] which Dr. Vermès has plausibly
explained[3] as referring not to ordinary brigandage but to joining the
Zealots in the struggle against Rome, since these were often called
'brigands' ($\lambda\eta\sigma\tau\alpha\acute{\iota}$);[4] and indeed John the Essene (if the peculiar form
of the word here used designates a member of the party) took up
arms and reached high rank in the war against Rome,[5] just as
monks (like Frederic the last Saxon abbot of St. Alban's Abbey) in the
Middle Ages left their monasteries and took to a life of violence.[6] The
suggestion cannot be discounted simply on the score that ordinary
brigandage may be intended because other monks preferred brigandage
or piracy; for the requirement of such an oath would be a natural
precaution at a time when the Essene order might have been seriously
embarrassed if many of its youthful members had been in active
opposition to the paramount power. The oath as thus interpreted
clearly precludes the identification of the Essenes with the Covenanters
if these are identical or even only connected with the Zealots.[7] The
latest Scroll, however, contains a rule that 'no man (sc. no Covenanter)
shall stretch out his hand to shed the blood of a Gentile for the sake of
possessions or gain; nor shall he take any of their possessions that they
may not blaspheme, except by order of the community of Israel'
(Z xiv 7–8). This rule does not imply that the Covenanters were

[1] Cp. de Vaux *Archéologie* 97–8 (who says that no coin has been found in any of the
caves).
[2] Josephus *War* II viii 7 § 142.
[3] In *JDU* 1960, 109[17].   [4] Pp. 238–9.
[5] Josephus *War* II xx 4 § 567 and III ii 1 § 11 ('Εσσαῖος, not 'Εσσηνός); Hegesippus
Historia III iii 3.
[6] Froude *Short Studies in Great Subjects III* [1877] 19   [7] Pp. 237–51.

forbidden to join forces with the Zealots; rather it means that no individual Covenanter may break away from the community to become a *sicarius*[1] operating as a free-lance against the Romans to satisfy private vengeance or obtain personal profit.[2] If the *Zadokite Documents*, in which this rule was laid down, were not composed till long after the First Revolt (A.D. 66–73),[3] it must be regarded as a prohibition of similar conduct on another but similar occasion, *e.g.* during the troubles *c.* A.D. 115 or at the time of the Second Revolt (A.D. 132–5).

The Essenes included no armourer in their number and indulged in no occupations likely to have military value; and they were allowed to carry a weapon solely for defensive purposes on a journey.[4] Far otherwise, the Covenanters would seem to have been both a religious and a military order,[5] and one of their books was devoted entirely to the glorification of war; here their equipment and manoeuvres and their expected conquest of the world by military means are exhaustively described.[6] Some few Essenes, of course, shared in the activities of the Zealots in the revolt against Rome (A.D. 66–73);[7] but these were the exception, mentioned because they were exceptional, probably youthful hotheads who could not be held back when their religion and their country were threatened by a foreign and pagan enemy. When therefore Josephus speaks[8] of their courage in enduring every conceivable torture at the hands of the Romans, he is evidently referring to such members of the order as these or to isolated members whom the Romans chanced to catch and tortured in order to obtain information from them. No evidence supports the assertion of Prof. Baron[9] that 'when later the Roman armies approached Jerusalem, 4000 of them, undoubtedly a majority, were amongst the most heroic of the besieged city. They fought to the last drop of blood: not one survived the catastrophe'; this is not history but historical fiction.[10] Conversely, the rules of the Covenanters were far remote from the military operations in which the majority of the order were engaged, although in all probability the more spiritual members would hold themselves aloof from such activities, even if they could not restrain the ardour of their colleagues. Indeed, reasons will be given hereafter for believing that the very purpose of the Covenanters was opposition to the acceptance of foreign rule as violating the sovereignty of God. These differences are so fundamental and far-reaching as absolutely to exclude any possibility of identifying the two parties,

---

[1] Cp. Hahn in *AOASH* XIV 135–8.   [2] Pp. 247–8.   [3] Pp. 367–9.
[4] Philo *Every Good Man* xii 78 and Josephus *War* II viii 4 § 125.
[5] S. pp. 439–41.   [6] Pp. 168–79.
[7] Hippolytus *Refutation* IX xxvi 2.   [8] In *War* II viii 10 §§ 152–3.
[9] In *Social History of the Jews*[2] II 50–1.   [10] Cp. Roth in *JTS*, NS X 90–1.

I

however close they may come superficially to one another; for two such groups, living at the same time within twenty miles of each other in a desert neighbourhood, could not have remained ignorant of and untouched by each other's theories and habits, if their origin and purpose had been the same.

This distinction in the attitude of the two societies to war is fundamental and in fact goes back to their very origins. It cannot be lightly dismissed by declaring that what Josephus says on this score must be called 'inconclusive and false';[1] he had personal knowledge of their way of life, their customs and their doctrines, and could have had no conceivable reason for falsifying his account of them. The Hasidaeans and the Essenes, who sprang from them, owed their origin to a profound antagonism to Hellenism as undermining the Mosaic, the national, religion; and, although they were ready to take up arms if and when the Seleucid rulers attempted to enforce Hellenistic practices by violence, they knew well that Hellenism was a subtle influence which could only be met by passive resistance. Armed resistance to it was virtually useless. When the intellectual influence of Hellenism was succeeded by the military power of Rome as the principal menace to Jewish ideals, the Jews were faced by a totally different threat, one aimed directly at the sovereignty of God over a sacred soil and a holy nation. This danger could not be met by passive resistance, and the new situation demanded new methods; a fresh party or parties, therefore, such as the party of the 'fourth philosophy' and the Covenanters, the Zealots and the *sicarii*, in due course sprang into being to meet it. Some Essenes, the sort of people who were always in opposition, would beyond doubt join the new society; they would see little difference between infiltration of foreign ideas and domination by foreign arms. The original Zadokites, who were opposed to Seleucid interference in Jewish affairs, and the early Covenanters, who sprang from them but were driven to action by antipathy to Roman domination, were obviously at the outset inspired by the same spiritual ideals as the Hasidaeans and the Essenes, and many of them might be too old to take part in active opposition to Rome or might still cling to outmoded notions of passive resistance. This element would always be present in the society; but, as the political and economic situation worsened, the militant party within it would gain the upper hand, and any quietist element would be submerged or suppressed and might eventually die out. The Covenanters, fired by the 'fourth philosophy' with 'an insuperable love of liberty and intolerance of any other rule but that of God',[2] were destined or indeed doomed by their very methods to bring about the ruin of their country and the destruction

---

[1] Schubert *Community* 76.
[2] Josephus *Antiquities* XVIII i 1 §§ 4–10 and 6 § 23.

of their nation. Briefly, both Essenes and Covenanters, though originally moved by similar aims, were in the course of their respective histories confronted by different perils and attempted to meet them by different methods. They must therefore be treated by the historian as distinct parties within Judaism.

Doctrinally, too, the Essenes and the Covenanters can be clearly distinguished. The Essenes totally rejected animal sacrifices, if Philo may be trusted,[1] as they did not recognize the priesthood of the Temple, but they maintained a connection with it at any rate in their early days[2] and sent gifts to it, although they did not take part in its worship.[3] Contrariwise the Covenanters, who too rejected the service of the Temple, although they held that sacrifices were in themselves of no avail in comparison with righteousness (D ix 3–5) and refrained from offering them in the present evil times (Z viii 11; cp. D xi 18–20), still regarded them as part of the ideal state of affairs which they expected to see restored (W ii 4–6)[4] and for which therefore they prescribed appropriate rules (Z xiii 27–xiv 1).[5] The Essenes were forbidden to take any oaths[6] other than that required on admission to the society; but the Covenanters, while forbidden to swear by the name of God, were allowed to take 'an oath of agreement' (Z xix 1, Rabin).[7] Also, the Essenes (perhaps under Greek influence) believed in the immortality of the soul,[8] whereas the Covenanters apparently believed in some sort of bodily resurrection as well as in eternal life, so far as the Scrolls show.[9] When therefore, unlike Josephus, Hippolytus says[10] that the Essenes believed also in the resurrection of the body, he is perhaps confusing them with the Covenanters.

Equally significant distinctions between the two parties were the importance attached by the Covenanters to the central figure of the Rightful Teacher, to whom no person of any kind corresponds in the Essene society, and the vital conception of the 'covenant' to which all Covenanters swore allegiance, whereas the Essenes according to contemporary accounts had no such institution or, if they had, attached but little importance to it (although some such conception was presumably implicit in their organization). Further, the Covenanters expected a Messiah or even two Messiahs having certain peculiar features not in accord with contemporary Jewish notions, whereas the Essenes either held the ordinary Jewish views on the subject or had rejected the whole conception;[11] and Josephus could hardly have failed

---

[1] In *Every Good Man* xii 75. [2] Josephus *Antiquities* XIII xi 2 § 311.
[3] *Ibid.* XVIII i 5 § 19 (s. Strugnell in *JBL* LXXVII 113–15).
[4] Cp. Ginzberg *Sekte* I 185 (4). [5] P. 68; cp. pp. 84–5.
[6] Josephus *War* II viii 6 § 135. [7] Cp. Matt. v. 34–7 and James v. 12.
[8] Josephus *Antiquities* XVIII i 5 § 18 and *War* II viii 11 §§ 154–8.
[9] Pp. 74–6. [10] In *Refutation* ix 27 § 1.
[11] Pp. 468–74.

to refer to so peculiar a doctrine as that of the two Messiahs if the Essenes had held it.

When the attempt is made to compare the Essenes with the Covenanters, allowance must be made for the fact that the former are known only from the scanty notices of writers who did not belong to their order, while the Covenanters are known only from their own writings.[1] Even so, the differences between the Essenes and the Covenanters cannot be lightly brushed aside, as Prof. Dupont-Sommer tries to do,[2] by declaring that Josephus was a tendentious historian who did not wish to include anything unpraiseworthy or unintelligible to his readers. He was, of course, biased where his political convictions were concerned; but these could hardly enter into the question when he was describing a religious group of which he had personal knowledge and of which he obviously had a high opinion. Many of these features are vital, and scarcely any of them can have been objectionable or incomprehensible to Greek or Roman readers. Even the doctrine of the Messiah, however objectionable to a Roman emperor, can hardly have been unintelligible to a Roman reader. On one occasion Josephus actually refers to the insurgents' hope that 'one of their own nation should be governor of the whole world'; and both Tacitus[3] and Suetonius[4] allude to the same expectation. Philo equally omits many such points from his description of the Essenes. Both writers therefore said nothing of them because they attached no importance to them or were unaware of them. Conceivably, then, the most that can be said, as Prof. Brownlee argues,[5] is that the Covenanters may have belonged to the same type of sect as the Essenes. That the Essenes were the parent body from which Judah and Saddok or Sadduk[6] broke away primarily on the question of opposition to Rome[7] and that subsequently their followers and successors developed other deviations from the norms of the Pharisees, is barely conceivable; for, even though Hippolytus derives[8] the Zealots, who are here taken to be connected with the Covenanters,[9] from the Essenes, the difficulty that the Essenes are not known to have had any specifically 'Zadokite' interests cannot be met. It is impossible if the Zadokite movement is rightly held to have been centred in Egypt for a large part of the 2nd and 1st centuries B.C.[10]

Finally Prof. Dupont-Sommer, the principal champion of the Essene theory,[11] unconsciously disproves it[12] if a plausible emendation

[1] Cp. Rowley *Scrolls* 11–12.   [2] In *Aperçus Préliminaires* 110–11.
[3] In *Histories* v 13.   [4] In *Vespasian* 4.
[5] In *BA* XIII 65; s. p. 105.   [6] Pp. 232–4.
[7] Cp. Jaubert in *NTS* VII 11–12.   [8] In *Refutation* IX xxi 2.
[9] Pp. 237–51.   [10] Pp. 226–37.
[11] Pp. 151–8.
[12] In *Écrits* 47–8 (where the meaningless $\Delta AK\Omega N$ is emended into $[\Sigma A]\Delta OYK[AI]\Omega N$).

which he proposes in the last clause of the description which Josephus[1] gives of the Essenes is accepted; for he now translates it as 'they live in no way different from, but as much as possible like, those [Sadducaeans (*i.e.* Zadokites)] who are called the Many'. If the Essenes only resembled the Zadokites, they could not be identical with them!

Accordingly, when every allowance is made, the differences far outweigh the resemblances between the Essenes and the Covenanters and, while the resemblances are incidental, the differences are fundamental; and other reasons for rejecting the identification of the two groups will appear hereafter.

7. THERAPEUTS

Dr. Vermès has recently attempted[2] to show that not only the Essenes and the Covenanters but also the Therapeuts are to be regarded as identical groups.

The Therapeuts have been identified with the Essenes on the ground that both names mean 'healers' ('*āsaiyâ*);[3] but, while the Greek term may mean this, it can also mean 'worshippers', which is equally plausible and is perfectly suited to the practice of these people, as described below. That, as Philo says,[4] they are so called 'inasmuch as they profess a healing art better than that current in towns, which cures only bodies while theirs treats also souls oppressed by grievous and well-nigh intolerable diseases' is too vague and imprecise to be taken as anything but playing with words rather than serious etymology; and he explains the name of the Essenes quite otherwise.[5] Philo seems also expressly to forbid the identification of these two groups, when he says[6] 'having discussed the Essenes, who in all things pursue the active life (τὸν πρακτικὸν βίον) . . . I will now at once go on to say also what is necessary about those who have embraced the contemplative life (τῶν θεωρίαν ἀσπασαμένων)'; and his two accounts show that he clearly distinguishes the purely contemplative life of those who were called Therapeuts from the ascetic but largely active life of the Essenes.

The Therapeuts, as Philo[7] and Eusebius[8] describe them (although the various accounts have been doubted),[9] were Jews living mostly beside the Mareotic Lake but settled also in small groups here and there elsewhere in (and even out of) Egypt, where they followed a mode of life not unlike that of the Essenes and the Covenanters. They did not live a common life in a 'monastery', however, but each member occupied a simple hut, in which a small apartment was set aside as a

[1] In *Antiquities* XVIII i 5 § 22.
[2] In *JDU* 1960, 97–115.
[3] Cp. Jastrow *Dictionary* I 93.
[4] In *Contemplative Life* i 2 (cp. ii 10–11).
[5] Pp. 100–1.   [6] *Ibid.* i 1.
[7] *Ibid.* i 2, ii 11–iv 39, viii 64–xi 90.
[8] In *Ecclesiastical History* II xvii 3–23.
[9] Cp. Schürer *Geschichte*[3] III 535–8.

'chapel or private sanctuary (σεμνεῖον ἢ μοναστήριον)', each hut being separate but not far distant from the next, and these huts were ranged about a central communal edifice, constructed to serve as meeting place, refectory and 'chapel (σεμνεῖον)'. Both men and women, 'most of them aged virgins . . . who have kept their chastity of their own free will in their ardent desire for learning', were admitted to the society; there they lived celibate lives, being separated even in the communal hall by a dividing wall so that they could hear but not see each other. Nothing is said of their initiation or training, except that novices chosen for merit served at the common meals in place of slaves, whom they refused to possess, considering all men to be free by birth. Having divested themselves of their wealth and entered the society, they followed no profane occupation, practised no craft and did no manual work. They had one garment of skin for the winter and another of linen for the summer, they wore a white robe on solemn occasions, and they used oil on their bodies. Rising at dawn, they began the day with prayer, facing the rising sun; they then devoted their time wholly to meditation and the study of the Scriptures, aided by commentaries 'composed by ancient founders of their order' and working out an allegorical exposition which they expressed in sacred hymns; and they ended the day's work with prayer at sunset. Then, on weekdays, they took their only meal alone in their huts, eating only cheap bread flavoured with salt or hyssop and drinking only water; some members, however, fasted for three or even six days on end in contemplative rapture. The members met only on the sabbath. Then all came together in the central hall for worship, at which they sat in silence ranged in order of age and keeping their hands concealed under their cloaks; the senior member who possessed the fullest knowledge of the doctrines which they professed gave an address, of which they expressed approbation by glances, nods and smiles, and disapprobation by pointing a finger of the right hand; after the address they gave the rest of the day to relaxation. They met for worship also 'after every forty-nine days'; this phrase has been taken either to mean that every fiftieth day was regarded as a 'jubilee' or to indicate the feast of Pentecost. On this occasion the members assembled in the evening and took their places in the order of their admission to the society with their attendants standing beside them, the men being on the right and the women on the left side (sc. of the dividing wall). When silence had been obtained, the presiding senior expounded a Scriptural subject by way of allegory and answered any questions which might be put to him; he then stood up and sang a hymn, either an old one or something which he had himself composed, and each member followed suit, as the Covenanters may have used their *Thanksgiving Hymns*[1]; they

[1] Vermès *Scrolls* 149.

then partook of supper, having the same fare as that provided on ordinary days. Members of both sexes then spent the rest of the night as a kind of vigil, singing sacred songs and dancing till dawn, when each went back to his own hut. Thus by 'healing' unruly passions and spiritual blindness, by making self-control the highest virtue and practising a solitary form of life, they devoted themselves wholly to the contemplation of God, 'the best and most divine part of philosophy'.

Clearly the Essenes and the Therapeuts lived very similar lives, but equally clearly many dissimilarities can be detected, so that they cannot be identified out of hand; but the relations of these two parties are no concern of the present enquiry. The same thing may be said when the Therapeuts are compared with the Covenanters; and here some brief discussion is necessary.

The play on 'healing' as supposed to be reflected in the Hebrew and Greek names of the two groups has been thought to be reflected in the Scrolls, in which healing is occasionally mentioned. So the author of one declares that 'the reward of all who walk in this spirit (*sc.* the spirit of truth) is healing (*marpē'*) and abundant peace with length of days' (D iv 6–7), and another announces 'I will be a snare for transgressors but healing (*marpē'*) for those who turn from transgression' (T ii 8–9); but the Hebrew word is different and cannot be linked with the Greek and Aramaic terms behind the two names, even if they are rightly interpreted, and the metaphor in any case goes back to the Old Testament, so that all three groups may have independently come upon it. It therefore has no value as evidence of identity.

Much is absent from both accounts, from that which Philo gives of the life which the Therapeuts lived and from that of the Covenanters as described in the Scrolls; but certain similarities and dissimilarities stand out. The former are the common meals and the meetings at which the members sat in order of seniority (although this is variously reckoned), the instruction given by the seniors, the intense study of the Scriptures and the composition of hymns, as also the observance of a jubilee or similar feast; but some of these are found in all types of coenobitic life, where they are necessary to maintenance of order, and others are simply characteristic of Jewish religious life. The latter are fatal to the identification of the two groups, apart from the fact that Philo himself keeps them apart. One group lived mostly in Palestine, while the other was settled principally in Egypt, and the accounts of neither throw out the least hint of intercommunication; both admitted women but, while the Covenanters raised families, the Therapeuts were strictly celibate; the Covenanters entrusted their personal property to the management of a special officer, whereas the Therapeuts would seem to have divested themselves of it (possibly leaving it to their families or friends) on joining their respective societies; the Covenanters (or at any rate a large number of them) lived together in a 'monastery', while the Therapeuts had their own separate huts or cells; the Covenanters met daily for their common meals, whereas the Therapeuts ate their meals alone, meeting only on certain specified occasions, principally the Sabbath, for public worship and a common meal; the Therapeuts eschewed meat as also the Covenanters did (Z xii 14), but the latter permitted the use of 'wine' (*tîrôš*)[1] while the former forbade it, drinking only water; the Covenanters spent the day in manual labour, while the Therapeuts devoted their entire time to spiritual exercises; the Covenanters kept vigil by relays every night, but the Therapeuts observed the custom only on the night following the Sabbath. Lastly, the fact that the Therapeuts put out their right hands to express disapprobation of a speaker has nothing to do with the prohibition of the Covenanters' uncovering their left hands at meetings.[2] Briefly, the differences outnumber and outweigh the resemblances, and the identification of the two groups cannot be maintained against them.

The Essenes and the Therapeuts and the Covenanters have many common features; and attempts have indeed been made to show that there may have been no Essenes as such but only a number of splinter-groups, Samaritan or Judaean or Egyptian Essenes, all springing from a widespread movement of Jewish or para-Jewish nonconformity[3], and that the need to reconcile the differences between the Judaean Essenes and the Covenanters disappears, as these last are but another of these splinter-groups.[4] The evidence is too confused to prove the theory, while the respective groups show enough differences clearly to distinguish them. The principal common feature is the ascetic life, whether contemplative or active; but the possibility must be considered whether this, however much the three groups may have indirectly or even directly influenced one another, is not due to borrowing by one from the other but is derived from an extraneous source known or accessible to all three groups.

8. ASCETIC MOVEMENTS

Epicurus (342–270 B.C.) founded a philosophic school which had already in the founder's lifetime attracted many Egyptian and Asiatic adherents; and not a few of the practices and doctrines of the Epicureans closely resembled those found in various groups of the 1st century A.D., including Essenes and Covenanters as well as Christians. The Epicureans lived in communities of both sexes,[5] which were held

---

[1] S. p. 513. Drinking *tîrôš* was not a violation of the Nazirite vow (P. Talmud *Nedarim* vii 1).
[2] Pp. 65–6.
[3] Black *Scrolls and Christian Origins* 48–74.
[4] Sparks in *Hibb. Journ.* LX 342.
[5] Pp. 259–60.

together by no other bond than the charm of mutual intercourse, they had the simplest fare of bread and water or cheese and wine, they apparently entrusted their property to supervisors[1] but did not practise communism, they liked rather 'to confer than to receive a benefit',[2] they avoided all culture, they regarded pleasure as lying in tranquillity and in freedom from distractions rather than in vigorous enjoyment, and devoted themselves to a life of moral purpose and philosophic study; they inculcated the due obedience of the inferior to his superior,[3] and they held that 'kinship with the flesh' was the cause of moral corruption in man[4] and that the death of the body was the end of everything for man. Porphyry also tells[5] of certain Egyptian philosopher-priests of the 1st century A.D. who sought out retreats where they could dwell in the sight of the gods, secure from human anxieties. They lived in solitude, mixing with other people only at religious assemblies or on festal occasions; they ate only bread seasoned with salt and spiced with hyssop and trained themselves to endure hunger and thirst; they renounced human toil and all other pursuits and gave their whole lives to the contemplation of divine things, holding that constant association with divine knowledge and inspiration delivered men from desires and subdued the passions and illumined the intelligence; and they passed their days in the worship of the gods, praising them morning and evening in hymns and psalms.

Epicureanism, starting in the 4th century B.C., lasted well into the 3rd century A.D.; and all three writers, Plutarch and Epictetus and Arrian, who gave accounts or inserted notices of it in their writings, lived c. A.D. 50–150, so that it would have been well known throughout the Graeco-Roman world just when the three Jewish movements were active. If then Philo and Josephus, who lived in the same age, were influenced, as many would hold, by the Greek model in their respective descriptions of the ideal life of the corresponding Jewish societies, these might similarly but independently have derived something, possibly much, from the same model while modifying what they took to suit Jewish racial and religious needs. That asceticism does not come naturally to Jews, even though traces of it can be detected in the Old Testament, supports this argument.

Like the Epicureans, both the Essenes and the Therapeuts seem to have been pacifist societies, whereas the Covenanters were a militant party; the problem, therefore, which requires examination is to discover the source of the militarism which colours much of the literature of the Covenanters.

---

[1] Oldfather *Epictetus* (Loeb) I iv 39.
[2] Plutarch *Moralia* 1097A (*non posse suaviter vivi* 15); cp. Acts xx. 35.
[3] Oldfather *Epictetus* (Loeb) I iii 7.   [4] *Ibid.* III xxi 3–4.
[5] In *de Abstinentia* iv 6–8.

HISTORICAL ALLUSIONS IN THE SCROLLS

1. Rightful Teacher and Wicked Priest

The story behind the Scrolls, which may enable them to be assigned to their proper place in history, must be picked out almost exclusively from two of them, although others occasionally provide some piece of fresh information or throw light on an obscure point already known from these two; these are the *Commentary on Habakkuk*, which conceals the principal historical episode behind the Scrolls, and the *War of the Sons of Light with the Sons of Darkness*, which under the guise of an apocalypse (though not an apocalypse in the strict sense; for such a work purports to recount history in the form of secret revelations, of which the *War* has none)[1] throws welcome light on the aspirations of the Covenanters. The *Zadokite Documents* give a date which, though useful, is not decisive and is indeed (if taken in its literal sense) too early, since it can be harmonized only with some, not with all, of the facts to which these documents may seem to allude;[2] and *Discipline* may contain hints by which the chief character in the story can perhaps be identified.[3] The *Thanksgiving Hymns* make but an uncertain contribution to the solution of the problem. Occasional pieces of information can be gleaned also from the various fragments; but these must be used with great caution, since the context is almost always wholly missing.

The *Commentary on Habakkuk* is not a commentary in the modern sense. As Dr. Cross says,[4] the Covenanters 'by perusing the Scriptures were able to find detailed descriptions of the events of current history'; but he also says[5] that 'the commentaries refer to events over a considerable period of history'. The first statement may be accepted without reservation, but the second must be seriously called in question; for a commentary of the former type is intelligible, whereas one of the latter will have neither rhyme nor reason. A commentator must be presumed to have some purpose: he may seek to explain an ancient text in the circumstances of the original author's own times or to treat it as reflecting the events of his own lifetime and so as conveying a message to himself and his contemporaries, but he can achieve neither end with a hotch-potch of allusions drawn from any and every period of the national history; and, if such a *farrago libelli* is required by any

---

[1] Cp. Van der Ploeg *Excavations* 174–5. [2] Pp. 311–6.
[3] Pp. 336–7, 343. [4] In *Library* 83. [5] *Ibid.* 85.

theory of interpretation, the possibility that the text has been mis-interpreted must always be borne in mind. The *Commentary on Habakkuk*, however, of which some two-thirds is almost perfectly preserved, can be shown to refer in almost every comment to the events of a very few years, scarcely a decade, of Jewish history; and it is a plausible pre-sumption that these are the events of the contemporary history, if not of the prophet, then of the Commentator himself. Since then the Com-mentator is demonstrably not trying to explain the prophecies of Habakkuk in the light of philological and archaeological research and to set them against their background in ancient history, he must be applying them to the events of his own age without regard to their orig-inal import; thus in his view they foretell the events of his own age and so serve in some sense as a political pamphlet or tract for the times.[1]

A few examples will show the commentator's method of using his text:

Habakkuk i 6: '*for lo! I raise up the Chaldaeans, that bitter and hasty nation.* Its interpretation points to the Kittians, who are swift and mighty in battle, destroying . . . [and subduing them] to the dominion of the Kittians; they . . . and do not put faith in [God's] statutes' (H ii 10-15);

Habakkuk i 10: '*then he sweeps by as a wind and shall pass over, and he makes his might his god.* Its interpretation points to the rulers of the Kittians, who pass on by the counsel of a guilty house, one before another; [their] rulers come one after another to lay waste the land' (H iv 9-13);

Habakkuk i 13: '*wherefore look ye* (!) *upon traitors and holdest thou thy peace when a wicked man swalloweth up one more*| *righteous than he?* Its interpreta-tion points to the house of Absalom and his counsellors, who were silenced, *i.e.* destroyed,[2] when the Rightful Teacher was chastised, and did not help him against the Man of Falsehood who rejected the law in the midst of their whole congregation' (H v 8-12);

Habakkuk i 15: '*therefore he sacrificeth unto his net and burneth incense unto his drag:* its interpretation points to the fact that they (*sc.* the Kittians) sacrifice to their standards, and their weapons are the object of their veneration' (H vi 2-5);[3]

Habakkuk ii 2: '*that he who reads may run:* its interpretation points to the Rightful Teacher, to whom God has revealed all the mysteries of the words of his servants the prophets' (H vii 3-5);

Habakkuk ii 4: '[*but the righteous shall live by his faith:*] its interpreta-tion points to all who do the law in the house of Judah, whom God will save from the house of doom because of their toil and their faith in the Rightful Teacher' (H vii [17]-viii 3);

---

[1] Cp. Del Medico *Énigme* 180, 192. [2] Pp. 271-2.
[3] Cp. Targum on Hab. i. 16.

Habakkuk ii 5–6: *'yea, but a wealthy man (?) is a traitor, a haughty man and that keepeth not at home; who openeth wide his throat like Sheol and like death cannot be satisfied but assembleth unto him all nations and gathereth unto him all the peoples. Shall they not all take up a parable against him and taunting riddles against him and say: Woe to him that increaseth what is not his!; how long shall he lade himself with pledges?* Its interpretation points to the Wicked Priest who was truly named when he took office; but, when he held rule in Israel, his heart was lifted up, and he forsook God and became a traitor to the statutes for the sake of wealth. He plundered and gathered the wealth of ruthless men who rebelled against God; he took the wealth of peoples, adding iniquity and guilt to himself, and conducted himself abominably in all impurity and uncleanness' (H viii 3–12);

Habakkuk ii 8: *'because thou hast spoiled many nations, all the remnant of the peoples shall spoil thee.* Its interpretation points to the last priests of Jerusalem, who have amassed wealth and gain from the spoil of the peoples; but at the end of the days their wealth with their spoil will be given over to the army of the Kittians, since they are the remnant of the peoples' (H ix 3–7);

Habakkuk ii 8: *'because of bloodshed and for the violence done to the land, to the city and to all that dwell therein.* Its interpretation points to the Wicked Priest, whom for the wrong done to the Rightful Teacher and his counsellors God gave over to his enemies to afflict him with a fatal blow in bitterness of soul, because he acted wickedly towards His elect' (H ix 8–12);

Habakkuk ii 12: *'woe to him that buildeth a town with blood and stablisheth a town by iniquity! Behold! is it not of the Lord of Hosts that the peoples labour for a trifle[1] and the nations weary themselves for vanity!* Its interpretation points to one who spluttered falsehood, who enticed many to build a city of delusion by bloodshed and to establish a congregation by falsehood for the sake of his honour, so that many labour in vain service and become pregnant with lying deeds, so that their toil is futile to the end that they enter into judgements of fire because they reviled and taunted the elect ones of God' (H x 5–13);

Habakkuk ii 15: *'woe to him that giveth his neighbour drink, that poureth out his fiery wine, even strong drink,[2] in order to gaze on their feasts.* Its interpretation points to the Wicked Priest who pursued the Rightful Teacher to swallow him up in the indignation of his wrath at (cp. W v 6)[3] the place where he was discovered[4]; and at the season of the feast of the rest of the Day of Atonement he appeared unto them to

---

[1] Cp. Septuagint at Jer. li. 48 (s. Driver in JSS IV 148).
[2] Cp. Driver *ThZeitschr*. XIV 133–5.
[3] Cp. Cooke *North-Semitic Inscriptions* 29 3–8 (where the same abnormal form is found twice beside the normal form of the same preposition in a Phoenician inscription).
[4] Pp. 272–3.

swallow them up and to make them to stumble on the fast day, the sabbath of their rest' (H xi 2–8);

Habakkuk ii 16: *Thou art filled with shame instead of honour; drink thou also and be as one uncircumcised. The cup of the Lord's right hand shall be turned against thee and foul shame shall exceed thy glory.*[1] Its interpretation points to the priest whose shame exceeded his honour inasmuch as he did not circumcize the foreskin of his heart but walked in ways of drunkenness to quench (his) thirst; and the cup of God's wrath will swallow him up to [heap disgrace] and pain [upon] him' (H xi 13–15).

These excerpts, which contain the principal details of the story lying behind the Scrolls, will suffice to show the nature of the comments in the *Commentary on Habakkuk*; other commentaries on *Hosea* and *Micah*, as also on the *Psalms*, are similar.

Two excerpts from a *Commentary on a Psalm* may be quoted here, since they throw some light on the same story:

Psalm xxxvii 32–33: '*the wicked watcheth the righteous and seeketh* [*to slay him. The Lord will not leave him in his hand nor*] *condemn him when he is judged.* Its interpretation points to the Wicked [Priest], who [sent to the Rightful Teacher] to slay him [and to make an end of the covenant] and the law. Yet, though he sent to him, God will not [leave him in his hand] nor [condemn him when] he is arraigned; but [God] will repay his due to that man by giving him over to the most ruthless of nations to execute [judgement] upon him' [APs.b i 1–4].

Psalm xxvii 14–15: '*the wicked have drawn the sword and bent their bow to cast down the poor and needy, to slay such as be upright in the way; their sword shall enter into their own heart and their bows shall be broken.* Its interpretation points to the wicked ones of Ephraim and Manasseh who seek to lay hands on the priest and his counsellors at the testing time which is coming upon them. God will redeem them (*sc.* the latter) from their power and afterwards they (*sc.* the former) will be given into the hand of the most ruthless of nations for judgement' (APs.b ii 1–5).

That this commentary (in which the verses are discussed out of order) is so badly damaged is a matter of the utmost regret, since it obviously refers to the same event or events; for another fragment speaks of 'the priest, the [Rightful] Teacher', thus almost certainly proving that the Teacher was a priest (APs.b ii 15).[2] It is thus shown that 'the wicked of Ephraim and Manasseh'[3] as well as the Wicked Priest were involved in the attempt 'to swallow up' the Rightful Teacher and further suggests that 'to swallow him up' means 'to slay him';[4] this interpretation of the verb is perfectly legitimate, since it often has this sense in the Old Testament.[5]

The story which can be consistently and reasonably reconstructed

[1] Cp. 1 Macc. i. 40.   [2] Pp. 275–6   [3] Pp. 295–7.
[4] Pp. 269–71.   [5] *E.g.* 2 Sam. xx. 19–20; Job viii. 18; Ps. cxxiv. 3.

from these works is approximately the following or something very similar.

A Teacher of Righteousness or Rightful Teacher (for the Hebrew expression is equivocal),[1] who seems to have been also a priest and at the same time the leader of a considerable party, is pursued by a Wicked Priest aiming 'to swallow him up', *i.e.* to destroy him together with his followers on the Day of Atonement; and he apparently succeeds in his purpose. At the same time a group called the 'house of Absalom' is 'silenced', *i.e.* 'destroyed',[2] and so is unable to come to the Teacher's assistance, while another group called the 'house of Judah' is rescued by God. The Wicked Priest and those who aid and abet him are clearly fellow Jews and therefore internal enemies; but the Teacher is at the same time troubled with external enemies called the Kittians, who carry death and destruction wherever they go.

The commentaries come from the same source as the other documents, which reflect a different aspect of the situation.

Both *Discipline* and the *Zadokite Documents* have already been discussed. The former describes a religious group living in community and calling themselves the 'sons (*i.e.* followers) of Zadok' (D ix 14 [!]; cp. Z v 7 vi 2) and also the 'Sons of Light' (D i 9 ii 16 iii 13, 24, 25), in contradistinction to their opponents in the world, whom they designate the 'Sons of Darkness' (D i 10);[3] this work does not say anything of a Rightful Teacher, but it does throw out hints which may perhaps indicate his name, as shown below.[4] The latter, which belongs to the same group of texts,[5] describes God's sending of a Rightful Teacher some 390 years after the exile 'to teach the last generations what He does to a last generation, a congregation of faithless men' (Z i 8); it says that 'all the men of war who took sides with the Man of Falsehood will be brought to an end about forty years after the gathering of the Unique Teacher (to his fathers)' (Z ix 39) and that those who, having embraced the 'new covenant', abandoned it will not be reckoned in the community of the people 'from the day when the Unique Teacher was' or 'is gathered (to his forefathers) until a Messiah shall arise from Aaron and from Israel' (Z ix 29). This last phrase clearly denotes a priestly Messiah and a lay Messiah and, taken in conjunction with other information discussed below,[6] seems to indicate that the Rightful Teacher or a successor of his line will reappear to combine the two offices, that of a priestly and of a lay Messiah, in his own person.

The *Thanksgiving Hymns* are psalms or hymns of thanksgiving for deliverance from a great conflagration and an overwhelming disaster;

[1] Pp. 257–8.
[3] Cp. p. 328.
[5] Pp. 29–30.
[2] Pp. 271–2.
[4] Pp. 336–7, 343.
[6] Pp. 471–6.

whether the conflagration is meant literally or metaphorically and what this disaster can have been will be discussed below.[1]

Finally the *War*, which has nothing to say of the Rightful Teacher or of the Wicked Priest, depicts the 'Sons of Light' engaged in a pseud-apocalyptic struggle with the 'Sons of Darkness' (W i 1); these last, who have been mentioned elsewhere in the Scrolls, here include the nations of the world, amongst whom the 'Kittians' take the leading place. In this war the 'Sons of Light' emerge or perhaps rather expect to emerge victorious over all their foes, in fact over all the world.

The identification of the Wicked Priest is made difficult by the considerable number of wicked priests known to history within the prescribed limits; that of the Rightful Teacher is rendered equally difficult for the opposite reason, the relative paucity or complete absence of suitable persons to play the part assigned to him. He must be an outstanding personage, a known teacher and a priest, the leader of a considerable religious and political party, which traces its origin to one Zadok;[2] he must be someone who is pursued by an internal enemy, also a priest, by whom he appears eventually to have been done to death with some of his followers, while others make good their escape, on the Day of Atonement; and he or his party must be capable of conducting organized resistance to an exceedingly powerful external enemy, who may also be regarded as a national enemy, attacking simultaneously from the north and the south.[3]

The *terminus a quo* for fixing the date of the Scrolls seems to be provided by the opening section of the *Zadokite Documents*, which say that 'in the epoch of wrath, three hundred and ninety years of (= after)[4] His (*sc.* God's) delivering them (*sc.* the Jewish nation) into the hand of Nebuchadnezzar king of Babylon, He visited them and made a root planted [aforetime] to shoot . . .; and they recognized their iniquity and knew that they were guilty men and were like blind men and like them that grope for a way for twenty years. Then God considered their conduct, how with a perfect heart they (had) sought him; and He raised up a Rightful Teacher for them . . . to teach the last generations what He does to a last generation, (which proves itself) a congregation of traitors' (Z i 5–8). The Captivity took place in 586 B.C., so that the date here indicated would seem to be 196 B.C.[5] There are however reasons for not assigning its literal sense to these 390 years,[6] which are clearly based on the number of days for which the prophet Ezekiel was bidden to lie on his left side bearing the iniquity of the house of Israel'.[7] Yet, however interpreted, these figures will give the earliest

[1] Pp. 302–3.   [2] Pp. 252–9.   [3] Pp. 203–5.
[4] Cp. Num. xxxiii. 38; 1 Kings vi. 1 and 2 Kings xxv. 27; Jer. lii. 31; Ezek. xxxiii. 21, xl. 1 (s. Wiesenberg in *VT* V 286–7).
[5] P. 133–6.   [6] Pp. 313–7.   [7] Ezek. iv. 5, 9 (s. Rabinowitz in *JBL* LXXIII 14).

possible date for the composition of the *Zadokite Documents*; for the author could hardly refer to an event which had not occurred at the time of its composition. That the *terminus a quo* contravenes that given by the test of radioactive carbon, namely *c.* 167 B.C., is no matter, for reasons which are given elsewhere;[1] so too the *terminus ante quem*, which has been fixed at A.D. 68 by the archaeologists, is by no means so secure as it seems, for reasons which will be given hereafter.[2] The dates of the events described in the Scrolls may therefore be discussed without attaching undue importance to any which may seem to have been pre-determined by such uncertain evidence.

These dates, although in themselves somewhat imprecise as the limits of the period within which those of the Scrolls must fall, are plausible enough and a working hypothesis may be based on them; but they must not be too closely pressed. Such a wide margin, however, is unsatisfactory, and every effort must be made to see whether and how far it can be narrowed down with a view to determining the exact date of the Scrolls. Since, then, neither archaeology nor palaeography, of which something will be said hereafter,[3] nor the only definite date mentioned in the Scrolls is sufficient for the present purpose, an attempt must be made to enucleate the story behind the Scrolls; for, if this can be recovered and identified, it will be decisive. The enquirer, however, finds himself in an exceedingly difficult position when he begins to search for the key to these esoteric mysteries in contemporary history; and his difficulties are increased by the fact that the authors of the Scrolls seem to have deliberately expressed themselves obscurely. They were addressing a small group whose secrets were not intended to be divulged to the uninitiated (D ix 17),[4] and they therefore concealed their meaning as best they could, resorting even to the use of pseudo-nyms and cryptograms.[5] In these circumstances, how can a modern scholar hope to discover the exact period in which he must look for the solution of the problem? Not unnaturally many answers have been given in the 2nd–1st centuries B.C. and in the 1st century A.D.; but three centuries, during which Jewish history is equally well known and for much of which Josephus is the main if not the only historian available, are a very wide field of enquiry. That a solution of the problem has been sought from the Babylonian captivity to the Crusades only shows how elusive the problem is.

2. PRE-CHRISTIAN IDENTIFICATIONS

Soon after the discovery of the Scrolls, Prof. Albright,[6] after a cursory study of a photograph of that containing *Isaiah A*,[7] announced

---

[1] Pp. 409–10.   [2] Pp. 394–6.   [3] Pp. 410–20.
[4] P. 54.   [5] Pp. 335–46.
[6] In *BASOR* CXVIII 6; cp. Yadin *Message* 34–5.   [7] Cp. Driver *Scrolls* 23.

that it must be assigned to a date *c.* 100 B.C. (between 175 B.C. and 75 B.C. as extreme limits). The contents of the Scroll, of course, have nothing to say on such a point, and so little is known of Hebrew palaeography in this period that it throws practically no light on the problem.[1] This conjecture, however useful it may have been as a working hypothesis, has bedevilled all subsequent discussion; for the date, thus lightly established, has been treated by subsequent writers as a historical fact and illogically used as proof of the pre-Christian date of all the Scrolls, although it has no necessary connection with that of any other Scroll.

Prof. Albright further announced[2] that 'the content of the new documents fits satisfactorily into the picture of Jewish life in the Maccabean age which we have from pseudepigraphical literature', and he went on to foretell that this would become 'increasingly clear when still unpublished material already identified in the Scrolls and fragments becomes available to scholars generally. Some of the new evidence is of the most extraordinary interest'. Appeals to unpublished documents are as rash as they are unconvincing, the prophecy has not been fulfilled and the statement is not borne out by close study of the texts.

Diverse attempts, based on Prof. Albright's hypothetical date, have been made to identify the episode just described in the 2nd and 1st centuries B.C., and the principal solutions put forward must now be described. Variations, equally numerous, of each solution have been proposed, but there is no need to set out and argue each in turn, since all are disproved by the same general considerations; the present discussion can therefore be restricted to certain typical identifications.

Prof. Seeligmann, the leader in the attempt to work out theory assigning the Scrolls to the 2nd century B.C., identifies the enemy called the 'Kittians' in the Scrolls with the Seleucid Greeks;[3] but he seems, after sketching it only briefly, to have abandoned it.[4] Now however Prof. Reicke and Prof. Rowley have both taken it up[5] and become its enthusiastic sponsors.

Following the late Prof. E. Meyer,[6] Prof. Rowley starts from the statement that 390 years after the captivity God visited His people and that they then wandered as blind men for twenty years (Z i 5–7); this seems to show that 390 years after 586 B.C. is 196 B.C., and that another twenty years added to this figure brings it to 176 B.C. These twenty years coincide almost exactly with the high-priesthood of Onias III, who came into office *c.* 198–195 B.C. and whom Antiochus IV Epiphanes de-

[1] Pp. 410–20.　　　　　　　　　　　　　[2] In *JQR*, NS XL 48.
[3] Cp. Michel *Maître* 125–62.　　　　　　[4] In *BO* VI 5–6.
[5] In *St. Th.* II 48–63 (Reicke) and *BJRL* XL 114–16 (Rowley); s. Rowley *Zadokite Fragments* 62–82.
[6] In *Abhandl. d. Preuss. Akad. d. Wissensch.* 1919 ix 13–14.

K

posed almost immediately after his accession in 175 B.C. This Onias, who was highly praised for his godliness and his hatred of wickedness and as a 'zealot for the laws',[1] remained loyal to the old faith when Antiochus sought to hellenize the Jews; but Menelaus, whom Josephus[2] calls 'a wicked and impious man' and who is also described as 'having the passion of a cruel tyrant and the rage of a savage beast',[3] was the leader of the hellenizing party. The high-priest's brother, Jesus (Graecized as Jason), had succeeded c. 174 B.C. in persuading the king by the promise of a large sum of money and his support of the royal policy to depose Onias and install himself as high-priest in his brother's place, though 'an ungodly man and no high-priest';[4] but in 171 B.C. Menelaus, by promising the king even larger sums of money, brought about the downfall of Jason and secured the high-priesthood for himself. He then procured the murder of Onias[5], who had sought asylum at Daphne, whence his emissary Andronicus decoyed him and treacherously slew him. The Wicked Priest, then, might 'with much appropriateness' be identified with Menelaus, and Onias might be taken for the Rightful Teacher.[6] Several small points are cited in favour of this identification.[7] First, Menelaus was apparently of the tribe of Benjamin and therefore not of a priestly family,[8] and he was also one of those who, abandoning Jewish national customs, adopted a Greek mode of life;[9] the authors of the Scrolls with their insistence on the legitimacy of the Zadokite priesthood would naturally be on the side of the legitimate priest Onias and would regard an illegitimate and hellenizing priest as a 'wicked priest'. Second, Menelaus, although he had promised a large sum of money to obtain the high-priesthood for himself, never paid it; this would well accord with the rapacity of the Wicked Priest, to which the *Commentary on Habakkuk* refers when it says that 'he became a traitor to the (*sc.* God's) statutes for wealth' (H viii 10–11). Third, Menelaus was said to have tolerated the many acts of sacrilege which Lysimachus committed in Jerusalem, while the *Commentary* describes that city as the place 'wherein the Wicked Priest wrought his abominable works and wherein he profaned the sanctuary of God' (H xii 8–9). Fourth, the *Commentary* adds that the Wicked Priest was punished for his sins when 'the horrors of evil diseases acted upon him and he paid the price of his misdeeds in the body of his flesh' and that 'God gave him over to his enemies to be afflicted with a fatal blow in bitterness of spirit' (H ix 1–2); this description of the

---

[1] 2 Macc. iv. 2; Josephus *Antiquities* XII vi 2 § 271.
[2] In *Antiquities* XII v 1 § 328 and ix 7 § 385.
[3] 2 Macc. iv. 25.   [4] *Ibid.* iv. 13.   [5] Cp. Charles *Daniel* 246–7.
[6] Cp. I Enoch xc 8 (s. Schonfield *Secrets* 75–6).
[7] Cp. Michel *Maître* 251–8, 293–8.
[8] 2 Macc. iii. 4 compared with iv. 23; s. Schürer *Geschichte*[3] I 195–6 and Marcus *Josephus* [Loeb] IV 120–1.
[9] Josephus *Antiquities* XII v 1 § 240.

Wicked Priest's end might be taken as an echo of the story that Antiochus V Eupator had Menelaus cast into a tower full of ashes, where he was suffocated to death.[1]

Two other points cited in favour of assigning the Scrolls to this period prove nothing. The first is the prohibition of marriage with a niece, of polygamy and divorce,[2] enforced by the Covenanters (Z vii 1, 9 xvi 8).[3] This might conceivably be aimed at Joseph, a member of the well-known Tobiad family; for Josephus relates[4] that he not only married his brother's daughter but also had another wife living at the same time. The same charge, however, can be brought against other persons within the prescribed historical limits, *e.g.* Herod the Great and several members of his family and certain prominent Jews in the following century.[5] The second is that many of those unwilling to give way to the hellenizing policy of the Seleucid kings took refuge in caves in the Judaean wilderness;[6] but this part of the country is riddled with caves which have been inhabited on and off throughout the ages, and nothing connects those in which the fugitives from persecution in the Maccabaean age took refuge with those in the cliffs round Qumrân.

So far as these details go, the identifications thus proposed are superficially attractive, but they are open to serious objections; and even the date, which seems unshakable, is but a broken reed.[7]

Nothing is known to suggest that Onias was regarded in any way as a teacher or that he was the leader of a war-party against a foreign enemy which had ravaged or was ravaging the country. Yet Fr. Michel, who shares this view of the Scrolls, can say[8] that, although historical truth does not allow the title of chief of the Hasidaean party to Onias, it allows him to be acclaimed leader of the 'Sons of Zadok' and Rightful Teacher; he thereby identifies one who was admittedly not a leader of a party with an admitted leader of a party. How then can the party have been described as 'like blind men, groping for a way' (Z i 6) *i.e.* leaderless, when they had a spiritual leader in the person of the high-priest? If, too, the Kittians are identified with the Seleucid Greeks, Onias cannot be the Teacher; for Onias was on friendly terms with the Syrian rulers,[9] while the Teacher was bitterly opposed to the Kittian enemy. Further, the murder of Onias is not said to have taken place on any Day of Atonement; if it had, such an outrage on Jewish sentiment would surely have been mentioned by any Jewish historian who recorded the event. Another difficulty is the assumed identification of the 'house of Absalom' and his partisans, who are supposed to have kept silence and not helped the Rightful

---

[1] 2 Macc. xiii. 5–8.
[3] Pp. 87–8.
[5] P. 87.
[7] Pp. 313–6.
[9] 2 Macc. iii. 1–2, 37–9, iv. 4–6.

[2] Cp. Segal in *JQR*, NS II 138.
[4] In *Antiquities* XII iv 6 §§ 186–93.
[6] 1 Macc. ii. 29–38; 2 Macc. vi. 11.
[8] In *Maître* 321.

Teacher when attacked by the Wicked Priest, with the Tobiad family, on the ground that the above-named Joseph, a member of that family and also a nephew of Onias, obtained the privilege of farming the taxes which had gone with the high-priesthood and so set himself up beside the high-priest as the most powerful person in the state[1]; but, even though the name of David's presumptuous son Absalom might be used as a pseudonym for this Joseph, the story conveys no hint of his having betrayed his uncle or of having made good his escape when attacked by his enemies. The assumption too, that he betrayed his leader by keeping silence on the fatal day rests on a mistranslation.[2] Further, 'the house of Judah, whom God will rescue from the house of doom because of their toil and their faith in the Teacher of Righteousness' (H viii 1–3), is left entirely out of the picture. Lastly, the Maccabaean allusions in the Scrolls, if they are rightly identified,[3] preclude a pre-Maccabaean date, *i.e.* any date before *c.* 165 B.C.

Fr. Milik[4] and Dr. Winter[5] cast Jonathan, fifth and youngest son of Mattathias the father of the famous Maccabaean brothers[6] who revolted against the Seleucid policy of hellenization, for the part of the Wicked Priest; and Fr. Sutcliffe has independently sought[7] to support this suggestion by adducing additional arguments in its favour.

The chronological problem is easily settled! The *Zadokite Document*'s 390 years from the captivity in 586 B.C. brings the date down to 196 B.C., and the Hasidaean party, who were so called for their 'loyalty' (*ḥeseḏ*) to the Law,[8] appear in 162–161 B.C. supporting Judas the Maccabee in his revolt against the Seleucid rulers of the country.[9] No exact dates can be given, as Jewish chronology for the period of the Second Commonwealth is notoriously inaccurate; but, if the party came into existence *c.* 180 B.C. and then 'they became like blind men and like them that grope for the way for twenty years' (Z i 6) until the Rightful Teacher appeared, the story would come down to *c.* 160 B.C., when Judas the Maccabee died and was succeeded by his brother Jonathan.[10] These figures, however, cannot be reconciled with any known Jewish chronology;[11] and no reason is adduced to show why the Hasidaeans should be regarded 'as blind men groping for the way' while they were allied to the victorious Judas and why the appearance of the Rightful Teacher should be equated with the succession of Jonathan, who *ex hypothesi* was the Wicked Priest, to be the nation's military commander and civil governor.

The *Commentary on Habakkuk* speaks of the Wicked Priest as one 'who

---

[1] Cp. Reicke in *St. Th.* II 45–70.
[2] Pp. 271–2.
[3] S. pp. 353–6.
[4] In *Dix Ans* [1957] 56–8.
[5] In *Hibb. Journ.* LVIII 53–60.
[6] Josephus *Antiquities* XII vi i § 266.
[7] In *Monks* [1960] 41–9.
[8] 1 Macc. ii. 42.
[9] *Ibid.* xiv. 6.
[10] 1 Macc. ix. 30.
[11] Driver in *Essays presented to S. H. Hooke* 62–77 (s. pp. 311–6).

was truly named when he took office; but, when he ruled in Israel, his head was lifted up, and he forsook God and became a traitor to the statutes for the sake of wealth. He plundered and gathered the wealth of ruthless men who rebelled against God; he took the wealth of peoples, adding iniquity and guilt to himself, and conducted himself abominably in all impurity and uncleanness' (H viii 8–11). This passage is referred to Jonathan on the grounds of his appointment, his name and his conduct.

When Judas died in 160 B.C., Jonathan succeeded him as military commander and civil governor,[1] but only when the Syrian general Bacchides finally departed two years afterwards is it said that 'he began to judge the people';[2] subsequently Alexander Balas nominated him high-priest in 152 B.C.[3] and Antiochus IV Epiphanes confirmed him in the office,[4] and he retained both offices till his death in 142 B.C. The successive appointments are then supposed to explain why the Commentator says that 'he took office' and also that 'he ruled'; but both verbs may equally well describe two aspects of the same operation, the first the entry upon office and the second the exercise of its functions.[5] That the Wicked Priest was one 'who was truly named when he took office' is taken as an allusion to David's faithful companion Jonathan, whose character is held to resemble that of this other Jonathan; for, although the name *per se* conveys no hint of loyalty, both Demetrius I Soter and Alexander Balas commended his 'loyalty' ($\pi i \sigma \tau \iota \nu$) to themselves.[6] Why, however, should the commentator praise the loyalty of a Jew to Gentile kings, who were merely flattering one whose loyalty was open to the highest bidder and whose assistance each was hoping to win? That the Wicked Priest 'forsook God and became a traitor to the statutes' and that he 'conducted himself abominably in all impurity and uncleanness' is referred to Jonathan's appointment as high-priest though not of the line of Zadok and, further, his acceptance of the office from a Gentile king; but the words, even when allowance is made for the venom of a political or religious opponent, surely are too much for the nature of the offence, which neither the strict author of *I Maccabees* nor Josephus denounces. That the Wicked Priest violated the Law inasmuch as 'he plundered and gathered the wealth of ruthless men who rebelled against God' and 'took the wealth of peoples' is only partly applicable to Jonathan. The historian says that 'he destroyed the ungodly (*i.e.* the hellenizers) out of Israel',[7] but he nowhere says that he appropriated their property; that he may have done so[8] is no argument for identifying him with the Wicked Priest.

[1] I Macc. ix. 30.   [2] *Ibid.* ix. 73.
[3] Josephus *Antiquities* XIII ii 2 § 45; I Macc. x. 18–20.
[4] I Macc. xi. 57.   [5] Cp. Neh. vi. 7.
[6] Josephus *Antiquities* XIII ii 2 § 45 and 3 § 48.   [7] I Macc. ix. 73.
[8] Sutcliffe *op. cit.* 43–4.

He did, however, seize considerable spoils from neighbouring peoples[1] and he accepted rich gifts from various rulers.[2] Clearly he did much 'for the sake of gain', which is denounced in the *Zadokite Documents* as one of three 'snares of Belial' (Z vi 10–11), but whether enough went into his own pocket to justify the commentator's charge can hardly be determined; much was booty taken by Jewish forces rather than his private loot. The offence, too, was one of which many priests under the Second Commonwealth were guilty.   That he personally took part in war, of which the Covenanters disapproved in a priest (cp. W ix 7–9), is not clear;[3] but such conduct may have come to be excused, like fighting on the Sabbath,[4] in the Maccabaean age, and the relaxation of such a rule may well have been tolerated for some while after it. Finally, soon after Jonathan's accession the Essenes, who had succeeded to the place of the Hasidaeans, became openly hostile to the Maccabaean party for the laxity of their observance of the Law, and this rivalry is supposed to be reflected in the clash between the Wicked Priest and the Rightful Teacher; but history gives not the least hint of any attempt by Jonathan 'to swallow up' (H xi 5) a teacher of any sort or of the other events in the story, and any such allusion loses its point in this connection if the Essenes are not identified with the Covenanters. The only point of contact comes with their deaths. The *Commentary on Habakkuk* speaks of the Wicked Priest as one 'whom God delivered into the hands of his enemies . . . ; they afflicted him with a fatal blow so that he ended his life in bitterness of soul because he had wronged His chosen ones' (H ix 9–12); and Jonathan fell into the hands of his enemy Trypho in Galilee and was murdered at his instigation.[5] Both therefore perished at the hands of their enemies, but many others did so; and the addition of the reason, namely 'because he had wronged His (*sc.* God's) elect', precludes such an identification, since the only Jews whom Jonathan treated harshly were the hellenizers and apostates whom he had driven out of the country and whom the Covenanters equally would have detested.

Support for Jonathan is sought[6] further in a large fragment of a *florilegium*, which is to the following effect: 'At the time when Jeshua finished praising and giving thanks in his praises, he said: *Cursed be the man that shall rebuild this city: with his firstborn shall he lay the foundation thereof and with his youngest son shall he set up the gates of it.*[7] And lo! cursed be the man of Belial who stands forth to be a fowler's snare

---

[1] *E.g.* Josephus *Antiquities* XIII iv 4 § 101 = 1 Macc. x. 86–7 (Ascalon); Josephus *ibid.* v 5 § 149 (Ascalon) and 10 § 179 (Nabataeans).

[2] Josephus *Antiquities* XIII iv 4 § 102 = 1 Macc. x. 89 (Alexander Balas); Josephus *ibid.* v. § 105 (Ptolemy VI Philometor); 1 Macc. xi. 57–8 (Antiochus VI Epiphanes).

[3] Cp. 1 Macc. xi. 21.

[4] Josephus *Antiquities* XIII v 9 § 171; 1 Macc. ix. 43–4.

[5] *Ibid.* XIII vi 6 § 209; 1 Macc. xiii. 49–50.

[6] Milik *op. cit.* 61–4; cp. Winter in *PQS* XCI 41–2.   [7] Josh. **vi. 26.**

for his people and a destruction to all his neighbours, and standing forth shall make [his son/sons(?)] rulers, that both of them may become weapons of violence; and they shall again build this city, and shall erect a wall and towers for it, to provide a refuge for wickedness [in the land and a thing of great shame] in Israel, a horrible portent in Ephraim and in Judah . . . ; and they shall bring about apostasy in the land and a thing of great shame among the sons of Jacob, [and shall spill] blood like water on the ramparts of Zion and in the bounds of Jerusalem' (AFl.d. iv 21–30).[1] Primarily the reference is to Jericho, but all interpreters admit that Jerusalem may or must be intended in the context;[2] for the consequence of rebuilding 'this city' is bloodshed in Zion and Jerusalem. The 'vessels of violence' in the Old Testament are Jacob's two sons Levi and Simeon;[3] and this has naturally suggested that the builders here are Jonathan, who began the rebuilding of the city,[4] and his brother Simon, who finished the work,[5] when Trypho was threatening the city _c._ 146 B.C. This suggestion, however, though superficially attractive, labours under the fatal objection that the 'man of Belial' will be Mattathias, 'the heroic and holy priest who gave the signal for revolt against the impious invader, the father of the glorious hero of the nation's liberation';[6] and it is inconceivable that the Covenanters, who modelled themselves on the Maccabaean heroes and often echoed their very thoughts,[7] should have spoken of him in such derogatory terms. The Commentator therefore must be referring to some other event, whether recorded or not recorded, in the history of the Second Commonwealth; and several such suggest themselves, especially as the text does not make clear who the subject of 'they built' is, whether father and son(s) or both sons alone, so that 'the gates of interpretation are open'. For example, Antipater father of Herod the Great in 43 B.C. repaired the ruined walls of the city after Pompey's departure[8] and Herod in 20–19 B.C. rebuilt the Temple and built also a palace for himself in Jerusalem;[9] or again Agrippa I _c._ A.D. 44 enlarged the walls of the city[10] and Agrippa II collected timber to underpin the sanctuary but was frustrated by the outbreak of the First Revolt in A.D. 66, during which John of Gischala used what he had got together for the construction of defensive towers.[11] None of these events, however, exactly fulfil the conditions of the commentary, especially as they leave the two sons (if rightly restored) who become 'vessels of violence' unidentified, and the question is best left for the

---

[1] Cp. Milik _op. cit._ 61[1].   [2] Cp. Allegro in _JBL_ LXXV 187.
[3] Gen. xlix. 5.   [4] 1 Macc. x. 10–11, xii. 36–7.
[5] _Ibid._ xiii. 10, xiv. 37.
[6] Dupont-Sommer _ap._ Milik & Strugnell _Ten Years_ 63–4.   [7] Pp. 353–5.
[8] Josephus _Antiquities_ XIV ix 1 § 156 and _War_ I x 3 § 199.
[9] _Ibid._ XV xi 1 § 380–75, 420 and _War_ I xxi §§ 401–2.
[10] _Ibid._ XIX vii 2 §§ 326–7 and _War_ II xi 6 § 218, V iv 2 § 151.
[11] Josephus _War_ V i 5 §§ 36–8.

moment unanswered, especially as a similar activity is ascribed elsewhere to the Splutterer of Falsehood (H x 9–10).[1]

The *Commentary on Habakkuk* refers also in several places to a priest,
who is generally taken, even if he cannot be proved, to be the Wicked
Priest. He is described as 'the priest who rebelled' (H viii 16), and the
text then adds that 'they worked on him [to] strike him with wicked
judgements and horribly evil sufferings, with acts of vengeance on the
body of his flesh' (H ix 1–2); but these remarks add nothing fresh and
may not even refer to the Wicked Priest. Another passage speaks of 'the
priest whose disgrace exceeded his glory because he did not circumcise
the foreskin of his heart but walked in the ways of utter drunkenness[2] to
quench his thirst; but the cup of God's anger will destroy him,
increasing his disgrace' (H xi 12–15); but the inference drawn from
this passage that, since Jonathan's brother and nephew were made
drunk and murdered at a banquet,[3] drunkenness was a vice of the
family to which Jonathan also was probably prone and that the priest
here meant was therefore Jonathan,[4] only shows to what desperate
straits the defenders of this identification are reduced. They invent a
slander to prove a theory!

The identification of Jonathan with the Wicked Priest must therefore
be abandoned;[5] the points of contact are either too vague or susceptible
of other explanations, the other figures in the story are left unidentified,
and the entire *mise-en-scène* is disregarded. That no attempt is made to
identify also the Rightful Teacher and the other persons involved in the
story in the same period only confirms the rejection of the theory as
inadequate to solve the problem.

Dr. Vermès[6] and Dr. Cross[7] put forward a different candidate for
the part of the Wicked Priest; this is Simon, another Maccabaean high-
priest (142–135 B.C.).[8] In 142 B.C., on the treacherous murder of his
brother Jonathan by Trypho's orders, Simon succeeded to the leadership of the Jewish nation; and at the same time, though not of the
line of Zadok, he secured the office of high-priest, in which Demetrius
II Nicator (145–138 B.C.), who had just come to the Seleucid throne,
confirmed him in order to win him from his friendship with Rome.[9]
In 140 B.C. Simon obtained a special decree legalizing what he had
done and providing that 'the Jews and the priests were well pleased
that Simon should be their leader and high-priest for ever, until a
faithful prophet should arise, and that he should be captain (*i.e.* military
commander) over them . . . and that he should take charge of the

---

[1] Pp. 307–9.   [2] Cp. Deut. x. 16 and xxix. 18 (which is misinterpreted).
[3] Josephus *Antiquities* XIII vii 4 § 228 and *War* I ii 3 § 54; 1 Macc. xvi. 16.
[4] Sutcliffe *op. cit.* 48.   [5] Cp. Michel *Maître* 228–33.
[6] In *Manuscrits* 92–100.   [7] In *Library* 95–119.
[8] 1 Macc. xiv. 1—xvi. 22; Josephus *Antiquities* XIII vi 1 § 187—vii 1 § 229.
[9] 1 Macc. xiv. 38–40.

sanctuary . . ., that he be obeyed by all, and that all instruments in the country should be written in his name, and that he should be clothed in purple and wear gold . . .; and that it should not be lawful for any of the people (*i.e.* the laity) or of the priests to set at nought any of these (things) or to gainsay the words that he should speak (*i.e.* to countermand the orders that he should issue) or to gather an assembly without him or to be clothed in purple or to wear a buckle of gold; but whosoever should do otherwise or set aside any of these things should be liable to punishment'.[1] By this means the office of high-priest, which had already been transferred in the person of Jonathan from the 'sons of Zadok', *i.e.* the descendants of Zadok[2], David's chaplain who had crowned Solomon, to the Hasmonaean family, *i.e.* the descendants of Judas the Maccabee, was continued in that family; and, although the high-priesthood in the house of Simon was in a sense provisional,[3] this family would rule until and unless God's spokesman declared against it at the end of the age. Dr. Cross then argues from the decree that 'there was opposition from *de facto* to *de jure* status for a non-Zadokite high-priestly house' patent in the threat of punishment directed against those who made a show of disobedience; and herein he sees the reason for the enmity between the Wicked Priest, whom he identifies with Simon, and the Rightful Teacher as leader of the party of the 'Sons of Zadok' (*i.e.* the Zadokites) of the Scrolls, whom he assumes to be the Essenes.

Meanwhile Demetrius was out of the way engaged in war with the Parthians and in the event their captive; and 'the land had rest all the days of Simon', while he consolidated his power.[4] In 138 B.C., however, Antiochus VII Sidetes, the late king's brother, invaded the kingdom and seized it and immediately afterwards sought to re-establish Syrian suzerainty over the Jews. The Jews, led by Simon's sons Judas and John, successfully resisted the Syrian encroachment. In 134 B.C., however, Simon and his sons, while touring the cities of Judah and looking to their defences in view of another Syrian attack which they expected, went down to Jericho, where they fell into a trap which Ptolemy the administrator of the district had organized and to which Antiochus was without doubt privy; they were invited to a great banquet, and Simon and Judas were murdered at it while John alone escaped.[5]

Dr. Cross connects these events with the description of the Wicked Priest's end, of which the author of the *Commentary on Habakkuk* says that 'God will deliver him into the hand of his enemies to afflict him with a mortal blow in bitterness of soul because he had wronged His elect' (H ix 10–12; cp. APs.a ii 2–4), adding that he was one 'whose shame

---

[1] 1 Macc. xiv. 41–5.
[2] Cp. Rowley *Men of God* 264[3] (where Zadok's origin is discussed).
[3] 1 Macc. xiv. 41.   [4] *Ibid.* xiv. 4–15.   [5] *Ibid.* xvi. 11–22.

exceeded his honour inasmuch as he did not circumcise the foreskin of his heart but walked in ways of drunkenness to quench (his) thirst; and the cup of God's wrath will swallow him up' (H xi 13–15).

The arguments cited in support of this opinion are as insubstantial as the identification is dubious. On the one hand, that the decree threatened punishment to any who should violate it was almost common form; decrees and laws as often as not carried sanctions without which they could hardly be enforced.[1] The Essenes are not known to have been interested in the Zadokite question; and this indeed seems, so far as negative evidence can be trusted, to have become dormant with the migration of the leading Zadokites to Egypt.[2] On the other hand, the identification of the Wicket Priest is the easiest part of the problem in view of the unfortunately large number of wicked priests available for the part in the whole period! The two passages cited from the *Commentary on Habakkuk* do superficially fit Simon; but how many other high-priests do they fit? Further, the Wicked Priest was engaged in an attempt 'to swallow up' (whatever that may mean)[3] a rival on or about the Day of Atonement; but there is no hint in any ancient authority that Simon had at any time in his life been involved in an attempt at murder on such an occasion and close to the precincts of the Temple. As his rival was attempting to usurp a priestly function, the memory of Simon's defence of his office would surely have been preserved in Sadducaean or Pharisaic circles. At the same time, the Wicked Priest is nowhere charged with usurping the offices of high-priest and king, nor is Simon ever charged with debauchery and apostasy[4]. The case, too, is not strengthened by supposing the statement that 'the Jews and the priests were well pleased that Simon should be their leader and high-priest for ever, until a faithful prophet should arise'[5] to be intentionally echoed in the comment that 'others will not grasp [instruction] until one shall arise who will teach righteousness at the end of the days' (Z viii 8); for the resemblance is hardly anything but verbal, Simon is not known ever to have been so engaged, and the idea itself is only part of the general Jewish expectation of a Messiah.[6] No other connection can be established between the two passages. The final test comes with the attempt to identify the Rightful Teacher, the 'house of Absalom' and the 'house of Judah', who were all involved in the affair of the Day of Atonement (H v 9 viii 1). The Teacher, who is the all-important character, and Judah are left out of the picture; and Absalom is half-heartedly equated with a man of the same name[7] of whom nothing is known except that he left two sons

---

[1] *E.g.* Josephus *Antiquities* XII iii 4 § 146 and v 4 § 254, XIV x 23 § 258; Ezra vi. 11–12, vii. 26 and Dan. iii. 6.
[2] Pp. 226–37.   [3] Pp. 269–71.   [4] Schreiden *Énigmes* 267.
[5] 1 Macc. xiv. 41.   [6] Pp. 480–3.   [7] In *Library* 115–16.

named Mattathias and Jonathan who were active *c.* 147–146 B.C.,[1] so that he could hardly have been contemporary with Simon. Finally, no attention is paid to the identification of the Kittians with the Romans, although Dr. Cross admits it in a note![2] The admission damns the theory; for not only were the Romans not 'trampling the land' (H iii 10) at any time during Simon's pontificate, but also he was on excellent terms with them.[3] If however the Covenanters were 'able to find detailed descriptions of the events of current history'[4] in the ancient Scriptures, they would have been bound to refer them all to the same historical period; passing arbitrarily from the Maccabaean to the Roman period would make the whole story unintelligible. If then 'the Kittians who were trampling the land' (H iii 9–10) were the Romans, the clash between the Wicked Priest and the Rightful Teacher could have taken place only when a Roman army was in occupation of Palestine; the admission therefore that the Kittians were the Romans would exclude any persons known to have lived in the Seleucid (*i.e.* pre-Roman) age, such as Simon the Maccabee and his contemporaries, from the picture.[5]

Prof. M. H. Segal derives[6] the Covenanters from the extreme 'pietists (*ḥăsîdîm*)', the so-called 'Hasidaeans', who had joined hands with the Maccabees in resisting the hellenizing policy of the Seleucid kings,[7] though only to obtain freedom to practise their own religion; for they had no nationalistic ambitions. When therefore Alcimus in 162 B.C. came to offer peace on behalf of the Seleucid king, who then was Demetrius I Soter (162–150 B.C.) and with whom he was on friendly terms (for he hoped to be nominated high-priest by him), they accepted his terms,[8] abandoning the Maccabees and supporting him as the 'only true representative of the Zadokite priesthood', as Prof. Segal describes him. Subsequently, when the Hasmonaean kings assumed the office of high-priest, they made common cause against them with the Pharisees and the scribes, who formed the moderate religious party and whom the people greatly revered. The Pharisees, like the Hasidaeans, did not oppose the political and military ambitions of the Maccabees and their Hasmonaean descendants so long as they did not clash with the strict observance of the Law; they thus were able to acquiesce in the Hasmonaean kingship but demanded the restoration of the Zadokite priesthood. A third party who would have objected to the Hasmonaean usurpation of the high-priestly office would be the descendants of the original Zadokites and their adherents, the remnants of the hellenizing party; these were the worldly-minded Sadducees who,

---

[1] I Macc. xi. 70, xiii. 11. [2] In *Library* 92–3.
[3] I Macc. xiv. 17–19, 24 xv. 15–21. [4] *Ibid.* 83.
[5] Cp. Michel *Maître* 228–33.
[6] In *JQR*, NS III 304–7 and *JBL* LXX 131–47.
[7] I Macc. ii. 42–8. [8] *Ibid.* vii. 13–18.

in view of the military successes of the Hasmonaeans as well as of their secularist and hellenizing policy, soon abandoned their opposition and became the chief supporters of the new dynasty.

The combined opposition of Pharisees and Hasidaeans to the Hasmonaean high-priests came to a head in organized resistance *c.* 140 B.C., shortly before or just about the time when Hyrcanus I assumed both high-priestly and civil functions, being the first person to combine them (135–104 B.C.); this would be the period when the party of the Covenanters, called 'a shoot from Israel and from Aaron' (Z i 5) as consisting of priests and laymen (Z vi 1–2), took shape. Thereupon Hyrcanus joined the Sadducees and began a brutal persecution of his opponents.[1] The Covenanters then became 'like blind men groping for a way for twenty years' (Z i 6), *i.e.* for half a generation, but while Hyrcanus was still in office, until a Teacher of Righteousness, a Zadokite and 'the priest whom God gave . . . to interpret all the words of His servants the prophets' (H ii 8–9; cp. APs.a ii 15), arose to help them *c.* 120 B.C.; with this end in view he organized his own party within that of the Hasidaeans, comprising priests and Levites and also laymen as well as a group called the 'house of Absalom' (H v 9), who could be identified with the prominent person of that name mentioned once or twice in connection with the high-priest Simon (142–135 B.C.).[2] Not all the Hasidaeans presumably joined the new party; many would probably resume their quietist mode of life and perhaps now formed the Essene order.[3] At the same time a great leader of the Pharisees, Simeon ben Sheṭaḥ, came to the fore as a vehement opponent of the Sadducees in the interpretation of the Law;[4] he was a brother of Salome Alexandra (76–67 B.C.)[5] and was famous for his wit,[6] and he was probably the 'Man of Falsehood' and the 'Man of Scorn'[7] so often mentioned as an enemy of the Teacher in the Scrolls.[8]

The next high-priest, Aristobulus I, who succeeded his father, held office for only one year, during which he assumed the title of king (104–103 B.C.),[9] but his brother who succeeded him, Alexander Jannaeus (103–76 B.C.), continued the persecution, in the course of which the Teacher of Righteousness was murdered, so that Jannaeus could be denounced by the Covenanters as the Wicked Priest;[10] and the

[1] Josephus *Antiquities* XIII x 5 § 288–6 § 298 and *War* I viii 8 § 67.
[2] 1 Macc. xi. 70 and xiii. 11; Josephus *Antiquities* XIII v 7 § 161 and vi 4 § 202 (if they are the same person).
[3] Cp.p. 113.   [4] P. Talmud *Sanhedrin* vi 4.
[5] P. Talmud *Berakoth* vii 2 and B. Talmud *Berakoth* 48a.
[6] Cp. Midrash R. *Genesis* xci § 3 and *Ecclesiastes* vii 12 § 1.
[7] Cp. Schubert in *TLz.* LXXVII 329–36 (where Alexander Jannaeus or John Hyrcanus is proposed for the Wicked Priest and Simeon Sheṭaḥ is put forward as both Man of Falsehood and Man of Scorn).
[8] S.pp. 294–8.   [9] Josephus *Antiquities* XIII xi 1 § 301 and *War* I iii 1 § 70.
[10] Cp. Brownlee in *BASOR* CXXVI 13–15, Delcor *Habacuc* 56–70 and Van der Ploeg *Excavations* 60–62, 169.

Teacher after his death, which his followers regarded as martyrdom, became a Messianic figure. During this civil war, which lasted six years, the Covenanters would have taken refuge, as the need arose, in the caves round Qumrân, where they would also have hidden their treasured books. Members of the same party might be the appeasers by whom Demetrius III Eucaerus was invited *c.* 88 B.C. to come to Jerusalem and rid them of the hated high-priest;[1] and members also probably of this party were amongst those who remained loyal to the king when Jannaeus succeeded in winning back the allegiance of some 6000 Pharisees.[2] When Jannaeus achieved final victory over his internal opponents would be the moment when such as survived of the Covenanters emigrated to Damascus; and indeed according to Rabbinic sources many of the defeated opponents of the priest-king took refuge there. This emigration was led by one surnamed the Star (a title taken from one of Balaam's oracles),[3] who interpreted the Law until the expected Messianic Teacher should appear (Z ix 8–10). The survivors ascribed their own escape to their loyalty to the Law and the disaster which had overtaken their fellows and allies to their transgression of the Teacher's covenant. The new leader therefore drew up a 'new covenant' enjoining a complete separation of the party from all other Jews, and those who accepted it settled down permanently in Syrian towns and villages (Z viii 6 ix 8, 37). Even so, they were not free from trouble, being torn by dissensions caused by some of the Pharisees who had fled with them and who now carried on an agitation to seduce them from the 'new covenant'. The *Zadokite Documents* apply a number of opprobrious epithets to these people and accuse them of abominable acts of wickedness, *e.g.* profaning the sanctuary by fornication and unjustly enriching themselves and making irregular marriages (Z vii 8 ix 16–17); these charges would be directed against the well-known leniency of the Pharisees in interpreting the Law.[4] When Jannaeus died and the Pharisees regained power, Alexandra was able to bring back the fugitives from his vengeance,[5] and the dissident members of the party might then have induced some of the Syrian exiles to return with them to Jerusalem; these would be those described as deserters 'who have no share in the house of the Law' (Z ix 37) and were threatened with fresh vengeance at the hands of 'the head of the Greek kings who is coming to execute vengeance upon them' (Z ix 20). This 'Greek king' would be Pompey who, having conquered all the Hellenistic kings of the neighbouring countries, was already looming on the horizon of Jerusalem, which he captured in 63 B.C.[6]

[1] S.pp. 292–3.
[2] Josephus *Antiquities* XIII xiv 2 § 379 and *War* I iv 5 § 95.
[3] Num. xxiv. 17.   [4] Pp. 138, 150.
[5] Josephus *Antiquities* XIII x 5 § § 288–6, 298 and *War* I viii 8 § 67.
[6] Cp. Bertholet in *BZAtW* XXXIV [1920] 35.

According to Prof. Segal, Jannaeus, who in wickedness outdid all the other priests who disgraced the high-priestly and royal offices[1] during these centuries, can be detected behind several of the passages in which the author of the *Commentary on Habakkuk* describes the Wicked Priest. For example, the Wicked Priest is described as one 'who was truly named when he took office but, when he held rule in Israel, his heart was lifted up, and he forsook God and became a traitor to the statutes for the sake of wealth. He plundered and gathered the wealth of ruthless men who had rebelled against Him (*sc.* God)' (H viii 8–11); so Jannaeus, who was made king because he was older than his brothers in age and superior to them in moderation, was afterwards puffed up with pride at his conquest of Gaza and Raphia and Anthedon in 96 B.C.,[2] while his ill-gotten wealth would be the spoils taken from neighbouring nations. The reference in 'the city is Jerusalem, wherein the Wicked Priest wrought abominable deeds and profaned the sanctuary of God' (H xii 7–9) will be to his introduction of mercenary troops into the Temple to quell a riot at the Feast of Tabernacles and to his general unfitness to perform priestly functions, which excited the populace against him.[3] The Wicked Priest was struck down 'by judgements of wickedness and horrors of disease and vengeance in the body of his flesh' (H ix 1–2), as Jannaeus on being defeated by the Arabs was thrust by a party mounted on camels into a gorge and barely escaped with his life, when presumably he sustained severe bodily injuries;[4] and, as Jannaeus on coming back to Jerusalem after this defeat was received with insults by the people and an outbreak of civil war, which caused him intense mortification,[5] so the Wicked Priest was given over to his enemies 'to afflict him with a fatal blow in bitterness of soul' (H ix 10–11). Lastly, the Wicked Priest was one 'whose shame exceeded his honour . . . and who walked in drunkenness to quench (his) thirst, and the cup of God's wrath will swallow him up to [heap disgrace] and pain [upon] him' (H xi 13–15), if this passage refers to the Wicked Priest; so Jannaeus in consequence of a drinking bout fell into a distemper from which he died within three years.[6]

In conclusion, Prof. Segal assigns the *Commentary* to a date in or shortly before 90 B.C. and the *Zadokite Documents* to one in or shortly before 63 B.C.; and he has recently assigned[7] *War* to the same period on grounds that permit (although they do not necessitate) so early a date.

[1] Cp. Strabo *Geography* XVI ii 40 (where Aristobulus is overlooked and Jannaeus is said to have been the first high-priest to call himself king).
[2] Josephus *Antiquities* XIII xiii 3 §§ 356–4 and *War* I iv 2 § 87.
[3] *Ibid.* 4 §§ 372–3 and *War* I iv 3 §§ 88–9.
[4] *Ibid.* 5 § 375 and *War* I iv 4 § 90.
[5] *Ibid.* 5 § 376 and *War* I iv 4 §§ 90–2.
[6] Josephus *Antiquities* XII xii 1 § 320–xv 5 § 404 and *War* I iv 1 § 85–4 § 106.
[7] In *Scr. Hieros.* IV 138–43.

This ingenious reconstruction of the history of the period, however attractive it may be at first sight, is entirely unsatisfactory; much of the picture is imaginary and many essential points are omitted.[1] Notably the 390 years from the Captivity cannot be fitted into the chronology of the period; and, if the Hasidaeans observed a lunar year, as the author of *Daniel* did,[2] they would be unlikely to have become the Covenanters, who preferred a solar year.[3] The high-priest Alcimus, of whom so much is made as the *fons et origo* of the Zadokite movement, though known to have been 'of the seed of Aaron', is nowhere said and can almost certainly be assumed not to have been of the line of Zadok.[4] No suitable character is suggested for the part of the Rightful Teacher; for this gap is not filled by belatedly conjuring up that Eleazar or Judah by whom Hyrcanus I was rebuked for holding the offices of both priest and king simultaneously, since this person can by no means sustain the role of the Teacher and indeed is of so little note that even his name is uncertain; and the whole story may be nothing but a legend.[5] No reference is made to the attack on the Day of Atonement by the Wicked Priest for the obvious reason that Jannaeus is not known to have attacked any one on that day; and, while the 'house of Absalom' which was silenced or destroyed is tentatively identified, nothing is said of the 'house of Judah' which escaped on the same occasion. Jannaeus, too, is never called 'priest' but only 'king' in Jewish literature,[6] as Dr. Roth has observed,[7] presumably because of his unpriestly character, while the Scrolls nowhere describe the Wicked Priest as 'king'; his name does not explain how he was once 'truly named'; and he did not suffer a 'fatal blow' at the hands of the Arabs, from whom he made good his escape, or of any other enemies. Also, however cruel and debauched he may have been, he is never charged with any crimes involving the violation of the sanctuary or breaches of the Law.[8] At the same time, the evidence for the flight of the Hasidaeans into Syrian territory, however probable it may be, is worthless; for it is given on the sole authority of a medieval scholiast on a disputed passage of the *Scroll of Fasts*,[9] which is discussed hereafter.[10] Also the stories about Simeon ben Sheṭaḥ, who is cast for the part of the Man of Scorn, are all late and historically worthless;[11] and the differences of doctrine and practice between the Sadducees and the Zadokites are blurred and in fact to all intents and purposes disregarded.

[1] Cp. Rowley in *BJRL* XL 133–7.
[2] Driver in *Essays presented to Professor S. H. Hooke* 84.
[3] Pp. 321–6. [4] Pp. 227–8. [5] Cp. Schürer *Geschichte*[3] I 271–2.
[6] *E.g.* B. Talmud *Kiddushin* 66a, Midrash R. *Genesis* xci § 3, *Numbers* xxii § 1, *Ecclesiastes* vii 12 § 1.
[7] In *Historical Background* 3[3]. [8] Schreiden *Énigmes* 257–62.
[9] Lichtenstein in *HUCA* VIII–IX 347–8. [10] Pp. 227–8.
[11] Cp. Schürer *op. cit.* I 279–80.

Another weakness of Prof. Segal's theory is the supposition that the Covenanters stood in a special relation of friendship to the Seleucid rulers; for the Scrolls give no hint of such a friendship in any passage, and indeed Damascus and Jerusalem were now controlled by mutually hostile governments. The Kittians are rightly identified with the Romans, who may perhaps be said to have been at the height of their power during the Hasmonaean period, as Prof. Segal claims; but that the Romans here meant are those of the Republican age cannot be sustained against the weight of evidence.[1] Further, although 'the rulers of the Kittians who pass on before one another by the counsel of a guilty house' may be the consuls and 'the rulers of [wickedness] come one after another to ravage the [country or land]' may refer to the pro-consuls and legates who pillaged the countries which they were sent out to govern, and although the Jews were much surprised at the Roman system of annual officers,[2] the 'guilty house' can hardly be the senate, which was never called a 'house' and did not in fact appoint the consuls. No attempt, too, is made to distinguish the 'Kittians of Asshur' from the 'Kittians in Egypt'. The supposition, too, that the activities of the Kittians as described in the *Commentary* were related solely to the general expansion of the Roman *imperium* and had no direct relation to the Jewish situation contradicts the *War*, in which they are clearly the principal enemy of the party;[3] and the Romans were too busily engaged elsewhere during this whole period to have occupied themselves in it with Palestine.[4]

A last desperate attempt to fit the story into this period is the suggestion, which Fr. Carmignac puts forward,[5] that the Rightful Teacher was not the Judah by whom Hyrcanus was rebuked but Judah the Essene. Only two things are known of this person, that he taught the art of foretelling future events to a number of disciples and that he predicted the death of Antigonus brother of Aristobulus I (104–103 B.C.);[6] but he in no wise fits the picture of the Teacher either as an interpreter of the Law or as the leader of a great religious and political party.

The final argument, which Prof. Goossens regards[7] as *un signe sûr de la solidité de la thèse* that the Wicked Priest must be sought among the Maccabaean priest-kings, is this: as the author of the *Commentary on Habakkuk* describes him as 'the Wicked Priest who was truly named when he took office; but, when he held rule in Israel, his heart was lifted up and he forsook God' (H viii 8–10), he must be one of those to whom the author of an apocryphal work refers when he says 'then

---

[1] Pp. 180–97.
[2] Cp. 1 Macc. viii. 15–16.
[3] Cp. Michel *Maître* 209–25.
[4] Schreiden *Énigmes* 226–71, 257–62.
[5] In *RSR* XXXI 159.
[6] Josephus *Antiquities* XIII xi 2 §§ 311–13 and *War* I iii 5 §§ 78–80.
[7] In *Flambeau* XXXIV 38–9.

there will be raised up unto them kings bearing rule, and they will call themselves high-priests of God; they will assuredly work wickedness in the holy of holies';[1] for these impious priest-kings were those Maccabaeans who held the double office.[2] The argument fails because the Wicked Priest is nowhere called a king, and history tells of many wicked priests, before and after, whether kings or not, with whom he can be identified; further, the Scrolls do not confirm the statement in the next verse that 'an impious king will succeed them'[3] and may, even must, be referring to some quite different period of history.

This solution of the problem, too, must be rejected; its contents as well as its omissions alike condemn it.

All these attempts to assign the Scrolls to the 2nd–1st centuries A.D., then, fail in the first instance for the particular reasons brought against each one of them, even though these are not all equally strong and the archaeological evidence is not unambiguous.[4] They are, however, reinforced by an objection which is common to each solution, that it is only partial. Their authors, relying solely on the *Commentary on Habakkuk*, are content to identify the Wicked Priest (which is the easiest part of the task; for in this period wicked priests are as common as righteous are rare), while the Rightful Teacher and the other characters are only half-heartedly identified or are even left out of account, and the Day of Atonement, which is a vital piece of evidence, is totally disregarded. The identity of the Kittians is assumed in accordance with the theory being argued and the evidence for it is not brought into the argument. At the same time no use has been made of the other Scrolls, even after the publication of all the relevant texts.

Secondly, the general objection may be brought against a date in this period that the Scrolls contain no reference to the characteristic social and political problems with which the Jews were then confronted; such negative evidence is in the circumstances of the times highly significant. At the beginning of the 2nd century B.C., as Josephus and *I Maccabees* make clear, the burning question which exercised the whole Jewish nation was hellenization and the outrages committed by their Seleucid overlords in their attempts to carry out this policy by force; and at its end, as *Jubilees* shows, it was still a live issue. The measures taken with this end in view are well known: the punishment of Jews found to possess copies of the Law with death and the burning of all copies taken, forbidding them to have their children circumcized, compelling them to desist from offering the regular sacrifices and to sacrifice swine in their stead, to eat unclean food and to defile Sabbath and feast-day, and finally setting up the 'abomination of desolation' in

[1] *Assumption of Moses* vi 1.   [2] Charles *Assumption of Moses* 20–21.
[3] Charles *ibid.* vi. 2.
[4] Cp. De Vaux *Archéologie* 89–90.

L

the Temple.[1] The apocalyptist, writing near the end of the 2nd century
B.C., was at pains to repair the consequences of this policy, which
continued into his own time; for example, he re-enacted the laws
regarding the observance of the Sabbath and punished its profanation
with death, insisted on circumcision and prescribed the severest penalties for its neglect.[2] Josephus refers[3] in the same connection to the habit,
adopted by Jewish youths under Seleucid pressure or persuasion, of
appearing naked at games in the amphitheatre, and the apocalyptist
expressly forbids it;[4] young Jews with this end in view had the external
signs of circumcision removed by a physician in order to conceal their
Jewish nationality,[5] and this last practice was still mentioned with
disapprobation in the 1st century A.D.[6] The same apocalyptist also
found need to forbid marital intercourse on the Sabbath and marriage
with a Gentile;[7] and the memory of this last prohibition, which
Rabbinic tradition assigned to the Greek period[8] when it might well
have been enacted in a moment of anti-Hellenic fanaticism (although
historians of the period had nothing to say of it), though apparently
abrogated, lingered on into the 2nd century A.D.[9] Yet the Scrolls say
nothing of these things.

According to the Scrolls, the Covenanters were engaged in a bitter
struggle on the one side with a cruel and ruthless enemy and on the
other side with their fellow Jews, whom they regarded as unduly lax
in their observance of the Law, if not as actual renegades. Yet the
Scrolls contain not a single allusion to the circumstances of the Seleucid
age. They describe the external enemy as ravaging the country and
worshipping their standards, a Roman practice which can hardly have
been known in Palestine before Pompey's capture of Jerusalem in
63 B.C. Only one instance of marriage with a niece and having another
wife at the same time has been found to fit into one of the proposed
solutions of the problem of the Scrolls,[10] although both are denounced
in them[11]; and they do not become common enough otherwise to call
for public condemnation before the age of the Herodian family and the
patriarchate of R. Gamaliel II.[12] That the Scrolls, reflecting none
of the characteristic problems confronting the Jews in the 2nd–1st
centuries B.C., were composed in that century, while referring to
practices and denouncing vices which only became prevalent long
afterwards, then, would be incomprehensible, even inconceivable.

These negative arguments are further strengthened by the positive

[1] 1 Macc. i. 41–64, ii. 15–22; Josephus *Antiquities* XII v 4 §§ 251–6.
[2] Jubilees i 6–13, ii 17–32, xvii 11–14, 26, 28.
[3] In *Antiquities* XII v 3 § 254.   [4] *Ibid.* iii 30–31.
[5] 1 Macc. i. 15; Josephus *Antiquities* XII v 4 § 241.
[6] *Assumption of Moses* viii 3.   [7] *Ibid.* i 8, xxx 3.   [8] B. Talmud *Sanhedrin* 46a.
[9] Mishnah *Nedarim* viii 6 (where eating garlic is an euphemism for sexual intercourse); cp. iv 10.
[10] P. 87.   [11] P. 91; cp. p. 11.   [12] Pp. 86–7.

arguments which can be drawn from the equipment and military dispositions which the author of the *War* describes; for these can be referred only to the Roman Imperial period, as argued hereafter.[1]

The champion of the late Roman Republican period is Prof. Dupont-Sommer.[2]

He begins by arguing that the party of the Covenanters arose in the Maccabaean period and that they were reformed about a century afterwards by the Rightful Teacher, after whose murder they migrated under the leadership of one called the 'Star', of whom the *Zadokite Documents* speak, to Damascus[3]; and he identifies the 'Kittians of Asshur' and the 'Kittians in Egypt', as they are distinguished in the *War* (which he assigns to this period), with respectively the Seleucids and the Ptolemies. Contrariwise, he identifies the Kittians in the *Commentary on Habakkuk*, which he regards as subsequently composed, with the Romans; for the term always stands *tout simple* without qualification in that work. This identification is based on three main points: first, that the Commentator's mention of 'the rulers of the Kittians who by the counsel of a guilty house pass on each before the other; their rulers come one after another to destroy the land' (H iv 10–13) are the series of rapacious proconsuls sent out from Rome to govern the provinces; second, that the description of them as a people 'who sacrifice to their standards and whose weapons are the object of their veneration' (H vi 4–5) refers to the Roman legions, since something of the sort was their established practice; and, third, that 'Kittians' stands for the Romans in the book of *Daniel,* where the usage is recognized by the two earliest ancient versions (Septuagint and Vulgate) and is generally admitted by modern scholars.[4]

Prof. Dupont-Sommer did not originally seek to identify the Teacher with any particular person, but he subsequently accepted[5] a suggestion put forward by Prof. Goossens[6] that he was the Onias called the 'maker of (magic) circles' or 'rain-maker', who was martyred in 65 B.C.; and he thinks that the Wicked Priest was now Hyrcanus II, who had two periods of office (78–69 B.C. and 63–40 B.C.), and now his brother Aristobulus II (69–63 B.C.)[7] although his final choice seems to be Hyrcanus.[8] Josephus tells[9] a story how Onias, who had obtained a great reputation for sanctity by having brought down rain during a prolonged drought by his prayers, which had been immediately answered, met his end. In the struggle with his brother for the office

---

[1] Pp. 180–97.   [2] In *Aperçus Préliminaires* 35–6 and *Nouveaux Aperçus* 33–61.
[3] Pp. 303–7.   [4] Pp. 197–8.
[5] In *VT* V 167–8; cp. Elliger *Habakuk-Kommentar* 273–4.
[6] In *Nouvelle Clio* VII 336–53.   [7] Cp. Brownlee in *BASOR* CXXVI 12–16.
[8] In *JS.* 1963, 208–12.
[9] In *Antiquities* XIV ii 1 §§ 22–24; cp. Mishnah *Taanith* iii 8 and B. Talmud *Taanith* 20b.

of king and high-priest Hyrcanus and his followers wished to avail themselves of this man's prayers and insisted that he should invoke God's curse on Aristobulus and his followers; but, instead of complying with their wishes, Onias stood forth in the camp and prayed to God to listen to the prayers of neither side engaged in a fratricidal struggle, whereupon the people immediately stoned him to death. Both Aristobulus and Hyrcanus met fates which tallied well enough with that of the Wicked Priest. The former was arrested and taken to Rome, where he was exhibited at Pompey's triumph in 61 B.C.; he escaped in 56 B.C. and reappeared in Palestine, where he created some excitement, but was soon retaken and sent back to Rome, dying there in prison from poison at the hands of Pompey's supporters in 49 B.C. Here the reader may find the 'fatal blow . . . in bitterness of death' and the 'cup of God's wrath' (H ix 11, xi 14–15) administered to the Wicked Priest for the injury which he had done to the Teacher. The latter, recognized by the Romans as high-priest but not as king, fell into the hands of the Parthians in 40 B.C. but was released by them and eventually fell a victim to the jealousy and ambition of Herod the Great, who had him put to death in 30 B.C., when an old man over eighty years of age.

The *Commentary on Habakkuk* says that 'at the season of the feast of the rest of the Day of Atonement he appeared unto them to swallow them up and to make them stumble on a fast-day, the Sabbath of their rest' (H xi 6–7). This is explained as meaning that Onias, the *ex hypothesi* Rightful Teacher who had been murdered in 65 B.C., rose again and reappeared to his followers at the capture of Jerusalem by Pompey on the Day of Atonement in 63 B.C., when he executed a terrible vengeance on his enemies; for Josephus[1] records that 12,000 persons perished on that occasion and that Absalom, uncle and father-in-law of the high-priest Aristobulus, was taken captive by the Romans. This would be the Absalom of whom the *Commentary* speaks when it says that 'the house of Absalom and his counsellors kept silence (*sic*)[2] when the Rightful Teacher was chastised, and they did not help him against the Man of Falsehood' (H v 9–11).

The theory is encumbered by the suggestion that the martyrdom of the Teacher inspired certain passages in the Old Testament, such as the Songs of the Servant in the *Deutero-Isaiah* and the prophecy in which the Lord pours a 'spirit of grace and supplication' on the inhabitants of Jerusalem (who seem to be represented as guilty of some murder) near the end of the Book of *Zechariah*,[3] as well as the Psalm beginning 'My God, my God, why hast Thou forsaken me?', the greatest of the so-called 'Psalms of the Passion'.[4] As Prof. Rowley says,[5]

[1] In *Antiquities* XIV lv 4 §§ 70–1.   [2] P. 271–2.
[3] Zech. xii. 10.   [4] Ps. xxii 2.   [5] In *Zadokite Fragments* 47.

that 'the writings of a persecuted sect about a martyred hero should have been incorporated in the Scriptures of those who were responsible for his martyrdom' is quite incredible; and that the insertions can have been made at so late a date as Prof. Dupont-Sommer thinks, namely in the latter part of the 1st century B.C., is almost equally difficult to believe, inasmuch as they are already present in the Septuagint. The acceptance or rejection of this suggestion, however, has no bearing on that of the theory itself.

Prof. Dupont-Sommer thus supposes that the party of the Covenanters came into being in the first quarter of the 1st century B.C. and that the Rightful Teacher, *i.e.* Onias, who was not its founder but its reformer, perished in 65 B.C. He also argues that the Commentator, in his references to the Wicked Priest, who is here at the same time equated with the 'Man of Falsehood' and the 'Splutterer of Falsehood',[1] was indicating two distinct Hasmonaean princes, namely the above-mentioned Aristobulus II and his brother, both predecessor and successor, Hyrcanus II; the choice between them was dictated to him in each section by the Biblical text on which he was commenting. These two would then be 'the last priests of Jerusalem who amassed wealth and gain from the spoil of the peoples; but at the end of the days their wealth with their spoil will be given over to the army of the Kittians, since they are the remnant of the peoples' (H ix 4–7). He further argues that the Commentator was aware of the death of Aristobulus but knew nothing of the captivity and death of Hyrcanus; for he was writing after the death of the former in 63 B.C. but while the latter was still in office, possibly shortly before 40 B.C. Although, however, the writings of the Covenanters were *ex hypothesi* composed in the middle of the 1st century B.C., the group maintained its vitality till *c.* A.D. 66, as shown by the existence of the monastery at Qumrân at the time of the First Revolt.

Finally, Prof. Dupont-Sommer supports his date by citing the evidence of the Moslem historian alShahrastânî,[2] who says that 'Arius . . . took his theory from the members of this sect (*sc.* the cave-men),[3] who lived 400 years before him and who devoted themselves to the practice of temperance and a simple life'.[4] The heresiarch was propagating his christological doctrine about A.D. 320 and died in A.D. 336; the sect from which he borrowed his doctrine, then, if the number of years was to be taken literally, would have flourished *c.* 80–65 B.C.[5]

On this reconstruction of the history of the period Prof. Dupont-Sommer[6] is able to reach the conclusion that 'the Galilaean Master, as he is presented to us in the writings of the New Testament, appears

---

[1] Pp. 308–10.   [2] P. 10.   [3] Pp. 9–13.
[4] Cp. De Vaux in *RB* LVII 422.   [5] Cp. Kahle in *VT* **I 46.**
[6] In *Aperçus Préliminaires* 121 and *Nouveaux Aperçus* 206–7.

in many respects as an astonishing reincarnation of the Teacher of Righteousness'; at the same time he is careful to disclaim having said that Jesus 'is nothing but an astonishing reincarnation of the Teacher of Righteousness'.

The objections to Prof. Dupont-Sommer's theory are as weighty as those which may be brought against any other pre-Christian date for the Scrolls; in fact, they are insuperable.[1]

The identification of the Kittians, however qualified, with the Seleucids and with the Ptolemies as well as with the Romans introduces an intolerable complication. The equation of these people with the Seleucids and the Ptolemies is discussed elsewhere, and the clear objections to it do not call for repetition.[2] That they stand for the Romans may be accepted, but the notion that the Republican Romans are meant must be rejected for reasons which will be given hereafter.[3] Here it will suffice to add that the Scrolls contain nothing that can be taken as the slightest hint of an allusion to the atrocities attributed to Pompey's troops at the capture of Jerusalem or to Jewish subjugation to Rome.[4]

The suggestion that the Teacher of Righteousness was Onias 'the rain-maker' is open to the same objection as the identification of him with the high-priest Onias III: he was not a character to sustain the part thus assigned to him. Indeed, if he were the Rightful Teacher, the failure of any reference in Jewish history to the most important event in his life would be totally unintelligible; and no hint that he was either a priest or the expected Messiah is found anywhere in Jewish literature.[5] It is also open to the objections that, although the Covenanters and therefore the Rightful Teacher were *ex hypothesi* Essenes, this Onias was not an Essene, and the Essenes, so far as known, had no such Teacher and that, while Onias was an orthodox Pharisee,[6] the Teacher was heterodox. That the Wicked Priest was Aristobulus or Hyrcanus would not be *a priori* impossible; but that he was both Aristobulus and Hyrcanus introduces difficulties of which the *Commentary* gives no hint.[7] That Hyrcanus is identified also with the Man of Falsehood only increases the confusion; and he seems indeed to have been unsuited to the parts assigned to him, having been a man who preferred a quiet life and one totally unfitted for office.[8] The supposition, moreover, that the brothers were the 'last priests of Jerusalem'

[1] Cp. Rowley in *BJRL* XL 126–33.   [2] Pp. 151, 199–200, 208.
[3] Pp. 169–216.   [4] Cp. Segal in *JBL* LXX 135–7.
[5] Cp. Michel *Maître* 276–80.
[6] B. Talmud *Ta'anith* 23a.
[7] Cp. Dupont-Sommer in *JS* 1963, 208–14 and 22 (where Hyrcanus is retained and Aristobulus dropped).
[8] Josephus *Antiquities* XII i 3 § 12, XIII xvi 1 § 407–2 § 408, XIV i 2 § 6, ix 2 § 158 and 5 § 179, XV vi 4 § 182 and *War* I v 1 § 109.

is demonstrably false.[1] If the Commentator composed his work shortly before 40 B.C., he must have known of many priests after them; and the 'last priests',[2] if they might be those massacred at the altar by Pompey's troops, could equally well be those massacred at the capture of Jerusalem A.D. 70, when the priesthood came finally to an end. Put briefly, the 'last priests' must have been the last priests.[3]

Another grave difficulty lies in the interpretation of the passage describing how the Wicked Priest pursued the Rightful Teacher with a view to swallowing him up. Professor Dupont-Sommer is compelled, in the interest of his theory, to translate this crucial passage: 'the Wicked Priest, who persecuted the Teacher of Righteousness so far as to swallow him up in the heat of his anger; and he (sc. the Teacher of Righteousness) appeared to them to swallow them up (sc. the Wicked Priest and his followers) at the moment of the sacred rest of the Day of Atonement and to make them stumble on a fast-day, the sabbath of their rest' (H xi 5–8); and he interprets this as meaning that the Wicked Priest persecuted and destroyed the Rightful Teacher, who however appeared after a resurrection in a kind of theophany and avenged his own (and his followers') fate by swallowing up (i.e. destroying) his enemies. This destruction of his enemies was ex hypothesi carried out by the Romans when Pompey took Jerusalem, as already said. The sudden and unheralded change of subject from the Wicked Priest to the Rightful Teacher, though intolerable to a western reader, is no valid ground of objection to the translation; Hebrew writers commonly indulged in such inconsequence. What is a serious objection is that the reader has to assume an interval of two years, which is in no way indicated in the text, between the two clauses if the first describes the murder in 65 B.C. and the second the reappearance and the vengeance in 63 B.C. The assumption, too, that 'appeared' connotes 'manifested himself in a theophany' is difficult.[4] The verb here used serves often enough in the Old Testament to describe the appearance of God in splendour, but it is nowhere so applied to a man, and the need to read into it the doctrine of a resurrection, of which there is otherwise no hint in the text, throws grave doubt upon this interpretation of it; and it can well enough mean simply 'appeared' (e.g. T v 32).[5] Stories of such mysterious appearances and reappearances are of course found. For example, Heliodorus and Apollonius in the 2nd century B.C. were connected with mysterious apparitions,[6] as also an impious Sadducee or Sadducaean was,[7] in the Temple; and this same Onias was thought to have reappeared seventy years after his death,[8]

[1] Michel ibid. 201–8.   [2] Josephus War I vii 4 § 148.
[3] Pp. 161, 297–8, 301–2; cp. Teicher in JJS V 51.
[4] Cp. Vermès in Cah. Sion. 1951, 64–5.   [5] Cp. Midrash R. Genesis XII § 4.
[6] 2 Macc. iii. 22–36 (Heliodorus) and 4 Macc. iv. 1–14 (Apollonius).
[7] B. Talmud Yoma 19b.   [8] B. Talmud Taanith 23a.

as Titus too was thought to have been raised from the dead.[1] That
Josephus refers to none of these stories, however, suggests that they
were not known or that he disbelieved them as absurd, and the Commentator does not give the impression that he was retailing absurdities
which educated men discredited; for the allusions in the Scrolls,
whenever they can be checked, are historically correct. The literature
of the period, too, nowhere recognizes a Messiah who has already
come.[2] Further, the date of the reappearance of Onias, in so far as it is
seriously meant, cannot be squared with that of Pompey's capture of
Jerusalem; and the story cannot be simply transferred *argumenti causa*
from one year to another. As then, there is no record that Onias was
the founder or reformer of a sect, so there is no valid evidence for his
reappearance or resurrection at the capture of the Holy City. The
argument is simply a conjecture *e silentio* and as such has no value.

The assumption that Pompey took Jerusalem on the Day of Atonement, too, is not beyond all doubt. Josephus puts[3] this event on a fast-
day, with which Strabo agrees,[4] while Dio Cassius assigns[5] it to the
Sabbath. The Day of Atonement is both the 'sabbath of sabbaths' and a
fast-day, falling in the month of Tishri (September-October), and the
sabbath can be a fast-day only when the Day of Atonement coincides
with it;[6] but Pompey is explicitly said not to have attacked the city
on the sabbath out of respect for Jewish scruples about fighting on that
day.[7] Whether the capture of the city took place even in that month
is not certain. Josephus says[8] that it was taken in the third month of the
siege, which is thought to have been Tammuz (July-August), although
the exact day of its commencement is not known; and the ninth day of
this month was a fast-day[9] (Tuesday or Wednesday). The late *Josippon*
puts the capture of the Temple on the seventeenth day of this month
(Wednesday or Thursday); but the evidence for this day is not known.[10]
The city was probably taken at some time between Tammuz and
Tishri, perhaps later rather than earlier; but the reference to the Day
of Atonement is probably an error, due to supposing that the fast-day
in question must have been that day.[11] Consequently, the exact date is
far too uncertain to be made the basis of an elaborate reconstruction.
Further, the passage in the *Commentary on Habakkuk* which mentions
the Day of Atonement gives no hint of anything remotely connected
with the events attendant on Pompey's capture of Jerusalem, *e.g.*
the desecration of the Temple, the slaughter of the priests at the altar

[1] B. Talmud *Gittin* 56b.   [2] Cp. Schonfield *Secrets* 70.
[3] In *Antiquities* XIV iv 3 § 66.   [4] In *Geography* XVI ii 40.
[5] In *Roman History* xxxvii 16.
[6] Cp. Friedlander *Jewish Religion*[4] 355 (s. Judith viii. 6).
[7] Josephus *Antiquities* XIV iv 2 § 4 and *War* I vii 2 § 146.
[8] Josephus *War* I vii 4 § 149 and V ix 4 § 397.
[9] Cp. Zeitlin *ap.* Weiss in *JQR*, NS XLI 153; s. *Megillat Taanith* 21–30.
[10] Breithaupt *Josephus Gurionides* iv 23.   [11] Cp. Schürer *Geschichte*[3] I 298–9.

and the massacre of the inhabitants of the city.[1] In any case, the whole discussion has no point in the context; for, although the Rightful Teacher was attacked on or near the Day of Atonement, Onias the 'circle-maker' was murdered apparently about the time of the Passover; they cannot therefore be identified.[2]

Further, the date given by alShahrastânî is suspiciously like a round figure,[3] which means little or nothing; he could have had no accurate or exact knowledge of the period, and Jewish historians far nearer the events which they described made no less serious mistakes in chronology. Not even Josephus himself was beyond reproach on this score.[4]

Briefly, a theory that may require multiple identifications and a miracle not recorded in history, and that is involved in an historical contradiction, makes too many assumptions and reads too much into the texts to command acceptance. It labours also under the difficulty, which besets all theories putting the Scrolls in the 1st century B.C., that the '390 years' after the Captivity (Z i 5) must be abandoned as a myth from the Old Testament;[5] and other reasons will shortly be given for excluding this entire century from consideration.[6]

Finally, those who accept the identification of the Essenes and the Covenanters and therewith the assignment of the story in the Scrolls to a pre-Christian date involve themselves in a fatal inconsistency. As Dr. Roth observes,[7] if the Covenanters are the Essenes, they cannot be dated before the 1st century A.D.; for Philo expressly asserts[8] that 'none of these (sc. the rulers of Palestine down to his own time), neither those who were extremely ferocious nor those who were deepdyed treacherous dissemblers, were able to lay any charge against the Essenes or "holy ones"[9] here described. Unable to resist the high excellence of these people, they all treated them as self-governing and freemen by nature'. Josephus similarly records[10] that Herod the Great held the Essenes in great honour. In other words, the Essenes suffered no persecution during the 2nd and 1st centuries B.C. This fact alone is incompatible with any persecution of them by Hasmonaean priest-kings or Seleucid rulers or even by the Roman authorities during the Republican age; it is compatible only with a persecution after the time of Philo, who was an old man in A.D. 40,[11] such as that of the Essenes by the Romans during the revolt of A.D. 66–73, to which Josephus alludes.[12]

[1] Josephus *Antiquities* XIV iv 4 §§ 70–2 and *War* I vii 5 §§ 150–4.
[2] *Ibid.* XIV ii 1 §§ 21–5.
[3] Cp. Dupont-Sommer *Nouveaux Aperçus* 209.
[4] P. 312; cp. Schürer *op. cit.* III 189–90.
[5] Cp. Bertholet in *B.z.At.W.* XXXIV 36–7.   [6] Pp. 312–6.
[7] In *JTS*, NS X 93.   [8] In *Every Good Man* xiii 89–91.
[9] P. 100.   [10] In *Antiquities* XV v 5 § 378.
[11] Schürer *Geschichte*³ III 489–90.   [12] In *War* II viii 10 §§ 152–3.

Philo's testimony cannot be set aside by pleading that 'rulers' or 'dynasts' (δυνάσται), as he calls them, refers in this connection only to secular or to religious rulers and excludes the other, whichever the argument requires; for, while Philo himself applies[1] this very term elsewhere to secular rulers, Josephus uses[2] it not only for such rulers of Asian, Syrian and Arab states but also for both secular and religious rulers of the Jewish state.[3] Consequently Jonathan and Simon, Hyrcanus II and Aristobulus II, are by this very term excluded from the part of the Wicked Priest who is described as having persecuted the Righteous Teacher, if the party led by him is held to be that of the Essenes. Here then is a dilemma: if Hyrcanus or Aristobulus, whom Josephus describes *eo nomine* as 'dynast', assaulted the Teacher who was *ex hypothesi* leader of the Essenes, neither could have been 'dynast' or ruler of the state (although each was in fact both high-priest and king); and the Teacher, if he was assaulted by either of them, could not have been an Essene (although he was in fact a Covenanter). Put in general terms, the dilemma is the following: if the Covenanters were the Essenes, they could not have been embroiled in a feud with the head of the state; or, if they were so embroiled, they could not have been Essenes. Consequently, unless both Philo and Josephus are mistaken in their picture of the Essenes, the feud between the Rightful Teacher and the Wicked Priest cannot be assigned to the Hasmonaean age; it can only be located in one in which such a clash can be conceived.

Finally, if the Zadokite line of the priesthood was maintained not in Jerusalem but in the so-called 'city of righteousness' in Egypt from the time when the pro-Seleucid Aaronite Alcimus came to the fore till the Romans put an end to Seleucid rule, when Boethus brought back the Zadokite interest to or revived it in Jerusalem, as Dr. Bammel suggests,[4] the quest for the 'Sons of Zadok', *i.e.* the Covenanters of Qumrân, in Palestine during this period is foredoomed to failure.

3. CHRISTIAN AND MOSLEM IDENTIFICATIONS

Dr. Teicher, abandoning a pre-Christian date, assigns the Scrolls to the first century A.D. He holds, reviving an old view,[5] put forward when only the *Zadokite Documents* were known and the Scrolls had not yet been found, that the Rightful Teacher was Jesus and that the

[1] In *On the Special Laws* I v 2 § 142.

[2] *E.g.* in *Antiquities* XIV iii 1 § 36 (Aristobulus II) and *War* I xix 1 § 365 (Herod the Great); cp. *War* VI x 1 § 438 (Melchizedek).

[3] Thackeray *Lexicon to Josephus* 195 (Syrians, Jews, Arabs; Cappadocia, Ammon, Adiabene, Parthia; Emesa; Aristobulus, Herod, Archelaus, Zeiphar, Zabeil, Iamblichus; Bazapranes, Pacorus).

[4] Pp. 226–37.

[5] Cp. Margoliouth in *Athenaeum* 4335 [2 xi 1910], 657–9 and *Expositor* VIII ii 499–517 and iii 213–35.

Wicked Priest, whom he identifies with the Man of Falsehood and the Man of Insolence,[1] was the apostle Paul, and that the Covenanters were the Jewish Christian Ebionites.

According to this theory, the Teacher of Righteousness,[2] whose title is regarded as coined by way of contrast to Isaiah's 'prophet that teacheth lies',[3] is Jesus, the 'true prophet' or 'the (only) prophet of truth' of Ebionite doctrine.[4] The identification is supported by recalling that the Teacher was one to 'whom God had taught all the secrets of the words of His servants the prophets' (H vii 4–5) that 'he might lead them (*sc.* God's people) in the way of His heart, making known to the last generations what He would do to a last generation, a congregation of traitors' (Z i 7–8), so that his coming, like the advent of Jesus, opened the way to salvation from sin and deliverance from God's wrath; for Jesus too claimed to have come to expound and to fulfil what the prophets had taught and to bring salvation to all men. Again, the Teacher had Messianic claims just as Jesus claimed to be the Messiah or Christ; and, as 'God will hand over the judgement of the heathen to His elect one (*sc.* the Teacher)' (H v 4), so 'the Lord Jesus' shall be revealed 'taking vengeance on them that know not God and on them that obey not the gospel of our Lord Jesus Christ'.[5] This last point is regarded as especially significant; for that not God but His elect will be the judge of mankind on the last day is not a Jewish but a Christian doctrine.[6] Further, the Messiah expected by the Covenanters is described as arising 'from Aaron and from Israel' (Z ix 29; cp. ix 10), namely as combining both the priestly and the lay or Davidic lines in his own person; this was explained by Charles[7] as meaning that this Messiah would spring from a non-priestly source on his father's side but from a priestly source on his mother's side. So the early church is said to have thought that Jesus had sacerdotal as well as royal blood through derivation from the tribe of Levi on His mother's side and from that of Judah on His father's side.[8]

The Wicked Priest[9] is identified as Paul; for, as the latter persecuted the followers of Christ in the synagogues of Damascus,[10] so the former 'persecuted (*sic*)[11] the Teacher of Righteousness to swallow him up' (H xi 5). The apostle is also the 'Man of Falsehood', who is then identified with the Wicked Priest; and the description of him as such and as 'one who was truly called when he took office; but, when he held rule in Israel, his heart was lifted up, and he forsook God and

---

[1] S. pp. 284–8.
[2] Teicher in *JJS* II 91–9, 122, 134–8, 140–1 III 53–4 V 52–3.
[3] Isa. ix. 14.   [4] Cp. Teicher *op. cit.* III 127–8.
[5] 2 Thess. i. 8.   [6] E.g. Jn. v 22.
[7] In *Apocrypha and Pseudepigrapha* I 795.   [8] Hippolytus *Refutation* ix 26.
[9] Teicher *op. cit* II 98, 122, 129, 141 V 55–9.   [10] Acts ix. 1–2.
[11] Pp. 269–70.

became a traitor to the statutes for the sake of wealth, and he robbed and gathered up the wealth of ruthless men who rebelled against God; he took the wealth of peoples, adding iniquity and guilt to himself' (H viii 8–12) is also applied to him. He it was who, being one of those 'which called on this name',[1] *i.e.* that of Jesus, began as a member of the Jewish Christian church but broke away from it when he organized the Gentile church. He it was, too, as he admits when he says 'I robbed others, taking wages of them to do you service',[2] who robbed the Gentile churches under false pretences by making collections amongst them for the maintenance of the Jewish Christian church. Further, as 'the Wicked Priest wrought abominable deeds in it (*sc.* Jerusalem) and defiled the sanctuary of God' (H xii 8–10), so Paul 'brought Greeks also into the Temple and hath polluted this holy place'.[3] The 'house of Absalom' and their adherents 'who kept silence (*sic*)[4] at the chastisement of the Rightful Teacher and did not help him against the Man of Falsehood' (H v 9–11) are taken for supporters of Paul; for, as Absalom is thought not to have opposed the Wicked Priest's attack on the Teacher, he and his followers can be those who did not oppose but even connived at Paul's high-handed treatment of the Jewish Christian church, which the Teacher here symbolizes, by striving to coerce it into giving up its national institutions and joining the Gentile church. Finally, as the Wicked Priest was given into the hands of his enemies for punishment, so Paul was martyred.

The Covenanters therefore might be those Jewish Christians who ultimately formed the Ebionite sect,[5] which perhaps arose as early as A.D. 35 and fled into Transjordan *c.* A.D. 70; they would then have taken refuge in a district strangely described as being in the 'vicinity' of Qumrân (for Pella, to which they went, lies 50 miles as the crow flies to the N.N.E. of Qumrân across the Jordan). These Ebionites were a small group who clung to the Mosaic law and retained certain Jewish practices such as circumcision and the observance of the Sabbath, denied the miraculous birth and divinity of Jesus (although a minority accepted the miraculous birth and worked out their own Christology), and used a Hebrew or Aramaic gospel but rejected the writings of Paul as an apostate; thus they called Paul the 'renegade from the law' and the 'pseudo-apostle',[6] employing a term of abuse which might be thought to resemble the 'splutterer of falsehood' found in the Scrolls (H x 9 Z ix 22).

The Ebionites took their name from a Hebrew word meaning 'poor men' (*'eḇyônîm*), which had perhaps been adopted by the early Christians on the strength of the Sermon on the Mount but had been generally

---

[1] Acts ix. 21.   [2] 2 Cor. xi. 8.   [3] Acts xxi. 28.
[4] Pp. 271–2.   [5] Teicher *ibid.* II 93–9, 123–4 V 58–9.
[6] Cp. Beveridge in Hastings' *ERE* V 139–45.

dropped by them and had then been applied by the Ebionites to themselves as reflecting their own circumstances. That the Covenanters of Qumrân are occasionally called 'poor men', *e.g.* in three passages describing the injury which the Wicked Priest has inflicted on them and foretelling that he will be treated as he has treated them (H xii 3, 6, 10), that their society is once called 'the congregation of the poor men' (APs. a ii 10), and that the final victory is won 'by the hand of the poor men whom Thou (*sc.* God) hast redeemed' (W xi 9; cp. xi 13, xiii 14), has suggested that the Covenanters as so called are demonstrably identified with the Ebionite Christians. The Hebrew term would then be used in the same way as the corresponding Greek word in the Pauline injunction 'that we should remember the poor; the same which I also was forward to do';[1] for one of Paul's offences in their eyes was *ex hypothesi* that by raising collections from the Gentile churches for the support of the 'Ebionites' he had caused a violation of their rule of evangelical piety, and the 'last priests who gathered wealth and unjust gain from the spoil of the nations' (H ix 4–5) would then be those ministers of the Ebionite church who had compromised with Paul and accepted the contribution of the Gentile churches. Another of Paul's supposed offences was that he had opposed the retention of Jewish practices such as circumcision and taught that the sacrifice of Christ had superseded the need for observing the Day of Atonement, inasmuch as 'at the fixed season of the rest of the Day of Atonement he appeared unto them to swallow them up and to make them stumble on the fast-day of their rest' (H xi 6–8). The opposition of the Hebrew Christians in Jerusalem was perhaps kept within bounds by Paul but broke out after his death into violent attacks on his teaching. Those who afterwards entered the 'new covenant' at Damascus were called in the *Zadokite Documents* the 'penitents of Israel' (Z vi 1) because they had lived in association with Paul's followers in Jerusalem; but now 'when the epoch is complete . . ., there shall be no union with the house of Judah' (Z vi 7). This covenant was then *ex hypothesi* a charter separating the Jewish Christian sect from the main body of Christians, who were to be treated henceforth as Gentiles.

Many traces of Christian doctrine are accordingly read into the Scrolls and cited to support this theory;[2] such are the doctrines of the community, of the spirits of good and evil, of the dual nature of man and original sin, of predestination and election, of the redemption of man from the consequences of sin, of the two manifestations of the Holy Spirit, of the future 'institution of the Holy Spirit' for making atonement for sin and securing divine favour, of the fulfilment of prophecy and the whole eschatological conception. Even the signs in

---

[1] Gal. ii 10.
[2] Teicher *ibid.* III 111–18, 139–50 IV 1–13, 49–58, 93–103, 139–53.

the margins of the Scroll of *Isaiah A* are claimed as marking Messianic passages and foretelling future events[1] and therefore as identical with those which Epiphanius describes[2] as being used to indicate Christological allusions;[3] and the inference is drawn that this scroll was copied by a Jewish Christian scribe.

Dr. Teicher seeks[4] to support his theory of the Christian origin of the Scrolls by invoking the fragmentary *Commentary on Joshua* already set out above.[5] This fragment, after citing the verses in which Moses is described as mediator between God and man[6] by way of prelude, introduces three *testimonia* from the Old Testament: first, God's promise to Moses that He will raise up one like himself to be a prophet for his people;[7] second, Balaam's prophecy foretelling the star out of Jacob and the comet out of Israel;[8] and, third, the promised blessing on Levi.[9] The points then made are the following: that the compiler's introductory formula, namely 'when he had finished giving praise and thanks with his songs of glory' is found also in Christian writings, notably in an apocryphal Coptic gospel;[10] that 'one of Belial' corresponds to the 'man of perdition', who is the antichrist, in the New Testament;[11] that 'Joshua' is here written 'Jeshua' to show that Jesus is meant; and that, whereas only Balaam's prophecy is applied in Jewish literature to the Messiah, all these passages are applied by Christian writers to Christ. The commentary is then regarded as a typological exposition of the text from *Joshua*,[12] in which Jericho is taken as a type of the pomp of this world under the tyranny of Satan against whom Jesus is waging a victorious war,[13] its fall is a type of Christ's victory over the antichrist,[14] and the 'one of Belial' is the antichrist who will restore the temple of stone in Jerusalem and the kingdom of the Jews (*i.e.* the fallen city) as the stronghold of wickedness.[15] The piece then is dated shortly after A.D. 70 or perhaps rather after A.D. 135, when Jerusalem was levelled with the ground.

The premises, however, will not bear the burden of proof laid on them. The introductory formula proves nothing; for 'when he had finished' occurs in similar contexts in the Old Testament[16] and the following verb depends on the context (from which the editor of the Coptic text supplies it; for the text is damaged at this point). The plea that 'one of Belial' has the same connotation as 'son of perdition',

[1] Teicher *ibid*. III 128–32.   [2] In *de mensuris et ponderibus* § 1.   [3] Pp. 527–31.
[4] In *Lit. Suppl.* LVII 160.   [5] Pp. 138–9.
[6] Deut. v. 25–6.   [7] Deut. xviii. 18–19; cp. Acts iii. 22–3.
[8] Num. xxiv. 15–17.   [9] Deut. xxxiii. 8–11; cp. Matt. x. 37.
[10] James *Apocryphal New Testament* 30.
[11] 2 Thess. ii. 3.   [12] Josh. vi. 26; (S. pp. 293–4).
[13] Cp. Migne *Patr. Gr.* XII 859 (Origen *in Librum Jesu Nave* vii 3).
[14] Cp. *op. cit.* VIII 271 (Augustine *Contra Faustum* xiii 31).
[15] Cp. *op. cit.* X 734 and 747 (Hippolytus *de Christo et Antichristo* vi and xxv).
[16] *E.g.* 1 Sam. xxiv. 17; Jer. xliii. 1.

whether right or wrong, proves nothing; for the priestly Messiah of the tribe of Levi is already depicted as conquering and binding Belial in the 2nd century B.C.[1] The claim that 'Jeshua' is here equivalent to Jesus, too, may be right or wrong but is not proved by the spelling; for it is a late form of 'Joshua', which is already used for Joshua the son of Nun in the Old Testament[2] and which the Septuagint's Ἰησοῦς for the same person confirms.[3] Lastly, that the typological use of *Joshua* is exclusively Christian is apparently true; but nothing precludes the possibility that it may have occurred in Jewish works now lost. The argument that what is not found in extant literature can never have existed is a common fallacy; and the Scrolls, if they can be proved Jewish and not Christian, will disprove it in this case.

The other arguments adduced in support of this theory, as cited above, can be shown to be equally unsatisfactory; and much of the contrary evidence is simply disregarded. Thus the disasters to which the *Commentary on Habakkuk* bears witness are rightly connected with the revolt against Rome in A.D. 66–70, since neither Antiochus IV nor Pompey laid the whole land waste; this work is therefore dated not long after the martyrdom of Paul *c.* A.D. 64, namely in A.D. 65–6,[4] though without regard to the sacrifice offered by the Kittians to their standards.[5] The *Zadokite Documents* are said *argumenti causa* to have been composed not long after Domitian (A.D. 81–96) and certainly not after A.D. 107;[6] the 390 *plus* 20 years from the Captivity, of which they speak, have therefore to be dismissed as merely symbolic figures, since they cannot be squared with these dates. Further, no evidence has been found for the existence of the Ebionites before A.D. 70;[7] and the first reference to them in history occurs *c.* A.D. 175.[8] The concealment of the Scrolls in the caves and the disappearance of the Ebionites could both theoretically be connected with the persecution of Diocletian in A.D. 303, during which orders were given that all religious books should be surrendered to the government;[9] but no evidence is adduced to show that the Covenanters were involved in that disaster.

What is equally important is that the practice and doctrine of the Ebionites, though resembling those of the Covenanters on many points, diverge so far on others that their identity cannot be maintained.[10]

The Ebionites, although they praised poverty and even sold their possessions for the common benefit[11] like the early Christians, developed

---

[1] Testaments *Levi* xviii 2–14; cp. Geffchen *Oracula Sibyllina* iii 63–75 (s. Charles *Apocrypha and Pseudepigrapha* II 381 n.).

[2] Neh. viii. 17.

[3] Exod. xvii. 9, 10, 13, 14 (and *passim*).

[4] Teicher *op. cit* III 55 V 59.

[5] Pp. 211–5.

[6] Teicher *op. cit.* II 138 IV 53–7.

[7] Epiphanius *Panarion* XXX ii 7.

[8] Irenaeus *adversus Haereses* I xxvi 2.

[9] Teicher *op. cit.* II 93–4.

[10] Schoeps in *ZR–Gg* III 332–6 and *ZAtW* LXIII 249–56; cp. Fitzmeyer in Stendahl *Scrolls* 208–31 (s. 292–3).

[11] Epiphanius *op. cit.* XXX xvii 1–3.

no system of common administration of members' possessions like the Covenanters nor any form of communism like the Essenes.[1] As the Covenanters had a leader called the 'Rightful Teacher' or simply the 'Teacher' (Z ix 50), so the Ebionites recognized a 'prophet', the 'true prophet' or 'only prophet of truth' (no new conception)[2], who also was called simply 'Teacher';[3] but, although their functions were similar, the Covenanters' Teacher was an unnamed person or one whose name was kept secret while the Ebionites' Teacher was openly called Christ. Further, this term is derived from the New Testament, where the Greek διδάσκαλος is loosely used for 'Rabbi', which means 'my master';[4] but the Hebrew term for 'teacher' (môreh), by which the Rightful Teacher is designated in the Scrolls, is a totally different one; also, it is an artificial term based on a metaphorical expression in the Old Testament.[5] What resemblance there is lies in the English, not the Greek or Hebrew, term, and it therefore affords no ground on which Jesus can be identified with the Teacher.[6] Again, the Covenanters' Teacher had several opponents, notably the Wicked Priest,[7] the 'Man of Falsehood' and the 'Man of Insolence',[8] all of them men; the adversary of the Ebionite Teacher was Satan, the 'prince of lies'. The *inimicus homo* or 'deceiver' was of course to the Ebionites the apostle Paul; but he was so as the adversary not of Christ but of James bishop of Jerusalem. Both Covenanters and Ebionites observed the ordinary Jewish lustrations; but, while the former allowed lustrations as washing away past contamination by the world but did not admit any type of baptism as beneficial or valid,[9] the latter practised baptism, 'for the remission of sins . . . so as to be born again',[10] *i.e.* Christian baptism. The novitiate of the Covenanters lasted for three but that of the Ebionites for six years. Both groups had common meals; but, while those of the Covenanters were the ordinary daily meals,[11] those of the Ebionites were apparently special occasions, if the use of such expressions as 'to take salt together'[12] and 'to break (bread)'[13] might be taken as indicating the nature of these meals. The Covenanters strictly forbade divorce,[14] but the Ebionites permitted both divorce and remarriage up to several times.[15] The Covenanters accepted all the Scriptures of the Old Testament with the possible exception of *Esther*; the Ebionites rejected parts of the Pentateuch as false additions and most if not all of the Prophets, although they occasionally cited them. The Ebionites

---

[1] Pp. 103–4.
[2] Cp. Testaments *Benjamin* ix 2.
[3] Pseudo-Clement *Homilies* ii 6; cp. Jn. xi. 28.
[4] Jn. i. 38.
[5] Hos. x. 12; s. pp. 257–9.
[6] Cp. Zeitlin in *JQR*, NS XLIII 165–6.
[7] Pp. 267–81.
[8] Pp. 284–7.
[9] Pp. 496–506.
[10] Pseudo-Clement *op. cit.* vii 8.
[11] Pp. 507–16.
[12] *Ibid. op. cit.* xiii 4.
[13] *Ibid. Homilies* xi 36 and *Recognitions* vi 15.
[14] Pp. 69, 87–8; cp. p. 11.
[15] Epiphanius *op. cit.* XXX xviii 2–3.

accepted a Hebrew *Gospel of Matthew*;[1] but no trace of any Gospel, Hebrew or Greek, has been found in the caves round Qumrân. The Covenanters recognized the duty of sacrifice (W ii 5–6 Z xiii 27), whereas the Ebionites rejected all sacrifices, holding that Christ had come to abrogate sacrifice in the Temple and therewith the priesthood as a relic of an age when sacrifices were required;[2] contrariwise, the Covenanters held the priesthood in high honour. Both groups believed in a form of dualism, modified by contact with monotheism; but, while that of the Covenanters was the mere antithesis of good and evil or of light and darkness,[3] the Ebionites believed not only in the doctrine of the 'two ways' but also in a system of 'syzygies' according to which everything existed in pairs (the smaller preceding the larger, the inferior the superior, the female the male, the evil the good, and so on).[4] All in all, the doctrinal differences far outweigh the resemblances, thus forbidding the identification of the Covenanters with the Ebionites on any such grounds.

The identifications of Jesus and Paul do not bear scrutiny. First, Jesus, being of the tribe of Judah,[5] could not have been in any natural sense a priest, as the Rightful Teacher perhaps was;[6] and the attempt to explain this term away by claiming that 'priest' in the Scrolls means not a 'sacrificing priest', although the restoration of animal sacrifices is clearly envisaged (Z xiii 27–xiv 1),[7] but 'a leader, a minister, a religious leader' and even an 'apostle',[8] is fraught with difficulties. Yet this objection is not fatal to the theory; for the possibility remains open that Jesus might have been called a priest in the Messianic sense, as he was in the New Testament,[9] or in an eschatological sense, as Elijah was long afterwards.[10] The argument however that Jesus, being of priestly descent on His mother's side (possibly through the priestly family of John the Baptist), could be the priestly (as well as the lay) Messiah would exclude the possibility of identifying Him with the Rightful Teacher, unless the Teacher too was a priest, which is denied,[11] so that the theory is inconsistent with itself. Also, no real evidence has come to light supporting the tradition that Jesus was of the tribe of Levi on the maternal side, so that He may be dissociated from the Teacher of Righteousness on this score. Also, though called 'Teacher' in the sense of 'Master' as a mode of address or appellation,[12] He is nowhere called 'Righteous Teacher'.[13] He and his followers frequented the Temple, while the Covenanters avoided it.[14] Most important and

---

[1] Irenaeus *adversus haereses* I xxvi 2 and Epiphanius *op. cit.* XXX iii 7.
[2] Epiphanius *op. cit.* XXX xvi 5–7.   [3] Pp. 550–62.
[4] Cp. Ecclus. xxxiii 15 xlii 24.
[5] Heb. vii. 13–14; cp. Matt. i. 1–16 and Lk. iii. 23–6.   [6] P. 129.
[7] Pp. 68, 84–5.   [8] Teicher *ibid.* II 131, V 54–5, 95–7.
[9] Cp. Heb. iv 14–16.   [10] Pp. 565–7.
[11] *Ibid.* II 97–8, 136 III 54–5 V 96.   [12] Mk. x. 17 and Lk. x. 25; cp. Jn. xi. 28.
[13] Zeitlin in *JQR*, NS XLII 166.   [14] Pp. 84–5.
M

fatal to the whole theory is that Jesus was crucified at the season of the Passover,[1] *i.e.* in the spring, whereas the Rightful Teacher was attacked in order 'to swallow him up' on the Day of Atonement (H xi 4–8), *i.e.* in the autumn. Second, Paul claimed to be of the tribe of Benjamin[2] and therefore could not have been a priest in the male line (and nothing is known of his descent on the female side), whereas the Wicked Priest was *eo nomine* such; and these facts cannot be evaded by supposing that 'priest' means 'apostle' in this connection. Further, whatever 'when he took office (*'ôm^e ḏô*)' and 'when he held rule (*māšal*) in Israel' may connote in the context, neither expression is in any conceivable form applicable to the apostle.[3] He can therefore hardly be identified with the Wicked Priest except on a singularly flimsy argument. Lastly, the whole picture of the relationship between Jesus and Paul is a travesty of the facts as recorded in the New Testament.

Other objections to the theory spring to the mind. That the Covenanters call themselves 'poor men' means nothing; the idea is obviously derived from the Psalms, whence it has become a common-place of religious literature. No characteristic Christian doctrine, such as that of the resurrection, is found in the Scrolls, and a total absence of texts or fragments of texts of the New Testament, such as have been found in the ruins of Ḥirbat alMird,[4] from the caves round Qumrân is left unexplained. The Ebionites, regarding Jesus as the Christ or Messiah who had come, died and risen again, looked for no other Messiah, certainly not for two Messiahs, such as the Covenanters expected at the end of the age.[5] The symbols found in the margin of the Scroll of *Isaiah A*, if they are rightly taken as marking passages of Messianic importance, are as likely to be Jewish as Christian in origin[6]; for what is Christological in this sense is also Messianic in the Jewish sense.[7] What may be either Jewish or Christian cannot logically prove the Scrolls either Jewish or Christian, and to use it for this purpose is a fallacy. No reasons are given to show why 'poor men' may not have its ordinary denotation in the *Commentary* as it has in the Psalter and in the rest of the Scrolls (W xi 9, 13 xiii 14 Z viii 4 xviii 19); and a perfectly good reason for the designation can be found.[8] The supposed description of the Gentile Christians from whom Paul raised contributions for the poor church at Jerusalem as 'men of violence' and the literal interpretation of his reference to 'robbing the churches' from which he raised such contributions reduce the whole theory to absurdity. Other difficulties are ignored, for example the problem of distinguishing the 'Kittians of Asshur' from the 'Kittians in Egypt',[9] the meaning of the

[1] Jn. xviii. 28 xix. 14. [2] Rom. xi. 1 and Phil. iii. 5.
[3] Schreiden *Énigmes* 78. [4] P. 23.
[5] Zeitlin in *JQR*, NS XLII 166. [6] Pp. 527–31.
[7] Zeitlin *ibid.* XLVI 130–1. [8] Pp. 54, 92–3.
[9] Pp. 197–216.

apocalyptic war, and the purpose of the Covenanters' peculiar calendar.[1] Herein perhaps wisdom is justified.

Two attempts, which may be cited as curiosities of historical research, have been made to find the historical background of the Scrolls in the Middle Ages. According to the first,[2] the Covenanters were the Jewish party of the 'Isâwites, whose founder 'Abû 'Isâ, killed in a revolt against the Caliph 'Abdu-'lMâlik ibn Marwân (A.D. 684–705), might be taken for the Rightful Teacher; his successor Yudghân declared himself the Messiah, and his successor Muskah, who in due course founded a rival party and tried to impose his views by force on the parent body but was defeated and slain, might have been the Man of Falsehood. According to the second,[3] the 'house of Absalom' might be a pseudonym for the followers of the younger brother of 'Anan, founder of the Qara'ite party; for the leaders of the Babylonian party c. A.D. 700 preferred him as exilarch over the head of his elder brother, whom they suspected of unorthodox views, whereupon 'Anan's adherents nicknamed his successful rival 'Absalom'. The Rightful Teacher might then be one Menahem ben Sârûq, who was 'attacked and thrown out of his house on the Sabbath day (most probably [that] after the Day of Atonement) by the great Jewish leader of (sic) Spain, Hasdai ibn Shafrut [who died c. A.D. 770–90]. It is probable that the persecution of Menahem was due to the accusation made against him that he was a Karaite'. These theories have little or nothing to commend them; they can be squared, even when the history of the periods involved is distorted, only with a few of the facts known about the Covenanters, and they reveal a total disregard of the vast bulk of evidence showing that the Scrolls must be assigned to a date between Alexander the Great or the Maccabees on the one side and the First or Second Jewish Revolt against Rome on the other side.

In conclusion, no solution of the problem of the Scrolls yet propounded brings conviction and all must be rejected. The general objections which have been raised against the typical solutions here examined, notably that none is based on a consideration of the whole evidence, are valid against all and any of the variant forms of them which have been put forward; they therefore do not call for special or particular examination.

[1] Pp. 316–30.
[2] Weis in *JQR*, NS XLI 137–42; cp. Schloesinger in *JE* VI 646.
[3] Zeitlin in *JQR*, NS XLI 264–5 XLII 152–5.

IV

COVENANTERS AND KITTIANS

1. Sons of Light and Sons of Darkness

The problem of the Scrolls cannot be definitely solved until several preliminary questions have been answered. These are the occasion and circumstances of the war in which the 'Sons of Light', as the Covenanters call themselves in this connection, are engaged with the 'Sons of Darkness' or the 'Kittians', as the enemy are variously styled, and in which they are destined to emerge victorious over the nations of the world, and the identity of this enemy.

The Scroll of the *War*, which is made up of two (W i 1–xiv 18, xv 1–xix 13) or even three (W i 1–ix 18, x 1–15, xiv 15, xiv 16–xix 13)[1] parts, contains elaborate descriptions of the organization and equipment, military training and tactical manoeuvres, of the host of the Sons of Light, from which much can be learned; for, although these descriptions are partly based on the practice of the ancient Hebrews as described in the Old Testament and the literature of the Maccabaean period, worked up in pseudo-apocalyptic form, they reflect also much that is evidently factual. If this residue can be traced to its source, it will throw considerable light on the period in which the works were composed.

The most convenient course will be to begin by examining the detailed description of the host of the Sons of Light, which Major-General Yadin, the son of Dr. E. L. Sukenik, to whom the *editio princeps* of the *War* is due, has shown to fit remarkably well what is known not of Hellenistic or Seleucid armies, even though reminiscences of these may be found here and there, but of the Roman Republican army; and he also remarks[2] that what is absent, *e.g.* chariots and elephants,[3] is nearly as significant as what is present in this work. At the same time other points, which will be discussed in due course, cannot be reconciled with this period and can be explained only in the light of the practice of the Imperial army, even though Republican customs may have left their mark far into the Imperial age.

The age of men serving in the infantry of the Sons of Light is lost; it may have been, as Prof. Dupont-Sommer suggests,[4] from twenty

---

[1] Cp. Rabin in Rabin & Yadin *Essays on the Dead Sea Scrolls* 31–47; cp. *Essays . . . in honour of E. L. Sukenik* 31–47.
[2] In *Message* 171–2. [3] Pp. 175, 210–1. [4] In *Écrits Esséniens* 195[1].

years upwards, at which civil duties seem to have begun (Q I *28* A i 8–9). That of the officers is to be between forty and fifty years; that of men in the ancillary services is fixed at twenty-five to thirty years, of the 'provosts' (?) at forty to sixty and that of camp-commandants at fifty to sixty years (W vii 1–3). The age of the cavalry is from thirty to forty-five or from forty to fifty years according to service and duties (W vi 13–14). The range of ages is thus the same as that for judicial officers in the communities away from Qumrân, namely twenty-five to sixty years (Z xi 1–2). The Old Testament gives twenty years as the lower age for military duties,[1] but nowhere fixes the upper limit, which is long afterwards given as forty years;[2] for the thirty to fifty years fixed for the service of the tabernacle,[3] not being military, cannot be cited in this connection, as it sometimes is.[4] Under the Roman Republic the age of service in the legion was from seventeen to forty-six years of age; but after 16 B.C. this period was reduced to sixteen successive years of service for legionaries and twelve years for the guards, but it was raised to twenty years in the legion and fifteen years in the guards in A.D. 5.[5] The basis of the ages given in *War*, except when based on the Old Testament, is unknown; and the comparison of them with the four stages of Essene initiation[6] is purely fanciful.[7]

No man who is physically disabled or ceremonially unclean, no one unwilling to face the hazards of battle (and therefore likely to demoralize his comrades),[8] and no women and children are admitted to the camps; and 'the place of the hand',[9] *i.e.* the latrines,[10] must be set at a distance of 2000 cubits, the distance between the Ark and the people in the wilderness[11] and the normal limit of a journey on the Sabbath,[12] from them, so that they may not be defiled by the presence of anything impure in them (W vii 3–8), in accordance with Biblical precepts.[13]

The army has also various semi-military officers and ancillary services attached to it, such as 'camp-commandants' (W iii 14; cp. Q II *42* 2, where the same title appears in a letter from Murabba'ât) and quartermaster's staff, parties to strip the slain and collect the spoil, because the ordinary soldier was forbidden to take booty,[14] to cleanse the ground, and so on (W vii 2–3); in the same way *fabri*, technicians and specialists, and other camp-followers accompanied the Roman army.

Here a small point may be made. The 'camp-commandant' bears

---

[1] Num. i. 3, xxvi. 2; cp. Rabin & Yadin *op. cit.* 75–9.
[2] Friedmann *Sifré debé Rab* II 197 (commenting on Deut. xx. 8).
[3] Num. iv. 3. [4] Gaster *Scriptures* 295.
[5] Alton in *Companion to Latin Studies* §§ 720, 742.
[6] Pp. 110–2. [7] Milik in *RB*, NS LXIV 589.
[8] Cp. Deut. xx. 8. [9] *Ibid.* xxiii. 13.
[10] Driver in *JTS*, NS VIII 142. [11] Josh. iii 4.
[12] P. 89. [13] Cp. Deut. xxiii. 9–14.
[14] Josephus *Against Apion* ii 29.

a title which is almost a literal translation of one for which Josephus is the earliest certain authority;[1] this is στρατοπεδάρχης, which corresponds to 'chief of the camp' in the Scroll (W iii 14). Most important of all, the Hebrew form reappears for the first time in a document assigned to the last year of the Second Revolt in A.D. 132–5 (II Q *42* 4).

Commanders and units in the *War* have their own 'standards (*'ôṭôṭ*)' called by a technical term taken over from the Old Testament.[2] These standards or banners vary in size with the importance of the unit to which they belong. The largest, that called 'the standard of the whole congregation', is 14 cubits (approximately 21 feet) long, and the smallest, that of a squad of ten men, is 7 cubits (approximately 10 feet 6 inches); these figures reflect the mystical value of 'seven', which appears elsewhere in this Scroll.[3] Each standard bears a suitable inscription; for example, the grand standard of the whole community is inscribed 'God's people' (*'am 'ēl*)[4] followed by the names of Aaron and the twelve tribes of Israel; those of the other units bear the names of the units and their officers, of the tribes composing it and their chiefs, and a suitable text. The standards of the Levitical units seem to have been similarly adorned, but the description only of that of the clan of Merari, which according to tradition was charged with the transportation of the Tabernacle,[5] and of its sub-clans has been preserved; obviously those of Gershom and Kohath have been lost from the end of the previous column, which is badly damaged.[6] The author also gives the texts for the standards of the various units which 'they shall write'[7] on them when they go out to battle, when they engage the enemy and when they come back to camp. These are in the case of the only Levitical unit preserved in the text, that of Merari,

on going out	on joining battle	on coming back
'God's Truth'	'God's Right Hand'	'God's Exaltation'
'God's Justice'	'God's Moment'	'God's Greatness'
'Glory of God'	'Terror of God'	'Praise of God'
'Judgement of God'	'Slain of God'	'Splendour of God'

Similar notices are provided for the standards of the secular units. These describe the units as God's when they march out and then announce

---

[1] In *War* VI iv 3 § 235; cp. Schubart & Schäfer *Spätptolemäische Papyri* 1822, 13 (where the word is restored in a document of the 1st century B.C.).
[2] Num. ii 2 and Ps. lxxiv 4; cp. *Yalqûṭ Sim'ônî* 931 on Ps. *l.c.*, where σήμαια (cp. Josephus *War* VI vi 1 § 316) is represented by the same Hebrew word.
[3] Cp. Dupont-Sommer *Hymnes* 192².
[4] Cp. 2 Sam. xiv. 13 (*'am 'ĕlôhîm*) and 1 Macc. xiv. 28 (Ασαραμελ; s. Van der Ploeg *Guerre* 81–2).
[5] Ginzberg *Legends of the Jews* IV 194.
[6] Num. iii. 21–39; s. Carmignac *Guerre* 60–1.   [7] S. pp. 180–1.

on engaging the enemy	on returning to camp
'God's War'	'God's Deliverance'
'God's Vengeance'	'God's Victory'
'God's Strife'	'God's Succour'
'God's Revenge'	'God's Support'
'God's Power'	'God's Joy'
'Recompence from God'	'Thanksgivings to God'
'God's Prowess'	'Praise of God'
'God's Destruction'	'God's Peace'

Clearly these legends on the standards, which recall the pass-words of the Maccabaean armies,[1] are all related to the occasion and are intended for the encouragement of and as rallying cries for the men serving under them (W iii 13–iv 14).

The legends or the key-words in them on the standards of the four military units are echoes of their respective names.[2] The key-word in the legend on that of the unit of 1000 (*'elef*) men is 'God's wrath (*'af 'ēl*)' and that referring to the centuries (*mē'ôt*) is 'from (*mē'ēt*) God is the might of war'; the legend on that of the unit of 50 (*ḥămiššîm*) men is 'the resistance of the wicked has ceased (*ḥādēl maʿămaḏ rᵉšāʿîm*)' and that indicating the unit of 10 (*'āśār*) men is 'shouts (as) of God to (the accompaniment of) a lute of ten strings (*'āśôr*)' (W iv 1–5).[3] This playing on words, trivial as it is, has some slight importance as emphasizing the extreme artificiality of the whole conception of the war as here depicted and as witness to the use of cryptograms and ciphers which has been detected also elsewhere in the Scrolls.[4]

The army has thirteen different trumpets to give the various commands in the fashion of the Old Testament,[5] each inscribed with a suitable legend or text, similar to those on the tribal rods in the desert wanderings.[6] These are the trumpets

for summoning the assembly, inscribed
   'Those summoned by God';
for summoning the chiefs or officers, inscribed
   'Princes of God';
for collecting points, command-posts or headquarters (cp. W v 3),[7] inscribed
   'God's array';
for men of renown, heads of families when they are gathered in the meeting place, inscribed
   'God's counsels for the holy council';

[1] 2 Macc. viii 23 xiii 15.
[2] Weis in *JQR*, NS XLI 149; cp. Carmignac *Guerre* 62–3.
[3] Cp. Ps. xxxiii. 2, cxliv. 9.   [4] Pp. 335–46.
[5] Num. x. 2–9.   [6] *Ibid.* xvii 17–18.
[7] Yadin *War* 86–7; cp. Kautzsch & Cowley, *Hebrew Grammar* 80–1.

for the camps, inscribed
'God's peace in the camps of the saints';
for the stages of their marches, inscribed
'God's prowess for the scattering of the foe and putting the
enemies of righteousness to flight and the restoration of His love
in (the defeat of) God's enemies';
for the battle-formations, inscribed
'Formations of God's detachments for His wrathful vengeance on
all the Sons of Darkness';
for summoning the skirmishers, when the 'gates of war'[1] are opened, to
sally forth against the ranks of the foe, inscribed
'Token of vengeance at God's appointed time';
for the slaughter, inscribed
'The hand of God's prowess in war to despatch all those wounded
in rebellion';
for an ambush, inscribed
'God's mysterious acts for the destruction of wickedness';
for pursuit, inscribed
'God has struck down all Sons of Darkness, (and) His anger will
not cease until all are destroyed';
for the return (!),[2] when they return from battle to rejoin the ranks,
inscribed
'God has recalled';[3]
for the return from the battle, inscribed
'God's rejoicings at the return of peace'

(W iii 1–11). The descriptions of these trumpets and the legends on
them for the most part explain themselves, but the number thirteen,
which is not a multiple of seven, is surprising.

The signals, called 'hands' (W viii 5, 7, 12 ix 7 xvii 11) from the old
method of signalling by hand,[4] or notes sounded on the trumpets
are not mentioned in immediate connection with them but only in the
course of describing an action. Some of the technical terms have not
been found elsewhere in Jewish literature so that their sense, except in
so far as it can be inferred from corresponding terms in the cognate
languages, is not altogether clear. The notes, which the priests give as
signals on the trumpets, are said to be drawn out, for forming the line
of battle, 'low and sustained' for the advance, 'sharp and intermittent'
to bring the fighting to a head, with a single fanfare on rams' horns 'to

---

[1] P. 176.
[2] Cp. Carmignac *Guerre* 52–3 (who plausibly suggests that *māšôḇ* 'return' is an
error for *ma'ăsāf* 'calling off' *sc.* the pursuit).
[3] Cp. 2 Sam. ii. 28 (s. Van der Ploeg *Guerre* 81).
[4] Yadin & Rabin *op. cit.* 99–100.

melt the heart of the enemy' and 'low and repeated' to recall the troops (W viii 5–14; cp. xvi 7)[1].

The heavy infantry carry rectangular shields, lances, javelins and daggers. The 'shield' (*māgēn*) is made of burnished bronze with a border of cable-pattern, a looped (?) decoration of inlaid gold and silver and bronze, and 'bands' (Hebr. *bāḏān* = Arab. *badan* 'orna-mented girdle') of precious stones set in a striped pattern.[2] The 'lance' (*rōmaḥ*) consists of shaft, socket and blade. The socket (which seems to be an extension of the blade gripping the end of the shaft) has three bands round it chased with a border of cable-pattern and a looped inlay above and below each band flanked by gems arranged in a similar pattern, and it is fluted between the bands (to prevent the blood running down over the handle); and the blade is of iron shining white and inset with golden ears of corn[3] running along the centre to the point. The 'javelin' (*ḥănîṭ*) is not described in detail; it seems to have been longer than the dart and therefore to have had a shorter range (cp. W vi 4–6).[4] The 'curved dagger' (*kîḏōn*) is of brightly polished iron; its blade itself is decorated with ears of corn of gold in *appliqué* work and provided with grooves running to the point on both sides, and the handle is of polished horn patterned with 'bands' (*bᵉḏānîm*) of gold and silver and gems in stripes (W v 4–14). The cavalry wear helmets and greaves and carry a round shield; the description of the rest of their equipment is unfortunately lost. The measurements of most of these weapons are added to the description of them; and these will be examined in detail hereafter, when the army as depicted in the *War* is compared with Seleucid and Roman models.[5]

The troops of the enemy and their equipment are not described; for, although a reference has been seen to light-armed and heavy-armed troops, the two terms thus translated have perhaps rather the general sense of 'men of low estate (*qallîm*)' and 'men of high rank (*nikbāḏîm*)' or the like (W xiv 11–12),[6] possibly 'privates' and 'officers'. At the same time, an allusion may here be seen to the Kittians, who are elsewhere described as 'swift (*qallîm*) and mighty men in battle' (H ii 12–13).[7]

Three 'standards' of light infantry support the front line; the first carry javelins and darts, the second shields and spears, and the third shields and daggers. These weapons are not described in detail, but the legends 'which they shall write' on them are duly recorded; these are 'Lightning flash of a spear for God's prowess' and 'Flaming sword

---

[1] Yadin & Rabin *War* 101–4; cp. Driver in *JTS*, NS VIII 142 and XIII 369.
[2] Cp. Driver in *JTS*, NS XI 369 and XIII 368.   [3] Cp. Zech. iv. 12.
[4] Yadin *War* 126, 129.   [5] Pp. 180–97.
[6] Van der Ploeg *Guerre* 158–9; cp. Gaster *Scriptures* 379, Dupont-Sommer *Écrits Esséniens* 205 and Carmignac *Guerre* 208.
[7] Cp. Yadin *War* 343.

consuming those slain for iniquity by God's judgement' on the javelins, and 'Firebrands of blood to fell those slain by God's anger' on the darts. The other weapons are not inscribed, but their purpose is explained in words reminiscent of the legends on the weapons just described; they are 'to fell those slain by God's judgement' and 'to subdue the enemy line by God's prowess' (W vi 1–6).

The shields (*māginnîm*) of the men forming the 'towers'[1] are said to be 3 cubits (4 feet 6 inches) long (W ix 12); their width is not given but will probably have been 1½ cubits (2 feet 3 inches), *i.e.* the same as that of the shields carried by the heavy infantry. These shields then are those of the ordinary legionary soldier, specially lengthened because of the exposed positions which the 'towers' occupy.

The cavalry, both men and horses, wear coverings for head and legs, *i.e.* helmets and greaves; and the men carry oval shields, lances 8 cubits (144 inches) long, bows and arrows, and darts of which the length is not given (W vi 14–16).

The organization and development, too, of the forces of the Sons of Light is carefully described in *War*, however uncertain some of the details may be; but Prof. Yadin's account,[2] which is here mostly followed, has thrown a welcome light on much that is obscure and so enabled certain fairly definite conclusions to be drawn from them.

The total number of the infantry is given as 28,000 men (W ix 4–5), of whom 7000 are skirmishers and 21,000 are troops of the line.

The troops of the line were distinguished from the skirmishers by their heavy equipment, which was standardized throughout the unit, and their relative immobility. The largest unit was that called a 'frontal formation', corresponding to a legion, regiment or brigade; it was arrayed in seven 'standards of battle' (W v 3, ix 10) or 'of the line' (W xvii 10), each consisting of 1000 men drawn up one behind another (W v 3–4) with 30 (?) cubits (*c.* 15 yards) between the lines (W v 16–17). Since each 'frontal formation' comprised 7000 men, the army had three such formations, drawn up abreast.

The lightly armed skirmishers were similarly organized in seven 'standards' according to their arms: 2000 slingers, 3000 throwers of darts, 1000 armed with lances and shields and 1000 with curved daggers and shields (W vi 1–6; cp. viii 1–3, 10–13). Each 'standard' therefore would consist of 1000 men, so that it corresponded roughly to a cohort or battalion. These skirmishers, who were posted between the lines of the frontal formations, issued in columns through 'gates' or gaps in the lines and took up positions, deployed in three successive arrays, between the opposing forces but beyond the range of the

---

[1] Pp. 191–2.
[2] In *War* 143–9 (light infantry), 149–61 (heavy infantry), 161–7 (cavalry), 167–80 (deployment in battle).

enemy (W iii 1, 7 vii 16 viii 3–4 xvi 3–4). Their purpose was to engage and destroy the enemy's skirmishing units, to exploit any local successes in breaching his lines, and to keep contact with his forces when in flight. The slingers began the engagement at long range and then fell back; the throwers of darts then advanced and discharged them at middle range and in turn fell back; and lastly the other two arrays engaged the enemy in close combat with respectively lances and daggers (W vi 1–6 viii 1–17; cp. xvi 1–8).

At each end of every line of heavy and light infantry 50 reḵeḇ were posted for the use of the 'men of the command ('anšê hassĕreḵ)', namely the regimental officers or the staff (W vi 10–11). This word has been taken to mean 'chariots',[1] which is its usual meaning in the Old Testament; and this is supported by the practice of the Macedonian army, in which chariots were employed in attack.[2] If, however, the model of the army in the *War* is the Roman army, as here argued, this meaning is impossible; for the Romans did not employ chariots except for ceremonial purposes, *e.g.* in a triumph. It must therefore here denote 'mounts'[3] (presumably in charge of grooms), held ready for the officers in case of need. This meaning of the word belongs to the Egyptian tradition of the Scrolls, being recognized by the Septuagint;[4] and, as it also accords with the Roman practice of having the officers mounted, it may be accepted here.[5]

The disposition of the cavalry is not altogether clear and something must be read between the lines where the sense is uncertain or supplied where it is defective. Its total number was 6000 horse (W ix 5–6; cp. vi 10) divided into two main groups, the first attached to the skirmishers and the second to the heavy infantry. The former consisted of 100 men riding on either flank of each of the 7 lines of skirmishers, making 1400 horse. The latter numbered 4600 men, divided into two groups; of these 100 were posted on either flank of each of the 7 lines of heavy infantry, which was thus protected by 1400 horse, and the remainder (whose number is not given but must have been 3200) were posted on either flank of the legion, *i.e.* 1600 horse on each wing. The total number then was 6000 horse, of which 500 were provided by each of the 12 tribes[5] (W vi 8–11). The cavalry with the skirmishers were younger and more lightly armed than the rest, obviously because they were required for more active operations (W vi 11–14).

The author also describes the five tactical formations which may be expected to result from a general attack, setting them down in a bare

---

[1] Bardtke *Handschriftenfunde* II 221.
[2] *E.g.* 1 Macc. viii. 6 and 2 Macc. xiii. 2 (where the chariots are 'armed with scythes').
[3] Dupont-Sommer *Écrits Esséniens* 195; s. Kuhn in *TLz.* LXXXI 25–8 and Van der Ploeg *Guerre* 105.
[4] 1 Ki. xvi. 9 and Isa. xxvi. 9; cp. Josh. xvii. 16, 18.   Cp. Rev. vii. 7.

list, which gives the appearance of being a series of headings taken over from a military handbook[1] (for example, such as Asclepiodotus, writing perhaps early in the 1st century A.D., inserts in his work), in the order in which they may be expected to develop.[2] These are a 'rectangle with towers' and 'enveloping arms with towers', an 'arc with towers' and a 'flat arc with projecting columns (*rāšīm*)',[3] and 'wings issuing from both sides of the line' (W ix 10–14). These dispositions are in all essential points the same as those of the Roman army, namely the 'long rectangle' (*frons longa* or *quadratus exercitus*), the 'arc' or 'wedge' (*cuneus*),[4] the 'pincers' for a double envelopment of the enemy (*forfex*), the 'serrated formation' of light units in the centre (*serra*), the 'wings' of the cavalry on the flanks (*alae*), and the so-called 'towers' (*turres*).[5] Only the *serra* and certain formations required in special circumstances are missing from the Scroll, since the situations in which they may be needed are not expected.

The 'towers' alone do not explain themselves. The author of *War* says that 'the shields of (the men posted in) the towers shall be 3 cubits long and their lances 8 cubits long.[6] The towers shall project beyond the line (of the main body) by 100 shields, and the face (*i.e.* side) of the tower shall consist of 100 shields; thus 300 shields shall run round the tower in the three frontal directions (*i.e.* on every side except the rear, which is open). Each tower shall have 2 'gates' (*i.e.* gaps or intervals), one on the right and one on the left' (W ix 12–14). These towers are four in number, since one is stationed on either flank of the two lines of which the *duplex acies* is composed; also the shields in each tower bear the name of that tower's guardian angels, and these angels are four in number, namely Michael, Gabriel, Sariel (or perhaps Uriel,[7] since the reading of the name is uncertain)[8] and Raphael (W ix 13–15).[9]

The order in which these successive positions are named follows the expected course of the battle.[10] The frontal formations, arrayed 7 deep, approach the enemy marching in 3 columns abreast. When within attacking distance, they abandon the defensive formation in depth and deploy in the long rectangle with 'towers' at the end of each line and cavalry on the flanks and in the rear; as there are four towers (W ix 15–16) and a middle 'gate', implying an even number of formations in the front-line through which priests emerge to encourage the

---

[1] Cp. Atkinson in *BJRL* XL 290–7.
[2] Aulus Gellius *Noctes Atticae* x 9 and Vegetius *Epitoma Rei Militaris* iii 20.
[3] Cp. Deut. xx. 9 (where *rŏ'š* is translated *cuneus* by Jerome).
[4] Cp. Polybius *Historiae* III xviii 8.   [5] Pp. 191–2.   [6] Pp. 182–3.
[7] Cp. I Enoch ix 1 (Michael, Uriel, Raphael, Gabriel).
[8] Cp. Yadin *op. cit.* 216–17.
[9] Dan. viii. 16, ix. 21 (Gabriel), x. 13, 21, xii. 1 (Michael); I Enoch vi. 7, xx. 6 (Raphael); Tobit iii. 17 *alq.* (Sariel).
[10] Yadin *op. cit.* 180.

troops and give the signal to attack (W vii 8–9), the new formation is not a *triplex acies*[1] but rather a *duplex acies*[2] with four 'frontal standards' or cohorts in the front and three in the rear. The skirmishers, who are stationed between and behind the lines, then emerge through the 'gates' in the ranks of the heavy infantry with a view to engaging the enemy in the order already described[3] and if possible softening his front, while the main body is deployed in the form of enveloping arms to immobilize his flanks; the arc will then engage his retreating centre and his flanks will begin to fall back, pursued by the ends of the arc coming forward in such a way that it is flattened; lastly, the whole enemy front will be engaged by advancing the ends of the arc (reforming the enveloping arms) and sending 'heads' (*i.e.* columns) of various units to destroy his lines, while 'wings', presumably squadrons of cavalry, are sent round and beyond his flanks so that he will be driven into an ambush where he can be surrounded and destroyed.

The text seems also to speak of forming an ambush (W ix 17–[?]); but, as it is here broken off at the bottom of the column, the entire description is unfortunately lost.

When the army confronts the enemy, seven priests clothed in special vestments recalling those of Aaron and his sons pass along the lines, the first exhorting the troops and the other six carrying trumpets for signalling orders; they are accompanied by seven Levites and preceded by three Levitical officers. When the priests blow their trumpets, parties of infantry will advance and take up their positions between the lines. When the 'gates of battle' (*i.e.* the gaps in the lines)[4] are opened, fifty warriors with shields will issue forth and take station behind the Levitical officers; then the rest of the troops will follow suit. When the priests give the signal, skirmishers will advance to positions between their own and the enemy lines (W vii 9–18; rest of column lost). The trumpets are sounded for the slingers, who discharge seven volleys of stones and fall back to their original positions. The priests then with the trumpets call out three companies of skirmishers to pass through the 'gates', who take up positions in lines flanked on either side by mounted troops; when the priests give the signal on the trumpets, these men drawing their weapons advance towards the enemy line. The priests then blow a loud fanfare lasting throughout the engagement, and 'all the trumpeters' blow a fanfare to strike terror into the enemy while the combatants hurl their javelins; when these cries die down, the priests continue to blow on the trumpets until seven volleys of javelins have been discharged and then give the signal for the troops to fall back on their own lines. This manoeuvre, similarly directed, is repeated by each of the three troops of skirmishers (W viii

[1] Gaster *Scriptures* 258.
[2] Yadin & Rabin *op. cit.* 191–2.
[3] Pp. 174–5.
[4] P. 176.

1–17; rest of column lost). When the enemy show signs of slackening their efforts, the host (?) wave their hands to urge the combatants to press the attack while the priests continue sounding the trumpets until the enemy is defeated; then, when they turn in flight, the priests sound a general summons on the trumpets to call out all combatant troops, who sally forth from the lines in six bodies and join those already engaged. On the signal being sounded by the priests, a general pursuit and slaughter of the enemy ensues; the priests then raise a shout of triumph from afar but do not approach the scene of the victory for fear of soiling their vestments with the blood of the slain (W ix 1–9).

The author of the *War* adds a number of addresses, psalms and hymns, for use on various occasions; these are the priest's allocution addressed to the troops before battle after the fashion prescribed in the Old Testament,[1] a hymn of victory (W ix [?]–xii 18), a thanksgiving prayer to God for victory recited by the priests and Levites and 'the elders of the order' (W xiii 1–xiv 1), and a thanksgiving hymn sung by the army after washing their bodies and changing their clothes on the morrow of the victory (W xiv 2–?).

The remainder of the *War* more or less repeats much that has already been said but gives a detailed account of a campaign 'against the king of the Kittians and all the host of Belial', in which 'God's lot (*i.e.* party)' are promised victory (W xv 1–3). The high-priest, priests and Levites begin by offering a prayer for victory[2] and reciting the instructions suitable to the occasion, after which the high-priest delivers an allocution, with which the Roman commander's *allocutio* on similar occasions may be compared,[3] urging the troops to quit themselves like 'men of valour' and promising them God's aid in overthrowing the enemy (W xv 4–xvi 1). The order of battle is then described. The priests will give the signal on the 'memorial trumpets' and the 'gates of war' will be opened, whereupon the columns on hearing the signal take their stations between the lines. At a second signal, when they are within bow-shot of the enemy line, each man raises his weapon, whereupon a general fanfare of trumpets accompanied by a battle-cry gives the signal to attack the enemy; the battle-cry dies down, but the priests continue sounding the trumpets so long as the battle continues (W xvi 3–9).

If Belial himself comes to the assistance of the Sons of Darkness and the infantry begin to suffer losses, the priests will give the signal for the second line to advance and for the first line to fall back, and the high-priest comes forward to address the troops (W xvi 11–xvii 9). The priests then give the signal for the line to be reformed. On receipt of a

---

[1] Cp. Deut. xx. 2–8.
[2] Cp. 1 Macc. iv. 30–3, ix. 44–6; 2 Macc. xv. 21–4.
[3] Gaster *Scriptures* 258–9.

second signal the troops advance within range of the enemy, and on hearing the Levites give a blast on the trumpets they launch the attack; as the battle-cry dies down the priests continue blowing the trumpets, the troops fall on the enemy and drive them before them (W xvii 10–15; rest of column lost). In this battle God intervenes on behalf of the Sons of Light 'and in the pursuit of Asshur the sons of Japhet will fall and the Kittians will be crushed with none [escaping]', whereupon all the ranks at a given signal will rally round the priests and put the Kittians to the ban; for 'the sun [will not] make haste to set on that day'[1] (W xviii 1–5). After the victory the high-priest, the priests and the Levites, the chiefs of the army and 'the men of command', whose identity is uncertain,[2] give thanks to God (W xviii 5–8). The rest of the *War* contains fragments of a thanksgiving hymn (W xviii 9–[?]) and what seems to be part of another allocution by the high-priest (W xix 1–13), which is perhaps here out of place.

The unreality, if not absurdity, of these battles is patent; the whole account smacks rather of the Chronicler's battles than of any real engagements which can actually have taken place. The suspension of all military work during the year of jubilee or sabbatical year is not enjoined in the Old Testament but is an exaggerated echo of the well-known reluctance of the Jews to fight on the sabbath,[3] which the Maccabaean commanders occasionally overruled, allowing defensive warfare on that day;[4] but the custom, which an apocryphal work explicitly prescribed,[5] was known to the enemies of the Jewish nation, who often took advantage of it.[6] The part played by the priests and the Levites is something utterly impossible in real warfare and clearly reflects battles in the latest parts of the Old Testament,[7] where a similar importance is ascribed to them.[8] The battle-cry, for which the signal was commonly given by trumpets,[9] was practised by the ancient Hebrews[10] as by other peoples,[11] and the shout of triumph or paean was equally well known in antiquity.[12] These are customs of no significance in the present connection; the author of *War* is simply drawing matter from common experience, even though he over-elaborates the picture in truly apocalyptic style, making it in many respects absurd.

---

[1] Cp. Josh. x. 12–14. [2] S. p. 175; cp. Yadin & Rabin *op. cit.* 177.
[3] Josephus *Antiquities* XIV iv 2 § 63, XVIII ix 2 § 319; *War* II xvi 4 §§ 392–4, IV ii 3 § 99 and *Life* 32.
[4] I Macc. ix. 43–4; Josephus *Antiquities* XII vi 2 § 276 and *War* II xix 2 § 517.
[5] Jubilees I 12–13.
[6] I Macc. ii. 38 and 2 Macc. v. 25–6, xv. 1; Josephus *War* I vii 3 § 146 and *Against Apion* i 21.
[7] *E.g.* Num. xxxi 6 and Josh. 9–10.
[8] *E.g.* 2 Chron. xiii. 14–15, xx. 14–28. [9] Josephus *War* III vii 27 § 265.
[10] Jud. vii. 20–2; I Sam. xvii. 20, 52; 2 Macc. xii. 36–7.
[11] *E.g.* Aeschylus *Persae* 395–402; 2 Macc. xv. 24–5; Livy *ab urbe condita* VII xxvi 3, Caesar *Bellum Civile* iii 92, Sallust *Catilina* lx 1–2.
[12] Psa. xli. 12; I Macc. iv. 24.

2. MILITARY MODELS

No one expects such a writer as the author of *War* to compile a serious military handbook exact in every detail, and everyone can see that the picture which he draws, however consistent it may for the most part be, contains some anachronisms and inconsistencies which cannot be fitted into contemporary practice, whatever that may have been. A part, if not much, of this inconsistency is caused by the necessity of adapting the account to the organization of the Israelite tribes in the wilderness.[1] On this score alone the professional Vegetius, who confuses the military institutions of many centuries, may perhaps be compared with him. Contrariwise the author of *War* leaves no doubt that he is describing Roman practice, even though he may occasionally seem to waver between Jewish and Roman, whether Republican or Imperial, customs; and here allowance must be made for modern ignorance of every detail of ancient practice.

The idea of inscriptions on the standards can hardly be referred back, as Dr. Gaster suggests,[2] to the Psalmist's 'in the name of our God we will set up our banners';[3] for this seems to be a modern (and by no means certain) rendering of the Hebrew expression. The texts on the standards do, however, recall Gideon's password and those which Judas the Maccabee on two occasions gave to his troops,[4] namely 'God's Succour' and 'God's Victory';[5] but too much stress must not be laid on these passwords, since they are something quite different from religious texts on banners and, although similar phrases occur on the Covenanters' standards, they recall similar if not identical phrases here and there in the Old Testament,[6] from which they may have been independently taken. Such an echo of Maccabaean custom, however, if Judas inspired these texts, would be characteristic of the Scrolls.[7] There is otherwise no hint of such inscriptions on standards before the Roman period; then the *signa* and *vexilla* of the Roman army had the name of the corps to which they belonged and those of the commander-in-chief or emperor inscribed on them. The *vexilla* were something in the nature of flags or might carry flags on which the name might be worked, *e.g.* in letters of scarlet; but sometimes a wooden *tabula* or medallion of metal carrying the inscription was attached to the standard.[8] This last practice explains what the author of *War* means when he says that 'they shall write' the inscriptions on their

---

[1] Cp. Yadin & Rabin *Scroll of the War* 38–40.   [2] In *Scriptures* 294.
[3] Psa. xx. 5.
[4] Jud. vii. 18 and 2 Macc. viii. 23, xiii. 15 (cp. Josephus *War* III v 3 § 86).
[5] Dupont-Sommer *Aperçus Préliminaires* 101–2.
[6] Cp. Jud. v. 23, Exod. xiv. 13, 2 Chron. xx. 17.   [7] Pp. 353–5.
[8] Vegetius *Epitoma Rei Militaris* ii 13; s. Reinach *ap.* Daremberg & Saglio *Dictionnaire des Antiquités* IV 1309–1316.

standards when going out to and coming back from battle:[1] the troops must be pictured as having a number of such placards suitably inscribed and ready to be fixed to the standards according to circumstances. The differences are that, while the length of these standards suggests banners, the Roman *signa* and *vexilla* were not banners although such might be attached to them;[2] and the Roman standards, unlike these, bore no religious mottoes. These differences, however, are not fundamental, being due to the exigencies of adapting a Roman institution to Jewish religious needs.

The trumpets throw considerable light on the date of the Scroll describing them. The ancient Hebrews, although they employed horns and trumpets for ceremonial or ritual purposes,[3] made no military or at any rate no formal military use of such instruments for signalling orders in the centuries spanned by the Old Testament. They used them only to give the alarm,[4] and they apparently had no highly developed method of signalling by them even in the Maccabaean wars;[5] their significance was still mainly religious, or to encourage their own men and terrify the enemy.[6] Trumpets, however, were well known to other nations of antiquity, including the Seleucid Greeks;[7] but it was principally the Romans who developed the practice of transmitting signals in battle by means of trumpets. The reason for the difference is that the Jews fought in close formations and therefore had no need for signalling to a distance, whereas the Romans fought in open formations which made signalling by banners and trumpets a necessity of battle.[8] The 'trumpet of assembly', while it echoes that of the Israelite host in the wilderness,[9] is here rather the *tuba concionis* of the Roman army. Further, the Greek historian Polybius,[10] writing in the 2nd century B.C., says that the Romans announced breaking camp by three signals on the trumpet: at the first tents were struck and the baggage was packed and collected for transport, at the second the pack-animals were loaded and all awaited the order to march, and at the third the troops marched out of camp. Long afterwards Josephus[11] in his account of the Roman army draws the same picture: the first trumpet gave the signal to the troops to leave their quarters, the second to make everything ready for the march, and the third to march out of camp. These signals obviously would represent ancient practice and would therefore have no value as evidence of the

---

[1] Cp. Targ. Jonathan at Num. ii. 3, 10, 18, 25.
[2] Cp. Van der Ploeg *Guerre* 81.   [3] Josephus *Antiquities* III xii 6 § 291.
[4] *E.g.* 1 Sam. xiii. 3; Am. iii. 6.   [5] *E.g.* 1 Macc. iv. 13, vii. 45, ix. 13, xvi. 8.
[6] *E.g. ibid.* iii. 54, iv. 40, v. 31, 33.
[7] *E.g. ibid.* vi. 33 (forming line of battle) vii. 45 (pursuit) ix. 12 (advance to attack); cp. 2 Macc. xv. 24–5 (advance).
[8] Yadin *War* 103.   [9] Num. x. 6.
[10] In *Historiae* VI xl 2–3.   [11] In *War* III v 4 §§ 89–91.

N

date of any Scroll describing them. The important point, however, is
that Josephus[1] elsewhere claims to have introduced the Roman
system of signalling with trumpets to the Jewish levies in Galilee when
training them in the winter of A.D. 66–7 for the revolt against Rome.
He says especially that 'he taught them the use of trumpets for the
charge and the retreat (σάλπιγγας προκλήσεως τε καὶ ἀνακλήσεως)';
these are the 'trumpets of pursuit' and the 'trumpets of recall' as used
by the Sons of Light (W iii 2 vii 13)[2]. In the end, the purposes to which
Josephus and the author of *War* assign the trumpets is singularly like
those which Vegetius postulates[3] in describing late Republican and
early Imperial practice, when he says that the Romans indicated by
means of them *utrum stare vel progredi an certe regredi oporteat, utrum longe
persequi fugientes an receptui canere*; but his evidence ought not to
be pressed since, writing in the 4th century A.D., he was apt to confuse
information relating to quite diverse periods. It would however seem
to confirm the view that *War* was reflecting what Josephus introduced.
That the system of signalling by trumpets is much elaborated in *War*
is no objection; for that is as much an apocalyptic as a historical work.
It is based on the stories in the Old Testament and on other Jewish
works, apocryphal and apocalyptic, while Josephus purports to be
writing Jewish history.

The helmet and greaves, which are not described, were worn also by
Roman troops. The helmet, which was worn only by the cavalry of the
Sons of Light, was the *cassis* of the Roman army. At the end of the
Republic that of the infantry was of metal; the cavalry, too, had one
of iron, which they might only occasionally use under the Empire.[4]
Greaves were worn by infantry and cavalry on both legs in the
Hellenistic army, but a single greave was worn under the Republic by
the legionary on the right leg; in Imperial times greaves were given up
by the rank and file of the infantry, though retained by centurions and
officers, and they were also worn by select mounted units in the
Imperial army, as the cavalry in *War* did (W vi 15).[5] Thus the practice
of the Sons of Light conforms in this matter approximately to that of
the Roman army under the Empire.

The rectangular shield of the heavy infantry, measuring $2\frac{1}{2}$ cubits
(3 feet 9 inches) by $1\frac{1}{2}$ cubits (2 feet 3 inches), like the Ark in the
wilderness,[6] is the *scutum*, measuring *c.* 4 feet by $2\frac{1}{2}$ feet, which was
carried by the Roman infantry in the late Republican and early
Imperial age.[7] The round shield of the cavalry (for the term translated

---

[1] In *War* II xx 7 § 579.   [2] Cp. Driver in *JTS*, NS XI 367–8.
[3] In *Epitoma Rei Militaris* iii 5; cp. ii 22.   [4] *E.g.* Josephus *War* III v 5 § 96.
[5] Yadin *War* 114–16; cp. Couissin *Armes Romaines* 350, 467–8 and Alton in *Companion to Latin Studies* § 731.
[6] Exod. xxv. 10.
[7] Polybius *Historiae* VI xxiii 2–5; cp. Van der Ploeg *Guerre* 90–1.

'round' is certainly not intended to describe it as made of calf's hide)[1] may be the circular *parma* of iron or leather rimmed with iron used by the early legionary cavalry[2] which however was discarded towards the end of the Republic,[3] when the oval shield (θυρεός) took its place.[4] This will be what the author of *War* meant; for 'round' in all probability does duty also for 'oval', for which no separate term is known in the classical language. So the Targum uses the corresponding Aramaic term for two or three different kinds of shield, including the large oblong or rather oval shield protecting the whole body.[5] If then these two shields are rightly identified, the author of *War* and Josephus[6] agree exactly in their descriptions. The former arms the heavy infantry of the Sons of Light with a rectangular shield and their cavalry with an oval shield; according to the latter the shield of the legionary soldier was an oblong θυρεός, while that of the cavalry was a θυρεός pure and simple. Since then θυρεὸς can describe a shield either oval or oblong,[7] the absence of any qualifying epithet here describing the shield as oblong shows that a different, *i.e.* an oval, shield must be meant. Thus

rectangular shield = oblong θυρεὸς
and   oval shield   = simple θυρεός,

as the author of *War* and Josephus respectively describe or call the two shields, so that they closely agree on this point.

The lance (*rōmaḥ*), said to be 7 cubits (10 feet 6 inches) long, corresponds to the *pilum*, a missile weapon nearly 7 feet long employed by the auxiliary troops from the Marian reforms onwards and by the legionaries when fighting in phalanx formations; the javelin (*ḥănîṯ*), 5 cubits (7½ feet) long, is probably the *hasta*, a shorter but heavier thrusting weapon which the *pilum* is recorded to have eventually displaced, since it was equally a thrusting weapon.[8] The dart (*zereq* or *šeleṭ*) would be the *hasta velitaris* or *jaculum* of the legionary cavalry; this was 4 feet long and was carried by the youngest and most active skirmishers each of whom had seven of them,[9] as those armed with them in *War* had (W vi 2, 4).[10] Accordingly, all these weapons are those of the late Republican or preferably the early Imperial Roman army, largely as Josephus describes them.[11]

Historically the most important of these weapons is the 'curved dagger' (*kîḏōn*). In describing it the author of *War* says that 'its length is 1½ cubits (= 27 inches)[12] and its breadth is 4 fingers (= 3 inches);

[1] Carmignac *Guerre* 100. [2] Yadin *War* 107–14.
[3] Couissin *op. cit.* 248–9. [4] Josephus *War* III v 5 § 96.
[5] Psa. xlvi. 10 ('*āgîlāh*, θυρεός) and xci. 4 (*sôḥērāh*, of which the meaning is disputed), 2 Chron. ix. 15, xi. 12, xiv. 7, xxv. 5 (*sinnāh*, θυρεός).
[6] In *War* III v 5 §§ 95–6. [7] Jones & McKenzie *Greek-English Lexicon* I 811.
[8] Yadin *op. cit.* 126–30. [9] Cp. Livy *ab urbe condita* XXVI iv 4.
[10] Yadin *op. cit.* 123–4. [11] In *War* III v 5 §§ 94–7.
[12] Cp. Jud. iii. 16.

and the "belly (*beṭen*)" is 4 thumbs (= 4 inches), and there are 4 hand-breadths (= 12 inches) up to the belly, and the "belly" is foot-shaped in this direction and in that direction for 5 hand-breadths or palms (= 15 inches)' (W v 12–14). The *crux* of the passage is the meaning of 'belly'.

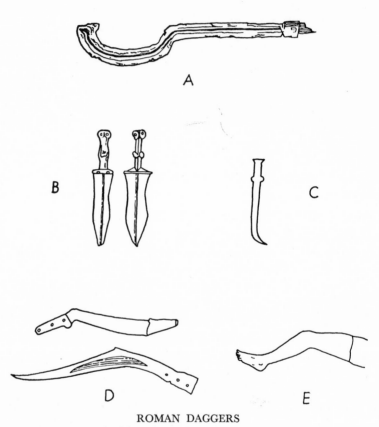

ROMAN DAGGERS

A. Byblian scimitar, ἁρπή (Contenau *Manuel d'Archéologie* II 862–3).
B. Roman *pugiones* (Couissin *Armes Romaines* 380).
C. Roman *parazonium* (Couissin *op. cit.* 385).
D. Curved daggers, *sicae* (Reinach *ap.* Daremberg & Saglio *Dictionnaire des Antiquités* IV 1301).
E. Human leg slightly flexed and tapering.

This is commonly supposed to be the sheath or scabbard,[1] which is impossible; for its position in the description shows it to be a part of the actual dagger, and a weapon having a blade 3 inches broad does not require a scabbard 4 inches in breadth. Further, the Hebrew word

[1] Van der Ploeg in *VT* V 380; cp. Yadin *op. cit.* 118.

for 'belly' nowhere means a 'case'; the word for 'house' (*bayiṭ*) is the proper term for such an object, if either of the two classical terms is not used. As Dr. Kuhn and Dr. Molin have recognized, apparently independently but at the same time,[1] the 'belly' is the 'bulge' or 'curve' of the blade. What then is meant by describing this weapon as 'foot-shaped' is, as Dr. Gertner has remarked, that it tapers like a leg or foot from the highest point of the curve towards each end,[2] *i.e.* one way to the point of the blade and the other to the socket of the handle. This tapering shows that the weapon can be used both for cutting and for thrusting and is therefore not an Oriental ἀρπή, as Prof. Dupont-Sommer suggests,[3] as this has disproportionate measurements and is only a cutting weapon.[4] It is rather a curved dagger with a handle of decorated horn into which a shaft at one end of the blade is fitted; the shaft and handle run straight for 12 inches, after which the blade curves upwards and then downwards for 15 inches to the point. The blade is 3 inches broad at its widest point, *i.e.* the centre, but its breadth is gradually reduced or narrowed down as it tapers towards each end, *i.e.* towards the point and the shaft of the handle; and the distance from the middle point of the blade on the inside of the curve is 4 inches to a line drawn on a level base from the tip of the blade to the handle. Further, as the blade is not said to be two-edged, it must be assumed to have only one edge.

Three short daggers, the *pugio* and the *parazonium*[5] and the *sica*,[6] were known to the Romans. The first does not call for consideration; for it had a straight, not a curved, blade. The second, which had a non-tapering blade with two edges, was introduced from Greece or the East towards the beginning of the Empire, when it was awarded as a *militiae decus* but was never carried as a fighting weapon by the ordinary soldier; it, too, therefore cannot be meant. The third was a curved dagger of Illyrian or Thracian origin, having a blade varying from 13¾ to 21¼ inches (so far as extant specimens show); it was not primarily a military weapon, although certain special units of the Roman army came to be equipped with it, but rather an assassin's instrument, being that which the *sicarii* had made notorious at Rome in the last century B.C. and which was not used in Palestine before the following century. What is here significant, however, is not so much the date of its introduction into Rome (for few Jews can have heard of the Catilinarian conspiracy) as that Josephus describes[7] it as the characteristic

[1] In *TLz.* LXXXI [1956] 30 (Kuhn) and *JSS* I [1956] 334–7 (Molin); cp. Driver in *JTS*, NS X 121 and XI 367–9.
[2] Cp. Van der Ploeg *Guerre* 180. [3] In *Écrits* 194¹.
[4] Cp. Contenau *Manuel d'Archéologie Orientale* II 863 (fig. 612).
[5] Couissin *Armes Romaines* 379–86.
[6] *Ibid., op. cit.* 493–4; cp. Daremberg & Saglio *Dictionnaire des Antiquités* IV 1300–1 and Pauly & Wissowa *Real-Encyclopädie* II 2184–5.
[7] In *Antiquities* XX viii 10 § 186 and *War* II xiii 3 § 254–5.

weapon adopted by the extremist groups of the Jewish rebels *c.*
A.D. 55–60 in their struggle against Rome. He speaks of them as then
'using daggers closely resembling the short swords of the Persians but
curved and similar to the weapons which are called *sicae* by the Romans',
and as carrying them concealed under their clothes. Both the 'dagger'
of the Scrolls and the *sica*, then, were curved daggers with a single edge
to the blade; and several such weapons presumed to be *sicae*, found at
sites in Europe, although they exceed the Jewish weapon in length,
otherwise have measurements almost exactly proportionate to those
which the author of *War* gives.[1] There can therefore be no doubt that

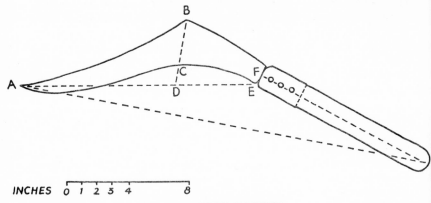

CURVED DAGGER

A—G total length of daggers	1½ cubits (27 inches)
A—E length of curve (*beṭen*) 'tapering either way'	5 spans (15 inches)
F—G length of shaft and handle (conjecturally restored)	
'up to the curve'	4 spans (12 inches)
B—C breadth of blade	4 fingers (3 inches)
B—D total depth of 'curve'	4 thumbs (4 inches)

the author of the *War* and Josephus are describing the same weapon;
and the coincidence suggests that they are referring to the same chain
of events. As then the historic weapon with which the heroic Mattathias
and his sons were armed when they hewed down the renegade Jew
who consented to offer sacrifice to a heathen deity was a sacrificial
curved 'chopper' (κοπίς),[2] so a 'curved dagger' (*sica*) became the
characteristic weapon both of the extremist rebels and of the Covenanters. These *sicarii* or 'brigands',[3] as Josephus calls them,[4] were in fact

---

[1] Cp. Driver in *JTS*, NS XI 367 and *Hibbert Journal* LX 352–3.
[2] Josephus *Antiquities* XII vi 2 § 270 and *War* I i 3 § 36; cp. Athenaeus *Deipno-
sophists* IV xvi 138–xvii 14 and Curtius *Life of Alexander* VIII xiv 29.
[3] Pp. 238–41, 245–9.   [4] *E.g.* in *War* II xvii 6 § 425.

only members of the anti-Roman parties who from the opposite point of view were styled 'zealots' by themselves after the Maccabaean proto-martyr who had been called a 'zealot for the law';[1] and, if the *sica* or curved dagger was the weapon not only of some of these but also of the Covenanters, these parties were likely to be either sub-groups of one and the same party or actually identical.

That the 'frontal formation' contains 7 'standards' of 1000 men each, namely 7000 men, whereas the Roman legion in Imperial times numbered only about 6000 men, is due to the author's predilection for the Biblical seven (cp. W i 14 ii 12 iv 10 v 3, 7, 16 vi 1, 2, 4, 8 vii 9, 14 viii 1, 13 ix 5 ix 5 xi 8) and is near enough to the legion for his purpose. Again, when he puts the cavalry at 6000 horse, he states that the figure is based on a calculation of 500 men to each of the twelve tribes (W vi 11; cp. ii 3), thereby committing a gross anachronism; for the twelve tribes had long ceased to exist as political entities, and he himself had said that only three were engaged in the campaigns which he was describing (W i 1; cp. iii 14).

The original theory, which has recently been revived, that the 'frontal formation' or principal combatant unit in *War* is the Hellenis-tic phalanx,[2] cannot stand up to exact study. Put bluntly, almost the only resemblance between the two bodies is that both are masses of armed men; but even so the numbers, as most other details, are entirely different. The phalanx consisted ideally of some 16,384 hoplites drawn up in 16 ranks of 1024 men each one behind another,[3] whereas the 'frontal formation' of the Sons of Light consisted of 21,000 men drawn up 7 deep. The phalanx had no sufficient space between the lines in which light troops could be stationed, not even space enough for the commander and his staff;[4] and the lines had no 'gates' or *intervalla* (although these were found occasionally before 400 B.C. in Greek armies)[5] through which such troops, if posted between them, could have emerged.[6] Its light troops, called peltasts, therefore were posted in the rear,[7] not between the lines. The equipment, too, of the two forces was quite different. The phalangite carried a small round shield 2 feet in diameter, while the heavy infantry in the 'frontal formations' had rectangular shields measuring 45 by 27 inches. The *sarissa*, a pike some 14 or even 16 cubits long, which needed two hands to wield it and with which the phalanx was armed,[8] is a totally different weapon from the lance 7 cubits long or the javelin 5 cubits long of the

[1] Pp. 243–4.
[2] Février in *Semitica* III 53–9 and Atkinson in *BJRL* XL 272–97.
[3] Asclepiodotus *Tactica* ii 7 iv 4.
[4] Tarn *Hellenistic Military and Naval Developments* 36–7.
[5] Van der Ploeg *Guerre* 115–16.   [6] Yadin *op. cit.* 135–6.
[7] Atkinson *ibid.* 294.
[8] Polybius *Historiae* XVIII xxix 3; cp. Tarn *op. cit.* 26–8.

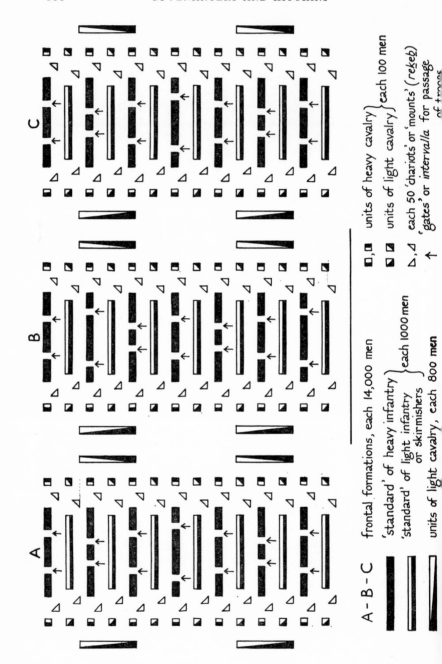

A – B – C   frontal formations, each 14,000 men

▬   'standard' of heavy infantry ⎱ each 1000 men

▭   'standard' of light infantry ⎰
     or skirmishers

    units of light cavalry, each 800 men

▣, ◩   units of heavy cavalry ⎱ each 100 men

◪, ◩   units of light cavalry ⎰

△, ◁   each 50 'chariots' or 'mounts' (*rekeb*)

↑   'gates' or *intervalla* for passage
    of troops

ORDER OF BATTLE OF THE SONS OF LIGHT, *duplex acies* (pp. 176–7).[1]

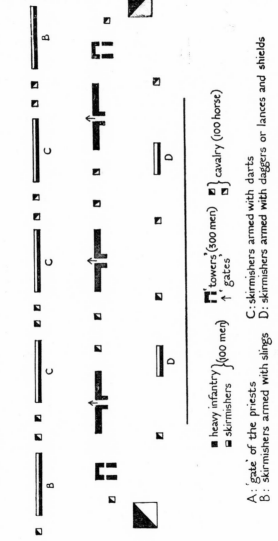
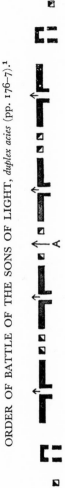

■ heavy infantry ⎫
⬚ skirmishers   ⎬ (100 men)

◨ 'towers' (300 men)
↑ 'gates'

◪ } cavalry (100 horse)

A: 'gate' of the priests
B: skirmishers armed with slings

C: skirmishers armed with darts
D: skirmishers armed with daggers or lances and shields

[1] Cp. Yadin, *Scroll of the War* 157 (reproduced as here modified by kind permission of the author).

heavy infantry in *War*; and the Hellenistic light infantry carried javelins, slings and bows,[1] whereas the skirmishers in *War* had slings or darts, lances or curved daggers. The characteristic broad-brimmed hat of the Macedonian infantry is absent. Further, the author of *War* nowhere refers to the chariots which supported the flank of a Hellenistic army or to the elephants (imported into the text solely by mistranslation)[2] which were employed by the successors of Alexander throughout the 2nd century B.C.[3] and were therefore well known to the Jews.[4]

The formations described in *War* are purely Roman. The 'frontal formation' of 7 lines containing 1000 men each made a unit of 7000 men; the former was the cohort and the latter the legion of the Roman army. This, as Marius (155–186 B.C.) reorganized it, had an average of 6000 men until Caesar reduced it to 3000 men.[5] So Herod's army investing Jerusalem in 37 B.C. was 'about 30,000 men' organized in 11 legions or divisions (for Josephus loosely uses technical terms), *i.e.* roughly 3000 men to the legion, in addition to 6000 mounted men and some Syrian auxiliary troops.[6] Augustus, however, restored the legion to a strength of 6000 men.[7] If then the Marian legion is out of the question as too early, Caesar's legion may be excluded on the score of numbers; consequently the Augustan legion must be what the writer is describing. The emphasis in *War* falls not on the three front-lines of the 'frontal formations', *i.e.* 3000 men drawn up abreast, but on the 7 lines of 1000 men each in depth, *i.e.* 7000 men, as constituting the ideal principal unit of the army of the Sons of Light; this, when allowance is made for the necessity of employing seven as a sacred number,[8] may be safely identified with the Augustan 6 cohorts in a legion of some 6000 men. Josephus supports this conclusion, when he describes[9] the 'phalanx' (as he calls the column of marching legions) as advancing in 6 files; for, when wheeled round to confront the enemy, they would be drawn up 6 lines deep. This number, too, corresponds to the 7 lines in depth of the 'frontal formation', when the substitution of seven for six on Biblical grounds is taken into consideration.[10]

The organization of the light infantry or skirmishers tells the same tale. The use of light troops fighting beside the heavy infantry was common to both Hellenistic and Roman armies. The Hellenistic serried phalanx, however, was drawn up in such close formation that the movement of troops within its ranks was impossible, as already

[1] Tarn *op. cit.* 20.   [2] Pp. 210–1.   [3] Tarn *op. cit.* 92–100.
[4] *E.g.* 1 Macc. i 17, iii. 34, vi. 30, 34, 35, 46, viii. 6; 2 Macc. xi. 4, xiii. 2, 15; 3 Macc. v. 1, 2, 10, 20, 38, 48.
[5] Alton *op. cit.* §§ 717–18; cp. Yadin & Rabin *op. cit.* 175–6.
[6] Josephus *Antiquities* XIV xvi 1 §§ 468–9.
[7] Alton *op. cit.* § 721; s. Van der Ploeg *Guerre* 89–90.   [8] S. p. 187.
[9] In *War* III vi 2 § 124.
[10] Cp. Rice Holmes *Caesar's Conquest of Gaul*[2] 588–9.

said,[1] whereas the structure of the Roman army was designed to allow it; so the *velites* stationed behind the *manipuli* in early days emerged through *intervalla* in their ranks to engage the enemy.[2] Both *velites* and cavalry, however, were withdrawn from the legion early in the 1st century B.C.,[3] but Augustus in his reform of 16–15 B.C. restored and refashioned these units. The *auxilia* were formed into cohorts, each divided into ten 'centuries', and they were named according to the arms which they carried (*sagittarii, scutati, contarii, funditores*, and so on). Such a cohort, called *cohors miliaria* as consisting of 1000 men, was usually *peditata*, consisting only of infantry; but it was sometimes *equitata*, when it was a mixed body of horse and foot, as the light forces in *War* were.[4] These *auxilia* were often the sole garrison of a province, especially in the east,[5] so that the Jews could not but have been familiar with them. The conclusion can hardly be avoided that these auxiliary cohorts were the model after which the 'standards' of 1000 skirmishers, posted between the ranks of the heavy infantry and emerging through 'gates in the battle-line' (W iii 7; cp. xvi 4), were drawn. This mixture of light and heavy troops as depicted in *War* is not Macedonian; it is typically Roman.[6]

The mysterious 'towers (*migdālôt*)', which are totally unknown in Greek armies and are a typically Roman device, have been thought to be the *turres ambulatoriae* used by the Romans in siege-operations;[7] these were wooden structures wheeled up to the walls of an invested city that missiles might be hurled from the upper storeys into it until positions on or near the walls were rendered untenable and the attackers could leap on to them. Such machines cannot be meant in the Scroll; this is not describing a siege, the descriptions do not tally, and the long lances are unsuitable for fighting in such a confined space. Alternatively, the 'tower' might be the 'tortoise' (*testudo*), also called a 'tower' (*turris*).[8] This was a device used by the Romans for attacking places whose walls were weak or low; the attackers approached them with the first rank holding their shields vertically in front of them while the second and third held theirs horizontally to protect them against missiles from above, like the shell of a tortoise, so that the walls could be breached under cover of them or scaled by clambering over the platform or roof formed by them. This device was known to the Jews of the 1st century A.D., since Josephus refers[9] to it twice (actually *eo nomine* in one place). Here too, however, the long lances of the *War* will have served no useful purpose, and none are

[1] Pp. 187–90.
[2] Yadin *op. cit.* 135–6.
[3] Parker *Roman Legions* 43.
[4] Yadin & Rabin *op. cit.* 181–2.
[5] Alton *op. cit.* § 723.
[6] Yadin & Rabin 161–2.
[7] Carmignac *Guerre* 131.
[8] Yadin *op. cit.* 167–80.
[9] In *War* II xix 5 § 537 (where it is called χελώνη 'tortoise'); cp. II iii 27 § 270 and VI i 3 § 27.

shown in ancient illustrations.[1] The 'tower' described here must have been rather an *ordre de bataille en carré* of which the three 'faces' (*i.e.* all but the open rear) presented a solid wall of overlapping shields against which the enemy might discharge their weapons or launch attacks to no purpose[2]; and in repelling these the long lance would be extremely useful. Such a 'tower' would cover the flanks of a legion changing position, it would enable fresh troops to be brought up and emerge through the 'gate' in order to take the enemy by surprise and throw them into confusion, and it would also support troops operating in no man's land between the opposing forces; it could also be employed in a retreat under fire.[3] A formation of this kind is perhaps the same thing as the *turris* which Cato is said to have described in his *de re militari* (now lost);[4] but the identification cannot be proved for lack of definite information.

Equally characteristic of the Roman army were the 'reserves' (*subsidia*), which were almost unknown in Greek or Macedonian armies[5] and were one of Caesar's innovations which continued into Imperial times;[6] and so, when the Sons of Light were pressed back in an engagement, the priests called up 'another formation, a reserve (*hălîfāh*) for the battle' (W xvi 12).[7]

The description of the cavalry in *War* agrees similarly but not so closely with Roman practice in the Imperial age.[8] In one Hellenistic army it had been numerous enough far to outnumber the Jews. Already however before the time of Caesar the legionary cavalry with a Roman legion of 6000 men numbered only 300 horse, and he almost abolished it, keeping only 200–100 horse with his reduced legion of 3000 men; and Josephus speaks[9] of only 120 horse with a legion under the Empire. Then, towards the end of the Republic, the legion became exclusively infantry, when its own proper cavalry was converted into mounted infantry for special duty, and the cavalry proper was made up almost entirely of auxiliary units; but under the Empire a complement of cavalry was again attached to every legion.[10] These are the conditions reflected in *War*, which has 1400 attached cavalry and 4600 independent cavalry, organized as 'wings' (W ix 11) like the Roman *alae* of cavalry with the legion, and broken up into very small units like the Roman cavalry at the end of the Republic and in the early years of the Empire.[11]

[1] Yadin *op. cit.* 173 (15).   [2] Dupont-Sommer *Écrits Esséniens* 198.
[3] Parker *Roman Legions* 256.
[4] Müller *Corpus Grammaticorum Latinorum Veterum* II 264, 716; cp. Aulus Gellius *Noctes Atticae* x 9.
[5] Tarn *op. cit.* 4, 9, 34; cp. Yadin & Rabin *op. cit.* 174.
[6] Cp. Rice Holmes *op. cit.* 587–8.   [7] Cp. Yadin *op. cit.* 160.
[8] 1 Macc. xvi. 4–7.   [9] In *War* III vi 2 § 129.
[10] Parker *op. cit.* 43 and Alton *op. cit.* §§ 713, 721.
[11] Cp. Yadin & Rabin *op. cit.* 178.

Such a battle-formation as that described in *War*, in which the infantry occupied the centre and the cavalry were posted on the flanks, was of course well known, being both Seleucid and Roman practice.[1] Yet it was not the invariable practice of Jewish commanders, since John Hyrcanus at any rate in one battle in which he was engaged did not follow it; for 'he divided the people (setting), the horsemen in the midst of the footmen'.[2] It was, however, the typical Roman formation, which in the present connection is highly instructive.[3]

In Caesar's time the Roman army marched in safe country in one long column: an *ala* of cavalry, then the legions, then auxiliary cavalry protecting flanks and rear. This order was also practically that adopted by Vespasian in the Judaean campaign, being then still customary, as Josephus expressly says.[4] In difficult country or when an attack might be expected, the army marched in four columns parallel to each other so that, if threatened, it could easily be reformed in battle-order. When it reached the point at which battle might be offered, a camp was formed as a base; here the dispositions of the troops were decided after consideration of the topography and the enemy forces. Since the organization had ceased after the Jugurthine wars (112–107 B.C.) to be manipular and came to be by cohorts, the increased size of the component units of a legion made it possible to draw up the army in one, two or three or even four lines. Caesar's usual formation was the *triplex acies*, in which four cohorts were placed in the first and three in each of the second and third ranks; when the *duplex acies* was chosen, the ten cohorts were equally divided between the two lines of battle. No order of battle is apparently known for the 1st century A.D., but Caesar's scheme was probably continued until the phalanx came back into use; Suetonius first used it against the Britons in A.D. 61, and it became the normal formation in the time of Hadrian (A.D. 117–38).[5] In the *War* the 'frontal formations' are drawn up like a Roman army marching under threat of attack, though not four but three abreast; and they are disposed as a *duplex acies* in battle, with the cavalry on the flanks.[6]

Briefly, the description of the forces, of their equipment, their composition and their manoeuvres, in *War* is that not of a Hellenistic but of the Roman army, and particularly of the Imperial period, although details of the Republican organization can still be detected in it. Even so, the description is as apt as it is accurate, except perhaps where elements from the Old Testament mar the picture; and that the *War* and Josephus, when they are in contact, can be shown to be in

---

[1] 1 Macc. iv. 7, vi. 38, ix. 11 and 2 Macc. xv. 20; Sallust *Jugurtha* xlix 6.
[2] *Ibid.* xvi. 7 (s. Abel *Livre des Maccabées* 279).
[3] Cp. Alton *op. cit.* § 733 and Parker *op. cit.* 252–6.
[4] In *War* II vi 2 §§ 115–26.   [5] Alton *op. cit.* §§ 731, 733.   [6] Pp. 176–7.

substantial agreement confirms this conclusion. To charge its author, therefore, with 'confusion in details' and to declare him 'incapable of distinguishing between what was of his own period and what had long been outmoded and given up'[1] completely misses the mark.

No Jewish writer can break away entirely from the history of his race, especially as it is told in the Scriptures, and its effect must always be considered even when it is not absolutely discounted. Naturally therefore its influence is seen in the terminology of the *War*, especially in the terms used for much of the equipment, which however often undergo or seem to undergo a subtle change of meaning: for example, the 'trumpet of assembly' does not perform exactly the function that it is said to have done in the wilderness, and the words for '(curved) dagger (*kîḏōn*)' and one of those for 'dart (*šeleṭ*)' perhaps do not denote exactly the same weapon as in the Old Testament. So too 'between-man', which is applied in the Old Testament to Goliath the Philistine 'champion' who came out between the lines to defy the Israelite army,[2] is here used for 'skirmisher', whether as posted between the ranks or as fighting between the opposed front-lines. That Goliath, however, was heavily armed does not prove that the 'between-men' in *War* were heavy infantry,[3] since the description of them proves beyond doubt that they were light infantry or skirmishers, while it was the heavy infantry who were armed somewhat like Goliath;[4] for *il faut distinguer la question d'origine et la question de valeur* and not let the one distort the other.[5] In the same way the classical word for a 'standard (*degel*)', which the Jewish colonists in Egypt in the 5th century B.C. used (just as the Romans used *vexillum*) for a military 'detachment' of unknown size,[6] here becomes the technical term for a 'cohort' of 1000 men. The numbers of the men constituting the various units, namely thousands and hundreds, fifties and tens, under their respective officers (W iv 1–5; cp. D ii 21–2 Z xv 4, and I Q *28* A i 29–ii 11) are introduced as pious echoes of the periods of the Old Testament and the Maccabaean revolt,[7] as so much in the Scrolls is;[8] for, although they are found in other armies including the Roman in some form or other, they do not entirely fit the author's military scheme. The predilection for seven, even when it is not in harmony with the author's model, is also evidence of his fondness for the Old Testament.[9] Or again, as in the military arrangements of the Old Testament and of the apocryphal literature,[10] priests play a large and often improbable part in the descriptions of the fighting in the Scrolls (W vii 9–ix 9 xvi 2–xvii 15); and this tradition

---

[1] Atkinson in *BRL* XL 295.   [2] 1 Sam. xvii. 4, 23.
[3] Atkinson *ibid*. 292.   [4] P. 173.
[5] Février in *Semitica* III 55.   [6] Cowley *Aramaic Papyri* xvi (Elephantine).
[7] *E.g.* Exod. xviii. 21, 25 (cp. Num. xxxi. 14, 48; 1 Chron. xiii. 1, xxvi. 26) and 1 Macc. iii. 5; cp. Josephus *Ant.* XII vii 3 § 301.   [8] Pp. 352–4.
[9] P. 187.   [10] *E.g.* Deut. xx. 2; 2 Chron. xiii. 12–14; 1 Macc. v. 67.

survives into the Mishnah, which speaks of 'the priests of the battle-line',[1] so that they are no ground for putting the Scrolls back into the 2nd century B.C.

That Jews such as Onias and Dositheus held important military posts under the Lagid Ptolemies early in the 2nd century B.C.,[2] whereas the whole Jewish nation was exempted on religious grounds from service in the Roman army, is well known, and it is certainly arguable that the Maccabaean leaders in the middle of the same century learnt much from the tactical knowledge of their compatriots in the armies of the Ptolemies;[3] but, even if the influence of Greek tactical works or of Cato's *de re militari* (published *c.* 175 B.C. but now lost) can be traced in *War*[4] (which is by no means certain; for the earliest tactical works have commonly been used by the latest writers, who often have nothing new to say), this may merely be something which has been handed down by tradition or learnt by study and which therefore throws no light on the date of the Scroll. What is decisive for this is the latest practice mentioned in a document such as *War*; for it cannot be dated before that event.[5]

In the Maccabaean wars the Jewish troops had been engaged only in guerilla warfare, and since then the Jews had had no opportunity of forming and training an army. Yet the author of *War* gives a quite elaborate picture of troops equipped with modern weapons and trained in modern methods of warfare; for, although much of the equipment and organization of the manoeuvres as described in the *War* can be traced back in particular details to the Old Testament or the post-Biblical works of the Maccabaean age, the general picture is that of the Roman army, whose equipment and tactical arrangements must have been tolerably well known to the Jews for some considerable time. This conclusion, however, does not mean that the composition of the *War* must be put in the Republican period; much that is described here may indeed be found in that period, but much will have continued in use far into the Imperial age, especially in outlying provinces of the Empire. Insurgents and rebels, too, are not likely to have had the most modern weapons for their use, as Josephus expressly remarks,[6] or to have been familiar with the latest tactical developments; and Josephus confesses[7] as much when he claims to have tried to train his levies in Galilee on the Roman model. He had been the first, according to his own account,[8] to see that the Roman legions owed their invincible might, to which Agrippa I had referred in his speech before the outbreak of the Revolt in A.D. 66 and which he had probably heard,[9] to

[1] Mishnah *Sota* viii 2.
[2] Josephus *Against Apion* ii 5.
[3] Février in *Semitica* III 59.
[4] Atkinson in *BJRL* XL 293–6.
[5] Yadin *op. cit.* 131.
[6] In *War* II xx 6 § 576.
[7] *Ibid.* II xx 7 §§ 578–9.
[8] *Ibid.* II xx 7 §§ 577–8.
[9] *Ibid.* II xvi 4 §§ 361–2.

their equipment, training and organization; and he began by instituting different ranks of soldiers and appointing officers of various grades over them. He called these by the Graeco-Roman titles of decurions and centurions, chiliarchs and general officers commanding legions; and the author of the *War* may have had them in mind when he spoke of similar commands in the army of the Sons of Light, although he changed them slightly to adapt them to those of the ideal units of Jewish history (W iv 1–5).

Professor M. H. Segal, seeking to assign *War* to the Maccabaean age, argues[1] that a knowledge of Roman military equipment, organization and manoeuvres, may well have reached the Jews before the 1st century A.D., brought back, for example, by members of Hasmonaean embassies sent to Rome; and, somewhat inconsistently, he goes on to urge that it is quite incredible that the author of *War* can have armed his own party, the Sons of Light, with equipment borrowed from the Roman 'Kittians' *i.e.* the sons of Belial. That Jews of the Maccabaean age may have had some knowledge of the Roman army is readily admitted; but that ambassadors are likely to have acquired detailed knowledge of it, *e.g.*, even of the size of the dagger, may be doubted and that forms of equipment, for example the *sica*, can have been discovered by them a century or so before their introduction into Rome may be safely denied. Ambassadors are not prophets! Old ideas die hard, and the date of a document depends as much on the latest as on the earliest fact or event mentioned in it. In this case, much that was old was probably retained as a link between past and present to keep alive the memory of the days before the Roman conquest in 63 B.C. and so to rekindle the ancient spirit of resistance after and in spite of the disaster of A.D. 70.[2] Further, the use of Roman equipment by the Sons of Light was but an example of turning the weapons of Belial against Belial and might well have the result of showing the party that, if they were to win the final Messianic war against Rome, they must be armed with as good and as modern weapons as the Romans.

Further, the author of the *War* is not a military historian but an apocalyptist describing an imaginary war depicted in terms of more or less recent or contemporary history, as it must of necessity be. In such cases it must be the author of the *War*, not Josephus, who is borrowing from the other, if indeed either is a borrower; for the practical training of troops in the field by an experienced officer would not be based on an apocalypse, whereas an apocalyptist might derive his information from a historian with military experience. Neither however is likely to have drawn anything directly from the other; yet the sober historian and the apocalyptic historian agree on many

[1] In *Scr. Hieros.* IV 143.   [2] Pp. 369–73.

military points. Such correspondences however as occur, being too close to be the result of chance, must reflect the same background; that can only be the First Revolt of A.D. 66–70 or 73. Josephus obviously obtained his information of this revolt partly from his own experiences in Galilee in the winter of A.D. 66–7 and partly from his acquaintance with the Romans, including their commanders, to whom he eventually went over. Contrariwise, the author of *War* could have had no personal experience of it; otherwise he would not be likely to have filled his account with such palpable absurdities, which can only have come from the history and literature of his nation. He might, however, easily have obtained all the information that he required for his purpose from conversation with or inquiry amongst members of his party who were fighting or had fought in the Revolt. In any case a work must be as late as the latest event or object described in it; the *sica* therefore brings the *War* down to a date after A.D. 55–60, when events are already beginning to advance inexorably towards the Revolt, and the method of signalling with trumpets, which Josephus claims to have introduced to the Jews, brings it down to *c.* A.D. 66–7, when he is training the Jewish levies in Galilee. The *War* therefore must reflect this Revolt,[1] whether it was composed during it or after its suppression; and reasons will be given below for preferring a date after it.[2]

3. KITTIANS OF ASSHUR AND KITTIANS IN EGYPT

The principal external enemy both in the *Commentary on Habakkuk* and in the *War*, described generally as a 'nation of wickedness' and as 'sons of darkness' or 'sons of Belial', are the 'Kittians', particularized as the 'Kittians of Asshur' and the 'Kittians in Egypt' (W i 2, 4); and their exact identification, geographically and historically, is of the greatest importance for the proper understanding of the Scrolls.

By origin 'Kittians' denotes the Cypriots, whose principal town was Citium (Kition);[3] but the name came to be applied loosely in the Old Testament to the inhabitants of the Mediterranean islands and coast-lands, and long afterwards it was used for[4] the people of the Phoenician coastal plain. It was also at times extended to include the Romans (which the ancient Versions often have)[5] and the Macedonians.[6] In the same way 'Asshur', which was properly Assyria, acquired an extended connotation in which Syria (which was a shortened form of

---

[1] Cp. Yadin *op. cit.* 222–7.   [2] Pp. 369–71.
[3] Josephus *Antiquities* I vi 1 § 128 and Migne *Patrol. Lat.* XXIII 1001/318 (Jerome *in Genesim* x 4).
[4] Eustathius *Commentarii in Homeri Iliadem* i 349 (K 409).
[5] Num. xxiv. 24 (Vulgate, Targum), Ezek. xxvii. 6 (Vulgate), 1 Chron. i. 7 (Targum), Dan. xi 30 (Septuagint, Vulgate); cp. Midrash R. *Genesis* xxxvii § 1.
[6] 1 Macc. i. 1, viii. 5 and Jubilees xxiv 28; Josephus *Antiquities* XI viii 4 § 326.

O

the same name) was included;[1] and it came also to be used occasionally for Rome,[2] which would however be out of the question if the identification of the Kittians with the Romans, as here maintained, should be accepted.

In view of these facts the 'Kittians of Asshur' have been taken for the Seleucid Greeks. Linguistically the suggestion is free from objection and superficially it is attractive; for the most part therefore it has been accepted without question or discussion. Mrs. Atkinson, however, has gone further and sought to prove[3] it by two arguments. First, following Dr. Gaster,[4] she translates the Hebrew words for 'pen (ḥereṭ) of life' (W xii 3) as 'charter (χάρτης) of life'[5] and, claiming this term as a 'significant Greek loan-word', argues that *War* must have been written in the Seleucid Greek period, in which it makes its first appearance. Unfortunately for this argument, the word here used has been confused with another of similar form but from a different root found in an expression meaning 'memorial inscription (ḥereṭ)' (TH i 24); this comes from an Aramaic verb occurring once in the Old Testament and also elsewhere in the Scrolls (D x 6, 8, 11 W xii 3).[6] As its root is widespread in the Semitic languages, a noun derived from it must be a genuine Semitic word, not a Greek loan-word. Further, even if this noun had been a Greek word, it would not necessarily prove a Seleucid date for any text which had it, as χάρτης was current both in Egypt in the 3rd–2nd centuries B.C.[7] and in Palestine in the 1st century A.D.[8], so that it was then well known. Second, she argues that the influence of the Greek tactical writers is so 'clearly traceable' in *War* that it can have been composed only in the Seleucid period. Reasons however have been given for suspecting that this influence may have been over-estimated; but, even if it has been correctly assessed, important writers impress their mark on others long after their own times, and the mark of these very writers can be traced in other works far into the Imperial age. The tactical authors chiefly cited (the Greek Asclepiodotus *c.* 100 B.C. and Onosander *c.* A.D. 50; the Roman Vegetius *c.* A.D. 400) cover a period of 500 years. Onosander describes many of the military practices found in the *War*,[9] whose author may have drawn his accounts of them from similar sources soon afterwards; Vegetius put his *Epitoma Rei Militaris* together from the

[1] Herodotus *Histories* vii 63 and Septuagint at Jer. xxxv. [xlii.] 2; cp. Jubilees xii 1 xlvi 6 (s. Zeitlin in *JQR*, NS XLI 61) and Lucian *de dea Syria* § 1 *alq.*
[2] *E.g.* Midrash R. *Genesis* xvi. § 4.   [3] In *BJRL* XL 280.
[4] In *Scriptures* 296 (s. Zeitlin in *JQR*, NS XLIX 30).
[5] Cp. Psa. lxix. 29 and 1 Enoch cviii. 3.   [6] Pp. 543–4.
[7] Is. viii 1 and Jer. xxxvi (xliii) 2, 6, 23 (Septuagint).   [8] 2 Jn. 12.
[9] For example *Strategicus* xvii (light-armed troops, javelin-throwers, archers and slingers, stationed in front of the legion), xix (gaps in the line for the light-armed troops to fall back), xxii (reserves), xxvi 1 (burying the dead), xxvi 2 (encouragement in defeat).

works of his predecessors, often displaying so little skill that the practices described by him can be assigned to no certain nation or period,
and the author of the *War* may have been equally imprecise in military
matters. The *terminus a quo* for this Scroll can be fixed only by reference
to some practice of which the introduction into Palestine can be
absolutely dated, *e.g.* the introduction of a new weapon such as the
sica[1] or of a new custom like signalling with trumpets;[2] the *terminus
ante quem* can be similarly determined only by reference to some
practice which is known to have been abandoned at a definite date
and thereafter to have passed out of human memory, and none is
known. Neither argument therefore offers any logical reason for
holding the Kittians to be the Seleucid Greeks.

This reasoning is supported by the impossibility of finding any
event comparable in all its aspects with the outrage on the Day of
Atonement to which the *Commentary on Habakkuk* alludes (H xi 4–8) in
the Seleucid period; it can only be so identified with a similar event
which Josephus describes in some detail as having happened at the
beginning of the war with Rome,[3] so that the enemy there called
Kittians must be the Romans of the Imperial age. This conclusion is
supported by three cogent and one clinching argument: first, it is
said that 'they come from afar, from the isles and coasts of the sea'
(H iii 10–11), by which not neighbouring Syria but distant Rome
must be meant, and that 'they consume the peoples like an eagle'
(H iii 11), which seems to be an allusion to the Roman eagles[4]; second,
the 'king of the Kittians' (W xv 2) cannot be any Greek or Seleucid
king since these are called 'kings of Greece' (Z ix 20);[5] and, third, a
fragment of a Scroll containing a *Commentary on Nahum* confirms this
conclusion by showing that the 'kings of Greece' (*i.e.* the Seleucid
Demetrius and Antiochus, both of whom it names) must have preceded
'the rulers of the Kittians' (ANa. iv 3). The Kittians, then, cannot have
been the Seleucid Greeks; they can only have been some or other of
their successors, *e.g.* the Romans. Consequently Prof. Dupont-Sommer's
attempt to take the 'Kittians of Asshur' as the Seleucid dynasty and the
'Kittians in Egypt' as the Ptolemies fails.[6] This identification is also
open to the improbability that 'Kittians', even when the term was
qualified by describing them respectively as 'of Asshur' and 'in Egypt',
could designate two different dynasties who were not of the same race
or family; and it would be intolerably awkward when the qualifying
terms were omitted, as they almost always are. That it sometimes

---

[1] Pp. 184–7, 196–7.
[2] Pp. 181–2.
[3] Pp. 267–81.
[4] P. 453.
[5] Cp. Dupont-Sommer *Écrits* 354–6.
[6] Cp. Allegro in *JBL* LXXV 93 and Burrows in *Oudt. Stud.* VIII 186–7.

designates also the Romans, as Prof. Dupont-Sommer holds,[1] only increases the confusion and therewith the improbability.

The only possible solution of the riddle is to assume that 'Kittians' designates the Romans wherever it occurs in the Scrolls; and this equation will be seen to satisfy all the conditions implicit or explicit in them.

The fragment of the *Commentary on Nahum* cited above speaks of 'the rulers of the Kittians', *i.e.* of the Romans, and the answer to the question who these 'rulers (*môšᵉlîm*)' are will provide one clue indicating whether Republican or Imperial Romans are meant. Here the *Commentary on Habakkuk* affords a vital piece of information, when it describes 'the rulers of the Kittians, who by the counsel of a guilty house pass on each before his peer; their rulers one after another come to destroy the earth' or 'the land' (H iv 10–13); the import therefore both of 'rulers' and of 'house' in this connection must be carefully considered.

The 'guilty house' has been supposed to be the Roman Senate of the late Republican period and the 'rulers' have then been taken to be the proconsuls whom it or occasionally the people sent out to govern the provinces; for the havoc which they wrought was notorious long before the end of the Republic.[2] The application of such an expression as 'guilty house' to Senate or people, however, is most improbable; for neither was drawn from a single house or family nor was ever so designated. The identification, however, has been buttressed by the suggestion that the Hebrew word here translated 'counsel' means rather 'council' (*'ēṣāh*)'; this would *ex hypothesi* exclude the Imperial period, when the Emperor himself appointed these officers.[3] This argument, too, has little force. The Hebrew word nowhere necessarily has a concrete denotation; in the Old Testament it means only 'counsel' and in the Scrolls it can always be rendered 'counsel' or 'deliberation(s)', and no passage can be found where it must unequivocally connote 'council' in the sense of a deliberative body.[4] If too the 'house' is the Senate, the addition of 'council' is otiose; the word must therefore mean 'counsel'. Further, from Pompey's capture of Jerusalem in 63 B.C. Syria was under a legate (whose correct title was *legatus Augusti pro praetore*). These officers followed one another in almost annual succession, Judaea was left under its own rulers (Hyrcanus II 63–40 B.C., and Antigonus 40–37 B.C.; Herod 37–4 B.C. and Archelaus 4 B.C.–A.D. 6), until the series of procurators began. These four persons between them ruled the country for nearly seventy years, which argues no rapid succession, and they did little damage; they can therefore hardly be recognized in another passage of the *Commentary* which speaks of 'the rulers of the Kittians, who despise the fortresses of the peoples and with mockery make sport of them; and they surround them with

[1] S. p. 154.
[3] Atkinson in *JSS* IV 240–4.
[2] Segal in *JBL* LXX 134.
[4] Cp. Elliger *Habakuk-Kommentar* 174.

a vast host to seize them . . . and they overthrow them because of the iniquity of those who dwell in them' (H iv 5–9). Lastly, these rulers were the representatives of a people 'who are trampling the land with [their] horses and their beasts of burden' (H iii 9–10). All this does not fit what is known of the Roman provincial governors at the end of the Republican period. Gabinius suppressed a small rising near Mt. Tabor in 57–6 B.C. and Crassus took a large sum of money from the Temple in 54 B.C.; and, when Caesar made Palestine a client-state in 40 B.C., the proconsuls ceased almost entirely to interfere in its affairs. That the same word for 'rulers (mšlm)' is a designation of the tribunes of the people in a Phoenician inscription of 8 B.C.[1] in itself proves nothing; but Jewish practice, by which the emperor and his officers are called 'rulers' (môšᵉlîm),[2] is decisive for the possibility of this usage in the Scrolls.

Dr. Vermès therefore must be right[3] in taking the 'guilty house' to be the house or family of the Caesars, which is often called the *domus Caesarum* by Latin writers of the 1st century A.D.; some of the persons so described are Augustus and Tiberius and the five Caesars together.[4] Even the emperors who followed the original Caesars, though not themselves sprung from that family, were called Caesars, *e.g.* Vespasian and Titus.[5] At the same time 'house' must not be so pressed as to restrict it to the Imperial household, *i.e.* the freedmen and favourites who played so large a part under the emperors during the 1st century A.D., even though the procurator Felix owed his appointment to a brother who belonged to this class;[6] it is simply a general term for the Imperial palace as the seat or centre of government, of which the commentator is not likely to have had any detailed knowledge. The 'rulers' then sent out by the 'guilty house', *i.e.* the emperors whether they were Caesars by blood or not, would be the legates or the pro-curators, whom they despatched to govern Palestine. There they followed each other in rapid succession, each outdoing the other in wickedness; such were the procurators Cuspius Fadus (A.D. 44–?) who was the best of them, Tiberius Alexander (A.D. ?–48) who had the two sons of Judah son of Hezekiah crucified,[7] Ventidius Cumanus (A.D. 48–52) who provoked three uprisings against his authority, Felix (A.D. 52–60) under whom rebellion became permanent, Porcius Festus (A.D. 60–2) who proved himself incapable of undoing the mischief wrought by his predecessors, Albinus (A.D. 62–4) whose guiding principle was the enrichment of himself by every means in

[1] Levi della Vida in *Africa Italiana* VI 4 (s. 8–9); cp. Atkinson in *JSS* IV 243–4.
[2] S. p. 202 n. 1.
[3] In *Cah. Sion.* v 65 and *Manuscrits* 86; cp. Teicher in *JJS* V 51.
[4] Tacitus *Annals* I x 5 and IV iii 1, Suetonius *Galba* 2.
[5] Pliny *Natural History* VII xlix 162.   [6] Atkinson in *JSS* IV 242–3.
[7] Josephus *Antiquities* XX v 2 § 102.

his power, and lastly Gessius Florus (A.D. 64-6) whose unbounded tyranny provoked the final outbreak terminating in the utter destruction of Jerusalem. The term would also include the legates sent on special missions; of these the best known were Vespasian, whom Nero appointed to suppress the incipient revolt in A.D. 66-7, and Titus who finally quelled it in A.D. 70. It would be singularly suitable to the last two, who each in turn became Emperor; for it was freely applied to the emperors in Rabbinic literature.[1]

A point, however, of great significance is the mention of 'the king of the Kittians' (W xv 2). This proves that the 'rulers (*môš͏elîm*)' cannot be the emperors[2] but must be the procurators, and it disproves the identification of the Kittians with the Republican Romans; they can therefore only have been those of the Imperial age.[3]

In the Scrolls 'wicked (*rāšā'*)' and 'wickedness (*reša', riš'āh*)' are terms frequently applied to the enemy. So the period preceding the appearance of the Messiah is the 'period of wickedness' (Z viii 9, xv 4; cp. Z viii 12, xix 7; H v 8), and the author of various hymns exclaims 'my feet stood in the region of wickedness' (T ii 12) and that 'snares of wickedness' were laid to catch him (T iii 36) while the '(most) wicked of peoples (?)'[4] hastened against him (T v 17), and he thanks God for his deliverance from 'wars of wickedness' (T vii 7; cp. vi 29); the enemy are similarly called a 'nation of wickedness' (W xiv 7), and the purpose of the war is 'to strike down wickedness' (W i 13; cp. iii 9) or 'to requite wickedness' (W xi 13-14), and at its end 'all nations of wickedness (*i.e.* the enemy and their allies) will be finished' (W xiv 7; cp. xv 2). Lastly, the Kittians are described figuratively as 'wickedness' (W xi 10-12), the 'nation of wickedness' stands parallel to 'king of the Kittians', when the final destruction of both is promised (W xv 2); and their commander is 'captain of the dominion of wickedness' (W xvii 2). Primarily 'wicked' and 'wickedness' here as elsewhere in the Scrolls import moral wickedness, but they gain added significance when considered in the light of Rabbinic literature; for there both terms regularly connote Rome and the Romans. So, on the one hand, the early Rabbis speak of 'Rome the wicked which is builded in Italy'[5] and *tout simple* of the 'kingdom of wickedness' for the Roman empire[6] and of the 'rulers of wickedness' for the Roman emperors or their subordinate officers;[7] and Titus, whom the *Sibylline Oracles* without naming him already call an 'unholy[8] king', is similarly designated 'the wicked

[1] *E.g.* B. Talmud Mishnah *Yadaim* iv 8 and Gemara *Baba Qamma* 38a (var. *mal̲k̲ût̲*).
[2] P. 201.   [3] Vermès *Scrolls* 123.
[4] Cp. Dupont-Sommer *Hymnes* 48⁶.
[5] Targum on Lam. iv. 22.
[6] *E.g.* Midrash R. *Genesis* ii. § 4 (s. Freedman & Simon *Midrash Rabba: Genesis* I 17⁵) and Exod. ix. § 13; B. Talmud *Berakhoth* 61b, *Shabbath* 130a (where a *quaestor* is mentioned), *Gittin* 57b, *Baba Qamma* 38a; Buber *Pesikta* 51a.
[7] *E.g.* B. Talmud *Baba Qamma* 38a (s. Jastrow *Dictionary* II 855).
[8] Geffchen *Oracula Sibyllina* 124 v 108.

one' in Jewish literature of diverse periods.[1] At the same time 'kingdom (*malkût*)' is used alone for the Roman empire apparently in the Scrolls (W xii 15 [?]) and often by the Rabbis;[2] and the Roman emperor is called by them 'king (*melek̲, malkâ*)', notably in the present connection both Vespasian and Titus.[3] On the other hand, these terms were apparently (for a negative proposition is hard to prove) never applied to any other enemy nation than the Romans before the 9th century A.D., when the Seleucid kingdom came to be called 'the wicked kingdom of Greece' (*malkût̲ Yāwān hārᵉšā'āh*).[4] Few therefore will doubt the possibility, even the certainty, that the authors of the Scrolls in their constant harping on these terms are but following common Rabbinic practice and are referring to the great war with Rome.

The Kittians are distinguished in the *War*, though not in the *Commentary on Habakkuk*, as the 'Kittians of Asshur' and the 'Kittians in Egypt' (W i 2, 4). No explanation of these two expressions is permissible which does not recognize that 'Kittians' must designate basically the same people, whoever that may be, in both expressions; the descriptive terms therefore must refer to two branches or groups of the same people. There is only one occasion within the prescribed period when such an equation is possible. In the winter of A.D. 66–7 Nero, alarmed at the reports of unrest reaching him from Palestine, ordered his most experienced military commander Vespasian to proceed to the East, there to assume command of the Vth and Xth legions and allied troops stationed in Syria and to take all necessary measures to suppress the revolt. Before leaving Achaea, where he was in attendance on the emperor, Vespasian despatched his son Titus to Egypt to fetch the XVth legion, which was in garrison at Alexandria, and any available auxiliary troops to join him in Palestine. Titus having reached Egypt after an unusually quick journey, mobilized the troops in that country and advanced by a forced march to Ptolemais (Acco), where his father soon joined him with the two legions from Antioch and considerable other troops and allied contingents.[5] The conclusion is difficult to resist that the 'Kittians of Asshur' (namely Syria, as said above)[6] means Vespasian's two Roman legions and the allied contingents based on Antioch and that the 'Kittians in Egypt' means the one legion and other troops stationed there whom Titus[7] brought from Egypt.

At this point a recently published fragment of a *Commentary on Isaiah*,

---

[1] *E.g.* Midrash R. *Exodus* ix § 13, *Leviticus* xxii § 3, *Numbers* xviii § 2, *Ecclesiastes* v § 4; B. Talmud *Gittin* 56b.
[2] *E.g.* Mishnah *Sotah* ix 15.
[3] Midrash R. *Lamentations* I v 31 and B. Talmud *Gittin* 56a–b (Vespasian); Schechter *Aboth dR. Nathan* 4 (Titus); Midrash *Genesis* lxiii § 8 and P. Talmud *Terumoth* 46b–c (Diocletian).
[4] Frumkin *Seder R. Amram* II 163, 2.
[5] Josephus *War* III i 3 §§ 6–8, iv 2 § 64, v 2 § 115.
[6] Pp. 197–8.   [7] Cp. Yadin & Rabin *Scroll* 258.

to which Dr. Roth[1] has drawn attention, is of some interest. The Commentator, after quoting the prophet's account of the Assyrian invaders' progress from Aiath to Jerusalem,[2] interprets it in the light of the events of his own time 'when he went up from the vale of Acco to fight against [the Jews] and up to the frontier of Jerusalem' (AFl. c iii 3–11). The antecedent to the pronoun is unfortunately missing, so that several possibilities lie open. Demetrius I Soter[3] cannot be meant;[4] for, although he was invited soon after his accession in 162 B.C. by the hellenizing party in Jerusalem to come and put an end to their oppression by their Maccabaean rivals, he himself made no attempt to go there in person but sent Nicanor with sufficient troops to enforce his will.[5] Demetrius III Eucerus[6] c. 88 B.C. advanced with an army to Shechem where he defeated Alexander Jannaeus but did not go on to enter Jerusalem, possibly because he was then also at war with his brother Philip.[7] Although, however, either Demetrius may be described as one 'who sought to enter Jerusalem by the counsel of the Seekers after Smooth Things' (ANa I 2), both periods are out of the question on general grounds.[8] Cestius Gallus, whom Dr. Hengel suggests,[9] actually forced his way into Bezetha, the northern suburb of Jerusalem, in the autumn of A.D. 66, but failed to take the temple-mount and fell back into a retreat which ended in disaster;[10] but Acco was only one stage in the route which he had taken (Antioch, Chabulon, Acco, Caesarea, Joppa, Antipatris, Lydda, Gibeon, Jerusalem), and the fragment gives no hint that the person to whom it refers not only entered Jerusalem but was also thrown out of it. The only other suitable occasion to which the Commentator can be alluding, as Dr. Roth has seen, must be Vespasian's advance on Jerusalem in A.D. 67–8. In A.D. 67 Vespasian, so soon as Titus had reached him at Ptolemais (Acco) with reinforcements from Egypt, 'being eager to invade Galilee' marched out of that city and pressed the campaign until early in A.D. 68 he was 'investing those in Jerusalem'; then 'after reducing the whole neighbourhood of Jerusalem' he returned to Caesarea and, being shortly afterwards proclaimed emperor on receipt of the news that Vitellius had been murdered, proceeded to Egypt and thence took ship for Rome.[11] He can therefore be properly said to have gone 'as far as the frontier of Jerusalem' and no further. Thus Vespasian inaugurated and Titus carried on the siege of Jerusalem and brought it to a successful con-

---

[1] In *Background* 35–6.   [2] Isa. x. 27–32; s. Burrows in *VT* VII 104–5.
[3] Rowley *Apocalyptic* 26; s. *JBL* LXXV 188–93 and *BJRL* XL 114–46.
[4] Cp. Cross *Library* 93–4.   [5] Josephus *Antiquities* XII x 4 § 402–5 § 412.
[6] Allegro in *JBL* LXXV 92.
[7] Josephus *Antiquities* XIII xiv 1 § 377–3 § 384 and *War* I iv 4 § 92–5 § 95 (s. Schürer *Geschichte*[3] I 282–3).
[8] Pp. 136–49, 288–93.   [9] In *Zeloten* 289–91.
[10] Josephus *War* II xviii 9 § 499–xix 9 § 555.
[11] *Ibid.* III vi 2 § 115 and IV ix 1 §§ 486–90, 2 §§ 588–91, xi 5 §§ 656–8.

clusion; their activities therefore exactly agree with those attributed in the *Commentary on Habakkuk* to 'the rulers of the Kittians, who despise the fortresses of the people . . . and surround them with a vast host to seize them, and they (*sc.* the inhabitants) are delivered into their hands in fear and dread; and they (*sc.* the rulers of the Kittians) overthrow them because of the iniquity of those who dwell in them' (H iv 5–9). During all this time, too, the Pharisees were for the most part 'seekers after smooth things', *i.e.* pro-Roman appeasers,[1] thus completing the comparison between the two pictures, in which Demetrius merely prefigures Vespasian.

The Commentator brings this event into connection with 'the end of the days' (AFl. c i 8). This is a phrase found often enough in the Old Testament, where it is applied to various historical events and especially to the Messianic age conceived as following the close of the existing order of things; and in the book of *Daniel* it refers now to the Macedonian empire and now to the Seleucid kingdom.[2] It is therefore not confined to any single epoch; and in the Scrolls it denotes the period when the Messiah will appear and bring victory to his people over their enemies. This may here be the victorious outcome of revolt against Rome, of which the date is inevitably postponed when it collapses in irretrievable disaster.[3]

Dr. Roth brings[4] another piece of a *Commentary on Isaiah* into connection with the same period. This sets out the prophecy that 'he shall cut down the thickets of the forest with iron, and Lebanon shall fall by a mighty one'[5] and explains it by saying that 'Israel and the humble ones . . . will be dismayed and [their hearts] will melt . . .; they are the warriors of the Kit[tians] . . .; by the hand of his great one[s] . . . Jerusalem, on his flight from before . . .' (AFl. c iii 3–9). The explanation of this passage by referring it to Vespasian is at first sight not obvious and may be thought strained; but what makes it worthy of consideration is that the Talmud refers[6] this very same passage of Isaiah to Vespasian's departure from his camp before Jerusalem on hearing of Nero's death. This was not in fact the occasion of Vespasian's departure[7] but is near enough to that event to satisfy Talmudic methods of interpretation; and the commentator's description of Vespasian's hurried withdrawal as a 'flight' is equally inaccurate.

The interpretation of these two texts is in their imperfect state of preservation extremely difficult, and the allusions to Vespasian uncertain; even however if they are here rightly taken, they cannot be used as definite evidence, although they may have some value as straws showing which way the wind blows.

---

[1] P. 94.
[2] Dan. ii. 28, x. 14 (s. S. R. Driver *Daniel* 26, 159).
[3] Pp. 474–5.
[4] In *Background* 37–8.
[5] Isa. x. 34; S. pp. 458–60.
[6] In *Gittin* 56a–b.
[7] Josephus *War* IV x 4 § 604.

In the *War* the principal enemy of the Sons of Light are the 'Kittians of Asshur' (namely Syria), while the 'Kittians in Egypt' drop out. The reason is obvious. Titus was the subordinate commander, and he brought only one legion with him; when therefore he effected a junction with Vespasian at Ptolemais, his command lapsed and his force, the inferior, was merged with the two legions which his father had brought from Antioch. When Vespasian left Palestine and Titus assumed the command, the 'Kittians' remained a single force under him with its base at Antioch, while Alexandria fell out of the picture. This picture, so far from disagreeing,[1] is in exact accord with that which the author[2] of the *War* draws. He speaks of a war 'first' with the neighbouring nations and the 'Kittians of Asshur' (W i 1–2), then 'after that war' of an advance against the 'Kittians in Egypt' (W i 3–4), and finally of an attack 'in due time' on 'the kings of the north' when 'Asshur shall fall and the dominion of the Kittians shall pass away' (W i 4–6). Exactly so, Vespasian advanced first from his Syrian headquarters, Titus joined him from Egypt, and their two forces were merged in a single army; and eventually a number of Syrian kinglets joined them.[3]

All the details concerning the Kittians in the *Commentary on Habakkuk* fit the identification with the Imperial Romans to perfection. The only objection which has been brought against this identification is that it contains no mention of or even allusion to the capture of Jerusalem by the Romans.[4] One reason for this omission would be that the principal theme of the *Commentary* is the quarrel between the Rightful Teacher and the Wicked Priest which, as argued below,[5] took place in A.D. 66, whereas Jerusalem was not taken till A.D. 70. The real answer to the objection, however, is that the description of the Kittians as 'sacrificing to their standards' (H vi 3–4) is in fact an allusion to that event, so terrible that no direct mention of it is possible.[6]

The Commentator in describing the Kittians says that 'they come from afar, from the coastlands' or 'islands of the sea' (H iii 10–11). These in the Old Testament and the apocryphal literature are the coastlands and islands of the Mediterranean sea, such as the Syro-Phoenician coast, Cyprus and Rhodes, Asia Minor and Macedonia; Greece and Italy, too, are included in these 'coastlands' by Rabbinic tradition.[7] The addition, however, of 'from afar' excludes the Syro-Phoenician coast,[8] which is the nearest of all these lands and islands to Palestine, even if the term is extended to include the Aegaean islands.[9] Further, although the Seleucids hired mercenary troops from 'the isles of the seas',[10] they could not be said themselves to come 'from afar';

---

[1] Cp. Driver in *JTS*, NS X 121 and XI 368–9.   [2] Rowley in *VT* IX 384–5.
[3] Pp. 219–20.   [4] Cp. Schonfield *Secrets* 102.   [5] Pp. 267–81.
[6] Pp. 211–15.   [7] Vulgate and Targum at Isa. lxix. 19 and Ezek. xxvii. 7.
[8] Michel *Maître* 135–6.   [9] Vermès *Manuscrits* 86.
[10] 1 Macc. vi. 29.

and no world-conquerors came from any of the other places within the historical limits within which the Scrolls must be dated except the Romans.[1] The Romans of the Hellenistic period cannot be meant; Judas the Maccabee found that 'they are valiant men and have pleasure in all that join themselves unto them and make amity with all such as come unto them',[2] whereas the Kittians are depicted as evil, avaricious and rapacious, cruel and ruthless. Those who are meant, therefore, must be the Romans of the Republican or Imperial age.

The Commentator then says that the enemy are 'swift and men of valour in battle, overthrowing [rulers who are brought under] the dominion of the Kittians' (H ii 12–14). The allusion here is surely not to the Seleucids but to the Romans; the Seleucids were hardly great conquerors or famous soldiers, although their cavalry may have given them mobility and speed, which however the use of elephants must have much impaired;[3] and no ancient author praises them for these qualities. Contrariwise the Romans, not the Seleucid Greeks, were the typical warriors of antiquity, and Josephus describes the legions as 'always swift to act' and speaks once or twice of the rapid movement of Roman troops.[4] Swiftness of movement, however, is as much part of the apocalyptic imagery in which the Commentator clothes the scene as actual fact; so the prophet, on whose work he is commenting, speaking of the Chaldaeans, calls them a 'hasty nation' and says that 'they fly as an eagle' (where the commentator may have seen an allusion to the Roman eagles), introducing a poetical figure found elsewhere in the Old Testament.[5] Again, the Commentator says of the Kittians that 'in counsel all their scheming is to do evil and with guile and deceit they proceed with all peoples' (H iii 5–6). The author of I Maccabees often cites instances of Seleucid bad faith[6], and this was also an ancient charge brought by Greeks against Romans.[7] It is however a charge that one nation always brings against another when they are at war.[8] Consequently, that Josephus happens to say nothing of Roman guile, although he often speaks of the ruses used by his compatriots against them in the course of the Revolt, has no significance.

The Kittians are also described as 'spreading their yoke and their tribute, (the burden of supplying) their food, on every people year by year, 'laying waste many' or 'great lands' (H vi 6–8). These words clearly refer to the burdens laid on the Jews not in all probability by the Seleucids but rather by the Romans; but an important point which

[1] Cp. Dupont-Sommer *Manuscrits* 35–6.   [2] 1 Macc. viii. 1–2.
[3] *E.g.* 1 Macc. i. 18.
[4] In *War* III v 7 § 106; cp. II xviii 10 § 503 and III iv 2 § 64.
[5] Hab. i. 6, 8; cp. Jer. iv. 13, xlviii. 40, xlix. 22.
[6] 1 Macc. i. 30, vi. 61–2, vii. 27–9, xi. 53, xii. 42–8, xiii. 14–19, xv. 27; cp. vii. 10.
[7] Cp. Livy *ab urbe condita* XXXIV xxiii 5–10.   [8] Cp. Michel *Maître* 132–3.

must be decided at the same time is whether the reference is to Republican or Imperial Rome.

The Ptolemies indeed collected tribute in cash from the cities of Palestine,[1] and the Seleucids from time to time made similar exactions both in cash and in kind and also demanded forced labour from their Jewish subjects,[2] as proved by special decrees by which exemptions and remissions were occasionally granted,[3] until Simon finally won release from all such impositions;[4] but the Seleucids can hardly be described as also 'laying waste many' or 'great lands'.

The Romans in 63 B.C. levied a fine of 10,000 talents on Jerusalem;[5] but this was a special imposition and not a tax levied 'year by year' and so does not justify the claim that 'the only possible way of accounting for the statements on the subject of tribute in the *Commentary* seems to be to assign its composition to the very end of the Hasmonaean period, after the Roman conquest had begun in 63 B.C. but before the final ratification of Pompey's *acta* by the Senate in 59 B.C.'.[6] The earliest reference to any form of regular taxation appears to be in Caesar's decree of 44 B.C. regularizing some dues, reducing others and prohibiting military exactions;[7] but these must soon have lapsed, when Palestine came under the rule of the Herodian family (37 B.C.–A.D. 6). A regular Roman taxation did not begin before A.D. 6–7, when Quirinius made the 'first enrolment', *i.e.* the first general valuation for purposes of taxation to which Judaea had been subjected by the Romans;[8] and this (if rightly dated) was when Judah the Galilaean rebuked his countrymen 'for consenting to pay tribute to the Romans' and raised the rebellion in which he met his end.[9] So too Tacitus tells[10] how in A.D. 17 *provinciae Syria ac Judaea, fessae oneribus, deminutionem tributi orabant*, which on one occasion they obtained. Throughout this period references to Roman tax-collectors become a common-place of contemporary literature.[11] Duties on exports and imports, and especially a tax levied in the markets of Jerusalem, which Herod had imposed and which Vitellius abolished on a visit to Jerusalem by way of winning favour with the Jews,[12] were another recurring source of irritation in the 1st century A.D. These burdens are recalled in Agrippa's reminder to the Jews in A.D. 66, on the eve of the Revolt, that Bithynians, Cappadocians and Pamphylians, Syrians and Cilicians, all alike paid tribute to Rome, that a third part of the inhabited world comprising all the nations along the Mediterranean shores sent tribute

---

[1] Josephus *Antiquities* XII iv 5 §§ 181–4.   [2] *Ibid.* XIII viii 3 §§ 246–7.
[3] *Ibid.* XIII ii 3 §§ 49–52 and iv § 128; cp. 1 Macc. x. 29–30 and xi. 28, 35–6.
[4] *Ibid.* XIII vi 7 § 213; cp. 1 Macc. xiii. 39.   [5] *Ibid.*XIV iv 5 § 78.
[6] Atkinson in *JSS* 244–6.   [7] Josephus *Antiquities* XIV x 5 § 201–6 § 207.
[8] Schürer *Geschichte*[3] I 510–43.   [9] Pp. 240–1.
[10] In *Annals* II xlii 7.   [11] Schürer *op. cit.* 473–9.
[12] Josephus *Antiquities* XVII viii 4 §§ 204–5 XVIII iv 3 § 90.

of all kinds in addition to their 'annual produce (ἐτεησίων καρπῶν)' contributed for eight months in every year to feed the populace of Rome, and that Egypt similarly paid a monthly tribute which exceeded the 'yearly tribute (ἐνιαύσιον φόρον)' of the Jews.[1] These words would not be exactly what Agrippa said but what Josephus put into his mouth long afterwards and so would reflect what people were then thinking and saying; and the Commentator would know and would have shared such opinions.

The laying waste of whole countries by the Kittians can also be assigned to the same period. Pompey's lieutenant Aemilius Scaurus indeed in 62 B.C. requisitioned corn in Palestine for the maintenance of the Roman army,[2] but equally Cestius in the course of the first campaign after the outbreak of the Revolt in the late autumn of A.D. 66 'sent out numerous foraging parties to the surrounding villages to collect corn' for his troops;[3] and throughout the war the Romans, in accordance with their reputation as *raptores orbis* who *ubi solitudinem faciunt pacem appellant*,[4] ravaged the country from end to end.

The Commentator, describing these same Kittians, tells also how '[on hills and] in level country they proceed to destroy and despoil the cities of the land' (H iii 1). The destruction of cities was not a characteristic operation of the Seleucid armies, although they were not unacquainted with siege-craft; these were rarely if ever compelled to reduce cities in Palestine by force of arms but the most part passed by them, if they were not bought off or received with open arms.[5] Again, Pompey in his campaign against Jerusalem destroyed no cities and did little material damage to Jerusalem itself and actually rebuilt a number of places which had fallen into ruins.[6] Scaurus was bought off by Aretas, so that Petra and the neighbouring towns were spared;[7] Gabinius reduced three fortresses by siege but did no damage to any other places and indeed, like Pompey, rebuilt a number of ruined places;[8] and Crassus, although he turned aside from the Parthian campaign to despoil the Temple in Jerusalem, did no other damage to any Judaean towns or villages.[9] Quite otherwise was the conduct of the Roman commanders in suppressing the Revolt in A.D. 66–73. In the late autumn of A.D. 66 Cestius Gallus and his legate Caesennius Gallus took six towns and numerous villages, plundering them and setting them on fire and killing any inhabitants whom they found;[10] only Sepphoris

[1] Josephus *War* II xvi 4 §§ 368, 382–6.
[2] Josephus *Antiquities* XIV v 1 § 80.   [3] Josephus *War* II xix 4 § 528.
[4] Tacitus *Agricola* 30; cp. Pliny *Natural History* VI xxv 182.
[5] *E.g.* Josephus *Antiquities* XIII viii 2 § 237–3 § 248; 1 Macc. vi. 48–54, x. 1.
[6] Josephus *Antiquities* XIV iii 1 § 34–iv 4 § 76.   [7] *Ibid.* v 1 §§ 80–1.
[8] *Ibid.* v 2 § 82–vi 4 § 104.   [9] *Ibid.* vi 1 §§ 105–9.
[10] Josephus *War* II xviii 9 § 503–xix § 516 (Chabulon, Joppa, Asamon, Aphek, Lydda) and 10 §§ 529–30 (Bexetha).

escaped a similar fate by opening its gates to him.[1] Vespasian and Titus carried out a similar campaign, in the course of which they took and destroyed twenty-six named towns and villages[2] and other unnamed places, while a few saved themselves by offering no resistance;[3a] thus, as Josephus[3b] says, the war spread over 'all the hill-country and the plains'. Finally, in A.D. 70 Lucilius Bassus reduced the fortresses of Herodium and Machaerus,[4] and Flavius Silva took and entered the ruined Masada, of which the garrison had committed suicide in the flames.[5] Some of these, of course, were not Jewish but Syrian towns, but would come within the Commentator's reference to 'the rulers of the Kittians who despise the fortresses of the people and laugh at them in mockery and surround them with a vast host, and in dread and fear they deliver themselves into their power' (H iv 5–8); but the terms are wide enough to include the whole process by which the Roman empire was built up. Too particular an application must not be given to expressions which are also applicable in a general sense. At the same time, few will doubt that the Commentator's allusion is not to the small number of places taken by the Seleucid kings or their commanders or to Pompey and his successors, but to the thirty-four named towns and villages and the unknown number of other places destroyed in the suppression of the great Revolt.

Further, these same Kittians 'trample the land with [their] horses and with their beasts' (H iii 10). These 'beasts' have been taken to be elephants;[6] and this interpretation of the word has been used to bolster up a Maccabaean date for the Scrolls, since Antiochus IV Epiphanes or rather his general Lysias employed elephants against the Jews.[7] Nowhere in Hebrew literature, however, is the word used in this sense; further, the cognate noun in the other Semitic languages does not designate the elephant, for which all have a totally different name of great antiquity,[8] found already in an Assyrian vocabulary.[9] That the Greek word for 'beast ($\theta\eta\varrho\iota\omega\nu$)' stands occasionally for the elephant in *I Maccabees* is well known;[10] but this is the only sense in which the

---

[1] Josephus *War* II xviii 11 § 510.

[2] *Ibid.* III vii 1 §§ 132–4 (Gabara), 31 §§ 289–306 (Japha), 33 § 316–36 § 339 (Jotapata), ix 2 § 414–4 § 431 (Joppa), x 4 §§ 492–502 (Tarichaeae); IV i 10 §§ 70–83 (Gamala), iii 2 § 130 (Jamnia, Azotus), vii 4 § 420–5 § 430 (Bethennabris), vii 6 § 438 (Abila, Julias, Besimoth), viii 1 § 443–2 § 451 (Thamna, Lydda, Bethleptenpha, Ammaus, Betabris, Caphartoba, Jericho), ix 1 §§ 486–9 (Adida, Gerasa) and §§ 551–4 (Bethela, Ephraim, Caphethra, Capharabis, Hebron).

[3a] *Ibid.* III ix. 8 §§ 543–61 (Tiberias); IV ii 5 §§ 112–20 (Gischala) and vii 3 §§ 410–18 (Gadara).

[3b] *Ibid.* IV ix 1 § 490.

[4] *Ibid.* VII vi 1 § 163 and 4 §§ 190–209.   [5] *Ibid.* VII ix 2 §§ 402–6.

[6] Stauffer in *TLz.* LXXVI 667-9 and Michel *Maître* 124.

[7] 1 Macc. iii. 34, vi. 30, 34–5, viii. 6; 2 Macc. xi. 4, xiii. 2, 15.

[8] Cp. Schreiden *Énigmes* 208-9.

[9] Muss-Arnolt *Concise Assyrian Dictionary* 803.   [10] 1 Macc. vi. 35–7, 43.

author of that work uses the word, so that the meaning is not in doubt in the single passage where the beasts in question have not already been called elephants.[1] In any case, as Fr. Sutcliffe argues,[2] Greek is no guide for Hebrew usage and certainly cannot prove an exception. The elephant, too, though used in war by Greeks, Macedonians and Persians, was distrusted by the Romans; on only two occasions did they even think of using them,[3] and no Roman commander ever employed them in Palestine. What is here meant, as Prof. Dupont-Sommer has shown,[4] is the train of draught-beasts (mules, asses, oxen) which transported the artillery and baggage of the Roman army in the field; and Josephus often speaks of these with their host of followers passing up and down the country.[5] This conclusion is in harmony with, even if it is not a proof of, a date in the 1st century A.D.

Finally, that the Kittians are the Roman legions at the time of the Revolt in A.D. 66–70 is put beyond doubt by the reference to their sacrificing to their military standards.[6] The enemy are described in the *Commentary*, as in the Targum,[7] as 'sacrificing to their standards, and their weapons of war are the objects of their reverence' (H vi 3–5). There is only one actual instance of such a sacrifice during the period within which the composition of this document must fall, although the adoration or veneration of the eagles as well as the offering of sacrifices to them are well-attested practices of the Roman legions.[8]

Explanations of the practice here ascribed to the Kittian army have been sought far and wide, in the empires of the East and in the Seleucid kingdom. All the customs cited under these heads, however, are open to objection on the ground either that they are not strictly parallel or that they are variously interpreted and therefore equivocal or even perhaps misinterpreted;[9] and other reasons for believing that the Kittians are not the Seleucids are so cogent that they may be excluded from the enquiry. This therefore is here narrowed down to a consideration of Roman practice.

During the Republican period no explicit mention of actual sacrifice to the standards can be found in the literary sources, although they seem as early as 494 B.C. to have been regarded as sacred objects, even as 'statues of the gods', as Dionysius Halicarnassensis says.[10] So too Livy tells[11] how certain soldiers and sailors in 210 B.C. bound themselves and their persons 'by the military standards and the eagles and the religious bond of an oath', and again, in 63 B.C. Catiline, according

[1] 1 Macc. xi. 56.
[2] In *Monks* 50–1.
[3] Reinach in Daremberg & Saglio *Dictionnaire des Antiquités* II 539.
[4] In *Manuscrits* 48–50.
[5] In *War* II xix 2 § 521 and 8 § 546, III vi 2 § 121 and § 125, V iii 5 § 132.
[6] Vermès in *Cah. Sion.* 1951, 68–9 and Driver in *JQR*, NS XLIV 3–11.
[7] Pp. 214–15.
[8] Cp. Tertullian *Apology* 18.
[9] Cp. Atkinson in *JSS* IV 255–62.
[10] In *Roman Antiquities* VI xlv 2.
[11] In *ab urbe condita* XXVI xlviii 12.

to Sallust,[1] set up a sort of shrine in his house for the eagle which Marius had carried in the Cimbrian campaign and 'which he (sc. Catiline) used to venerate on setting out to commit murder', as Cicero says;[2] but this eagle had become the object of Catiline's veneration not as a symbol of Rome's military power but as having once belonged to the great soldier who was honoured as the prototype of a revolutionary democratic leader. Clearly, however, under the Republic the eagles were regarded as 'very honourable' or 'precious objects' and even 'as statues of gods'; and so Dio Cassius, referring to events in 53 B.C., says[3] that 'a small chapel, in which a golden eagle is enshrined', was carried round by the Roman army.[4]

The practice of the army in the Imperial age was similar or the same; for example, Tacitus[5] says that the standards were kept in the commander's tent or in similar quarters, for example in domo Germanici in A.D. 14, and that they had the value of sanctuary; and Josephus calls[6] the standards 'sacred objects' which were a guarantee of victory. Accordingly, Munatius Plancus, threatened by mutinous troops in the same year, 'sought safety in religion, having embraced the standards and the eagles', and was saved by the intervention of the standard-bearer, with the consequence that 'the altars of the gods' were not profaned by bloodshed. Tacitus confirms[7] their deification when Germanicus in A.D. 16 hails the appearance of a flight of eagles as 'Roman birds, the proper numina of the legions', and again when Antonius Primus in a riot in A.D. 63 speaks of 'the standards and the gods of the wars', even if he barely identifies the one with the other. Normally, too, when foreign kings did homage in the field, the ceremony took place before the standards. So the Armenian king Tiridates I in A.D. 63 in one account was invested with the crown 'between the military standards and the vexilla' and in another took the omens in the same ceremony 'facing the standards and the effigies of the emperor'.[8] So too oaths were sworn apud signa at the conclusion of a treaty.[9] On other similar occasions the standards were adored. Thus Plautius Silvanus, who died at some time before Vespasian's accession, records on an inscription how he brought 'kings who were unknown or were hostile to the Roman people to adore the Roman standards'.[10] The most important of these occasions for the present purpose is one, which Suetonius reports,[11] at which the Parthian king Artabanus III in A.D. 70 'adored the eagles and the Roman standards and the busts

[1] In Catilina 59.   [2] In Catilinarian Oration I ix 24; cp. II vi 13.
[3] In Roman History XL xviii 1.
[4] Cp. Reinach in Daremberg & Saglio Dictionnaire des Antiquités IV 1324–5.
[5] In Annals I xxxix 4, 7.   [6] In War III vi 2 §§ 123–4.
[7] In Annals II xviii 2 (Germanicus) and Histories iii 10 (Antonius Primus).
[8] Suetonius Nero 13 and Tacitus Annals XV xxiv 3.
[9] Tacitus Annals XV xvi 1.   [10] Dessau Inscriptiones Latinae Selectae II 986.
[11] In Caligula 14; cp. Vitellius 2.

of the Caesars'; for Dio Cassius in the parallel Greek account says[1] that he was compelled 'to sacrifice to the busts of Augustus and Gaius'. This last passage is the only place in which sacrifice is mentioned; and it is offered to the busts of the deified emperors, not to the military standards.

This evidence, drawn from literature, as Mrs. Atkinson has now shown,[2] can be supplemented by that of both Republican and Imperial coins. Several of these in the former period, of which the earliest is dated in 218/7 B.C. and the latest in the Social War of 91–88 B.C., show a young man standing in the company of a soldier or soldiers before a spear (representing the military standard) or before the standard itself with a pig; he is evidently taking the oath as a recruit and is going to sacrifice the pig to the deified standard or eagle. This evidence can be supplemented by a coin of the latter period in which the empress Julia Domna (who died in A.D. 217) is shown offering a sacrifice in her capacity as *mater castrorum* in front of two military standards.

That the actions described in the passages here cited from Greek and Latin literary sources were accompanied by sacrifice would seem then to be beyond doubt. What may now be asked is this: granted that the Jews had known of the custom of offering sacrifice to the standards and might even have handled coins depicting it from their earliest contact with the Romans, why should they have totally disregarded it for several centuries and then suddenly shown themselves aware of it in A.D. 70? The answer must be that they thought nothing of it but regarded it, so far as they did think of it (for the admission of recruits into the Roman army in Palestine could not have been a common event and would not in any case have been normally attended by civilian bystanders; and few people would perhaps have understood the scene as depicted on foreign and often worn coins) as a heathen custom which had to be tolerated, and that they only took offence when it was brought forcibly and flagrantly to their notice.

If then the Jews did not normally allow themselves to be unduly upset by this practice, to what did they object? The answer may well be found in one or other of certain events which Josephus relates. The first was when some Jewish students tore down the golden eagle which Herod had set up over the great gate of the Temple at the instigation of two Rabbis who paid for their rashness with their lives;[3] and the second was when Pontius Pilate provoked a riot by introducing the Roman standards into Jerusalem by night and was compelled to withdraw them.[4] These stories would seem to show that the Jewish

---

[1] In *Roman History* LIX xxvii 3.   [2] In *JSS* IV 246–55.
[3] Josephus *Antiquities* XVII vi 2 § 149–4 § 167 and *War* I xxxii 2 § 648–4 § 655.
[4] *Ibid.* XVIII iii 1 §§ 55–9 and *ibid.* II ix 2 § 168–3 § 174.

P

populace would be roused to fury not by any regular habit of the Romans, to which familiarity had bred indifference, but only by some extraordinary outrage, and to suggest that, although the Commentator was describing the Romans in general terms, he was prompted to do so not by their normal practice but by some singular and particular outrage on his religious sentiments, for example a threat to the sanctity of the Holy City or the Temple. Sacrificing to the standards alone was not sufficient; the rite had to be performed in some sacred place, where the offence would be aggravated by the fact that the standards carried the effigy of the emperor.[1] These two episodes, however, involve no sacrifice; while therefore they show popular reaction to such outrages, neither can be the event here intended.

Only one suitable occasion can be found. In the autumn of A.D. 70, when the buildings of the Temple and its precincts were on fire, the Roman soldiers 'conveyed the emblems into the sanctuary and set them up over against the eastern gate, sacrificed to them there and proclaimed Titus Caesar', as Josephus has recorded,[2] in an outburst of emotional fervour. The Greek word here used may denote any kind of emblem, including the bust of the emperor, who however is not mentioned; the standards, however, must be meant, since Titus is being hailed as *imperator*, not as emperor. This act was exceptional, in fact unique, and was without doubt intended as an outrage to avenge the prolonged and bitter resistance which the Jews had offered to the Romans. No similar outrage is recorded in Jewish history, even on the occasions of the capture of the Holy City by Nebuchadrezzar and by Pompey, and it rankled so bitterly in Jewish memories that Titus was ever afterwards called 'the wicked one';[3] and there is no other event in recorded history to which the Commentator is likely to be or can be alluding.

That other references to this event can be detected in more or less contemporary history is therefore not surprising;[4] but what is significant is that it is again brought into connection with the same prophecy of Habakkuk of the Old Testament.[5] R. 'Aqîbâ, commenting on God's command that 'Ye shall not make (other gods) beside Me',[6] says 'Ye shall not behave towards Me as others behave towards the objects of their reverence; when prosperity comes to them, they say: Therefore they offer sacrifice to their net . . .'; and he uses a noun for 'objects of reverence' derived from the very same root as that which the commentator on Habakkuk uses.[7] Again, the Targum (or Aramaic paraphrase) of Jonathan ben Uzziel explains the same words of Habakkuk

---

[1] Josephus *Antiquities* XVIII iii 1 § 55 and *War* II ix 2 § 169; cp. Michel *Maître* 147.
[2] In *War* VI vi 1 § 316.
[3] Pp. 202–3.
[4] Cp. Wieder in *JJS* IV 14–18.
[5] Hab. i. 16.
[6] Exod. xx. 23.
[7] Lauterbach *Mekilta de-Rabbi Ishmael* II 277.

as meaning 'therefore he sacrifices to his weapons and offers incense to his standards'.[1] R. 'Aqîbâ was executed by the Romans at the beginning of the Second Revolt c. A.D. 132, and Jonathan ben Uzziel, to whom the Targum is traditionally ascribed, flourished at the beginning of the Christian epoch; the Targum, however, though it contains much early matter, is a largely composite work which does not seem to have reached its present form before the 4th–5th centuries A.D. It has, too, other contacts with the Scrolls,[2] and the conclusion can hardly be avoided that these three comments on Habakkuk's words, couched in similar language, are in some way or other connected. This connection can only be that the idea of seeing a reference to sacrificing to military standards in the prophet's words is born of deep pondering over the disaster of A.D. 70 and the attempt to account for it in the teaching of the ancient prophet.

The arguments, or many of the arguments, here adduced can superficially be turned by pleading, for example as Prof. Goossens has done,[3] that the Roman legions must have sacrificed to their legions on other occasions before A.D. 70, even if no record of their having done so has been preserved, since the practice is *sûrement très ancien chez les Romains*, indeed an ancient one of totemistic origin. This type of reasoning can be extended indefinitely and then invoked against each piece of evidence in turn; and *sûrement* betrays the weakness of the argument. He who protests most is most in doubt! The *argumentum e silentio*, too, is notoriously weak and on every occasion on which it is prayed in aid it strains credulity further, until it eventually reaches breaking point; thus in the end it defeats itself. Moreover, the historian must rely on facts, not on fictions; for the argument from totemism is nothing but a piece of special pleading. Contrariwise, the cumulative argument, which is here employed, gains force with each additional piece of evidence adduced; when every point is met and every statement explained, it becomes so convincing that, even though it may not amount to absolute proof, the explanation can properly be used as the basis of the next stage in the argument.

One other point, which in itself is unimportant but which gains significance in the light of the foregoing discussion and therefore perhaps deserves a passing mention, is this,[4] that the Covenanters applied the prophecy that 'Lebanon shall fall by a mighty one'[5] to the Kittians (AFl. c iii 2–8 4–6), while R. Johanan ben Zakkai takes it as referring to Vespasian and the Romans.[6] The application of the same text to each of these people does not prove their identity but shows

---

[1] Lagarde *Prophetae Chaldaicae* 467.   [2] Pp. 456–7, 471–2; cp. pp. 387–8.
[3] In *Nouvelle Clio* IV 151–2 and *Flambeau* XXXIV 35–6.
[4] Roth in *JSS* VII 74-5.   [5] Isa. x. 34; s. pp. 458–60.
[6] B. Talmud *Gittin* 56a-b.

that it must not be regarded as inconceivable in the thought of the
1st and 2nd centuries A.D.

In conclusion, then, 'Kittians' stand for the Imperial Romans in
the Scrolls as 'Babylon' stands for imperial Rome in the New Testament; the reason was the same in both cases, namely the side that
anti-Roman sentiments if openly expressed might call down Roman
vengeance.[1]

4. HISTORIC AND CONFEDERATE ENEMIES

The forces of the Sons of Light are said to consist of the tribes of Levi
(which here enjoys the precedence customarily granted by the Covenanters to priests and Levites), Judah and Benjamin[2]; and they are collectively designated 'the sons of the wilderness' (D viii 12–14). This title
is intended to distinguish them as representing the community living
at Qumrân on the edge of the wilderness' of Judah from those members
of the group[3] here described as 'the exiles of the Sons of Light from the
wilderness of the peoples',[4] by which Damascus and the surrounding
country must be meant;[5] and the campaign will not open until the
two groups have been reunited in a single army. The enemy are the
'Sons of Darkness', contemptuously called the 'host of Belial' (W i 2–3).
Each side is supported by various beings from another world. Ranged
on the side of the Sons of Light and assisting them in various capacities
are 'gods' (W i 10–11 xiv 15–16 xvii 7; cp. T x 8 xviii 3) and 'divine
warriors' (W xv 14), 'holy angels' (W vii 6; cp. xii 7) and 'holy beings'
(W vi 8–9; cp. T iii 22 iv 25 x 34 xi 12); but the Sons of Darkness are
assisted only by 'messengers (angels) of mischief' (W xiii 12; cp. D iv 12
Z ii 4).[6]

The human enemies of the Sons of Light are described as the 'troops
of Belial, seven nations of destruction' (W xi 8–9), counted by the
historic number of Israel's enemies;[7] and this 'army of Belial' consists of
the Kittians of Asshur and in Egypt, who are further subsumed under
'Sons of Japhet',[8] of Edomites and Moabites, Ammonites and Philistines,
and of 'the kings of the north' (W i 1–7)[9]. At the same time the war is
also depicted as involving the most distant nations of the known
world.[8]

The nearest of these enemies, with whom the Sons of Light had to
contend and who must therefore be fitted historically into the picture,
were the 'children of Ammon (and perhaps Amalek)',[10] Edom and

[1] Cp. pp. 132, 348–9.
[2] Cp. Testaments *Dan* v. 10 (Judah and Levi) and *Benjamin* xi 2 (Benjamin).
[3] Pp. 63–5, 67–71, 303–8.   [4] Cp. Ezek. xx. 35.
[5] Cp. 1 Ki. xix. 15.   [6] Cp. Yadin *War* 209–11.
[7] Cp. Deut. vii. 1 and Acts xiii. 19; s. pp. 223–4.   [8] Pp. 223–4.
[9] Cp. Dan. xi. 15–19.   [10] Carmignac *Guerre* 2.

Moab, and the Philistines (W i 1–2). These four nations were Israel's historic enemies in Hebrew literature, and to some extent their names might have been merely borrowed from that source to lend verisimilitude to the picture;[1] and in the same way Judas Maccabaeus warred with the Ammonites and Idumaeans and the Philistines.[2] The insurgents in the revolt against Rome, however, had to deal with the same four nations; that they are named in the *War* then very possibly reflects contemporary history. Agrippa, by origin an Idumaean, whose kingdom lay along the ancient territory of Ammon, supported the pro-Roman party in Jerusalem against the insurgents and on several occasions furnished the Romans with contingents for use in suppressing the revolt.[3] In A.D. 66 Machaerus, in territory that had been now Ammonite and now Moabite, was a constant anxiety whether in Roman hands or in those of rival insurgent groups; for it was too important to be left in uncertain possession.[4] In A.D. 66–7 Simon bar Giora, one of the insurgent leaders who had established himself at Masada, harried the territory of the Idumaeans (approximately that of the ancient Edomites), whom he had found troublesome, possibly because they had Roman sympathies, and again in A.D. 68 he overran their country and stripped it bare for having aided the rival Zealots.[5] In that year, too, John of Gischala, seeking support against his rivals, introduced a party of Idumaeans into Jerusalem where they did much damage and whence they were induced only with great difficulty to depart.[6] Finally, in A.D. 70 the Idumaean rulers sought to save themselves by making separate terms with the Romans; but Simon succeeded for the moment in checking their efforts, and nothing is heard of them again in this connection. Evidently, however, they were a thorn in the side of all the rival parties, and their treachery at the end would have moved the Covenanters to hatred of them.[7] Lastly, on the coast Ascalon, which had been an independent state since 104 B.C. and had long been hostile to the Jews, as well as Anthedon and Gaza, had been well-known Philistine cities. In A.D. 66 the Jews had to attack both for their pro-Roman attitude, and shortly afterwards the people of Ascalon had risen and massacred 2000 of the local Jewish population; again, in A.D. 67 the Zealots fell on the same towns but were beaten off by the inhabitants at the second attempt to gain an entry, thanks to Roman aid.[8] A member of a patriotic party, such as the

[1] Cp. Ps. lxxxiii. 7–9 and Dan. xi. 41.
[2] 1 Macc. v. 1–8, 65–8; cp. Jubilees xxiv 28–32 xxxviii 1–14.
[3] Pp. 219–20.
[4] Josephus *War* II xviii 5 § 485, IV vii 6 § 439 and 9 ix § 555, VII vi 1 § 163–vi 4 § 209.
[5] *Ibid.* II xxii 2 §§ 652–4, IV ix 5 §§ 515–19 and 10 § 556–12 § 584.
[6] *Ibid.* IV iv 1 § 224–vi 1 § 365 and ix 11 §§ 566–8.
[7] *Ibid.* VI vii 2 §§ 378–81; cp. VII viii 1 § 267.
[8] *Ibid.* II xviii 1 § 460 and 5 § 477, III ii 1 § 9–3 § 28.

Covenanters were, might well feel himself surrounded by the historic enemies of his nation on all sides.

Here Dr. Roth makes a point,[1] which is worth consideration. The author of the *War*, quoting Balaam's prophecy of the doom of the Gentiles,[2] changes 'Edom shall be a possession' into 'the enemy shall be a possession' and omits 'Seir also shall be a possession' (W xi 6–7). This respect for the feelings of Edom would have been strange before the conversion of the Edomites to Judaism at the end of the 2nd century B.C. and unthinkable during the reign of the hated Edomite, Herod; but it would have been natural during the revolt against Rome (A.D. 66–70), when the Zealots invited the Idumaeans into Jerusalem to assist them against their priestly opponents.[3] That the writer, having introduced Edom into the list of the nations' enemies (W i 1), may here contradict himself, as Dr. Zeitlin observes,[4] is hardly a serious objection. Such inconsistency is common enough, especially in Jewish apocalyptic literature. So 'Asshur' in the *War* is now Assyria (W ii 12), now the enemy in a general sense (W xi 11 xvii 2 xix 10), and now Syria as occupied by the Romans (W i 2); and similarly the author of the apocryphal book of *Baruch* speaks in one verse of 'Nabuchodonosor king of Babylon' as having taken Jehoiachin captive and applies the very same name and title in two subsequent verses pseudonymously to the Roman emperor Vespasian.[5] The author of the Scroll would be going no further; in the one place he would be taking the names of Israel's ancient enemies as part of the 'stage-scenery' borrowed from the Old Testament[6] for the description of Israel as surrounded by hostile nations and transferring them *en bloc* from the historical to the apocalyptic plane without regard to detail,[7] while in the other he would be avoiding a downright denunciation of a nation which was temporarily on friendly terms with his party. Possibly, however, and even probably the reason why the writer avoids the mention of Edom and Seir is that he does not wish to run the risk of calling down the vengeance of the Roman authorities on his party; for these two names are common cryptograms for Rome in Rabbinic literature.[8]

If the identification of the Kittians with the Roman enemy at the time of the first Revolt is accepted, that of 'the kings of the north' (W i 4) ceases to be a problem. These enemies must be rulers of kingdoms or principalities living on the northern frontier of Palestine and likely to be allied with the Romans in the great struggle which the *War* depicts.

---

[1] In *Background* 50–1.
[2] Num. xxiv. 17–19.
[3] Josephus *War* IV iv 1 § 224–vi 1 § 353.
[4] In *JQR*, NS XLIX 232–3.
[5] I Baruch i. 9, 11–12 (s. Charles *Apocrypha and Pseudepigrapha* I 574–6).
[6] *E.g.* Ps. lxxxiii. 6–8; Jer. xxv. 20–22.
[7] Cp. Jubilees xxxvii 10 and 1 Macc. v. 3–8, 65–8.
[8] *E.g.* Midrash R. *Exodus* xxxv. § 5 (Edom = Rome) and Friedmann *Sifré debê Rab* 343 on Deuteronomy xxxiii. 3 (Seir = Rome).

Such 'kings', if the Kittians were the Seleucid Greeks, could not have been the Seleucid kings,[1] who would already be *ex hypothesi* the rulers of the 'Kittians in Asshur';[2] and there was only one Seleucid king at any one time. The suggestion that they were the Seleucid and allied kings[3] would be plausible only if the Seleucid kings were probable on other grounds; as they are out of the question,[4] this identification cannot be accepted. In 64 B.C. Syria was annexed by Pompey and made a Roman province, although the old dynasty lingered until Philip II made a brief appearance on the scene as its last king *c.* 56 B.C.; but 'chief of the kings of the Greeks' (Z ix 20) as a title for Pompey[5] is unlikely at any time. From then on till the end of the 1st century A.D. the neighbouring principalities enjoyed a fitful independence; and, whatever their proper titles might be, whether kingdoms or tetrarchies, these petty states were commonly called 'kingdoms' and their rulers 'kings' by contemporary Greek and Roman historians.[6] Their loyalty to Rome, however, though for some time very uncertain, was much strengthened when princes of the Herodian family were put in charge of several of them.[7] Such were Ituraea proper and the successor-states into which it was divided, Abilene, Trachonitis and Auranitis, Calchis, Emesa and Commagene, and others further to the north and east.

The rulers of all these petty states naturally found it in their own interests to do what Rome wished, and such a course tended naturally to commit them to actions hostile to the ever-rebellious Jewish nation on their southern flank. Already in 47 B.C. Herod had caught and executed Hezekiah,[8] the father of Judah the Galilaean or Gaulonite who had been one of the founders of the 'fourth philosophy',[9] and Herod's great-great-grandson Agrippa II king of Chalcis and of other tetrarchies had done everything in his power to check the incipient revolt in A.D. 66 and to contain it after its outbreak, even going so far as to send troops into Jerusalem to support the moderate party.[10] He sent aid to the Romans when Cestius had led them into a trap;[11] and he only arrived too late, being forestalled by a small party of Romans, to save Tiberias from the insurgents.[12] Early in A.D. 67 he joined Vespasian at Antioch with his own forces[13] and on a subsequent

---

[1] Del Medico *Énigme* 363.
[2] Cp. 1 Macc. viii. 5.
[3] Van der Ploeg in *VT* V 394.
[4] Pp. 197–216.
[5] Dupont-Sommer in *Semitica* V 41–57.
[6] *E.g.* Dio Cassius *Roman History* xlix 32 and Tacitus *Annals* xii 23 (Ituraea); Josephus *War* II xi 5 § 215, xii 8 § 247 and *Life* xi 49 (Abilene); Josephus *War* II xii 8 § 247 (Trachonitis, Batanaea, Gaulonitis); Josephus *Antiquities* XVIII v 4 § 135 (Emesa); Josephus *Antiquities* XX v 2 § 103, viii 4 § 158, and *War* II xi 6 § 221, xii 1 § 223 (Chalcis); Josephus *War* VII vii § 219 (Commagene).
[7] Cp. Schürer *Geschichte*³ I 707–25.
[8] Josephus *War* I x 5 § 204.
[9] *Ibid.* II xvi 2 § 336–xvii 17 § 407.
[10] *Ibid.* II xvii 4 §§ 417–21 and 6 §§ 481–6.
[11] *Ibid.* II xviii 9 §§ 500–3.
[12] *Ibid.* II xxi 8 §§ 632–3.
[13] *Ibid.* III iii 4 § 29.

occasion furnished other troops.[1] Throughout the Revolt he remained
on friendly terms with the Romans, from whom he received various
favours,[2] and was wounded fighting on their side at Gamala;[3] and
finally he and Titus went together to Rome to salute the new emperor
when Galba succeeded to the throne in A.D. 69.[4] Antiochus king of
Commagene and Soaemus king of Emesa similarly supported the
Romans with troops in their campaign against the Jewish rebels;[5]
and in A.D. 72–3 Antiochus, when accused (apparently falsely) of disloyalty to Rome, fled and was welcomed as an old friend by Vespasian.[6]

These kinglets, rulers of neighbouring petty states who owed their
thrones to the Romans and depended on them for the continued
enjoyment of their kingdoms, had naturally done all they could to
assist the paramount power in suppressing the Revolt; they could
therefore well be 'the kings of the north' whom the author of the *War*
includes amongst the enemy. From a practical point of view, even after
the defeat of the Kittians, the campaign to conquer the world could not
be brought to a satisfactory conclusion unless the remaining danger
from the north was removed, and the final victory would not be complete until the nation had wreaked its vengeance on all its historic
enemies.

Such an identification of 'the kings of the north' is surely preferable
to searching for the Biblical sense of the expression.[7] A phrase, whatever
it may originally have denoted, is not bound to have the same connotation whenever and wherever it occurs; that must always fit the
actual context. Here an echo of the Maccabaean wars may be detected
in 'the kings of the north'; for in the book of *Daniel*, which refers to
that struggle, mention is made of 'the king of the north' who has ill-
treated the Jews and is doomed to destruction.[8] This was Antiochus IV
Epiphanes, whose hellenizing policy was the cause of the Maccabaean
revolt. His fate, that 'he shall stumble and fall and not be found',
might be thought to foretell that of 'the kings of the north', who had
assisted the enemies of the Covenanters, and after their downfall as
after his the Messianic age might be expected to begin; for many
echoes of the Maccabaean achievements and ideas can be traced in the
Scrolls.[9]

This explanation of 'the kings of the north' throws light on a passage
in the *Zadokite Documents*, which speaks of a time when every man did
what he liked and the people rebelled against the Lord; and He said
that 'their wine is the venom of serpents and the cruel poison of asps:[10]
the serpents are the kings of the nations, and their wine is their ways;

[1] Josephus *War* III iv 2 § 68.   [2] *Ibid.* III ix 7 § 443–8 § 461 and x 10 §§ 540–1.
[3] *Ibid.* IV i 3 §§ 14–16.   [4] *Ibid.* IV ix 2 §§ 498–500.
[5] *Ibid.* II xviii 9 §§ 500–3 and III iv 2 § 68.
[6] *Ibid.* VII vii 3 §§ 239–40.   [7] Cp. Jer. xxv. 26.
[8] Dan. xi. 2–45.   [9] Pp. 353–5.   [10] Deut. xii. 8.

and the poison of the asps is the chief of the kings of the Greeks (*Yāwān*), who comes to wreak vengeance upon them' (Z ix 19–20). The necessity of playing on the use of homonyms for 'poison' (*rō'š*) and 'chief' (*rō'š*) obscures the meaning; but the author seems to be referring to the wickedness of the Jewish nation which has brought down the wrath of God on their heads. Obviously 'the kings of the Greeks', taken apart from the context, can designate Philip and Alexander of Macedon or the Seleucid rulers of the Syrian state carved out of their empire or the kinglets of the petty Syrian and neighbouring states of the first century A.D.[1] The first group is out of the question; for neither Philip nor Alexander come into the historical picture into which the Scrolls must be fitted. The second group is equally unsuitable, inasmuch as they are a series of rulers following one another on their thrones, whereas the context demands a number of synchronous rulers under a common chief or leader; and Antiochus IV Epiphanes, who has been suggested as a Seleucid *i.e.* Greek king and one who may be said to have come 'to wreak vengeance upon them',[2] *i.e.* to punish the Jews for their transgression of the Law,[3] must also be excluded since he seems to have been acting against them alone and not as 'the chief of the kings of the Greeks', *i.e.* a leader of a confederacy of Syrian kinglets. Only the third group can be meant, namely the Syrian kings and princes listed amongst the allies of the Romans in the war against the Jews in A.D. 66–73; and this too seems to have been regarded in contemporary Jewish thought as a punishment inflicted by God.[4] Further, the Romans as 'Kittians', who were reckoned amongst the descendants of 'Javan (*Yāwān*)',[5] could properly be grouped with if not actually subsumed under 'the kings of the Greeks (*Yāwān*)', especially as the emperor was often styled 'king (*melek*)' by Jewish writers,[6] and their 'chief' would be, as Hölscher has argued,[7] the Roman emperor, whether Vespasian or Titus according to the occasion which the writer might have in mind; for the former, coming to take command of the forces in Syria at the outbreak of the Revolt, disposed also of 'many allies from the neighbouring kings' and the latter, when he massed his forces for the siege of Jerusalem, not only had his father's legions but was also 'attended by the contingents supplied by the allied kings in greatly increased strength and by a considerable body of Syrian auxiliary troops'.[8] If this explanation of the reference to 'the kings of the Greeks' is right, the writer intends a *double entente* of a kind common enough in the Scrolls: he is hinting at one and the same time at the Maccabaean revolt as the prototype of the events of his own time and at the revolt

---

[1] Torrey in *JAOS* XXV 302–11.   [2] Kahle *Opera Minora* 109.
[3] Cp. Dan. ix 11–12 and Assumption of Moses viii 1–5.
[4] Cp. 2 Baruch xx. 2 and 2 Esdras (IV Ezra) vi. 18–20.
[5] Gen. x. 4.   [6] Pp. 202–3.   [7] In *ZNtW.* xxviii 44.
[8] Josephus *War* III i 3 § 7 and iv 2 § 68 (Vespasian), V i 6 § 42 and ii 1 § 47 (Titus).

against Rome in A.D. 66–73 as posing the greatest problem of the time through which he has lived.[1]

5. GLOBAL WAR

The war, which is depicted as spreading almost to the furthest corners of the known world, will begin with an attack by the combined forces of the Sons of Light, represented by the three tribes which alone remained faithful to David,[2] namely Judah and Benjamin with Levi (W i 2), on the Sons of Darkness nearest to them, *i.e.* Israel's historic enemies: Moab and Edom, the Ammonites (and possibly the Amalekites)[3] and also the Philistines, supported by the Kittians with their confederate forces and 'such as do wickedly against the covenant'.[4] Then 'after the (*sc.* this) war they will go up (*i.e.* attack) from there (*sc.* the scene of these campaigns) [(as) a mighty host (cp. W i 11) against] the Kittians in Egypt'; and 'in due time it (*sc.* the mighty host) will go forth[5] in mighty fury[6] to fight against the kings of the north' (W i 1–4), *i.e.* the petty Syrian kinglets aiding the Roman forces.[7]

The actual length of the war is nowhere explicitly stated but seems to have been pictured by the author as 40 years;[8] these may be divided into 2 main stages,[9] one of 6 years of mobilization as for a 'war of obligation' or holy war from which none are exempt,[10] followed by 1 'year of release' in which no work is done (W ii 6) and another of 33 years of warfare (W ii 9); and a series of 7 'separate campaigns' take up these 33 years, one of 9 and two of 10 years each (W ii 10–14) *plus* the 4 'years of release' which will fall within this period. Thus the preparatory work and active service occupy 35 years (W ii 9), to which 5 'years of release' must be added. These will occur at the end of every sixth (not at the end of every seventh)[11] year;[12] in other words, every seventh year will be a 'year of release', in which no fighting may take place. Obviously, therefore, a 'year of release' would occur in the middle of the fifth campaign; but the Covenanters would only be following early Maccabaean custom in observing the Sabbath without regard to the operations of the enemy.[13] Regarded from another point of view, the 40 years may be divided into 35 years of active work

---

[1] Pp. 353–5.
[2] 2 Chron. xi. 12–13; cp. Testaments *Simeon* vi 3 (Χετταῖοι, possibly the Kittians), *Dan* v. 7, 10 (Judah and Levi) and *Benjamin* xi 2 (Benjamin).
[3] P. 216.   [4] Pp. 216–18.
[5] Driver in *JTS*, NS X 120–1 and XI 368.
[6] Cp. Dan. xi. 44.   [7] Pp. 218–20.
[8] Cp. Rost in *TLz.* LXXX 205–8.   [9] Cp. Yadin *War* 6–7, 18–20, 33–5.
[10] Mishnah *Sotah* viii 7; cp. Yadin & Rabin *Scroll* 35, 65, 67–70.
[11] Gaster *Scriptures* 293.
[12] Deut. xv. 1, xxxi 10 (where the 'year of release' is put 'in the course of' the seventh year) and xv. 9 (where it is the seventh year).
[13] 1 Macc. ii. 29–38.

plus 5 'years of release'; and these 35 years may be artificially divided into 5 periods of 7 years of civil and military activity connected with the war, just as the final struggle consists of 7 campaigns. Thus forty and seven are basic figures in the calculations determining the length of the war.[1]

The series of campaigns staged against the various enemies is arranged on the following scheme:

year 1: Aram Naharaim (= Mesopotamia);
year 2: the 'sons of Lud' (= Lydians, *i.e.* Asia Minor);
year 3: the rest of Aram, Uz, Hul, Togar (error for Gother = Gether)[2] and Mesha (as in some ancient versions of the Pentateuch for Mash);[3]
years 4–5: Arpachsad;
years 6–7: all the 'sons of Asshur' (= Assyrians) and the Persians and the Easterners 'as far as the Great Desert';
year 8: the 'sons of Elam';
year 9: the 'sons of Ishmael and Keturah'.

For the next ten years the war will be continued against 'all the sons of Ham according to [their clans in] their settlements' and for the last ten years against 'all [the sons of Japhet (cp. W i 6 xviii 2) in] their settlements', as the text is generally restored (W ii 10–14).[4]

The last battle will fall into three 'lots', *i.e.* phases:[5] in the first three the Sons of Light will prevail, in the next three the Sons of Darkness will gain the upper hand, but in the seventh God will intervene to bring victory to His party (W i 12–15). Here too 'seven' is the key-number to the phases to which the final campaign will fall; and its reappearance in other respects in connection with this war suggests that it may in some way reflect contemporary history.

These years, following a 'time of distress' (W i 11–12),[6] will be a 'time of salvation for the people of God' (W i 5)[7] when those who have cast in their lot with the 'Sons of Belial' will suffer eternal destruction. Great 'discomfiture' will fall on the 'sons of Japhet', *i.e.* the Syrian kinglets,[8] when 'Asshur' (*i.e.* the Roman legions in the north) left without help will collapse and 'wickedness' (*i.e.* the Roman empire)[9] will pass away and none of the Sons of Darkness will survive.

The names of the nations against whom the seven campaigns will be launched are taken from the Table of Nations at the beginning of

[1] S. p. 117; cp. Van der Ploeg *Guerre* 71–3.   [2] Gaster *Scriptures* 293.
[3] Gen. x. 23; cp. Albright in *Studi Orientalistici in onore di Giorgio Levi della Vida* I 2–3.
[4] Cp. Carmignac *Guerre* 40.   [5] Yadin *ap.* Van der Ploeg *Guerre* 67.
[6] Cp. Dan. xii. 1.
[7] Cp. Frumkin *Seder R. 'Amrām* II 163, 2–3 (where *'ēṭ sārāh* and *tᵉšû'āh* are contrasted in reference to the Maccabaean revolt).
[8] Cp. Driver in *JTS, NS* XI 369.   [9] Pp. 202–3.

the Pentateuch[1] and are evidently intended, however loosely, to comprise all possible enemies surrounding Israel and so to indicate global war on an apocalyptic scale. The hosts of Edom and Moab and Ammon and of the Philistines, named at the outset as comprising the inner ring of her historic enemies (W i 1–2)[2] but not mentioned again here, must not be supposed to have been already destroyed[3] (for nothing has been said of their defeat); they are subsumed under their parent stock: the first three under Ishmael and Keturah representing the (mostly Semitic) peoples to the east and south of Palestine,[4] and the fourth and last under the 'sons of Ham', whose descendants are said to be Canaan and Egypt, with which Philistia is included.[5] The 'sons of Japhet' will comprise the 'Greeks', who include now the Seleucids[6] and now, as here, their Roman successors, the 'Kittians of Asshur' with the 'Kittians in Egypt' (W i 2, 4, 6), since these are the descendants of Javan, *i.e.* Greece,[7] together with their northern allies.[8] The *War* begins and ends with the Kittians; their devastation of Palestine (H iii 9–11) is the cause of the war and only when they have been finally defeated and given over to slaughter '[when] the sun is hastening to set'[9] will the High Priest be able to give thanks to the God of Israel for their final deliverance from the 'hosts of Belial' (W xviii 1–6).[10] The outer circle of enemies, in which Assyrians and Persians and the Far East are grouped together, points to the heyday of the Parthian empire whose furthest boundaries were the Euphrates and the Indus, the Hindu Kush and the Indian Ocean.[11] They are added because victory, though achieved, will not be final until all the nations of the world allied or subject to the principal enemy, the Roman empire, have also been overthrown.

This picture of the war, and not least its duration, is of the utmost importance. The total length is obviously based on that of the wanderings in the wilderness,[12] *i.e.* forty years of toil followed by rest in the promised land[1] corresponding to forty years of war followed by the Messianic peace; it is also the Messianic period, as recently promulgated, which seems to have been derived primarily from the same source but also to represent certain recurrent periods which can be traced in Jewish history in the 1st century B.C. and the 1st century A.D.[13] The periods of seven years into which the whole period may be broken up are somewhat artificial and in themselves immaterial; but the number

---

[1] Gen. x. 1–32.   [2] Pp. 216–7, 476–7.   [3] Van der Ploeg 73–4.
[4] Gen. xxv. 1–4 (Keturah) and 13–15 (Ishmael).
[5] Gen. x. 6, 13–14.   [6] P. 223.   [7] Pp. 220–2.
[8] Cp. Gen. x. 2–4 (where the 'sons of Japhet' include Yavan and the 'sons of Yavan' include the 'Kittim', *i.e.* Kittians).
[9] Josh. x. 13.   [10] Cp. Testaments *Simeon* vi 3.
[11] Dupont-Sommer *Écrits* 188.
[12] Exod. xvi. 35, Num. xiv. 33–4, Deut. ii. 7, viii. 2–4, xxix 5.
[13] Pp. 342–3, 475–6.

gains significance when the seven campaigns making up the whole war and the seven phases of the final struggle are taken into consideration in the light of the other factors mentioned in connection with it and in the circumstances of the time. The principal enemy, as already said, were the 'Kittians of Asshur' and the 'Kittians in Egypt' (W i 2, 4), *i.e.* invaders from respectively Asshur (Syria) and Egypt; and they included 'such as do wickedly against the covenant' (W i 2),[1] who would be not dissident members of the community but any Jews who collaborated with the enemy[2] (for the term is indefinite). Only one war in recorded Jewish history conforms to these requirements: that it lasted seven years, that the enemy invaded the country simultaneously from Egypt and Syria and were accompanied by 'the kings of the north', that all the nation and not only the army were engaged in it, and that traitors or deserters played a notable if ignominious part in it. This was the First Revolt (A.D. 66–73); it lasted just seven years and involved the entire population, as a 'war of obligation' would do.[3] During it, too, the leading parties, Sadducees and Pharisees, were notoriously pro-Roman,[4] and both Josephus and a number of other Jews, actually went over at various times to the enemy.[5] Finally, seven years of distress before the coming of the Messiah became a part of the Messianic picture.[6]

Thus the *War* echoes reality in this as in other respects, even though it does not depict a real war; and, since no one can suppose that its author can be anticipating or foretelling the First Revolt, it must have been written after that struggle. Some time must then be allowed for the dispersed Jews and especially the party of the Covenanters to return to some sort of normal life; the suggestion may then be hazarded that the work was perhaps composed during the reign of Domitian (A.D. 81–96), who at one time and another persecuted the Jewish race,[7] especially attempting to extirpate the descendants of David,[8] with whom the Covenanters perhaps claimed a connection;[9] its purpose would then be to encourage them to look forward to ultimate victory over their hated persecutors under the leadership of the Messiah. Alternatively, it might lie behind the events of A.D. 113–16, when the Jews in several neighbouring countries were once again in ferment and Palestine itself was not entirely free from disturbance;[10] the author, however, gives no hint that he had any expectation or knowledge of the troubles of those years.

---

[1] Cp. Dan. xi. 32.   [2] Cp. Van der Ploeg *Guerre* 57.
[3] Pp. 222–3.   [4] P. 94.
[5] Josephus *War* III viii 2 §§ 345–408, IV x 7 §§ 622–9 (Josephus); IV vi 3 §§ 377–80, vii 3 §§ 410–12, V x 1 §§ 420–3, xiii 2 §§ 534–40, VI ii 2 § 113–3 § 121, viii 2 §§ 382–5 (unnamed deserters).
[6] Midrash R. *Song of Songs* II 13 § 4.   [7] Suetonius *Domitian* 12.
[8] Eusebius *Ecclesiastical History* iii 19–20.   [9] Pp. 356–8.   [10] Pp. 370–1, 382–3.

SONS OF ZADOK

1. ZADOKITES AND BOETHUSIANS

If the historical background of the Scrolls is the First Revolt of the Jews against the Roman *imperium* (A.D. 66–73), as the Roman evidence which they afford seems to indicate, the next questions must be to enquire whether the Jewish evidence contained in them indicates any body or party in the Jewish community to which the origin of the Covenanters of Qumrân can be traced and whether there is any episode which can be discovered in the history of the same period corresponding to that outlined in them.

As Dr. Bammel has privately suggested, some coherence can be given to the complicated chain of events following the murder of Onias III and the hitherto unravelled origin of the Zadokites if the history of the rival Jewish temple at On in Egypt is taken into consideration; and the probability that all these events may have been in some way connected is greatly increased by the chronological coincidences which have just been worked out.

When Onias III, who was 'zealous for ancestral customs',[1] was murdered *c.* 170 B.C., his son Onias (IV) was too young to succeed to his father's office, which Jason and Menelaus (though not a priest) held each in turn by bribing the Seleucid ruler to appoint him to it. Shortly before the end of the Maccabaean revolt *c.* 162 B.C. Alcimus was nominated to the office by the king but could not enter upon it till the collapse of the revolt in 161 B.C., when Judas Maccabaeus was defeated and killed. Alcimus had indeed been welcomed by the Hasidaean party, to whom he had offered peace and freedom of worship in the king's name; but he soon alienated their sympathy not only by his hellenizing tendencies but also by hunting down the surviving Maccabaeans and surrendering those whom he caught to the vengeance of the king's officers.[2] He then further incensed the Hasidaean party by pulling down the wall of the inner court of the Temple. Consequently he and his adherents came to be called the 'lawless' and the 'ungodly'; and he himself shortly afterwards suffered a stroke and died *c.* 160 B.C.[3] The office of high-priest then remained vacant for

---

[1] 2 Macc. iv. 2.
[2] 1 Macc. vii 10–20, ix. 25–6; Josephus *Antiquities* XII x 1 § 391–3 § 401.
[3] 1 Macc. ix. 54–6; Josephus *Antiquities* XII x 6 § 413.

seven years, until the Maccabaean Jonathan was elected; when he was murdered in 142 B.C. his brother Simon succeeded him, and John Hyrcanus I in due time followed him in office (135–105 B.C.),[1] combining it with that of king in despite of the Pharisees.[2]

Meanwhile Onias (IV) had been conveyed by or had gone with a number of those who remained loyal to his father's memory to Egypt, where a considerable Jewish colony already existed; and Alexandria became their home. Then c. 154 B.C. he obtained permission from the Egyptian king to rebuild a disused temple at On (Leontopolis) near Memphis in the nome of Heliopolis, to dedicate it to the God of the Jews for the use of his fellow countrymen and to appoint 'priests of his own race (ἐκ τοῦ ἰδίου γένους)' to serve it.[3]

This is a point of great importance. Alcimus is described in several places as derived 'from the seed of Aaron'[4] but nowhere as sprung from the family of Onias; and, as Onias could not appoint foreigners as priests, the statement that he wished to appoint priests 'of his own race' can refer only to priests of his own (Zadokite) family as distinct from the present (Hasmonaean) line of priests in Jerusalem. If this argument is correct, the inference from this insistence on his Aaronite descent and the corresponding failure to say anything of a Zadokite connection must be that Alcimus, though descended from Aaron (for the Pharisees were content with Aaronite priests),[5] was not a descendant of Zadok, to whose family Ezekiel had designed to restrict the priesthood.[6] This conclusion is supported by the appeal, which Onias made,[7] to Isaiah's prophecy that 'there shall be five cities in the land of Egypt that speak the language of Canaan (i.e. Hebrew) and swear to the Lord of Hosts: one shall be called the City of Destruction. In that day there shall be an altar in the midst of the land of Egypt and a pillar at the borders thereof'.[8] Symmachus in his translation calls this city the city 'of the sun (ἡλίου)' and the Targum calls it 'the house of the sun (bêt šemeš)',[9] while many Hebrew manuscripts and the Talmud have 'sun (heres)' instead of 'destruction (heres)';[10] clearly the place intended is On, i.e. Heliopolis[11] or Leontopolis, where Onias had built his rival temple. Why however is the name rendered πόλις ασεδεκ 'the city of righteousness (haṣṣedeq)' by the Septuagint? This hitherto unsolved problem can now be solved: the name was given

---

[1] Josephus Antiquities XX x 3 §§ 237–40.   [2] Ibid. XIII ix 2 §§ 259–66.
[3] Ibid. XII ix 7 § 388, XIII iii 1 § 62 4 § 79 and x 4 § 185, XX x 3 §236, War VII x 2 § 422–3 § 432.
[4] 1 Macc. vii. 14; Josephus Antiquities XII ix 7 § 387 and XX x 3 § 235.
[5] B. Talmud Qiddushin 66a.
[6] Ezek. xl. 46, xliii. 19, xliv. 15–16, xlviii. 11–12.
[7] Josephus Antiquities XIII iii 1 § 63 and War VII x 3 § 432.
[8] Isa. xix. 18–19.   [9] Cp. Jer. xliii. 13 (Septuagint).
[10] De Rossi Variae Lectiones Veteris Testamenti III 22.
[11] Cp. Gen. xli. 50 (Septuagint).

to it by the Jews residing there as recalling the founder's great-great-grandfather (?) Simon the 'Just'[1] or rather the 'Rightful', *i.e.* Zadokite (*ṣaddîq*), a former high-priest who presumably owed his title to some dispute about the Zadokite succession and from whom Onias III was descended; thus it indicated that this city was the place where the true Zadokite priesthood, which Onias and not Alcimus represented, was maintained. The Septuagint translators, who lived and worked in Egypt, alone knew the local tradition, which they preserved in their rendering of the sacred text, and so the Zadokites or Covenanters long afterwards called themselves the 'sons of righteousness (*ṣedeq*), as heirs of the same tradition. Naturally therefore the place is called 'the city of *ḥeres*' and not 'of *heres*', namely of the 'sun' or the 'lion' and not of 'destruction', in the Covenanters' copy of *Isaiah* found in Cave I at Qumrân (Is. A xv 25).

All this in turn explains what follows. When the Seleucid kingdom came to an end and Jerusalem was taken by Pompey in 63 B.C., some if not all of the Zadokites in Egypt, whose ancestors had emigrated out of opposition to the Seleucid kings on account of their support of the rival non-Zadokite priesthood in Jerusalem, would seem to have come back; for a certain 'Alexandrian priest' named Boethus, who appears from his title to have come from the very place where Onias (IV) is known to have settled in Egypt, is now found in Jerusalem with a following of adherents called Boethusians.

The date of the formation of this party has long been a matter of dispute, inasmuch as the traditional chronology seems to put it too soon[2]; but a small adjustment will correct this. A story, which has generally been regarded as apocryphal but which may contain a grain of truth, tells how a disciple of Simon the Just or Rightful (*ṣaddîq*) named Antigonus of Socho had a long line of disciples succeeding each other in pairs (which are obviously artificial)[3] and how two rival parties, the Boethusians (whose founder was an otherwise undescribed Boethus) and the Sadducaeans (who took their name from a similarly otherwise undescribed Zadok) sprang from the fourth generation of teachers.[4] If then Simon the *ṣaddîq* was not Simon I high-priest in the middle of the 3rd century B.C., as Josephus thought,[5] but his grandson Simon II, high-priest *c.* 200 B.C., as Rabbinic references indicate,[6] the chronological difficulty disappears. One of the third generation of disciples was Simeon ben Sheṭaḥ (*c.* 90–70 B.C.), so that the fourth generation would have flourished *c.* 70–40 B.C.; and the principal

---

[1] Josephus *Antiquities* XII iv 1 § 157.
[2] Cp. Ewald *Geschichte*[3] IV 358[1] and Geiger *Urschrift und Uebersetzungen der Bibel* 30.
[3] Mishnah *Aboth* i 2–18.
[4] Goldin *Rabbi Nathan* 39 § 5.
[5] In *Antiquities* XII ii 5 § 43.
[6] Marcus *Josephus* [Loeb] III 732–6; cp. Michel *Maître de Justice* 302.

teacher of the fifth generation, Hillel, flourished *c.* 30 B.C., according to tradition a century before the destruction of the Temple in A.D. 70.[1] These dates agree remarkably well with two facts: that the 'Alexandrian priest' Boethus would not be likely to have come to Jerusalem before the downfall of Seleucid rule, *i.e.* before Pompey's capture of Jerusalem in 63 B.C. (since his party had originally fled to Egypt to escape from another foreign, *i.e.* Seleucid, rule), so that he could be father of the Simon whom Herod created high-priest and whose daughter Mariamme he married *c.* 24 B.C.[2], and that the Boethusian party would seem to have been formed in consequence of disputes arising out of the teaching of the fourth generation of teachers *c.* 70–40 B.C.

Another significant fact in this connection is the late tradition that Boethus had one named Zadok associated with him in some way in founding the party of the Boethusians;[3] for it at once prompts the question whether this otherwise unknown Zadok may not be the Saddok or Sadduk the partner of Judah son of Hezekiah in the formation of the party of the 'fourth philosophy' which has been shown to have been connected, if not identified, with that of the Covenanters of Qumrân.[4]

Only a few doctrines of the Boethusians are known. First, Antigonus is said to have taught his disciples 'Be ye not like slaves, who serve their master for the sake of compensation; rather be like slaves who serve a master with no thought of compensation, and let the fear of Heaven (*i.e.* God) be upon you, so that your reward may be double in the age to come'. A subsequent generation of disciples disputed this lesson, on the grounds that a workman would not work all day and receive no reward in the evening and that, if their ancestors had known that there was a future life and a resurrection of the dead, they would not have so taught. Thereupon they renounced the Law and a twofold schism of Sadducees (or Sadducaeans) and Boethusians broke out.[5] The teaching which caused this schism seems to be echoed in a passage in one of the Scrolls which says: '[Let there be] eternal hatred towards the men of perdition on account of their deceitful spirit (in concealing their wealth and not surrendering it to the society),[6] by abandoning (your) wealth and (the produce of) manual labour to them as a slave (does) to him who rules him and shows humility towards his taskmaster; and let a man be zealous for the ordinance (of God) and His time, for the day of vengeance, so as to do what is acceptable in every thing to which hand may be put and in all His Dominion, as He has commanded; for everything done by him He will accept. Apart from God's will [and

---

[1] B. Talmud *Shabbath* 15a.   [2] Josephus *Antiquities* XV ix 3 §§ 320–1.
[3] Nemoy *Kitâb al-Anwâr wal-Marâqib* of alQirqîsânî I ii (I ii 7); s. pp. 260–1, 264–5.
[4] Pp. 99–100.   [5] Goldin *Rabbi Nathan*, 39 § 5.
[6] Cp. Dupont-Sommer *Écrits Esséniens* 111.[4]

Q

favour] one shall have no pleasure' (D ix 21–25); for this implies working for God, as a slave works for his master, without expecting material payment for the work done. This story has hitherto been rejected as a late and pious fiction, on the ground that the Sadducees are said not to have believed in a resurrection and therefore not in recompense and punishment hereafter;[1] but, if the people meant are not the Sadducees but the Saducaeans or Zadokites, who were believers in some form of future life with rewards and penalties,[2] this objection cannot be sustained. Second, the Pharisees and the Boethusians differed in their interpretation of the rule that 'ye shall bring the sheaf of the first-fruits of your harvest unto the priest: and . . . on the morrow after the sabbath the priest shall present it (sc. before the Lord').[3] The Pharisees took 'sabbath' here to be first day of Passover, regardless of the day of the week on which it might fall, i.e. 15 Nisan, so that 'the morrow of the sabbath' would be 16 Nisan;[4] they therefore assigned an unnatural (and probably incorrect) sense to 'sabbath'. Contrariwise, the Boethusians, having a calendar in which the month always began on a Wednesday and the feasts consequently all fell on the same day of the week, so that 15 Nisan on which Passover always began was invariably a Wednesday, held that 'the morrow of the sabbath' was the day after the sabbath following the octave of that feast, namely Sunday 26 Nisan.[5] This indeed is the natural explanation of the phrase and probably thereupon reflects the old sacred calendar;[6] and it is of great importance in the present connection as proving that the Boethusians observed the same calendar as the Covenanters and the Qara'ites.[7] Third, while the Pharisees allowed the ceremony of waving willow-branches and carrying them in procession round the altar in the Temple on the seventh day of the Feast of Tabernacles to be held even when this fell on a sabbath,[8] the Boethusians objected to this concession as profaning that day.[9] The attitude of the Covenanters to this ceremony is not known; but it would probably never have fallen on a sabbath according to their calendar as it could not in accordance with that of 'Ananites, who were in some sense descended from them.[10] This objection may also be reflected in alBîrûnî's reference to attempts to construct a calendar under which the difficulty would not arise.[11]

---

[1] Schürer Geschichte[3] II 408–11.   [2] Pp. 71–2, 74–5, 85–6.
[3] Lev. xxiii. 10–11.   [4] Mishnah Menahoth x 3 (s. Danby Mishnah 506[1]).
[5] Cp. Efendipulo Judah Hadassi: Sefer Eshkol hakkofer 41b § 98 (citing David b. Marwan alMuqammaṣ as his authority).
[6] Cp. Deut. xvi. 9; s. Driver & White Leviticus 94 and Burnaby Jewish and Muhammadan Calendars 197–200.
[7] S. pp. 9–10, 321–3; cp. Goudoever Biblical Calendars 19–29.
[8] Mishnah Sukkah iv 1–7.   [9] B. Talmud Sukkah 43b.   [10] Pp. 11, 320–1, 334–5.
[11] Sachau Chronologie Orientalischer Völker von alBêrûnî 283–4 = Chronology of Ancient Nations of alBîrûnî 277–8.

Once again, then, the Boethusians seem to have shared an opinion which may reasonably be held to be Zadokite in origin. Fourth, the Boethusians were regarded as a cause of disaster by the Rabbis[1] and were even charged with being 'heretics (*mînîm*)' in a dispute regarding the announcement of the appearance of the new moon;[2] and this, being a matter of importance in fixing the dates of the principal feasts, also connects them with the Zadokites.

Accordingly, the majority of the recorded points on which the Boethusians differed from orthodox Pharisees arose out of the calendar, which was a matter of prime importance also to the Zadokites or Covenanters; and on all or most of them they would seem to have adopted Zadokite customs. Thus the only facts known about the Boethusians tend inevitably to connect or identify them with the Zadokites.[3] At the same time they put them in the very period in which the Zadokites or Covenanters are depicted as active in the Scrolls; they are the link connecting the old Zadokites in Egypt with the new Zadokites in Palestine. If this reconstruction of the origins of the Zadokites and Boethusians is accepted, it argues an element of truth in late traditions connecting the two parties with one another[4]; and one of these was that 'in the time of those kings (*i.e.* John Hyrcanus I and Alexander Jannaeus) the sect of the Qara'ites, who are also called *Ṣaddûqîm* and Boethusians, began'.[5] The Zadokites and the Boethusians are here more or less rightly assigned to a common origin in the 2nd century B.C. and identified with the Qara'ites, although these are *eo nomine* put historically far too far back.

Meanwhile, in the confused political and religious situation following the Maccabaean wars, another party had sprung into prominence, called unfortunately by a name which was to all intents and purposes the same as that of the Zadokites or Sadducaeans; these were the well-known Sadducees. The origin of their name has been much discussed, but the opinion now generally accepted is that it too is derived from Zadok the priest;[6] for they were the wealthy and aristocratic and above all things high-priestly party amongst the Jews. In the times of Nehemiah and Ezra many of the common priests and some of high-priestly lineage had married women of mixed or even foreign blood,[7]

---

[1] B. Talmud *Pesachim* 57a.

[2] Mishnah *Rosh ha-Shanah* ii 1 (*mînîm*) and B. Talmud *Rosh ha-Shanah* 22b (Boethusians).

[3] Cp. Margoliouth in *Expositor* VIII iii 234.

[4] Cp. Poznański in *RÉJ* XLIV 171–2 citing Yefet ben 'Ali on Genesis i. 14 and Villars *Abulfathi Annales Samaritani* p. 160 ll. 10–15 (where *Ba'ûnây* must be an error for *Ba'ûṭây* = Boethusians and *Saddûqây* means Sadducaeans = Zadokites).

[5] Embden & Filipowski *Liber Juchassin . . . R. Abraham Zacuti* 13a; cp. Trigland *Diatribe de Secta Karaeorum* 16–17.

[6] Geiger *op. cit.* 23–33.

[7] Ezr. ix. 1–2 (common priests), Neh. xiii. 4 (high-priest Eliashib) and 28 (Eliashib's son).

and the Sadducees might well have taken the name as a protest against the laxity of some of their number and with a view to emphasizing the purity of their own descent; they would think Zadok's blood, however much diluted, as likely to flow in their own veins as those of their rivals, whose leader was Onias (IV), while the name would not only counter the claims of the Zadokites in Egypt but would at the same time sustain their own pretensions at home. These Sadducees became politically important when Hyrcanus I (135–105 B.C.) adopted their views out of antipathy to the Pharisees,[1] although all the high-priests from Onias III had been Hasmonaeans, until Herod appointed the Zadokite Simon to that office;[2] and during the next two centuries (except while Alexandra had authority) the Sadducees were the dominant party in the state. Then the Pharisees began to gain the upper hand, although the high-priests were mostly Sadducees,[3] in the last two decades before the Revolt of A.D. 66–73, after which these disappeared from the scene as a political party, lingering on only in the uncertain notices of Rabbinic literature.[4]

Consequently, when Boethus and his followers the (Egyptian) Zadokites or Boethusians (*ex hypothesi*) attempted to revive Zadokite interest in Jerusalem, it had become little else than a piece of antiquarian lore; the (Palestinian) Zadokites or Sadducees were firmly seated in power in Jerusalem, the high-priest was their nominee and nothing could be done to dislodge them. In these circumstances the party of the Boethusians would have died out but for one fact. Opposition to Roman domination, voiced by the Pharisees in 63 B.C., was revived[5] and in 47 B.C. Hezekiah, who though called the 'arch-brigand' was probably actuated by political motives, presumably dislike of foreign rule, ravaged the Syrian frontier of Palestine, was caught by Herod and executed with a number of followers.[6] Some twenty years afterwards his son Judah with a certain Saddok or Sadduk reformed the old or formed a new party which differed from the Pharisees only in its fanatical insistence on the rule of God and in open opposition to Rome; he staged an abortive rising in 4 B.C. and another in A.D. 6, ostensibly over the question of Roman taxation,[7] when he was caught and executed[8]. Here the old Zadokite and Boethusian party with its outworn slogan could find a fresh lease of life: the Boethusians, sprung from a party which had preferred exile in Egypt to Seleucid, *i.e.* foreign, interference in Jewish affairs and therefore opposed to the Pharisees, as traditionally tolerant of foreign and especially Roman rule, and to the Sadducees for the same reason (for Hyrcanus I had done everything possible to foster friendly relations

[1] Josephus *Antiquities* XIII x 5 § 288–6 § 298.   [2] *Ibid.* XX x 3, § 238–5 § 249.
[3] Schürer *Geschichte*[3] II 201.   [4] Pp. 260–6.
[5] Josephus *Antiquities* XIV iii 2 § 41.   [6] Pp. 219.
[7] Pp. 207–9.   [8] Pp. 201–2.

with Rome)[1] and also for their usurpation of the high-priesthood (as being of rival Zadokite origin). Possibly they also resented the close connections which their leader Boethus and his family had forged with the Idumaean, *i.e.* foreign, Herod and his family; and the attitude of his son Joazar in opposing Judah over the question of taxation in A.D. 6[2] would naturally be sympathetically inclined to the new party and ready to join it, as formed with the express object of resisting foreign (*i.e.* Roman and possibly also Herodian)[3] rule. The name, too, of the co-founder Saddok or Sadduk[4] (for Judah's name served another purpose)[5] would facilitate the fusion of the two parties on economic as well as political and religious grounds in a new Zadokite party with common and indeed virtually identical aims.

All this would explain what Josephus[6] meant by declaring that the 'fourth philosophy' was 'imported ($\grave{\epsilon}\pi\epsilon\acute{\iota}\sigma\alpha\varkappa\tau\sigma\varsigma$)' and 'unusual ($\grave{\alpha}\sigma\nu\nu\acute{\eta}\theta\eta\varsigma$)' and that its founder was 'a teacher of wisdom in no respect like the others ($\sigma\sigma\varphi\iota\sigma\tau\grave{\eta}\varsigma$ $\sigma\grave{\upsilon}\delta\grave{\epsilon}\nu$ $\tauo\~\iota\varsigma$ $\check{\alpha}\lambda\lambda\sigma\iota\varsigma$ $\pi\rho\sigmao\epsilon\sigma\iota\varkappa\acute{\omega}\varsigma$)'. The doctrine was 'imported' because it derived from the Zadokite party in Egypt, whence Boethus had brought it back to Palestine, and it was 'unusual' because it challenged the prevalent theory of the Zadokite line in Palestine, which it regarded as 'impure'; and its teacher was unlike others not only because he contradicted current beliefs of the Sadducees and Pharisees but also because he was ready not merely to refuse to recognize Roman suzerainty but also to die for his loyalty to scriptural doctrine on the subject, whereas the two ruling parties were only too eager to compromise with foreign rule. At the same time the suggestion that the society of the Covenanters was originally formed in Egypt and remained there for over a century would readily explain why no Jewish historian made any reference to them before the middle of the 1st century A.D.

The history of the period as thus reconstructed agrees perfectly with the discoveries of the archaeologists as interpreted by them. First, some moment between the flight of Onias (IV) and his supporters into Egypt and the years when Hyrcanus I was persecuting the Pharisees would be the occasion when such of the original Zadokites who had not fled into Egypt might find themselves driven to seek a refuge in the Judaean wilderness; for, though Zadokite in name, they were not Sadducees but Pharisees in doctrine.[7] These were the very years when the buildings at Levels IA and B at Qumrân were being erected. Second, the years between Judah's first and second rebellions, when he and his party disappeared from the scene, were actually those in

---

[1] Josephus *Antiquities* XIII ix 2 §§ 259–66.
[2] *Ibid.* XVIII i 1 §§ 2–9.
[3] Pp. 99–100.
[4] Pp. 242–3, 260.
[5] P. 279.
[6] In *War* II viii 1 § 118.
[7] Pp. 76–8, 94–5.

which the buildings at Level II were reconstructed after their destruction by an earthquake during Herod's reign.[1]

Although however the Boethusians had apparently been merged in the party of the 'fourth philosophy' of Judah and Saddok or Sadduk, the party still retained and cherished Zadokite aspirations, as shown by the Scrolls; indeed, the maintenance of Zadokite or Sadducaean (as distinct from Sadducee) interests was inextricably bound up with intolerance of foreign rule, since the Sadducees and the Pharisees were hand in glove with the Romans. The need to defend and push Zadokite interests becomes apparent when the list of the high-priests from the beginning of Herod's reign in 37 B.C. till the destruction of Jerusalem in A.D. 70 is considered; for during these years two (the first and the last) were of humble origin, only five were not of high-priestly families, only six (Simon, Joazar, Eleazar, Simon Kantheras, Elionaios, Joseph Kabi) were of the Egyptian Zadokite line (the first four sons and the last two sons of Boethus), while the rest, nineteen in number, were almost exclusively Sadducees.[2] That only six out of these thirty-two high-priests were Zadokite or Sadducaean as against nineteen Sadducees shows how they were losing ground before the Sadducees and goes far to explain the strongly Zadokite tone of the Scrolls.

Such a fusion of the three parties will explain several hitherto unresolved difficulties. First, the puzzling mixture of religious or Zadokite and militaristic or anti-foreign (*i.e.* anti-Roman) interests in the Scrolls,[3] the former predominant in *Discipline* and the *Zadokite Documents* and the latter in the *Commentary on Habakkuk* and the *War*, is now seen to reflect the two strains in the party's composition. Second, the Boethusians are nowhere mentioned in history after the 1st century B.C. and 'Boethusian' and 'Sadducaean (*ṣaddûqî*)' are used as interchangeable terms in Rabbinic literature,[4] because the two parties were in fact one. Third, at the end of the Revolt in A.D. 73 some six hundred surviving *sicarii* fled into Egypt to escape the vengeance of the Romans,[5] who thereupon suppressed the Jewish temple at Heliopolis;[6] obviously the survivors were making their way to the old headquarters of the Zadokite movement, and the Romans destroyed the place 'lest they (*sc.* the *sicarii*) might again collect in force and draw others away with them'. The action therefore of the Romans was not a piece of wanton destruction; they seriously wished to prevent a desperate rump who refused 'to confess that Caesar was

---

[1] Pp. 37–8.
[2] Schürer *Geschichte*[3] II 216–20; cp. Smallwood in *JTS*, NS XIII 14–34.
[3] Pp. 439–41.
[4] *E.g.* Tosefta *Yoma* i 18 (Boethusian) = B. Talmud *Yoma* 19b (*Ṣaddûqî*) and Tosefta *Sukkah* iii 16 (Boethusian) = B. Talmud *Sukkah* 48b–49a (*Ṣaddûqî*); cp. B. Talmud *Erubin* 68b–69a.
[5] Josephus *War* VII x 1 § 46.   [6] *Ibid.* 2 § 421 and 4 §§ 433–5.

their lord', *i.e.* who were animated by the same motive as the party of the 'fourth philosophy', from making it a centre of future disaffection. Fourth, in spite of the Roman action numerous Ṣaddûqîm were still living in Egypt, where they were called Qara'ites, in the 13th century A.D.[1] All these facts, taken together, explain the traces of Egyptian influences which can be detected in the Scrolls and the preservation of a copy of the *Zadokite Documents* in a synagogue in Egypt.[2]

One other factor connecting the Zadokites with Egypt may here be mentioned. This is that the Hebrew (but not the Greek) *Ecclesiasticus*, composed *c.* 190–180 B.C., has a hymn, interpolated in the last chapter and found in no other version, which consists of fifteen verses giving thanks to God for the benefits conferred by him on the Jewish race; one of these is

'Give thanks to Him who hath chosen the sons of Zadok for priests; for His mercy endureth for ever.'[3]

The whole poem requires careful consideration in the light of the Scrolls;[4] but the significant points in the present connection are that the thanksgiving for the Zadokite priesthood appears to be unique in Hebrew literature and that it is found only in a Hebrew manuscript recovered from the same synagogue as the *Zadokite Documents* in Cairo.

In the heyday of the Rabbinic period, when the Rabbis as successors of the Pharisees and the scribes had become the dominant party, the opinions of the Zadokites or Covenanters were generally condemned. The Rabbis indeed may have suspected that the fanaticism of the Zadokites, who had absorbed the extremist party of the Pharisees and their Zealot followers, had been largely responsible for the disasters which had befallen the nation. The memory, then, of Zadokite intransigence and of Zadokite deviations from strict orthodoxy, which must often have been resented by straitlaced Pharisees,[5] probably lies behind the indignant outburst of R. Joshua ben Hananiah (*c.* A.D. 80–120) that 'the plagues of the Pharisees are destroying the world';[6] for so orthodox a Rabbi is not likely to be reproaching 'the strictest sect of the Pharisees' of his own time in such words. In the same spirit the Rabbis declared that 'the city of the sun' or 'the lion' was doomed to destruction;[7] and finally the Massoretes in the spirit of the Pharisees tampered with the sacred text and altered 'the city of the sun' or 'of

---

[1] Maimonides on *Abhoth* i 3. [2] Pp. 14–15.
[3] Ecclus. li. 12 (i).
[4] Cp. Lévi *L'Ecclésiastique* I xlvii–lv (where the peculiarities of the hymn are examined but not satisfactorily explained).
[5] Cp. Roth *Background* 69. [6] Mishnah *Sotah* iii 4.
[7] B. Talmud *Menahoth* 110a (where Alexandria is named as the place in which the Egyptian altar is said to have been built).

the lion (*ḥeres*)' into 'the city of destruction (*ḥeres*)', as it is read to this day in synagogue and church[1].

Briefly summarized, the argument up to this point is that those who wanted to maintain the purity of the Zadokite lineage of the priesthood split into two parties after the deposition or the murder of Onias III, when his brother and successor divided the nation into two camps by his Hellenizing policy; and the next two high-priests, not being Zadokite by birth, intensified their opposition. The less strict group, which was ready to come to terms with the Seleucid kings and to tolerate their interference in the high-priesthood, remained in Palestine; there they controlled, even if their representatives did not always hold, the high-priestly office and there they ultimately became the wealthy and aristocratic but unspiritual Sadducees of the New Testament. Many of the stricter group were unwilling to put up with foreign, originally Seleucid, interference in spiritual affairs, especially as seen in the appointment of non-Zadokite high-priests, and emigrated to Egypt; there they kept the (as they held) true Zadokite line alive until their successors were able to come back to Jerusalem after the overthrow of the Seleucid rule by the Romans in 63 B.C. Others of this last group perhaps remained in Jerusalem until they too were driven out, *e.g.* after the execution of Judah in A.D. 6–7; these would perhaps be the founders of the community at Qumrân, if this grew up during the period of Roman rule. Thus the Zadokites in Egypt and the Hasidaeans and after them the Essenes in Palestine represented parallel movements of protest against foreign interference in spiritual affairs and corruption in the high-priesthood; and the absence of the Zadokites for some 100 years will explain why no references to them can be found in Jewish literature before the 1st century A.D. Boethus, the leader of the Egyptian group, however, compromised himself in the eyes of his followers when he sought to advance the ends of his party, called after him the Boethusians, and the interests of his own family by playing into the hands of the hated, half-foreign and Idumaean, Herod. Thereupon the bulk of the Boethusians made common cause with the extreme anti-foreign, now anti-Roman, wing of the Pharisees, the so-called party of the 'fourth philosophy' under Judah and Saddok or Sadduk; and together they formed the party which in due course was merged with or became the Sons of the Covenant, the so-called Covenanters of Qumrân, and their ranks in the course of the century were swelled by the adherence of large numbers of malcontents who, whatever their individual grievances were, saw a chance to exploit them in the general hatred of Rome. Meanwhile, the successors of the Zadokites who had been left behind in Egypt when Boethus led his own followers back to Jerusalem formed

[1] Pp. 227–8.

Zadokite and therefore anti-Roman 'pockets of resistance' in Egypt, with which not a few Zealots and *sicarii* sought refuge after the suppression of the revolt against Rome in A.D. 73.

That some links are missing in the chain of argument here put forward is readily admitted; and these in the present rate of knowledge cannot and perhaps never will be made good. It does however provide an answer, however hypothetical, to several questions which have never been answered: for example, why was On called the 'city of righteousness' by the Septuagint, what eventually became of the party settled there, what place did the Boethusians fill in Jewish history (for they must have been of some importance to be mentioned in it), what happened to the 'fourth philosophy' in the century following the formation of this party, why *sicarii* sought refuge in On and why the Romans destroyed it after the First Revolt? It also goes far to fit the Covenanters into the history of the period.

2. ZADOKITES AND ZEALOTS, ASSASSINS AND BRIGANDS

In seeking to find the historical circumstances behind the story which can be elicited from the Scrolls, the conditions which must be fulfilled are those of a period of Jewish history under the early Roman empire when political authority was still in the hands of the priesthood, so that they could procure the death of a religious and political leader opposed to their views, and when revolt made Roman military intervention imminent. The leader of the party with whose affairs the Scrolls are concerned must be a person of some importance with a considerable body of followers, capable of organizing and leading the resistance of his party and of the nation to external enemies while harassed at the same time by internal rivals or adversaries who eventually brought about his downfall or death.

The main authority for the detailed history of the events leading up to the First Revolt (A.D. 66–70 or 73), of its terrible course and catastrophic termination, is the Jewish historian Josephus, who wrote his account many years afterwards. Here a word of caution is necessary. Josephus as the son of a priest was naturally inclined to sympathize with the priests, who (or of whom at any rate the elders) with the Sadducees and Pharisees were almost unanimously opposed to the Revolt. They had nothing to gain and all to lose from it, and in their opinion it could only result in the destruction of the Temple and the Holy City and in the ruin of the country; and after his capture by the Romans he went over to their side. He wrote his history, too, with Greek and especially Roman readers, whom he was especially anxious to please, always in mind; and this necessity increased his bias against all who had presumed to defy the Roman government. So Milman remarked[1] that 'Josephus, writing to conciliate the Romans both to his own person and to the miserable remnant of his own people, must be received with some mistrust. He uniformly calls the more obstinate insurgents, who continued faithful to the cause which he had deserted, by the odious name of robbers'. Actually the insurgents were rather, as Dr. Roth describes them,[2] 'patriotic (however misguided) revolutionaries', so that to some extent whatever Josephus says about them must be reversed vis-à-vis anything in the Scrolls which is thought to refer to them (in so far as they may be held to be or to include or to be connected with the Covenanters). For, while doing lip-service to the duty of respecting what he calls the 'truth of history',[3] he declares[4] that his purpose in writing his work has been 'to console the vanquished and to deter those eager for revolution'; and these motives throw light on the presumed purpose of the author of the scroll of the War, who seems to have been animated by the opposite desire to revive the broken spirits of his party (and also perhaps of his fellow-countrymen) after the collapse of the Revolt and to encourage them or their successors to make a fresh attempt at some propitious moment when they might hope for final success.

Throughout the 1st century A.D., in the difficult years preceding and even during this Revolt, Palestine was distracted by the activities of charlatans and quacks, religious and revolutionary leaders, who summoned the nation to throw off the Roman yoke in the name of religion;[5] and it was also harassed by the ravages of brigands masquerading as patriots and of patriots turned brigands and by the quarrels of rival political leaders. Josephus names several such groups:[6] these are the 'brigands (λῃσταί)', the 'assassins (σικάριοι)', who are so called from the curved dagger which they carried,[7] and the Zealots. All these may be included among those whom he calls 'insurgents', which is a general term for the whole body of rebels against Rome. The sicarii, first mentioned in the New Testament,[8] were, as Josephus depicts[9] them, revolutionaries 'who committed murders in broad daylight in the heart of the city (i.e. Jerusalem)'; and they were amongst the first 'to set the example of this lawlessness and cruelty to their kinsmen, leaving no word unspoken to insult and no deed untried to destroy the victims of their conspiracy'. He says[10] somewhat similarly of the Zealots, whom Wellhausen[11] calls the theokratische Aktionspartei of the Revolt, that 'they

[1] In History of the Jews II 255.
[2] In Background 4–5.
[3] In War I 5 § 16.
[4] Ibid. III v 8 § 108.
[5] Josephus Antiquities XX v 1 § 97–99 = Acts v. 36 (Theudas) and Antiquities XX viii 6 §§ 167–72 and War II xiii 5 §§ 261–3 = Acts xxi. 38 (Egyptian impostor); cp. Matt. xxiv. 24–6.
[6] In War II xiii 2 §§ 253–4.
[7] Pp. 183–7.
[8] Acts xxi. 38.
[9] In War II xiii 3 § 255 and VII vii 1 § 262.
[10] Ibid. VII viii 2 §§ 268–70.
[11] In Israelitische und Jüdische Geschichte⁸ 331–2.

excelled in this (*sc.* utter lawlessness), being a class which justified its name by its actions; for they copied every evil deed, nor was there any previous villainy recorded in history which they failed zealously to emulate. Yet they took their title from their professed zeal for virtue, either in mockery of those whom they wronged, so brutal was their nature, or reckoning the greatest of evils good'. He describes[1] yet another group as 'another horde with purer hands but unholier intentions', who equally disturbed and destroyed the peace of Jerusalem; some were deceivers, others deceived, but both alike 'under pretence of being inspired fostered revolution and persuaded the populace to act like madmen and led them out into the wilderness under the belief that God would there give them tokens of divine deliverance.' These will perhaps have included adherents of the 'fourth philosophy' and even Covenanters, to whose 'purer hands but unholier intentions' the historian seems to be bearing unwilling witness.[2] How exactly these various groups, including the Covenanters, may have been related to one another is a difficult question which must now be discussed and, if possible, answered.

Reasons have already been given for believing that the Covenanters had the closest affinity with the Pharisees of all the Jewish parties[3] (according to Rabbinic tradition twenty-four in number)[4] which were active during the 1st century A.D.; and Mr. Del Medico has drawn attention[5] to the movement called the 'fourth philosophy', an offshoot of the Pharisees, which Josephus briefly mentions in connection with that party.[6]

This movement took its origin with the family of a certain Ezekias (Hezekiah) whom Josephus describes[7] as 'the arch-brigand who with a very great horde was overrunning the districts of the Syrian frontier'; he was there hunted down and summarily executed *c.* 47/6 B.C. by Herod the Great at the beginning of that monarch's career. His son Judas (Judah), who was probably the same person as the Judas who became one of the founders of the party of the 'fourth philosophy', since both he and Menahem son of Judah the 'sophist'[8] who claimed the leadership of the revolt aspired to royal honours,[9] immediately after Herod's death in 4 B.C. raised a revolt which seems to have been abortive; for nothing is heard of him for the next ten years. He rebelled again in A.D. 6–7, being probably that same Judas of Galilee who 'rose up in the days of the taxing and drew away much people after

---

[1] In *War* II xiii 4 §§ 258–9.
[2] Cp. Grintz *ap.* Rabin & Yadin *Essays in memory of E. L. Sukenik* 11–18.
[3] Pp. 76–8, 94–5; cp. Farmer *Maccabees Zealots and Josephus* 32–3.
[4] P. Talm *Sanhedrin* x 5.
[5] In *Deux Manuscrits* 12–13.   [6] Pp. 99–100.
[7] In *War* I x 5 § 204; cp. *Antiquities* XIV ix 2 § 159.   [8] Pp. 252–3, 343–4.
[9] Josephus *Antiquities* XVII x 5 §§ 271–2 (Judah son of Hezekiah) and *War* II xvii 9 § 444 (Menahem son of Judah).

him'; he also perished and all, even as many as obeyed him, were dispersed.[1]

The exact moment when the 'fourth philosophy' came into existence can hardly be determined. It must have taken shape after Pompey's capture of Jerusalem in 63 B.C., following which Boethus apparently came to Jerusalem; and some time must be allowed for the alienation of his followers caused by his playing into the hands of Herod the Great, who became king in 37 B.C. Judah would have been only a child when his father Hezekiah was executed and in middle age at the time of his first rising in 4 B.C.; he must therefore have been well over 50 years of age at the time of his second rising,[2] which cost him his life in A.D. 6–7. He might have brooded over his father's fate during his boyhood, when he would have known of and perhaps have formed contacts with the Boethusians[3], and have been gathering a party of young malcontents round himself between c. 25 B.C. and 4 B.C., when it would have been ripe for action; for the abortive rising of that year would not be likely to have been the work of a solitary rebel but one which had the backing of a number of followers. The formation of the party can therefore be assigned approximately to the last quarter of the 1st century B.C.

Judah, called the Galilaean or Gaulonite (as having come from Gamala in Golan),[4] was 'a teacher of wisdom ($\sigma o \varphi \iota \sigma \tau \dot{\eta} \varsigma$)[5] with a private following, having nothing in common with the others (*i.e.* Sadducees, Essenes and Pharisees)', as Josephus says[6] in his description of the Jewish parties in his time; and a certain Saddok or Sadduk was associated with him in resisting Roman attempts to enforce taxation. Their party agreed in all respects with the Pharisees except that they cherished also an unconquerable passion for liberty and would tolerate no other lord or master but God alone, in strict accordance with the Scriptures;[7] such principles naturally brought them into conflict with Rome and would make the centres of government, Jerusalem and generally any large city, unsafe for them, as the fate of 'the Galilaeans whose blood Pilate had mingled with their sacrifices' proved.[8] In these circumstances taxation would become a burning problem; for the payment of taxes, apart from the economic aspect, was tantamount to recognizing the Roman *imperium* as the legitimate government.[9] The lawfulness of such recognition lies behind the question put to Jesus, 'whether it is lawful to pay tribute to Caesar or not';[10] for the Pharisees expected that by His answer He would embroil Himself either with the Roman authorities or with the anti-Roman elements amongst the

[1] Acts v. 37. [2] Cp. Roth *Background* 7[1]. [3] Pp. 228–34.
[4] Josephus *Antiquities* XVIII i 1 § 4 (Gaulonite); *Antiquities* XX v 2 § 102, *War* II viii 1 § 118 and xvii 8 § 433 (Galilaean).
[5] Pp. 343–4, 473–4. [6] In *Antiquities* XVIII i 6 § 23 and *War* II viii 1 § 118.
[7] Deut. xvii. 15. [8] Lk. xiii. 1–3. [9] S. pp. 207–9.
[10] Matt. xxii. 17–21, Mk. xii. 14–17, Lk. 21–5 (cp. xxiii. 2).

Jewish populace. Taxation would also fall heavily on the Covenanters, who were 'poor men' (H xii 3, 6, 10), although it is not mentioned in their literature; and they evidently shared the principles of the 'fourth philosophy', to which the *War* gives expression when it foretells 'a time of victory for the people of God and a period of dominion for the men of this party . . . when the dominion of the Kittians shall vanish' (W i 5–6).

After Judah's death in A.D. 6/7 the party must have gone underground for a while, since no reference is made to it for another forty years. The leaders of the party during this period of exile were Judah's two sons, Jacob (James) and Simeon (Simon), who in their turn followed the examples of their grandfather and their father and rebelled *c.* A.D. 46–48; but the renegade Jewish procurator Tiberius Alexander caught them and had them crucified.[1] Once again the party went underground for another twenty years, emerging again in A.D. 66, when another of Judah's sons named Manaemus (Menahem) led a group of friends and 'other bandits' up from Masada to Jerusalem to take command of the incipient revolt; and there the 'brigands' and the Zealots established themselves as his bodyguard.[2] Clearly Judah's party of the 'fourth philosophy' under his three sons, the Zealots and the so-called 'bandits (λῃσταί)', were closely connected if not identical bodies during the years leading up to the First Revolt.

Thus the party of the 'fourth philosophy' disappears from view on three separate occasions: for ten years after Judah's first unsuccessful rising (4 B.C.–A.D. 6/7), for forty years from his execution till the rising of his two elder sons (A.D. 6/7–A.D. 46/8) and for twenty years[3] from their crucifixion till the emergence of his third son to claim the leadership of the Revolt (A.D. 46/8–66). Where those who escaped went on these occasions is not known, but the neighbourhood of the Dead Sea was the obvious hiding place; there fugitives from society had concealed themselves in past ages, and there the Essenes already had their peaceful retreat at Engedi.[4] This suspicion is strengthened by archaeology, which has revealed the significant fact that the buildings at Qumrân, which had been destroyed in 31 B.C., were actually rebuilt and reoccupied while Archelaus was on the throne (4 B.C.–A.D. 6), namely during the first of these three periods. Dr. Roth then may well be right[5] in assigning the reconstruction and reoccupation of the 'monastery' at Qumrân to the fugitive members of the 'fourth philosophy'; and, if the suggestion is right, it at once brings the party of the 'fourth philosophy' into connection with the Covenanters of Qumrân.

[1] Josephus *Antiquities* XX v 2 § 102.
[2] Josephus *War* II xvii 8 §§ 433–4 and 9 § 44.   [3] Pp. 274–5.
[4] Pp. 109–10.
[5] In *Background* 24–5.

Prof. Rowley has disputed[1] this suggestion on the ground that it would be 'remarkable for the Romans to suppress the revolt of Judah and immediately afterwards permit the surviving rebels to establish themselves in the imposing headquarters at Qumrân'; but he may be overestimating the number and importance of the defeated and dispirited rebels and the strength of the newly rebuilt ruins of Qumrân, as he is certainly forgetting that the Romans similarly permitted two or three other very strongly fortified places to be seized and occupied by armed groups of insurgents early in the Revolt[2] and made no attempt to recover them till the very end.[3] Where the survivors of Judah's party lay hid during the second period (A.D. 6/7–A.D. 46/8) is also unknown; but the neighbourhood of the Dead Sea would again be a likely place. During the third period (A.D. 46/8–A.D. 66) they were at Masada; for that was the place from which Judah's third son Menahem went up to Jerusalem in A.D. 66, when 'brigands' from Masada and Zealots in Jerusalem were his escort and supporters.[4] On this occasion, then, these and the adherents of the 'fourth philosophy' were brought into connection with one another, operating from the same base.

Lastly, Menahem's relative Eleazar son of Jair[5] to all intents and purposes declared himself an adherent of the 'fourth philosophy' when he exclaimed that 'we swore long ago not to serve the Romans or any other gods';[6] for this was the party's watch-word.[7]

Josephus seems to refer to the Sadduceans or Zadokites *eo nomine* only twice.[8] The person so designated is a certain Ananias 'Sadouki (*Σαδουϰι*)', who after the murder of Menahem and the flight of the survivors of his party from Jerusalem in the autumn of A.D. 66 became involved in the treacherous massacre of the Roman garrison which had evacuated Herod's palace on condition that their lives would be spared (when their commander Metilius alone saved himself by accepting circumcision), and who soon afterwards was in Galilee plotting to undermine the position of the historian, then in command of the levies there, and to have him recalled, presumably because he was already suspected of pro-Roman sympathies. The word has been taken as a patronymic and translated 'son of Sadok',[9] but its form is that of a gentilic or appellative term; it must therefore be equivalent to the Talmudic *ṣaddûqî* which means both 'Sadducee' and 'Sadducacan' (*i.e.* Zadokite).[10] Here it cannot designate one of the priestly and

[1] In *VT* X 228.
[2] Josephus *War* II xvii 2 § 408 (Masada) and xviii 5 §§ 485–6 (Machaerus).
[3] *Ibid.* VII vi 1 § 163 (Herodium) and 4 §§ 190–209 (Machaerus), viii 5 § 304–ix 1 § 401 (Masada).
[4] Pp. 274–5.   [5] P. 269.   [6] Josephus *War* VII viii 6 § 323.
[7] Pp. 99–100.   [8] In *War* II xvii 10 §§ 449–56 and xxi 7 §§ 623–31.
[9] *E.g.* Thackeray *Josephus* [Loeb] II 499, 565 and Hengel *Zeloten* 374².
[10] Pp. 261–4.

2. ZADOKITES AND ZEALOTS, ASSASSINS, BRIGANDS 243

aristocratic Sadducees, as Ananias was a Pharisee,[1] and must be taken to mean 'Sadducaean' or Zadokite; for Ananias was clearly anti-Roman in outlook. If this argument is right, the important conclusion may be drawn that these two terms, namely 'Sadducee' (Σαδδουκαῖος) as denoting a member of the aristocratic and high-priestly party and 'Sadducaean' (Σαδουκι) as denoting a follower of Judah and Saddok or Sadduk, are distinguished by the historian as they are not distinguished in Talmudic literature, where the same term is used for both 'Sadducee' and 'Sadducaean', i.e. Zadokite (ṣaddûqî).[2]

The title by which the Zealots were called or called themselves[3] was of Biblical origin, as Dr. Roth has remarked,[4] being based on the story of Phinehas son of Eleazar who checked the plague at Baal-Peor by thrusting his spear through the Hebrew man and the Midianite woman whom he had married; so by taking the law into his own hands 'he was zealous for his God and made atonement for the Israelites'.[5] So Mishnaic law provided that 'if a man steals a vessel belonging to the Temple or invokes a heathen god (?) in a curse or marries an Aramaean woman, the Zealots may fall on him';[6] clearly, they regarded themselves and perhaps were regarded as entitled to take the law into their own hands in the case of certain religious offences. Further, the elaboration of the story of Phinehas in the Midrash is of considerable interest in the present connection; for there he is described as concealing the head or blade of his spear 'in his bosom' as he went to slay the offenders,[7] just as the sicarii are described as carrying their daggers 'in their bosoms' concealed under their garments when bent on assassination.[8] Clearly, as Dr. Roth says,[9] both Zealots and sicarii modelled themselves on Phinehas, the former in his mental outlook and the latter in his mode of action. Dr. Roth at the same time draws attention[10] to another significant point, that the story of Phinehas in the Old Testament immediately follows Balaam's prophecy about 'a star out of Jacob' and his mysterious reference to 'ships from the coasts of Kittim',[11] whom some ancient versions here identify with the Romans.[12] Thus both Zealots and sicarii seem to be brought into connection with the Covenanters, whose characteristic weapon was a curved dagger and whose enemies were the 'Kittim', i.e. the Romans and who were buoyed up by Messianic hopes.[13]

This same term had already acquired a special significance in

---

[1] Josephus Life xxxix 197. [2] Pp. 261–4.
[3] Josephus War II xxi 1 § 651 and IV iii 9 §§ 160–1. [4] In JSS IV 335–6.
[5] Num. xxv. 1–15; cp. 1 Macc. ii. 26, 54 and Ecclus. xlv. 23–4.
[6] Mishnah Sanhedrin ix 6. [7] Midrash R. Numbers xx § 25.
[8] Josephus War II xiii 3 § 255 and xvii 6 § 425. [9] In JSS IV 335–6.
[10] Ibid. 336. [11] Num. xxiv. 15–24.
[12] Pp. 197–8. [13] Pp. 467–8.

Maccabaean times, when the high-priest Onias III, described as 'a zealot for the laws',[1] became a martyr to his faith; and Mattathias, the father of the Maccabees, was praised 'because his zeal was kindled'[2] when he called on any 'who was a zealot for the customs of their forefathers and the service of God' to raise the standard of rebellion against those who would compel him to worship false gods;[3] but no party of that name is mentioned before the 1st century A.D. That some such party of resistance was formed out of opposition to the Seleucid rulers, against whom the Maccabees rebelled, and continued underground during the early years of the Roman occupation is probable even if it cannot be proved. Hezekiah is likely to have represented a party, although none such is mentioned; and similarly Judah and Sadduk may have worked on 'Zealot' elements, since the Zealots seem to have emerged as a party about this time, inasmuch as the name already has a definite political connotation by A.D. 30–33.[4] Nothing else, however, is heard of them *eo nomine* as a group till the outbreak of the Revolt in A.D. 66; for their attitude to Roman rule must have made residence in Jerusalem and other big cities difficult if not impossible.[5] Then Judah's third son Menahem, so far from being on bad terms with the Zealots,[6] took them as his bodyguard when he marched up to the Temple in royal state to claim the leadership of the Revolt in the autumn of A.D. 66,[7] so that the 'house of Judah' which supported the Rightful Teacher may be properly brought into connection with them;[8] and the fiercest of the Zealots were, like Hezekiah and Judah, of Galilaean origin.[9] Left leaderless in the city after the murder of Menahem and the flight of Eleazar son of Jair, the Zealots attached themselves to various leaders, *e.g.* Eleazar son of Gion or Simon[10] and John of Gischala.[11] This John indeed seems to have been an opponent of the Covenanters as he was not always a member of the Zealot party;[12] but he may have once belonged to 'them and afterwards left[13] them as he twice caused secessions from the ranks of the Zealots.[14]

Many Zealots, however, remained faithful to their old allegiance; so Simon and Jude, apparently brothers of Eleazar son of Jair, distinguished themselves amongst the Zealots in the last desperate battles in Jerusalem.[15]

Two or three objections have been brought against the identification

[1] 2 Macc. iv. 2.
[2] *Ibid.* ii. 24.
[3] Josephus *Antiquities* XII vi 2 § 271.
[4] Pp. 245–7.
[5] Roth in *JSS* IV 336–7.
[6] Pp. 274–5.
[7] Pp. 268–9.
[8] Cp. De Medico *Deux Manuscrits* 125.
[9] Josephus *War* IV ix 10 § 558.
[10] *Ibid.* IV i 1 § 225; V i 2 §§ 5–10, vi 1 § 250.
[11] *Ibid.* IV ix 10 §§ 558–9, 564, 570; V vi 1 § 250, xiii 1 § 528.
[12] *E.g., ibid.* IV iii 13 §§ 214–5.   [13] Pp. 291–7.
[14] *Ibid.* IV vii 1 §§ 389–97 and V i 2 §§ 5–6; cp. xii 1 § 528.
[15] *Ibid.* VI i 8 § 92 (Simon and Jude) and ii 6 § 148 (Simon).

of the Covenanters with the Zealots. First, Dr. Zeitlin argues[1] that, if the Covenanters are held to be the followers of Judah and Saddok or Sadduk, the founders of the 'fourth philosophy', they cannot have been Zealots since this term can have had no recognized political connotation till 'after the Jewish victory over the Romans' in A.D. 66; for Josephus does not introduce it before that event. The description, however, of the disciple Simon as the 'Zealot' or 'Cananaean' in the New Testament (unless the Evangelists have been guilty of an anachronism) puts it back by a quarter if not half a century;[2] for it implies the formation of the party before A.D. 30–33, in fact to the very period when the party of the 'fourth philosophy' must have been in process of becoming merged in that of the Zadokites or Covenanters. Second, Dr. Wernberg-Møller finds it strange[3a] that Josephus makes no reference to the Zealots' use of a peculiar calendar such as they must have had if they are taken to be the Covenanters. One or two stories, however, which the historian tells[3b] about the Zealots seem to imply such a calendar; and the reason why the historian says nothing of it is surely that he looks on them with intense dislike and is not concerned to give any account of their doctrines except in so far as they affect the Revolt. So, even when purporting to summarize the teaching of the 'fourth philosophy', he contents himself with citing a single divergence from orthodox Pharisaism, namely the intolerance of any other rule but that of God, which he regards as the cause of the war and the ruin of the Jewish state. Further, the Covenanter was required to be 'zealous for the Law' (D ix 23; cp. D iv 4 T ii 15 xiv 4) exactly as the Zealots were so called for 'their zeal for God and the Law'.[4] Lastly, that the Covenanters and the Zealots may not be identified because of their very different philosophies is a false antithesis; not all Covenanters were pacifists, as Ananias 'Sadouki' (if this appellation is rightly explained)[5] by his behaviour and *War* by its glorification of the 'holy war' show, and so presumably not all Zealots were necessarily fanatically militant. Zeal can and does take many different forms even within a single party or organization.[6]

Whether the 'brigands ($\lambda\eta\sigma\tau\alpha\iota$)', of whom Josephus often speaks, are to be identified with either of these groups is not absolutely clear but is highly probable in some if not in all passages.[7] Certainly Josephus describes Hezekiah, the father of the founder of the 'fourth philosophy' and the rebel who perished in 47 B.C., as the 'arch-brigand',[8] and the

---

[1] In *Tradition* II 183–4.
[2] Mat. x. 4, Mk. iii. 18 (Cananaean) = Lk. vi. 15 and Acts i. 13 (Zealot).
[3a] In *JJS* IX 218.
[3b] For example in *War* II xviii 9 §§ 443–5 (Zealots); cp. II xiii 3 § 255 and xvii 6 § 425, IV vii 2 § 402 (*sicarii*).   [4] Hippolytus *Refutation* ix 26; cp. 28.
[5] Pp. 272–3.   [6] S. pp. 439–41; cp. Gal. i. 13–14.
[7] Cp. Roth in *JSS* IV 332–3, 347–8.   [8] Pp. 239–40.

R

sicarii, who are the same group as or a sub-group of the Zealots, are described as 'another group of brigands' or simply as 'brigands'.[1] Josephus also says[2] that Manaemus (Menahem) took a number of 'brigands' with him as a bodyguard when coming up to Jerusalem and that he had the Zealots as escort at his entry into the Temple, and he elsewhere describes[3] those who perished with him on that occasion as a 'mob of brigands' or as the 'brigands with him'[4]; and he also says that the *sicarii* were under the command of Menahem's relative Eleazar son of Jair.[5] This term, then, being sufficiently imprecise, perhaps served not only for brigands in the strict sense but also loosely for any groups of whom the historian personally disapproved, now the slaves, malcontents and ruffians,[6] who joined this or that party as much for their own as for any patriotic ends and now the regular insurgents, especially the members of the two principal groups involved in the Revolt; only the context may show whether insurgents, Zealots or *sicarii* (in so far as these can be distinguished), or ordinary bandits, are meant in any given passage.

Fanatical opposition to Rome had already flared up in 47 B.C., when the 'arch-brigand' Hezekiah rose, was caught and executed, in Galilee,[7] and it grew in intensity as the years passed, and the rising of Hezekiah's son Judah against paying taxes is mentioned in the New Testament.[8] Possibly too the 'brigands ($\lambda\eta\sigma\tau\alpha\iota$)' mentioned in several places in the Gospels, where the word is commonly translated 'thieves' or 'robbers', may have been not criminals in the ordinary sense but political offenders. Those whom Jesus drove out of the Temple with the money-changers[9] were perhaps, as Dr. Roth argues,[10] political agitators, although the suggestion is not free from objections; and the two crucified with Him[11] may well have been condemned for some political offence, *e.g.* engaging in activities likely to embroil the Jewish ruling classes with the Roman government, even though they are also described as 'malefactors ($\varkappa\alpha\varkappa\omicron\tilde{\upsilon}\rho\gamma\omicron\iota$)'.[12] Such passages would then be witnesses to the continuing activity of these people, who were contemptuously but incorrectly called 'brigands' from the time of Judah's rising to that of the First Revolt, which were crucial years for the Zadokite movement.

If then not only the Zealots but also the 'brigands' (as Josephus used the term) were well known *c.* A.D. 30–33, being mentioned in the Gospels, Jesus would have been fully aware of their activities and might already have seen the menace which they would become and

---

[1] Josephus *War* II xiii 2 § 254 and xvii 6 § 425.   [2] In *War* II xvii 9 § 444.
[3] In *Life* v 21, xi 46.   [4] S. p. 249 n. 2.
[5] In *War* VII viii 1 § 253.   [6] Josephus *War* IV ix 3 § 508 ($\delta\omicron\tilde{\upsilon}\lambda\omicron\iota$ and $\pi\omicron\nu\eta\rho\omicron\iota$).
[7] Pp. 239–40.   [8] Acts v. 37.
[9] Mk. xi. 15–17; cp. Mt. xxi. 12–13 and Lk. xix. 45–6.
[10] In *Novum Testamentum* IV 174–81.
[11] Mt. xxvii. 38 and Mk. xv. 27.   [12] Lk. xxiii. 32–3.

even have divined that they would eventually provoke the Romans into retaliation. No great prescience would be needed in one who knew his fellow-countrymen to foresee that they would not stop until they had brought down ruin on their own heads; history would tell him what form that ruin would be likely to take. Passages in the Gospels, therefore, referring to the destruction of Jerusalem,[1] which did not take place till A.D. 70, might not necessarily have been written up after the event.

The *sicarii* were apparently a group closely connected with Judah the Gaulonite or Galilaean who, as Josephus relates,[2] was 'eager for revolt (*sc.* against Rome)'; for he says[3] also that 'in those days the *sicarii* combined against those who consented to submit to Rome and in every way treated them as enemies' and that 'the people joined them in the revolt and took part with them in the war with Rome, only however to suffer worse atrocities at their hands'; and elsewhere he says[4] that it was not until Gessius Florus was procurator (A.D. 64–6) that 'the nation began to grow mad with this distemper', *i.e.* the anti-Roman movement. Judah's followers, however, were not apparently called *sicarii* until Felix was procurator (A.D. 52–65), when their daring outrages in Jerusalem again attracted attention. Their first victim then was the high-priest Jonathan; and his death was followed by many other murders.[5] They also took part in the riots in Jerusalem, including the assault on the Temple, immediately after the outbreak of the Revolt in the autumn of A.D. 66.[6] They too and others were in Masada towards the south-western end of the Dead Sea when Mena-hem's relative Eleazar son of Jair and his followers took refuge there after the murder of Menahem,[7] and there they held out to the bitter end and committed mass-suicide in A.D. 73[8] in preference to falling into Roman hands;[9] for, like the followers of Judah and Saddok or Sadduk, they steadily refused to acknowledge Caesar as lord to the very end.[10] Lastly, Josephus assigns[11] the same motive of self-interest for the conduct of both parties during all these disastrous years; he asserts that the followers of Judah and Sadduk committed every sort of crime and brought ruin to the nation 'in pretence indeed for the public welfare but in reality for hopes of gain to themselves' and that the *sicarii* used their claim to be resisting enslavement by Rome as 'a pretence and a cloak for their own cruelty and avarice'. These

---

[1] *E.g.* Matt. xxiv. 15–22, Mk. xiii. 14–17, Lk. xxi. 20–24.
[2] In *Antiquities* XVIII i 1 § 4; cp. *War* II viii 1 § 118.
[3] In *War* VII viii 1 §§ 253–8.   [4] In *Antiquities* XVIII i 6 § 25.
[5] Josephus *War* II xiii 3 §§ 254–7.
[6] *Ibid.* II xvii 6 §§ 425–9.   [7] *Ibid.* II xvii 9 § 447.
[8] *Ibid.* VII viii 1 § 252.   [9] *Ibid.* VII vii 2 § 275–ix 1 § 410.
[10] *Ibid.* VII x 1 §§ 418–19.
[11] In *Antiquities* XVIII i 1 § 7 and *War* VII viii 1 § 256.

two statements strengthen the suspicion that the followers of Judah and Sadduk and the *sicarii* must in the end have been or become identical.[1]

The *sicarii* and the Zealots seem at the same time to be so interconnected that their eventual identification can hardly be doubted. Indeed, almost the only distinction between them is that, although both were connected with Masada,[2] during the Revolt the Zealots were active for the most part (except for occasional sallies) within the city of Jerusalem, while the *sicarii* operated mostly (from the time at any rate when the city was completely invested) in the surrounding country (although they occasionally appeared in it).[3] The Zealots would seem at the outset to have been a more conciliatory group which had some respect for law or at any rate for the forms of law in preference to political assassination, so that they would be closer to the 'fourth philosophy' than to any of the more militant groups,[4] but in the end they proved themselves no less violent.[5] The *sicarii* regularly behaved themselves equally ill, 'leaving no word unspoken, no need untried to destroy the victims of their conspiracy'[6] and readily assassinated their political opponents.[7] While then the Zealots were the backbone of the Revolt and the organized force behind it, the *sicarii* were the riff-raff of the population who were operating primarily for their own selfish ends and who also played the part of free-lances in the struggle with Rome as much to cover their own nefarious activities as to advance the common cause. Consequently the Covenanters would seem to have been warned against repeating their offences while they were free to join such a movement as that of the Zealots.[8] When therefore Milman wrote[9] that 'the *sicarii* were the most extravagant of the school of Judas the Galilaean' and that 'the bold and lofty tenets of Judas the Galilaean none the less inspired their ideals', he was not far from the truth.

In conclusion, the three parties, however they differed in origin and function, were or became in actuality one. Josephus so regarded them; for according to him Menahem's followers might be called either Zealots[10] or 'brigands',[11] the *sicarii* were but 'another horde of brigands',[12] and *sicarii* were loyal to his relative Eleazar to the end.[13] That ultimately 'Zealots' and *sicarii*, both of whom

---

[1] Cp. Hengel *Zeloten* 91–3.   [2] P. 250.
[3] *E.g.* Josephus *War* II xvii 6 § 425 (*sicarii* in the city) and IV ix 5 § 514 (sally of Zealots from the city).
[4] *Ibid.* IV v 4 §§ 334–44.   [5] Pp. 238–9.
[6] *Ibid.* § 262.   [7] *Ibid.* II xiii 3 § 256.
[8] Cp. Hahn in *AOASH* XIV 136–7.   [9] In *History of the Jews* II 206, 240.
[10] In *War* II xvii 9 § 444.   [11] In *Life* iii 21.
[12] In *War* II xiii 3 § 254; cp. xvii 6 § 425.
[13] *Ibid.* VII viii 1 § 253.

Hippolytus derives from the Essenes,[1] became interchangeable terms,[2] therefore, was as natural as it was inevitable.

How then did these groups stand to the Covenanters?

First, Zealots and 'brigands' and *sicarii*, who flourished at the same time during the formative years of the society of the Covenanters, were animated by the same fanatical hatred of a foreign enemy as the Covenanters, the former of the Romans and the latter of the Kittians, who were none other than the Romans.[3] Again, both the *sicarii* and the Covenanters used the characteristic curved dagger, the former as an instrument primarily of assassination and the latter as a weapon of legitimate warfare; and the 'brigands' similarly carried a 'small dagger (ξιφίδιον)'[4] concealed under their clothes for the purpose of political assassination.[5] Further, the Zealots elected one Phanni (Phineas) to be high-priest (actually the last high-priest) by lot,[6] although the procedure was unconstitutional, since the office was hereditary; and they chose him not so much for his humble origin as because he bore a name honoured in Zealot circles.[7] This action would seem at once to connect them with the Covenanters, who too used the lot for a variety of purposes, including the election of members (D vi 15–23, I Q *28A* i 9) and officers (I Q *28A* i 16–17) of their society, so that it might seem to them a natural and obvious method of election, especially as it had Biblical authority.[8]

Second, the Zealots and *sicarii* resembled the Covenanters in the ease with which they seem to have formed splinter-groups.[9] For example, the *sicarii* had been troubled by Theudas and an Egyptian pseudoprophet[10] some years before the Revolt,[11] and during it a party of Zealots led by Eleazar son of Simon and three others broke away from the main body;[12] so the Covenanters suffered much from 'the splutterer of lies who led many astray to build a city of vanity at the cost of bloodshed and to set up a community by treachery' (H x 9–10)[13] and Damascus was the scene of a schism in their body.[14] Dr. Roth identifies[15] the Egyptian pseudoprophet with the 'splutterer of lies'; but no shred of evidence supports the identification. Too much stress, too, must not be laid on these dissensions; for political and religious groups have always been plagued by them.

[1] In *Refutation* IX xxvi 2.
[2] *E.g.* B. Talmud *Sanhedrin* 82a-b and 106b, where Phinehas is classed with the 'zealots (qannā'īn)' but called a 'brigand (listā'āh)', and Schechter *Aboth deR. Nathan* 20 (siqārīn) = 32 (qannā'īn).
[3] Pp. 197–216. [4] Josephus *Antiquities* XX viii 5 § 164.
[5] Pp. 183–7. [6] Josephus *War* IV iii 7 § 153–86 § 155 (cp. iii §§ 160–1).
[7] P. 243. [8] *E.g.* 1 Chron. xxiv. 5–xxvi. 19.
[9] Roth in *JSS* IV 339–40. [10] Pp. 238–9, 249.
[11] Josephus *Antiquities* XX v 1 §§ 97–8, viii 6 §§ 169–72 and *War* II xiii 5 §§ 261–3; cp. Acts v 36 xxi 38.
[12] Josephus *War* V i 2 §§ 5–6. [13] Pp. 296–7.
[14] Pp. 306–10. [15] *Ibid.* 339.

Third, Zealots and brigands and the *sicarii*, Menahem and Eleazar, alternatively or simultaneously throughout the Revolt occupied Masada which remained in rebel hands till the very end of the Revolt;[1] thus, lying on either side of Qumrân, they could have maintained easy contact with the Covenanters or with any amongst them who wished to take part with them against the common enemy.[2]

That the Zealots, whose extreme wing was the *sicarii*, and the Covenanters may be in some sense identified[3] will also explain why these last called themselves or were called 'poor men' (H xii 3, 6, 10). This term had a twofold application, a political and a religious. The Zealots and *sicarii* and other insurgent groups made a point of 'fostering revolutionary changes' and stirring up the poor against the rich and of thus winning their adherence in the struggle in which they were engaged as much against wealthy, priestly and aristocratic, pro-Roman sympathizers and rival insurgent groups as against the Romans;[4] and their rival Simon bar Giora outbid all in his political programme by promising freedom to any slaves who joined him.[5] Also, all the religious parties or sects, Essenes and Christians at the same time and the Qara'ites long afterwards,[6] emphasized poverty as a virtue conducive to personal holiness. The Covenanters were no exception to this rule; for *Discipline* shows the value which the spiritual members of the society gave to detachment from worldly goods, while the military members of the order must have been alive to the necessity of raising recruits among the impoverished proletariat and the dispossessed peasantry in order to carry on the struggle against rival parties and foreign enemies. Consequently 'poor men' was partly a religious and partly a political title adopted to attract the populace.

In conclusion, absolute certainty on the identity of these parties is unobtainable and the identification of them as here argued cannot be proved. The adherents of the 'fourth philosophy' and the Zealots, the *sicarii* and the 'brigands', are known only in their political aspects from the picture drawn by a historian strongly prejudiced against them; contrariwise, the Covenanters, to whom the historian does not refer as a group because he seems to have regarded them spiritually as a sub-group of the Essenes,[7] whom he has described *eo nomine* in detail and politically as a branch of the Zealots, whom he detests, can be studied only in theological texts composed by the spiritually minded members of their own society, who are concerned to present it in the

---

[1] Josephus *War* II xvii 2 § 408 (insurgents), 8 §§ 433–4 (Menahem), 9 § 447 (Eleazar), xxii 2 § 653 (brigands); IV vii 2 §§ 399–404 (*sicarii*), ix 3 § 504 (brigands), ix 5 § 516 (*sicarii*), ix 9 § 555 (brigands); VII viii 1 §§ 252–3, 2 §§ 275–6, 4 § 297 (Eleazar and *sicarii*).
[2] Roth in *RQ* II 83.   [3] Cp. Klausner *Hisṭoriyah* V 332–40.
[4] *E.g.* Josephus *War* II xiii 4 § 259 and 6 §§ 264–5, xvii 6 § 427.
[5] *Ibid.* IV ix 3 § 508 and 4 § 510.   [6] Szyszman in *ZR-Gg.* XI 373–80.
[7] Pp. 105–6.

most favourable light and whose accounts are as valuable as monkish records for the events of contemporary secular history. The argument, however, seems to show that the followers of the 'fourth philosophy', the Zealots, the 'brigands', now co-operating and now quarrelling, acting now in concert and now as distinct groups, can hardly be dissociated and ought in all probability to be regarded as overlapping, connected or even identical with the Covenanters, whether jointly or severally; for no clear distinction can now be consistently traced between the various groups, and whatever may have existed at the outset will have become blurred and altered during the course of the struggle. Some of these groups, those most clearly defined and most strongly organized, would provide the spiritual and political back-ground of the opposition to foreign rule, without which it could never have attained coherence or would soon have collapsed. Thus 'exegetes (ἐξηγηταί)' and 'teachers of wisdom (σοφισταί)' i.e. interpreters of the Law and the Scriptures, such as the priestly chief of the Covenanters was (H ii 7–9), not only stirred up the disaffection of the 'populace (πλῆθος)' but also with their own hands performed deeds calculated to provoke Roman vengeance, courting martyrdom[2] in the hope of a future life like the Covenanters (T vi 29–34)[3] and many others in the 1st century A.D.[4] Various named teachers of the resistance were similarly called 'teachers of wisdom', exactly as the leader of the Covenanters was known as the 'Rightful Teacher (môrēh ṣedeq)'.[5] Other groups, such as the sicarii, inspired by the same teachers and in turn inspiring the 'populace (πλῆθος)' to join them, loosely knit but goaded by a common economic distress as much as by anything else into open insurrection, were the militant extremists who formed the guerilla-fighters and partisans of the 'resistance',[6] which but for their cooperation would have sunk into futile speculation. At the same time, that a fanatical anti-Roman Pharisee is described as a 'Zadokite (Σαδουκι)'[7] and that the Covenanters of Qumrân, who are depicted as fanatically opposed to the 'Kittians', i.e. the Romans,[8] are similarly called Sons of Zadok or 'Zadokites', inevitably connects the Pharisaic group of Ananias the Σαδουκι with the Zadokites of Qumrân, although these can be shown to have been at variance with the Pharisees on a number of theological and legal points. Such a fusion of disparate elements in a single society is no matter for surprise; history shows other examples of societies at once spiritual and political, religious and militant.[10]

[1] Josephus Antiquities XVII ix 3 § 216 and War I xxxiii 2 § 648, II i 3 § 10.
[2] Hengel Zeloten 263–77.   [3] Pp. 71–2, 74–5.
[4] E.g. Rev. xx. 4–6.   [5] Pp. 257–8.
[6] P. 248.   [7] Josephus Antiquities XX viii 5 § 160.
[8] Pp. 197–216.   [9] Cp. Buchanan in HUCA. XXXI 103–5.
[10] P. 440.

3. JUDAH AND SADDOK OR SADDUK

Josephus describes the 'arch-brigand Hezekiah's son Judah as a very clever sophist' or 'teacher of wisdom' and his son Menahem simply as a 'sophist' or 'teacher of wisdom (σοφιστής)'; the epithet is probably intended to distinguish the father as the inspirer of the 'fourth philosophy' and the intellectual leader of the movement from the son as only carrying on its traditions.[1] This is a term which Josephus elsewhere applies[2] to masters of the law; for example, he so describes two teachers or Rabbis, as they may be called[3] (for the title was already well known in the 1st century A.D.),[4] who were distinguished as 'having a very great reputation for an accurate knowledge of the national laws and customs'; and Jesus is similarly called a 'sophist' by Lucian,[5] a satirist of the 2nd century A.D. The application of this term, which seems to have had little or no derogatory or contemptuous implication at this period, cannot be exactly defined; but it obviously implies a person of intellectual tastes and a teacher, presumably one holding theories or views on Jewish life which he endeavours to transmit to his disciples.[6] Further, a Palestinian tradition[7] speaks of people 'wise in fixing New Years and new moons and in calculating months and years, reckoners (sôfisṭîn) of the beginning(s) of the months so as to fix the feasts in their seasons'; and this use of the term is especially important in view of the Covenanters' preoccupation with the calendar.[8] The title seems therefore to be designed to bring out both Menahem's function as the head of a party with its own peculiar calendar (cp. T i 23–5)[9] and that of the Rightful Teacher, whose title is itself of Biblical origin,[10] as qualified as much to teach his followers right ritual observances as to expound the society's own interpretation of the Scriptures.

The family of Hezekiah perhaps attached some importance to the hereditary principle, based on their unswerving opposition to Rome; indeed, this had resulted in the death of five of its members, two of whom (and possibly others) enjoyed the title of 'sophist' or 'teacher of wisdom'.[11] So the title of 'Rightful Teacher' was apparently borne not merely by one individual but by several distinct persons; for the author of the *Zadokite Documents* says of one that God had considered His people's deeds 'and raised up a Rightful Teacher for them' to lead them in the way which He desired (Z i 7), and of another that the

---

[1] Cp. Roth *Background* 28[1].
[2] In *War* I xxxii 2 §§ 648–9.
[3] Roth *op. cit.* 7; cp. Zeitlin in *JQR*, NS XLVIII 254.
[4] *E.g.* Matt. xxiii. 7, 8 and Jn. i. 38, 49 iii. 2, 26 vi. 25; cp. Mk. x. 51 and Jn. xx. 16.
[5] Lucian *de Peregrini morte* 13.
[6] Cp. Roth *op. cit.* 7–8.
[7] Targum on 1 Chron. xii. 32.
[8] Pp. 316–30. Roth *op. cit.* 60[2].
[9] Pp. 323–81, 343–4, 357.
[10] Hos. x. 12.
[11] Pp. 240, 269.

princes and nobles will not grasp instruction 'till the appearance of
one who shall teach righteousness at the end of the days' (Z viii 10).
Clearly one Teacher, if not several, had already come and perhaps
had died and another who should teach righteousness at the end of
the age was still expected.[1] Briefly, then, as there were two 'sophists',
Judah the founder of the 'fourth philosophy' and his son Menahem,
the one long dead and the other still alive when the Revolt broke out,
so there might be two 'rightful teachers', one whom God had raised
up and another who should come afterwards. The coincidence of titles
in time and place cannot be overlooked; and, as these two enjoyed the
title of 'sophist', so Eleazar son of Jair, another descendant of Judah
and a 'relative (προσήκων)' of Menahem, was qualified to be called a
'teacher of righteousness', if his final speech may be trusted,[2] whatever
his personal character was. The *double entente* in the term is but one of
several such plays on terms and is therefore probably intentional;
the danger was thereby avoided of revealing the leader's name, but
the true interpretation of the expression would be seized by the
initiated Covenanter while it remained secret to anyone uninitiated in
the mysteries of the order.

Accordingly, Lagrange was probably not far wrong[3] in connecting
the group called the 'Sons of Zadok' in the *Zadokite Documents* (which
alone of the Scrolls was known when he put forward the suggestion)
with the party which looked to Saddok or Sadduk,[4] the colleague of
Judah 'the sophist' or 'teacher of wisdom' in promulgating the 'fourth
philosophy', as their founder or rather co-founder. The party would
then have taken his name rather than that of Judah partly because
Judah's death already had contributed to the eclipse of his name, and
partly because the name of Zadok might give them a spurious appearance of antiquity and respectability, since it recalled 'the priests, the
Levites, the sons of Zadok' of whom the prophet Ezekiel had spoken[5]
as also perhaps Simon the Just.[6] What is important here, however, is
that the author of the *Zadokite Documents* has deliberately altered
Ezekiel's words to read 'the priests, the Levites, and the Sons of Zadok'
(Z v 7), inserting 'and' to distinguish the priests and Levites from the
'Sons of Zadok'. That this is no textual accident but a deliberate
alteration is proved by his explanation; for he goes on to say that 'the
priests are the penitents of Israel who have gone forth from the land
of Israel, and the Levites are those who are joined with them, and the
Sons of Zadok are the elect of Israel, called by name who will arise at
the end of the days' (Z vi 1–2). The writer is projecting himself into

---

[1] Pp. 474–6. [2] Josephus *War* VII viii 6 §§ 323–36, 341–88.
[3] In *Le Judaïsme avant Jésus-Christ*[2] 332–3; cp. Del Medico *Deux Manuscrits* 63–4, 92–3.
[4] Cp. Farmer *Maccabees Zealots and Josephus* 34–5.
[5] Ezek. xliv. 15. [6] S. pp. 228, 258.

the past and foretelling the future, when the party would be in exile and split; but his purpose is clear. He here describes as Sons of Zadok the lay members of the society as distinct from the priests. That 'Sons of Zadok' denotes elsewhere also the priestly members (D v 2, 9; I Q 22A i 2) is no matter; once again, such a *double entente* is only too characteristic of the Scrolls. The title thus served a double purpose: it connected the society with Zadok the priest through its priestly members, thus recalling those 'sons of Zadok' whose ancestor had supported David and crowned Solomon and whom alone Ezekiel regarded as of the true priestly line, and at the same time it described the lay members by the name of 'Zad(d)ok' their co-founder. The order might thus be called 'Sons of Zadok' in a double sense. Yet Judah's name was not entirely forgotten; it survived in the 'house of Judah', which became the designation of the family of Menahem and Eleazar son of Jair[1] as leaders of the party and of their immediate circle (H viii 1 Z iv 11).[2] Whether Menahem may have had the blood of the tribe of Judah or of king David in his veins to justify the title on another ground is not known but is conceivable; certainly he affected the royal style and perhaps claimed royal privileges.[3]

That the lay members of the party are called Sons of Zadok as the followers of Judah's colleague Saddok has one important consequence. They could not have been so described before the 1st century A.D., when the only recorded Zadok to whom the title could be referred was the priest of that name; the title as applied to laymen would be intelligible only when a lay Zadok was known from whom it could have been derived. The only suitable layman of that name in history is this Saddok or Sadduk, Judah's colleague in the 'fourth philosophy'; and any document containing the name as alluding to this person must be dated in or after his period, *i.e.* in the 1st century A.D.

Twice in the Scrolls the name of Zadok appears in suspicious circumstances. First, although the Covenanters are properly called 'Sons of Zadok' (Z v 7 vi 2; cp. D v 2, 9 and elsewhere), they are once called the 'Sons of the Zadok (*haṣṣāḏôq*)' by an apparent solecism (D ix 14). This phrase has of course been emended into the obvious 'Sons of Zadok (*Ṣāḏôq*)'[4] or 'sons of righteousness (*ṣeḏeq*)',[5] which both occur elsewhere (*e.g.* D v 2, 9 Z v 7 vi 2 D iii 20, 22), or 'the sons of the righteous one (*haṣṣaddîq*)';[6] but *difficilior lectio potior* is a rule of interpretation which, even if it is apparently unknown to Hebraists, suggests caution in emendation. The reading is simply a *double entente* designed, like the many *formae mixtae* which the Massoretes have introduced into the text of the Old Testament as offering a choice of

---

[1] Cp. Del Medico *Énigme* 349, 356-7.   [2] Josephus *War* VII viii 1 § 253.
[3] Pp. 356-8.   [4] Ginsberg *ap.* Brownlee *Discipline* 37.   [5] Kuhn *Konkordanz* 185.
[6] Cp. Midrash R. *Leviticus* i § 3, where 'Zadok' (as meaning 'righteous') is given as a title to 'Aaron the priest'; s. Wernberg-Møller *Discipline* 90-2.

alternative readings, to leave an ambiguity. It can be read 'Sons of Zadok (*Ṣāḏôq*)' and so recall the Covenanters' connection with Zadok, David's chaplain to whose line Ezekiel restricts the priesthood, and Saddok or Sadduk the co-founder of the party of the 'fourth philosophy' with whom the Zadokites seem to have been merged;[1] or it can be read 'sons of the rightful one (*haṣṣaddîq*)' and so bring the famous Zadokite high-priest Simon the Just (*haṣṣaddîq*) into connection with the Covenanters.[2] At the same time it perhaps hints at the title of 'the sons of the just' or 'righteous ones (*ṣāḏeqān*)' which the author of *Jubilees* gives to the righteous descendants of Noah by way of contrast to the 'sons of perdition' under Satan's dominion;[3] for *Jubilees* is connected with the Scrolls through the peculiar calendar which is common to them both and which the Rightful Teacher is bound as σοφιστής to maintain as revealed in all its details in that book.[4] Second, a historical passage, speaking of David's sin with Bathsheba, excuses him on the ground that he had not read 'the sealed book of the Law in the ark of the covenant' because it had not been opened 'till the appearance of Zadok' (Z vii 6). An allusion to David's chaplain of that name is improbable; and a reference to the high-priest Hilkiah, the finder of the book of the Law in Josiah's reign,[5] can only be read into the text by emending it to 'till the appearance of < the son of > Zadok' on the assumption (which is not confirmed by the Old Testament) that Hilkiah may have been of Zadokite lineage.[6] The alteration of the text is again unnecessary; for the writer is surely referring to Saddok or Sadduk the co-founder of the 'fourth philosophy'. So he implies that, as David was in ignorance of the Law which would not be revealed, *i.e.* rightly expounded, until Zadok, *i.e.* Saddok or Sadduk, should found the party of the 'fourth philosophy' and therewith that of the Covenanters who had their own exposition of it (cp. Z vi 2–5), so Israel had strayed in ignorance of the Law 'till the appearance of one who shall teach what was right (*haṣṣeḏeq*)' (Z viii 10), namely the Rightful Teacher (cp. Z i 7, ix 53), to whom God had given power 'to expound all the words of His servants the prophets' (H ii 8–9); and those who accepted his teaching became the 'sons of righteousness (*ṣeḏeq*)', namely the Covenanters of Qumrân (D iii 20,22).

The significance of this continual harping on 'righteousness, rightfulness (*ṣeḏeq*)' and terms derived from it is that they are all key-words in the vocabulary of the Covenanters, who have given it various shades of meaning, historical and political as well as moral and theological, reflecting the circumstances of their own society. Nothing, however,

[1] Pp. 239–41.   [2] Pp. 228–9.   [3] Jubilees x 3–6.
[4] Pp. 318–26.   [5] 2 Ki. xxii 8; s. Ginzberg *Sekte* I 28.
[6] Kohler *ap.* Rabin *Zadokite Documents* 18–19.

indicates that the Rightful Teacher must have been actually named
Zadok,[1] even if someone of that name may have held the office, *e.g.*
Saddok or Sadduk for a while after the death of his colleague Judah.
At the same time the Teacher is described as a 'righteous one' (*ṣaddîq*) by
a slight modification of the vowels (D ix 14); for the authors of the Scrolls
loved to play on the various forms and senses of the root, namely 'lawfulness' or 'righteousness (*ṣedeq*)' and 'justice, just measure (*ṣᵉdāqāh*).'

The title of 'Teacher (*môreh*)', too, had a long history. It seems to have
been coined by playing on two expressions in the Old Testament. The
first[2] is that translated *cum venerit qui docebit vos iustitiam* by Jerome and
similarly in the other ancient Versions but 'until He comes and rains
righteousness (*yōreh ṣedeq*) upon you' in the Revised Version; the
second[3] is that translated *qui dedit vobis doctorem iustitiae* by Jerome and
similarly in the Targum but 'for He giveth you the former rain in just
measure (*môreh liṣᵉdāqāh*)' by the Revisers. The divergent translations
are due to an ambiguity in the meaning of the verb, which can be used
of discharging concrete objects such as weapons or rain and also of
issuing instructions or the like. Naturally the Covenanters will have
taken these expressions in the sense assigned to them by Jerome, who
was dependent on Rabbinic authority and the ancient Jewish exegetes,
and based the title of their 'teacher (*môreh*)' on it.

Further, Dr. Roth has suggested[4] that these two passages, which
seem to have inspired the Teacher's title, may have yet another
significance. The first[5] goes on to speak of the coming disaster like
that once inflicted on Israel for past misdeeds by a Moabite king and
the second[6] depicts invasion under the figure of a plague of locusts and
a subsequent restoration when 'the years that the locust hath eaten'
will be made good. Both situations are comparable with that in
Palestine at the time of the Roman suppression of the First Revolt,
while the promised restoration may reflect the Covenanters' hope of a
similar restoration after it. The suggestion would be plausible if
previous leaders of the party had borne a different title or different
titles and that of Rightful Teacher had been coined for its leader at
the time of the Revolt; but nothing is known on this point. In another
sense, it seems intended to reverse the title of the 'teacher of lies',
whom two of the prophets denounce (cp. H xii 11).[7]

A contributory factor in the choice of this title for the Teacher
might well have been the prophecy of the Servant of the Lord, of
whom the author says:

'through the travail of his soul he shall be flooded <with light>
(and) through his humiliation he shall win full justification (*ṣedeq*);

---

[1] Rohmer in *Colloque de Strasbourg* 129.   [2] Hos. x. 12.
[3] Jo. ii. 23.   [4] In VT XIII 91–5.   [5] Hos. x. 13–15.
[6] Jo. ii. 24–6.   [7] Isa. ix. 14 and Hab. ii. 18.

(so) that my servant justify (*yaṣdîq*) many
and himself bear the punishment of their iniquities';[1]

for these words were echoed down the ages, being applied in each successive generation to some just man or Messianic figure who suffered an unjust fate. So in the 1st century A.D. the expectation of a just sufferer can be clearly traced,[2] and history tells of various just men wrongfully done to death, such as James the Just[3] and Zacharias son of Baris.[4] Such memories could easily play a part in the choice of a title for the leader of a party in that century; for the Jews always loved to play on words and names and saw no incongruity in mingling ancient tradition with present fact.

This title, which since the recovery of the *Zadokite Documents* has been commonly translated Teacher of Righteousness (*môrēh ṣedeq*), may also be rendered 'right guide' in the sense of 'true expounder of the law'[5] and 'true teacher'.[6] In fact, a *double entente* underlies the term, so that its full force cannot be brought out by any single word in a foreign language. On the one hand, the Commentator explains the prophet Habakkuk's 'justice doth never go forth; for the wicked doth compass about the righteous'[7] by saying 'he is the Righteous Teacher' (H i 11-13) in allusion to his maltreatment at the hands of the Wicked Priest; and the Teacher is elsewhere identified with 'the Staff (*i.e.* Ruler) who interprets the Law' (Z viii 8), while his function is 'to lead them (*sc.* Israel) in the way of His (*sc.* God's) heart and to teach the last generations what He will do to the last generation, the congregation of the faithless' (Z i 8). The title can mean also 'Rightful Teacher',[8] as 'son of righteousness' and 'king of righteousness' connote respectively a legitimate son and a lawful king in Phoenician inscriptions;[9] and that this is the prevalent meaning of the title is proved by the usage of one writer who elsewhere employs this title (Z i 7 x 53) but speaks of the coming of 'one who shall teach righteousness' or 'what is rightful' when he wishes to emphasize his function as distinct from his office (Z viii 10). So too the Messiah expected by the party is once called the 'Messiah of Righteousness' or 'Rightful Messiah' (A Fl. a i 1); he is the Messiah regarded by the Covenanters as the rightful or legitimate Messiah in contrast to the Messiah expected by orthodox Jews. From this point of view, then, the Teacher is the legitimate or authorized teacher[10] whom Israel must follow rather than any other,

---

[1] Isa. liii 11 (s. p. 443).
[2] *E.g.* Wisdom of Solomon ii 12–20 and Acts vii. 52.
[3] Josephus *Antiquities* XX ix 1 § 200.　　　　[4] Josephus *War* IV v 4 §§ 334–5.
[5] Gaster *Scriptures* 14–15, 309.　　　　[6] Teicher in *JJS* II 97–8.
[7] Hab. i. 4.　　　　[8] Cp. Jer. xxiii. 5 and Zech. ix. 9 (*saddîq* = 'lawful').
[9] Lidzbarski *Kanaanäische Inschriften* 20 ix 1 (cp. Cooke *North-Semitic Inscriptions* 29 9) and Dunant *Fouilles de Byblos* I 30 *1141* 6–7.
[10] Cp. Sutcliffe *Monks* 253[18].

the successor of Judah and Saddok and the leader of the 'Sons of Zadok' who include 'all who know righteousness' (Z i 1) and all 'sons of righteousness' (D iii 20). Thus 'righteousness, rightfulness (*ṣedeq*)' is a key-word at one and the same time hinting at the party's historical link with Zadok the priest and Simon the Just or rather Rightful (*i.e.* Zadokite) high-priest and with Saddok or Sadduk their co-founder with Judah, at the truth of their interpretation of the Law in all its strictness, and at the legitimacy of their claim to overthrow the Roman *imperium* under the leadership now of the 'Rightful Teacher' or eventually of their own rightful or legitimate Messiah.

Long afterwards the Rabbis of the Talmudic age applied Hosea's expression to the prophet Elijah as the forerunner of the Messiah;[1] and eventually the Qara'ites in the 9th and 10th centuries A.D. gave the title in the very form in which it appears in the Scrolls to the same prophet for the same reason.[2] It thus connects the Covenanters with the Qara'ites, and the allusion in the Talmud shows that this line of thought must not be regarded as having been interrupted by the eclipse of the Covenanters; it is seen rather to have been continuous throughout the Talmudic age and so supports other evidence for the view that the group must have remained in existence, however small and insignificant, till their re-emergence in the Qara'ite group in the 8th century A.D.[3]

The Teacher's alternative title of the 'Unique (*yāḥîd*) Teacher' (Z ix 29, 53) is another *double entente* of the kind so dear to the Covenanters; for it at once connects him with the 'unity', *i.e.* the 'community' (*yaḥaḏ*), of the Covenanters and makes his position clear as their sole authority in spiritual matters and specifically in the interpretation of the Law. At the same time it sets them firmly in the Rabbinic period; for in Rabbinic literature the same term designates a teacher who stands alone in his opinions[4] and who, even though they may not be preferred to those of the majority, is qualified to be the head of a community.[5] The expression therefore is perfectly justifiable and must not be emended out of the text on grounds either of grammar[6] or of import.[7]

Once the title of 'Teacher' appears without qualification in the Scrolls (Z ix 50), as Jesus is occasionally addressed or described as Teacher (διδάσκαλος)[8]; this Greek title has also been found on a Jewish ossuary dated in the early part or middle of the 1st century

---

[1] Cp. Mishnah *Eduyoth* viii 7 w. B. Talmud *Bekhoroth* 24a.
[2] David alQûmisî on Joel ii 23 and Jephet ben Ali on Hosea ii 5, 16 (s. Weis in *JQR*, NS XLI 135–7).
[3] Pp. 9–12, 264–6.   [4] B. Talmud *Berakhoth* 9a.
[5] *Ibid. Taanith* 10b.   [6] Cp. Segal *Mishnaic Hebrew Grammar* 182–3.
[7] Cp. Neher in *Colloque de Strasbourg* 48–54.
[8] *E.g.* Matt. xxiii. 8 and Jn. xiii 13 and *passim* (cp. Josephus *Antiquities* XVIII iii 3 § 63, if the passage is genuine).

A.D.[1] That nothing is known of it before this time seems to indicate that it may have been a coinage of that century.

4. SADDUCEES, SADDUCAEANS AND ZADOKITES

The question must now be asked whether the Sadducaeans, *i.e.* the followers of Judah and Zadok, who are here identified with the Sons of Zadok or Zadokites, *i.e.* the Covenanters of Qumrân (and therefore distinguished from the Sadducees of the New Testament), can be traced anywhere else in literature,[2] and whether such allusions as may be found in any way confirm this identification.

The Christian Jewish apologist Justin Martyr (*c.* A.D. 100–165) includes[3] 'Sadducees' and 'Baptist Pharisees' in a list of heretical Jewish groups. Since neither the Sadducees nor the Pharisees of the New Testament could have been regarded as heretics, as Dr. Black argues,[4] he must have been thinking of the Zadokites of the Scrolls as a splinter-group of the Pharisees which attached notable importance to baptism, although he wrongly took them to be two groups through confusion with the two similarly named orthodox groups mentioned in the New Testament. That Justin subsequently speaks of the Pharisees as 'the chiefs of the synagogue'[5] shows that he is well aware of the distinction, which the addition of 'Baptists' in the passages under discussion puts beyond doubt. Then Hegesippus, a Jewish convert to Christianity alive at the time of the Second Revolt (A.D. 132–5) and the author of a book on Jewish groups from which Eusebius quotes extracts, who as a Palestinian might have had access to good sources of information, names 'Essenes, Galilaeans, Hemero-baptists, Masbothaeans, Samaritans, Sadducees, Pharisees';[6] and subsequent writers repeat this list each with variations.[7] Here the 'Galilaeans' can only be the followers of Judah the Galilaean, who with Saddok or Sadduk founded the 'fourth philosophy' as an offshoot of the Pharisees;[8] and this identification is confirmed by the fact that 'Sadducaean' and 'Galilaean heretic' are interchangeable terms in the Talmud.[9] At the same time, if the Covenanters have been rightly identified with the Zadokite or Sadducaean followers of Judah the Galilaean and his colleague Saddok or Sadduk,[10] they are here explicitly distinguished from the Essenes by a writer who may well have been personally acquainted with members of these parties.

Next, the writer known as the Pseudo-Clement, describing the Jewish parties of the 1st century B.C. and the 1st century A.D. in a

[1] Sukenik *Jüdische Gräber* 17–18.　[2] Cp. Bammel in *ZAtW*. LXXI 265–70.
[3] In *Dialogue against Trypho* § 80.　[4] In *Scrolls* 48–52.
[5] *Ibid.* § 137.　[6] Eusebius *Ecclesiastical History* IV xxii 7.
[7] Cp. McGiffert *Nicene and Post-Nicene Fathers* NS I 200 (14).
[8] Pp. 99–100.　[9] P. 261.　[10] Pp. 253–8.

work composed in the 3rd century A.D., says[1] that 'the first schism was that of those who were called Sadducees, who arose about the time of John (sc. the Baptist); these, as more righteous than others, began to separate themselves from the assembly of the people'. The only 'righteous' but schismatic 'Sadducees' would be the 'Sadducaeans' or Zadokites who came into prominence c. 25 B.C., formed a party which separated itself from the main stream of Jewish orthodoxy and remained actively in opposition till A.D. 70.[2] In a similar strain Ephraem the Syrian, who died in A.D. 373, adds[3] the Galilaeans 'who are always wandering' as well as the Samaritans and Ebionites, amongst others, to the list of heretical groups 'in the midst of Israel'. These three groups are interesting; for the 'Galilaeans' are clearly the group which Hegesippus describes under the same name, i.e. the Zadokites or Covenanters, who seem to have had Samaritan connections;[4] and the 'Ebionites', i.e. the 'poor men (*'ebyônîm*)', may be either the Covenanters who often speak of themselves as such,[5] here treated as distinct from the Galilaeans (although the different names may merely reflect the different aspects of the same group), or perhaps the Essenes, who are known to have made a cult of poverty and whom Hegesippus includes in his list.[6]

Two Latin fathers of the church clearly distinguished the Sadducees of the New Testament from the Sadducaeans or Zadokites of the Scrolls. First, Filaster[7a], who died c. A.D. 397, held that the *Sadducei* were a heretical baptizing sect derived *a Saddoc homine Iudaeo*,[7b] who was a disciple of Dositheus;[8] these people were clearly surely not the Sadducees but the Zadokites. Second, Jerome distinguished two homonymous sects. These were *Sadducaei . . . qui interpretantur iusti et ipsi vindicant sibi quod non erant* and who believed in the spirit, in angels and in the resurrection, and another group equally called *Sadducaei* who accepted none of these doctrines and taught also that the soul perished;[9] the former must be the Zadokites or Sadducaeans, while the latter are clearly the Sadducees.

Long afterwards the Jewish writer alQirqîsânî,[10] a member of the Qara'ite party which apparently traced its origin to the Covenanters of Qumrân, describes a group whom he calls 'Sadducaeans' (who too can have no connection with the Sadducees of the New Testament) in one of his works; amongst other things he says that 'the Sadducaeans, whose leaders were Zadok and Boethus,[11] appeared after the Rabbanites

[1] In *Recognitions* i 53–4.   [2] Cp. Schoeps in *ZRGg*. III 335–6.
[3] Aucher & Moesinger *Evangelii concordantis expositio facta a sancto Ephraemo* 287–8.
[4] Pp. 391–2.   [5] Pp. 92–3, 160–1.   [6] Pp. 112–3.
[7a] In *Diversarum Haereseon Liber* § 5; cp. Eisler in *Occident and Orient* 135.
[7b] Cp. Ibn Ḥazm *ap*. Poznański in *JQR*. xvi 766–8.
[8] Cp. Epiphanius *Panarion* XIV ii 1; s. pp. 78–80, 262–3.
[9] Migne *Patrolog. Lat*. XXVI 163–4 [179] and 165A [181].
[10] Nemoy *Kitāb al-Anwār wal-Marāqib* I ii 7 (marriage with niece) and vi 1 (calendar);
s. Nemoy *Qaraite Anthology* 50 (cp. Bammel in *ZAtW*, NF LXXI 265–70).
[11] S. pp. 228–31.

. . .; Zadok was the first to expose the Rabbanites and to disagree with them, writing books . . . and . . . attacking them. He adduced no proofs of anything that he said but restricted himself to bare assertions, except in two matters, namely the prohibition of marriage with a niece on either side', and he says further that 'they prohibited divorce, though permitted by the Scriptures; and they reckoned the month at thirty days'. There is here some historical confusion, but the identification of the historian's Zadok (Saddok or Sadduk) with the Zadok of the *Zadokite Documents* can hardly be doubted; for these documents expressly forbid marriage with a niece[1] and second marriages (Z vii 1-2, 9-10). Also, both the *War* and *Discipline* distinctly imply that the Covenanters used a calendar in which the month had only thirty days (D x 4 W ii 1-2); for, if they followed the reckoning in *Jubilees*, they counted their solar year of 364 days as consisting of four quarters of 90 days each (*i.e.* 3 months each of 30 days) *plus* an additional day at the end of one month in each quarter to make up the full number.[2]

The question which now naturally forces itself on the attention is this: have the Zadokites or Sadducaeans left any traces of themselves in purely Jewish literature? The answer is not easily given; for the only too often inconsistent notices found in Jewish works, notably in the Talmud, on almost every conceivable (and indeed inconceivable) subject, the inconclusive and illogical arguments used by the authors or compilers to establish their conclusions and their total lack of historical sense, make them most unsatisfactory sources of information. Hitherto scarcely any trace of the Zadokites has been found or even suspected in Jewish literature other than the Scrolls; but, when what can be gleaned about them there and the hints which Josephus throws out about Saddok or Sadduk are combined, the need to compare all this with the notices in such compilation as the Talmud, both Mishnah and Gemara, regarding the 'Sadducees' or 'Sadduceans' (*Ṣaddûqîm* or *Ṣaddûqîn*) becomes imperative. That these people appear often to be called 'heretics, sectarians (*mînîm*)' in the Talmud (where the terms appear to be interchangeable, if the manuscripts and editions may be trusted) and may even be rated as Gentiles[3] is also significant in the present connection: for it throws doubt on the common assumption that the *Ṣaddûqîm* are everywhere, despite inconsistencies and contradictions, the Sadducees of the New Testament.

The Talmud says in several places[4] that the *Ṣaddûqîm* believe in only one world and no future life,[5] and in another it says[6] that the

---

[1] Cp. Poznański in *JQR.* XVI 766-8 (where Ibn Ḥazm is said to have spoken of a Jewish sect of the same name as prohibiting marriage with a niece).
[2] Pp. 229, 264-5, 323-6.   [3] B. Talmud *Erubin* 68b.
[4] B. Talmud, Mishnah *Berakoth* ix 5 (var. *mînîm*), Gemara *Shabbath* 152b-153a (var. *mînâ*) and *Sanhedrin* 91a (var. *mînîm*).
[5] So also Josephus *War* II viii 14 § 165.   [6] B. Talmud *Sanhedrin* 38a (var. *mînîm*).
S

Ṣaddûqîn hold that there are 'many ruling powers in heaven'. Clearly
the former can only be the Sadducees of the New Testament who say
'that there is no resurrection, neither angel nor spirit'[1] (*i.e.* who do
not accept the developed angelology of the period); the latter are
equally clearly the Zadokites, whom the Scrolls depict as believing in
rewards and punishments in the next world and in angels and spirits
controlling the destiny of every individual man.[2] That the *Ṣaddûqîn*
are said to deny the existence of God[3] is not true of either party; it is
perhaps an exaggeration of the charge which Josephus brings[4] against
the Sadducees, that 'they do away with fate, holding that there is no
such thing and that human actions are not achieved in accordance
with her decree but that all things lie in our power, so that we ourselves
are responsible for our well-being while we suffer misfortune through
our own thoughtlessness'; so far from this being true of the Zadokites,
these come very close to regarding man as predestined by God to good
or evil and as being therefore virtually incapable of escaping their pre-
ordained fate.[5] Another difference on the same plane is that the
Ṣaddûqîm seem to have held dualistic views;[6] nothing of the sort can
be traced to the Sadducees, whereas dualism is characteristic of the
Zadokites as depicted in the Scrolls.[7]

The *Ṣaddûqîm* are described in various places as engaged in a number
of petty ritual and legal controversies with the dominant party, who
are the Pharisees; but the nature of these disputes and what is known
of their history is not usually enough to show whether Sadducees or
Zadokites are meant, unless external evidence can be cited to answer
the question. For example, when the *Ṣaddûqîm* are said not to admit
all the laws which the Pharisees[8] regard as binding, the reference is
clearly to the Sadducees' acceptance of only the written law and their
rejection of the oral tradition of the scribes and Pharisees; for Josephus
refers[9] expressly to this distinction between the two parties. So too a
ṣaddûqî court of law which is said to have acted in ignorance of the
law[10] can hardly have been one composed of Sadducees; but the
Zadokite Documents contain specific provisions for cases in which the
priest may be ignorant of the law (Z xv 6–8).

In other passages only the Zadokites can be meant. When a *Ṣaddûqî*
is said to become a Pharisaic 'associate' (*ḥāḇēr*),[11] he is most likely to
have been a Zadokite; for the 'associations' (*ḥăḇurôṯ*) are described as
having been organized on lines very like the Zadokite communities,[12]

---

[1] Acts xxiii 8; cp. Matt. xxii. 23; Mk. xii. 18; Lk. xx. 27.
[2] Pp. 74–5.   [3] B. Talmud *Yeḥamoth* 63b (var. *mînîn*).
[4] In *Antiquities* XIII v 9 § 173; cp. *War* II viii 14 § 165.
[5] Pp. 71–2.   [6] *E.g.* B. Talmud *Hullin* 87a.
[7] Pp. 550–62.   [8] B. Talmud *Sanhedrin* 33b and *Horayoth* 4a.
[9] In *Antiquities* XIII x 6 § 297.   [10] B. Talmud *Sanhedrin* 52b.
[11] B. Talmud *Niddah* 33b–34a.   [12] Pp. 95–9.

and a Sadducee 'associate' is most improbable. The opinion, too, that daughters of the Saddûqîm, if they follow their fathers, must be regarded as Samaritan women,[1] is interesting in view of the Samaritan influence which can be detected in the Scrolls;[2] but too much must not be read into this point, since 'Samaritan' is often used merely as a synonym for 'heretical' in reference to the opponents of the prevalent Pharisaism. So, for example, Origen brings the two together when he says[3] that the 'Σαδδουκαῖοι or Samaritans' accept only the Pentateuch; he is inaccurately identifying the Sadducees' acceptance of the written law of the Pentateuch alone (as distinct from the oral law of the Pharisees) with the Samaritans' unorthodox rejection of all the Scriptures other than the Mosaic law of the Pentateuch. Again, the Saddûqîm are said to intensify the restrictions on the Sabbath;[4] but the Sadducees, although very severe in carrying out the penal laws,[5] are nowhere said to have increased the burdens on the Sabbath, whereas this practice is characteristic of the Zadokites.[6] Again, a Saddûqî rebukes the Pharisees because 'in a deed of divorce ye write the name of the ruler (sc. the Roman emperor) together with the name of Moses';[7] editors of the tractate in which this story appears are at a loss to explain the point,[8] since the Sadducees are nowhere stated to have been anti-Roman. The difficulty vanishes so soon as Saddûqî is here seen to designate a Zadokite, since the Zadokites appear in their writings as fanatically opposed to Kittian i.e. Roman rule;[9] and that the same Saddûqî is further described as a 'Galilaean heretic' supports the identification, since Galilee is known to have been the home of the founder of the Zadokite party.[10] Further, the Saddûqîm seem to have insisted that Pentecost must always fall on a Sabbath;[11] but this is possible only with a year of 364 days like that of the Zadokites.[12]

The Saddûqîm are accused also of misapplying or misinterpreting Scripture;[13] this charge, which seems in no way to fit the Sadducees, is singularly applicable to the Zadokites, who have left commentaries expressly designed to present their own peculiar views. The Saddûqîm are also charged with carelessness in the matter of books and writings 'which defile the hands';[14] this charge is equally applicable to the

---

[1] Mishnah Niddah iv 2; cp. B. Talmud Niddah 33b.
[2] Pp. 391–2.　　　　　　　　　　　　[3] In contra Celsum i 49.
[4] B. Talmud Erubin 68b–69a.　　　　[5] Josephus Antiquities XX ix i § 199.
[6] Pp. 88–90.
[7] Mishnah Yadaim iv 8; cp. Zeitlin in JQR NS XLIX2298–9.
[8] Cp. Lisowsky Jadajim 79.　　　　[9] Pp. 197–16.
[10] Pp. 239–41.
[11] Mishnah Hagigah ii 4 (s. Danby Mishnah 213)and Menahoth x 3; cp. B. Talmud Menahoth 65a where this peculiarity is ascribed to the Boethusians (s. p. 230).
[12] Pp. 319–22.
[13] E.g. P. Talmud Berakoth II i 5 (2) 10a, B. Talmud Berakoth 7a, 10a and Yoma 56b–57a.
[14] Mishnah Yadaim iv 6.

Zadokites, since many if not most of the works found in the caves round Qumrân are vulnerable to it.[1] Lastly, the actual writings of the Saddûqîm are condemned as uncanonical;[2] this charge too fits the Zadokites rather than the Sadducees. The only known works of the Sadducees are probably *Ecclesiasticus* which is sometimes condemned (although it seems to have been revised with Pharisaic intent), and *I Maccabees* (to which *II Maccabees* appears to have been intended as a Pharisaic counterpart), which is nowhere condemned, so that the Sadducees are unlikely to have been singled out for their unorthodox literature; contrariwise, the surviving writings of the Zadokites contain much that cannot have been approved by the Rabbis and is often frankly heterodox. Here then as in the other cases it is not the Sadducees but the Zadokites who are meant.

On chronological grounds, too, the *Saddûqîm* now may and now must be not the Sadducees but the Zadokites. Such a conclusion, already established on other grounds,[3] agrees with the evidence of the Qara'ite alQirqîsânî who describes[4] the old Jewish groups in the following order: Samaritans, Rabbanites (*i.e.* Pharisees), Sadducees, 'cave-men' (*maǵârîyah*),[5] Christians, schools of Hillel and Shammai;[6] and when he adds that Zadok and Boethus were the leaders of the Sadducees, he must mean the Sadducaeans or Zadokites, the followers of Judah and Saddok or Sadduk, if these are identical with the Covenanters, *i.e.* the 'cave-men', as argued above.[7] Elsewhere the *Saddûqîm* are named in discussions or disputes with Joshua ben Hananiah (c. A.D. 90–130), with the Palestinian R. 'Ammî (c. A.D. 300) and with the Babylonian Rabâ (A.D. 299–352).[8] Since the Sadducees of the New Testament are generally thought to have ceased to exist as a party with the cessation of the priesthood after the destruction of the Temple in A.D. 70, they are not likely to have been involved in controversies with these scholars or at any rate with the last two of them; the persons here meant by *Saddûqîm* must then be the Zadokites, who will have lingered on as a distinct and recognizable group till their absorption into the Qara'ites in the 8th century A.D.

Thus a slender thread runs through the Talmud, connecting the Covenanters or Sons of Zadok through the *Saddûqîm* with the Qara'ites. This at once gets rid of the need to suppose that all the Scrolls must have been written before the end of the First Revolt (A.D. 66–73); any or all of them could have been composed after it if the Covenanters were still in existence.

---

[1] Pp. 387–9   [2] B. Talmud *Sanhedrin* 100b.   [3] Pp. 240–56.
[4] Nemoy *Kitâb al-Anwâr wal-Marâqib* I 10–12 (I ii §§ 5–9, 11) = Nemoy in *HUCA* VII 325–8.
[5] Pp. 9–10.   [6] Cp. Kahle *Geniza* 24.   [7] Pp. 229, 240–3, 260–1.
[8] B. Talmud *Shabbath* 88a–b (Rabâ), *Erubin* 101a (Hananiah), *Sanhedrin* 91a ('Ammî).

Another point of contact may here be added. The Zadokites described themselves occasionally as 'men of the Law'[1] and as 'the house, *i.e.* party, of the Law' (Z ix 35–8), while the Qara'ites called themselves 'disciples of the Law'[2] or 'masters of the Law'[3]; and the similarity of these appellations seems to support the suggestion that the two groups must be identified.

Further, Dr. Wieder has drawn attention[4] to two points connecting the Covenanters both with the Sadducaeans and with the Qara'ites. First, the Covenanters' exegetical methods of interpreting the text of Scripture were taken over by the Qara'ites; for they too used the principle of *gêmaṭr*ᵉ*yâ* (extracting a meaning from the numerical values of the letters composing a word),[5] and they also applied Biblical names and expressions to persons and events of their own times.[6] For example, the Qara'ite alQûmisî at the end of the 9th or beginning of the 10th century A.D. applied 'Ephraim feedeth on wind and followeth after the east wind'[7] to the Jews of the Dispersion who conformed to the principles and precepts of the Rabbanites, on the ground that their ordinances and feasts would pass away like the wind; for according to him Ephraim stood for all Israel, while Assyria and Egypt designated the lands of the Dispersion. In the same way Japhet ibn 'Alî (A.D. 950–90) made Nineveh a cryptic name for Baghdad and took 'the man of the spirit'[8] (which for him meant 'madman') and 'wine, a treacherous dealer'[9] for Mohammed and then explained 'no more of thy seed shall be sown'[10] as referring to the Arab rulers of Baghdad descended from the prophet; and he also held that those 'that shall bite thee' and 'that shall vex thee'[11] were the Qarmatians who overran the Moslem world in the 10th century A.D. Many other examples of this type of interpretation, to which the writings of certain prophets especially lend themselves, can be found.[12] Second, the famous Jewish commentator Abraham ibn Ezra in the 12th century A.D. used 'Sadducaean doctors' almost as a term of contempt for the Qara'ites,[13] affirming that 'these commentators have desecrated the sanctuary' by their misinterpretation of Scripture. Thus the wheel comes full circle: Zadokites and Covenanters, Sadducaeans and Qara'ites, had the same attitude to the Rabbanites, who condemned them both as heretical, and the same exegetical methods; and the identification of the Sadducaeans with the Qara'ites at the same time

---

[1] Milik in *RB*. NS LXIII 60–1.
[2] Marmorstein in *Livre d'Hommage à la Mémoire du Dr. Samuel Poznański* p. 144 l. 12.
[3] Mann *Texts and Studies* II p. 1150 l. 15.
[4] In *Between East and West: Essays dedicated to the Memory of Bela Horovitz* 75–105.
[5] Pp. 339–40, 357–8.   [6] *E.g.*, pp. 313–6, 458–9.   [7] Hos. xii. 1.
[8] *Ibid.* ix. 7.   [9] Hab. ii. 5.   [10] Nah. i. 14.
[11] Hab. ii 7.   [12] Cp. Wieder in *JQR*, NS XLVII 97–113, 269–92.
[13] Gallé *Daniel avec Commentaires* 141 (Dan. xi. 31).

identifies them with the Covenanters, with whom they are closely connected and may virtually be identified on quite other grounds.

Why these people are not called 'Sons of Zadok' but only *Ṣaddûqîn* in the Talmud is not far to seek. The *double entente* in 'Sons of Zadok' as denoting in the first instance the priestly line of Zadok and secondly the Covenanters as members of a party whose co-founder with Judah was called Zadok would prevent an orthodox Jewish writer from applying this term to any person or party suspected of heterodoxy; for he might appear to be referring to the line of Zadok the priest and not to the followers of Zadok the founder of an unorthodox sect and so to be imputing heresy to one of the most respected figures of the Old Testament.

Such a dual use of a name or title, however much it may mislead historians, rarely troubles contemporary society, and it is not uncommon at the present time; for example, an 'Old Catholic' may be a member of an English family which maintained its allegiance to Rome in spite of the Reformation, or an adherent of the Church of Utrecht which separated itself from Rome in 1724, or one of the party which broke away from Rome in 1870; and 'English Catholic' and 'Anglo-Catholic' create only wilful confusion. The multiple use of titles is a commonplace of ecclesiastical history.

The argument has now reached a point at which the identification of the 'Sons of Zadok', as the Covenanters are commonly called in the Scrolls, with the followers of the 'fourth philosophy' founded by Judah son of Hezekiah and a colleague named Saddok or Sadduk (Zadok) at the turn of the century may be regarded as reasonably certain. Once again, then, the Scrolls are seen against the background of the 1st century A.D.; for no suitable person of this name can be found in any other period of the Second Temple.

VI

REVOLT AND RUIN

1. Murder on Mount Ophel

Mr. Del Medico, following up Lagrange's identification of Zadok with Saddok or Sadduk,[1] seems to have come nearest to finding the answer to the question: who was the Rightful Teacher? He has suggested[2] that Manaemus (Menahem), who was a son of Judah the 'sophist' or 'teacher of wisdom', already mentioned,[3] and who was murdered or whose murder was procured by Eleazar son of the high-priest Ananias (Hananiah) and captain of the Temple, was the Rightful Teacher and that this Ananias was the Wicked Priest of the *Commentary on Habakkuk*; he further suggests that the 'house of Absalom' designated the followers of Menahem's lieutenant Absalom who was murdered at the same time and almost on the same spot, and that the 'house of Judah' designated those followers of Menahem who on the murder of their leader escaped to the fortress of Masada close to the western shore of the Dead Sea. Josephus has recounted[4] the story in some detail, and a careful study of his account shows that it agrees so remarkably with the allusions in the *Commentary on Habakkuk* that no doubt can remain but that he and the Commentator are narrating or alluding to the same event. The Wicked Priest, however, as Dr. Vermès has suggested,[5] must be Eleazar, the leader of the radical party amongst the priests in Jerusalem, not his father Hananiah (if the Hananiah murdered a few days before Menahem was the same person),[6] as Mr. Del Medico thinks. Unfortunately Mr. Del Medico did not or could not prove his suggestion and Dr. Vermès apparently withdrew his,[7] so that the theory was overlooked or set aside by every subsequent writer on the subject, obviously because it conflicted with the weight of opinion in favour of a date in the 2nd or 1st century B.C.

The revolt broke out in the late summer of A.D. 66, when Eleazar, 'a very bold young man' (as Josephus calls him),[8] aided and abetted

---

[1] Pp. 253–6.
[2] In *Deux Manuscrits* 124–9, 132–40 and *Énigme* 181–8, 342–57.
[3] Pp. 241–2; cp. Hengel *Zeloten* 338, where the genealogy of the family is set out.
[4] In *War* II xvii 8 § 433–9 § 448.
[5] In *Cah. Sion.* IV [1950] 200; cp. V [1951] 66.　　　　　　[6] Pp. 277–8.
[7] Cp. *Manuscrits* [1953] 69, 89 (where he assigns the *Commentary on Habakkuk* to 65–63 B.C.).
[8] *Ibid.* 2 § 409.

perhaps by a certain Zechariah (if the Talmud may be trusted),[1] persuaded some priests and many of the people against the wishes of the hierarchy to withhold the customary sacrifices for the Emperor and the Roman people; this was tantamount to a declaration of war, which could not be overlooked by the paramount power. Meanwhile, Menahem and a party of followers went down to the fortress of Masada, from which the Roman garrison had lately been expelled by the insurgents, and equipped themselves with weapons from Herod's armoury there. Thus armed, one day soon afterwards they marched up to Jerusalem, where the fort known as Antonia had already fallen into the hands of the insurgents and the Roman garrison with its Jewish sympathizers was being besieged in the strongly fortified royal palace in the Upper City. Menahem at once assumed command of the insurgents and directed the siege. The bulk of the garrison soon capitulated, although the Roman troops held out for some short while in the fortified bastions; and some of the leaders, who had taken refuge in the palace, were hunted down by the triumphant patriots and Hananiah (possibly the same person as the former high-priest and father of Eleazar) was amongst the slain.[2] If he was the father of Eleazar, his death would exclude the possibility of his being the Wicked Priest of the Scrolls.

Menahem, now over sixty years of age (for his father had been executed in A.D. 6–7),[3] evidently claimed the leadership of the Revolt partly in virtue of his seniority and partly as the prerogative of his family, which had given so many sons to the cause of Jewish independence.[4] He therefore could not yield what he regarded as his rightful place to the young upstart captain of the Temple, though a high-priest's son. Eleazar for his part had started the revolt by his bold action and was not going to see himself pushed aside by the newcomer; feeling his position threatened, he set about rousing supporters against him. When then Menahem, who had come up to Jerusalem 'like a king' and had succeeded in making himself extremely unpopular by his high-handed conduct in the city, forced a way into the Temple 'swaggering . . . and robed in royal attire' with his followers in arms 'intending to worship', they seized their opportunity. They saw in his action an attempt to claim royal and perhaps also priestly privileges (since he was or claimed to be also a priest) after the fashion of the Hasmonaean priest-kings. Eleazar, inflaming the populace with such charges, easily fomented a riot and several casualties occurred. Menahem and his party offered a brief resistance but, seeing themselves assailed by a multitude, fled wherever they could. Menahem

---

[1] B. Talmud *Gittin* 56a.
[2] Josephus *War* II xvii 2 § 408 and 8 § 433–9 § 441.
[3] Cp. Roth *Background* 7[1].　　　　　　　　　[4] Pp. 239–41.

made his way down Mt. Ophel, where he was caught in hiding and dragged 'into the open', tortured and killed. His chief of staff (ὑπηρέτης, which Josephus or his translator uses in its classical sense in accordance with his custom) Absalom with a small party was similarly taken nearby and murdered; but Eleazar son of Jair (Hebrew *Yâ'îr* = Latin *Jairus*) or Ari,[1] a 'descendant (ἀπόγονος)' of Judah (the Galilaean) and a 'relation (προσήκων)' of his son Menahem,[2] and a few followers 'having run away secretly (λάθρα ἀποδράντες)' took refuge at Masada. This Eleazar lived to maintain the tradition of his family and to become in due course the last hero of Jewish independence, being one of those who committed suicide at Masada in A.D. 73 when escape was seen to be hopeless.[3] These events took place shortly before if not actually on 10 Tishri, the Day of Atonement, in A.D. 66.[4]

Now the central fact in the history of the group at Qumrân was an episode which took place on the Day of Atonement. This is described in the *Commentary on Habakkuk* in speaking of the conduct of 'the Wicked Priest who pursued the 'Rightful Teacher to swallow him up in the vexation of his rage at the place of his discovery; and at the period of the season of the Day of Atonement he showed himself to them (*sc.* the Teacher's supporters) to swallow them up and to bring them to the ground on a fast-day, the sabbath of their rest' (H xi 4–8). This passage clearly reflects a clash, almost certainly a fatal clash, between the Teacher and the Wicked Priest on the or a Day of Atonement and immediately recalls the similar clash between Eleazar the high-priest's son and Menahem the 'teacher of wisdom' on or near to the Day of Atonement; but the Commentator seems by his wording to be trying to depict the Wicked Priest's action as a deliberate attempt to provoke the Teacher and his party into violating the Day of Atonement by taking up arms albeit in self-defence.[5]

A few linguistic and grammatical points of vital importance for the right understanding of this crucial passage must now be considered. The verb in the first sentence here rendered 'pursued' means literally 'followed after (to overtake)' and cannot connote 'persecuted', as it is commonly mistranslated in this section;[6] the preposition absolutely excludes such a translation.[7] It will then describe the pursuit of Menahem when he fled from the precincts of the Temple on to Mt. Ophel. What 'to swallow up' means is not entirely clear; for the Hebrew verb can mean either 'to confound' or 'to destroy', which is a

---

[1] Cp. Niese *Flavii Josephi Opera* VII 30 (where the variant 'Ari' is given in brackets, apparently without manuscript authority).
[2] Josephus *War* II xvii. 9 § 447 and VII vii. 3 § 253.
[3] *Ibid.* VII ix 1 §§ 389–401.   [4] Pp. 281–4.
[5] Cp. Milik & Strugnell *Ten Years* 67–8.
[6] *E.g.* Dupont-Sommer *Manuscrits* 38.
[7] Cp. Brown-Driver-Briggs *Hebrew Lexicon* 922–3.

meaning found in a number of passages in the Old Testament.[1] Here
'to destroy him' may be accepted, at any rate provisionally, since it
seems to be supported by a fragment which speaks of 'the Wicked
Priest who sent . . . to kill . . . of the land . . .; and God will pay his
recompense by delivering him into the power of the most ruthless of the
peoples . . .' (APs. c i 2–5). This passage is unfortunately badly mutilated
but can be assumed, at any rate provisionally, to be referring to the
same episode. Also, the Commentator refers the prophet's 'w o e...
b e c a u s e o f t h e b l o o d s h e d a n d f o r t h e v i o l e n c e d o n e
t o t h e l a n d, t o t h e c i t y a n d t o a l l t h a t d w e l l t h e r e i n'
to the Wicked Priest 'whom for the wrong done to the Rightful Teacher
and his counsellors God gave over to his enemies . . . , because he
acted wickedly towards His elect' (H ix 8–12); and the comparison
of these two passages clearly implies that the Teacher's blood
had been shed, *i.e.* that he was killed by the Wicked Priest or his
followers (cp. T ix 8–9).

The interpretation of these expressions here put forward is further
supported by certain verbal resemblances between the Hebrew and
Greek accounts of this episode. The Wicked Priest pursued the Rightful
Teacher 'in the vexation of his rage', while the mob which Eleazar
incited against Menahem and his supporters was acting 'to gratify
angry passions (ἐπὶ τὰς ὀργάς)'; and the Teacher was pursued 'to the
place of his discovery', *i.e.* where he was discovered in concealment,
while his enemies dragged Menahem 'into the open (εἰς τὸ φανερόν)',
i.e. from the place where he was discovered concealing himself.[2] That
these two expressions are somehow or other correlative can hardly be
accidental, and the conclusion forces itself on the reader that the
Commentator and the historian are describing one and the same event;
and the historian is known to have been in hiding in the inner court
of the Temple at the moment,[3] so that the riot may have taken place
in the outer court.[4]

Next, the statement that 'he (*sc.* the Wicked Priest) pursued after
the Rightful Teacher to swallow him up' (H xi 4–5) is followed by
'and . . . he appeared (*hôfîaʿ*) to them to swallow them up' (H xi
7–8); the two clauses are closely parallel, and the obvious conclusion
is that the subjects are not different but the same, namely the Wicked
Priest. The meaning must then be that the Wicked Priest, after
despatching the Teacher, immediately proceeded to appear before or
to show himself in some way to the Teacher's followers, whom too he
intended to despatch. Alternatively, the force of the verb may be that
the Wicked Priest, having disposed of the Teacher, then 'showed him-

---

[1] *E.g.* 2 Sam. xx. 20, Hos. viii. 8, Hab. i. 13, Lam. ii. 5, Jb. ii. 3.
[2] Pp. 272–3; s. Driver *ap.* Roth *Background* 71 and in *JTS*, NS XIII 369.
[3] Josephus *Life* v 21.   [4] Roth *op. cit.* 62–3.

self' in his true colours, *i.e.* as one 'whose heart was lifted up' (H viii
10) not as a priest of God but as a political assassin, by murdering him
and his followers on the spot. The character of the Wicked Priest,
who had not been true to his name (H viii 8–10), is in harmony with
this interpretation of the verb; and the connotation thus given to it,
though rare, is well established. For so Jesus ben Sirach, describing a
man's enemy, says that 'whenever he comes with thee, he does not
reveal himself to thee and, if thou fallest, he does not throw himself
down to help thee. So long as thou standest, he does not show himself
(*sc.* his true nature); and if thou art tottering, he cannot contain himself'.[1] The parallelism between the two passages is so close as to leave
no doubt about the possibility that this must be the meaning of the
verb. This explanation of the passage has also the advantage that it gets
rid of the apparent tautology of saying that the Wicked Priest pursued
the Rightful Teacher 'to swallow him up' (H xi 5) and that he appeared
to them (*i.e.* him and his followers) 'to swallow them up and to bring
them to the ground' (H xi 7–8)'; for, if the preposition has a different
force in each clause (as it may have in the style of the Old Testament),[2]
it describes in the first the pursuer's aim and in the second the activity
by which[3] his true character stood revealed, in other words that he
revealed his true nature by destroying them.

Josephus further reports[4] that Menahem's enemies also caught and
massacred 'his lieutenants together with Absalom, the most eminent
supporter of his tyranny'. Here the commentator, quoting the prophet's
'Wherefore look ye upon traitors and holdest thy peace, when a
wicked man swalloweth up one more righteous than him?'[5] refers these
words 'to the house of Absalom and his counsellors, who were silenced'
or 'destroyed at (the time of) the chastisement of the Rightful Teacher
and did not help him against the Man of Falsehood' (H v 9–11). These
two passages, which Dr. Vermès and Mr. Del Medico have brought
together, cannot be taken apart from one another and can be explained only as describing the same episode, but their essential identity
has been missed in consequence of a mistranslation: the Hebrew text,
in which the verb may be variously interpreted according as it is
vocalized, says in reference to Absalom's followers that 'they were put
to silence (*nādammû*)' or 'destroyed (*niḏᵉmû*)', not that 'they kept
silence (for the verb is not in the active but in the passive voice).[6] Here
the Commentator catches up the prophet's 'thou holdest thy peace',

---

[1] Ecclus. xii. 15 (Hebrew text).
[2] Cp. Isa. liii. 8 and Psa. cix. 34 (where *min* 'from' means both 'in consequence of'
and 'without').
[3] Kautzsch & Cowley *Hebrew Grammar* § 114 *o* (4).
[4] In *War* II xvii 9 § 448.   [5] Hab. i. 13.
[6] Cp. Brown-Driver-Briggs *Hebrew Lexicon* 198–9; cp. Driver in *Sefer Tur-Sinai* 9*
and *JTS*, NS XIII 370.

of which God is the subject, by 'who were put to silence' in the sense of 'destroyed', which he applies to Absalom and his party. The parallelism is obviously not verbally exact; but the Commentator is not expounding prophecy as in a modern commentary and, having no interest in philology, is content with a verb of equivocal sense yielding a *double entente* linking the comment to the passage on which he is commenting, while simultaneously it gives a hint of the meaning which those whom he addresses will understand. The comment thus fits the prophecy to the scene. The supposition, too, that 'Absalom' is a pseudonym taken from David's disloyal son[1] for some unknown traitor who betrayed the Teacher at the critical moment is needless; the commentator reckoned Absalom a traitor, as he showed by linking the prophet's 'traitors' to his comment that 'they (*sc.* the house of Absalom) did not help him (*sc.* the Teacher)' when he was being hunted to his death. Absalom was running away, like Eleazar ben Jair, when he was caught and killed. Once again commentator and historian are in complete agreement.

Josephus also reports[2] that Eleazar son of Jair, a relative of Menahem, escaped with some supporters from the massacre and made his way to Masada; so the Commentator speaks of 'all doers of the law in the house of Judah whom God was saving[3] from the house of judgement because of their toil and their faithfulness to the Rightful Teacher' (H viii 1–3). What he means is that Eleazar, a descendant (grandson or grand-nephew) of Judah the original 'teacher of wisdom', and other members of his family and party who had remained faithful to the Law as expounded by them escaped to a place of safety. He prudently gives no hint that Eleazar and his followers, like the 'house of Absalom', in fact, 'secretly (λάθρα)' ran away and so betrayed their leader; for Eleazar was presumably Menahem's successor, whose wrath he would not wish to incur. What 'house' or 'place of judgement' (*bêt mišpāṭ*) means is not quite clear; for the expression is apparently unique. What it cannot be is a 'court of law (*bêt dîn*)';[4] this makes no sense in the context, which is referring to the place where a murder took place in daylight. The expression seems to be chosen partly to avoid anything savouring of a court of law and partly as echoing 'the place of his discovery (*bêt geʹlôṭô*)', where the Teacher and his followers are said to have been attacked (H xi 6), *i.e.* Mt. Ophel; it thus describes this as the 'place of doom'[5] where the Wicked Priest and his party caught their opponents and executed savage vengeance on them by a kind of lynch-law. This interpretation of the expression has the advantage that it

---

[1] Cp. Winter in *PQS* XCI 38–9.   [2] In *War* II xvii 9 § 447.
[3] Cp. pp. 277–8.   [4] Zeitlin in *JQR*, NS XLI 38.
[5] Brownlee in *BASOR* CXXVI 14 (where however the text is referred to a totally different episode).

agrees with its use in a subsequent passage, where it described the place
where God will execute His sentence on the nations, *i.e.* Mt. Zion, which
is full of His justice (H x 3–4)[1]; here it has a good, there a bad sense.
That the allusion is to the murder on Mt. Ophel is confirmed by the
description of those to be saved as 'all the doers of the law in the house
of Judah' (H viii 1), *i.e.* all the survivors of the massacre; for this was the
last occasion on which any of the party would survive. The Commentator could not at this time have known that 'all' the house of Judah
was doomed, being extinguished at Masada in A.D. 73. The author of
the historical part of the *Zadokite Documents*, however, did know this; for
he declared that 'when the epoch is completed, according to the number
of these years, there shall be no participation with the house of Judah;
each must stand on his own watch-tower' (Z vi 7). What he meant was
that the surviving Covenanters 'at the end of the age' in which they
were living, *i.e.* in the last Messianic struggle, would not be able to rally
round the 'house of Judah', *i.e.* the leading family in the movement,
which by then was extinct, but would be compelled each to rely on
himself. Hence the *War* contains no reference to this family.

The Commentator says that the Wicked Priest sought not only 'to
swallow him up' (H xi 5) but also 'to swallow them up' (H xi 7),
referring in the first case to the Rightful Teacher, who was in all
probability murdered, and in the second to his followers, some of
whom perished while others escaped destruction. An echo of this very
expression can be found in one of the *Thanksgiving Hymns*, whose author
giving thanks for his escape from an undescribed danger, exultantly
exclaims 'so I will answer him' or 'them that slander me',[2] as the verb
means in the context, or 'that seek to swallow me up',[3] as it may
allusively be translated (T ix 8; cp. vii 5). The *double entente* clearly
hints that the author of the hymn in question was one of the 'house of
Judah' who made good their escape on the fatal day.

Yet, however close the accounts are of the outrage on Mt. Ophel
which the historian and the Commentator give, some divergencies due
to their different points of view naturally remain.

Josephus on the one hand gives a straightforward description of the
scene which leaves the distinction between Menahem and Eleazar
perfectly clear. The Commentator's interest, on the other hand, is
centred not on the dead but on the living Rightful Teacher. He says
that the Wicked Priest pursued the Teacher 'to swallow him up . . . at
the place of his discovery' (H xi 5–6). In other words, he mentions
only the Wicked Priest's intention to kill the Teacher, leaving the fact
that he had been killed to be inferred from the prophet's mention of

[1] Cp. Isa. xxxiii. 5.
[2] Cp. Driver in *JTS* XXXIII 40–1 and LXI (NS XIII) 369–70.
[3] Cp. Isa. xlix. 19.

'bloodshed' and from his own reference to 'the place of his discovery', which would otherwise be pointless. He does not say explicitly 'and he swallowed him up' because his interest lies not so much in the identity of the individual Teacher as in the continuance of the office in the person of the ideal Teacher who lives on in accordance with the principle that 'the king is dead; long live the king!'; for 'He (sc. God) built a sure house for them (sc. the Covenanters) in Israel, such as had not appeared aforetime even till now' (Z v 5). He has however already thrown out another hint of his meaning, that Menahem had in fact perished, by saying that the 'house of Judah' would escape destruction (H viii 1–2); this was Eleazar ben Jair, nephew of Menahem, and his supporters. Those who knew the events at first hand would have no difficulty in understanding the allusion and would have long ago known what had happened to Eleazar. The Commentator's reluctance to say clearly what he meant was natural in the circumstances of the Revolt and without doubt intentional; those who knew the facts would read between the lines and understand the allusion, while those outside would learn nothing of the society's secret lore. He was following the trend of the times, for an obvious reason;[1] for it was a mark of political literature under the Roman empire that it should not carry its meaning on its face.[2] The danger inherent in revealing revolutionary secrets is well illustrated by the story of the 'oracle', as the Romans regarded it, that the Jews expected one of their own race to become ruler of the world; for Josephus tells how, when taken as a prisoner before Vespasian, he hastened to forestall the risk of betraying his countrymen by applying it to the Emperor himself.[3]

That the Rightful Teacher and Manaemus (Menahem) are one and the same person satisfies most, if not all, of the necessary conditions; but four objections to their identification must be faced before definitely accepting it.

First, that Josephus says nothing of the 'covenant' into which the Covenanters, whose leader was the Rightful Teacher, entered[4] is easily explained; the historian is concerned not to describe the internal affairs of the religious community involved in the dispute but to tell the story of the disaster which was brought on the nation by the Revolt. Second, the point has been made that Josephus nowhere affords any indication that Manaemus (Menahem) succeeded his brothers in the leadership of the Zealots after their death in A.D. 46–8[5] but implies rather that he appeared as 'an unsavoury character, even to his fellow Zealots'. Naturally the historian has nothing to say on the first point; for he

---

[1] Cp. pp. 348–9.   [2] Syme *Tacitus* 29.
[3] In *War* III viii 9 §§ 399–408 and VI v 4 §§ 312–3.
[4] Michel *Mattre* 285.   [5] Rowley in Hempel & Rost *Von Ugarit nach Qumran* 187–90.

was not writing the history of the Zealots and had no interest in the internal affairs of the party. The inference that Manaemus became their leader, however, is plausible; for, unless he had been a Zealot leader, he could not have marched up to the Temple in the autumn of A.D. 66 with an escort of Zealots. Third, that Manaemus was not a *persona grata* with the Zealots misrepresents what Josephus says.[1] His words are that Manaemus, 'taking the Zealots (τοὺς ζηλωτὰς) as an escort with him', went up to Jerusalem to take command of the rebels; in other words, these Zealots, namely the bulk of the party who had been in hiding by the Dead Sea and without doubt had gladly answered the call to arms, were his enthusiastic supporters. The people to whom he appeared an 'unsavoury character' were Eleazar the high-priest's son and his partisans; they thought that 'after revolting from the Romans for love of liberty, they ought not to sacrifice this liberty to a Jewish hangman and put up with a master who, even if he were to abstain from violence, was anyhow far beneath themselves'. Eleazar and his party, if they were Zealots, were a rival group who thought that, having started the Revolt, they ought to lead it and were unwilling to surrender the leadership to one who had not struck the first blow and who in their opinion was inferior in station to themselves; for they included the younger members of the aristocratic and priestly families who resented foreign rule and the older members of these classes who hoped by taking their side to exercise a restraining influence on them. Fourth, while the Scrolls almost certainly make the Teacher a priest (H ii 7–10, Pb ii 15; cp. H vii 4–5), neither Josephus nor the Talmud says that Manaemus or Menahem was one; and Josephus nowhere gives the title of priest to any member of his family.[2] In exactly the same way, however, Alexander Jannaeus is never described by him as a priest or as high-priest, even when offering sacrifices; he either calls him 'king'[3] or gives him no title. So too he does not say that Eleazar son of Hananiah was a priest; he is simply described as 'acting as captain (στρατηγῶν)', *sc.* of the troops garrisoning the Temple,[4] even though as a high-priest's son he must have been a priest. The reason is in each case obvious: the historian, who came of a distinguished priestly family,[5] would not give the priestly title to priests of whose activities he vehemently disapproved as defiling the sacred office. The argument from silence never carried under weight; and here the silence may be intentional.

In what sense Menahem was a priest is a much vexed question. If such, he might have been a 'common priest' (for Eleazar and his

---

[1] In *War* II xvii 9 §§ 443–4.   [2] Dupont-Sommer *Écrits Esséniens* 411.
[3] In *Antiquities* XIII xii 1 § 320 and xiii 5 §§ 372, 398 and also *War* V viii 3 § 304 and VII vi 2 § 171.
[4] In *War* II xvii 2 § 409.   [5] Josephus *Life* i 1.

partisans considered him 'far below themselves'),[1] or he might not
have been so described if he had not been in the habit of exercising
priestly functions in the Temple.[2] That the family of Menahem had
been settled for several generations in Galilee would not debar it from
being a priestly family, even an Aaronite of the Zadokite line[3]; for,
although the families of practising priests lived in or in the immediate
neighbourhood of Jerusalem, many whose members had long ceased
to exercise priestly functions might well be living elsewhere, and the
number of persons qualified must have long exceeded that of those
required for the service of the Temple. Alternatively, Menahem has
been thought to have been a priest elected by the community of the
Covenanters, such as the Essenes are sometimes supposed (probably
erroneously)[4] to have had.[5] Or he might have received the appellation
from his followers as a title of honour, as various persons in the Old
Testament received it, not as consecrated priests of the line of Aaron
but as princes or others who performed priestly functions;[6] somewhat
similarly the corresponding Aramaic title was occasionally used to
translate the Greek term for 'elder'.[7] Or again Menahem perhaps took
or received the title of priest for the same reason as Jesus was styled
a priest in the New Testament, namely in virtue of the priestly character
belonging to Israel's king;[8] for he clearly claimed a royal privilege
when he came up to Jerusalem in royal style and entered the Temple
in royal robes. Or lastly, he might have been an 'eschatological priest',
as Elijah was expected to be when he returned as the Messiah.[9] In any
case, that Menahem's relative Eleazar ben Jair, who had escaped when
his uncle was murdered on Mt. Ophel, lived on as 'Eleazar the priest' in
Jewish folk-lore[10] may be some indication that the family had a priestly
origin.[11] Whether all these suggested reasons are rejected or any one of
them is accepted as approximating to the true reason, the combined
title of 'teacher' and 'priest' surely recalls the Chronicler's description of
the time, though long past, when 'for long seasons Israel hath been
without the true God and without a teaching priest (*kōhēn môreh*) and
without law; but when in their distress they turned back unto the Lord
God of Israel and sought him, he was found of them';[12] for the Rightful
Teacher will certainly have been regarded by his followers as exactly
fulfilling these conditions.

---

[1] Josephus *War* II xvii 9 § 443.   [2] Cp. Roth *Background* 55–6.
[3] Lévi in *RÉJ.* LXI 165.   [4] Strugnell in *JBL* LXXVII 110–11.
[5] Josephus *Antiquities* XVIII i 5 § 22; s. Schürer *Geschichte*[3] II 571.
[6] *E.g.* Gen. xiv. 18 (Melchizedek), Jud. xviii. 4 (young Levite), 1 Sam. i. 9,
ii. 11, xiv. 3 (Eli); 2 Sam. viii. 18 (sons of David).
[7] Teicher in *JJS* III 131–2.   [8] Heb. v. 5–6; cp. Psa. cx. 4.
[9] Hengel *Zeloten* 161–2.   [10] Breithaupt *Josephus Gurionides* vi 57–8.
[11] Cp. Roth in *PQS* XC 108–9 (suggesting that Menahem's nephew Eleazar may
have been confused with Eleazar son of the high-priest Hananiah).
[12] 2 Chron. xv. 3–4.

Further, according to both Midrash and Talmud,[1] Menahem was a name given to the expected Messiah; but, although the Scrolls nowhere indisputably declare in so many words that the Teacher was the expected Messiah, the inference is plausible enough, as argued below,[2] and may therefore be accepted.

These are all points which cannot perhaps be definitely settled in the present state of knowledge; but neither objection is sufficiently serious to outweigh the evidence for the identification which is here maintained. Both the Rightful Teacher and Manaemus or Menahem were exponents of a philosophy or doctrine which had the same end in view and both had a large body of followers; both were connected in some way with a certain Judah, who had a considerable following, and both had as their lieutenant an Absalom who was murdered; both were harassed by internal and external enemies and both were murdered on or at the times of the Day of Atonement.

That the Wicked Priest is rightly identified with Eleazar captain of the Temple rather than with his father Hananiah the high-priest[3] is supported by certain slight indications which emerge from a careful study of the Hebrew and Greek accounts of these events. First, he is nowhere called 'high-priest' but always simply 'priest' (H viii 8, 16 ix 9 xi 4, 12 xii 2, 8). Second, Eleazar, whose rash action was the spark which kindled the Revolt, is said to have been 'a very bold ($\theta\rho\alpha\sigma\acute{\upsilon}\tau\alpha\tau\sigma\varsigma$) young man';[4] and his character as thus depicted closely resembles that of the Wicked Priest, inasmuch as 'when he held rule in Israel, his heart was lifted up' (H viii 9–10). Third, the verb stating that 'he held rule ($m\bar{a}\check{s}al$)', in itself a purely general term,[5] is one which appears otherwise to refer only to secular office;[6] it would therefore be applicable to Eleazar's office as captain of the guard in charge of the Temple which he held, although he was also a priest. Fourth, the Wicked Priest is further described as one 'who was called by the name of truth' or 'a true name at the beginning of his appearing on the scene' or 'entering an office' (H viii 8–9); here the reference to Eleazar is unmistakable. As already said, his bold action had precipitated the Revolt and as its instigator he would have been welcomed by Menahem and his party as an ally and supporter, rightly called 'Eleazar', which means 'God has helped (us)' sc. by providing a timely reinforcement. When however the ambitions of these two leaders clashed, Menahem's followers would see reason to change their minds about him; for, far from being one whom God had sent to help them as a heroic champion of the 'truth',[7] i.e. of their particular type of revolutionary ideology, as

---

[1] Pp. 356–8.
[2] Pp. 471–5.
[3] P. 267.
[4] Josephus *War* II xvii 2 § 409.
[5] Cp. B. Talmud *Baba Metzia* 75b (where it is applied to a wife who dominates her husband).
[6] Dupont-Sommer in *VT.* V 122.
[7] Cp. Ecclus. xlvi 1.

T

he had seemed at the beginning of his Revolt, 'he showed himself' in his true colours[1] (H xi 7) by murdering their leader and so became the Wicked Priest *par excellence* in their eyes. Fifth, the Commentator says that 'the Wicked Priest wrought abominable deeds in it (*sc.* Jerusalem) and defiled the sanctuary of God' and also 'stole the wealth of the poor' in the cities of Judah (H xii 7–10). So in Jerusalem, soon after the outbreak of the Revolt in A.D. 66, the leading priests and the party in favour of peace occupied the Upper City while Eleazar and those eager for rebellion had fortified themselves in the Lower City near the Temple; and, while the rebels sought to gain control of the Upper City, their opponents were trying to seize the Temple and to expel 'those who were polluting the sanctuary'.[2] Eleazar, too, was responsible for the riot in the Temple when he drove out Menahem and his followers and also for the massacre of the Roman garrison in a fort in Jerusalem after its capitulation on being promised that their lives would be spared; then the city was 'polluted by such a stain of guilt as could not but arouse a dread of some visitation from heaven', and 'the massacre took place on the Sabbath, a day on which from religious scruples Jews abstain even from the most innocent acts'.[3] Further, this description of Eleazar's activities falls in with the statement that his father Ananias the high priest had 'very wicked servants who joined themselves to the boldest sort of the people and went to the threshing-floors and took away the tithes due to the priests by violence and did not refrain from beating such as would not give these tithes to them';[4] for his son Eleazar presumably was cognizant of and probably also implicated in such and similar outrages and would without doubt have had his share of the wealth accruing from them.[5]

A possible objection to his identification may be found in a statement in the *Commentary on Habakkuk*, which speaks of him as one 'whom God, for his sin against the Rightful Teacher and the men of his counsel, gave into the hands of his enemies to afflict him with a fatal blow in bitterness of soul, because he had dealt wickedly with God's chosen one' (H ix 9–11), whereas Josephus has nothing to say of Eleazar's fate. According to the historian, after the murder of Menahem Eleazar resumed or assumed command of the Jewish insurgents in Jerusalem and was mainly responsible for the treacherous massacre of the Roman garrison in the bastion, where they had surrendered when he had granted them a safe-conduct to leave the city. Subsequently he apparently became one of the commanders appointed to undertake the direction of the war in the south; this is the last notice which Josephus has of him.[6] As he is not mentioned again, the probability is that he,

---

[1] Pp. 270–1.   [2] Josephus *War* II xvii 5 §§ 422–4.   [3] *Ibid.* 10 §§ 449–55.
[4] Josephus *Antiquities* XX ix 2 §§ 205–7.   [5] Roth *Background* 20–1.
[6] In *War* II xx 4 § 566 (s. Thackeray *Josephus* II 540).

like other insurgent leaders,[1] did not survive the war and therefore came to a violent end during the siege or in the final conflagration. The medieval *Josippon* says that he committed suicide or was killed towards the end of the Revolt;[2] but this work, which may have been compiled perhaps as late as the 9th century A.D., perhaps confuses Eleazar son of Hananiah with Eleazar son of Jair,[3] and no uncorroborated statement in it can be trusted.

Another curious point is that Absalom and Judah are here called by their proper names and not by pseudonyms or descriptive phrases as other characters in the Scrolls are designated. Such an occasional use of the real name is no matter for surprise as it has Biblical authority; for 'Egypt (*Miṣrayim*)' is once similarly used in the *Book of Daniel* for the country of that name and not as a pseudonym for some other country.[4] The reason, too, why the author of the *Commentary* uses the real names here is not far to seek: both are not only equivocal in themselves by virtue of their associations in the Old Testament but also remininiscent of various heroes of the Maccabaean wars, which are often indirectly recalled in the Scrolls.[5] Such would be Judas Maccabaeus as well as Judah son of Chalpî[6] and Absalom the father of Mattathias and possibly also of Jonathan,[7] and another undescribed Absalom,[8] who all played parts in them. In the same way Zadok the co-founder of the party is called not by a pseudonym but by his own name; the reason obviously is that the name was extremely common and especially that 'Sons of Zadok' was an equivocal expression which might refer to priests of the line of the historic Zadok, whether those of the community or others who claimed to be of the true priestly line, or to the members of the community as a whole, as an elect and in a spiritual sense a priestly body (Z v 7; cp. D ix 14).[9] None of these names, therefore, would betray any esoteric secret which the party did not wish to be known. At the same time, on the one hand, as Absalom was dead, no harm could come from openly giving his name. On the other hand, only a hint of Eleazar's identity was possible as he was still alive and, if he was named, might well be hunted down and killed; it was therefore only half-revealed, while remaining half-concealed, in his grandfather's very common name.

The outrage took place on Mt. Ophel, which lay on the obvious line of flight from the city and the Temple along the Wâdi-'nNâr to the region of the Dead Sea. Dr. Roth therefore pertinently draws attention[10]

---

[1] Josephus *War* III ii 2 § 219 (John the Essene), IV vi 1 §§ 359–63 (Niger the Peraean), VII v 6 § 154 (Simon bar Giora) and ix 1 §§ 389–401 (Eleazar ben Jair).
[2] Breithaupt *Josephus Gurionides* vi 56–7.   [3] Cp. p. 275 n. 11.
[4] Dan. xi. 8 (s. Wernberg-Møller in *JJS* IX 217).   [5] Pp. 353–5.
[6] 1 Macc. xi. 70 (cp. Josephus *Antiquities* XIII v 7 § 161.)
[7] 1 Macc. xiii. 11 (cp. Josephus *Antiquities* XIII vi 4 § 202).
[8] 2 Macc. xi. 17.   [9] P. 254.   [10] In *Background* 80–1.

to the importance apparently attached by the Covenanters to the prophecies of Micah; for several portions of a *Commentary on Micah* have been recovered from one of the caves.[1] One speaks of the Splutterer of Falsehood[2] and of 'the Rightful Teacher, who [will teach the Law to] his [council] and to [all] who offer themselves freely to be added to the elect of [God, who do the Law] by the counsel of the community, (and) who will be rescued from the day of [judgement]' (I Q *14* viii 4–x 9);[3] and another applies the prophecy that 'thou [shalt sow but not] reap, thou [shalt tread the olives but shalt not anoint (thyself) with oil; and] thou shalt not drink the new wine [of the vintage]'[4] to the 'last generation' (I Q *14* xvii–xix 2–5), presumably those who opposed the Covenanters (cp. Z i 8). Unfortunately no piece of the intervening passage, in which the prophet says 'and thou, O tower on rough and rocky ground, hill of the daughter of Zion, unto thee shall it come; yea, the former dominion shall come to the daughter of Jerusalem,'[5] nor of the commentary on it, has been discovered; for this address to Mt. Ophel would have played into the hands of the Commentator, who could well have brought it into connection with the murder of the Teacher; for the 'sophist' Manaemus (Menahem) and his lieutenant Absalom are described as having been chased on to this very hill and then murdered on it.[6]

The key-points in this historic episode may now be set down in parallel columns, as the two authors have described them, in order to bring out their significance relative to one another:

Commentary on Habakkuk	*Jewish War*
An unnamed	Manaemus,
Rightful Teacher	described as a 'sophist',
with Messianic aspirations	'decked in royal attire',
pursued	hunted
'to the place where he was discovered'	'into the open'
with intent 'to swallow him up'	and murdered on Mt. Ophel
by	by
an unnamed	Eleazar son of the high-priest
Wicked Priest, 'whose heart was lifted up' when he took office',	⎰ and therefore a priest, 'a very rash young man' and 'acting as captain of the Temple',
on 'their'	near the

[1] P. 17.   [2] Pp. 307–9.   [3] On Mic. i. 5–7.
[4] On Mic. vi. 15.   [5] Mic. iv. 8.   [6] Pp. 268–9.

Day of Atonement,	beginning of Tishri,
during a 'Kittian' invasion;	during war with Rome;
the 'house' or party of Absalom	Absalom and other followers
treacherously failing to help the Teacher,	while trying secretly to escape
'silenced' or 'destroyed'	massacred
and	and
	⎧ Judah's grandson
the 'house of Judah'	⎨ Eleazar ben Jair
	⎩ with a few followers
saved by God.	saved by a 'stealthy' flight.

No such series of coincidences can be found anywhere else in ancient, certainly not in Jewish, history, and these can hardly be fortuitous. All therefore who refuse to admit any connection between the events tabulated in these two columns and hold that on examination 'the whole remarkable series of parallels dissolves into nothing'[1] must go beyond a shadowy 'dissolution' which rests on dubious interpretation and seek a comparable set of events to explain the resemblances; the quest is hopeless, a counsel of despair![8]

2. DAY OF ATONEMENT

The murder of the Teacher is said in the *Commentary on Habakkuk* to have occurred 'at the period of the season of the Day of Atonement . . . on a fast-day, the sabbath of their rest' (H xi 6–7).[2]

The first point is to decide to whom the pronoun in the description of the murder as 'the sabbath of their rest' refers. The Commentator may mean that the Teacher was killed on the 'sabbath of rest' of his opponents, *i.e.* on the orthodox Day of Atonement; or he may mean that his party were harried on their own 'sabbath of rest', *i.e.* on the day observed by themselves as the Day of Atonement, which will not necessarily have been that of the orthodox party. A divergence between the calendars of the parties may have come about in one of two ways: either the Pharisees may have decreed a 'postponement (*d⁽ᵉ⁾ḥîyāh*)' of one of the annual feasts or fasts for reasons of expedience and so have caused a dislocation of the year's calendar, such as the strict Covenanters may have refused to accept,[3] or the Covenanters may have followed a different, namely the solar instead of the lunisolar, calendar.[4] Which reason may have been the cause can be plausibly inferred; for while little is known of the actual practice of 'postponement' at this time, the Covenanters are proved to have had

---

[1] Rowley in Hempel & Rost *Von Ugarit nach Qumran* 188–9.
[2] Cp. Friedlander *Jewish Religion*[1] 355.
[3] Cp. Oberman in *JBL.* LXXV 293–4.   [4] Pp. 323–6.

their own calendar. Unfortunately, however, the date of their Day of Atonement, as distinct from the orthodox date, cannot be determined, as the precise correlation of the heterodox calendar of the Covenanters to that of orthodox Judaism is unknown;[1] the presumption is perhaps that it will have been a day reasonably close to 10 Tishri.

The second point is to decide, if possible, on what day the episode which Josephus describes will have actually occurred; and this depends not only on his words but also on another question of the calendar in the 1st century A.D. Josephus says[2] that the date of the previous event described by himself (the evacuation of the palace by the Roman garrison following Menahem's assumption of the command of the insurgents) was 6 Gorpiaeus and that 'on the following day' Ananias (Hananiah), presumably the high-priest, and his brother were murdered by Menahem's followers; he then goes on to say[3] that Manaemus was so puffed up and brutalized by his success in driving out the Roman garrisons and by the murder of his rival the high-priest that he became an insufferable tyrant and that the party of Eleazar, son of the murdered man, laid plans to be rid of him. Clearly time must be allowed for Menahem's increasing unpopularity to make him intolerable and for plans to remove him to be discussed and prepared.

Whether the murder took place on 10 Tishri, the orthodox Day of Atonement, however, depends on the quite different question: what was 6 Gorpiaeus? Gorpiaeus was the sixth month in the Tyrian calendar, which Josephus often used, and 6 Gorpiaeus in it in A.D. 66 would be approximately 14 Tishri,[4] which would be too late for the murder if it fell after the orthodox Day of Atonement (10 Tishri) in the Jewish calendar. Normally, however, in giving dates Josephus uses the Tyrian names of the months for the names of the corresponding Jewish months in combination with the Jewish (not the Tyrian) calendar,[5] so that Gorpiaeus (6th Tyrian month) is merely substituted for Elul (6th Jewish month); in this case 6 Gorpiaeus = 6 Elul would fall nearly five weeks before 10 Tishri (7th Jewish month). This day would not necessarily be too early. An interval of such duration for Menahem to render himself so unpopular that his murder became inevitable is no unreasonable assumption; that it may have taken place on 1 Tishri (New Year's Day),[6] the day on which Aaron is recorded to have died,[7] is a pure guess, and it may equally well have been committed on 10 Tishri (Day of Atonement). In any case, if the

---

[1] Cp. Roth in *PQS* XC 109–110.   [2] In *War* II xviii 8 § 440–9 § 441.
[3] *Ibid.* §§ 442–3.
[4] Zeitlin in *JQR*, NS X 270 and XLVIII 254–5 and Dupont-Sommer in *Évidences* IX 19; cp. Niese in *Hermes* XXVIII 203–4 (where it is equated with 24 September).
[5] Schürer *Geschichte*[3] I 746–60.
[6] Del Medico *Énigme* 186, 356–7 and *Mythe* 97.
[7] Num. xxxiii. 38.

murder was not committed on that very day, it happened so near to it that the Commentator could reasonably describe it as having happened on it. That Josephus in his circumstantial account of these events says nothing of a murder on the Day of Atonement, which he would surely have mentioned if a murder had then been committed, is strong evidence against supposing that Menahem was murdered on the orthodox Day of Atonement; the murder must then have taken place on some other day, which might have been a divergent Day of Atonement as observed by the Covenanters.

Another reason in favour of supposing that a heterodox Day of Atonement is meant may be found in the Commentator's statement that 'he (sc. the Wicked Priest) showed himself (in his true character)[1] to them (sc. the party of the Rightful Teacher) to swallow them up and to make them to stumble on a fast-day, the Sabbath of their rest' (H xi 7–8); for 'he' is clearly contrasted with 'them' and 'their' in this passage. Its purport then is that the Wicked Priest sought to provoke the Rightful Teacher's followers into meeting violence with violence and so profaning their own sacred day.

This type of pseudo-synchronism, whereby events are assigned by pious fancy to a certain day or year although they are known to have occurred on different dates, is characteristic of Jewish traditions. In just this way, for example, R. 'Aqîbâ was commonly held to have been executed by the Romans on the very day on which R. Judah the patriarch was born;[2] but in actual fact the former perished in A.D. 132 and the latter was not born till A.D. 135.[3]

Two objections which Dr. Zeitlin has urged[4] must be mentioned, even if they are rejected. He holds that the Revolt broke out in the autumn of A.D. 65 (not A.D. 66),[5] and that Josephus was here using the Tyrian (not the Jewish) calendar. If 6 Gorpiaeus in the Tyrian calendar corresponded to 3 Tishri in the Jewish calendar in A.D. 65, it would have corresponded to 14 Tishri in A.D. 66; thus the murder of Menahem after that date would have occurred some days after the orthodox Day of Atonement on 10 Tishri. These arguments, however, are too uncertain to outweigh the equation of the dates here adopted; and, if they were valid, they would not necessarily be fatal to the supposition that Menahem was murdered on or sufficiently near to the Day of Atonement to support a belief fostered by religious propagandists, with little care for the truth, that he was actually murdered on that day. The possibility, too, always remains that Josephus or his translator made a mistake when rendering the original Aramaic text of his

[1] Pp. 270–1.   [2] Midrash R. *Ecclesiastes* I v 1.
[3] Cohen *ap*. Freedman & Simon *Midrash Rabba* VIII 16⁹.
[4] In *JQR*, NS X 74–80, XLVIII 254–5, XLIX 233.
[5] In *Megillat Taanit* 88.

Jewish War into its present Greek form; if so, the actual date of the murder will have been irrevocably lost, and any reconstruction of the history of the event within reasonable limits becomes possible.

3. RIVAL GROUPS AND LEADERS

Certain characters of secondary importance, concealed under pseudonyms, occur here and there in the Scrolls; they can perhaps be identified, though only in very tentative fashion. Some of these seem to resemble the 'quacks and deceivers' or 'impostors and deceivers' and so on, who during these momentous times misled numbers of people, often claiming divine inspiration.[1] All these without doubt were driven to rebel by the same fundamental causes as those which inspired the rebellions of Hezekiah, of Judah and of Simeon and Jacob, as well as of Menahem; these were discontent with economic conditions and intolerance of Roman rule, to which objection was taken as an infringement of the sovereignty of God.[2]

The identity, however, of most of the pseudonymous persons in the Scrolls must be sought not in the first but in the second half of the 1st century A.D., amongst the rivals striving for the leadership in the Revolt of A.D. 66–73; some of these will have been contemporary with the Rightful Teacher, and others will not have come into prominence till after his death and the flight of his relative Eleazar son of Jair to Masada, where he was in command of the insurgents. Then and afterwards various rivals continued to dispute the leadership of the Revolt and the control of Jerusalem and their quarrels, continued even while the Romans invested Jerusalem, ultimately brought ruin to the city and the nation.

The *Zadokite Documents* speak of a time, when the Rightful Teacher had appeared, when 'traitors turned aside in the way'; that was the time 'when the Man of Insolence, who spluttered words designed to lead Israel astray and made them go astray in a pathless wilderness' so that 'they sought smooth things and chose delusions . . . and made men to transgress the covenant and to set law at nought . . . and pursued them with the sword and fomented disputes among the people. So the anger of God was kindled against their congregation so as to make all their rabble desolate' or 'to lay waste all their wealth' (Z i 8–17); and further on, speaking of those who have rejected the Law, they say that 'they shall be judged in the same manner as their fellows who turned aside with the Men of Insolence because they spoke falsely against the laws of righteousness (*ṣedeq*) and rejected the covenant (of God)[3] and the firm agreement which they had drawn up

---

[1] Pp. 238–9; cp. Josephus *Antiquities* XX viii 6 §§ 167–72. [2] Pp. 239–41.
[3] Cp. Rabin *Zadokite Documents* 38–9 and Kuhn *Konkordanz* 37[4] (noting that 'of God' has been erased in the manuscript).

on oath in the land of Damascus, which is the new covenant; and neither they nor their families shall have any portion in the house of the Law' (Z ix 34–8). The same people are also mentioned twice in a fragment of a *Commentary of Isaiah* whose author, interpreting the prophet's denunciation of them 'that rise up early in the morning that they may follow strong drink and tarry late at night until strong wine inflame them'and of those 'who have rejected the Law of the Lord and have despised the word of the Holy One of Israel' and[1] referring them to 'the end of the days', *sc.* his own times, says of the former 'these are the Men of Insolence' and of the latter 'This is the congregation of the Men of Insolence who are in Jerusalem' (AIs. e ii 1–10). Individually the 'Man of Insolence' and the 'Men of Insolence' cannot be identified with any known person or persons; but the group to whom the writers are so cryptically alluding is obvious. They were those opponents of the Zadokites who had rejected the 'laws of righteousness (*ṣedeq*)', namely the Zadokite interpretation of the Law,[2] who had done everything possible to antagonize the mass of the populace in Jerusalem to them before and during the Revolt, and who had supported the 'Seekers after Smooth Things', namely the rich and highly placed Pharisees and Sadducees whose policy was one of appeasement of Rome at all costs.[3] God, however, had punished these as he would punish all other opponents of the party; all four passages, therefore, though referring to events before the destruction of Jerusalem which had been their punishment, were written after that event.

One of the most mysterious characters in the Scrolls is the person called the 'Man of Falsehood' or 'Lies', who appears in several places. Whether he is the same person as the 'Splutterer of Falsehood' (if this is a title) and the 'Man of Insolence' cannot be decided; but the general care taken by the authors of the Scrolls in the use of their special terms militates against the identification.

The *Commentary on Habakkuk* refers a denunciation in that prophet 'to [the] traitors with the Man of Falsehood, because they did not [listen to the words of] the Rightful Teacher (coming) from the mouth of God, and to the traitors [to] the new [covenant], because they were not loyal to the command of God [and profaned] His holy name' (H ii 1–4); and it refers in another passage 'to the house of Absalom and his counsellors' who were 'put to silence[4] when the Rightful Teacher was chastised and did not help him against the Man of Falsehood who rejected the Law in the midst of their whole congregation' (H v 9–12). This passage does not necessarily imply that the Man of Falsehood must be identified with 'the Wicked Priest who pursued the Rightful Teacher to swallow him up' (H xi 4–5); it can

---

[1] Isa. v. 11, 24.   [2] Pp. 257–8.   [3] P. 94.   [4] S. pp. 271–2.

indicate simply that he was present as a confederate, aiding and abetting him in the murder. The only other passage where he is mentioned is found in the *Zadokite Documents*; this says that 'from the day when the Rightful Teacher was gathered (to his fathers) until all the men of war who went aside with the Man of Falsehood (is) about forty years' (Z ix 39). This passage tells nothing of the life or death of the Man of Falsehood but deals solely with his followers, of whom the last survivors will not die until a whole generation has passed away, *i.e.* till early in the next century; and this would be perfectly possible if some of them were young men when the Revolt broke out.

The Man of Falsehood was then an associate as well perhaps as a rival of the Wicked Priest, and he was notorious for treachery; this suggests that he had once been a waverer between the pro-Roman and anti-Roman parties or between the various groups into which the insurgents were split, who had let each think that he was on their side while he played for time to see which way the wind would blow, seeking only his own advancement at whatever cost of bad faith, one who perhaps had become a follower of the Teacher but had afterwards deserted him, possibly out of jealousy if he was an ambitious man who coveted the leadership of the party.

One who might conceivably be regarded by extremists as a waverer was Agrippa II,[1] who was on friendly terms with the Jewish leaders and with the Roman authorities and often sought to mediate between them; and one consequence of his attitude was that the *sicarii*, who at the outbreak of the Revolt were acting in concert with the Zealots and Menahem's followers, burnt down his palace.[2] He could on chronological grounds have been denounced in the *Commentary on Habakkuk*, if this was composed *c*. A.D. 70–3[3]; but he then received a considerable extension of territory and ceased to intervene in Jewish affairs (when the only known event in his life is that Josephus corresponded with him),[4] although he lived on till *c*. A.D. 100. Another character cast for the part of the Man of Falsehood is Eleazar captain of the Temple;[5] but, if he is the Wicked Priest, the identification becomes unlikely, especially as the title does not entirely fit what is known of him. Further, neither of these persons can have been or seems to have been a former member of the party who has turned traitor. Eleazar son of Gion or Simon, too, might come into the picture.[6] He was apparently a member of the moderate anti-Roman

<hr/>

[1] Del Medico *Énigme* 130–1, 354–5.
[2] Josephus *War* II xvii 1 §§ 406–7, 4 §§ 414–21, 6 § 427, xviii 5 § 483 and 9 § 502, xix 3 §§ 523–6; III ix 7 § 443 and 8 § 456; IV i 3 § 14 and 8 § 456; V i 5 § 36; cp. *Antiquities* XX ix 6.
[3] Pp. 361–5.   [4] Josephus *Life* lxv 359–69.   [5] Del Medico *Deux Manuscrits* 136.
[6] Josephus *War* II xx 3 §§ 564–5; IV iv 1 §§ 224–5; V i 1 § 5 and § 7, i 3 § 15 and 4 § 21, iii 1 § 99, vi 1 § 250 (cp. xiii 1 § 528).

group who had Zealot leanings (for he had a bodyguard of Zealots) and had acquitted himself well against the Romans in the winter of A.D. 66, when Cestius had been routed at Beth-horon[1]; but his arrogance had made him personally unpopular. In the winter of A.D. 67 he was a party to the admission of the Idumaeans (possibly not Idumaeans in the strict sense but Jewish settlers in the northern part of their country)[2] into Jerusalem in pursuance of a political advantage over his rivals. He afterwards split the party and formed his own faction among the Zealots; and at the Passover in A.D. 70, being in control of the Temple, he admitted a number of citizens to worship within the sacred precincts. Finally, when the situation was well-nigh desperate, he patched up his quarrel with the main body of the Zealots and brought his own followers back into the fold. His respect, however, for the service of the Temple would make it unlikely that he had ever been a member of the inner circle of the Covenanters, who had cut themselves off from it;[3] and the Covenanters would have no reason to blacken the memory of one who had purged his desertion by rejoining the party.

One of the most prominent leaders of the Revolt, whom Josephus describes[4] in terms which correspond exactly with this nickname and all that it implies, is John of Gischala. The historian records nothing of his movements before or at the time of the murder of Menahem, so that he may well have been a former supporter. He first mentions him in the late autumn of A.D. 66, when he crossed his path in Galilee, as a 'brigand' who from acting alone had succeeded in collecting a considerable body of followers and had even engaged in plundering that district; shortly afterwards, 'having got up a very crafty swindle', he formed a monopoly of oil and amassed a fortune. He then quarrelled with the historian, who had been appointed commander in Galilee in the winter of A.D. 66-7, and fell back on his native town, which he induced to join the Revolt against the Romans; when Titus approached the city and offered terms, John promised to persuade the citizens to accept them if the Romans would respect the Sabbath but, having received the promise, he slipped away with a few supporters to Jerusalem, leaving the city to its fate. In Jerusalem he won the confidence of the younger men by deceiving them about the strength of the Roman forces, although the older men saw through him; there, supported by the Galilaean extremists among the Zealots, he made himself leader of the war-party. His next exploit was to feign friendship with Ananus, the leader of the moderate anti-Zealot party, and then to betray his confidence to the Zealots, who invited the Idumaeans[5]

---

[1] P. 375.   [2] Pp. 84–5.   [3] Roth in *JSS* IV 345[1].
[4] In *War* II xxi 1 § 585–2 § 594; IV ii 1 § 84–4 § 111, iii 1 § 121–2 § 128 and 13 § 208–v 2 § 325, vii 1 §§ 389–97, ix 10 §§ 558–63; V iii §§ 98–105, x 4 §§ 439–441, xiii 1 § 528 and 6 §§ 562–5; VI ix 3 §§ 433–4.
[5] Cp. pp. 216–8, 222.

into Jerusalem to help them maintain their position; these, thus introduced into the city, slaughtered the guard and then murdered both Ananus and Jesus the high-priest. John thereupon assumed despotic power, in which he was supported by the most depressed elements of the populace. In the spring of A.D. 70, when the situation was becoming desperate, the moderate Zealot Eleazar son of Gion or Simon opened the gates of the inner Temple to admit worshippers at the Passover, whereupon John broke in by a ruse and beat up the defenders; he then attached himself to the Zealots, and the two parties combined to bid defiance to Simon bar Giora, who was occupying the Upper and much of the Lower City. Notwithstanding their mutual rivalries, each party allowed free licence to the other to attack all 'enjoying wealth or rank' in order to replenish their coffers; and John did not even shrink from the sacrilege of plundering the sacred treasury. Finally, both John and Simon were taken prisoners at the capture of Jerusalem in A.D. 70; Simon was executed when Vespasian and Titus celebrated their triumph in Rome, while John implored his captors to spare him and was .condemned to imprisonment for life. Thus John was, as Josephus[1] describes him, an intriguer as unscrupulous as he was crafty, 'a ready liar and clever at obtaining credence for his lies, making a merit of deceit', he was 'a charlatan, and one extremely subtle in character' and 'a man of extreme cunning'. Few, even after every allowance for the historian's personal animosity against one who had opposed and deserted him,[2] could have so fully deserved to be called the 'Man of Falsehood' as John of Gischala; and that he was not afraid to commit sacrilege in pursuit of his aims may explain why the Commentator says of the Man of Falsehood that 'he spurned the Law' (H v 11-12). Here a *double entente* may be seen; for the phrase, while meaning primarily that the Man of Falsehood had flouted the Law by committing sacrilege, may also contain a covert allusion to his abandonment of the Teacher's exposition of the Law. Josephus only mentions him when he first crosses his path. However, that John was originally a member of the Zealot party (and perhaps therefore also a Covenanter) and stayed with them when the Revolt broke out, having seen a chance to cover up his own misdeeds and to advance his fortunes by opposition to Rome, that he abandoned it and subsequently rejoined it, even though he did not remain with it to the end, is well within the bounds of possibility.

Another character denounced in the Scrolls is the 'Lion' or rather the 'Young Lion of Wrath', as the expression ought to be translated; for the point, though small, is important for the light which it throws on

---

[1] In *War* II xxii 1 §§ 585-6; IV ii 1 § 85, iii 13 § 208, ix 10 § 558; cp. VII viii 1 §§ 263-4.
[2] Cp. Milman *History of the Jews* II 264.

he problem of identifying the person who is thus described. He it nowhere mentioned in any of the main works so far published but appears in two fragments of commentaries on prophetical books. The first, a *Commentary on Hosea*, of which only two imperfect lines have been preserved, speaks in the first of 'the young lion of wrath . . . to crush (?) him like a roaring lion (?)' and refers in the second to '. . . the last priest, because he stretched out his head to strike a blow in Ephraim' (AHo. 1–2). The second is a *Commentary on Nahum*, of which the beginning is lost. The subject of the first surviving comment is '[Demet]rius king of Greece, who sought to enter Jerusalem by the counsel of the Seekers after Smooth Things . . . the kings of Greece from (the time of) Antiochus till the appearance of the rulers of the Kittians'[1]; it then speaks of 'the Young Lion of Wrath who used to smite amongst his great ones and his counsellors' and '. . . by the Seekers after Smooth Things, when he used to hang men alive . . .'; and it declares his prey to be 'the wealth which the [priests] (cp. H ix 4)' or 'the [magnates][2] of Jerusalem amassed' (ANa. I 2–11).

The key to the second passage has been sought in the statement that 'he used to hang men alive'; and so its editor Mr. Allegro,[3] assuming that hanging alive connoted crucifixion, thought that the Young Lion of Wrath was the priest-king Alexander Jannaeus who crucified an immense number of his opponents, priests and laymen alike, on a single day and enriched himself with their property,[4] and that the Seekers after Smooth Things were his enemies the Pharisees.[5] This interpretation of the passage, however, is not so straightforward as it seems at first sight to be. First, the offence of which Jannaeus was guilty was an extraordinary act committed on a single occasion, whereas the Hebrew tense here used normally describes repeated or habitual activity in prose and a single act in past time only in poetry.[6] Second, the connotation of 'hanged alive' is far from clear; for the expression occurs nowhere else in Hebrew or Jewish literature before the medieval period. The ancient Hebrews used neither crucifixion nor hanging as modes of execution. Crucifixion is not mentioned in the Old Testament, although the Septuagint interpret hanging as crucifixion in one place in the story of Haman,[7] improbable as this seems on a tree 50 cubits (75 feet) high; and the latter is ascribed only to foreigners.[8] The Hebrews hung only the bodies of offenders after execution, *i.e.* when dead, to expose them as an additional indignity to public gaze,[9] when according to the Mishnah they were suspended

[1] Pp. 93–4, 204–5.   [2] Cp. 2 Ki. x. 6.   [3] In *JBL* LXXV 92.
[4] Josephus *Antiquities* XIII xiv 2 §§ 379–83 and *War* I iv 6 §§ 96–8.
[5] Cp. Rabin in *JJS* VII 3–11.   [6] Teicher in *JJS* VII 4 (2).
[7] Esth. vii. 9 (where the Septuagint have 'crucified', though elsewhere 'hanged').
[8] Gen. xli. 13 (?) and 2 Sam. xxi. 12.
[9] Deut. xxi. 22–3, Josh. viii. 29 x. 26, 2 Sam. iv. 12.

'after the manner of butchers'.[1] Hanging however perhaps became a Jewish mode of execution in the post-Biblical period, *e.g.* when eighty women were 'hanged' for witchcraft at Ashkelon;[2] for crucifixion of women would be most unusual. At the same time 'hanged' might be loosely used for 'crucified', as when the Jews are charged with having killed Jesus 'hanging him on a tree';[3] but the phrase is a conscious echo of the Old Testament.[4] In this way the Hebrew verbs for 'hanged (*tālāh*)' and 'crucified (*ṣālaḇ*)' came to be almost interchangeable terms in Rabbinic literature,[5] although Philo still employed different Greek verbs for 'hanged' (*e.g.* for scourging) and 'impaled'.[1] Contrari-wise, hanging men up (*sc.* alive) as a form of torture or for scourging[6] is mentioned not only in the Old Testament[7], which says that 'princes were hanged up by their hands' (presumably by foreign oppressors), but also in both Midrash and Talmud, *e.g.* to extract their wealth from them;[8] in such cases crucifixion would have been useless, as the victims would almost certainly have died (for very few exceptions are re-corded),[9] and the secret of their wealth would have been lost with them. That this is what 'hanged alive' in all probability means in the passage under discussion is supported by one of the only two other passages in Rabbinic literature in which it occurs. In the one[10] a commander is described as ordering the execution of a subordinate officer by hanging him alive; but, as the punishment is not further specified, it throws no light on the expression. The other[11] is a comment on the Biblical law that 'if a man has committed a sin worthy of death and he be put to death, thou shalt hang him on a tree';[12] this is usually supposed to mean that he shall be put to death and that his body shall afterwards be exposed on a tree to public gaze. The expositor here quoted, however, explains it as meaning 'possibly they hang him on a tree after the manner of the kingdoms'; he clearly means not that the victim shall be crucified[13] but that he shall be hanged before death on a tree and be left there to die. This explanation agrees with the description of the punishment as 'after the manner of the kingdoms', *i.e.* heathen nations; for the Romans (and presumably other races) both crucified and hanged persons condemned to death. They also hanged them alive for various forms of punishment and torture, of

---

[1] Mishnah *Sanhedrin* vi 4 (s. Danby *Sanhedrin* 90–3).   [2] *Ibid.* vi 4.
[3] Acts v. 30 x. 39; cp. Gal. iii. 13.   [4] Deut. xxi. 22–3.
[5] *E.g.* Tosefta *Sanhedrin* ix 7 (s. Rengstorf *Jebamoth* 203–4); cp. Ibn Ezra on Genesis xxvii 39 and Qimhi on Isaiah liii. 12.
[6] Ezr. vi. 11.   [7] Lam. v. 12.
[8] *E.g.* Midrash R. *Lamentations* iii 65 § 9; B. Talmud *Gittin* 37b *Baba Qamma* 62a and *Baba Bathra* 47b.
[9] *E.g.* Josephus *Life* 75.
[10] Zeitlin in *JQR*, NS XLVII 75–81, XLVIII 75–6, 391–9.
[11] Friedmann *Sifré debé Rab* I 114b § 221.   [12] Deut. xxi. 22–3.
[13] Wieder in *JJS* VII 71–2.

which *pendentem ferire* and many similar expressions are adequate evidence. Since then hanging men alive for various purposes must have been a practice well known to the Jews, the expression may be taken here as meaning what it says. Consequently 'the Young Lion of Wrath ... used to hang men alive' may be read as referring not to someone who like Alexander Jannaeus put a large number of Jews to death by crucifixion on a single occasion, but to one who made a practice of torturing his fellow Jews by this means in order to get possession of their wealth.

Further, the mention of the 'last priest' in the first passage, on the assumption that the person meant is not the last priest whom the writer happens to have known but the last high-priest of history (namely Phanni son of Samuel, elected in the autumn of A.D. 67),[1] shows that the Young Lion of Wrath as contemporary with him cannot be a figure of the 2nd or the 1st century B.C., for example Alexander Jannaeus,[2] but must be sought in the last part of the 1st century A.D.

The Young Lion of Wrath, although he must be sought in the 1st century A.D., cannot have been Titus, as Dr. Schonfield suggests.[3] Certainly Titus was a young man, only about twenty-four years old when he took Jerusalem, he was contemporary with the 'last priests', and he had allowed the mutilation and crucifixion of a number of Jewish prisoners.[4] However, that the Covenanters can have expected him to listen to the Rightful Teacher or to help the Teacher in his extremity and that the dissidents of the party can have been described as going aside with him is inconceivable; and the title is hardly compatible with the character which Titus is known to have borne. Alternatively Eleazar son of Hananiah, the rash young priest whose bold action touched off the Revolt, might conceivably be meant if he were not in all probability the Wicked Priest;[5] and the description of the Young Lion of Wrath, so far as it goes, fits neither Eleazar nor the Wicked Priest.

The character of Simon bar Giora, as Josephus[6] depicts it, agrees well with the title of the 'Young Lion of Wrath'. At the outbreak of the Revolt he was a 'youth' or 'young man' but distinguished as less cunning than John of Gischala 'though excelling him in physical strength and audacity'; he cherished high ambitions and aspired, if Josephus may be trusted, to despotic powers, and he had a revolutionary programme which included promises of freedom to slaves and rewards to free men if they would join him. Though nowhere said to be either a *sicarius* or a Zealot, he was closely in league with the extreme anti-Roman groups. In the autumn of A.D. 66 he was operating

[1] Josephus *War* IV iii 8 §§ 155-7.
[2] Dupont-Sommer in *JS* 1963, 205-6.   [3] In *Secrets* 96-7.
[4] Josephus *War* V xi 1 §§ 449-51 and 2 § 455.   [5] Pp. 267, 277-9.
[6] In *War* II xix 2 § 521; IV ix 3 §§ 503-8, 7 §§ 535-7, 8 §§ 540-2; V x 2 §§ 439-41, xiii 1 §§ 527-33.

with the insurgents in the neighbourhood of Jerusalem and in the summer of A.D. 66 he was with the 'brigands' at Masada;[1] but after a quarrel with them (possibly over the question, amongst others, of women in the camp)[2] he left the place and formed his own band of followers with whom he overran the villages, became a terror to the towns, and even descended into the lowlands where he wrought havoc in the countryside, collecting supplies and training his followers for an assault on the Zealots in Jerusalem. When these seized his wife, who was living there, as a hostage, he advanced on the city 'like any wounded beast', torturing and killing all whom he caught outside the gates. So soon as he had forced an entry into the city, he joined battle with John on one side and with Eleazar on the other; and both Simon and John arrested and tortured any wealthy Jews on whom they could lay their hands in order to extract their wealth from them. Simon even went so far as to murder his patron Matthias, by whose help he had gained an entry into the city, and any other prominent people who stood in the way of his cupidity or his ambition. Ultimately, as already said, Josephus[3] at the end sums up his character by asking 'what outrage did he refrain from inflicting on the persons of those free men who had made him a despot?' That he speaks of Simon as raging like a 'wounded beast' and that the *Commentary* describes the Young Lion's prey as the wealth amassed by priests or magnates in Jerusalem surely makes this identification probable.

It now becomes quite clear why '[Deme]trius king of Greece' (*i.e.* a Seleucid Demetrius) is brought into connection with the Young Lion of Wrath in this fragment of a commentary and whether Demetrius I Soter (162–150 B.C.)[4] or Demetrius III Eucerus (*c.* 96/5–89/8 B.C.) is meant.[5] The former, invited by a group of malcontents which included a number of the Hasidaean party, to come and relieve them from the tyranny of the rival Maccabaean party, sent three expeditions which eventually reduced the whole country and occupied Jerusalem.[6] He however can hardly be meant, since he made no attempt to enter Jerusalem in person; for Nicanor represented[7] him. The latter, when Alexander Jannaeus by his cruelty had driven the Jews into rebellion, was invited by the Pharisees *c.* 88 B.C. to come and rid them of the hated priest-king; he came and drove him out of the city but almost immediately withdrew his forces, whereupon Jannaeus re-entered Jerusalem.[8] Thus on this occasion *c.* 88 B.C. the 'seekers after smooth things' or 'appeasers' were those Pharisees who invited a foreign enemy into the Holy City to rid themselves of a

---

[1] Cp. p. 250.   [2] Roth *Background* 43–4.
[3] In *War* VII viii 1 § 265.   [4] Rowley in *JBL* LXXV 188–91.
[5] Allegro *ibid.* 92; cp. Dupont-Sommer *Écrits Esséniens* 281.
[6] Josephus *Antiquities* XII x 1 §§ 391–2 and 2 § 395; cp. I Macc. vii. 5–7, 12–13.
[7] S. p. 204.   [8] *Ibid.* XIII xiii 5 § 376 and *War* I iv 4 § 92.

native tyrant; as such they were the prototypes of the 'Seekers after Smooth Things' of A.D. 66–70[1] who, true to their party's history of peace[2] at any price, were opposed to war *à outrance* against Rome.[3] These were the ruling classes, as well as Pharisees and Zealots, who had connived at the introduction of Simon into the city in order to rid themselves of John.[4] In the same way Jannaeus became a prototype of Simon; for, although Demetrius had defeated him, he was brought back by a band of 6000 compatriots and admitted into Jerusalem, where he proceeded to wreak a terrible vengeance on his enemies, of whom he hanged 800 alive and whose wives and children he butchered before their eyes, just as Simon, when admitted by the ruling classes into the city with a horde of Idumaean allies, 'haughtily consenting to be their despot . . . treated those who had invited him no less as his enemies than those whom he had been invited to oppose' and robbed and murdered all the leading citizens to his heart's content.[5] Further, Demetrius III, like Vespasian, only approached but did not enter Jerusalem[6]; the allusion thus serves to indicate the event which it apparently conceals. The purpose of the passage, then, is one which appears often elsewhere: it is to indicate the present in terms of the past, comparing the events of a previous struggle with those of the present revolt.

A fragment of a Scroll, which may have been a *testimonium* of some sort, perhaps refers to these two men. After a more or less inexact recitation of the promise to Levi which Moses is reported as including in his final blessing pronounced over Israel,[7] it goes on to say: 'At the time when Joshua finished praising and giving thanks with his prais e then he said: C u r s e d b e t h e m a n w h o (r e) b u i l d e t h t h i s c i t y : w i t h t h e l o s s o f h i s f i r s t - b o r n s h a l l h e l a y t h e f o u n d a t i o n t h e r e o f, a n d w i t h (t h e l o s s o f) h i s y o u n g e s t s o n s h a l l h e s e t u p t h e g a t e s o f i t . '[8] And lo! a man accursed, one of Belial, will arise to be a fowler's snare to his people and (a cause of) destruction to all his neighbours. And . . . the two of them will become instruments of violence; and they will again build . . . for it a wall and towers to provide a refuge for wickedness . . . in Israel and a horrible thing in Ephraim and Judah.[9] [They will perform] (a work of) pollution in the land and of great blasphemy (?) among the sons of. . . . [They will spill] blood (?) like water on the rampart of the daughter of Zion and in the circuit of Jerusalem' (AFl. d iv 21–30). The connection between the two pieces is not clear; but the first is perhaps prefixed to introduce Levi's name. The second does not contain the name of

---

[1] Cp. Roth in *PQS* XC 118–19. [2] Pp. 93–4.
[3] Josephus *War* II xvi 2 § 338 and xvii 2 § 410–41 § 418; cp. xxii 1 § 648.
[4] *Ibid.* IV ix 11 §§ 570–4.
[5] *Ibid.* IV ix 11 §§ 575–6; cp. V xiii 1 §§ 527–33. [6] Pp. 203–5.
[7] Deut. xxxiii. 8–11. [8] Josh. vi. 26. [9] Hos. vi. 10.

U

Jericho, which the original curse has, clearly because the writer intends to apply it to a different city; this may well have been Jerusalem.

The editor's suggestion that these three figures are the high-priests Alexander Jannaeus (103–76 B.C.) and his two sons Hyrcanus II (75–67 and 63–40 B.C.) and Aristobulus II (67–63 B.C.) is at first sight attractive.[1] The outrages committed by the former and the rivalries of the latter are equally well known; and these last are said also to have committed many 'wicked murders'.[2] Hyrcanus, too, in 47 B.C. obtained permission from Caesar to rebuild the walls of Jerusalem and soon afterwards carried out the work;[3] but any value that this argument may have had is weakened by a divergent account[4] in which Antipater is made the hero of the story. In default too of any definite historical notice the suggestion can be neither proved nor disproved.

Another solution of the problem, therefore, which has also the advantage of explaining the names of the two patriarchs in whose hands 'weapons of violence' are said to be, may be tentatively offered, especially as it accurately fits the circumstances of the 1st century A.D. The commentator, too, may have been citing the earlier period with the intention of comparing but not identifying it with the later and so of bringing out the wickedness of his own age.

The two patriarchs in the Old Testament who wielded 'weapons (instruments) of violence' were Simeon and Levi,[5] known as typical Zealots (qannā'îm) in Rabbinic literature[6]; and the suggestion therefore springs to the mind that the words are a covert allusion to Simon bar Giora and John of Gischala, whose father's name was Levi.[7] The statement then that the two of them 'shall erect for it (sc. Jerusalem) a wall and towers' will refer to the activities of Simon bar Giora and John of Gischala during the First Revolt. Many, possibly most, of the Zealots had stayed in Jerusalem after the murder of Menahem, whom they had supported in his attempted coup d'état, and eventually threw in their lot some with Simon and others with John. Those with John 'converted the temple of God into their fortress and refuge from any outbreak of popular violence and made the sanctuary the head-quarters of their tyranny'.[8] Then, when his Idumaean allies threw him over and introduced his rival Simon into the city, John and his Zealot followers strengthened their position 'by erecting four huge towers in order to increase the elevation from which their missiles were discharged' and so kept the newcomer at bay,[9] while Simon

---

[1] Cp. Dupont-Sommer Écrits 366–7.
[2] Diodorus Siculus Bibliotheca Historica xl 2.
[3] Josephus Antiquities XIV viii 5 § 144 and ix 1 § 156.
[4] Josephus War I x 3 § 199 and 4 § 201.
[5] Cp. Gen. xlix. 5.   [6] Hengel Zeloten 183.
[7] Josephus War II xx 6 § 575 and xxi 8 § 585, IV ii 1 § 85.
[8] Ibid. IV iii 7 § 151.   [9] Ibid. IV ix 12 §§ 577–84.

apparently at the same time erected similar structures.[1] However, quarrels broke out amongst them and they split into rival factions; of these one under Eleazar son of Gion (or Simon) occupied the inner court of the Temple, while the other joined Simon bar Giora who 'occupied the Upper and a large part of the Lower City', and both harrassed John who with his followers was entrenched in the inner court of the Temple. As thus placed they carried on their internecine strife, and they killed not only many combatant members of their respective parties but also many innocent citizens, so that 'the blood of all manner of corpses formed pools in the court of God'.[2] Caught between the cross-fire of the rival factions, John 'actually misappropriated the sacred timber for the construction of engines of war', and, taking the beams which had been collected for the underpinning of the Temple, 'had them cut and made into towers, which he then brought up and placed in the rear of the inner court, opposite the western hall, where alone this was practicable', hoping thereby to overcome his rivals; but the approach of the Roman army forestalled his attempt.[3] The parallelism of fortifications and towers and the picture of bloodshed in the heart of Jerusalem strongly suggest that Josephus and the Commentator are dealing with the same events. In his view these leaders who built up the fortifications of Jerusalem in bloodshed for their own evil purposes were as bad as Hiel who, when he rebuilt Jericho, 'laid the foundation thereof with the loss of Abiram his first-born and set up the gates thereof with the loss of his youngest son Segub';[4] and the two sons can be disregarded, being merely incidental to the punishment. The Covenanters, though willing to throw themselves into Jerusalem and defend it against the Romans, were now outside and could afford to denounce those inside who were fortifying it against each other rather than against the Romans.

That these two characters are in all likelihood rightly identified, the Man of Falsehood as John of Gischala and the Young Lion of Wrath as Simon bar Giora, seems to be supported by a *Commentary on the Psalms*, of which a small fragment has survived. This speaks of 'the wicked ones of Ephraim and Manasseh, who seek to lay hands on the priest and his counsellors in the time of purgation' and says that God will redeem them from their power 'and afterwards they (*sc.* the wicked ones) will be delivered' or 'will deliver themselves into the power of the most ruthless of nations for sentence' (APs. b ii 3–5). These cannot be taken as respectively Hyrcanus II and Aristobulus I[5], if the situation must be sought in the 1st century A.D., as here argued. The reference is rather to John and Simon: the former came from Gischala,

---

[1] Josephus *War*. VI viii 1 § 377. [2] *Ibid*. V i 2 § 5–3 § 18.
[3] *Ibid*. V i 5 § 36–6 § 39. [4] 1 Ki. xvi. 34.
[5] Dupont-Sommer in *JS* 1963, 214–9; cp. 223–4.

which though then in Galilee lay within the bounds of ancient Ephraim,[1] and owed his position to Zealots from Galilee;[2] the latter had his home at Gerasa in territory once occupied by the tribe of Manasseh[3] and had been governor of the toparchy of Acrabatene, also in Ephraim, from which he had been expelled and had gone to join the 'brigands' at Masada.[4] Both had made a practice of maltreating and murdering priests;[5] and both eventually gave themselves up to the Romans, who sentenced John to lifelong imprisonment and Simon to death.[6]

These operations 'to rebuild a city of vanity in bloodshed', while they recall a similar rebuilding of Jerusalem by an enemy in the Maccabaean wars,[7] were the work of a leader or leaders 'who led many astray . . . that they might come to judgement of fire' (H x 10–13), i.e. who led the people into rebellion and so made them the cause of their own undoing and the destruction of Jerusalem by fire in A.D. 70, confirm the identification of these persons; for, as Josephus said, 'the sedition subdued the city and the Romans the sedition . . . , and all the tragedy of it might properly be ascribed to her own people'.[8]

Another obscure fragment of the *Commentary on Nahum* seems also to deal with these two persons. It refers the prophet's 'Woe to the bloody city! It is full of lies and rapine'[9] to 'the city of Ephraim, the Seekers after Smooth Things at the end of the days, who walk in lies and falsehood' (ANa. II ii 1–2), during whose time 'the city of Ephraim', i.e. Jerusalem under the domination of John, will be harassed by discord and the sword of the Gentiles, captivity and exile; then 'the simple ones of Ephraim will flee from the midst of their assembly and forsake those who mislead them and join themselves to Israel', while the Seekers after Smooth Things will be like Nineveh (*ibid.* iii 5–8). Jerusalem will then be no 'better than Amon (*sc.* No-amon) that was situated among the rivers, that had the waters round about her'[10]; for 'Amon is Manasseh and the rivers are the nobles of Manasseh' (*ibid.* iii 8–9). No-Amon's allies, Ethiopia and Egypt, Put and Lubim, are then used as figures for 'the wicked ones of her [host], the house of Peleg, who have joined themselves to Manasseh' (*ibid.* iv 1); for 'she was carried into captivity at the end of the days, when his 'kingship (*malkûtô*)'[11] over Israel will fall . . . ; his wives, his children and his household, will go into captivity' with 'the wicked ones of Ephraim . . . whose cup will come after Manasseh' (*ibid.*

---

[1] Josephus *War* II xxi 1 § 585 (s. Roth in *JSS* IV 342–3).
[2] *Ibid.* IV ix 10 § 558.   [3] *Ibid.* IV ix 3 § 503.   [4] *Ibid.* IV ix 3 § 504.
[5] *Ibid.* V xiii 1 §§ 529–33 (Simon) and VI ii 1 § 110–2 § 113 (John).
[6] *Ibid.* VI ix 3 § 433.   [7] 1 Macc. i. 33–7.   [8] In *War* V vi 1 § 257.
[9] Nah. iii. 1.   [10] *Ibid.* iii 8.
[11] Cp. Josephus *War* IV vii 1 § 390 (where John is described as μοναρχίας προσποιούμενος) and § 395 (where τοῖς ἐναντιωθεῖσιν Ἰωάννης ἀντεβασίλευσεν).

iv 4–6). The passage may well reflect the destruction of Jerusalem in A.D. 70 and also the execution of Simon and imprisonment of John. The allusion in the 'house of Peleg' is obvious. He was one of the sons of Eber, the eponymous hero of the Hebrew race who was called Peleg, which means 'division', because 'in his days the earth was divided';[1] the name therefore, while recalling the divided Hasmonaean house,[2] may indicate a party seceding from the main body of the Covenanters. The allusion will then be to 'the house of Peleg, who went out from the holy city and put their trust in God in the period of Israel's transgression and polluted the sanctuary but returned unto God' (Z ix 6–7). The subjects of the last two verbs are uncertain; but what would seem to be implied was that the 'house of Peleg', i.e. the dissident group, seeing that they had been misled, rejoined the main body of the Covenanters in exile when the Revolt collapsed.

If then one of the 'wicked ones of Ephraim and Manasseh' is John of Gischala, Dr. Roth's suggestion may well be right[3] that the priest in the description of them as persons 'who seek to lay hands on the priest and his counsellors' but 'God will redeem them from their power' (APs. b ii 3–5) is Phineas (Phanni) son of Samuel, the last high-priest. He was the nominee of the Zealots who had chosen him as an illiterate person and therefore a man of the people and had irregularly elected him to the office of high-priest by lot,[4] which could perhaps be easily rigged, thus using a method of election employed by the Covenanters for the admission of new members of their society (D vi 15–23; cp. ix 7–8) and for appointment to priestly office in it (I Q 28A i 15–17)[5]; and, since he officiated in the Temple, he must have been closely associated with Eleazar son of Gion (or Simon), who was in control there.[6] There was however a running feud between Eleazar and John with considerable loss of life, so that Phanni would have been an object of enmity and might well have met the fate of other high-priests who incurred John's displeasure;[7] fortunately for him, however, the quarrel was patched up in face of the growing Roman menace, while Eleazar did not lose his life in the course of the quarrel and could be properly described as 'redeemed' by God.

Other priests mentioned in the Scrolls are 'the last priests of Jerusalem, who amassed wealth and gain from the spoil of the peoples; but at the end of the days their wealth with their spoil will be given over to the army of the Kittians' (H ix 4–7); these will include the Wicked Priest himself, inasmuch as 'he . . . became a traitor to the statutes for the sake of wealth. He plundered and gathered the wealth

---

[1] Gen. x. 24. [2] Dupont-Sommer ibid. 216–7.
[3] In Background 38–40; cp. PQS XC 116–17.
[4] Josephus War IV iii § 152–8 § 156.
[5] Pp. 286–8. [6] Ibid. V iii 1 §§ 98–105 and vi 1 § 250.
[7] E.g. ibid. IV v 2 §§ 315–16 (Ananus and Jesus).

298   REVOLT AND RUIN

of ruthless men who had rebelled against God; he took the wealth of peoples' (H viii 10–12). Ananias father of Eleazar, was 'great at amassing money' and also 'he had very wicked servants who joined themselves to all the bullies and went round the threshing floors, seizing the tithes which belonged to the priests by violence and not refraining from beating any one who would not surrender the tithes to them',[1] while his son Eleazar (who was *ex hypothesi* the Wicked Priest) would without doubt have had his share of his father's ill-gotten wealth; and Ananus, another high-priest, and his party were 'corrupted by bribes'.[2] The wealth of the Temple,[3] too, which the priests managed and controlled and which they did not hesitate to use for their own personal advantage,[4] should be added to their private wealth. Here clearly is 'the spoil of the peoples' and 'the wealth of ruthless men', which the last priests and others had got into their hands and which ultimately fell to the Romans.[5]

These stories of the rapacity of the rival leaders may explain the rule, to which Mr. Del Medico has drawn attention,[6] requiring the Covenanters 'to hold themselves aloof from the impure wealth of wickedness in (the matter of) that which is vowed and devoted (to God) and of the wealth of the sanctuary' (Z viii 12); for the prohibition is directed against carrying off tithe and converting the wealth of the Temple to private use, as these persons seem often to have done.

In conclusion, then, as the 'Man of Falsehood' and the 'Young Lion of Wrath' take rank next in importance after the Wicked Priest among the enemies of the Rightful Teacher in the leadership of the Covenanters, so John of Gischala and Simon bar Giora come next after Eleazar son of Hananiah as the rivals of Menahem's nephew and successor for the leadership of the insurgents in the revolt against Rome.

4. JERUSALEM AND DAMASCUS

If the events to which the *Commentary on Habakkuk* alludes are indeed those of the First Revolt against the Romans, notably the siege and destruction of Jerusalem in A.D. 70, one or two passages in the *Thanksgiving Hymns* become intelligible. The author is returning thanks to God for his deliverance from a great disaster, which he describes by saying that 'soldiers encamped against me, they surrounded me with all their weapons of war; they discharged arrows without intermission and flashing fire-brands that consumed the timbers' (T ii 25–6). These words can but reflect scenes during the siege of Jerusalem. For example, when Jerusalem was divided between three rival factions, the Upper and much of the Lower City being

[1] Josephus *Antiquities* XX ix 2 §§ 205–7.
[2] Josephus *Life* 39 § 196.
[3] Josephus *War* VII v 5 §§ 148–52.
[4] *Ibid.* VI viii 3 §§ 387–91.
[5] Pp. 35–6.
[6] In *Énigme* 259–60.

held by Simon bar Giora while the outer court of the Temple was in the hands of John of Gischala and the inner court in those of Eleazar son of Gion or Simon, their cross-fire made the positions not only of the rival combatants but of everyone else so dangerous, with javelins raining down from above and hand-missiles and shots from catapults, quick-firers and stone-throwers, discharged upwards, that many even of the priests and the worshippers in the Temple were killed.[1] On one occasion Titus himself, riding round the walls, narrowly escaped death from a hail of arrows which flew past him.[2] The Romans, too, were well equipped with similar artillery, notably the Xth legion with its famous engine for hurling large rocks to a great distance, with which they constantly harassed the defenders and the inhabitants of the city; they also had archers who came close up to the walls, discharged their arrows and withdrew to a safe distance.[3] Thus pressed and harassed, the Jews ultimately found themselves entirely surrounded by a wall which the Romans had constructed round the city and which, fully manned, prevented the escape of fugitives from it.[4]

The author of the *Hymns* then goes on to say 'I took up my post[5] at the frontier of wickedness ... and blasts of defeat beset my footsteps ...' when 'arrows of destruction flew without chance of being returned ...; and Belial's torrents flowed over all the high (stepped) wings (of the porches) with (?) fire consuming all their ivories, destroying all woodwork both fresh and dry in their courses until nothing was left of their substructures; it ate (its way) through the foundations of clay, and the bases of the hills became a burning mass' (T iii 24–31). This passage, neither more nor less ludicrous than others in this work, when examined in detail yields valuable information.[6] The 'frontier of wickedness' may be explained as the front-line of the Roman troops advancing to the assault, since 'wickedness (*riš'āh*)' regularly connotes the Romans in writings of this age;[7] and the arrows flying 'without chance of being returned', though an echo of the Old Testament,[8] will be Roman arrows, such as Marius and Caesar had devised, whose heads broke off or bent on impact so that they could not be re-used against those who had discharged them.[9] The 'high (stepped) wings (of the porches)' are clearly the 'pilasters and lintels (παραστάδες καὶ ὑπέρθυρα)' of the porches opening on the courts of the Temple, while the structures flanking the gates of the Temple 'like shoulders (ὥσπερ ὦμοι)' are not necessarily excluded;[10] for the picture is evidently composite, and all

---

[1] Josephus *War* V ii 1 § 5–3 § 20. [2] *Ibid.* ii 2 §§ 54–66.
[3] *Ibid.* vi 2 § 263 and 3 §§ 269–72.
[4] *Ibid.* xi 4 §§ 466–8, xii 2 §§ 510–3 § 511 and 4 §§ 522–3.
[5] Cp. 1 Sam. xvii. 16 and Jer. xliv. 4, 14.
[6] Cp. Driver in *JTS*, NS XIII 373–7. [7] Pp. 202–3.
[8] Jer. l. 9. [9] Alton in *Companion to Latin Studies* 469.
[10] Josephus *War* V v 3 § 201 (pilasters and lintels) and 4 § 207 (flanking structures).

were set on fire by the Romans. The lintels were perhaps especially in the author's mind. These consisted of five tiers, each composed of two rows of superimposed wooden beams and one course or layer of stone, so that the timbers could be said to be destroyed 'out of their channels' or 'courses (*mippalgéhem*)', *i.e.* that the two rows of beams were burnt out between every course of unburnt stone; and each tier projected one cubit beyond that beneath it so that they resembled inverted steps.[1] Thus they would seem aptly to fit the description; for 'wing (*'ăgāf* or *'aggāf*)' was the technical term for the framework and mouldings, *e.g.* of a city-gate, and could have been used if required for those of the Temple.[2] The porches and the Temple contained also much valuable carved woodwork,[3] some probably salved from previous buildings but much of it necessarily new[4]; it might then properly be described as 'fresh and dry'. The 'ivories (*šen'abbîm* = *šenhabbîm*)' are reminiscent of Solomon's temple;[5] but, although nothing is known of such decorations in Herod's temple, the βαρβαρικὰ σκεύη with which it is said to have been adorned[6] may well have included plaques of ivory affixed in panels on the walls. Lastly, the 'substructures (*šôtîm* for *šātôt* in post-classical usage)'[7a] will be those under the porches and other buildings undermined by the fire as, fanned by draughts of air, it sweeps along the numerous subterranean passages running under the courts and the Temple;[7b] and the 'beaten platform of earth' can only be the artificially levelled terrace supporting the Temple itself and all the adjacent buildings.[8] So again 'on one occasion John of Gischala undermined the Roman works and left them suspended'; then 'having introduced timber smeared with pitch and bitumen, he set the whole mass alight. The props being consumed, the mine collapsed in a heap and the earthworks fell in with a tremendous crash. First dense volumes of smoke arose with clouds of dust, the fire being smothered by the wreckage: but, as the materials which crushed it were eaten away, a vivid flame now burst forth'.[9] Yet again, at one time the Jews set fire to the Roman battering engines and the Romans 'with their wicker-shields ablaze' were 'enveloped in flames' as they attempted to save their artillery.[10] On another occasion the Jews themselves set fire to one portico of the Temple, whereupon the Romans set the adjoining portico on fire, whence the flames spread for a consider-

---

[1] Mishnah *Middoth* iv 7.

[2] Levy *Neuhebräisches u. Chaldäisches Wörterbuch* I 23 (s. Driver in *JTS*, NS X 125 and XIII 373–7).

[3] Josephus *Antiquities* XV xi 3 § 395 and 5 § 416, *War* V v 2 § 190.

[4] Cp. Josephus *War* V i 5 §§ 36–8 (fresh beams of cedar-wood collected for repairing the Temple but diverted to defence-works); s. Ezek. xxi 3.

[5] 1 Ki. x. 22.   [6] Josephus *Antiquities* XV xi 3 § 402.

[7a] S. pp. 423–4.   [7b] *Ibid*. XV xi 7 § 424 and *War* VI iii 3 §§ 370–3.

[8] *Ibid*. XV vi 5 § 39 and *War* V v 1 §§ 184–9; Mishnah *Middoth* iv 6.

[9] Josephus *War* V xi 4 §§ 469–73.   [10] *Ibid*. xi 5 §§ 477–81.

able distance.[1] A few days afterwards, the Jews caused great losses to the Romans by filling the space between the rafters and ceiling with dry tinder, bitumen and pitch; then, when the Romans arrived, they set it alight, so that the flames shot up on every side and the fire 'spreading far and wide, instantly enveloped even those already doomed to some other form of death'.[2] Next, the Romans set fire to porticoes and gates, and the Jewish defenders found themselves encircled by fire; deprived of all energy, they made no efforts to ward off or extinguish the flames, which continued to burn throughout that day and the following night.[3] Then a soldier snatched up a brand from some burning timber and, hoisted up by his fellows, hurled it through a low door giving access to the chambers surrounding the sanctuary, when this caught fire; and 'the roar of the flames streaming far and wide mingled with the groans of the falling victims'. Titus made unavailing efforts to save the Temple by getting the flames under control, but a soldier thrust a fresh firebrand in the darkness of the night into the hinges of the gates, and the blaze became uncontrollable. So 'owing to the height of the hill and the mass of the burning poles one would have thought that the whole city was ablaze'; and again 'you would indeed have thought that the temple-hill was boiling over from its base, being everywhere one mass of flame, but yet that the stream of blood was more copious than the flames and the slain more numerous than the slayers'.[4] Finally, the Romans fired what buildings still stood unburnt.[5] Such were the scenes which Josephus saw and described, and such might be those from which the author of the *Thanksgiving Hymns* might have escaped.

Two other passages in the Scrolls seem to allude, however indirectly, to the same event. The author of the *Commentary on Habakkuk* interprets the prophet's announcement that 'the stone shall cry out from the wall and the beam shall respond from its timber'[6] as referring to the destruction of the Temple; for he goes on to explain that its ministers, the 'last priests of Jerusalem' and with them the 'Wicked Priest', have so abused their office that the prophecy must be taken as foretelling the ruin of 'the house of judgement' or 'doomed house,'[7] whose sentence God will deliver in the midst of many' or 'mighty nations and from whom He will take it up for judgement and in whose midst He will condemn it and punish it with fire and brimstone' (H x 1–5). Here a *double entente* may be detected: the Temple on Mt. Zion is the seat from which God pronounces sentence and also the victim of that sentence, inasmuch as it is involved in the guilt of those who have misused it. At the same time the sentence is regarded as reserved for the Mes-

---

[1] Josephus *War* VI ii 9 §§ 164–7.   [2] *Ibid*. iii 1 §§ 177–86.
[3] *Ibid*. VI iv 1 § 228 and 2 §§ 232–5.   [4] *Ibid*. iv 5 § 249–7 § 266.
[5] *Ibid*. v 2 §§ 281–4.   [6] Hab. ii. 11.   [7] Pp. 272–3.

sianic age; for the Temple has already been destroyed. Again, the author of the *War*, in a passage which is unfortunately much damaged, says: 'and He will ensure their safety in the conflagration . . . , (though) tested in the crucible, and will sharpen its weapons of war; and they shall not grow blunt till [the final end of] wickedness. Do you then remember the sentence [on Nadab and Abi]hu, sons of Aaron; by passing judgement on them God displayed His holiness in the eyes of [the people and] He firmly attached [Eleazar] and Ithamar to Himself for a covenant of everlasting [priesthood]' (W xvii 1–4).[1] Nadab and Abihu were consumed by fire for their presumption in offering 'strange fire' before the Lord; and as they were destroyed, so will the Kittians and their allies, the enemies of God's people, perish after their final victory in the Messianic age. In both passages, then, fire is introduced in a somewhat forced fashion; and this reason can only be that the authors' respective pictures of the eventual punishment of the party's and the nation's enemies is coloured by some recent experiences which is still vividly before their minds. Both writers are projecting the past into the future, using their own experiences to give colour to their description of the Messianic end.

There can therefore be little doubt that the various passages quoted above reflect the burning of the Temple and the Holy City by the Romans, who are the personification of 'wickedness' in the eyes of the Covenanters,[2] in A.D. 70. There is therefore no need to follow Mr. Del Medico in supposing[3] that Vesuvius, whose famous eruption occurred in A.D. 79, was in the writer's mind in these or any other passages which refer to a fire or conflagration (D iv 13–14, H x 3–5, T viii 30); he was concerned with some disaster which had befallen himself and his own people, not with one which had overwhelmed distant cities in Italy. At the same time the doctrine of a universal conflagration, though of Iranian origin, seems to have become widespread in this decade, as Dr. Vermès has noted;[4] but the allusions in the Scroll are too definite for such a conflagration preceding or accompanying the end of the age,[5] to which not only the burning of Rome in A.D. 64[6] and Jerusalem in A.D. 70,[7] as well as numerous fires in Rome,[8] but also Vesuvius[9] and Etna[10] in eruption, may have lent colour. Although, too,

---

[1] Lev. x. 1–2 and Num. iii. 4.   [2] Pp. 202–3.

[3] In *Deux Manuscrits* 139–40 and *Énigme* 192, 442; cp. 161, 192, 287, 354, 472.

[4] In *Cah. Sion.* IV [1950] 14–21, 197; cp. *Communauté* 207.

[5] Josephus *Antiquities* I ii 3 § 70; 1 Baruch iv 35; Adam and Eve xxix 4–5 xlix 3; Sibylline Oracles iii 84–5 iv 115–18, 125–7, 159–61, 173–4 v 211–13, 155–61, 273–4, 512–31; 2 Pet. iii. 5–10 and Rev. viii. 5–7; Hippolytus *Refutation* ix 27 § 3 (Essene belief in a universal conflagration accompanying the last judgement).

[6] Tacitus *Annals* XV 38–41 and Suetonius *Nero* 38.

[7] Geffchen *Oracula Sibyllina* iv 125–6, v. 150–4.

[8] Suetonius *Titus* 8; Tacitus *Histories* I ii 2–3, III 71; Dio Cassius *Roman History* lxvi 21, 24.

[9] Pliny *Epistles* VI 6 and 20.   [10] Geffchen *op. cit.* iv 80–2.

as Prof. Rowley remarks,[1] 'when general terms are used, it is always dangerous to read particular references into them', yet general ideas owe their inception to particular events, whose application it may be equally dangerous to disregard. Each case must be decided on its merits. Nebuchadrezzar, Alexander the Great and Seleucus are not known to have destroyed the Temple and the Holy City by fire, Antiochus IV Epiphanes burnt only parts of the city (not including the Temple)[2] and Pompey is known to have done them no harm; Titus alone, so far as historical records show, destroyed both by fire. What other events than this last and most famous conflagration can have inspired the vivid pictures of destruction by fire which the author of the *Thanksgiving Hymns* has drawn? None so suitable can be found.

That Damascus and its neighbourhood are mentioned in a number of passages as a place in which the Covenanters can and do take refuge is another argument for assigning the Scrolls to the 1st century A.D.

The city lay not far from the home of Hezekiah's family, which sprang from Galilee,[3] and members of the party founded by that family might naturally have sought safety there on various occasions during its checkered history, *e.g.* after the risings of 47 B.C., of 4 B.C. and A.D. 6–7, and during the troubles of A.D. 46–8, when the neighbourhood of the Dead Sea was or might be thought to be unsafe.[4] The fugitives after these outbreaks would probably be few and could therefore easily escape the notice of the authorities in a large and populous city, which already had a considerable Jewish population, even though they were liable to become the victims of sudden pogroms.[5] Damascus, however, was probably a safe refuge for Jews only intermittently. It was under Seleucid rule from the end of the 4th century till the middle of the 1st century B.C. except for a brief period *c.* 280 B.C., when it came into the hands of Ptolemy II Philadelphus king of Egypt. It fell *c.* 85 B.C. to the Arabian king Aretas and remained his till occupied by Pompey's legate in 64 B.C.; and it apparently remained a part of the Syrian province till the reign of Caligula (A.D. 37–41), when it was put under an 'ethnarch', *i.e.* a viceroy of another Arabian king named Aretas.[6] This city certainly cannot have been a safe place of refuge for members of a Jewish party whose main principle was hatred of foreign rule, which it was prepared to press *à toute outrance*, when it was either under hellenizing Seleucid kings or under Roman proconsuls or legates; contrariwise, it might be such for Jewish refugees (except for occasional outbursts) when it was under

[1] In *Zadokite Fragments* 57 (5).
[2] Josephus *Antiquities* XII v 4 § 252; cp. 1 Macc. i 31.
[3] *Ibid. War* I x 5 § 204 and II iv 1 § 56; s. pp. 239–41.
[4] Cp. Roth in *Évidences* LXV 40–1.
[5] Josephus *War* II xx 2 §§ 559–61 and VII viii 7 § 368 (where 18,000 Jews with their wives and families are said to have been massacred).   [6] 2 Cor. xi. 32.

Arabian rulers. The first Arabian period, however, is unlikely in view of the difficulty of equating the Kittians with the Romans of the Republican period and of locating the persons and the principal episode in the Scrolls in it.[1] Consequently the second Arabian period must be accepted, especially as it had very large Jewish colonies in the 1st century A.D.,[2] with whom the Covenanters could have safely sought refuge. Possibly, too, Damascus was connected in the minds of the Covenanters with vague notions of a Messianic appearance in the north, as their use of the prophecy of Amos might seem to suggest (Z ix 7–8);[3] and echoes of such an expectation can be found both in the New Testament[4] and in Rabbinic literature.[5]

The notion, which has been put forward as the only means of avoiding this conclusion, that Damascus does not indicate the city of that name but is borrowed from the Old Testament[6] as typifying a place of exile, wherever that may be, or has not a real but a figurative sense, e.g. as denoting Qumrân[7] or the Nabataean kingdom,[8] in which that place lay, is unlikely, because those who went there journeyed from 'the land of Judah' (Z viii 6; cp. vi 1) to 'the land of the north' (Z ix 4); and, if the real Judah is meant, as it must be since Qumrân lay within its territory, the real Damascus too is likely to be meant. Indeed, no reason for such a device is apparent except modern inability to understand the ancient allusion, and the place itself bears no resemblance to either district. The reference to and deliberate alteration of the prophet's description of exile 'beyond Damascus' into exile 'from my tent (sc. God's house in Jerusalem) to Damascus' (Z ix 5) points to a real place; both places are on the same level of reality. The improbability is increased by the terms in which the author of one of the Thanksgiving Hymns speaks of it. He says 'I praise [Thee, O Lord]; for thou hast put me at a source of flowing streams in a dry land and (at) a spring of water in a parched land, and by channels watering a garden . . . (?), a plantation of firs and pines with cypresses for Thy glory, trees of life by a mysterious fountain, hidden amid trees lapping water' (T viii 4–6). That this description can refer to 'Ain Fäšhah, the spring near Qumrân, is highly improbable,[9] if only because the trees here named can never have grown there; and it would grossly exaggerate the quantity of water available at that place. The place

---

[1] Pp. 197–216.
[2] Acts ix. 1–25 and Gal. i. 17; Josephus War II xx 2 § 561 and VII viii 7 § 368.
[3] Am. v 26–7.
[4] E.g. Matt. xxvi. 32, Mk. xiv. 28 xvi. 7, Acts viii. 1–9.
[5] Cp. Wieder Judean Scrolls and Karaism 5–48.
[6] Cp. Am. v. 27 and Zech. ix. 1.
[7] Cross Library 59–60; cp. de Vaux Archéologie 87–9.
[8] North in PQS LXXXVI 37–48.
[9] Bardtke in Gott und die Götter (Festschrift für Erich Fascher) 44–55; cp. TLz. LXXXV 265–6.

described can only be Damascus, famous for its springs and gardens, described by one who must have lived, if he is not actually living, in that city; so it has been sung by Arab poets, and so an English writer describes it as a city lying on the fringe of the parched wilderness, as 'the paradise of the Arab world', where 'the chief gardens spread between walnuts and poplars, and the water rushes by them, swift and cold'.[1] As a corollary to the passage quoted above, the paucity of allusions to the wilderness in the *Thanksgiving Hymns* takes on a special significance. The view that the real Damascus is meant is further supported by an obscure allusion in an apocalyptic work, written *c.* A.D. 88–100, to a migration of Jews 'to the region of Tyre and Sidon'[2], *i.e.* to Syrian cities in the north. The only possible inference from these facts is that the *Hymns* cannot have been composed at Qumrân and must therefore be assigned to a period after the evacuation of the fort or monastery there, when their author or authors lived in some other place (cp. T iv 8–9);[3] that will have been Damascus or its neighbourhood.

Damascus moreover has a special significance in the Scrolls as a city of refuge or exile for the Covenanters and as the place where their society was re-formed; and the proof of its reconstitution may be found in the allusion to two distinct covenants which appear in certain Scrolls.

Here attention must be drawn to a very important point, which has been generally overlooked; this is that *Discipline*, which alone of the Scrolls can be dated before the Revolt,[4] speaks always and only of a simple covenant, whether as a 'covenant of God' (D v 8 x 10) or as 'the covenant of the community' (D viii 6), which members of the society enter.[5] Contrariwise, only those Scrolls which must be dated during or after the Revolt[6] speak of a 'new covenant'. Thus the *Commentary on Habakkuk* refers cryptically to 'those who acted treacherously with the Man of Falsehood; for they did not [pay heed to the words of] the Rightful Teacher at the mouth of God' and then goes on to speak of 'those who acted treacherously against the new [covenant and] were not loyal to the covenant of God' (H ii 1.4). Whatever else this passage imports, it shows clearly that there were two covenants, an old and a new; and it hints at the identity of the person behind the breach.

The *Zadokite Documents* further speak of 'those who turned aside in Israel, who went forth from the land of Judah and sojourned in the land of Damascus' (Z viii 6) and of those 'who entered the new covenant in the land of Damascus' (Z viii 15); and they say that 'when the two houses of Israel were separated, Ephraim became ruler

---

[1] G. A. Smith *Historical Geography of the Holy Land* [25] 674–6.
[2] Ascension of Isaiah v 13   [3] Pp. 37–8, 365–7.
[4] Pp. 360–1.   [5] Pp. 54–5.   [6] Pp. 52–3, 72–4, 361–5, 367–9.

over Judah; and all who turned aside were delivered to the sword, while those who held fast (*sc.* to the covenant or the Law) escaped to the land of the north' (Z ix 4). This last passage, in its first clause, clearly alludes to the division of the kingdom in the 10th century B.C., comparing the breach then effected with the present rift in the nation. Then 'Israel rebelled against the house of David' and 'there was none that followed the house of David but only the tribe of Judah',[1] so that Israel greatly outnumbered Judah; now 'Israel' (*i.e.* those Jewish parties which in the eyes of the Covenanters had weakened the Law) ruled the nation if only by force of numbers, while 'Judah' (*i.e.* the Covenanters as members of the 'house of Judah', namely the party of Judah the Galilaean from whom the Rightful Teacher sprang) alone remained, a powerless minority, faithful to the Law as interpreted by the Teacher. Or again, as once Israel and not Judah forsook the Lord,[2] so now 'Israel' was faithless and 'Judah' faithful to the Law. The second clause defines the occasion as one on which those who abandoned the cause of the Covenanters perished while those who were loyal escaped to the north. This would be when the 'house of Judah', *i.e.* Eleazar grandson of the same Judah and his followers, fled after the murder of Menahem from Jerusalem to Masada; for many others of them may be supposed to have made their way northwards, ostensibly to organize resistance, raise recruits and amass money and munitions of war, if not also to ensure their own safety and that of their families, among the Jewish colonies in various Galilaean and Syrian cities. Their headquarters, as the other two passages make clear, was Damascus; and there they drew up a new covenant.

Damascus was evidently chosen not so much for its own importance as a capital city, but because, when the Revolt broke out, it was not under direct Roman rule and also as it had a large Jewish colony.[3] The new covenant would be intended partly to meet the new conditions of life in a large city but especially to bind the party together afresh and to strengthen the loyalty of any waverers or dissidents amongst their number; for, as successive waves of refugees arrived, quarrels would inevitably break out. So the *Zadokite Documents* speak of 'those who entered the new covenant in the land of Damascus but turned back and became traitors and strayed from the well of living water' (Z ix 28), and describe how 'they spoke apostasy against their rightful statutes (*ḥuqqê haṣṣedeq*) and rejected the covenant and the pact which they had sworn to observe in the land of Damascus; that is the new covenant' (Z ix 37). They then describe those still loyal to the principles of the society as 'those who love Him (*sc.* God) and revere Him to a thousand generations, those of the "house of division" who went forth from the holy city and leaned upon God in the time when Israel sinned and

[1] 1 Ki. xii. 19–20.   [2] 2 Chron. xi. 10–11.   [3] P. 52.

made the sanctuary unclean; but they (*sc.* those who were loyal) turned to God'[1] (Z ix 45–7);[2] for, having left the doomed city, they had no share in the pollution of the Temple for which the rival factions fighting in its courts were solely responsible.

The cause of this breach in the ranks of the Covenanters can perhaps be guessed, even if it cannot be proved, from three notices in the Scrolls. The first speaks of 'those who acted treacherously with the Man of Falsehood' and goes on apparently to connect them with 'those who acted treacherously against the new [covenant and] were not loyal to the covenant of God' (H ii 1–4); the second tells how 'the house of Absalom . . . did not help him (*sc.* the Rightful Teacher) against the Man of Falsehood who rejected the Law' (H v 9–11); and the third refers to 'all the men of war who turned back' or 'went aside with the Man of Falsehood' (Z ix 39). Thus the new covenant is connected with the Man of Falsehood and his military followers and through him with the murder of the Teacher; and this brings it into connection with the events arising out of the outbreak of the Revolt. Was the cause of the breach, then, a fundamental division of opinion regarding the question whether the proper course was to stay behind in Jerusalem (like Ananias the Σαδουκι and many of the Zealots)[3] and hold the city against the Romans or to abandon it (like Eleazar son of Jair and his followers) and continue the struggle in the country? Those who slipped 'secretly' away could be charged with cowardice;[4] but those who remained behind would incur the guilt of profaning the Temple by fighting in its very courts.[5] What began as a practical problem arising out of a quarrel between two factions in the city would then have been continued as an ideological dispute on a very different plane amongst the exiles. One party would regard the defence of the holy city as a supreme act of heroism and self-sacrifice; the other would denounce the shedding of blood in fratricidal strife in the precincts of the Temple as sacrilege and would look upon its inevitable consequence, the destruction of both Temple and city, as the penalty of that sacrilege.

The schism, thus begun, would seem to have been continued and actively fomented by a leader or leaders who too were pseudonymously described by their opponents. Such perhaps was the person called the Man of Scorn or Scoffing or rather Man of Insolence (for the Hebrew term has approximately the same force as the Greek ὕβρις, by which the Septuagint often render it)[6] and, if he is not a distinct person, the 'Splutterer of Lies' or 'Falsehood'. This last expression,

---

[1] Cp. Isa. xix. 22.   [2] Cp. Rubinstein in *VT* VII 359–60.
[3] Pp. 242–3.   [4] Pp. 269, 272.
[5] *E.g.* Josephus *War* IV iii 12 § 201, v 1 § 313 and 4 § 343; cp. *ibid.* V ii 1 § 110.
[6] Buhl *BZAtW* XXVII 81–6.

however, ought perhaps to be translated '(he) who splutters falsehood' since it seems in form to be rather an epithet than a straight title. Both expressions, too, seem to be applied to one and the same person; this is certainly not the anti-Messiah,[1] since they clearly designate a real person (unless this person may have been regarded as the anti-Messiah, which seems improbable).[2]

The *Commentary on Habakkuk* speaks of 'one who spluttered falsehood, who led many astray to build a city of vanity in blood and to set up a congregation of sin by lies . . . so that they will come to fiery judgements because they reviled and reproached the elect of God' (H x 7–13). In a similar strain the author of the *Zadokite Documents*, loosely identifying 'the last generation, the congregation of traitors' who had rejected the Rightful Teacher and the dissident minority which broke away from the covenant, declares that 'they are those who turned aside from the path', namely at the time concerning which 'Israel hath behaved himself stubbornly like a stubborn heifer'[3] was written, 'at the appearance of the Man of Insolence who spluttered waters of falsehood at Israel and caused them to go astray in a pathless wilderness' (Z i 8–10), and so on; that 'those who built the wall and daubed it with spittle[4] did not understand these things (*sc.* why the kings of the north and their allies should attack Israel), because one walking like wind and raising storms and spluttering falsehood at men spluttered (falsehood) at them, so that God was angry with His whole congregation' (Z ix 21–2); and that 'all who reject the Law (*sc.* the Law as interpreted by the Covenanters) shall have no part in the house (*i.e.* party) of the Law (*sc.* the society of the Covenanters). They shall be judged like their fellows who turned away with the Men of Insolence; for they spoke error against the righteous statutes, and rejected the covenant and pact which they had sworn (to observe) in the land of Damascus, namely the new covenant; and they and their families shall have no portion in the house (*sc.* party) of the Law' (Z ix 34–7). Further, the compiler of a fragmentary exposition of *Micah*[5] asks 'What is the transgression of Jacob? is it not Samaria?' and refers the threat that Samaria will be utterly ruined to him 'who splutters falsehood, [who himself leads astray the] simple (*i.e.* the loyal members of the community)'; and he goes on to ask 'what are the high-places of Judah? are they not Jerusalem?' and refers this figure to 'the Rightful Teacher who himself [teaches the Law to] his council and to all who offer themselves freely to be added to the elect of [God, doers of the Law] in the council of the community, who will be saved from the day of [judgement]' (I Q *14* viii–x 1–9).

---

[1] Mowinckel & Anderson *He that cometh* 272–3.   [2] Pp. 486–91.
[3] Hos. iv. 16.   [4] Ezek. xiii. 10–12.   [5] Mic. i. 5–7.

Obviously the Man of Insolence and 'he who spluttered falsehood' are one and the same person; for each is said to splutter falsehood and to lead men astray. Who these are whom he leads astray is equally clear. He 'who spluttered falsehood' is like Samaria, the cause of Jacob's going astray after idols long ago, while the Rightful Teacher is compared to the 'high-places of Judah', namely Jerusalem; in other words, as Samaria had been the evil rival of Jerusalem in past ages, so the Man of Insolence was now the evil rival of the Teacher. The rivalry of the Man of Insolence took the form of inducing 'those who built the wall and daubed it with spittle' not to join the Teacher's party and those who rejected the 'new covenant' not to remain loyal to him. Having thus led many astray, the Man of Insolence sought 'to build a city of vanity in blood and to set up a congregation in lies', *i.e.* to build up a false and schismatic party even at the cost of bloodshed. A *double entente* of the kind so frequently occurring in the Scrolls may perhaps be detected here. On the one hand, an indirect allusion may be intended to those who seem elsewhere to be denounced for rebuilding the fortifications of Jerusalem[1] in order to gain an ephemeral advantage in the unceasing quarrels between the rival parties during the First Revolt. On the other hand, the direct allusion in 'those who built the wall and daubed it with spittle' can hardly be to these operations, if only because the walls of the city can never have been literally repaired 'with spittle';[2] this will then be a mere figure of speech[3] for those who made a pretence of observing the Law as interpreted by the Covenanters but in fact flouted it. Like the Pharisees, they made a 'fence' about it; but by their laxity in interpreting it they showed how shoddy their work of safeguarding it had been. In the same way the 'city of vanity' is not a real city such as Agrippa II is said to have rebuilt;[4] it may indirectly refer to Jerusalem, whose walls hastily rebuilt during the siege proved inadequate to keep out the enemy, but directly, as the parallel 'congregation' shows, it is a body of men, *i.e.* the schismatic body which the Man of Insolence had formed, partly of members of the Pharisaic party and partly of those who had joined the Teacher, at the expense of the main body of Covenanters.[5] In this work he was not alone; for the plural 'Men of Insolence' shows that he had associates in seducing members from their allegiance (Z ix 36). His identity remains unknown; for neither Josephus nor any other contemporary writer has anything beyond one or two passing references to the Zadokites or Covenanters and not a single notice concerning the party's internal affairs. The Scrolls however show the leader of the

---

[1] Winter in *PQS* XCI 39–40.
[2] Cp. Hermann *Ezechiel* 80. [3] Cp. Vermès *Manuscrits* 98.
[4] Del Medico *Deux Manuscrits* **137**; cp. Josephus *Antiquities* XX ix 4 § 211 (Caesarea Philippi, renamed Neronias).
[5] Delcor *Habacuc* 35.

X

secession to have been a man prepared at the cost of bitterly antagoniz-
ing his former colleagues 'to set up a community by lies' *i.e.* to build up
a new community inspired by his own teaching and principles which
the main body of the old members could but regard as 'lies', and 'to
build a city of vanity' *i.e.* to set up a new centre for his heretical group.
The Commentator, an orthodox member of the society at Qumrân,
would regard this new but heretical centre, wherever it might be,
not as 'a city of righteousness'[1] but as a 'city of vanity', even though
its own adherents might think of it as a 'new Jerusalem'[2] in a spiritual
if not in a geographical sense.

   If then the 'Man of Insolence (*'îš lāṣôn*)' is rightly taken as the same
person as 'he who splutters lies', a suggestion which Dr. Gertner has
made deserves consideration, namely that the now accepted interpretation of the title ought to be given up in favour of 'Man of Deviation,
Deviationist' or the like; for the root can bear this meaning and the
character will be well reflected in the new translation.

   In conclusion, the allusions in the Scrolls to a migration to or an
exile in the north, to a rift or rifts within the ranks of the Covenanters
and to a 'new covenant' replacing the old covenant, can all be explained
in the light of the events of the Revolt of A.D. 66–73; but the details,
including the identity of the persons behind the secession, are of
necessity obscure and, while some can be more or less plausibly guessed,
others will perhaps never be elucidated.

   [1] Isa. i. 26.   [2] Cp. Rev. iii. 12, xxi. 2.

VII

CHRONOLOGY AND CRYPTOGRAMS

1. ZADOKITE CHRONOLOGY

The series of arguments here put forward has inevitably pointed to the identification of the Covenanters, from whose party the Scrolls emanate, with the Zealots whose activities seem to have been behind the First Revolt (A.D. 66–73); and, if this conclusion is accepted as correct, such chronological notices as the Scrolls contain must indicate the same historical period.

Attention has already been drawn to the statement at the beginning of the *Zadokite Documents* that God had visited Israel in 'the three hundred and ninetieth year of[1] His giving them into the hand of Nebuchadnezzar king of Babylon . . . ; and they were like blind men and groping for a way for twenty years, and God . . . raised up a Rightful Teacher for them to guide them in the way of his heart' (Z i 5–7). This date taken literally, as shown above,[2] comes to 196 B.C. and another twenty years brings it down to 176 B.C.: these years seem to correspond almost exactly to the period for which Onias III held the office of high-priest (*c.* 198–175 B.C.). This Onias, the first person called a 'zealot' and the protomartyr of the Zadokite party, however, cannot be the Rightful Teacher, who must have lived in the time of the First Revolt, if only for historical reasons which are argued elsewhere.[3] At the same time chronological calculations do not necessarily indicate any date early in the 2nd century B.C.; for, although this calculation is approximately correct in the ordinary reckoning, other and incorrect reckonings, which yield very different results, are known to have been current in the 1st century A.D. Those scholars like Schechter,[4] therefore, who apply modern chronology to these figures are as likely to be wrong as right just because they are right.[5]

The 390 years seem to be based on the 390 days for which the prophet Ezekiel was bidden to lie on his left side as signifying the duration of the exile of Israel and Judah[6] (however that figure may have been

---

[1] Cp. Jer. lii. 31 and II Chron. xxxiv 8; s. B. Talmud *Abodah Zarah* 9a-b (where *'aḥar* 'after' and *leḥorban habbayiṭ* 'of the destruction of the Temple' have virtually the same sense).
[2] Pp. 133–4.   [3] Pp. 280–1.   [4] In *Documents* I xii (s. p. 136).
[5] Cp. Margoliouth in *Expositor* VIII ii 504–7, Meyer in *Abhandlungen d. Preussischen Akademie d. Wissenschaften* 1919 xi 13–14 and Hölscher in *ZNtW.* XXVIII 40–6.
[6] Ezek. iv. 4; s. Lagrange in *RB*, NS IX 331.

reached).[1] Symbolic and round figures, however, are rarely and indeed often cannot by their very nature be exact, as other examples in this very period show. Thus Josephus reckons[2] the period of the Return from the Exile (538 B.C.) to the time of Aristobulus I (105–104 B.C.) at 471 or 481 instead of 433 years, apparently thinking of it as roughly 'seventy weeks' (*i.e.* 490 years)[3] after the Biblical model;[4] and he puts[5] the duration of the temple at Leontopolis at 343 instead of 243 years, regarding the period very inaccurately as a triple jubilee ($7 \times 7 \times 7 = 343$ years).[6] In these cases the deliberate use of symbolical figures wrecks the chronology; in others the errors seem to be the consequence of sheer miscalculation. For example, Josephus gives[7] the number of years from the deportation of the Jews in 597 B.C. to the accession of Antiochus V Eupator in 164 B.C. as 504 instead of 433 years, *i.e.* 71 years too many, and that of those from the same event to the destruction of Jerusalem by Titus (A.D. 70) as 639 instead of 607, some 30 years too many. In the same way the Hellenistic Jew Demetrius reckons 573 instead of 500 years from the captivity of Israel (722 B.C.) to the reign of Ptolemy IV Philopator (222–204 B.C.).[8] Thus the chronology of the Second Commonwealth seems to have been subject both to traditional miscalculations and to inaccuracies due to the use of symbolic figures.[9]

Two ancient calculations are here of particular importance.[10]

R. Jôsê, who flourished in the 2nd century A.D. and to whom the established and semi-official chronology of Hebrew and Jewish history was commonly ascribed, calculated the following figures for the period of the Second Commonwealth:[11]

Semi-exile (3/4 Jehoiakim–11 Zedekiah)			..	18	
Exile (586 B.C.–538 B.C.) ..	..	..	..	52	
Persian rule (538 B.C.–332/1 B.C.)		..	..	34	years;
Seleucid rule (332/1 B.C.–166 B.C.)		..	..	180	
Hasmonaean rulers (166 B.C.–37 or 35 B.C.)		..	103	
Herodian kingship (37 or 35 B.C.–A.D. 68 or 70)		103	

and his son Ishmael, when consulted,[12] re-affirmed them, although they reduce 608 to 472 years. The principal error lies in the earlier period in the figures for the Persian period, for which Jewish historians had no sufficient information; and this error in some form or other

[1] Cp. Cooke *Ezekiel* 64.
[2] In *War* I iii 1 § 70 (471) and *Antiquities* XIII xi 1 § 301 (481).
[3] Dan. ix. 24.   [4] Eisler *ap.* Thackeray *Josephus* III 627.
[5] In *War* VII x 4 § 436.   [6] Eisler *ibid.* 627.
[7] In *Antiquities* XX x 2 §§ 234 and *War* VI iv 8 § 270.
[8] Clement *Stromateis* I xxi 141 (where however the text is uncertain).
[9] Cp. Schürer *Geschichte*[3] III 189–90 and Driver in *Studies presented to Professor S. H. Hooke* 62–77.
[10] Cp. Lagrange in *RB*, NS IX 330–1 and de Vaux *ibid.* LVII 428–9.
[11] Neubauer *Mediaeval Jewish Chronicles* II p. 66 ll. 1–3 (*Seder 'Olam* §30).
[12] B. Talmud *Abodah Zarah* 8b.

vitiated all ancient Jewish chronology, while sheer miscalculation increased the confusion. In these circumstances the author of the *Zadokite Document* could not have had access to the true figures and therefore could not, except by the merest chance, have brought 390 years after 586 B.C. to 196 B.C.

An alternative explanation of these 390 years, therefore, may be put forward.

A group which prided itself on the possession of a divergent calendar[1] would be likely to have also a divergent era, if a suitable one could be found, to complete its peculiar system. Indeed, some other calculation seems to be demanded by the discrepancy between the description of these 390 years at the beginning of the *Zadokite Documents* and the known picture offered by the historical facts of the period from 586 B.C. to 196 B.C.; it presupposes a period of unrelieved gloom depicting those who came back from the Exile as a mere 'remnant' and discounting the ideal period from that event till the supposed end of the epoch (Z i 3–6). Dr. Roth,[2] therefore, arguing from these facts, has suggested that, as 'Kittians' stands for Romans,[3] so 'Nebuchadnezzar king of Babylon' may stand for some other king of Babylon into whose hands Jerusalem can be said pseudonymously to have been given. He proposes two suitable persons: these are Alexander the Great and Seleucus I, one of his commanders who succeeded to a part of his empire. The former marched down the Phoenician and Philistine coast in 332 B.C., when Tyre and Gaza fell to him after two hard sieges, made himself master of Egypt and then retraced his steps and occupied Babylon in 331 B.C., pursuing a career of conquest from then onwards till his sudden death in 323 B.C.; the latter at the division of Alexander's empire obtained Babylon but was driven out of it and was not able to re-establish himself as king of Babylon till 312 B.C. Two eras thus came into use; some of the Syrian towns, *e.g.* Ptolemais (Acco), dated events from Alexander's death in 323 B.C.,[4] but the Jews commonly used the Seleucid era, the so-called 'era of contracts', which began in 312 B.C. Both the authors of the *Books of Maccabees*[5] and Josephus[6] used this last system. The choice by the Covenanters of Alexander's conquest of Palestine rather than his death would be easy to explain. According to a somewhat improbable story which Josephus recorded,[7] Alexander when passing through Palestine visited Jerusalem, where he was honourably received by the high-priest and the whole priesthood in splendid vestments and escorted to the

---

[1] Pp. 323–6. [2] In *Background* 53–4.
[3] Pp. 197–216. [4] Schürer *Geschichte*[3] II 112.
[5] *Ibid.* I 32–40.
[6] In *Antiquities* XII v 3 § 246 and ix 3 § 363, XIII vi 7 § 213.
[7] In *Antiquities* XI v 8 §§ 329–39.

CHRONOLOGY AND CRYPTOGRAMS

Temple; there he was shown a copy of the book of *Daniel* (which is an obvious anachronism, so that this part of the story at any rate must be an embellishment of the truth or sheer fiction), in which he found a prophecy declaring that 'one of the Greeks should destroy the Persian empire'[1] and saw a reference to himself in it;[2] thereupon he offered sacrifice to the God of the Jews, exempted them from taxation in every seventh year and allowed them to observe the laws of their ancestors. This story is generally regarded as apocryphal, even though Persian princes seem often to have offered sacrifices in the Temple;[3] but Josephus shows that the story, whether true or false, must have been current in the 1st century A.D. and may well have been generally believed, so that it may be accepted for the purpose of the present argument. As then the privileges mentioned in it were precisely those for which the Covenanters were contending against Rome,[4] they might be expected to prefer an epoch dated from Alexander the Great to the 'era of contracts' which rested on a Seleucid and therefore heathen base and was used by all other Jews (including both Pharisees and Sadducees, to whom they were bitterly opposed) in giving the date of an event or a document. Thus one conqueror of Babylon and Jerusalem would be substituted for another such conqueror.

This substitution of a pseudonym is not an unknown device; so, for example, as Alexander the Great is here represented *ex hypothesi* under the name of 'Nebuchadnezzar king of Babylon', so Vespasian and his son Titus are represented under those of 'Nabuchodonosor king of Babylon and his son Baltasar' in an apocryphal work written shortly after A.D. 70 and therefore approximately contemporary with the Scrolls on the present argument.[5] The reason for both substitutions is obvious, namely the danger of throwing out any hint which might suggest a threat of immediate rebellion against the Roman Empire; in the same way Josephus hastened to explain away the famous 'oracle' that the Jews expected some one of their own race to become ruler of the world by referring it to the emperor Vespasian, however improbable such an allusion might be.[6] The *Zadokite Documents*, then, if Nebuchadnezzar is taken as a pseudonym for Alexander and the 390 years are a Biblical figure used as a round number to yield an approximate date, do but follow a literary convention of the 1st century A.D.

The chronology of the later period must be similarly reckoned with the exception of the inclusion of the 26 years of direct Roman rule, which Jewish chronologists omit, as the following figures show:

---

[1] *E.g.* Dan. viii. 5–8, 20–22.
[2] Cp. Josephus *War* II xvi 4 §§ 392–3.
[3] Cp. Schürer *Geschichte*³ II 300–5.   [4] P. 373.
[5] 1 Baruch i. 10–12 (s. Hitzig in *Hilgenfeld's Zeitschrift* III 267).   [6] S.p. 274.

Greek and Seleucid rulers (331 B.C.–166 B.C.) .. 180⎤
Hasmonaean priests and kings (166 B.C.–63 B.C.) 103 ⎬ years.
[Roman governors (63 B.C.–37 B.C.) .. .. 26] ⎪
Herodian kings (37 B.C.–A.D. 70) .. .. 107⎦

The figures are again erratic, as the simplest calculation shows; and the omission of the Roman period, though here restored, seems surprising. It was, however, known to the Jewish chronologists but was passed over because they regarded it as a discreditable episode in their history of their people, although they claimed to have been treated by them as 'allies' (an obvious euphemism for subject-allies).[1] Contrariwise the Covenanters, much as they disliked Roman domination, could not leave out these years. They were the formative age in the history of their society, when Boethus had come back with other Zadokites from Egypt to Jerusalem[2] and when Hezekiah, the ancestor of the leaders against Rome, had raised the standard of revolt at the cost of his life,[3] and they would be almost within the memory of not a few members of the party who were still alive. According to these figures, then, the 390 (reckoned as 180+103+26+81) years from Alexander's entry into Jerusalem in 331 B.C. would terminate in A.D. 44 and another 20 years corresponding to those in which 'they (*sc.* the nation or the Covenanters) were like blind men and those groping for a way' would bring the closing date down to A.D. 64; but A.D. 44 approximates closely to A.D. 46 and another 20 years brings the date down to A.D. 66, which were both crucial years for the Covenanters; for *c.* A.D. 46–8 Judah's two sons James and Simon rose against the Romans and being caught were executed, whereupon their brother Menahem the 'teacher of wisdom', who was *ex hypothesi* the Rightful Teacher, succeeded to the leadership of the party; he then went apparently into hiding in the neighbourhood of the Dead Sea for 20 years,[4] during which it was left to all intents and purposes leaderless (although Menahem was perhaps organizing it behind the scenes for the coming struggle), *i.e.* groping like blind men, until he emerged at the end of these 20 years, *i.e.* in A.D. 66, to claim the leadership of the Revolt.[5] These 20 years, too, although they are factual, are also symbolical; for the Teacher's active mission will have begun in the 20th year of his becoming leader of his party as that of Nehemiah is said to have begun[6], while they can at the same time be regarded also as half a Messianic period.[7]

In conclusion, if the starting point is taken to be Alexander's conquest of Palestine (and visit to Jerusalem), in 332/1 B.C., from which

---

[1] B. Talmud *Abodah Zarah* 9a.   [2] Pp. 228–9.
[3] Pp. 329–40.   [4] P. 241.   [5] Pp. 268–9.
[6] Neh. i. 1.   [7] Schubert *Community* 105–6.

the Alexandrian era is usually reckoned, the figure of 390 years, interpreted in the light of the only chronology that its author can have known, comes close enough to the crucial years in the history of the Covenanter as here depicted to be accepted as factual. Thus the interpretation of the chronology, being in harmony with the historical reconstruction, goes far to confirm it.

2. SOLAR AND LUNAR CALENDARS IN JUDAISM

Most religious groups like to regard themselves not only as deriving their origin from some famous name but also as in some sense a peculiar people; with this end in view they perpetuate old or create new customs which differ from those of their neighbours, whether based on history or designed for some special social, religious or nationalist, purpose.

Thus the Jews seem at various periods of their history to have had two different calendars, the one ancient and sacred and the other secular and modern; and such a dual system can be traced throughout the period of the Second Commonwealth.[1]

A cryptic poem at the end of *Discipline* enshrining the rules governing the rotation of the seasons and therefore controlling the Covenanters' calendar speaks of them as an 'engraved ordinance' (D x 6; cp. T i 33–4); this is a clear echo of the 'heavenly tablets' on which the ordinance in *Jubilees* prescribing the date of the Feast of Weeks (Pentecost) is said to have been inscribed.[2] These two passages cannot be dissociated, but the explicit and detailed account in *Jubilees* must be the source of the reference in *Discipline*, which is too allusive of itself to convey its meaning to the reader; the former could not have been derived from anything so vague as the latter, while the latter is unintelligible except in the light of the former. The mention of this 'engraved ordinance', by recalling the 'heavenly tablets', has another importance beyond that of determining the relation of the two working to one another: it hints at the source of the Covenanters' calendar and so enables a very difficult passage to be explained.

The author begins by saying that he will continue to bless God 'during the periods which 'ālef has prescribed. At the beginning of the dominion of light throughout its circuit and when it withdraws itself into its prescribed abode, at the beginning of the watches of darkness, when He opens his storehouse and sets it (*sc.* darkness) over the world (?) as well in its circuit as when it withdraws itself before the light, when the luminaries (*sc.* the sun and the moon) appear in the holy zenith[3] as well as when they withdraw themselves into an abode' or

---

[1] Cp. Finegan *Light from the Ancient East*[2] 570–87 and Driver in *Studies presented to Professor S. H. Hooke* 77–83.
[2] Jubilees vi 17, 19.   [3] Cp. Hab. iii. 11.

'mansion of glory, when the fixed seasons enter into the days of the
new moon He renews (*yāḥēḏ*) their circuit (*sc.* that of the sun
and the moon) at the time of their conjunctions (*massōrôṯām* for
ma'ăsōrôṯām) one with another; when they renew themselves, the *M*
is great (*i.e.* important, significant) for the holiest things and the
letter' or 'sign of *N* for the opening (*i.e.* beginning)' or 'revealing of
His deeds of unfailing love for ever, at the beginnings of the seasons in
every period that may be. At the beginning of the months according
to their seasons and holy days in their ordered sequence, as a memorial
at (each of) their seasons I will bless Him with the offering of my lips
according to the prescribed ordinance engraved[1] to eternity. At the
beginning of the years and during the rotation of their seasons, when
the prescribed period of their sequence is finished, each day in its due
turn, as one (is linked) to another, (namely) season of harvest to
summer-fruits and season of sowing to season of green herbs (and)
the seasons of the years to their weeks, and at the beginning of their
weeks to the season of release, as long as I am the prescribed ordinance
as engraved shall be on my tongue as the fruit of praise and the appointed portion of my lips'[2] (D x 1–8). The author then declares that he
will ever continue to offer praise and thanksgiving to God, describes
how he will behave himself towards other men and towards God and
how his justification is in God's hands; and finally, he confesses man's
unworthiness before God, 'inasmuch as he is earth of His kneading
and his due fate is to be food for worms, inasmuch as he is moulded[3]
only of potter's clay (*m'ṣawwār raq ḥōmer qôrēṣ*) and his impulse is
earthy; what answer can the clay and what is made with the hand by
the potter's craft (*qōreṣ*)[4] give (to the potter) and what sort of counsel
does he understand?' (D xi 21–2).

The usual or official Jewish calendar is generally held to have been
lunar, having 354 days in the year;[5] but there is considerable evidence
that a solar calendar too of 364 days had long been recognized in
theory[6] if not employed in actual practice. This calendar, which was
apparently of Phoenician origin, went back probably to the building
of Solomon's temple and, in spite of efforts to abrogate it, continued
long in use beside the old agricultural lunar calendar, when its heathen
origin came to be forgotten[7]; and so Judah the Persian, a medieval
Jewish heretic, maintained that 'the Israelites have always reckoned
by solar years'.[8] The solar calendar, too, was widely used: the Egyptians

[1] S. pp. 543–4.   [2] Cp. Hos. xiv. 3.
[3] Cp. Gen. ii. 7; s. Wiegand in *ZAtW* X 87–93 and Hempel *ibid.* NF XI 289 and
also Driver in *JBL* LIII 273–4.
[4] Cp. Jb. xxxiii. 6.
[5] Cp. Psa. civ. 19 (used by the Rabbis as the proof-text for a lunar year).
[6] Jubilees vi 30 (year of 52 weeks) and I Enoch lxxxii 6 (year of 364 days).
[7] Morgenstern *Fire upon the Altar* 38–9, 98.
[8] Poznański in *RÉJ* L 18–19.

had it, Caesar introduced it into Rome in 46 B.C. and Augustus extended its use to the Asiatic provinces of the Empire. The Covenanters, however, presumably adopted the solar calendar out of antagonism on the one hand to those orthodox groups which, like the author of *Daniel*, clung to the old lunar calendar and from whom they differed on a number of other doctrinal points, and on the other to the leaders of the nation who were willing to go so far in compromising their Judaism as to accept the Hellenistic lunisolar calendar. At the same time, if they came from Egypt,[1] they would have been familiar with the solar calendar as more accurate and less impracticable than either of the other two.

Actually the antithesis between lunar and solar years is too clear-cut and simple, since the orthodox Jewish year, like that of the Babylonians and Syrians, is lunisolar (for only Moslems keep a purely lunar year): the beginning of the months and therefore of the year and the dates of the annual feasts depended on the moon (for the commencement of the month was governed by the first visibility of the new moon, and the consequent error was in all probability corrected by intercalation, though mentioned in no early text), but the length of the year in months and days was determined by the sun. The real question then is on which, on the sun or on the moon, the emphasis falls. The author of *I Enoch* and *Jubilees*, followed by the Covenanters, laid it on the part played by the sun, while the Rabbis in accordance with ancient belief[2] regarded the influence of the moon as decisive; to this extent then the difference between orthodox and unorthodox practice can be treated as that between a lunar and a solar year.

The calendar of the priestly school, however, which was responsible for the Priestly Code and which exercised a strong influence on the composition and redaction of other parts of the Old Testament, was that which subsequently re-appeared in *I Enoch* and *Jubilees*; and Enoch was reputed to have originated or at any rate transmitted it, since 'he was the first to write a testimony, and he testified to the sons of men among the generations of the earth and recounted the weeks of the jubilees and made known to them the days of the years and set the months in order and recounted the sabbaths of the years'.[3] This passage incidentally explains why the principal seasons were called by the Covenanters 'fixed seasons of testimonies' (D i 9, iii 10); the reason was either that they celebrated the great occasions in history on which God had testified to His power in Israel[4] or that Enoch had given his testimony to them when he transmitted them in writing to succeeding generations.[5]

---

[1] Pp. 226–37; cp. Atkinson in *BRL* XL 286–7.
[2] Psa. civ. 19 and Ecclus. xliii. 6–7.   [3] Jubilees iv 17–18; cp. vi 38.
[4] Van der Ploeg in *BO* VIII 115[4].   [5] Barthélemy in *RB*, NS LIX 201–2.

As the author of *Daniel*, whom Philo and Josephus followed on this point,[1] preferred the lunar calendar[2] as a bulwark against the increasing Hellenization or secularization of Jewish society, so the Covenanters clung to the old sacred solar calendar. The first threat to this sacred calendar had already come before the Exile from the Babylonian calendar, whose names for the months had long displaced the old West-Semitic names. The next danger came from the Hellenistic calendar; so Antiochus IV Epiphanes had sought 'to change the times and the law',[3] which was the prerogative of God.[4] When in course of time this danger ceased to be pressing, the author or redactor of *I Maccabees*, though a staunch Maccabaean, could regularly use the secular Seleucid era in assigning dates to the events which he was recording. The special rules regulating the occurrence of the annual feasts were therefore laid down according to the author of *Jubilees* 'lest they (*sc.* the members of his party) forget the feasts of the covenant and walk in conformity with the feasts of the gentiles after their error and after their ignorance',[5] thereby celebrating them on the wrong days; and such rules according to the Covenanters were 'the hidden things in respect to which all Israel had gone astray in the matter of His (*sc.* God's) holy sabbaths and His glorious appointed times' (Z v 1). The purpose of both passages is perfectly clear: to condemn the abandonment of the old sacred calendar and the adoption of the new, secular and foreign, calendar in its place.

The texts now available have enabled several scholars, notably Mlle. Jaubert and Fr. Barthélemy, Dr. Winter and Dr. Talmon, to solve a number of problems which have hitherto been centred in *I Enoch* and *Jubilees* but which are latent in both the Old and the New Testaments; but it is the Scrolls from which the impetus has come to reopen the whole question of the calendar.

In the Old Testament many of the principal events in the Priestly Code fall on or were assigned to the same three days, Sunday[6] and especially Wednesday[7] and Friday,[8] on the assumption that eight months (Nisan, Iyar, Tammuz, Ab, Tishri, Marcheswan, Tebet, Adar) have 30 days and four (Sivan, Elul, Kislev, Shebat) have 31 days each; this is a calendar in which basically every month consists

---

[1] Van Goudoever *Biblical Calendars* 73-4.
[2] Cp. Driver *op. cit.* 84.
[3] Dan. vii. 25 (s. Jaubert *Cène* 50-1); cp. 1 Macc. i. 41-3.
[4] Dan. ii. 21.   [5] Jubilees vi 35.
[6] Gen. vii. 11 (beginning of Flood).
[7] Gen. viii. 5 (mountains uncovered after Flood), 13 (waters dried up), 14 (ground dry); Num. xxxiii. 3 (departure from Egypt); Exod. xl. 1 (erection of Tabernacle); Num. x. 11 (departure from Sinai).
[8] Gen. viii. 4 (ark on Ararat); Exod. xii. 3 (choice of Pascal lamb), xvi. 1 (arrival at Sin); Num. i. 1 (numbering of Israelites), xxxiii. 8 (death of Aaron); Deut. i. 3 (discourse of Moses); Josh. iv. 19 (entry into Canaan).

of 30 days and which is put approximately right by the addition of
1 intercalary day in each period of 3 months.[1] In keeping with the
principles of the Priestly Code, the prophecies of Ezekiel fall pre-
ponderantly on Sunday,[2] only two on Wednesday[3] and two on Friday,[4]
and none on any other day (if variant readings may be adopted in
three passages). The Chronicler exhibits the same peculiarity; and,
when the rule appears to be broken by beginning the building of the
Temple 'in the second day of the second month', the text is proved
corrupt by the omission of the day from some Hebrew manuscripts and
three of the ancient Versions.[5] The books of *Ezra* and *Nehemiah*
prefer Wednesday[6] but recognize also Friday[7] and Sunday,[8] to which
they assign only one event each. This concentration of events on the
same three days in the Priestly Code (to which all the passages cited
from the Hexateuch belong), in the prophecies of Ezekiel and in the
work of the Chronicler or of his school, cannot be accidental. Further, a
similar peculiarity reappears in *Jubilees* in the dates of the principal
events in the lives of the patriarchs; these fall exclusively on Sundays[9]
and Wednesdays.[10] All these facts, those in the Old Testament as well
as those in *Jubilees*, cannot be dissociated from the corresponding fact
that the principal feasts are allocated to these three days (the Passover
and the Feast of Tabernacles with its octave to Wednesday, the Day
of Atonement to Friday, the Feast of Weeks to Sunday)[11] in the same
work.[12] Annually recurring feasts, however, will fall regularly every
year on the same day of the week only if the year is exactly divisible
into weeks; such a year cannot be a lunar year with 354 days but
must be a solar year of 364 (7×52) days.[13] The authors or compilers of
I Enoch and *Jubilees* therefore made the year a solar year of exactly 364
days,[14] choosing this figure for dogmatic reasons rather than the correct
$365\frac{1}{4}$ days; and the Covenanters, using this calendar, ensured that the
seven principal feasts of the year followed each other at intervals of
seven weeks.[15]

Further, the Feast of Weeks according to *Jubilees* always fell in the

---

[1] Pp. 325-6; s. Charles Apocrypha and Pseudepigrapha II 22.
[2] Ezek. i. 1 (iii. 15-16), viii. 1 (one var. Hebr. MS.), xx. 1, xxix 1, xxxi 1, xxxii
1; cp. xxxiii 21.
[3] *Ibid.* xxix 17, xxx 20 (Heb. MSS.), xxxii 17 (LXX).
[4] *Ibid.* xxiv. 1, xl. 1.   [5] 2 Chron. iii. 2 (LXX, Vulg., Pesh.).
[6] Ezr. vii. 9 (Ezra's departure from Babylon), x. 16-17 (meeting for putting away
of foreign wives), Neh. viii. 2 (fresh assembly of people).
[7] Ezr. vii. 9 (Ezra's arrival in Jerusalem), Neh. ix. 1 (day of penitence).
[8] Ezr. viii. 3 (departure from Ahava).
[9] *Jubilees* iii 17, xiv 1, xv 1, xvi 12-13.   [10] *Ibid.* iii 32, vii 2, xii 16, xvi 1.
[11] Cp. pp. 10-11.   [12] Jaubert in *Cène* 28-39.
[13] Jubilees vi 36-8 (where the lunar calendar is said to disturb the seasons); cp.
I Enoch lxxiv 10-12, lxv. 2.
[14] II Enoch xiv 1 (s. Charles *op. cit.* II 23, 459).
[15] Vermès *Scrolls* 44.

middle of the third month,[1] *i.e.* 15 Sivan. Contrariwise, according to the Pentateuch the Feast of Weeks fell 50 days after the offering of the first sheaf of barley 'on the morrow of the sabbath', *i.e.* the Sabbath of Passover,[2] and was celebrated on 6 Sivan. The problem is to reconcile this discrepancy, which depends on the meaning assigned to 'the morrow of the sabbath'; this was a well-known matter of dispute between the Pharisees and the sect of the Boethusians.[3] The Pharisees, for whom the year was a lunar year of 354 days with months of 29 or 30 days, so that the feasts did not necessarily always fall on the same day of the week, interpreted 'the morrow of the sabbath' to be the second day of the feast, taking 'sabbath' as denoting the first day of the feast (14 Nisan), which was a day of rest, and 'the morrow of the sabbath' to be the second day of the feast, *i.e.* 15 Nisan; they then counted 50 days from this day (assigning 29 days to Nisan and 30 to Iyar), and (excluding the first and last days from the 50 days in their calculation) they celebrated the Feast of Weeks (otherwise Pentecost, the feast of the 50th day) on 6 Sivan. Contrariwise, the Boethusians, holding 'sabbath' to mean an ordinary sabbath, maintained that the sheaf was to be offered on the day after the sabbath, *i.e.* the Sunday in the week after the feast (26 Nisan),[4] which is the natural and therefore probably the original meaning of the phrase;[5] they then (assigning 30 days to both Nisan and Iyar and reckoning 49 days from the day of the offering of the sheaf, namely 26 Nisan, and including the first and last days of the 50 days in their calculation or, alternatively, counting 49 days from the day after the offering of the sheaf, namely 27 Nisan) held that Pentecost, falling 'seven sabbaths' after this day,[6] would begin on the day after the sabbath; this according to *Jubilees* was 15 Sivan.[7] On the one hand, therefore, if the sabbath in the 'morrow of the sabbath' is envisaged as falling within the week of the Passover, it cannot have fallen on 26 Nisan, which is too late; on the other hand, if the year began with the first day of Creation (Sunday), a sabbath could not fall on 25 Nisan nor a Sunday on 26 Nisan.[8] All attempts to solve the dilemma have broken down on this fundamental impasse; only by assuming the coexistence of two different calendars can it be resolved.

The dilemma can then be resolved by assuming that the calendar of *Jubilees*, like that of the 'cave-men' (*i.e.* the Covenanters) according to alBîrûnî,[9] began on the fourth day of the week (Wednesday), on which God had made the greater and lesser luminaries.[10] This assumption

[1] Vermès *Scrolls* xv 1, xvi 12–13.
[2] Lev. xxiii. 15–16; cp. Deut. xvi. 9.
[3] B. Talmud *Menahoth* 65a–66a; s. p. 230.
[4] Pp. 230–1.
[5] Jaubert in *VT* III 257–8.
[6] Lev. xxiii. 15.
[7] *Jubilees* xv 1, xliv 4–5.
[8] Jaubert *ibid.* III 250–1.
[9] P. 10.
[10] Gen. i. 14–19.

has two consequences. First, the 'cave-men' in accordance with it would put the beginning of their festal calendar on 1 Nisan, showing that they regarded that day as the beginning of the year.[1] Josephus alludes[2] to this custom when he says that 'Moses appointed that Nisan should be the first month for their (*sc.* the Hebrews') feasts'; and it is illustrated by the Mishnaic saying that 'the New Year for kings and feasts is on 1 Nisan'.[1] This day was presumably chosen to avoid anything that savoured of the orthodox calendar, whereby the ordinary New Year's Day fell on 1 Tishri[3] without any regard to the day of the week. Second, the Passover on 15 Nisan would now fall on a Wednesday, 25 Nisan on a Saturday and 26 Nisan on a Sunday. This assumption thus solves the problem of the Feast of Weeks or Pentecost; for, since Nisan and Iyar had each 30 days, if the calculation of the 50 days starts not from the sabbath of Passover but from the sabbath which follows, this feast will fall on Sunday 15 Sivan.[4] A number of other considerations confirm that in *Jubilees* the place of the Sabbath is taken by Wednesday. So, while its author declares that anyone who goes on a journey or performs certain other prohibited actions on the Sabbath shall die,[5] thus doing lip-service to the orthodox law of the Sabbath, the only day of the week on which the patriarchs never do travel is the fourth day, *i.e.* Wednesday; and Jacob and Laban actually desist from their journeyings and do nothing on that day.[6] Thus, although their Feast of Weeks (15 Sivan)[7] falls on Sunday and the Day of Atonement (10 Tishri)[8] on Friday, the Passover (15 Nisan) and the Feast of Tabernacles with its octave (22 Nisan)[9] fall on Wednesday.[10]

A calendar, however, having a year of 364 days soon goes wrong, falling short by some 50 days in 40 years, which upsets the cycle of feasts tied to the seasons of the year; but how the error was rectified by those who used it is not known. Two suggestions have been made: one is to suppose that the year of jubilee was not in fact a year but an interval of time between two jubilees, allowing the loss of 50 days to be made good by inserting 49 days (for the author of *Jubilees*, like some Jews[11] and the Samaritans,[12] made every jubilee a period of 49, not 50, years)[13] after the harvest at the end of every 40 years;[14] another is to suppose that 35 days were intercalated in every cycle of 28 years, as a certain R. Eliezer (writing probably in Palestine in the 9th

[1] Talmon in *Scr. Hieros.* IV 172.
[2] In *Antiquities* I iii 3 § 81.
[3] Mishnah *Rosh ha-Shanah* i 1.
[4] Barthélemy in *RB*, NS LIX 199–201.
[5] *Jubilees* 1 12–13.
[6] *Ibid.* xxix 5–7.
[7] *Ibid.* xv 1, xvi 1, xliv 1–7.
[8] *Ibid.* xxxiv 18.
[9] *Ibid.* xlix 1 (Passover) and xxxii 27–30 (Tabernacles).
[10] Jaubert in *VT* III 252–4.
[11] B. Talmud *Nedarim* 61a (R. Jehuda).
[12] Neubauer in *JA* VI xiii 393/427.
[13] Charles *Jubilees* lxvii; s. Dillmann & Ryssell *Exodus u. Leviticus*[3] 665 (on Lev. xxv 8).
[14] Zeitlin in *RÉJ* LXXXIX 349–59.

century A.D.) says.[1] Neither method would entirely get rid of the deficit (which would actually be $61\frac{1}{4}$ days at the beginning of the 49th year), as the Jews were well aware; and their own explanation of it was that 'in the days of sinners the year will be shortened'.[2] In other words, the deficit was regarded as a punishment for following a heathen custom,[3] namely the adoption of the Hellenistic or secular lunisolar calendar.[4] Further, even if the first year of the calendar began with the full moon, as the 'cave-men' believed,[5] such an arrangement could not be reproduced in the next year with a solar year of 364 days, since 12 lunar months have only 354 days; and the author of *Jubilees* was equally well aware of this fact,[6] since he charged the moon with arriving 10 days too soon every year. He was therefore compelled to make the year begin with the sun, to which he twice refers as controlling the year, the seasons and the feasts.[7] Accordingly he preserved the memory of the Covenanters' ideal year beginning with the sun to explain why their year began on Wednesday; thus the 'full moons' fixing the beginning of the years and months were to a certain extent notional rather than factual.[8]

The Covenanters were no exception to the general rule of peculiar societies; as they had their own era,[9] so they had their own calendar 'according to the finding of the members of the new covenant in the land of Damascus' (Z viii 15), where it was perfected. Accordingly they were required 'not to transgress a single one of God's provisions in (the matter of) their periods and not to advance their times nor to lag behind in any of their appointed seasons' (D i 14–15),[10] and twelve laymen and three priests at the head of the society were to be 'perfect in all that is revealed in the whole Law in the practice of truth and righteousness and justice . . . and in walking with all men in the measure of truth and in the proper reckoning of the time' (D viii 1–4); and God made His covenant with the ancestors of the nation and of the society 'by revealing to them hidden things wherein all Israel had gone astray; and He laid open before them His holy sabbaths and His glorious appointed seasons, His righteous testimonies and His true ways and the requirements of His desire, which a man shall do and by which he shall live' (Z v 1–2), and all members of the society were bound 'to observe the sabbath-day according to its specification and the appointed seasons and the fast-day according to the finding of the men of the new covenant' (Z viii 15). The 'exact interpretation' clearly

---

[1] Finegan *Light from the Ancient Past*[2] 586–7 (s. Friedlander *Pirkê de Rabbi Eliezer* 34).
[2] I Enoch lxxx 2–8.   [3] P. 319
[4] Cp. Barthélemy in *RB*, NS LIX 201–2 and Jaubert in *VT* III 254–5.
[5] P. 10.   [6] Jubilees vi 36.
[7] *Ibid.* ii 9, iv 21; cp. I Enoch lxxiv 12.   [8] Jaubert in *VT* III 255–6.
[9] Pp. 313–15.   [10] Cp. I Enoch lxxiv 12.

refers to the society's peculiar interpretation of the rules fixing the dates of the sabbath and the recurring feasts of the annual cycle.

What is meant by 'advancing their times' and 'lagging behind in any of their appointed seasons' is clear, as Dr. Obermann has shown.[1] The Pharisees claimed the right to adjust the times and dates of the recurring feasts and fasts for reasons of expediency or convenience. For example, if New Year's Day (1 Tishri) was due to fall on Sunday or Wednesday or Friday, it was postponed to the following day if that was a *dies licita* or advanced to the preceding day if it was not such; similarly the Day of Atonement (10 Tishri) if due on Sunday or Tuesday or Friday and the Passover if due on Monday or Wednesday or Friday were similarly shifted to a suitable day. The 'Ananites,'[2] however, postponed feasts or fasts only if they fell on a sabbath to the following Sunday, while the 'cave-men' required New Year's Day and Passover to be observed only on Wednesdays.[3] Or again, if in the 12th month (Adar) the crops were not far enough advanced to be reaped or the lambs not big enough to be sacrificed in four weeks' time, *i.e.* in the middle of the first month (Nisan), a month (Adar II) was intercalated between Adar and Nisan so that the Passover might be delayed for a month; the 'Ananites, however, intercalated a month after the preceding month, *i.e.* Shebat (Shebat II).[4] So too, if the fast of 9 Ab was to fall on a sabbath, when fasting was prohibited, it was deferred till the next day.[5] Or lastly, the evening sacrifice on 14 Nisan was put back, *i.e.* advanced, by two hours so that it would not clash with that of the eve of the Passover.[6] Too much emphasis, however, must not be laid on these adjustments because little or nothing is known of them in practice in the 1st century A.D.; they are mentioned only as showing how easily the orthodox and the Covenanters' Day of Atonement might have failed to coincide if the two groups did not agree about advancing or postponing the date, even if they did not have completely different calendars. In any case, the injunction not to advance or retard any of the fixed feasts may be read as a protest by the Covenanters against the current practice of the Pharisees in adjusting them for reasons of calendrical convenience.

That the basis of the Covenanters' calendar was a solar, as Schechter hinted long ago,[7] in place of the orthodox lunar year can easily be proved from the Scrolls. The proof, as Dr. Winter has shown,[8] is

[1] In *JBL* LXXV 292–3.
[2] Sachau *Chronologie Orientalischer Völker von alBêrûnî* 53–9, 275, 283–7 = *Chronology of Ancient Nations of alBîrûnî* 61–9, 268, 283–7.
[3] Pp. 9–10, 321–2.
[4] Cp. B. Talmud *Rosh ha-Shanah* 6b–7a, 8a, 19b–20a.
[5] P. Talmud *Shekalim* iv 1.
[6] Mishnah *Pesahim* v 1; cp. B. Talmud *Pesahim* 58a.
[7] In *Documents* I xvi, xix–xxi; cp. Talmon in *Biblica* XXXII 549–66.
[8] In *VT* VI 215–17.

furnished by the *War's* figures for the rotation of the priestly courses. The heads of the priestly families, as laid down in the Old Testament, were 22 or rather 24[1] (if the correct text is followed),[2] so that each family's periods of duty in the Temple were apparently based on a year of 48 weeks, since each family did duty for 2 weeks in the year; and Josephus[3] and the Talmud[4] reflect the same arrangement. Contrariwise, according to the *War* the heads of families were 26 in number (W ii 2), so that their 2 weeks' course of duty every year must be based on a solar year of 52 weeks.

This proof that the Covenanters must have followed a calendar with a year of 52 weeks is reinforced by another discovery. Lists of priestly courses are mentioned in Jewish literature,[5] and one on a small sherd containing portions of three lines found at Caesarea has been known for some time; and now a fragment of another on skin found in Cave VI contains the ends of eight lines of text, of which the beginnings can fortunately be restored from the corresponding Biblical list.[6] The importance of this last discovery is that it confirms the observance of twenty-six (instead of twenty-four) courses by the Covenanters; for the author of the list allows for two additional courses of priests serving four periods between them, two being put at the beginning and two at the end of the list.[7] That the Covenanters recognized the discrepancy is proved by the discovery in Cave IV of another fragmentary text giving an apparently orthodox list of the priestly courses;[8] but whether this represents an attempt to reconcile the discrepancy between the orthodox and unorthodox lists or is merely a piece of lip-service to orthodoxy cannot unfortunately be made out, so badly damaged is the text.

Briefly, then, during the 1st century A.D. any month within certain limits might have 29 or 30 days[9] in order to make up a lunar year of 354 days, but in the time of Gamaliel II (A.D. 80–115) the practice that the months should alternately have 29 and 30 days became usual;[10] either method could give or gave a year of the required length. Contrariwise, the Covenanters' year of 52 weeks implied a solar year of 364 (which came near enough to the approximately true solar year of $365\frac{1}{4}$) days[11]. This year was also the sacred year of the authors of *Jubilees* and especially of *I Enoch*; there it is prescribed as one in which

---

[1] Cp. Talmon in *Scr. Hieros.* IV 169.
[2] 1 Chron. xxiv 7–18; cp. Neh. x. 3–9, xii 1–7, 12–21 (s. Ryle *Ezra and Nehemiah* 293–4); cp. Tosefta *Ta'anith* iv 2 and B. Talmud *Ta'anith* 27a.
[3] In *Antiquities* VII xiv 7 § 365.   [4] B. Talmud *Taanith* 27a–27b.
[5] *E.g.* Tosefta *Taanith* ii 1.   [6] 1 Chron. xxiv. 7–18.
[7] Talmon in *Scr. Hieros.* IV 168–76.   [8] Milik in *VT, Suppl.* IV 24–25.
[9] Cp. Mishnah *Rosh ha-Shanah* iii 1 (any month with 30 days) and *Arakhim* ii 2 (4 months of 30 days and 8 months of 29 days).
[10] Kühn *Galeni Opera* xxvii 23; cp. I Enoch lxxviii 15–16.
[11] Cp. II Enoch xiv 1.

Y

every month had 30 days (which would give a year of 360 days) but in which one day was added to every quarter, bringing it up to 364 days.[1] Clearly these 4 intercalary days were disregarded, when the length of the month was stated, as affecting only 4 months in the year. Accordingly, the length of the Covenanters' months agrees with the statements of the two Qara'ite writers alQirqîsânî and Jāfět ibn 'Alî that the 'Sadducaeans' reckoned 30 days to the month; for these people, who cannot for various reasons be the Sadducees of the New Testament, may once again be identified with the Zadokites or Covenanters of Qumrân. These calculations, however arid they may seem, will presently gain fresh interest when the problem of solving the ciphers in the Scrolls is reached.[2]

This solar calendar, having been reflected in the Priestly Code[3] and adopted in *Jubilees*,[4] and therefore once regarded as sacred, again became through its adoption by the Covenanters and the Qara'ites a heresy; and so the author or compiler of a late midrash, which was perhaps completed in the 9th century A.D., could speak of 'the heretics (*mînîm*) who calculate neither the new moons nor the courses of the stars'.[5] These people can hardly be Christians[6], as the editor has suggested, but may well be the Covenanters or rather their successors the Qara'ites, who alone still clung to a solar calendar.

According to the earliest sources in the Old Testament the agricultural year began with ploughing in the autumn,[7] while the religious year began in the spring;[8] but this occasion might be celebrated, at any rate according to late priestly custom, in the autumn[9] when the sabbatical year was always held to begin.[10] The Seleucid year began in the spring in Palestine but with the Syrians in the autumn,[11] while both Josephus[12] and the Mishnah[13] put the beginning of the religious year in the spring and that of the civil year in the autumn. The Covenanters naturally harked back to ancient religious practice and reckoned the year from the harvest (D x 7),[14] which began in April around Jericho and ended elsewhere late in May; thus their calendar once again agreed with that of *Jubilees*, whose author made the solar year begin with the first month,[15] *i.e.* Nisan (March-April).

Orthodox Jews counted the day and therewith the Sabbath from sunset to sunset; and the next question is to decide whether the

---

[1] Jubilees vi 29–32, 38 and I Enoch lxxxii 11.   [2] Pp. 335–406.
[3] Cp. Gen. vii 11 w. viii 14 (making the deluge last 12 months *plus* 10 days or 364 days); s. Skinner *Genesis* 167–8).
[4] Jubilees vi. 32.   [5] Midrash *Tehillin* on Ps. xxviii. 5.
[6] Braude *Midrash on Psalms* ii. 466.
[7] Exod. xxiii 14–16 (E) and xxiv 22 (J).   [8] Exod. xi. 2 (J).
[9] Lev. xxiii. 23–5 (P) and Numb. xxix. 1–6 (P).   [10] Lev. xxv. 8–10 (P).
[11] Schürer *Geschichte*[3] I 32–40.   [12] In *Antiquities* I iii 3 § 81.
[13] In *Rosh ha-Shanah* i. 1   [14] Cp. Ettisch in *TLz.* LXXXVIII 189–94.
[15] Jubilees vi 23.

Covenanters followed the usual custom of their fellow Jews or whether they differed from them in this as in other matters of the calendar.

With a solar calendar the day begins at daybreak, and traces of this usage are preserved in the Priestly Code;[1] if however the calendar is lunar, the day is reckoned from sunset, as elsewhere in the Old Testament after the triumph of the Law. The Rabbis, therefore, leaning to a lunar calendar, naturally made the day begin with the preceding nightfall; they based this practice on the statement that 'there was evening and there was morning, one day' at the creation of the world[2] and further supported it by citing the order of a man's daily actions as implicit in the Old Testament, which speaks of the times 'when thou sittest in thy house (*sc.* in the evening) and when thou walkest in the way (*sc.* in the morning) and when thou liest down (*sc.* at night) and when thou risest up (*sc.* at dawn)';[3] for here evening is put before morning. That the author of *Discipline* starts with light (D x 1), puts day before night (D x 10) and inverts these clauses, saying 'at the beginning of going forth (*sc.* in the morning) and coming in to sit down (*sc.* in the evening) and rising up (*sc.* at dawn) and when lying down in thy bed (*sc.* at night)' (D x 13–14),[4] is therefore significant; for in each case he puts morning before evening, as also the author of *War* does (W xiv 13–14). Whereas, too, according to ordinary Hebrew usage the 'going forth' of the sun and its 'coming in' connote respectively sunrise and sunset, the Covenanters reverse the words in these idioms; for them the 'coming in of light' is morning and the 'going forth of light' is evening (T xii 4–7). Dr. Zeitlin's objection,[5] that 'the outgoings of the day' commonly denotes the following day,[6] has no bearing on the point at issue; for 'went forth' is equivocal, and the end of one day is the beginning of the next day. The Covenanters, too, did not necessarily follow the prevailing linguistic usage. Dr. Zeitlin further cites[7] a rule in the *Zadokite Documents* which seems at first sight to contradict the inference that their day may have begun at dawn; this says 'let no man do any work on the sixth day (*i.e.* Friday) from the time when the sun's orb is distant from the gate by its fulness (*i.e.* just before touching the western horizon in the evening); for it is He (*sc.* God) who said: Keep holy the sabbath day and hallow it[8]' (Z xiii 7). This seems to suggest that the Sabbath and therefore every other day must begin in the evening. The objection, however, is purely superficial; the purpose of the rule is to ensure that the Covenanters shall keep holy the night of Friday (as ordinary orthodox Jews do) as well as the whole following day and night (*i.e.*

---

[1] *E.g.* Exod. xii. 6, 18 and Lev. vii. 15 xxiii. 32 (s. Dillmann *Genesis*[6] 22).
[2] Gen. i. 5.
[3] Deut. vi. 7.
[4] Cp. Isaiah A xxxvii 28.
[5] In *JQR*, NS XLIX 225, 234–5.
[6] *E.g.* Tosefta *Shabbat* iii 5.
[7] In *Zadokite Fragments* 17–18.
[8] Deut. v. 12.

their own peculiar Sabbath). They must not abate one jot or tittle of the old law while at the same time keeping their own law: they thus in this as in other respects[1] increased the burdens laid by the Rabbis on men's shoulders, outdoing the Pharisees in the stringency of their requirements. Indeed, the exception approves the rule; for what would have been the need for this elaborate description of the beginning of the Sabbath if it had been normal? Finally, as Prof. Ginsberg has remarked,[2] whether the Sabbath began on Friday evening or Saturday morning would be immaterial, since the astronomical calendar and that in daily use would not necessarily agree; in theory the Covenanters might observe one by way of doing lip-service to orthodox use,[3] while in practice they followed another calendar.

The probability then is that the Covenanters will have counted the day from dawn to dawn.[4] This conclusion is supported by Mâsawaihi (Meshwî) al'Ukbarî, a dissident Qara'ite c. A.D. 850, who is said to have held that the day began at sunrise;[5] the inference then is that this heterodox custom came down from the Covenanters to the Qara'ites, who had many points of contact with them. It can be traced, too, in the Synoptic Gospels and perhaps also in the fourth Gospel.[6]

Consequently 'Sons of Light' would be a suitable appellation for a party who held that the day began with daylight just as 'Sons of Darkness' would be for a rival party who held that it began with the onset of darkness.[7] Thus a *double entente*, such as the Covenanters loved, would underlie the names which they bestowed respectively on themselves and on their opponents.

Another possible divergence between the Pharisees and the Zadokites may here be mentioned[8] although the Scrolls do not touch on it; for it illustrates their chronological differences. This is their respective interpretations of 'between the two evenings', the phrase used to describe the time for the sacrifice of the Paschal lamb[9] and of the evening burnt-offering,[10] for the lighting of the lamps in the Tabernacle[11] and for the appearance of the quails in the wilderness.[12] The normal view, which may be taken to be that of the Pharisees, was that it meant from 'a half after the eighth hour' to 'a half after the ninth hour' (approximately 2.30–3.30 p.m.)[13] or 'from the ninth to the eleventh hour' (approximately 3–5 p.m.)[14]: in other words, from the moment

---

[1] Pp. 86–91.   [2] In *JBL* LXXII 260.
[3] Pp. 326–7.   [4] Talmon in *Scr. Hieros.* IV 188–93, 198–9.
[5] Poznański in the *RÉJ* XXXIV 169–76.
[6] Cp. Finegan *Handbook of Biblical Chronology* 9–10.   [7] Talmon in *Scr. Hieros.* IV 193.
[8] Cp. Charles *Jubilees* 255 (where 'Sadducees' will be a misnomer for 'Sadducaeans' or Zadokites).
[9] Exod. xii. 6, Lev. xxiii. 5, Num. ix. 3, 5, 11.
[10] Exod. xxix. 39, 41, Num. xxviii. 4, 8.
[11] Exod. xxx. 8.   [12] Exod. xvi. 12.
[13] Mishnah *Psahim* v 1.   [14] Josephus *War* VI ix 3 § 423.

when the sun began to decline until it set. The author of *Jubilees*, however, says that the Passover must be observed 'between the evenings, from the third part of the day to the third part of the night', *i.e.* round about sunset, and that the Paschal lamb must be slain not 'during any period of light but during the period bordering on the evening',[1] *i.e.* soon after sunset. Further, Abraham ibn Ezra records that the *Ṣaddûqîm*, who presumably must here be the Sadducaeans (Zadokites), or 'heretics (*mînîm*)' held that the meaning of 'between the two evenings' was the last of the 'three evenings' which they recognized;[2] this would apparently be the last period of the evening, from sunset to the final disappearance of the light. As the same expositor elsewhere calls[3] the Qara'ites 'Sadducaean doctors' and as the Qara'ites (like the Samaritans) are known to have taken 'between the two evenings' in this last sense,[4] Abraham ibn Ezra's *Ṣaddûqîm* cannot have been the Sadducees; they must therefore have been the Zadokites or Covenanters of Qumrân.

Lastly, in the Old Testament the night seems to be divided into three watches,[5] but the Roman system of four watches is found in the New Testament;[6] and Josephus uses this last system even in references to the Old Testament.[7] The two systems were warmly debated in the synagogue: R. Eliezer *c.* A.D. 90 declared that three watches were customary in the Temple and *c.* A.D. 160 R. Nathan still declared that this was the proper system, while Rabbî advocated a night of four watches.[8] The only allusion to such a system in the Scrolls is contained in the rule that 'the Many shall stay awake in community for a third of every night throughout the year to read aloud from the Book (*sc.* the Scriptures) and to study law and to bless in community' (D vi 7–8); this implies the division of the night into three shifts or watches.[9] Clearly the system of three watches was a relic of the old sacred calendar, while one of four watches was that of the new secular calendar; the Covenanters then in this and in other matters still clung to ancient custom.[10] The divergence, however, cannot be used to prove that *Discipline* must be dated before A.D. 70,[11]

---

[1] Jubilees xlix 10–12.
[2] On Exod. xii. 6 (where *Ṣaddûqîm* appears in some and *mînîm* in other editions); cp. Friedmann *Mechilta de-Rabbi Ismael* 5b–6a (suggesting that this is an ancient interpretation of the phrase here discussed).
[3] On Dan. xi 31 (s. p. 265).
[4] Trigland *Diatribe de Secta Karaeorum* 27 and Reland *Dissertatio de Samaritanis* § 22.
[5] Exod. xiv. 24; 1 Sam. xi. 11 (morning watch); Jud. vii. 19 (middle watch); cp. Lam. ii. 19 (night the beginning of the watches).
[6] Mk. xiii. 35 (four watches); cp. Matt. xiv. 25 (fourth watch).
[7] In *Antiquities* V vi 5 § 223; cp. XVIII ix 6 § 350.
[8] Tosefta *Berakoth* i 1 and B. Talmud *Berakoth* 3a–b.
[9] Cp. Talmon in *RQ* II 482–4.
[10] Cp. Strack & Billerbeck *Kommentar* I 688–91.
[11] Rabinowitz in *VT* III 180–1.

even though such a date can be maintained on other grounds; for evidence of the recognition, if not the regular observance, of a threefold division of the night can still be found long after A.D. 70.[1]

Thus the Covenanters had their own era, their own system of years and months, and their own day and night; and traces of all these peculiarities can be found elsewhere in the 1st century A.D.

The use of a divergent calendar and of different systems of reckoning time would have the advantage of enabling the Covenanters to keep themselves in some sense separate from their fellow Jews; but it would also have the disadvantage of hindering or preventing their participation in the services of the Temple[2] and might even produce serious clashes. It might therefore be one reason why they had retreated into the Wilderness of Judah (cp. D viii 13–14, ix 20 W i 2).[3]

3. DIVERGENT CALENDARS IN THE CHURCH

The assumption of these two calendars, that of *Jubilees* and the Scrolls and that of the orthodox Pharisees and Rabbis, goes far to solve the dilemma of the discrepant dates in the accounts of the crucifixion of Jesus. This can only be resolved by assuming that the Synoptists must have had a calendar in which the Passover must fall on a Wednesday, that is the old sacerdotal calendar of *Jubilees* and the Scrolls, while the author of the Fourth Gospel is following the official calendar of the Pharisees and the Rabbis, in which the feasts fall not on a fixed day but on any day of the week.[4] That both Covenanters and Christians had Galilaean connections supports the notion that they may have used the same calendar.

The problem of the date of the Crucifixion is well known. The Synoptists[5a] represent the Last Supper in some respects as a Paschal meal;[5b] if therefore they are following the official Jewish calendar, Jesus will have held the Last Supper on the evening of 14 Nisan and have been crucified on 15 Nisan. These two days, however, leave no time for all the events of the week of the Passion. Contrariwise, that according to the Fourth Gospel, when Jesus was taken before Pilate, the Jews refused to enter the judgement-hall 'lest they should be defiled, but that they might eat the Passover'[6] does not necessarily refer to Friday 14 Nisan, the eve of the Passover;[7] for, since impurity contracted by entering a heathen house lasted seven days,[8] the appearance before Pilate might have taken place on the Thursday, 13 Nisan.

---

[1] B. Talmud *Berakoth* 3a–b. [2] Yadin *War* 187–8.
[3] Talmon in *Script. Hieros.* IV 166–7.
[4] Cp. Jaubert in *NTS* VII 1–30; cp. Goudoever *Biblical Calendars* 224–30.
[5a] Matt. xxvi. 17–19, Mk. xiv. 12–16, Lk. xxii. 7–20. [5b] S. pp. 512–5.
[6] Jn. xviii. 28. [7] Jn. xix. 14.
[8] Strack & Billerbeck *Kommentar* II 838–40.

If then the Synoptists and the Fourth Evangelist are thinking of the same Passover, the discrepancy cannot be reconciled.

Mlle. Jaubert, however, has shown[1] that the discrepancy disappears on the assumption of two different Passovers, the one calculated according to the old sacerdotal (solar) and the other based on the official (lunar or rather lunisolar) calendar.[2] In the former the Passover can fall only on a Wednesday, whereas in the latter it falls on a different day in every year; but in this the day of the Passover must have been on Friday because Jesus rose on 'the third day',[3] which according to the unanimous testimony of the Evangelists was a Sunday.[4] The events of the Passion then may now be tabulated in accordance with such a double calendar:

Sacred (solar) calendar of Synoptists Nisan		Official (lunar or lunisolar) calendar of Fourth Gospel Nisan
Saturday, 11	Arrival of Jesus at Bethany: anointing of His feet at supper	8
Sunday, 12	Entry into Jerusalem and return to Bethany to sleep	9
Monday, 13	Departure from Bethany	10
Tuesday, 14 (Eve of Passover)	Last Supper	11
Tuesday– Wednesday	Jesus arrested and taken before the high-priest	
Wednesday, 15 (Passover)	Meeting of Sanhedrin to procure His death	12
Thursday, 16	Meeting of Sanhedrin to condemn Him; Jesus sent before Pilate and then to Herod	13
Friday, 17	Jesus condemned by Pilate and crucified; His body taken from the cross so as not to defile the Sabbath	14 (Eve of Pass-over)
Saturday, 18 (Sabbath)		15 (Passover)
Sunday, 19	Resurrection[5]	16

This reconstruction, according to which the Passion will have lasted

[1] In *Cène* 79–136.   [2] Cp. Goudoever *ibid* 268–73.
[3] I Cor. xv. 4.   [4] Matt. xxviii 1, Mk. xvi. 2, Lk. xxiv 1, Jn. xx. 1.
[5] Matth. xxvii 63, Mk. viii 31 ('after three days'); Matth. xvi 21, xvii 23, Mk. ix 31, x 34, Lk. xviii 33, xxiv 7, 46 ('on the third day'); s. pp. 332–3.

two and a half days, allows ample time for the various events (all of which are not here set out) crowded into the period of time between the Last Supper and the Crucifixion, including two separate sessions of the Sanhedrin. The summoning of this body would itself have taken some length of time, since twenty-three members were required for a *quorum* in capital cases; and two sessions were necessary, since a verdict of guilty might not be given on the day on which sentence of death was pronounced.[1] Consequently, a capital trial could not be held on the eve of a feast lest sentence might have to be pronounced on the feast-day. That the synoptic tradition has some authority is further shown by the fact that several Fathers of the Church reflect it; for example, Epiphanius[2] (c. A.D. 315–403) says that at dawn on Wednesday the Lord was arrested and on Friday He was crucified.

The scheme, however, is not free from difficulties.[3] For instance, it explains why no Paschal lamb at the Last Supper is mentioned in the fourth Gospel but not why it is not mentioned in the three Synoptic Gospels.[4] Also, it requires several assumptions to which objections have been taken:[5] (i) that Jesus came to Bethany on the Sabbath; (ii) that, when the author of the Fourth Gospel said that 'Jesus six days before the Passover came to Bethany',[6] he meant that six full days would intervene (*i.e.* that Jesus came there seven days before the feast in modern usage); and (iii) that, when the Synoptist says just before describing the arrival at Bethany, that 'after two days is the feast of the Passover',[7] he similarly implied that two full days would intervene between that of which He was speaking and that on which the feast would be celebrated. None of these objections are fatal. Jesus might have come from some place quite near after sunset to Bethany[8]; or, if He came from Jerusalem, the journey of 45 minutes on foot would have been perfectly feasible between sunset and a late supper.[9] Two full days intervene between 11 and 14 Nisan (eve of Passover) as six between 8 and 15 Nisan. Usually, however, both the first and the last day are included by ancient writers in such calculations;[10] but a comparable divergence in calculation appears when Jesus (as He apparently does) counts four[11] and the Rabbis six[12] months from seed-time to harvest (Marcheswan to Nisan).[13] The difficulty therefore in the Fourth Gospel disappears if the author is assumed to be using the

---

[1] Mishnah *Sanhedrin* i 4, iv 1.   [2] In *de Fide* xxii 1.   [3] Cp. Jaubert in *NTS* VII 1–30.
[4] Cp. Rowley in *BJRL* XLIV 148; and Hempel in *ZAtW* LXX 141–2.
[5] Jeremias in *JTS*, NS X 132–3.   [6] Jn. xii. 1.
[7] Matt. xxvi. 2, Mk. xiv. 1.   [8] Jaubert *Cène* 112[2].
[9] Cp. Josephus *Life* 44 § 220 (where dinner is going on at the 2nd hour of the night); s. Kraus *Talmudische Archäologie* III 29–31.
[10] Cp. Matt. xvii. 23, xx. 19 = xxvii. 63.   [11] Jn. iv. 35.
[12] P. Talmud *Taanith* 64a.
[13] Namely Marcheswan, (Kislev, Tebet, Shebat, Adar,) Nisan; cp. Driver in *Studies presented to Professor S. H. Hooke* 68–9.

short method of counting time; but strict accuracy or consistency in such matters cannot and must not be expected of Oriental writers, especially when they are describing events by no means recent and may also be fixing them by an obsolete calendar.[1] Further, the Evangelists were compelled by the ambiguities inherent in the use of the two calendars, when speaking of 'the preparation', to define what day they meant. Accordingly, the Synoptists added 'that is the day before the Sabbath' or 'and the Sabbath drew near'[2] to show that they meant not Tuesday, the eve of the Passover, which always fell on a Wednesday in the old sacred calendar, but Friday as the eve of the Sabbath in the same week; and in the same way the author of the fourth Gospel said 'the preparation for the Passover'[3] to show which eve he meant, although the Passover and the Sabbath happened to coincide in that year in the secular calendar, but subsequently said simply 'the preparation' as the story showed clearly what he meant.[4]

The only remaining objection to this theory lies in the Synoptists' statement that the Last Supper was held on 'the first day of unleavened bread, when they sacrificed the Passover'.[5] According to the orthodox secular calendar the Paschal victim was killed before sunset on the eve of the Passover, i.e. the afternoon of 14 Nisan, but eaten between sunset and midnight of the same day, which was counted in the orthodox reckoning as falling within the day of the Passover, i.e. 15 Nisan;[6] and this on the same reckoning was the 'first day of unleavened bread',[7] since the day was held to run from sunset to sunset.[8] If, however, the Synoptists, using the sacred calendar, counted the day from morning to morning,[9] the victim would be both killed and eaten on the same day, the eve of their Passover, i.e. 14 Nisan; and this would be for them the 'first day of unleavened bread',[10] since unleavened bread began to be eaten on the same evening 'according to the precise determination of the seven days' of the Feast of Unleavened Bread.[11] Thus the assumption that the Synoptists were following the old calendar removes the inconsistency with which they have been charged in giving the date of the Last Supper.[12]

Such a use of two divergent calendars will also account for the statement that the Wicked Priest's attack on the Rightful Teacher took place 'at the season of the fixed feast of the rest of the Day of Atonement . . . on the fast-day (i.e. the Day of Atonement)[13] of the Sabbath of their rest' (H xi 6–8); for the addition of the pronoun

---

[1] Cp. Jaubert *Cène* 113–15.   [2] Mk. xv. 42 and Lk. xxiii. 24.
[3] Jn. xix. 14.   [4] Jn. xix. 31.
[5] Mk. xiv. 12; cp. Matt. xxvi. 17 and Lk. xxii. 7.   [6] Exod. xii. 6, 8.
[7] Lev. xxiii. 5–6, Num. xxviii 16–17; cp. Josephus *Antiquities* III x 5 § 249.
[8] Cp. Gen. i. 5, Ps. lv. 18, Dan. viii. 14.   [9] Pp. 320–2.
[10] Exod. xii. 18; cp. Josephus *War* V iii 1 § 99.   [11] S. R. Driver *Exodus* 95.
[12] Chwolson *Passahmahl* 3; cp. Box in *JTS* III 359.
[13] Cp. Acts xxvii. 9.

would imply that 'they' (whichever party might be meant) was using a different calendar from the other party.[1] An allusion to this divergence has been detected also in a fragment of another commentary which speaks of '[the congregation of] the poor ones who have accepted the fixed season of the fast (*i.e.* the Day of Atonement) and will be delivered from all the snares of [Belial]' (APs.a 9–10). The reason for this divergence is that the Day of Atonement in the solar calendar of *Jubilees* and therefore of the Covenanters was tied to a Friday; but, as alBîrûnî remarks,[2] it could never fall on this day in the orthodox lunar calendar.[3] In the week of the Passion, as here outlined, the two Passovers are three days apart; this interval is apparently the least possible. Obviously, when for example the tenth day of the seventh month, *i.e.* the Day of Atonement, is permanently tied to the sixth day of the week, it changes every year in relation to the date fixed by the sun's course; synchronization cannot be guaranteed and ideally the fast may fall on any day of the week. The actual difference depends on the distance of the year in question from the nearest leap-year, which is designed to adapt the lunar year to the solar period (although it does not entirely fulfil its purpose); the discrepancy therefore may range from three to twenty-five days.[4] It cannot however be definitely fixed for any given year, as nothing precise is known about the incidence of intercalation in the 1st century A.D.;[5] and the difficulty in this case is increased by the fact that the year of the Crucifixion is uncertain.[6] The theory, therefore, however attractive it may be, must remain only a hypothesis until these two points can be cleared up.

That the Evangelists may perhaps be making practical use of the solar calendar in the last part of the 1st century A.D. is not without significance; it inevitably suggests that the only other known instance of its actual use, that by the Covenanters, may be assigned approximately to the same period of time. Further, the problem was apparently a practical one in both Jewish and Christian circles in this and the following century; for the apostle Paul had need to chide[7] the Galatians because, as he said, 'ye observe days and months and seasons and years'; long afterwards, too, the Syriac chronicler Gregory bar Hebraeus recorded[8] that in A.D. 825 (two years after that in which the patriarch Timotheus had died)[9] a dispute had broken out at Tiberias in which the orthodox party amongst the Jews were accusing the 'Ananites (*i.e.* Qara'ites) of dishonouring the Sabbath in favour of

---

[1] Pp. 281–4; cp. Talmon in *Biblica* XXXII 553–4.
[2] Sachau *Chronologie orientalischer Völker* 283 = *Chronology of ancient Nations* 277.
[3] Jaubert *Cène* 53–4.   [4] Talmon in *Scr. Hieros.* IV 180–1.
[5] Cp. Wiesenberg in *JJS.* XI. 82.   [6] Cp. Hempel *loc. cit.* 143.
[7] Gal. iv. 10.
[8] Abbeloos & Lamy *Gregorii Barhebraei Chronicon Ecclesiasticum* I 365–6.
[9] Pp. 8–9.

Wednesday. All these facts are witness to a persistent cult of the ancient solar calendar in certain Jewish and in Christian circles, possibly as guardians of the old sacred point of view. They are witness also to the interesting fact that this calendar had been transmitted from the old priestly school, which had been responsible for compiling or editing much of the Old Testament, through the party whose sectarian literature included *I Enoch* and *Jubilees*, the Boethusians, the Covenanters and the early Church, down to the 'cave-men' of the 9th-10th centuries A.D.

The difficulties which the use of two different calendars may or must have caused are no reason for rejecting the suggestion here made;[1] for the practice is well known in the East. The Christians of the 2nd century A.D. did not all celebrate Easter on the same day, and various Eastern churches clung to the Julian calendar and refused to observe the Gregorian calendar when it was introduced in A.D. 1582, and its introduction into Greece in A.D. 1924 was fiercely resisted by the so-called 'palaeohemerologists', namely the supporters of the old calendar; and the calendar still followed by the monks of Mt. Athos is now 13 days behind that used in the rest of Greece. These facts would seem to show, as Fr. Van der Ploeg argues,[2] that the Covenanters' use of an old sacerdotal calendar was probably a purely sectarian matter.

4. CIPHERS AND CRYPTOGRAMS

The preoccupation of the Covenanters with the calendar had another importance, that the authors of the Scrolls hinted at their own peculiar calendar in ciphers or cryptograms, in which at the same time they were apparently seeking to convey other esoteric but significant information. That they should have used this method of transmitting information is nothing surprising, being in keeping with their own practice; for Cave IV has yielded several documents in cipher and cryptograms.[3]

The Rabbis are known to have employed two devices of this sort. The first is that called *nôṭārîqôn*, which is the substitution of single letters, generally the initial letter, of a word by way of abbreviation for the whole word; this is a very old practice, of which examples can be found not only on Aramaic and Phoenician inscriptions and on Jewish coins of both Revolts (A.D. 66–70 and A.D. 132–5)[4]; it is described in the Mishnah,[5] and examples occur in it[6]·and in the Tosefta.[7] The second is called *gîmāṭr'yâ* (that is 'geometry'); this consists of adding

[1] Del Medico *Mythe* 267–8.
[2] In *Excavations* 128–9.
[3] Pp. 17, 19.
[4] Driver in *Textus* I 112–4 and IV 76–8.
[5] Mishnah *Shabbat* xii 3.
[6] In *Maaser Sheni* iv 11.
[7] In *Berakoth* vii 20.

up the numerical values of the letters (for the letters of the alphabet served also as numerical symbols in default of an adequate system of ciphers) in a word and identifying any two words whose letters yielded the same total number. Examples can be found both in the Old Testament[1] and in the Mishnah[2] (c. A.D. 180). These devices had various purposes: they might fit a word into a small space on a coin or save labour and time in copying a text; they might be a mere literary embellishment, a means of avoiding the profanation of the divine name or of conveying esoteric information.

A case of abbreviation in the Scrolls to avoid profanity is in the prohibition of swearing 'by '*ālef* and *lāmed* and by '*ālef* and *dālet*' (Z xix 1), where the first pair stand for '*l[hym]* = '*ĕlôhîm* 'God' and the second for '*d[ny]* = '*ădônāy* 'Lord'. So the Rabbis wrote '*yôd hē*' = *Yh[wh]* and even "*ālef* without *dālet*' = '*[lhym]* as substitutes for respectively 'Jehovah' and 'God'.[3]

In *War* only one instance, which has no significance, of playing on the letters of words as a literary device has been detected (W iv 1–4).[4]

The author of *Discipline*, describing the virtues which members of the community at Qumrân must cultivate, speaks of the state to which they aspire as one 'in which none shall walk in the stubbornness of his heart to go astray after his own heart and his own eyes and his own impulsive desire, but '(*ālef*)–'(*ālef*)–*m(êm)* shall circumcize the uncircumcision of desire and the stiff neck in the community' (D v 3–5).

These three mystical letters are of course drawn from the text of the passage itself, being the initial letters of the key-words indicating the purposes of the society; its members offer themselves 'for holiness to '(*ahărôn*) Aaron' to be a 'household of '(*ĕmet*) truth' (D v 6) in returning to the 'law of *m(ōšeh)* Moses' (D v 8). Thus the initial letters of these three words, two proper names and one common term, are the basis of the cipher (אמת); but in themselves they still make no sense and have no point. As Dr. Brownlee explains them,[5] however, they indicate who will circumcize the uncircumcized heart and this, as the Old Testament shows, is in the first instance God;[6] the words for which they will stand, then, on the principle of *nôṭārîqôn* will be '(*ădônāy*) '(*ĕlôhêhe*)*m* 'the Lord their God' or the like. At the same time this abbreviation appears to be unusual if not unique, and the circumcizer of the heart is not always God but is sometimes the people[7] (H xi 13); accordingly '(*ālef*)–' (*ālef*)-*m(êm)* may be read as standing also for '(*anše hā*)'(*ĕ*)*m(et)* 'the men of truth' as one of several designa-

---

[1] Driver *Semitic Writing*[2] 235; cp. *Textus* I 114–31 and IV 78–94.
[2] Mishnah *Aboth* iii 19 and *Uktzin* iii 13.
[3] Mishnah *Shebuoth* iv 13; Tosefta *Berakoth* vii 20.　　　[4] P. 176.
[5] In *Manual of Discipline* 49–50; *JQR*, NS XLV 155–6.　　　[6] Deut. xxx. 6.
[7] Cp. Deut. x. 16 and Jer. iv. 4.

tions of the members of the community (H vii 10, T [ii 14] xiv 2). Their real point, however, is to be hinting at '$(ab\check{s}\bar{a}l\hat{o}m)$ '$(el'\bar{a}z\bar{a}r)$ $m('nah\bar{e}m)$ 'Absalom, Eleazar (and) Menahem', the three leading members of the society listed in the reverse order of their importance. These are Menahem the Rightful Teacher, Eleazar son of Jair his kinsman and successor and Absalom his chief lieutenant, the leaders of the society whose duty it would be to see that the people's hearts were duly circumcized.

In another passage, in the poem on the year at the end of the same work, the author says: 'during the ages which '$(\bar{a}lef)$ has prescribed . . ., when the luminaries shine from the holy zenith at the time when they are brought together into a mansion of glory at the entry (coming) of the fixed seasons into the days of the new moon, He (sc. God) renews their circuit (rotation) at the time of their conjunction with one another; when they renew themselves (are newly in conjunction), the M is great (significant) for all that is most holy and the sign/letter of N is for the unlocking of' or 'to serve as the key to His eternal acts of enduring love' (D x 1–4).

As Dr. Brownlee has observed,[2] the '$\bar{a}lef$ must here be an abbreviation of some term representing the subject of '(he) has prescribed'; this can only be '$(\bar{e}l)$ or '$(\check{e}l\hat{o}h\hat{i}m)$ 'God' or some similar word, as the reference to 'His eternal acts of enduring love' at the end of the passage shows.

Next, Prof. Bowman, whose translation has been followed, has the credit of finding the proper clue to the passage[3] by recognizing after Dr. Obermann[4] that it contains an attempt to harmonize the conceptions of a solar and a lunar year,[5] and he offers the following explanation of it, based on Samaritan sources; he justifies the assumption of such an origin for the passage by observing that the Samaritan priests claim that they, unlike the established post-exilic priesthood, are of true Zadokite lineage[6] as the Covenanters' priesthood claims to have been, and that the Samaritan Chronicle known as the *Tolidah* has affinities with *Jubilees*, from which the Covenanters are thought to have derived their solar calendar.

A partial eclipse of sun and moon occurs every month but is not normally visible, being known generally by calculation. However, a major conjunction, the so-called 'nodes' of the moon, takes place twice a year, in spring and autumn, when the orbit of the moon intersects the ecliptic of the sun. This conjunction is the basis of the Samaritan calculation for fixing the dates respectively of the 'assembly of Passover' ($\textit{\d{s}imm\hat{u}\underline{t} pesa\d{h}}$) on 15 Shebat, a feast celebrated 60 days before

---

[1] Cp. Bardtke *Handschriftenfunde* I 93.   [2] In *Discipline* 38.   [3] In *PQS.* XCI 23–37. [4] In *JBL.* LXXV 295.   [5] Cp. Ecclus. xliii. 2–10. [6] Cp. Gaster *Samaritans* 56–7. The Zadokite lineage of the Samaritan priesthood, however, is doubtful (s. p. 80).

the Passover proper (15 Nisan), and the 'assembly of Booths (ṣimmûṭ sukkôṯ) on 15 Ab; for the Samaritans reckon the full moons of Nisan and Tishri to fall 60 days respectively after the vernal and autumnal conjunction of the sun and the moon. That the Scrolls, like *Jubilees*,[1] suggest a division of the year into four quarters rather than two halves is no matter; for *I Enoch* similarly shows its division into two halves,[2] which must lie behind the Covenanters' calendar. Thus 'the entry (coming) of the fixed seasons to the days of the new moon' will correspond to the 'assembly of Passover', which is described as 'the opening (gate) to the days of the festive and joyous seasons, by which in all places the calculations for the beginning of months and feasts are determined'.[3] Accordingly *M* will be an abbreviated substitute for *m(ā'ôn)* 'mansion' or, as Prof. Bowman prefers, for *m(igdōl)* 'castle; constellation' (as often in Samaritan liturgical poems), *i.e.* the 'mansion' or constellation in which the conjunction takes place. This can happen only when sun and moon are in one 'mansion' or 'constellation'; and it was 'important for all that is most holy' because it was essential both for fixing the feasts, which concerned not only the Temple but also the priests, who were responsible for the calendar and the cult, and for the welfare of the community of the Covenanters, who were 'a society of all that is most holy', *i.e.* a most holy society (D viii 5–6). Here then there is a slight *double entente*, as so often in the Scrolls; for 'holy of holies' or 'all that is most holy' refers both to the sacrifices which are often so called in the Old Testament and to the community which is so described in the present work. In the following clause *N* may stand for *n(e'ĕsāf)* 'gathered, brought together' or for *n(e'ĕmān)* 'sure', as Ginsberg has suggested;[4] accordingly the clause may be translated 'and (it is) a sign brought together (grouped)' or 'and (it is) a sure sign for the opening of' or 'for a key to His eternal acts of enduring love'. Here probably *mā'ôn* 'mansion', and *n(e'ĕsāf)* 'grouped together' are the true keys to the cryptogram (*M* and *N*), since both words occur already in the passage (D x 3); in the same way all three abbreviations in the previous passage find an explanation from the passage itself. This possibility is essential in the primary but not in the second or subsequent interpretations; for otherwise the reader is left entirely without a clue and will be unable even to begin to solve the riddle.

Two or three small points remain to be noticed. The Hebrew word for the 'unlocking' of or the 'key' to God's acts of enduring love is derived from the same root as the Samaritan word for the 'opening' or 'gate' of the festive and joyous seasons; and the Hebrew noun for 'new moon' and the verb in 'when they renew themselves' are

---

[1] Pp. 325–6.   [2] I Enoch lxxii 3.
[3] Cowley *Samaritan Liturgies* I 436, 39b.
[4] In Brownlee *op. cit.* 51.

cognate with the Samaritan word for 'new moon; conjunction'. Also
the proper Hebrew term for the moon's renewing of itself (*hiṯḥaddēš*) is
avoided and an ambiguous word is used; this may be read according
to the vocalization either 'he renews' (*yāḥēd*) or 'he unites' (*yaḥēd*)
with, as it happens, little difference to the sense in the present context;
the latter is the ordinary verb for 'united' (Hebrew *yiḥēd* = Aramaic
yaḥēd), while the latter is a rare word for 'renewed' (Samaritan
ḥaddēd = Arabic *ḥaddada*). The *double entente*, however, has the
advantage that the author, while appearing to use a correct Hebrew
form, seems to be hinting at a Samaritan custom which accords with
that of his own party.

Convincing, however, as this interpretation may be, it is not the
whole answer to the riddle; and much information can still be extracted from the passage.

Accordingly, although the '*(ālef)* can be attached to '(he) has
prescribed' and, as argued above, indicate God as its subject, it may
also be read in combination with *m(êm)* and *N* as forming a cipher;
thus taken together, these three letters may be read as a
cryptic indication of '*āmēn* 'amen', which is an ancient divine appellation[2] and a familiar liturgical term (cp. D i 20, ii 10, 18). This term
may then be taken as standing *extra constructionem*, as it sometimes does
elsewhere[3] (although of itself it makes no sense in the context), since
according to the device of *gîmāṭr'yâ* it has the value of $1+40+50 =$
91;[4] this is the numerical value of the letters in *YHWH 'DNY* (namely
$10+5+6+5 = 26$ and $1+4+50+10 = 65$, making 91 when added
together[5]) *i.e.* 'Lord Jehovah' and in *H* (= *YHWH*) *'LHYM* (namely
5 and $1+30+5+10+40 = 86$, making 91 when added together)
i.e. 'Lord God'.[5] It will thus provide the name of God as an alternative form of the subject for '(he) has prescribed' and give the number
of the days in every quarter of the year in the solar calendar of *Jubilees*,
where they are given as $90+1 = 91$,[6] which multiplied by 4 yields
364, *i.e.* a solar year of 364 days.[7] Briefly both *nôṭārîqôn* and *gîmāṭr'yâ*
according to these explanations yield the same result.

Alternatively, if '*(ālef)* is disregarded as merely indicating God as
the subject of '(he) has prescribed' and *M* and *N* are taken alone,
they can be explained as abbreviations of *mê nōaḥ* 'waters of Noah',
as the Deluge is sometimes called;[8] or, read as numbers, they stand
respectively for 40 and 50, to which again *Jubilees* offers a ready key.
Its author (following the story of the Deluge) says that it lasted 40 days
and nights and that, when its waters subsided, God gave what *Genesis*

---

[1] *E.g.* Ecclus. xliii. 8.   [2] Isa. lxv. 16; cp. 2 Cor. i. 20.
[3] P. 347.   [4] Pp. 347-8.
[5] Cp. Hurwitz *Mahzor Vitry* 97 § 126.
[6] Cp. Finegan *Light from the Ancient Past* 586-7.
[7] Jubilees vi 38 (s. pp. 369-73).   [8] Isa. liv. 9.

calls a 'sign' (which is expressed by the same Hebrew word as in the passage just quoted from *Discipline*) to Noah and his sons as 'a covenant for ever' that there should never again be a flood on the earth and that 'for this reason it is written and ordained on heavenly tablets that they shall celebrate the Feast of Weeks once a year in this month, to renew the covenant every year';[1] this Feast (otherwise called by the Greek name of Pentecost)[2] was held on the 50th day after the Passover. Not only does the author of *Jubilees* thus connect the institution of this Feast with the 'waters of Noah', but also alQirqîsânî in his account of the Sadducaean party expressly says[3] that their reckoning of the month at thirty days was derived from 'the story of Noah', thus once again connecting the Sadducaeans with the Covenanters.[4] On these interpretations the cipher is seen to connect the calendar of *Jubilees* doubly with that of the Covenanters.

Alternatively again, these two letters may be taken as abbreviations of *m(ā'ôr)* 'luminary' and *n(îsān)* 'Nisan', the name of the first month of the year; the line may then be translated 'when they renew themselves, the great luminary *(mā'ôr)* for the holy of holies and the sign of N(isan) for the revelation of His *(sc.* God's) unfailing acts of love', even if the grammar is slightly strained, though not beyond contemporary usage.[5] As thus interpreted, the passage alludes to the Covenanters' preference for a solar to a lunar and for a sacred or ecclesiastical to a civil or secular calendar. That the solar year is meant is clearly shown by the mention of the 'great luminary'[6] which is known to designate the sun (cp. T xii 5);[7] for all the emphasis here falls on it, while only a subordinate position is assigned to the moon, inasmuch as 'he *(sc.* the sun) will be at the beginning of the seasons in every epoch, at the beginning of moons with their seasons and holy days in their ordered sequence' (D x 5). Here again the 'holy of holies' may be the 'days of holiness' or holy days, *i.e.* fixed feasts, or the holy community. Contrariwise, Jesus grandson of Sirach (apparently a Sadducee whose book has been revised in the interests of a dominant Pharisaism), although he begins by praising the sun, equally clearly reflects a lunar year: for, writing *c.* 190 B.C., he says that 'the moon also is in all things for her season, for a declaration of times and a sign of the world; from the moon is the sign of the feast-day'[8] (cp. D i 14–15), whereas the unknown author of the scientific section of *I Enoch*, writing not long before 110 B.C. (although he tries to reconcile

---

[1] Jubilees v 25–7, vi 15–18, 24; cp. Gen. vii. 4, 12, 17, ix. 12–17.
[2] Tobit ii. 1.
[3] In *Kitab al-Anwār wal-Marāqib* I [vi 18; cp. Yafet ben 'Ali on Genesis i 14 (s. Poznańsky in *RÉJ* XLIV 171–8).
[4] Pp. 259–66.
[5] Cp. Segal *Mishnaic Hebrew Grammar* 183 § 377 and 192–3 § 390 (see D iv 13, 15).
[6] Brownlee *Discipline* 39.   [7] Gen. i. 16; cp. I Enoch lxxii 2.
[8] Ecclus. xliii. 6–7.

the two systems) asserts emphatically that 'the sun and the stars bring in all the years exactly, so that they do not advance or delay their position (cp. D i 14–15) by a single day but complete the years with perfect justice in 364 days'.[1]

The mention of Nisan has a similar import, being the first month of the sacred year, that in which God brought Israel out of Egypt by a signal mark of His 'unfailing love';[2] hence it can be described as appointed 'for the revelation' or 'opening' (*i.e.* beginning) of His acts of unfailing love', such as He had shown to the ancestors of the race (Abraham, Jacob, Moses, David) and had only withdrawn because of its apostasy but which He might be expected to renew in favour of those who repented and joined the society of the Covenanters. Like the compiler of *Discipline*, the author of the same section of *Enoch* says that 'first there goes forth the great luminary, that is the sun; . . . In this way he rises in the first month in the great gate (*i.e.* zodiacal sign), which is the fourth gate';[3] here again the 'great luminary' and Nisan are brought together. Further, Josephus speaks[4] of two New Year's Days, one in Nisan 'as to all the solemnities which they (*sc.* the ancient Hebrews) observed to the honour of God' and another in Tishri 'as to selling and buying and other ordinary affairs', while the Mishnah speaks of four New Year's Days, including Nisan (March-April) as that 'for (Israelite) kings and feasts' and Tishri (September-October) as that 'for the years (*sc.* of foreign kings)'.[5] Both clearly refer respectively to an old Israelite sacred and a foreign secular calendar, the former that in which the annual cycle of feasts beginning with Passover commenced on 1 Nisan in the spring and the latter that in which the civil year commenced on 1 Tishri in the autumn.[6]

The Jews seem to have adopted the civil year towards the end of the exile.[7] The old sacred year however survived into or was revived in the Maccabaean period, presumably as a protest against the use of a secular year, which would have been disliked as foreign and heathen;[8] for Asia Minor and northern Syria mostly (Damascus and the Arabs excepted; for their year began in spring) had calendars in which the New Year fell in the autumn.[9] This passage then, as here explained, harks back to the Maccabaean age as exhibiting what the Covenanters can but have regarded as the ideal practice, extolling the old sacred solar calendar in protest against Pharisaic acceptance of the new Hellenistic, lunisolar, civil calendar as the toleration of a heathen custom; at the same time it brings the calendar of *I Enoch* into connection with that of the Covenanters.

[1] I Enoch lxxiv 12; cp. Jubilees ii 9, iv 21. [2] Exod. xv. 13.
[3] I Enoch lxx ii 4–6. [4] In *Antiquities* I iii 3 § 81.
[5] In *Rosh ha-Shanah* i 1. [6] Cp. Schürer *Geschichte*[3] II 48.
[7] Schiaparelli & Benecke *Astronomy in the Old Testament* 119–20.
[8] Schürer *op. cit.* I 33–7. [9] Ideler *Chronologie* I 393–476.

Z

Accordingly, the primary purpose of the author of the hymn at the end of *Discipline* is to show that the old sacred calendar used by the Covenanters is an ordinance of God; for what he describes in it are called 'the periods (of time) which '*ālef* (namely God) has prescribed' (D x 1). He starts with 'the beginning of the dominion of light' and goes on to the moment 'when it (*sc.* darkness) is withdrawn before' or 'by reason of light' (D x 1–2), proceeding from morning to morning; he thus shows that the day is reckoned from morning to evening, not from evening to morning.[1] Next, he tells of 'the shining of luminaries (*i.e.* sun and moon) from the holy zenith'[2] and how 'He (*sc.* God) unites (*yaḥēd*)' or 'renews (*yāḥēd*) their circuit(s) when they are gathered into a mansion of glory at the time of their junction with one another' (D x 3–4); here he refers to the nodes of the moon, thus hinting at a reconciliation of solar and lunar years.[3] He goes on to bring these (*sc.* sun and moon) 'when they renew themselves' into connection with *M* and *N*, namely with 40 and 50, thus showing that he is thinking of a solar year of *c.* 360 (not a lunar year of 354) days;[4] and he connects 'the beginning of the months with their fixed feasts' and the 'holy days in their ordered sequence' (D x 5) with this year, showing that these feasts depend on the sun, as in the old sacred calendar.[5] He then describes the seasons of the year, joining reaping to the fruits of summer and sowing to green herbs (D x 7); since reaping of barley begins in the plains in Palestine in April[6] and sowing is done there as everywhere in the autumn, he is making the year begin in the spring, again as in the sacred calendar, and not in the autumn as in the secular calendar.[7] Lastly, he joins 'the seasons of years to their weeks (of years)' and 'the beginnings of their weeks to a season of release' (D x 7–8), clearly alluding to the old 'sabbatical year' and the 'year of release' which the compiler of the Priestly Code in the Old Testament includes in his sacred calendar[8] and which the author of *Jubilees* re-enacts.[9]

Further, as Dr. Brownlee argues,[10] the acrostic '*āmēn* has a secondary Messianic import. First, the initial '*ālef* indicates God as 'one' (*'aḥad*), the first as well as the last;[11] so the Rabbis say 'God is one (*'aḥad*) and His name is one (*'aḥad*)'.[12] Then *M* for '40' may be taken as referring to the 40 years between the death of the Rightful Teacher and the coming of the Messiah,[13] the 40 years of the Messianic war[14] and

---

[1] Pp. 326–8.
[2] Cp. Hab. iii. 11.
[3] Pp. 337–8.
[4] Pp. 322–6.
[5] Jubilees ii 9; cp. vi. 36–7.
[6] Paterson in Hastings' *DB* I 49–50.
[7] Pp. 326, 341.
[8] Lev. xxv. 2–7 (Sabbatical year), 8–55 (year of release).
[9] Jubilees l 3–4.
[10] In *NTS* III 22–3, 199–203.
[11] Cp. Isa. xli. 4, xliv. 6, xlviii. 12 and Rev. i. 8, 11.
[12] Buxtorf & Fischer *Lexicon Chaldaicum Talmudicum et Rabbinicum* 133.
[13] Pp. 475–7
[14] Pp. 224–5

generally to the 40 years of the Messianic period;[1] and N for '50' may equally well refer to the jubilee after 49 years,[2] *i.e.* in the 50th year,[3] with its typological significance for the Messianic age.[4] Second, the initial *'ālef* may still stand for *'(ēl)* 'God'; but M may be the abbreviation not only of *m(āšiaḥ)* 'Messiah' but also *m(ā'ôr)* 'luminary' as a title of the high-priest, and N may stand for the *n(ēzer)* 'crown' worn by him. This interpretation is supported by a passage in a fragmentary Scroll called the *Benediction of the Priests* to the effect that 'He *(sc.* God) will make thee *(sc.* the priest) holy among His people and to be a [great] luminary *(mā'ôr)* [for a light to] the world by knowledge[5] and to illumine the countenances of many [by understanding of life; and He will make thee] a crown *(nēzer)* for the Holy of Holies' (I Q *28* B, 3 iv 27–8; cp. T vii 25, ix 26–7). The Messianic allusion is clear;[6] for the same theme is applied by the apocalyptists to the priestly Messiah,[7] and Jesus takes it up and applies it to His followers in the world.[8]

In the third place, here as in the case of the previous cipher, no obvious reason for the adoption of a cryptogram to indicate the old sacred calendar by the Covenanters suggests itself; it can neither have embroiled them with the Jewish authorities (except for the possibility of a clash on feast-days) and it certainly cannot have imperilled them with the Romans. An ulterior purpose may therefore be suspected: this is that it too conceals the names of members of the society's leading family. So *'ālef* may be taken as the initial letter of *'(el'āzār)* and $M \ldots N$ as those of *m(e)n(aḥēm)*, namely Menahem and Eleazar; these two were the sole surviving members of the famous family of anti-Roman rebels sprung from Hezekiah and Judah, and the publication of their names in view of their known Messianic claims would assuredly have put them in danger of Roman vengeance. The use of the first letter of a name as an abbreviation is common enough; and that of the first two letters is no matter of surprise, being found elsewhere in the Scrolls (Z xix 1).[9]

This explanation of the cipher to indicate the names of Menahem and his nephew and successor Eleazar as concealed in a hymn on the rotation of the seasons can now be seen to connect Menahem with the Rightful Teacher. As his father Judah may have been,[10] so Menahem is called a σοφιστής or 'teacher of wisdom', as the Greek word may be translated; in the form, however, of the Hebrew and Aramaic *sôfistôs* or *sôfisṭâ* it means 'mathematician', such as one who is concerned with

---

[1] Pp. 471–5.
[2] Lev. xxv. 8–12.
[3] Cp. Charles *Book of Jubilees* lxvii–lxviii (§ 18).
[4] Cp. Isa. lxi. 1–6.
[5] Cp. Isa. xi. 2.
[6] Cp. Barthélemy & Milik *Discoveries* I 12 (where parallel passages are cited).
[7] *E.g.* Testaments *Levi* iii 3, xviii 3, 9.
[8] Matt. v. 14–16.
[9] Pp. 336–7.
[10] Cp. Thackeray *Josephus* II 492[2].

the calendar must be;[1] the initial letters of Menahem's name are worked into a poem intended to prescribe what calendar the group must observe; and the Rightful Teacher is head of a group whose members have promised 'not to advance their seasons nor to fall behind with any of their fixed feasts' (D i 14–15),[2] which must be celebrated in accordance with this very calendar as that 'which *'ālef* has prescribed' for the group's observance (D x 1–8). The wheel comes full circle.

A curious echo of this cipher is found in the Scroll of *Isaiah A*, where the prophet's 'thus saith the Lord, the Holy One of Israel and his Maker: ask me of the things that are to come (*'ôtîyôt*)' has been altered (apparently deliberately) to 'thus saith the Lord, the Holy One of Israel, the Maker of the signs (*'ôtôt*): ask me' (Is. A xxxviii 7),[3] in allusion to the 'sign (*'ôt*) of *N*', which is the last letter in 'amen' (*'āmēn*), the cipher indicating the number (91) of the days in any one quarter of the solar year. This allusion also gives point to the apostle Paul's 'even so we, when we were children, were in bondage under the elements of the world';[4] for 'the elements' or rather 'rudiments (*στοιχεῖα*) of the world' are the 'letters' used as ciphers with cosmological significance as indicating the calendar which had regulated the seasons of the Christian's life under the old dispensation and still regulated that of the Covenanters.[5]

Certain objections to the interpretations of these mysterious letters, here put forward, must now be met.

First, Prof. Dupont-Sommer argues[6] that 'which *'ālef* has prescribed' (D x 1) is an impossible translation, as the sign for *'ālef* is run together with the verb and not separated from it by the usual space dividing words. The objection has little if any force. That it is so written may be intentional, a device to heighten the mystery; or it may be accidental, as elsewhere the first letter of a word is joined to the previous word by a copyist's slip (*e.g.* D vi 13).

Second, Dr. Wernberg-Møller argues[7] that not *M* (the sign of the letter) but *mêm* (the name of the letter) would be expected; but examples of such usage are known.[8] That the final, not the initial (or medial), form of *M* is here employed is nothing surprising. The use of a final letter as an abbreviation is not absolutely excluded[9], but a possible reason for it is that it is a scribal error; for there are instances of medial for final (D x 14, T xii 4, 6, 8) as of final for medial (D x 14, T ii 22) forms in the Scrolls. That the *N* is an initial form and is

---

[1] P. 252.   [2] P 324.
[3] Isa. xlv. 11.   [4] Gal. iv. 8.
[5] Barthélemy *ap.* Brownlee in *JQR*, NS XLIII [1952–3] 198–200 and Brownlee in *NTS* III [1957] 206–7.
[6] In *VT* II 234.   [7] In *Discipline* 143.   [8] Pp. 336–7.
[9] Cp. Levias in *Jew. Encyclop.* I 40(4).

followed by a space is no proof that the rest of the word has been accidentally left out, as Dr. Zeitlin supposes,[1] since abbreviations are normally so treated; and the writer, if he had accidentally failed to finish the word, would surely either have run on without a gap or have inserted the missing letters above the line, so that the space or gap would seem to have been intentional. Dr. Wernberg-Møller also objects[2] that 'the *mêm*' ought to be treated not as a masculine but as a feminine word; but the objection rests on a misunderstanding of Hebrew usage. The rule is that the letter is treated as feminine *quâ* name but can or may otherwise be treated as masculine; so, for example, Rabbinic writers say "*ālef* complained to God that *bêt* was preferred to it', using a feminine form of the verb, but 'one *'ālef-bêt*' with a masculine form of the number in the sense of 'one acrostic chapter' (*sc.* of *Lamentations*).[3]

The interpretation here proposed, therefore, conforms to Hebrew usage and avoids both a false concord (involved in supposing *hm* to be a plural pronoun)[4] and the introduction of the Pythagorean doctrine of fifty as a sacred number;[5] this is not only out of place in so intensely Jewish a document, although Philo refers to it,[6] but also leaves $M = 40$ without explanation.[7]

These two ciphers, the one quadruple and the other octuple, may then be accepted as supplying three pieces of information (the subjects of the clauses in which they stand, the aims of the Covenanters or their calendar as the case may be, and the names of the party's presumably contemporary leaders); they do so with scarcely any violation of Hebrew usage, and they convey information which fits perfectly into the picture here drawn. That all this is mere matter of chance is inconceivable; and, if it is conceivable, it carries conviction with it, inasmuch as another series of multiple interpretations is in the highest degree improbable.

This method of indicating the name of the Rightful Teacher in *Discipline* is backed by another, equally cryptic, in the *Commentary on Habakkuk*, which describes the 'swallowing up' of the Teacher 'at the season of the fixed feast of the rest of the Day of Atonement' and 'on a fast-day, the sabbath of their rest' (H xi 6–8). The description of the Day of Atonement as a 'fixed feast' and a 'fast' and as a 'sabbath' accords with its nature; it was a fast-day which recurred regularly on the same day of the year (10 Tishri) and a 'sabbath of sabbath-observance'[8] but it is never described as a day of 'rest' or 'repose', as it

---

[1] In *JQR*, NS XLIII 148–50 and XLIX 18–19. [2] *Ibid.* 143.
[3] Levy *Neuhebräisches u. Chaldäisches Wörterbuch* 1 89–90.
[4] Zeitlin *ibid.* XLIX 18.
[5] Dupont-Sommer *Nouveaux Aperçus* 152–4 and *Écrits Esséniens* 112.
[6] In *Contemplative Life* viii 65. [7] Cp. Driver in *JTS*, NS IX 96–7.
[8] Lev. xvi. 31, xxiii 32.

is here. What is the reason for this peculiar appellation? Mr. Del Medico[1] draws attention to the euphemistic use of 'rest' for 'death' in late Rabbinic literature[2] and suggests that the word is chosen here to describe this Day of Atonement as that of the death of Menahem and his followers. This explanation of the expression is not certain; but a *double entente* may lie behind it if 'repose, rest' (*mᵉnûḥāh*) may here be taken also as a play on words designed to recall 'Menahem' (*mᵉnaḥēm*), the name meaning 'comforter'[3] of the Teacher 'laid to rest'[4] on that day. This is not so far-fetched as it may seem; for, although the two Hebrew words have absolutely no philological connection, exactly the same play occurs in the story of Noah, on which the Covenanters' calendar is based; there the author of *Genesis*, explaining Noah's name, declares that 'he called his name Noah (*nōaḥ* = 'rest'), saying: This same shall comfort us (*yᵉnaḥămēnî*) for our work and the toil of our hands'.[5] That the explanation is unscientific is no matter;[6] Rabbinic exegesis pays no heed to the niceties of philology[7]

5. Contemporary Literary Devices

That such devices as those here assumed can be found throughout Hebrew literature is well known.[8] When therefore Dr. Zeitlin urges[9] that *nôṭārîqôn* and *gîmāṭrᵉyâ* are medieval practices which must not be invoked in interpreting the Scrolls unless these are accepted as medieval documents, the facts are against him. Both devices can be traced from the Exile, through the whole period of the Second Commonwealth; they reached their fullest development, if not their most extensive employment, in the 1st and 2nd centuries A.D. and continued into the Middle Ages.

Instances of conveying information by means of or deducing it from ciphers can be found in both Testaments. Examples already occur in the Old Testament: the number of Abraham's trained bands equals the sum of the numerical value of the letters in his steward Eliezer's name, and the number of the days, as given by the Septuagint, during which the prophet Ezekiel is bidden to lie on his left side is the sum of the number of the letters in the Hebrew words for 'days of siege';[10]

---

[1] In *Énigme* 356.
[2] Cp. Ps. xcv. 11 w. Jb. iii. 13, 17, which may have suggested this usage.
[3] Cp. Midrash R. *Lamentations* I xvi 51 (on Lamentations i 16).
[4] Cp. Isa. lvii. 2, Job iii. 17, Dan. xii. 13.
[5] Gen. v. 29; cp. Midrash R. *Genesis* xxv. 2.
[6] Cp. Goldschmidt *Sēfer hayyāšār* 14.
[7] Cp. Brownlee in *BA* XIV 60–76 and Driver in *JTS*, *NS*. IX 97–8.
[8] Cp. Marcus in *JNES* VI 109–15.
[9] In *JQR*, NS XLIII 191–2 and XLIII 147–8.
[10] Gen. xiv. 14 and Ezek. iv. 4–8.

and the names of Nebuchadnezzar and Antiochus Epiphanes have the same numerical value (423) when written in Hebrew letters.[1]

The system must certainly have been fully developed by the end of the 1st century A.D.; for the New Testament contains several instances. For example, the author of the *Gospel according to St. Matthew* divides the genealogy of Jesus into 3 groups each containing 14 names;[2] these are based on the sum of the values of the letters in the name of David ($d = 4 + w = 6 + d = 4$).[3] So, too, the author of the Greek *Apocalypse* cryptically reveals the name of the beast by giving the numerical value of the Hebrew letters making up the emperor's name, whether 616 or 666;[4] for it comes out as Nero, according to the spelling, whichever reading is adopted.[5] The same writer begins by declaring that his message is 'from him which is and which was and which is to come . . . and from Jesus Christ who is the faithful witness, the firstborn of the dead . . . ; to him be glory and dominion for ever and ever. Amen. Behold! he cometh with clouds . . . Even so, Amen. I am Alpha and Omega, saith the Lord God, . . . the Almighty'; and he goes on to tell how he saw 'seven golden candlesticks and in the midst of the seven golden candlesticks one like unto a son of man . . .', who said to him 'I was dead and behold, am alive for evermore, Amen, and have the keys of death and hell'.[6] The writer begins and ends with 'amen', which is to all intents and purposes otiose; but he immediately plays on this word when speaking of the 'faithful witness', so that the reader at once suspects something cryptic.[7] If then the passage is clothed in Hebrew words, the three letters making up 'amen' (namely *'ālef*, *mêm* and *nûn*) become insistent: the first is the initial letter of 'I (*'ănî*)', of 'Alpha (*'ālef*)' and of 'last (*'aḥărôn*)'; the second is that of 'Christ (*māšîaḥ*)', of 'candlesticks (*m⁽nôrôṯ*)' and 'angels (*mal'ăḵîm*)', of 'keys (*mafṯēḥôṯ*)' and 'dead (*mēṯ*)' and of 'death (*māweṯ*)'; and the third is that of 'faithful (*ne'ĕmān*)'.[8] Finally 'amen' serves as a substitute for the speaker's name in 'these things saith the AMEN';[9] for the Hebrew letters for *'āmēn* have the same value as those for certain names of God.[10] This cipher, then, as based both on the initial letters of the keywords and on their numerical value and as arranged in such a way that the words beginning with those letters are distributed amongst the various clauses, recalls that in *Discipline*; thus each illustrates the other.

The more or less contemporary Judaeo-Christian *Sibylline Oracles*

---

[1] Cornill *Daniels Siebzigwochen* 31; cp. Dan. i. 1 (where the spelling of Nebuchadnezzar, being unique in this book, is obviously designed to yield the desired number).
[2] Matt. i. 17.   [3] Gfrörer *Heilige Sage* I 9.
[4] Rev. xiii. 18 (*Nrw Qsr* = 616, *Nrwn Qsr* = 666).
[5] Cp. Lehmann in *Stud. Patr.* IV 133–4.
[6] Rev. i. 4–18.   [7] Jaubert in *VT* III 257.
[8] Cp. Isa. xlix. 7.   [9] Rev. iii. 14; cp. Gal. iv. 3–11.
[10] P. 339.

have a somewhat different device. They indicate the Roman emperors by the numerical values of the initial letters of their names according to the Greek enumeration.[1] So too the Christian father Irenaeus (c. A.D. 130–200) plays with the initial letters and the numerical value of letters, including those of 'amen';[2] and the Rabbis often resort to the practice to convey secret information.[3]

These fanciful but mysterious methods of playing with letters and numbers gratified their authors' desire to indulge an innate ingenuity and to create a sense of mystery; but they were used also as a means of preserving or conveying information in times of mortal peril. Indeed, the Mishnah refers explicitly to marking hidden treasure with only initial letters to conceal its nature 'in the times of danger'.[4] Writers, however, had little or nothing to fear under the Seleucid kings, except during fitful and brief periods of acute persecution, or under Republican Rome. Contrariwise, persecution and oppression were ever-present dangers under Herod the Great and the early Roman emperors; and these were just the years when the Covenanters were active. During this century, when they were in constant opposition to Rome through their refusal to pay taxes and to tolerate the dominion of any other ruler but God, a series of their leaders from a single family lost their lives in the cause of freedom.[5] Herod's cruelty had been only too well known[6] (if only because he had had Hezekiah executed),[7] but Rome was equally terrible if not so unpredictable. The claim of Jesus to be the expected Messiah was kept secret for this reason and not revealed till relatively late in His ministry. Again, as the tension increased and the First Revolt became imminent, prominent people like Menahem and his relative Eleazar would be in constant danger, not only because of their revolutionary activities but in consequence of their royal and Messianic claims; for the names of Menahem's grandfather Hezekiah and father Judah would inevitably connect them with the Jewish royal family, especially as the Romans were well aware that the Jews expected one of their own race to rise up and become ruler of the whole world.[8] The Covenanters, too, sharing this hope, refer explicitly to the 'dominion of Israel over all flesh' (W xvii 7–8). The Roman authorities, therefore, would have watched their movements carefully and would not have been slow to strike down any member of their family who might give them the least cause for taking action. That this was a real danger became apparent soon afterwards, at the very

---

[1] Geffchen *Oracula Sibyllina* 105 v 36–44 (Vespasian represented by 'seventy', Titus and Trajan by 'three hundred', Domitian by 'four', Nerva by 'fifty').

[2] Harvey *S. Irenaei Libri quinque adversos Haereses* I 127–64.

[3] *E.g.* Midrash R. *Genesis* i 13 xii 9; B. Talmud *Shabbath* 103b–104a.

[4] Mishnah *Maaser Sheni* iv 11.   [5] Pp. 239–41.

[6] *E.g.* Matt. xvi. 16–17; Josephus *Antiquities* XVII vi 4 § 167 and *War* I xxiii 4 §§ 654–5.

[7] Josephus *War* I x 5 § 204.   [8] Cp. p. 274.

time when the *Apocalypse* was being written, whether under Nero or under Domitian, when too persecution was rife; for both Vespasian and Domitian made attempts to have all who claimed descent from David sought out and put to death[1] in order that the whole Jewish royal family might be eliminated as a possible focus of rebellion. The authors of the Scrolls, therefore, had as good reasons as the author of the *Apocalypse* to employ ciphers and cryptograms to conceal their meaning; for the policies of a Nero or a Domitian made caution and secrecy a matter of life or death.

A hint that *Discipline* may actually have been composed at such a time may be discovered in a passage where again the author has attempted to conceal the sense, though for a different purpose. In condemning a member of the society who blasphemed the name of God, he says that such a person shall be put out of the community 'if he curses either through being frightened in consequence of distress or for any (other) reason that he has' (D viii 1); here the Hebrew text is barely grammatical and hard to understand, especially as 'he curses' has no object. Clearly 'either through being frightened in consequence of distress (*'ōw lᵉhibbā'ēṭ miṣṣārāh*)' is a deliberate re-arrangement of an original 'God in time of distress (*'ĕlôhîm bᵉ'ēṭ ṣārāh*)' to avoid introducing the name of God in a derogatory sentence;[2] the clause as thus corrected will run 'if he curses God in time of distress (*sc.* persecution) or for any (other) reason that he has'. This means of concealing the divine name in such a context is found also in the Massoretic text of the Old Testament;[3] and the threat recalls what Josephus says[4] of the Essenes and St. Paul's confession that 'I punished them oft in every synagogue and compelled them to blaspheme'.[5] Here the 'time of distress' refers to fear of persecution, which can never have been far off in Roman Palestine during the 1st century A.D.; and this incidentally confirms a date in that century for this Scroll, inasmuch as religious persecution was quite unknown in the Republican age and was only introduced into Rome when the worship of the emperors was threatened by other religions.

Such fantastic methods of conveying esoteric information naturally do not commend themselves to modern readers, but they are known Jewish devices; such riddles can only be unravelled by reversing the methods by which they have been constructed, and the information so obtained may be regarded as genuine. In these speculations, however far-fetched they and the explanations here offered may appear to be, the Covenanters must be regarded as but the forerunners of medieval Rabbis in their ghettos and monks in their monasteries, whiling away

---

[1] Eusebius *Historia Ecclesiastica* iii 12, 19.
[2] Cp. Wernberg-Møller *Discipline* 112–13.   [3] 1 Sam. iii. 13.
[4] In *War* II viii 10 §§ 152–3.   [5] Acts xxvi. 11.

their time devoting a sadly misplaced ingenuity and subtilty to spinning the cobwebs of theology.

6. SCROLL OF FASTS AND ROLL OF HONOUR

Attention may here be drawn to the document called the *Scroll of Fasts*, since it is an indirect witness to the importance attached to Menahem after his death.

This curious document, written in the Aramaic language in the last half of the 1st or the first half of the 2nd century A.D.,[1] so far from prescribing a number of fast-days, as its title implies, gives a list of days 'on which one may not fast and on some of which one may not beat the breast', *i.e.* indulge in public lamentation. These days are days of national victory and the like, given in the *Roll* in the historical order of their occurrence; here they are presented in the order of the calendar in accordance with Dr. Zeitlin's arrangement and interpretation.[2]

The list starts with three days in the pre-Hasmonaean period. The first is that on which the 'continual offering' was established; this seems to be the holiday instituted on the return from the Babylonian captivity in the memory of the dedication of the Second Temple in 516 B.C. The second cannot be identified. The third is that on which the wall of Jerusalem was dedicated, presumably on some occasion in the same period.

This list is followed by one recording sixteen days in the Hasmonaean or Maccabaean period. With three of these Judas Maccabaeus, with one his son Simon, and with three John Hyrcanus and his sons, are connected directly in a military capacity; the rest, so far as they can be identified, refer to celebrations arising out of various successes won against the Seleucid kings who then ruled Palestine.

Three dates are those of episodes in the Roman Imperial period before the outbreak of the great Revolt. The first is the occasion when Pilate was forced by the indignant populace to remove the effigies of the Roman emperor which he had brought into Jerusalem; the second refers to the annulment of the edict to set up Caligula's statue in the Temple on the report of his death in A.D. 41; the third refers to the rebuilding of the wall of Jerusalem which Agrippa I undertook but which Claudius forbade him to finish in A.D. 42–3.

The next period is that of the Revolt of A.D. 66–70 and is therefore of some interest for the present investigation. It contains ten public holidays, which cannot all be certainly identified but which must be fully set out with such explanations as are possible.

[1] Cp. Farmer *Maccabees Zealots and Josephus* 153, 157–8, 192–3.
[2] In *JQR*, *NS* X 237–43, 91–115.

Sivan 14: 'the tower of the fort was captured'. On this day the 'rebels', as Josephus called them,[1] mounted the porticoes connecting the fort, which was called Antonia, with the Temple and forced the main Roman garrison to evacuate Jerusalem; and Menahem may have taken part in this operation.[2]

Sivan 21 or 25: 'the tax-collectors were removed from Judah and Jerusalem'. When Florus withdrew his troops, the Jews withheld the tribute against Agrippa's advice.[3]

Ab 15: 'the day of fetching wood (for the altar)'. On 15 Ab, one of the days on which the community went out into the country to collect wood for the altar, the *sicarii* attacked the above-mentioned fort and after a two days' siege the garrison, consisting of a Roman detachment and a number of pro-Roman citizens, was massacred and the place itself was burnt down.[4] The event is probably mentioned because it was the first clash with Roman troops after the outbreak of the Revolt, though otherwise not significant.

Elul 17: 'the Romans evacuated Jerusalem'. On this day Menahem 'having become leader of the revolt' compelled the Romans, whom Agrippa had called into Jerusalem to restore order, to leave the city.[5]

Elul 22: 'they began to slay the wicked'. Menahem's followers then massacred any Roman stragglers whom they caught in the forts where they had taken refuge.[6]

Tishri 3: 'the appellations were removed from the documents'. Josephus records no such event; not improbably, however, so soon as the Roman troops had been expelled from the city, the insurgents would remove the name and titles of the reigning Emperor from public notices and substitute that of the high-priest, since this was a cherished privilege which the Maccabees had wrested from the Seleucid kings.

Kislev 9: 'there is a public holiday'. No reason for this holiday is known.

Tebet 28: 'the assembly sat in judgement'. When Cestius and his troops had been driven out of Jerusalem in the previous month, the 'brigands' (as Josephus here calls the Zealots) secured the adherence of Roman sympathizers in Jerusalem partly by persuasion and partly by force and, 'having met in the sacred precincts', appointed general officers (amongst whom the historian Josephus was included) to take command in various theatres of war against the Romans.[7]

Shebat 2: 'there is a holiday'. No reason for this holiday is known.

Adar 12: 'the day of *Ṭiriyôn*'. The most plausible explanation, perhaps, of this reference is that it celebrates the day on which the

---

[1] In *Life* v 21.
[2] Josephus *War* II xv 6 §§ 330–2.
[3] *Ibid.* xvi 5 § 404.
[4] *Ibid.* xvii 7 § 430.
[5] *Ibid.* 8 §§ 433–9.
[6] *Ibid.* § 440.
[7] *Ibid.* xx 3 § 562–4 § 568.

newly appointed commanders commenced the training of the *tirones* or recruits for the coming campaign; the reason for making it a feast-day was not so much this as that it probably represented a victory of the anti-Roman Zealots over the pro-Roman parties, who would only reluctantly take such measures. Indeed, Ananus the high-priest, who had planned to bring the Zealots round to a policy of moderation, immediately fell a victim to their violence.[1]

Adar 17: 'the Gentiles rose against the refugees of Sepphoris in the provinces of Chalcis and of Beth-Zabdai, but deliverance came to the Jews.' Sepphoris and other towns in Galilee were notoriously pro-Roman and, like Damascus, had expelled or massacred the local Jewish population on the arrival of Vespasian, fearing that they would follow the example of the Zealots and bring down the vengeance of the Romans on themselves; Josephus, therefore, on taking up his command in Galilee, tried but failed to reduce Sepphoris and 'the one refuge for the persecuted inhabitants was in the cities which he had fortified'.[2]

If the holidays in this last group are here connected with the proper events, they run from the summer of A.D. 65 to the spring of A.D. 67, when the list comes to an abrupt end. The calendar, then, is a record of successes against foreign rulers, reflecting the views of some group holding the rule of God alone and not that of any earthly power to be acceptable. It begins by giving a list of Maccabaean successes: such are the day on which Antiochus left Jerusalem, that of the victory of Judas over Nicanor, that on which the Greek decrees were annulled, that on which the tribute from Judah and Jerusalem was discontinued, that on which the Greek garrison evacuated the city, and so on. Each of these has its almost exact counterpart in the list of successes against Rome from the summer of A.D. 65. That it comes to an end with the spring of A.D. 67 suggests that the party from which it emanated had then suffered an eclipse. What was this party? The decisive factor in answering this question is that, as Judas Maccabaeus has more successes (namely three) credited to him than any other leader in the Seleucid wars, so Menahem has more than any others (namely two or perhaps three) credited to him in the war against Rome; in fact, he is almost the only leader who is known by name and can be identified, and it comes to an end almost immediately after his death, which occurred late in A.D. 66. The list is continued after his death only till a date early in A.D. 67, when the pro-Roman Sepphoris was giving trouble.[3] The reason for the inclusion of this event in the calendar was perhaps, as Dr. Roth suggests,[4] that Sepphoris and Beth-Zabdai lay astride the home-county of Judah the Galilaean or Gaulonite[5] on

---

[1] Josephus *War* xx 7 §§ 577–82 and xxii 1 §§ 647–51.   [2] *Ibid*. III iv 1 §§ 59–63.
[3] *Ibid*. II xviii 11 § 510, xxi 7 § 629 and 10 §§ 645–6.   [4] Pp. 239–41.
[5] In *Background* 26.

the way to Damascus, to which some of Menahem's followers, *i.e.* the Covenanters, may have escaped when Jerusalem fell and when Eleazar son of Jair escaped after the murder of his uncle to Masadah. Any action to keep open the roads to Damascus would earn the gratitude of the Covenanters; and Damascus spelled the end of the party of the Covenanters as a politically effective body.

Menahem would seem, then, to have been a person of considerable importance, who played no small part in events which his followers did not hesitate to compare with those of the Maccabaean revolt; in the same way the authors of the Scrolls, in writing of the events in which the Rightful Teacher was engaged, always had comparisons with that struggle at the backs of their minds.

That events of the Maccabaean wars and those of the Revolt are thus balanced in the *Scroll of Fasts*, the 'roll of honour' of the Zealots (who have been not inaptly called the neo-Maccabaean party)[1] or Covenanters, illustrates the methods of the authors of the Scrolls; and it is one which becomes well known long afterwards, when the principle that 'the deeds of fathers are a sign to sons' is a favourite one with the Jewish scholars. In the Scrolls a number of passages seem to be inexplicable except on the assumption of a *double entente* in which a reference to two events can be read, the one in the time of the Maccabees and the other in that of the Revolt; this schematization reflects the authors' desire to use past history as a justification of the Covenanters' present policy of resistance and as an earnest of future success. So Onias III, the proto-zealot and first martyr of the Maccabaean cause, foreshadows the murdered Rightful Teacher,[2] and the name of 'Zealot' becomes the symbol of the challenge to foreign customs[3] and is adopted by the party pledged to resist Roman authority to the very death;[4] and the Maccabaean 'zeal for the law'[5] is echoed in the Covenanters' 'zeal for rightful judgement' (D iv 4; cp. ix 23). Only two personal names are mentioned, those in the 'house of Judah' and the 'house of Absalom', obviously because they recall Maccabaean heroes of the same name, so that no danger can be directly caused by their mention to those who bear them.[6] The Maccabaeans were confronted by 'the king of the north' and the Covenanters by 'the kings of the north',[7] and the historic enemies surrounding the Maccabees are echoed in those who encircled the Covenanters.[8] The famous curved chopper with which the first blow was struck in the Maccabaean revolt reappears as the curved dagger of the Covenanters and the Zealots,[9] the pass-words of the former are echoed in the mottoes on the

[1] Hausrath *ap.* Farmer *op. cit.* 26.
[2] P. 226.
[3] Josephus *Antiquities* XII vi 2 § 271.
[4] Pp. 186–7.
[5] I Macc. ii. 58.
[6] P. 279.
[7] Pp. 218–20.
[8] Pp. 216–18.
[9] Pp. 186–7.

standards of the latter,[1] and their respective arrangements are in many respects comparable and indeed identical, notably in the organization of their armies[2] in Biblical fashion under commanders of thousands and hundreds, fifties and tens.[3] The Maccabaean warriors are 'volunteers for the law',[4] just as the Covenanters are 'volunteering to carry out all the statutes of God' (D i 7–8); and both alike are called 'God's people (*'am 'ēl*)' (W i 5 iii 13).[5] Antiochus IV had occupied Jerusalem (cp. ANa. ii 3–4) as Titus would do, Demetrius III Eucerus foreshadowed Vespasian in his advance on Jerusalem, which neither entered;[6] and on both the former occasions 'great men'[7] or other traitors[8] played the same part as the Seekers after Smooth Things did on the latter.[9] Further, the adoption of the sacred calendar in place of the civil calendar is reminiscent of the Maccabaean preference for the old as against the new calendar which the Pharisees observed; and even the use of proof-texts has been traced back to the Maccabaean age.[10]

As the age of the Maccabaean revolt was a 'time of trouble',[11] so was that of the final struggle against the Kittians or Romans representing the embattled powers of wickedness[12] in 'time of distress' (W i 11–12), coming 'at the end of the days' (H ii 5 ix 6);[13] and as the old Hasidaean or Maccabaean heroes 'whose leader is Judas Maccabaeus, keep up war and are seditious, not suffering the kingdom to find tranquillity',[14] so the Covenanters are depicted as maintaining a forty years' war against the enemies of their race and faith. As the Maccabaeans at the beginning of their revolt against their hellenizing Seleucid overlords refused to fight on the sabbath,[15] so the Covenanters would refrain from war in the 'year of release (W ii 8–9); as the Hasidaeans and Maccabees had sought to save their lives by hiding in caves in the wilderness,[16] so the Covenanters settled in the wilderness to save their souls (D viii 12–14); both Maccabaeans and Covenanters in prayer and exhortation before battle recalled past deliverances wrought by God (W xi 1–4, 9–12);[17] as the Maccabaeans received angelic assistance 'when the battle waxed strong',[18] so the Covenanters would in the last phase of their struggle with Rome be aided by 'the angels of His (*sc.* God's) dominion' (W i 14–15; cp. xii 4–9); and, as the Maccabaean Simon had wrested exemption from taxes from the

---

[1] Pp. 170–1. [2] Pp. 195–6.
[3] 1 Macc. iii. 57; cp. Josephus *Antiquities* XII vii 3 § 301.
[4] 1 Macc. ii. 42 (πᾶς ὁ ἑκουσιαζόμενος τῷ νόμῳ).
[5] 1 Macc. xiv. 28 (s. Yadin & Rabin *Scroll of the War* 44).
[6] P. 292. [7] Dan. ix. 27. [8] Pp. 247, 365.
[9] Pp. 93–4. [10] P. 527. [11] Dan. xii. 1.
[12] Pp. 202–3. [13] Dan. x. 14. [14] 2 Macc. xiv. 6.
[15] 1 Macc. ii. 32, 36, 38.
[16] 1 Macc. ii. 29, 31, 41, 2 Macc. v. 25.
[17] 1 Macc. iv. 8–11 vii. 40–42 2 and 2 Macc. xii. 15 xv. 22–24.
[18] 2 Macc. x. 29–30.

Seleucid kings,[1] so Judah the Galilaean had risen against the threat of taxation by the Roman authorities.[2]

In other words, the references to the Maccabaean age in the Scrolls are not primary but secondary; they do not describe an actual conflict or actual events but contain hints of the ideal course which the Covenanters as heirs and successors of the Maccabaeans must keep ever before their eyes.

Josephus seems in the same way to go out of his way to draw attention to parallel episodes in the Maccabaean revolt and in that against Rome by emphasizing similar details;[3] but the comparisons are never directly made, since they would not be likely to commend him or his work to the Romans, while the bare notice of the details would be sufficient to bring the point home to Jewish readers. The cause of both revolts was the love of 'liberty', for which the same word is used in reference to both events;[4] self-defence on the Sabbath in defiance of the strict letter of the Law is sanctioned in both cases;[5] the rebels in both were ready to die for the Law, for example the seven brothers who refused to eat swine's flesh in the Maccabaean revolt and the two Rabbis who were responsible for defying Rome by tearing down the golden eagle from the Temple,[6] and to commit suicide rather than fall into the hands of their enemies;[7] Simon Maccabaeus besieged Greeks and Jews in the citadel of Acra and starved them out as the insurgents and the *sicarii* besieged and massacred the Roman garrison with their Jewish supporters in the fort of Antonia on the outbreak of the revolt;[8] the humble petitions not to defile the Temple addressed to Heliodorus and to Petronius were both such as to move the 'pity' of those who heard them;[9] and both Antiochus and Titus, when they plundered the Temple, carried off the very same instruments of worship amongst the spoils which they took.[10]

This balancing, which can hardly be accidental,[11] of the events of the two revolts, that of the 2nd century B.C. and that of the 1st century A.D., against one another and implicitly if not explicitly comparing the details in them was evidently a commonplace of the historical writing and a part of the *mystique* of the period; the Covenan-

[1] 1 Macc. x. 29–35, xiii 3, 39; *Antiquities* XIII vi 7 § 213.
[2] Acts v. 37.   [3] Cp. Farmer *op. cit.* 47–158.
[4] Josephus *Antiquities* XII xi 2 §§ 433–4 and XVIII i 1 §§ 9–10.
[5] 1 Macc. ii. 40–1 and Josephus *Antiquities* XII vi 2 §§ 276–7; Josephus *War* II xix 2 §§ 517–18.
[6] 2 Macc. vii 1–40 (cp. 1 ii 50, 2 viii. 21); Josephus *Antiquities* XVII vi 3 §§ 158–9.
[7] 2 Macc. xiv. 37–46; Josephus *War* VII viii 6 §§ 324–6 and 7 § 385–9 § 397 (cp. *Antiquities* XIV xv 5 §§ 429–30 and *War* III vii 34 § 331, viii 7 §§ 387–91, VI v 7 §§ 387–91).
[8] 1 Macc. xiii. 49–50; Josephus *War* II xvii 7 § 430.
[9] 2 Macc. iii. 14–21; Josephus *War* II x 4 §§ 195–8.
[10] 1 Macc. i. 20–3; Josephus *War* VII v 5 §§ 148–51.
[11] Farmer *op. cit.* 82–3.

ters and the authors of the Scrolls, therefore, were in this respect as in others the children of their age. That could only be the 1st-2nd centuries A.D.

7. MENAHEM IN RABBINIC LITERATURE

The Revolt of A.D. 66–73 was due to several causes, some economic and others nationalistic, especially that the Roman *imperium* was an affront to the kingship of God and that it rendered void the Messianic hope; for the insurgents were inspired not merely by intolerance of any other lord or master than God[1] but also by the belief and hope, which Josephus mentions,[2] that 'at that time one from their country would become ruler of the world, whom they took to be a native of their own race'. This Messianic expectation was shared in some sense or other by most Jewish groups, including that from which the Scrolls emanated. This group expected two Messiahs called the 'Messiahs of Aaron and Israel' (D ix 22; cp. Z ix 29), namely a priestly and a lay or Davidic Messiah,[3] as the Midrash explains the prophet's 'two sons of oil'.[4] The Rightful Teacher is nowhere explicitly mentioned as the present or future holder of such an office, and the identification has been much disputed;[5] but parallel passages referring to a period of waiting 'till the appearance of one who shall teach righteousness at the end of the days' (Z viii 10) and 'till the appearance of the Messiah of Aaron and Israel' (Z ix 29) come near to indicating a time 'at the end of the days' in which the two offices, that of the Teacher and that of the Messiah, will be combined in a single person, whether the Teacher killed on the Day of Atonement or a successor. Passages in the Talmud and Midrash, which Mr. Del Medico cites,[6] go further in this matter; for a Messianic *aura* hangs about the person of Menahem in both.[7] These contain discussions concerning the Messiah, when he will come, what his name will be, and how long he will reign.[8] First, the Messiah seems to be described as the offspring of the patriarch Judah, he is said to have been born on the occasion of the destruction of Jerusalem and to have been called the 'comforter (*m'naḥēm*)'.[9] Second, in a scholastic dispute[10] one Rabbi gave his opinion, that the son of David, *i.e.* the Messiah, would not come 'until judges and magistrates

[1] Josephus *Antiquities* XVIII i 6 § 23 and *War* II x 1 §§ 184–5 and 4 §§ 195–7.
[2] *Ibid.* VI i 4 §§ 312–13; cp. Tacitus *Histories* v 13 and Suetonius *Vespasian* 4.
[3] Pp. 468–72.
[4] Zech. iv. 14; s. Midrash R. *Lamentations* I xvi 51.
[5] Cp. Rowley *Zadokite Fragments* 53[2].
[6] In *Deux Manuscrits* 138–9.   [7] Cp. Hengel *Zeloten* 299–302.
[8] Cp. Gressmann *Messias* 449–62 (s. Dalman *Aramäische Dialektproben* 14–15).
[9] Midrash R. *Genesis* lxxxv. 1 and *Lamentations* I xvi 51; cp. *Esther*, Prologue 11 § 5.
[10] B. Talmud *Sanhedrin* 98a–99b and p. Talmud *Berakhoth* ii 5; cp. Midrash R. *Lamentations* I xvi 51.

should disappear from Israel' (cp. Z ix 40), *i.e.* until the series of the Roman legates and procurators had come to an end. Third, what his name will be comes to be debated, and the pupils of the various Rabbis propose or play on their own teachers' names, which obviously reflect no tradition; they are merely attempts at currying favour. Then someone points out that 'there are those who say that his name is Menahem son (*i.e.* grandson)[1] of Hezekiah'. This alone of the names proposed is a historical name, and the addition of the grandfather's name argues an element of tradition behind it; and the Hezekiah here meant can only be Ezechias (Hezekiah), the brigand whose grandson bore that name. Fourth, the length of the Messiah's period is debated, and round figures are suggested such as 40 or 70 or 400 years; of these the first may contain a reference to the 40 years of the Scrolls,[2] if it is not merely one of the common round numbers of the Old Testament. Finally, Rabbî declares that the period will be 'three hundred and sixty-five years according to the number of the days of the sun', *i.e.* the solar year. Third, a late Midrash describes a person named Menahem who went forth with his 'pupils' clad in 'silk of gold', *i.e.* royal attire, to Jerusalem and was involved in a quarrel in which his 'brother Judah and an Eleazar were engaged on his side in an affray with one Hanan.[3] The story dimly reflects the outbreak of the Revolt. It shows that the memory of Menahem son (not brother) of Judah the Galilaean, who attired in royal state and supported by his relative Eleazar had disputed the leadership with another Eleazar son of the high-priest Hananiah,[4] must have lingered on; for the Hezekiah of this story cannot have been king Hezekiah (as the Rabbis supposed), if only because he had no known son of that name.

That the Rightful Teacher is also called a 'shoot (*ṣemaḥ*) of David' in two fragments of Scrolls (AFl.b i 3–4 and c i 11) may perhaps not be without significance in the present connection; for that expression, though based on a Biblical saying,[5] does not occur in this actual form in the Old Testament, where it is a rare Messianic title. As then Zechariah applied the noun alone to Zerubbabel as the expected restorer of the Davidic dynasty,[6] so the Covenanters coined this new expression to apply to their own Messiah whom they expected to restore the nation's fortunes; and in so doing they would surely have remembered what the Rabbis had noted, since the device of *gîmāṭryâ* was familiar to them,[7] that the numerical value of the letters in *ṣemaḥ* and *m'naḥēm* was the same (namely 138).[8] That they also taught that the Messiah so called came from Beth 'Arba', possibly the modern

---

[1] Cp. Brown-Driver-Briggs *Hebrew Lexicon* 120.   [2] Pp. 472–7.
[3] Schechter *Agadath Shir Hashirim* 46–7 viii 12; cp. B. Talmud *Hagigah* 16b.
[4] Pp. 267–81.   [5] Jer. xxiii. 5.
[6] Zech. iii. 8, vi. 12.   [7] Pp. 339–40, 342–3.
[8] P. Talmud *Berakoth* ii 5 and *Sanhedrin* 98b; Midrash R. *Lamentations* I 16 § 51.

AA

'Urtâs between Bethlehem and Qumrân,[1] is therefore not without its own significance. Describing their Teacher as a *ṣemaḥ* of David from Beth 'Arba' would therefore preserve the memory not only of his Davidic claims but also of his actual name and home.

All these several lines of argument converge on Menahem son of Judah son of Hezekiah and the Rightful Teacher as the future Messiah and thus identify them. The Scrolls throw out a cryptic hint that the Teacher, who is the leader of a party using a solar calendar, is named Menahem and perhaps imply that he or a successor bearing the same title will be the Messiah who will appear after 40 years. Josephus records that Manaemus, a 'teacher of wisdom', had a grandfather and father who were called respectively Ezechias and Judas and that he had royal pretensions. Correspondingly the Rabbis preserved dim memories of a Menahem who came from the neighbourhood of Qumrân, who claimed Davidic descent and was sprung from a Hezekiah and a Judah and who was regarded as the Messiah whose coming in 40 years was expected; he also belonged to a party which observed the solar year and had been involved in the Revolt which terminated in the destruction of Jerusalem. That on one account they made him son instead of grandson of Hezekiah and in another connected his birth and not his death with the Revolt would be matters of indifference to them; the use of 'son' for 'grandson' was not unknown even in the Scriptures, and the death of R. 'Aqîbâ and the birth of R. Judah were suitably if incorrectly brought together.[2] The Rabbis had little historical sense and were not writing history but inventing theology! If the two differences are discounted, these three persons can hardly be dissociated.

These coincidences, like many others to which attention has already been drawn, can hardly be accidental; and some weight may be given to both Talmud and Midrash which, even though they contain much that is purely fictitious, also embody a certain amount of genuine tradition.

[1] Cp. Yadin in *ILN* CCXXXIX [4.xi.1961] 775.
[2] P. 283; s. p. 357 n. 1.

VIII

HISTORY OF THE SCROLLS

1. Date of the Scrolls

The composition, copying and recopying, of the Scrolls must have been spread over a considerable period of time; their very number, whether only three hundred or even as many as four hundred or more,[1] makes this necessary. The considerable differences in the scripts of the various Scrolls, too, argue some development, even though this provides no scale by which the absolute dates of the individual documents can be established, if only because a sequence is not a chronology.[2] Some of the literature from the caves round Qumrân may go back to the very beginnings of the community, whether in Egypt before Pompey's conquest of Jerusalem or in Palestine soon after that event, when Judah son of Hezekiah and Sadduk or Saddok were forming their party,[3] but the bulk of it must belong to the early Christian or post-Christian age; for no evidence has been produced to show that the Covenanters as a body were extinguished with the destruction of the Temple in A.D. 70.[4]

Jewish religious refugees in Egypt or groups like the pseudo-monastic community at Qumrân could hardly have existed without copies of their sacred scriptures, in this case the Old Testament and a number of Jewish writings derived from it; and the work of copying the Scriptures would have been the earliest and principal task of the community's members, as of Christian monks, throughout its existence. Nothing is known of the archetypes from which the Biblical Scrolls are derived. They may have been obtained from the Temple, as Dr. Rengstorf has suggested;[5] but official texts must have been far too precious to have been extensively lent out to copyists; and they would not be likely to have been lent to dissident bodies settled away from Jerusalem. The variations in the orthography, e.g. between the texts of the two parts of *Isaiah A* and between these and that of *Isaiah B*,[6] also tell against the supposition that the Covenanters can have had access to official copies or have used single copies of individual works representing any unified trad-

---

[1] Pp. 16, 18–19, 21–2. [2] P. 415.
[3] Pp. 240–1. [4] Cp. De Vaux in *RB*, *NS* LI 229–36.
[5] In *Allgemeine jüdische Zeitschrift* XV iii [1957], 21; cp. Segert in *Arch.Or.* XXV 674.
[6] Kahle *Handschriften* 72–81.

ition. The lack of standardization may be due to differences of dialect or may simply reflect the whims of not very skilful copyists introducing the spelling of their own times, as Babylonian and Assyrian scribes are known to have done in copying archaic texts; but it suggests that these copies amongst the Scrolls must have been made before the final establishment of the received text of the Old Testament between the 2nd-3rd centuries B.C. and the 2nd century A.D. Their archetypes then will have been texts in the hands of religious groups or even of private persons, of which a certain number must always have been in circulation. However this question is answered, the community's early need of copies of the Scriptures and the palaeographical evidence are enough to suggest, if not to prove, the priority of *Isaiah A* over the other Scrolls; but that it shows signs of being badly worn at the ends by much use proves nothing, since this wearing or rubbing may have been caused not by length but by amount of use and lack of care in handling it.

That *Discipline* appears to quote the *Psalms of Solomon* (D x 6, 8, 9),[1] which are dated *c.* 50 B.C., gives *prima facie* a date before which it cannot have been composed or compiled. A body like the Covenanters would not, at any rate at the outset, require a *corpus* of written rules; the first regulations, only gradually evolved, would be simple and easily remembered. Elaborate written rules would come late, a consequence of increasing membership, maturing reflection and stabilization, and perhaps also waning enthusiasm. That *Discipline* is a very early work, even though it is certainly the earliest of the non-Biblical works that have survived more or less complete, is therefore very improbable. Two facts support this conclusion. First, it speaks itself of 'the first laws by which the men of the community began to be disciplined' (D ix 10). Second, its attention to minute details argues long observation of such points and argues a time when principles were becoming submerged under trivialities; and the codification of a society's rules is likely to be the end rather than the beginning of a process, betraying not so much experiment as experience. Thus *Discipline* might well have been put together when the society was being flooded with politically-minded and even criminal recruits and when its spiritually inclined members were becoming afraid that its rules and precepts might go by the board; but nothing in it suggests that the Revolt had yet broken out. This would be at a time when the expectation of two Messiahs (D ix 11), based on these two brothers (or their predecessors) had not given place to that of one Messiah (Z ix 10, 29 xv 4), which followed the elevation of Menahem to the leadership of the society.[2] At the same time the ciphers (D v 5, x 4) indicate Menahem as already the leader of the community;[3] he could not have become

---

[1] Cp. Psalms of Solomon xv 5.   [2] Pp. 472–3.   [3] Pp. 336–7, 343.

that before the execution of his two brothers *c.* A.D. 46–8[1] and he himself was murdered in A.D. 66,[2] so that it must have been composed during these twenty years. It speaks, too, of 'the covenant' (D i 16, 18, 20 ii 10, 18 v 2, 3, 9, 10, 20 vi 15), the 'covenant of God' (D v 8, x 10) and the 'covenant of the community' (D viii 16), while the *Commentary on Habakkuk* and the *Zadokite Documents* talk of 'a' or 'the' new covenant (H i 3–4 as restored; Z viii 15 ix 28, 37), so that it must be dated before them; for the covenant *tout simple* must be the original, the old, covenant and as such will obviously have been prior to any 'new covenant' into which the society or any of its members may subsequently have entered.[3] Lastly, the extraordinary parallelism between *Discipline* and the various recensions of the *Two Ways* argues a clear connection between them and therefore points to a date somewhere in the middle of the 1st century A.D.[4]

The *Commentary on Habakkuk*, like the *War*, was clearly written when hostility to the Romans, here called the Kittians, was at a pitch that it had not reached even after Pompey's conquest of Jerusalem.[5] It describes the murder of the Rightful Teacher, who is *ex hypothesi* Menahem, in A.D. 66, and it refers to the 'new covenant' (H i 3) and to the sacrifice offered by the legions to their standards in A.D. 70; but it contains no hint of the final disaster in A.D. 73.[6] It cannot therefore be dated before the outbreak of the Revolt in that year nor before its collapse in A.D. 70; but, being only a short work, it might well have been put together, if conditions permitted, during the lull between that date and the mopping-up of A.D. 73, while the Romans were still trampling the country and memories were still as fresh as they were bitter. The reference in the promise that the party's enemies would be destroyed 'by fire and brimstone' (H x 3–5), while recalling the destruction of Sodom and Gomorrah[7] long ago, would also reflect the recent burning of Jerusalem in A.D. 70, thus giving poignancy to the promises.[8]

One of the most important factors for determining the date of the *Commentary on Habakkuk*, as several writers have remarked, is the use of the tenses. For example, Fr. Van der Ploeg,[9] following others who have made the same or similar points,[10] argues that everything said about the Rightful Teacher and the Wicked Priest is described in the perfect tense, *i.e.* as having already taken place in past time, but that the operations of the Kittians are set out in the imperfect (present-future) tense or in the participle, *i.e.* as still happening or as going to

[1] P. 241.
[2] Pp. 267–9.
[3] Pp. 52–3, 72–4, 305–8.
[4] Pp. 552–8.
[5] Cp. Schreiden *Énigmes* 205–7.
[6] Pp. 211–14.
[7] Gen. xix. 24; cp. Ezek. xxxviii. 2 and Psa. xi. 6.
[8] Pp. 299–303.
[9] In *BO* VIII 10 and *Colloque de Strasbourg* 25–35.
[10] *E.g.* Segal in *JBL* LXX 136–7, Brownlee in *BASOR* CXXVI 16, and Vermès *Manuscrits* 81.

happen; and that this distinction is observed also in various other references to actual events. He then draws the conclusion that the Commentator intends to portray certain events as already past and others as in course of taking place or as still future. Accordingly, as the Kittians cannot be the Seleucids but must be the Romans (as he rightly holds), they cannot yet be in Palestine, although they may be expected to appear there at no distant date; the Commentary therefore must be dated after the Maccabaean struggle with the Seleucid oppressor but before the Roman capture of Jerusalem in 63 B.C.

Although the observation of these facts is as acute as it is correct, the conclusion drawn from them rests on a fallacy; for the imperfect tense is equivocal. It may describe anything still incomplete (past or present or future) in Biblical Hebrew, although its application to past time has fallen almost entirely into desuetude in the Mishnah, where it is hardly found except with a modal force.[1] Such a use, however, may be expected in works written in a pseudo-Biblical idiom, and it is found here and there possibly in the *Commentary* (*e.g.* H ix 5; cp. vi 1 with vi 10) and certainly in the *Hymns* (*e.g.* T ii 11–13, 16 iv 6–8); consequently the possibility of its employment in the *Commentary* cannot be ruled out of court. The tense therefore does not prove the time of the event which the verb describes. Further, if the argument were valid, it would lead nowhere; for no attempt by a Wicked Priest 'to swallow up' a Rightful Teacher and no offering of sacrifices by a foreign enemy to their standards are recorded in the whole period which the theory postulates.

The argument from the tenses, however, far from being for these reasons valueless, is not only in harmony with the attempt to assign the *Commentary* to the closing years of the First Revolt (A.D. 66–73) but even allows the time of its composition to be determined within reasonably narrow limits.

On the one hand, the *Commentary* cannot have been written before or during the opening months of the Revolt, if the Rightful Teacher and the Wicked Priest are respectively Menahem and Eleazar, captain of the Temple; for Menahem and his lieutenant Absalom were murdered soon after the outbreak of the Revolt, in the autumn of A.D. 66, and the Commentator describes the pursuit of the Teacher by the Priest and the silencing of the 'house of Absalom' by verbs in the perfect tense, *i.e.* as events already past. In the same way the Commentator describes the fate of the Wicked Priest in the perfect tense, saying that 'God has delivered him into the hands of his enemies to afflict him with a fatal blow' (H ix 9–11), so that he may be regarded as dead; so too, although nothing definite is known of the death of Eleazar, he is very unlikely to have survived the Revolt.[2] When there-

---

[1] Segal *Mishnaic Hebrew Grammar* § 314.   [2] Pp. 278–9.

fore the Commentator changes from the perfect to the imperfect tense in describing the priest (if the Wicked Priest is here meant) as one 'whose shame exceeded his glory because he did not circumcize the foreskin of his heart but walked in ways of drunkenness that[1] his thirst might be removed and the cup of God's wrath might swallow him up' (H xi 12–15), he is not necessarily describing something still future; the swallowing up is only future in relation to the shame which has exceeded the glory. The escape, too, of the 'house of Judah', *i.e.* Eleazar and his supporters, is described in the imperfect tense but is not necessarily future; the Commentator is speaking of 'all who did the law in the house of Judah, whom God wished to save from the doomed house[2] because of their toil and their faith in the Rightful Teacher' (H viii 1–3), and His saving of these persons is regarded from the point of view of one contemporary with and perhaps a witness of their salvation. Another reason for thus referring to an event which, as the writer must have known, has already happened is that he regards it as still in some sense incomplete or potential; he is describing it as God's purpose which has been only partly fulfilled by the salvation of the party on Mt. Ophel in A.D. 66 and is still being fulfilled and will only be finally fulfilled when the 'house of Judah' comes back to lead their people to the Messianic victory 'at the end of the days'.

On the other hand, the Commentator generally speaks also of the Kittians in the imperfect tense to describe both their characteristic habits and their present activities, *e.g.* when he says that 'the Kittians were' or 'are trampling the land' (H iii 9–10). If he is writing between A.D. 60 and A.D. 73, either of these translations is possible, since the Roman operations are known to have continued with intermissions during the whole of this period; the frequentative past or present is permissible and no compelling need arises to take it here as implying future time. Once he uses the participle, when he describes the Kittians as 'sacrificing to their standards' (H vi 4). The participle's primary function is to describe the subject as being in a state of activity or passivity without reference to the time of either, past or present or future, and it may refer to a single act or to repeated acts.[3] Accordingly, the Commentator is here generalizing from a single act: aware of the sacrifice by the Roman troops to their standards in A.D. 70, he describes the practice as a general habit.[4] Further, when the Commentator refers to 'the last priests of Jerusalem who were collecting wealth and booty from the spoil of the peoples, but towards the end of the days their wealth was being delivered into the hand(s) of the army of the Kittians; for they are all who survive of the peoples' (H ix 4–7), he must mean that 'the last priests . . . were collecting wealth and booty'

---

[1] Cp. Brown-Driver-Briggs *Hebrew Lexicon* 775b (n. 1).
[2] S. pp. 272–3.   [3] Segal *op. cit.* §§ 322–5.   [4] Pp. 211–14.

till the moment when fate overtook them; for, as he could only know that these were the 'last priests' when all was over, so their collection of wealth would be over when he described how it fell into enemy hands.[1] He cannot be predicting that it 'would be delivered'[2] but must be describing how it 'was being delivered' into the hands of the Kittians when he was composing his work; for the same tense must surely have the same force in two immediately parallel and consecutive clauses. That this is his meaning is proved by contemporary history; for the wealth of the Temple fell only gradually into enemy hands. So, even before the capture of the whole city, the Romans obtained a very considerable amount of money and other valuables from the burning Temple[3] and when they destroyed the public treasury, in which the richest citizens had also deposited the contents of their ruined houses;[4] and on another occasion two priests sought to buy their own safety by delivering some of the treasures of the Temple to them.[5] Then again, when the Romans took the city by storm, much treasure was discovered in subterranean passages;[6] and, some time afterwards, when Titus returned from a tour of the Eastern provinces, huge quantities were still being dug up in the city or recovered through information given by prisoners to the Romans,[7] when vast treasures were removed also from the Temple itself and taken to Rome.[8] Much of this was of course the public treasure; but few will doubt that, as ordinary citizens had transferred their private wealth to the public treasury for safety, so priests probably had hidden theirs in the Temple or had smuggled out of the city what they had not hidden in it. The uncovering of all this wealth would then have been for the Romans a task of months if not of years, especially if treasure had been buried all over the country, as the Scroll of Copper would indicate.[9]

Accordingly, the author of the *Commentary on Habakkuk* will have known the principal events of A.D. 66–70, including some that occurred after the capture of Jerusalem, but not of the final collapse of the Revolt at Masada; for he says nothing of the death of Eleazar and his companions in A.D. 73. He must therefore have composed his work in these three years. The tenses which he uses, in so far as they are not dictated by those of the texts on which he is commenting, agree with this conclusion. If he was an eye-witness of the events of the siege, he would be one of those who made good his escape from the doomed city during the last few weeks or days before its destruction, as a certain number succeeded in doing by devious routes;[10] when he

[1] Cp. Schreiden *op. cit.* 327. [2] Cp. Rowley in *VT* X 228.
[3] Josephus *War* VI v 1 § 271 and vi 1 § 317.
[4] *Ibid.* VI v 2 §§ 281–2. [5] *Ibid.* VI viii 3 §§ 387–91.
[6] *Ibid.* VI ix 3 § 432. [7] *Ibid.* VII v 2 §§ 114–15.
[8] *Ibid.* VII v 5 §§ 148–51. [9] Pp. 35–6.
[10] *E.g.* Josephus *War* VII vi 5 § 210.

composed it cannot be further defined. Who he may have been is unknown; he may have been Eleazar son of Jair, as Dr. Roth suggests;[1] but the conjecture cannot be proved.

Whether the *Thanksgiving Hymns* are the work of a single or of several authors is a disputed point.[2] They seem, on grounds of style, to read as the work of one person, but of one who does not always make clear whether he is describing his own experiences or those of the community to which he belongs; but this point is of relatively slight importance, since the experiences described are likely to have been shared as often as not by him with them. He also often does not make clear whether he is presenting his own work or is at times incorporating that of others; but the freedom with which he uses the Old Testament and the apocryphal literature, so far as quotations from these can be identified, suggest that he may not have been so original as he may at first sight appear. If then he is a single person, he must have been one of some importance,[3] one who regards himself as an inspired leader and teacher in the community of which he is a member. Thus, addressing God, he declares that 'Thou hast set me in the territory of wickedness (*riš'āh*)' (T ii 8) and 'I will become a spirit of zeal against all Seekers after Smooth Things' (T ii 15); and he goes on to say that 'Thou has set me up as a standard for the elect of righteousness and a mediator of knowledge in respect to wonderful mysteries, to make proof of men of truth and to test men fit for rebuke' (T ii 13–14; cp. iv 27–8), since he has been rescued from the clutches of the Seekers after Smooth Things (T ii 31–3). Clearly the 'elect of righteousness (*ṣedeq*)' are the members of the Zadokite community,[4] the 'territory of wickedness' is a country under Roman rule,[5] and the Seekers after Smooth Things are the appeasers ready to compromise with Rome rather than continue the struggle against it, as elsewhere in the Scrolls.[6] Meanwhile, all his friends have been dispersed (T iv 8–9), and he has been driven from his country 'like a bird from her nest' and is living in a 'strange land' (T v 5), which can be no other than Damascus and its neighbourhood,[7] where traitors are all round him (T v 22; cp. ii 9–10).[8] However, he goes on to say that 'Thou (*sc.* God) hast set me up as a strong tower' or 'as a tower of refuge on a wall raised high; and Thou hast erected my building on a rock,[9] and everlasting foundations are my base, and all my walls have become a well-tried rampart which cannot be shaken' (T vii 8–9); and he adds that he has become 'a father of loyal sons and a foster-father to men who are a sign',[10] *i.e.* the Covenanters or Zadokites who have been

---

[1] In *Évidences* LXV 39–40. [2] Cp. Holm-Nielsen *Hodayoth* 316–31.
[3] Cp. Dupont-Sommer *Hymnes* 10–20 and Mansoor *Hymns* 45–9.
[4] S. p. 450. [5] Pp. 202–3. [6] Pp. 93–4.
[7] Pp. 303–7. [8] Pp. 247, 354. [9] Pp. 458, 519.
[10] Cp. Zech. iii. 8.

appointed to be a sign and proof of God's displeasure with Israel (cp. Z i 8), while those who have slandered him and attacked him have been scattered 'like chaff before the wind' (T vii 20–23). Here the allusion is to the rift in the party which seems to have broken out amongst the exiles after the destruction of Jerusalem.[1] Then, once again addressing God, he says that 'Thou hast opened a well-spring for them amid channels [of water]' (T viii 21), by which Damascus again must be meant,[2] and that 'my soul has delighted in the multitude of Thy mercies, and I have answered my detractors' or 'those who have sought to swallow me up' (T ix 8), if an allusion to the outrage inflicted on the Rightful Teacher (H xi 5) may be detected here.[3] Finally, he declares that 'Thou has not put my support in gain and wealth . . . nor made any creature of flesh, (even) an army of warriors, the source of my strength'[4] (T x 22–4); he thus clearly dissociates himself from those teachers who have taken up arms and so brought ruin on their country. At the same time the author puts forward more or less clearly Messianic claims for himself. He describes the birth of a 'wonderful counsellor'[5] who will be born at the same time as the 'serpent', *i.e.* the anti-Messiah (T iii 7–12);[6] this 'wonderful counsellor' is apparently intended as the last Rightful Teacher, who may nor may not be the author himself according to the time that the Messianic age is delayed. He says too 'I have shone with a light sevenfold [that of the sun]' (T vii 24), thus postulating for himself (if the text is rightly restored) something characteristic of the Messianic age when the light of the sun is expected to be seven times as bright as at other times.[7] Mostly clearly of all, he applies the old Messianic title of the 'branch (*nēṣer*)'[8] to himself in several passages, which puts his meaning beyond doubt.

In spite of all these allusions the author's identity cannot be established; only a few general conclusions can be drawn from the hints which he throws out. He was probably, if not certainly, a member of the family of Menahem, who too had Messianic pretensions;[9] he was not one of those who had taken up arms against Rome; he had survived the destruction of Jerusalem in A.D. 70, a disaster of which he had perhaps been an eye-witness; he remained implacably opposed, however, to all who would acquiesce in foreign rule and was one of those members of the Zadokite party who escaped into exile and became their leader. He was therefore not the founder of the party[10] but rather its re-founder after its dispersion in exile.

The *Thanksgiving Hymns* therefore must have been composed after

[1] Pp. 305–10.
[3] Pp. 270–3; cp. Driver in *JTS* XXIII 40–1.
[5] Isa. ix. 5.
[7] B. Talmud *Sanhedrin* 91b on Isa. xxx 26.
[9] Pp. 277, 356–8; cp. pp. 472–4.

[2] Pp. 303–5.
[4] Cp. Matt. xxvi. 52.
[6] Pp. 486–7.
[8] Isa. xi. 1.
[10] Dupont-Sommer *Hymnes* 11.

A.D. 70, and probably after the final disaster at Masada in A.D. 73; for, although they seem to contain no allusion to this event, the intervening years are an unlikely period for their composition. The author seems to be always looking back to an age that is past, and his air of relief suggests a time when suspense and danger are over. Such a date, though not proved by the absence of any reference to the Temple and its services, is consonant with it. If then the author is rightly regarded as a or the Rightful Teacher,[1] he will have been Eleazer's unknown successor; and the time of their composition would be between the final collapse of the Revolt in A.D. 73 and the persecutions of the Jews by Vespasian and Domitian,[2] and while the Neronic myth, which was apparently known to the author, was still current.[3]

The *Zadokite Documents* which, having survived (except for some very small fragments)[4] only on two mediaeval manuscripts, cannot be brought into the palaeographical scheme;[5] their date therefore can be fixed only by internal evidence, whether that of external events or that of their relationship to the other Scrolls. In any case they must be dated after the alteration of the original 190 days for which Ezekiel is bidden to lie on his side, as given by the Septuagint, to 390 years (cp Z i 5)[6] which the Massoretic text has;[7] in other words, they can be dated only after the date of the Septuagintal translation of Ezekiel, which must have been made at some time in the 2nd century B.C. They must also probably be dated after the disputes between the schools of Hillel and Shammai in the 1st century B.C., since some of these seem to be reflected in them;[8] but such influence must not be pressed, as it cannot in its very nature be assigned to any very precise date. The legal section implies the loss of the *ius gladii*, which the procurator Coponius (A.D. 6–9) took away from the Sanhedrin[9] except for religious offences[10] (although Jewish tradition wrongly put this act 40 years before the destruction of the Temple in A.D. 70, *i.e.* approximately A.D. 30)[11] and to which the statement that an offender must be executed 'by the statutes of the Gentiles (*bᵉḥuqqê haggôyîm*)' alludes (Z x 1); they therefore must be dated after this event. If the Nebuchadnezzar, whose capture of Jerusalem serves as the *terminus a quo* for the 390 years till the appearance of the Rightful Teacher (Z i 5–7), is not the Babylonian king of that name but Alexander the Great pseudonymously so called as also having taken Jerusalem,[12] the *terminus post quem* for this work will be A.D. 46 or there-

---

[1] Sukenik *ap.* Sczyner in *VT* X 109; s. Yadin *Message* 108.
[2] Pp. 225, 348–9, 370; cp. Schürer *Geschichte*³ I 660–1.   [3] Pp. 489–91.
[4] Pp. 18–19.   [5] Pp. 14–15.   [6] Pp. 346–7.
[7] Pp. 311–15.   [8] Ezek. iv. 5, 9.   [9] P. 70.
[10] Josephus *War* V ii 4 §§ 125–6; s. Juster *Les Juifs dans l'Empire Romain* II 127–49 and Lengle in *Hermes* LXX 312–21.
[11] P. Talmud *Sanhedrin* 18a, 24b and B. Talmud *Sanhedrin* 41a.
[12] Pp. 313–16.

abouts. Further, they cannot be dated before the time of R. Eliezer ben Hyrcanus (A.D. 50–120); for they cite the Messianic period as defined by him.[1] If the reference to a redeeming Messiah, which has been detected in one passage (Z xviii 8–9), is correctly interpreted, these documents or this part of them must have come under Christian influence and cannot be pre-Christian; for no such doctrine is known in Judaism.[2] Also, the *Zadokite Documents* contain numerous rules modifying those in *Discipline*, which are aimed at members of the party living in community, in such a way as to adapt them to the needs of members living in the world, *i.e.* in Damascus and the neighbourhood. When Covenanters began to settle there is not known; small parties may have sought safety there on various occasions,[3] but the principal migrations must have taken place about the time of the Revolt of A.D. 66–73. Thus, while *Discipline* speaks of a 'covenant', the *Zadokite Documents* refer not only to this but also to a 'new covenant', which must of course have been a successor to the original covenant;[4] the *Zadokite Documents* must therefore come after *Discipline*, which has been assigned to *c.* A.D. 46–66 on independent grounds.[5] The references, too, in these documents to the Temple by no means prove that they must have been composed before its destruction in A.D. 70;[6] for the rules regarding sacrifices and other offerings (Z xiii 27–xiv 1) may be but wishful thinking, echoes of an ideal state which has passed away and will never recur, as the rules of the Priestly Code must have been. Again, the author of these documents, after describing the 'sure house in Israel'[7] which God has built for Israel in the community of the Covenanters (Z v 5), goes on to say 'when the epoch is finished . . . there shall be no incorporation in the house of Judah, but each man must stand on his own watch-tower' (Z vi 7). He will here be describing the time when the 'house of Judah' *i.e.* the family of Judah son of Hezekiah, the founder of the party,[8] had become extinct; his youngest son Menahem had been murdered in A.D. 66[9] and his grandson or great-nephew Eleazar ben Jair had perished at Masada in A.D. 73.[10] Then 'each man must stand on his own watch-tower' means that the exiles in isolated groups must rely on themselves to maintain the old spirit and not look to the parent body which had been dispersed after that disaster (to which the Hebrew text seems to allude), in order that they might not be taken alive by the Romans.

The description of Jerusalem as being 'at that period . . . without king and without prince and without judge and without arbitrator' (Z ix 40) is significant; for the terms, though partly taken from the

---

[1] Pp. 476–7.
[2] Cp. Ginzberg *Sekte* I 333–40, 357–61.
[3] Pp. 303–5.
[4] Pp. 305–6.
[5] Pp. 360–1.
[6] Rabinowitz in *VT* III 180.
[7] Cp. Num. xii. 17, 1 Sam. ii. 35, xxv. 28, 1 Kings xi. 38.
[8] Pp. 239–40.
[9] Pp. 268–9.
[10] Pp. 278–9.

Old Testament[1], are apparently chosen to include every sort of ruler and governor who may have held office during the Second Commonwealth, *i.e.* military leaders and civil governors and rulers,[2] priest-kings and half-Jewish kings, as well as judges of various grades,[3] including those presiding over courts of limited jurisdiction as permitted under Roman rule. The list therefore would seem to indicate a time when the entire Jewish administration had been swept away, namely following the disaster of A.D. 70. Also, Eisler has drawn attention[4] to an interesting rule which reflects the conditions of this period; this is the provision that 'no man shall have intercourse with a woman in the Holy City (*sc.* Jerusalem), that the city of the sanctuary may not be defiled by their impurity' (Z xiv 4). Such a rule would have been as impracticable as it would have been unintelligible at any time when Jerusalem was occupied by a teeming Jewish population, pulsating with life, as it was even during the siege (A.D. 68–70); and it would have been pointless after A.D. 135, when Hadrian razed the walls and ploughed up the very soil, forbidding Jews to visit the country even as pilgrims.[5] It could have been incorporated in the society's rules only between A.D. 70 and A.D. 135, when the city lay waste but was still a place of pilgrimage for pious Jews.[6] Further, the *Zadokite Documents* refer to an event as 'from the day of the gathering of the Unique Teacher (*sc.* to his fathers) . . . about forty years' (Z ix 39). If the allusion is to the death of Menahem in A.D. 66, these documents cannot have been composed before *c.* A.D. 106, or, alternatively, if it is to that of Eleazar ben Jair in A.D. 73, the earliest possible date for them will have been *c.* A.D. 113, shortly before the abortive rising of A.D. 115–17; they can hardly have been composed after these years, since they reflect a period of untroubled peace with no hint of coming turmoil and rebellion. Lastly, if the Interpreter of the Law is rightly taken to be Moses, the *Zadokite Documents* in which he is mentioned cannot be dated after the early years of the 2nd century A.D.; for *Moses redivivus* disappeared from Rabbinic literature about that time, when Jesus began to be called the 'second lawgiver' by Christians[7]. All the evidence, then, points to the period between A.D. 106 and *c.* A.D. 115 for that in which the *Zadokite Documents* must have been composed.

The *War* cannot be dated so early as *c.* 50 B.C.–A.D. 50.[8] It may

[1] Hos. iii. 4 (king, prince); cp. 1 Bar. ii. 1 (judges, kings, princes).
[2] Cp. 1 Macc. x. 37 (ruler) and xiv. 41–2, 47 (leader, captain, ethnarch).
[3] Cp. 1 Esdr. viii. 23 (judges and justices).
[4] In *Occident and Orient* 123.
[5] Justin Martyr *Apology* I xlvii 6 and Eusebius *Ecclesiatical History* IV vi 3, Mishnah *Taanith* iv 6 and B. Talmud *Taanith* 29a; s. Schürer *Geschichte*[3] I 691–3.
[6] Cp. Moore in *HTR* IV 330–77 (where the Covenanters as the party of the Zadokite Documents are dated *c.* A.D. 79–86).
[7] S. p. 480.　　　　　[8] Yadin & Rabin *War* 244–6.

reflect features of the Roman Republican army, but it reflects also those especially of the Imperial age. It describes the curved dagger imported into Palestine c. A.D. 55–60 and military practices introduced among the Jewish forces in A.D. 66–7 in preparation for the coming struggle;[1] and it requires the heads of the community to be 'recruiting soldiers of all the tribes of Israel through the countries of the Gentiles' (W ii 6–7), just as Josephus describes[2] how in the winter of A.D. 66–7 'he levied an army of upwards of a hundred thousand young men' which he trained and had 'ready for action', when 'each town sent out one half of its levy on service and kept the remainder back to provide them with supplies'. Thus the *War* describes something which, though past, must have been remembered by persons still living, while it at the same time anticipates what R. 'Aqîbâ is said to have done at the beginning of the Second Revolt (A.D. 132–5).[3] This exaggeration was an outcome of the dreams with which the Jews buoyed up their hopes between the two Revolts; it would have been equally out of place before the First as after the Second Revolt. In the same way it describes a pseudo-apocalyptic struggle based on the experience of a national war which can only be the First Revolt of A.D. 66–73, although in fact it is looking not backward but forward, being designed as a visionary struggle to bring consolation for past defeat by the promise of future victory and 'dominion over all flesh' (W xvii 8–9). The text says further, first that the war would take place 'when the exiles of the Sons of Light came back from the Wilderness of the Peoples[4] to encamp in the Wilderness of Judah' (W i 3) and, second, that neither boy nor woman shall enter the camp 'when they sally forth from Jerusalem to do battle' (W vii 3–4). Thus the *terminus a quo* will be some years after the end of the First Revolt, when the exiles have commenced straggling back into the neighbourhood of Jerusalem, and the *terminus ante quem* will be Hadrian's edict forbidding Jews to reside in Jerusalem.[5] The *War* will then be one of the latest Scrolls, since time must be allowed for the depression resulting from total defeat to be shaken off and for a new generation to grow up and dream again of world-wide victory, as the Romans *eo (ipso) tempore* suspected![6] Possibly the attempt of Domitian (A.D. 81–96) to exterminate all who survived of the line of David[7] turned the party's thoughts once again to war as a desperate remedy for an intolerable situation. It may have been composed in time to inspire the risings of c. A.D. 113–16 or perhaps that of A.D. 132–5, certainly not afterwards; for none of the early Covenanters will have been alive and active after that date.

This last conclusion seems in harmony with another fact, which Dr.

[1] Pp. 168–97.　　[2] In *War* II xx 6 § 576 and 8 §§ 583–4.
[3] Del Medico *Énigme* 370–1.　　[4] Cp. Ezek. xx 35.
[5] P. 369; cp. p. 70.　　[6] Tacitus *Histories* V 13 and Suetonius *Vespasian* iv 5.
[7] Pp. 225, 348–9.

Roth has noted,[1] that several hundred *sicarii* provoked a rising in Egypt soon after the capture of Masada in A.D. 73; taken prisoners, they endured every kind of torture, steadily refused to acknowledge Caesar as lord and met a heroic death.[2] Here *sicarii* may well include Zealots and Covenanters; for all these groups had occupied the place separately or together at various times during the Revolt,[3] and all the parties engaged in it would inevitably have become almost indistinguishable in the last desperate stages of the struggle. The stoic heroism, too, of the rebels in Egypt and their refusal to acknowledge any other ruler but God were characteristic of the Zealots and the Covenanters.[4] The story then is witness to the existence of such groups, refugees from Palestine, in Egypt after the collapse of the Revolt. Who were responsible for the next rising in Egypt under Trajan in A.D. 115–17 (when also Libya and Cyrenaica as well as Palestine and Mesopotamia were involved) is not known; but the spirit of Zealots and Covenanters obviously inspired it. The significance of such risings in the present connection is that they suggest the existence of groups of Covenanters, for whose encouragement and guidance in exile the *Zadokite Documents* may well have been composed, between A.D. 73 and A.D. 135. They may also account for the presence of a copy (although a late copy) of these texts in the Qara'ite synagogue at Cairo; for copies would hardly have been taken there if there had been no one interested in possessing them in Egypt.

As then the old apocalyptic literature had inspired the original Zealots,[5] so the Scrolls served a similar purpose; for, while *Discipline* and the *Zadokite Documents* were directed to the spiritual aims and practical organization of the society of the Covenanters, the *Commentary on Habakkuk* and the *Thanksgiving Hymns*, even though primarily historical, were ultimately aimed, as the *War* was, at keeping alive the opposition to foreign rule and fostering the hope of final victory. This view of their purpose agrees with the dates to which the various documents are here assigned: *Discipline* to the years between A.D. 46–8 and A.D. 66, the *Commentary of Habakkuk* to A.D. 70–3, the *Thanksgiving Hymns* to a time not long after A.D. 73, the *War* and the *Zadokite Documents* to some time between A.D. 106 and A.D. 115 and certainly not after A.D. 132–5.

The relative order of the Scrolls as here worked out on historical grounds is supported by the development which the doctrine of the consummation of the age undergoes, as Dr. Rabinowitz has argued[6] (although his order cannot be accepted exactly as it stands, and his

---

[1] In *Background* 51.
[2] Josephus *War* VII ix 1 §§ 389–401.
[3] P. 250.
[4] Josephus *ibid.* VII x 1 §§ 416–19.
[5] Cp. Harford *Talmud and Apocrypha* 193–4.
[6] In *VT* III 175–85.

dates in the Maccabaean age for the Scrolls must be rejected out of hand).[1]

In *Discipline* the consummation is presented as not yet imminent but as something which is in course of preparation though still some years distant; so the compiler says that 'they (*sc.* the Covenanters) shall do this year by year throughout the days of the dominion of Belial' (D ii 19) and 'all they who are not reckoned in His (*sc.* God's) covenant shall be set apart . . .; and He will rid the world of all those who despise His word' (D v 18–19), and again 'when these things come to pass, the council of the community will have been established in truth as an eternal plantation, a holy house for Israel . . . ; these will serve the purpose of grace to make atonement for the earth and to decree the condemnation of wickedness, that there may be no wrong-doing' (D viii 4–10). The *Commentary on Habakkuk* is witness to some anxiety that the consummation may be delayed; so the Commentator says that 'the last age may be protracted beyond anything that the prophets have foretold; for the mysteries of God are cause for wonder' (H vii 7–8), and he speaks of 'the men of truth, those who fulfil the Law, who do not relax their efforts for the service of truth even when the last age is delayed to their distress; for God's ends will come about in due course, even as He has determined . . . by the mysteries of His wisdom' (H vii 10–14). In the Admonition, *i.e.* the opening sections of the *Zadokite Documents*,[2] the lessons of history from the Deluge to the restoration from the Exile are a guarantee that a consummation will take place at no distant date. So the writer urges his readers to listen to his message; for 'from the day when the Unique Teacher was gathered (*sc.* to his forefathers in the grave) until all the men of war . . . are consumed (will be) about forty years; and in that epoch the wrath of God will be kindled against Israel . . . ; but those who have turned from the transgression of Jacob, who keep God's commandments, shall speak each to his fellow to bring him to righteousness . . . ; and God shall listen to their words, and a book of remembrance shall be written before Him for those who fear God and think upon His name, until salvation and righteousness (victory) is revealed for those who fear God. Then ye shall again discern between righteous and wicked, between him also who serves God and him who has not served him' (Z ix 39–44). Here the consummation is expected within the lifetime of those who are still alive. So too the Laws contained in the same work[3] are 'for the epoch of wickedness, until the Messiah of Aaron and Israel shall arise' (Z xv 4; cp. xix 7), and they contain a rule that 'all who enter the covenant for the Israelites shall bring their sons, who reach (an age) to enter the ranks of those who are enrolled, to swear the oath of the covenant' (Z xix 6); these imply therefore that the

---

[1] In *VT* VIII 391–404.   [2] Pp. 51–2.   [3] Pp. 52–3.

consummation is in sight, but that members must still train their sons in the rules of the order and arrange for their admission to it. Lastly, the author of *War* makes the commander addressing his troops say 'now is the heart that was melting turning to a well-spring of hope; Thou (*sc.* God) has done unto these (*sc.* the enemy) as Thou didst unto Pharaoh and the captains of his chariotry at the Sea of Reeds' (W xi 9–10); and he says in the thanksgiving for victory 'blessed be Thy name, O God of [mercies]; for Thou hast done great and wonderful deeds. . . . Thou it is who hast determined [this] time for us, and this day Thy glory has shone upon us . . . ; ensuring perpetual redemption, removing the enemy from us that he may be no more' (W xviii 6–12). Here the author can depict victory as happening or even as having happened and the climax of the end as imminent if not actually present; for he is in effect describing what has not yet happened but is imminent as though it has happened, as prophets and poets constantly do.

If then the *Thanksgiving Hymns* are left aside (for they are concerned with the personal experiences of the author or authors and make no reference to the consummation of the age), the order of the Scrolls as already determined on quite other grounds (*Discipline, Commentary on Habakkuk, Zadokite Fragments, War*) is amply confirmed by the arguments drawn from the doctrinal development here examined in outline.

The approximate dates here proposed for the individual Scrolls may now be summarized in the following table:

Discipline	.	A.D. 46/48–66
Commentary on Habakkuk .	.	A.D. 70–3
Thanksgiving Hymns .	.	A.D. 73–81 (?)
Zadokite Documents ⎫	.	
War . . ⎭		A.D. 96–132

Thus the chronological order of the Scrolls, as here argued from their historical contents, tallies with that which has been established on palaeographical, linguistic and doctrinal grounds,[1] although the absolute dates are totally different; only the *Zadokite Documents* (of which the two parts may not come from the same period) must be excepted from the palaeographical comparison, inasmuch as they have been preserved only in medieval copies.[2]

2. CONCEALMENT OF THE SCROLLS

The final questions may now be asked: why and when the Scrolls were put away in the caves round Qumrân, and whether they were deposited in them all at the same time or at different times.

[1] Cp. p. 480. [2] Pp. 14–15.

The problem of the Scroll of Copper may be discussed first and separately from that of the Scrolls on leather or parchment; for there is no necessary or logical connection between them. All that has been argued and perhaps proved is that the list inscribed on it refers to a real, not a mythical, treasure and that the language (so far as it has been studied) permits a date in the 1st century A.D.[1] That the cave, in which it was found rolled away in a corner, also contained fragments of Scrolls on leather might be purely fortuitous.

That this treasure was Essene property or that it had been entrusted for safe custody by the authorities to the Essenes who were forbidden to have great possessions or even to handle money, or belonged to the Covenanters, in view of their claim to be a religious or ascetic corporation of 'poor men',[2] would seem highly improbable.[3] It would not be likely to have been the property of the insurgents, to whichever party they belonged; for the quantity would seem to exceed anything that they could have extorted from rich Jews before or obtained by capture from the enemy after the outbreak of the Revolt.[4] It can only have been the accumulated wealth stored in the Temple, where the national treasure will have been deposited with that of the Temple itself[5] and where the wealth of many private persons is said to have been banked, as often in antiquity;[6] for the horror of sacrilege will have to some extent protected it from robbery and pillage. The occasion will have been the First rather than the Second Revolt; for, while such huge sums are known to have been amassed in the long peace between Pompey's capture of Jerusalem in A.D. 63 and the outbreak of the First Revolt in A.D. 70,[7] little can have been accumulated in the lean years between the destruction of Jerusalem in A.D. 70 and the outbreak of the Second Revolt in A.D. 132. During the former period, too, references to the wealth of the Temple and Jerusalem occur here and there in contemporary literature,[8] while none can be found in the latter.

On this assumption the time when the treasure was concealed is easily fixed within very narrow limits. The imminence and in any case the outbreak of the Revolt would compel its custodians to take immediate measures for storing it in places of safety; for they could have had no illusions about the coming struggle. This vast operation could hardly have been undertaken, even by night, while the Romans were in actual occupation of Jerusalem and also controlled all the surrounding country; it could only have been carried out when they were

---

[1] Pp. 30–6.   [2] Pp. 54, 92–3, 103–4, 260.
[3] Cp. Dupont-Sommer in *RHR* CLI 22-36.
[4] *E.g.* Josephus *War* II xx 3 § 564 (where Cestius is described as losing a considerable sum of money to Eleazar son of Simon).
[5] Cp. Kuhn in *RB*, NS LXI [1954] 193–205 and *T.Lz.* LXXXI [1956] 541–6.
[6] Pp. 32–3.   [7] Pp. 32–3.
[8] Cp. Schürer *Geschichte*[3] II 266–71.

at a distance. On the one hand, the Jews had already seized Masada in the summer of A.D. 66;[1] Metilius and the troops under him garrisoning Jerusalem capitulated in August;[2] and Cestius, defeated at Beth-horon in November, fell back on Antipatris some way to the north.[3] Thus Jerusalem and the districts to the south of the city were for the time being clear of Roman troops; and these (if Bethshean and the Samaritan Gerizim are eliminated from the list)[4] are the very districts in which according to the Scroll the entire treasure was hidden away, namely in Jerusalem and round the north end of the Dead Sea.[5] On the other hand, in June A.D. 68 Vespasian visited Jericho and the Dead Sea[6] and then proceeded to invest Jerusalem, surrounding it so completely that 'all egress . . . was cut off'.[7] Thus the treasure must have been put away between the winter of A.D. 66 and the summer of A.D. 68,[8] the only time when the places where the bulk of it was stored were free of Roman troops; and the Scroll containing the record of the treasure would have been compiled and hidden at the same time. This would not necessarily be the time when the sectarian and other Scrolls were put away in the caves at Qumrân; but a date c. A.D. 100, which has been suggested,[9] would certainly be too late, if only because no satisfactory reason can be found for the operation at that time.

The reason why the treasure was hidden only in Jerusalem and in certain localities round the head of the Dead Sea now becomes apparent. The Romans, after being driven out of Jerusalem and the district to the south-east of the city, never fell back behind an arc running roughly through the southern slopes of the hill-country of Ephraim (Caesarea-Antipatris-Scythopolis), so that no localities to the north of Jerusalem would be safe from their incursions; and the low-lying country to the south-west of the city offered no suitable sites (e.g. hills with inaccessible caves) for the concealment of vast quantities of treasure. The only suitable area was the south-east, where the wild and little frequented ravines running down to the Dead Sea afforded all that was needed for such a purpose.

An inventory of all this treasure with a list of the places where it was hidden, drawn up in detail and recorded on durable material (cp. SC xii 10–13), would have been absolutely necessary; no one could remember all the details and no one who had the information might survive if the struggle lasted many years. Such an important record could not have been entrusted to the Covenanters as a body; for, even though they might have been regarded as a group of people unlikely to betray a trust, being sworn to keep secret the mysteries of their own

[1] Josephus *War* II xvii 2 § 408.
[2] *Ibid*. xvii 10 §§ 451–54.
[3] *Ibid*. xix 7 § 540–9 § 555.
[4] P. 30.
[5] Cp. Allegro *Treasure* 63–119.
[6] Josephus *War* IV viii 1 § 450 and 4 § 477.
[7] *Ibid*. ix 1 §§ 486–80; cp. §§ 550–5.
[8] Cp. Allegro *op. cit.* 123–4.
[9] Milik in *RB*, NS LXVI 322.

society (D ix 17), and even though they might have enjoyed a reputation for loyalty similar to that of the Essenes, who preferred to endure torture and even death rather than to reveal anything to the Romans,[1] entrusting such important information to a large community would inevitably increase the risk of leakage. The fewer who know something important, the greater the security! The caves round Qumrân must have been well known to many people, and the safest, the only safe, course would be to charge some trustworthy person with the duty of hiding the record in some secret place; the person selected would be someone well acquainted with the Wilderness of Judah and the shores of the Dead Sea, one who would slip quietly out of Jerusalem and hide the list in a cave known only to himself and perhaps a few trustworthy colleagues, who were sworn to secrecy. If then any other party or parties came at some time or other to leave a collection of Scrolls in the same place, they might come and go without noticing an odd piece of metal lying coiled up in some dark corner of the cave.

Yet with all these precautions this risk was always present: whereas, if one hiding place was found, the others might escape notice, the discovery of a list of them all would be fatal to the whole treasure. In this connection the last clause of the Scroll gains significance; for it contains the curious statement that 'a copy of this document (sc. of the Scroll) and its interpretation (pĕrûš) and their measurements and a description of each single piece' is buried at the mouth of the hole of the 'pit' (SC xii 10–13). This note raises the question whether the Scroll is not in some form of cipher; for the purport of an 'interpretation' is not otherwise apparent. The employment of such a device would be by no means improbable, being already known in the 1st century A.D. when it was being used by the Covenanters for their own purposes;[2] and then or in the 2nd century A.D., when it was employed by other Jews for stuff hidden at one or other of the two Revolts,[3] it could obviously serve to make assurance doubly sure. A number of people would necessarily know where this or that deposit was concealed (for many persons would have been engaged in the operation), whereas very few might know where everything was or where the key to the inventory was, hidden alone in the 'pit'; this was perhaps a pit connected with the drainage of the altar in the Temple[4] where no one would think of looking for such a document. Anyone, too, who found it by chance in such a place would never think of connecting it with the detailed list lying hidden in a cave at Qumrân. If this explanation of the 'interpretation' is correct, it will confirm the genuineness of the Scroll; for no one is likely to have forged a document in cipher together

[1] Josephus *War* II viii 10 §§ 152–3.
[2] Pp. 335–46.
[3] Mishnah *Maaser Sheni* iv 11.
[4] Cp. Allegro *op. cit.* 169–70.

with its key. At the same time it will suggest that the attempt to find the treasure will be futile until the key to the Scroll is found!

Incidentally, the list on this Scroll twice speaks of 'documents (*sᵉfārîm*)' as part of the buried treasure, one document being hidden in a pitcher '[in the inner] chamber of the platform of the double gate, facing east, in the northern entrance (buried), three cubits (from the surface)' (SC vi 4–5), and the rest being put 'in the drain-pipe (?) in the eastern path to the treasury, beside the entrance' (SC viii 3). These notices are very important if the text is meant to be taken in the literal sense. First, the presence of sacred vessels and vestments (as the 'garments' must surely be)[1] in the list proves that the deposits must have come from the Temple; second, since both localities are apparently situated in the city (for that is where the 'double gate' and the 'treasury' will have been), they indicate that the official copies of the Scriptures and other documents were hidden in Jerusalem and not in caves over-looking the Dead Sea. If too the Scrolls in the caves had come from the Temple, they would have been mentioned in this list together with their hiding places. The copies of the Scriptures found amongst the Scrolls were therefore not official and possibly not even officially approved texts; they might even have been texts actively disapproved or even forbidden by Rabbinic standards.[2]

The question of the deposit of the sectarian Scrolls (D, H, T, W, Z) and of such other Scrolls, many or few, as may have belonged to the Covenanters, must now be discussed and, if possible, answered.

The first problem is the date of the deposit of the Scrolls in the caves round Qumrân; and this seems unfortunately to be one of which no exact solution can be found in the present state of knowledge.

Dr. Roth thinks[3] that the exile of the Covenanters in Damascus was due to the events following the death of Herod the Great in 4 B.C., when Judah the Galilaean or Gaulonite[4] collected a small force at Sepphoris in Galilee and raised a revolt, which was speedily suppressed, whereupon he disappeared from the scene;[5] the place to which he fled, though not named, might well have been Damascus, which was not far from Galilee and where there was a large Jewish colony. There he may well have lain hid for some years, since nothing is heard of him until he reappears in Palestine leading the opposition to the payment of taxes to Rome. The party may then be supposed to have occupied and restored the ruins at Qumrân at this time and used them as a base of operations against the Romans, until Judah was caught and executed in A.D. 6–7.[6] The historical part of the *Zadokite Documents*, which speaks of 'a covenant and a pact which they (*sc.* the Covenanters,

---

[1] Allegro *op. cit.* 142.
[3] In *Background* 25–7, 33–4.
[5] Josephus *Antiquities* II iv 1 § 56.

[2] Pp. 386–8.
[4] P. 239.
[6] Acts v. 37.

or some of them) made in the land of Damascus' (Z ix 37) will have been composed at this time. This requires members 'to observe the sabbath-day according to its specification and the feasts and the day of the fast' (Z viii 15) *i.e.* to observe the group's peculiar calendar; and it will presumably have contained a solemn undertaking to reform and redeem Israel from the Roman yoke at the earliest possible opportunity. The same work goes on to say that 'when the Unique Teacher is gathered (to his fathers) until all the men of war who return come to an end (will be) about forty years . . . and in that period God's wrath will burn against Israel' (Z ix 39–40). Here the 'unique teacher' is *ex hypothesi* Judah;[1] and if 'forty years' (though inspired by the Old Testament, like so much in the Scrolls)[2] is meant in a historical sense, it will denote the period from A.D. 6–7 to A.D. 46/8, *i.e.* from the death of Judah till those of his two sons Simon and Jacob.[3] These 'men of war', who apparently went into exile with the Teacher but came back with the Man of Falsehood,[4] would then be some of Judah's followers who, having supported his first abortive revolt in 4 B.C. and escaped with him into exile, quarrelled with him there and formed a rival party under one of their members as a new leader; and the reason why God was angry with Israel during these 'forty years' would be that the people had not rallied to Judah's support during his absence nor welcomed him on his return, foreseeing fresh trouble if such a firebrand or his successor with his turbulent followers were re-instated in their midst. Meanwhile, Menahem was perhaps lying low somewhere in the Wilderness of Judah; and this suggestion would explain why the apocalyptic war would take place 'when the exiled party of the Sons of Light return from the Wilderness of the Peoples to encamp in the wilderness of Jerusalem' (W i 3). Eventually, when Eleazar son of the high-priest Hananiah provoked the Revolt, Menahem seized Masada and established some sort of authority in the surrounding districts,[5] which his followers maintained till the final destruction of the fortress in A.D. 73;[6] for this was a much stronger place than Qumrân and further from the Roman lines. He resided here, administering the district in a rough and ready manner and raiding recalcitrant settlements in the neighbourhood while himself harassed by intermittent engagements with the Romans; meanwhile members of the group must be pictured continuing their literary work, copying the Scriptures and composing such of the Scrolls, *e.g.* the *War* and *Thanksgiving Hymns*, as cannot have been composed before this period. The community then may have hidden the earlier works so

---

[1] Cp. Roth *Background* 73–4 (s. Winter in *PQS* XCI 132–3).
[2] Cp. Ezek. iv 6.
[3] Josephus *Antiquities* XX v 2 § 102.
[4] Pp. 305–10.
[5] Josephus *War* II xvii 8 § 433–4.   [6] *Ibid.* VII viii 1 § 252–ix 2 § 406.

soon as the Revolt broke out and added the later works to them just
before or soon after the final disaster; but they will probably have
waited to put the whole collection into the caves not long before finally
withdrawing their forces to Masada in A.D. 72–3.

This reconstruction of the history of the early years of the Covenanters is open to serious objections. Damascus is certainly mentioned in
the Scrolls as a place of refuge for the Covenanters (D viii 6 ix 28, 37).
Although, however, Sepphoris and Galilee, which were the scene of
Judah's rising, are close to Damascene territory and Damascus had a
large Jewish population,[1] it would be a very unlikely retreat for Judah
and his followers; for, as Varus the proconsul of Syria had defeated
him and his followers while his colleague Caius occupied Sepphoris,
they would hardly take refuge in the very province which was under
the control of these two highly placed Roman officers, while the
Jewish residents there would hardly welcome so dangerous a party of
fanatical anti-Roman refugees. In fact, Damascus would be a tolerably
safe place of refuge for Jewish revolutionaries only after its transference,
for which Gaius (A.D. 37–41) was responsible, from direct Roman rule
to that of a viceroy of a local Arabian king.[2] Also, according to Dr.
Roth,[3] Judah and his followers after the rising of 4 B.C. disappeared
from the scene for this whole 'decade', during which they resided at
Damascus and the *Zadokite Documents* were composed there. After these
'eight or ten years' they returned to Palestine and entered into occupation of the ruins at Qumrân, where they proceeded to organize the
rising of A.D. 6; alternatively, after its collapse and Judah's consequent
execution by the Romans 'his followers took up residence for the first
time at Qumrân'.[4] Alternative solutions of a problem, however, cannot
be accepted as satisfactory. Further, either of those here discussed
presupposes too early a date for the Scrolls, which its author makes
no attempt to justify or prove; it conflicts, too, with his date for the
Zadokite Documents which he assigns to a period after the outbreak of
the Revolt in A.D. 66.[5]

The date at which the Romans took and destroyed the fort or
monastery at Qumrân, whether in A.D. 68 or in A.D. 73 or in any other
year about that time,[6] has no material bearing on that of the deposit
of the Scrolls in them. The Scrolls seem to have and indeed must have
been written at various times, some before and others after its destruction. Since too the Sadducaeans or Zadokites, *i.e.* the Covenanters, can
be traced from the 1st century A.D. continuously through the Talmud
down to the 8th century A.D.,[7] the deposit may theoretically have
been made at any time within that period. The possible or probable

[1] Acts ix. 1–22 and 2 Cor. xi. 32–3.   [2] Pp. 303–4.
[3] Roth *Background* 26.   [4] Pp. 240–1.
[5] *Ibid.* 46–8.   [6] Pp. 394–9.   [7] Pp. 259–66.

date of the composition of each Scroll is the earliest possible date for its deposit, and this has now been settled;[1] but this does not fix the absolute date of the deposit. The Scrolls may in any case have been deposited in the caves singly or in groups or altogether; but this is a question which cannot be answered on the available evidence. The remaining problem of date therefore is the exact *terminus a quo* and the *terminus ante quem*, namely the earliest and latest possible or probable dates of the deposit. These too cannot be precisely fixed, but certain general conclusions throwing some light on the problem can be reached.

That the Scrolls must have been written and copied and hidden in the caves by the Covenanters themselves while still living in the monastery or at any rate able to obtain access to the caves has not and hardly can be proved; that no Scroll can have been composed or copied and therefore hidden after the destruction of the 'monastery' and the dispersion of the community has been disproved. These arguments, therefore, cannot prove, as Fr. de Vaux thinks,[2] that all must have been put away before A.D. 68, when in his opinion Qumrân was taken by the Romans;[3] and the suggestion that the Romans must be held responsible for tearing them up into thousands of fragments[4] is but a counsel of despair, being quite unproved.

Cave III affords one scrap of evidence which may throw some light on the date when the Scrolls (or at any rate those of which fragments have been found in this cave) will have been put away. According to the archaeologists who opened it, the remains of some forty jars and numerous fragments of parchment from Scrolls were found lying on the ground and afterwards the several pieces of the Copper-Scroll were uncovered 'hard up against the inner wall';[5] the obvious conclusion is that the Copper-Scroll was already there when the jars with the Scrolls in them were brought into the cave. If then the Copper-Scroll was engraved and put into the cave between A.D. 66 and A.D. 68,[6] the other Scrolls were most probably hidden in it after that date. This argument is strictly valid only for the Scrolls in Cave III; but that their concealment must have taken place a considerable time after this date is supported by two arguments. The Covenanters would hardly have left the Scrolls in the caves when they fled before the Romans (whether in A.D. 68 or A.D. 73) and they could hardly have taken them with them on their flight;[7] for this would in all probability have been hasty and disorganized.

Dr. Kahle has also drawn attention[8] to one or two other points which may be helpful. First, he has detected what looked like two letters of

[1] Pp. 359–73.   [2] In *Archéologie* 82–4.   [3] Pp. 394–9.
[4] De Vaux *ibid.* 78[1].   [5] Allegro *Treasure* 19–20.
[6] Pp. 374–7.   [7] Cp. Schreiden *Énigmes*, 190–1.
[8] In *Handschriften* 18, 58–9; cp. *TLz.* LXXV 537–40 and *VT* I 40.

the Syriac alphabet on a fragment of leather which was being cleaned; this alphabet had hardly been evolved and certainly had not come into general use before the middle of the 1st century A.D. This however will not necessarily have been the *terminus a quo*, since these letters may have been subsequently added; but the addition must surely have been made before the deposit in the cave. Second, a few *papyri* written on both sides have been found among the Scrolls; these seem therefore to represent *codices* which did not come into general use in the East before the 1st–2nd centuries A.D., so that they could hardly have been put away before that period. Thus the earliest *terminus a quo* for the concealment of these would be a date late in the 1st century A.D.[1] The *terminus ante quem* is equally difficult to determine; but here again Dr. Kahle cites[2] a point which in his opinion may throw some light on the problem. He observes that nothing written on parchment has been found in the caves. This, which is thought to have been invented not long before the 2nd century B.C., is found in regular use amongst Jews as also amongst Christians by the 4th century A.D. and must of course have been used for some considerable time before becoming common. If the Scrolls had been put away after such a date, some manuscripts on parchment would have been expected among them. Unfortunately, this absence of parchment can hardly be said to indicate any very definite date, and even the existence of a parchment bearing a Greek text dated in 195 B.C. proves nothing definite;[3] Greeks may have employed it long before Jews. It certainly permits the assumption that the Scrolls were perhaps deposited in the caves while the use of parchment was still uncommon; but, being an *argumentum e silentio*, even this conclusion has little value. The date, too, of the leather, which has been put slightly before the time of the documents from Murabba'ât (*c.* A.D. 132–5), is too uncertain to afford any real assistance.[4] Further, Roman pottery of the 1st–3rd centuries A.D. has been found in the caves,[5] showing that they may have been entered during that period; but those who deposited it in the caves might have been survivors of the original Covenanters or their successors who had returned to Qumrân after a certain lapse of time to resume their old manner of life,[6] or they might not have had anything to do with the Scrolls. All these considerations, taken together, would seem to show that the Scrolls could have been deposited in the caves in the 1st or even in the 2nd century A.D.; and that is all that they prove.

The recovery of fragments of the Septuagint (presumably a relic,

---

[1] Cp. Ezek. ii. 10 and Rev. v. 1; s. Birnbaum *Scrolls and Palaeography* 15.
[2] *Ibid.* 57–8. [3] Cp. Birnbaum *op. cit.* 16.
[4] P. 408. [5] Pp. 18, 38, 40–1, 402–3.
[6] Cp. Schreiden *op. cit.* 156.

direct or indirect, of the party's early sojourn in Egypt),[1] in Cave IV
(if it is rightly identified), too, may contribute something to the
solution of the problem. These fragments all came from the old Greek
translation which preceded that which Aquila, a convert to Judaism,
made in the 2nd century A.D. The use of the old version had been
officially recognized by the Jewish authorities, but it was eventually
displaced by Aquila's work which at once became the authorized
translation for Greek-speaking Jews; the reason apparently was that
Christians had been using that of the Septuagint for controversial
purposes, and the Jewish authorities preferred one which they thought
safe.[3] Mr. Del Medico, following this line of argument, has therefore
suggested[4] that the fragments of the Septuagintal version found in the
caves came from copies which had been discarded after the introduction
of Aquila's version; they could not be left anywhere or even destroyed,
being in a sense sacred texts, inasmuch as they contained the name of
God, but might as such be deposited in a g^eníẓāh with other disused
Jewish writings. Copies of the old version could not be thus put away
until the new one had come into circulation c. A.D. 130–40, which
therefore would be the earliest possible date for their deposit in the
caves.

Accordingly, Mr. Del Medico,[5] who assigns the *Commentary on
Habakkuk* to a date c. A.D. 74–8 and *Discipline* to one c. A.D. 90–110,
thinks that the bulk of the Scrolls may have been put away in the
caves by A.D. 115, shortly before the revolt against Trajan (A.D.
113/4–16);[6] the *War* and the *Hymns* can then have been hidden at
the same time. Consequently, the *Zadokite Documents*, in saying 'from
the time when the Unique Teacher was gathered (to his fathers) . . .
about forty years' (Z ix 39) would be referring to the murder of
Menahem in A.D. 66; for forty years after that, taken as a round number,
would be A.D. 106, which is not too long before c. A.D. 113/4–16.
Alternatively, if the 'unique teacher' was not Menahem who was
murdered in A.D. 66 but his nephew (and presumably successor)
Eleazar son of Jair who committed suicide at Masada in A.D. 73, forty
years after this event would be A.D. 113; this would be close enough
to the abortive rising of A.D. 113/4–16, when the last survivors of the
First Revolt might have met their ends. If this suggestion is right, it
brings the date of the latest event mentioned in the Scrolls down to
c. A.D. 115, and the apocalyptic war expected to take place after these
forty years would reflect the vain hopes which inspired the rising of
A.D. 113/4–16. In this case, the concealment of the Scrolls in the

---

[1] Pp. 226–37.   [2] P. 20.
[3] Cp. Swete & Ottley *Introduction to the Old Testament in Greek* 30–4.
[4] In *Énigme* 262–4.   [5] In *Deux Manuscrits* 103–5, 139–40.
[6] Spartianus *de Vita Hadriani* V 2.

caves must probably be postponed to some date after these years, when they might have been hidden away in view of Bar Cochba's rebellion (A.D. 132–5).

The reason for concealing the Scrolls in the caves has been much discussed; but a fairly clear answer to the question seems to be now within sight.

That the Scrolls were intended for the use of the occupants of the caves, as Dr. Cross thinks,[1] seems entirely improbable. What use, for example, could the limited number of inhabitants (whoever they may have been)[2] of any one cave have had for numerous copies of any single given text, odd books of the Septuagint, tables of the rotation of the priestly duties, lists of personal names, and so on? Whatever Cave I may have been, a number of similar collections in similar positions precludes any such possibility; and no one would put away a library intended for regular use in so inaccessible a place or disperse it over a number of such places, where no facilities for study can have existed.[3] Archives are equally improbable; for, although these were often stored in jars,[4] the inaccessibility of the caves would make them unsuitable even for such a purpose; and the caves in fact contained extremely few deeds and documents but large literary and religious works, which would not normally be stored with archives of any sort.

A different and obvious explanation of the discoveries at Qumrân, as Fr. de Vaux has argued,[5] is that the caves were chosen as hiding places where valuable property might be kept safe. These caves must have been well known to all who had at any time lived by the Dead Sea, e.g. brigands and robbers, fugitives from justice or religious or political oppression, hermits and others fleeing from the world, Essenes and Covenanters and many like them; and some of these groups may have been settled there from times long past. If then the Covenanters had had their headquarters at Qumrân almost from the start, they would presumably have had many occasions during their checkered history when they would have found the caves useful hiding places for themselves and their property;[6] but even this explanation of the deposits at Qumrân is not free from objection, as argued below.[7]

Accordingly, if the reason for the deposit was not military, e.g. the circumstances of the First Revolt, as Fr. de Vaux thinks,[8] it might have been persecution by the Roman government.

The early years of the 2nd century A.D. were a troubled period for the Jews of Palestine, who suffered much at the hands of their Roman overlords, even if their sufferings were due largely to their

[1] In *Library* 18.
[2] Pp. 46–8.
[3] Cp. Kahle in *VT* I 38–40.
[4] Pp. 7, 391.
[5] In *RB*, NS LVI 593–6.
[6] Cp. 1 Macc. ii. 29–38.
[7] Pp. 384–5.
[8] In *Archéologie* 82–4.

own fault. Foreign rulers had indeed long before this age sought to break their spirit by proscribing their literature. So Antiochus IV had long ago attempted to have all Jewish books on which he could lay hands consigned to the flames,[1] and so the Romans in the time of R. 'Aqîbâ (whom they put to death c. A.D. 132) were said to have proscribed Jewish literature;[2] and its destruction is implicit in the story of the martyrdom of R. Hananiah ben Teradion and other scholars under Hadrian[3] and in the disappearance of certain named books at that time.[4] In the same way Diocletian (A.D. 245–313) proscribed Christian books;[5] for this was an obvious way of silencing troublesome people whose national or religious continuity was based on a sacred literature. The Covenanters' fundamental doctrine of opposition to Rome would have made them ever liable to persecution and have compelled them to keep hiding places ever in mind; there their revolutionary and potentially dangerous literature might safely be hidden.

Any such reason, however, for depositing the Scrolls in the caves round Qumrân, whether invasion by a foreign enemy or persecution by a foreign ruler, is not entirely satisfactory. On the one hand, the care with which these Scrolls, several hundred in number,[6] seem to have been packed and the arduous task of conveying them and stowing them in almost inaccessible caves secretly and safely must have required leisure for careful planning and time for the execution of the plan when made; and neither will have been available with a swift and ruthless enemy overrunning the country and searching every nook and cranny for fugitives and munitions of war. On the other hand, if the Scrolls were being concealed in time of persecution by a hostile government, they would scarcely have been put by their owners in caves in immediate proximity to their own headquarters; these would at once have attracted attention and been searched. In either case, too, the risk of treachery would have been considerable, especially if rumours were abroad that untold wealth had been concealed with the Scrolls in the caves. The Covenanters in such circumstances would surely have sought to smuggle their treasured possessions out of the country to some neighbouring place of safety; such would be Damascus with its large Jewish colony or Egypt whence their society had sprung,[7] where it still had successors[8] and where copies of some of the Scrolls have actually been found.[9] Lastly, such solutions leave unexplained the absence of any copy of *Esther* alone of the books of the Old Testament (as also of *Judith* and *I*

---

[1] 1 Macc. i. 56–7.   [2] B. Talmud *Berakhoth* 61b.
[3] B. Talmud *Abodah Zarah* 17b–18a.
[4] Juynboll *Chronicon Samaritanum* 51 = 189 xlvii § 246.
[5] Eusebius *Ecclesiastical History* VIII ii 4–5.   [6] P. 359.
[7] Pp. 226–37.   [8] Pp. 13, 370–1.   [9] Pp. 14–15.

Maccabees amongst apocryphal works) from the caves; and any solution of the problem must take also this fact into consideration.

Dr. Roth has suggested[1] that the reason for the absence of *Esther*, if not accidental, is that its author tolerates and even favourably regards the rule of a foreign power; it would then be in conflict with one of the principal tenets of the Covenanters, who recognized no other ruler but God. This reason cannot be accepted; for, as Dr. Zeitlin has argued,[2] the authors of *Ezra* and *Nehemiah* and of *Daniel*, of which fragments have been found in the caves,[3] speak equally well of Babylonian and Persian rule. The reason why no copy of *Esther* was included amongst the Scrolls in the caves (if not a mere matter of chance) must be that it was not regarded by the Covenanters in the same light as the rest of the Old Testament. It does not contain the divine name or title (as transmitted in the Massoretic text, though not as translated by the Septuagint)[4] and has indeed no great spiritual or religious value; and it was not, perhaps for that reason or partly for it, subject to the same rule of purity[5] as other books of Scripture.[6] It might be read publicly by any Jew, except a deaf-mute or feeble-minded person; even a minor might read it (though subsequently forbidden to do so) or a woman (except when menstruating) in the home,[7] and the reader might sit or stand to read it.[8] Lastly, the custom prevailed and in fact was prescribed, that at the feast of Purim, at which the roll of *Esther* was publicly read, the people should drink until they could not distinguish between 'Blessed be Mordecai!' and 'Cursed be Haman!'[9] If too the feast of Purim was a Pharisaic innovation connected in some way with the reform of the calendar, the Covenanters would have had an additional reason for rejecting the book dealing with it.[10] It was probably the last book admitted to the canon; for, even when R. 'Aqîbâ (*c.* A.D. 70–132) had declared it to be inspired,[11] doubts were not entirely dispelled and its canonicity continued to be discussed.[12] Similarly, it found no place in the earliest Christian lists, such as those which Melito (A.D. 170) and Gregory Nazianzus (*c.* A.D. 391) have left, while Origen (A.D. 253) appends it at the end of his list; and Athanasius (*c.* A.D. 373) says that it was not classified as canonical but was included with other books which might be read for instruction.[13]

---

[1] In *Background* 34. [2] In the *JQR*, NS XLIX 12–13.
[3] P. 19. [4] Esth. vi. 1.
[5] B. Talmud *Megillah* 7a.
[6] Del Medico *Énigme* 262; cp. Mishnah *Kelim* xv 6 and *Yadaim* iii 5 (s. Danby *Mishnah* 626⁴) and also B. Talmud *Shabbath* 15a.
[7] Mishnah *Megillah* ii 4, P. Talmud *Megillah* 30a–b and B. Talmud *Megillah* 19b–20a.
[8] *Ibid.* iv 1. [9] B. Talmud *Megillah* 7b.
[10] Bowman in *PQS* XCI 26, 30–1. [11] B. Talmud *Megillah* 7a.
[12] P. Talmud *Megillah* 70b and B. Talmud *Megillah* 7a.
[13] Ryle *Canon of the Old Testament* 213–18.

The same or similar reasons will also account for the absence of
Judith and of other apocryphal works of equally little spiritual value
from the caves; for such works might easily have failed to commend
themselves to the puritanical Covenanters and have therefore been
excluded from their libraries, wherever they were living.[1] In any case,
the absence of *Esther* would only have the negative value of allowing
the caves to be regarded as a *gᵉnîzāh*; for it was the only book of the
Old Testament which was generally held to have none of that sanctity
which would normally require the deposit of an unwanted copy of a
document for preservation in such a place.[2]

Accordingly, Mr. Del Medico has revived[3] the suggestion, made
some years ago,[4] that the caves were a 'burial place (*bêṭ gᵉnîzāh*)' where
books and documents which were considered uncanonical or undesir-
able or had gone out of use might be deposited out of sight and harm.[5]

The canon of the Old Testament seems to have been completed for
all practical purposes *c.* 100 B.C.; but doubts and disputes regarding
the canonicity of individual books, based on the presence of inconsistent
passages or contradictions of passages in other parts of Scripture or
of opinions savouring of heresy, lingered on well into the 1st if not the
2nd century A.D. Works of doubtful canonicity then came to be withdrawn from use and put away in some secret place; these were called
'concealed' or 'apocryphal' books, and the place of the deposit was
called a 'place of concealment (*bêṭ gᵉnîzāh*)'. Such books were *Ezekiel*,
Proverbs, Ecclesiastes, Song of Songs, Esther, and perhaps also *Jonah*,[6] as
well as other works not found in the Jewish canon. At the end of the
same century, however, Josephus[7] seems to have found them all in
the canon as known to him; and even those about which the greatest
doubts still lingered had been officially recognized as canonical by
c. A.D. 180.[8]

The use of the *gᵉnîzāh* soon came to be extended to include a different
category of books besides those regarded as uncanonical.[9] These were
in the first instance incorrect copies of the Scriptures or copies which
contained corrections above a certain number on any given page,
e.g. a medial form of a letter in a final position or a final form in a
medial position;[10] secondly, translations of canonical books which did

[1] Cp. Bardtke *Handschriftenfunde* II 118–19.
[2] B. Talmud *Megillah* 7a; s. Del Medico *Énigme* 24.
[3] In *Deux Manuscrits* 93 and *Énigme* 23–7; cp. Albright in *Studies in honour of C. H. Dodd* 164³.
[4] Sukenik *Megilloth Genuzoth* I 10 and II 20; cp. Dhorme in *CRAIB-L* 8 iv 1949, 97–8.
[5] Cp. Mishnah *Shabbath* xvi 1.
[6] Ryle *op. cit.* 202–12; cp. Schürer *Geschichte*³ I 307–11.
[7] In *Against Apion* i 2, 8.   [8] Mishnah *Yadaim* iii 5.
[9] Cp. Talmon in *Textus* II 14–5 (where the texts known as φαυλότερα and κοινά or *vulgata* are described).
[10] P. Talmud *Megillah* i 9/8.

not follow *verbatim* the official text; and thirdly, subversive or heretical books, which would include all sorts of other documents, *e.g.* a contract of marriage or divorce dated by the year of a Roman emperor[1] or by a witness signing his name in Greek letters.[2] Books in the hands of unbelievers were excepted. They ought to be destroyed but might be passed through a flame of fire; if however they had been written by a Jew, a *g^enîzāh* was the proper place for them.[3] Books and documents put away in a *g^enîzāh* which are named in Rabbinic literature include a worn copy of the Law,[4] sacred writings in other than the Hebrew or Greek language[5], a *targûm* (Aramaic translation or paraphrase) of *Job*,[6] a book of genealogies[7] and a medical work;[8] and a single defective letter could condemn a phylactery.[9]

All the documents found in the caves exhibit the defects listed above or similar defects.[10] The copies of the Scriptures are without exception in some way imperfect; for example, the Scroll of *Isaiah A* has been torn and resewn, and the text not only contains numerous erasures and corrections but also does not entirely conform to Rabbinic tradition, *e.g.* in the use of medial and final forms of letters;[11] others contain mistakes, *e.g.* in the misuse of these letters (T ii 22 xii 3, 6, 8, 26)[12] and corrections, some have been rolled up backwards or inside out, and all show marks of injury. The phylacteries[13], too, do not conform to Rabbinic norms and are marred by the omission of clauses and even of verses.[14] The non-Scriptural works, for example *Ecclesiasticus* which might not be read[15] (*i.e.* publicly read; for its contents were well known to the Rabbis, who often quote it) and the *Targum on Job* (which has recently been reported but not yet published),[16] come under the Rabbinic ban; for all who read 'external (*i.e.* extra-canonical and therefore heretical) books' are condemned with those 'who have no share in the world to come'.[17] Genealogical works, too, of which samples have been found at Qumrân, are similarly banned.[18] Briefly, the lists of condemned works in the Talmud might almost have been based on the collections hidden in the caves round Qumrân, so closely do they tally.

Here a passage in the Talmud which speaks of 'external (*i.e.* un-

---

[1] Cp. Q II 101–3 no. 18 (acknowledgement of a debt dated in the 2nd year of the emperor Nero).
[2] Mishnah *Yadaim* iv 8; P. Talmud *Gittin* i 43b, ix 30b.
[3] B. Talmud *Gittin* 45b. [4] *Ibid. Megillah* 26b.
[5] Mishnah *Shabbat* xvi 1.
[6] B. Talmud *Shabbath* 115a; cp. Mishnah *Yadaim* iv 5.
[7] *Ibid. Pesachim* 62b. [8] *Ibid.* 56a.
[9] Mishnah *Menahoth* iii 7 and B. Talmud *Menahoth* 34a; cp. Friedmann *Sifré debé Rab* 75a § 36 (Deut. vi. 9). [10] Del Medico *Deux Manuscrits* 44–7.
[11] Burrows *Scrolls* I xxii (incorrect *m* frequent). [12] Sukenik *Scrolls* 40.
[13] Pp. 17, 19, 21. [14] Kuhn *Phylakterien* 25–6.
[15] B. Talmud *Sanhedrin* 100b. [16] P. 390.
[17] Mishnah *Sanhedrin* x 1. [18] P. 20.

canonical) books' as 'books of heretics' which may not be read acquires exceptional importance; for a variant reading for 'heretics' (*mînîm*), as in several other places, is 'Sadducaeans (*ṣaddûqîn*).[1] The Sadducees of the New Testament cannot be meant, since they are not known to have had their own writings or have left none intact; only the Sadducaeans, *i.e.* the 'Sons of Zadok' or the Covenanters, can be meant.[2] The books so described therefore may well have been or at any rate have included copies of the Scrolls found at Qumrân; that a *targûm* on *Job* has been found at Qumrân and that one is mentioned in the Talmud as a condemned book[3] is therefore significant in the present connection.

The rules for depositing such works in a *gᵉnîzāh* were numerous, varied and detailed. For example, a defective or damaged copy of the Law ought to be put away beside the tomb of a scholar or of his pupil, wrapped in pure linen and enclosed in a jar of earthenware.[4] In other respects the procedure, especially in the case of a copy of the Law, varied: in some countries it was wrapped in pure linen and carried to a *gᵉnîzāh* beside a cemetery, in others it was kept in safe custody in a chamber attached to a synagogue until it could be carried by a pilgrim to the Holy Land and be buried there beside a scholar's bones. Some of the provisions bear a remarkable resemblance to the conditions in which the Scrolls have been found. Many of the Scrolls so far found conform to one or other or several of these rules. They have been wrapped in linen and stored in jars and have been found carefully put away in safe places of concealment. All were fully qualified for interment in a *gᵉnîzāh*, and the caves were proper places to serve as a *gᵉnîzāh*, until the opportunity arose finally to dispose of them, in accordance with Rabbinic prescription.[5]

This explanation of the hiding of the Scrolls, however, still leaves unexplained why they have been found in ten or eleven caves; many *gᵉnîzôt* in the ordinary sense are as inexplicable as many libraries are at Qumrân.[6]

If the Rabbis after fixing the Canon decided to collect and dispose of all unstandardized, imperfect or damaged, copies of the Scriptures and other heterodox writings throughout the country or to compel their owners so to dispose of them, they could hardly have achieved their purpose all at once; for outbursts of religious zeal are apt to be sporadic and their operation intermittent. On such occasions works would be collected first from conspicuous centres, while those from outlying places would come in gradually and late. Consequently,

---

[1] B. Talmud *Sanhedrin* 100b (s. Wünsche *Babylonischer Talmud* II 214); cp. *Megillah* 24b.
[2] Pp. 260–1.   [3] P. 387.
[4] P. Talmud *Megillah* xxvi 2 and B. Talmud *Megillah* 26b.
[5] Cp. Rabin in *Scr. Hieros.* IV 159–61.   [6] Cp. de Vaux *Archéologie* 80–1.

parties would go out to hide them in the *gᵉnîzāh* on which they had decided, for example this or that cave at Qumrân, at suitable times, *e.g.* when a good number of manuscripts had been brought together; and the different burial parties might not always go to the same cave, since their instructions would necessarily be vague.[1] Which cave was used would be immaterial so long as all these ceremonially dangerous texts were safely put away where they might not 'defile the hands', as the Rabbis said, nor be defiled if they contained the divine name; one cave or a dozen caves would serve this purpose equally well.

That the literature found in the caves was predominantly that of the Covenanters would be explained by two facts: that the Sadducaeans (*Ṣaddûqîm*), who were *ex hypothesi* the Covenanters, were the principal 'heretical sect' in early Rabbinic times, and that the caves round Qumrân were of all places the most obvious *gᵉnîzôt* for such literature as theirs. The absence of any copies of *Esther* from the caves, therefore, confirms other indications[2] that they were not a mere hiding place for sacred books from the Temple or from the synagogue of any ordinary Jewish community[3] but *gᵉnîzôt* for books or copies of books disapproved or condemned for this or that reason; for it was not included amongst books condemned to be thus put away, because it was thought not to contain the name of God[4] and was regarded as of doubtful canonicity.

At the same time, that much of the literature in the caves seems to have been that of the Covenanters does not prove that all of it must have been theirs. On the one hand, the Covenanters would be unlikely to have required several and even many copies of books in one place, such as were found in the caves, in an age when few people read and most listened to books being read to them; but they might have brought copies of the Greek Old Testament with them from Egypt (where *ex hypothesi* they had once lived),[5] even if they had little use for them as all must have understood Hebrew perfectly well. On the other hand, the Rabbis, if they were bent on collecting all imperfect, unstandardized or incorrect, copies of the Scriptures and other writings which did not conform to the rules which they had prescribed would pay little regard to the sources from which they came; they would gather them all together and dispose of them on each occasion in the same cave or group of caves. This explanation will also account for the presence in the caves of early texts which may be dated on palaeographical grounds (so far as palaeography can be trusted) before the formation of the society of the Covenanters; they might be ancient texts, both sacred and profane, *e.g.* versions of

[1] Cp. Del Medico *Énigme* 205–6.   [2] Pp. 384–5.
[3] Cp. Josephus *Antiquities* XVI vi 2 § 164.
[4] Actually the divine name seems to have been deliberately eliminated from the Hebrew text (s. Driver in *Textus* I 119–20).   [5] Pp. 226–37.

CC

scriptures[1] and registers[2] which had come at some time or other into the possession of the Covenanters or which, having come from Temple or synagogue in the confusion of the Revolt and its aftermath, had been condemned by the Rabbinical authorities as not conforming to their newly defined standards of correctness and were deposited in the caves with other collections, of which those of the Covenanters constituted the bulk.

A factor which will have contributed to this end will have been the growing insistence on orthodoxy by the Rabbis from an early date and especially between the destruction of Jerusalem (A.D. 70) and the councils of Yabneh (A.D. 90 and A.D. 118); for this will in all likelihood have been followed by 'purges' here and there, as Dr. Kahle suggests,[3] the result of official pressure or of local fanaticism. So already Gamaliel I, the teacher of St. Paul, had ordered an Aramaic Targum on *Job*[4] which was brought to him for a decision, as it was doubtfully canonical, to be buried under a heap of bricks or mortar, and his grandson Gamaliel II declared that he would give orders for such a work to be 'hidden';[5] and early in the following century R. Tarphon, a contemporary of R. 'Aqîbâ (c. A.D. 70–132), declared that he would burn the books of the 'heretics' (*mînîm*) or 'Sadducaeans' (*Ṣaddûqîm*) as well as the *gilyônîm* (apparently apocalypses or Gospels).[6] Allusions to such a banning of 'external' (*i.e.* extra-canonical) writings, including those of the *Ṣaddûqîm*, are found here and there in Rabbinic literature.[7]

At the same time, a contributory factor may have been the gradual extinction of the dwindling communities of Covenanters dispersed among various Syrian and Palestinian centres by death or by the reabsorption of those unable to continue their resistance to orthodox pressure. Such a failure to resist would have compelled little groups of survivors to dispose of their compromising literature in accordance with Rabbinic law and custom; and they would be as careful in the preparations which they made for concealing their Scrolls in the caves as the Rabbis were when they put away condemned literature in a *g⁽e⁾nîzāh* to avoid profaning the name of God. So they would leave their valued Scrolls solemnly interred as though in holy ground, in the hope of better days when their society might come to life again and, recovering the writings in which the records of past heroism and the hopes of future success were enshrined, might be inspired by studying them to renew the struggle against an *imperium* which

[1] Cp. Eusebius *Ecclesiastical History* VI vi 1 (Origen's 'long-hidden versions')

[2] Cp. Josephus *Against Apion* i 7; Mishnah *Yebamoth* iv 13 (archives at Jerusalem) and *Kiddushim* iv 5 (archives at Sepphoris).

[3] In *T.Lz.* LXXIV 94 and LXXV 540; cp. *Handschriften* 59–61.

[4] S. pp. 387–8.   [5] B. Talmud *Shabbath* 115a.

[6] *Ibid.* 116a.

[7] *E.g.* Mishnah *Sanhedrin* x 1; P. Talmud *Pe'ah* i 1; B. Talmud *Shabbath* 116a; *Gittin* 45b, *Sanhedrin* 100a (*mînîm* var. *Ṣaddûqîm*).

infringed the sovereignty of God. Thus the Scrolls would be 'closed and sealed till the time of the end,' as Daniel had been bidden to do with the record of his visions.[1] Which may have been the reason for depositing the Scrolls in the caves round Qumrân, if either is indeed the true reason, is likely to remain as unknown as are the sources of the various collections which have been found in them.

Evidence can be found in the 1st century A.D. for similar procedures in caring for books. So Moses in an apocryphal work,[2] generally dated between A.D. 7 and A.D. 30,[3] says to his destined successor Joshua: 'Now I declare unto thee that the time of the years of my life is fulfilled, and I am passing away to sleep with my fathers . . . ; and do thou receive this writing that thou mayst know how to preserve the books which I shall deliver unto thee; and thou shalt set them in order and anoint them with oil of cedar and put them away in earthen vessels in the place which He (sc. God) made from the beginning of the creation of the world, that His name should be invoked till the day of repentance wherewith the Lord shall visit them in the consummation of the end of the days.' Dr. Kahle, quoting these words, argues[4] that the Scrolls seem to have been similarly interred, not hastily against impending invasion but ceremoniously in accordance with regular custom; but no trace of cedar-oil has been found with the Scrolls, although its use has been conjectured.[5] The jars in which the Scrolls were found might be those in which they had always been stored, or others of a similar type copied from them[6] packed with special care whenever they were being transferred from one place to another to safeguard them against damage on the way. In the same way the Scroll of Copper includes 'a jar, in it one written document (sēfer)' amongst the treasures which it lists (SC vi 4–5). This passage, too, has some importance as evidence for the continued use of the ancient practice of storing documents in jars in the 1st century A.D. Both passages also suggest that conformity with Talmudic rules is not inconsistent with a date long before the age of the Talmud.

Lastly, according to a late Arabic work known as the *Samaritan Chronicle* an air of mystery had come to hang about certain caves at or in the neighbourhood of Qumrân by the time of the Second Revolt (A.D. 132–5).[7] Hadrian, it relates, while besieging Jerusalem, was warned by two Samaritan youths, if he wished to subdue the whole region, to send 'troops to seize and hold Jericho and Lydda and also carefully to close the entrances to the caves, so that no one might take anything into them, but not to approach them himself alone; and then

---

[1] Dan. xii. 9.
[2] Assumption of Moses i 15–18.
[3] Charles *Assumption of Moses* lv–lviii § 11.
[4] In *Das Altertum* III 35–6.
[5] Bruce *Second Thoughts* 27.
[6] Cp. pp.402–7.
[7] Juynboll *Chronicon Samaritanum* 17 (= 187) xlvii §240.

to occupy Bethlehem and so to cut off the supplies being sent from there to Jerusalem'. The *Samaritan Chronicle* is far from being a trustworthy record, but it may occasionally preserve the memory of a historical fact. This story, therefore, in so far as it may be accepted, seems to imply that the caves in this district were known long afterwards to contain something of value to the Samaritans, from which they were willing to divert the attention of the enemy even at the cost of the surrounding towns. This could hardly be the wealth of Jerusalem; but it might or even would rather be sacred writings, possibly even the Scrolls (for the Samaritans and the Covenanters had not a few affinities).[1] In that event, some Scrolls might have been deposited in the caves before A.D. 132–5, with which the other facts here mentioned would agree.

All this reconstruction of the concealment of the Scrolls is naturally conjectural; but some attempt must be made to account for the presence of the Scrolls, as well as that of the Copper-Scroll, in the caves round Qumrân in view of the inadequacy of the current theories. The conjectures, however, are all in accord with known Jewish practices.

Whatever the reason for concealing the Scrolls in the caves round Qumrân may have been, their nature is as clear as their background is intelligible. They were primarily the text-books of an ascetic religious group, whose overriding doctrine was the kingship of God; the copies of the Scriptures, *Discipline* and the *Zadokite Documents*, were directed to the moral and spiritual edification of its members. The fanatical belief in the sovereignty of God with its corollary, an unconquerable passion for liberty, soon had practical results; these were manifested in the withholding of tribute due to a human ruler, and such a policy if continued could but bring open rebellion in its train. So a religious group became a political party; asceticism begat fanaticism, which in turn bred civil war and rebellion. The party, becoming involved in a struggle, which was both religious and national, against the Roman *imperium*, began searching the Scriptures for precedents to justify the taking up of arms. The prophets, notably Habakkuk 'denouncing in succession the rapacious violence of the Chaldaeans, the suicidal policy pursued by them in establishing their dominion, the dishonesty and cruelty by which the magnificence of their cities was maintained, the barbarous delight with which they reduced to a state of helplessness the nations that fell under their sway, their irrational idolatry'[2] offered texts which could without much violence to context and sense be applied to the Roman invaders of the Commentator's own day; but he restricted himself to the first two chapters because the third had little that suited his purpose. The author of the *Commentary on Habakkuk* adapted these ancient prophecies to the description of the

---

[1] Pp. 87, 260, 322, 337–8, 391–2, 426–7, 429, 467.
[2] S. R. Driver *Literature of the Old Testament*[9] 338.

events of his own time and used them as a guarantee of future success, both national and personal: as the Chaldaeans had been punished, so the Romans would be punished for their arrogance and cruelty; as the enemies of the nation had been punished, so the enemies of the Covenanters would be punished. These perhaps rather than any desire to heal the breach between the Sadducaeans or Covenanters and the Zealots, as Mr. Del Medico suggests,[1] were the motives which animated the author of this work; for the way in which he spoke of the enemies of the party was not one that was likely to cast oil on troubled waters. The *Hymns*, like many of the Biblical Psalms, were expressions of gratitude for deliverance from a great disaster and provided justification of the Commentator's interpretation of Habakkuk's prophecies; and the *War* held out the promise of eventual victory in the manner of an apocalypse, when all the injuries done to the nation by the Romans would be finally avenged. Throughout the Scrolls echoes of the Maccabaean struggle can be detected,[2] reminding the party of a previous revolt which had been successful and by its success seemed to provide a guarantee that the present revolt would be equally successful. The Scrolls by their appeal to the past justified the present and provided a guide to the future, so that despair might be turned to hope. Here another reason may be found for putting the Scrolls out of sight in the caves round Qumrân: the Rabbis, fearful of a repetition of the disaster of A.D. 70, would be only too glad to be rid of such compromising documents, of which several were composed with the express purpose of keeping the anti-Roman spirit alive and provoking just such another rebellion.

The theory here maintained, that the caves were some sort of *gᵉnîzāh*, would go far to account for the conditions in which the Scrolls were found to have been put away and for the types of literary and other documents recovered from them; for these might have been concealed as potentially dangerous from a political or a theological point of view or as the treasured possessions of a religious and political group which ran the risk of extinction. The explanation, too, whichever form of it is adopted, suits both historical and technical conditions late in the 1st or early in the 2nd century A.D.

3. ARCHAEOLOGICAL PROBLEMS

Objections to a date for the Scrolls in the 1st or 2nd century A.D. and therefore to the identification of the central historical event described, however allusively, in them with that which Josephus reports as having taken place on Mt. Ophel in the autumn of A.D. 66[3] have been raised under several heads, of which the archaeological is the most important.

[1] In *Deux Manuscrits* 192.   [2] Pp. 353–5.   [3] Pp. 267–81.

The facts on which the archaeological objections are based may be accepted without any reservation; what may and indeed must be disputed are the inferences drawn from them. They clash with the historical notices in the texts themselves; but the internal evidence afforded by a document must take precedence over any external evidence. Some of these inferences are possible but not inevitable, others are dubious or even logically untenable.

I. The notion that the 'monastery' at Qumrân must have been destroyed in the summer of A.D. 68 rests on the supposition that the series of coins of the Revolt found in Level II[1] does not go on after that year.[2] Hence Prof. Rowley says[3] with some approximation to the facts that 'since the hundreds of coins in the lower level [i.e. Level II] were all coined before the fall of Jerusalem, and all of those found in the higher level [i.e. Level III] were coined after that Fall, it is virtually certain that the destruction of the earlier of these buildings took place very close to that Fall', and again that the date of the demarcation between these two structures is 'drawn with precision in that year A.D. 68 by a series of Jewish coins running down to that year, and a number of Roman coins from that year to A.D. 73. It seems impossible to escape the conclusion that the change of structural plan for the building and the change of occupiers belonged together and that the year 68 was the year that saw that change'. Fr. de Vaux even goes so far as to say[4] that *lorsque cette explication s'accorde avec les données d'histoire, l'hypothèse est démontrée*, having forgotten that the historical records say nothing of the destruction of Qumrân in A.D. 68 by the Romans; in other words, the *données d'histoire* are historical fiction! Even the discovery of a solitary coin of the second year of the Revolt (A.D. 67–8) in the neighbouring ruins at 'Ain Fäšḫah in no wise strengthens the argument;[5] and, however watertight it may at first sight look, it is seen when closely examined to be quite unsound.

In fact, what the coins prove is by no means clear or decisive.[6] The latest coins found in the 'monastery' (Level II) are five Jewish coins of the third year of the Revolt (Apr., A.D. 68–Mar., A.D. 69), none of the fourth (Apr., A.D. 69–Mar., A.D. 70) and only one of the fifth (Apr.–Sept., A.D. 70)[7] year[8]. The reason for this sudden cessation of Jewish coins would not necessarily be that the Jews had been driven out of the place; for Jerusalem was completely invested by the Romans

---

[1] Pp. 37–41.
[2] De Vaux in *RB*, NS LXIII 565–9; cp. *Archéologie* 29–32.
[3] In *TICP* IV (*Mélanges Bibliques*) 346 and Hempel & Rost *Von Ugarit nach Qumrân* 189–90; cp. *Scrolls from Qumran* 17.
[4] In *RB*, NS LXVI 99–102.   [5] *Ibid.* 245–6.
[6] Cp. Bardtke in *TLz.* LXXXVII 816–7.
[7] Yadin in *JLN* CCXLV [31. x. 1964] 696.
[8] Cp. Roth in *Num. Chron.* VII ii 91–100 (where the reckoning of the years on the coins of the Revolt is discussed).

by mid-summer A.D. 68,[1] all egress from the city was stopped and coins minted there could not have been conveyed in any quantity to outlying places. The rarity of coins of the last two years in collections[2] suggests that the mint was going out of operation; bullion would be running short (possibly removed to places of safety in the country) and conditions in the city would not have been conducive to minting coin on a large scale.[3] The discovery of two coins of the second and one of the fourth year of the Revolt at Masada does not refute this argument; for, so far from being 'evidence that in A.D. 69–70 there was full intercourse between Jerusalem and Masada, undisturbed by the Roman legions',[4] it proves only that someone carrying these three coins was once there. A local mint, too, might even have been set up outside Jerusalem. Otherwise, the Jewish garrison would have obtained both money and food by raiding the countryside, cutting off parties of Roman stragglers or intercepting convoys, as Cestius had been caught at the very beginning of the Revolt.[5] This state of affairs would also account for the presence of Roman coins of A.D. 67–8 in the fort which succeeded the 'monastery' (Level III); they might as well have been seized by the Jews in such a raid and brought there by them as by a Roman garrison, since 'nothing about the coins reveals that they were left by a Roman garrison',[6] and Roman coins were the principal currency in Palestine almost as much before as after the destruction of Jerusalem in A.D. 70.

The truth is that a deposit of coins is largely a matter of chance, and what it can prove is strictly limited. Coins do not go out of circulation and are not deposited in an archaeological site immediately after being minted, and they may remain current for a very long time in remote districts. That a maximal period of circulation is 150 years[7] is by no means a fact; for example, dollars of the Austrian empress Maria Theresa (A.D. 1717–80) were found by the British army to be the only currency accepted by the Arabs when war broke out in A.D. 1914. A large mass of coins found *in situ* will establish the general trend of its occupation, but neither many nor few will fix a precise date. Accordingly, Fr. de Vaux puts the case fairly[8] when he says that the Jewish coins *à elles seules* do not prove that the Jews evacuated Qumrân in A.D. 68 and that the Roman coins *à elles seules* do not prove that the Roman garrison occupied it in the same year;[9] but he surely goes too far in claiming that, since the two groups of coins are exactly

---

[1] Josephus *War* IV ix 1 §§ 486–90; cp. V ii 3 §§ 67–70.
[2] Cp. Madden *Coins of the Jews* 197, 206 and Reifenberg *Ancient Jewish Coins*[2] 32.
[3] Cp. Roth in *IEJ*. XII 42–6.   [4] Kadman in *IEJ* VII 61–5.
[5] P. 375.
[6] Teicher in *Lit. Suppl.* LVII 160; s. *Antiquity* XXXVII 25–30.
[7] Bardtke in *TLz*. LXXXV 269–70.   [8] In *Archéologie* 35–6.
[9] Cp. Kanael in *Eretz-Israel* V 164–70.

divided between two superimposed levels, the Jewish in the lower and the Roman in the upper, the place then changed hands. The facts can be otherwise explained; and the use of one point susceptible of alternative explanations to establish another is tantamount to falling into the fallacy of equivocation. All that can be said is that the evidence of the coins is consistent with either A.D. 68 or A.D. 73 for the abandonment of the buildings by the Jews and the occupation of them by a Roman garrison.[1]

II. Another argument supposed to prove the abandonment of the 'monastery' at Qumrân by the Jews and its occupation by the Romans in A.D. 68 is that the buildings, after having been burnt, appear to have been adapted to a different purpose.[2] Not only does a distinct type of pottery come into use, but the occupants seem also to have cut up some of the common rooms of the main building of the complex into barracks, using only the most easily fortified portion of this building and leaving the remainder of the site in ruins. The elaborate water-system of the earlier settlement, not being required by the reduced company, was by-passed by a 'crude canal dug helter-skelter' through installations of the second period of occupation to connect with a single cistern in the south-east.[3] Thus altered, the buildings were put to a different purpose, serving as a military post which was maintained for some few years towards the end of the 1st century A.D.[4] This description, so far as facts are recorded, may be accepted, but no evidence has been produced to show that the alterations were made not by the Jewish occupants themselves but by the Romans; for the argument that the change-over from Jewish to Roman coins means that new occupants must have taken possession of the 'monastery' has been shown to be not necessarily sound. Further, the description of the alterations as 'crude' and 'helter-skelter' does not suggest Roman work; and what need is there to suppose that everything called 'Roman work' must have been the work of Roman hands? Not every Gothic building is the work of Goths! The supposition that the 'Roman' alterations were the work of the Jewish occupants of the 'monastery' would not be absurd; for the Jews were thoroughly familiar with Roman military structures, and many might have been employed, willing or unwilling, on building them; and the half-Jew Herod knew how to fortify buildings so as to make them as nearly as possible impregnable.[5] The Jewish levies, too, when the Revolt broke out, showed themselves apt pupils in Roman military methods, and

---

[1] Cp. Bardtke *Handschriftenfunde* II 71–3 (A.D. 68) and Schonfield *Secrets* 38–40 (A.D. 73).
[2] De Vaux in *RB*, NS LXIII 567; s. Rowley in Hempel & Rost *op. cit.* 189–90.
[3] Pp. 38, 41.   [4] Cross *Library* 47–8.
[5] Josephus *War* I xxi 10 §§ 419–21, VII vi 2 §§ 173–6 and viii 3 §§ 285–93.

the *War* confirms their aptitude.[1] The final argument, that the Romans will have militarized the 'monastery' as 'a military outpost to watch over the northern half of the Dead Sea'[2] would of course be possible if that had been necessary after their capture of the place, whenever that may have been, *e.g.* after A.D. 73; that it was militarized as 'a forward post to protect Jericho against the centres of a guerilla resistance southward in the desert of Judah'[3] is incredible. The 'monastery' lay on a spur projecting into and overlooking the narrow plain along the edge of the Dead Sea and so commanded only the coastal route, which led nowhere; contrariwise the heights behind it, while preventing its occupants from exercising any effective control over the desert routes which were invisible from the 'monastery', would enable it to be effectively overlooked and its occupants to be held in check!

These arguments against the theory of the abandonment of the 'monastery' by the Covenanters and its destruction by the Romans in A.D. 68 are reinforced by the silence of the historical records, which throw out no hint of such an event.

First, Josephus says[4] only that Vespasian visited the Dead Sea 'to explore the lake' and that, having established camps at Jericho and Adida (a small place situated about 20 miles to the north-west of Jerusalem), he returned to Caesarea to await news from Rome. If he had gone on to Qumrân and, finding a Jewish garrison there, had attacked it, it would surely have been desperately defended, as Masada was in A.D. 73, and in the end seriously damaged or even razed to the ground. Not even the presence of a number of arrows in the buildings would have proved that they had been attacked by a military force: for, as Dr. Teicher has pointed out,[5] they were not scattered outside the walls or in the open courtyards but were collected together in certain rooms, so that they were as likely to have belonged to the occupants as to the attacking force. Further, if desperate fighting had taken place, if the buildings had been demolished and the garrison massacred, Josephus would surely have mentioned such a disaster in his detailed account of the events of A.D. 68, as he mentions[6] the fate of many other places in the course of that and of other campaigns.

Second, the only other evidence cited for such a campaign involving the capture of Qumrân by a Roman unit is the discovery there of a coin which is supposed to prove that *Legio X Fretensis* must have

[1] Pp. 193–6.
[2] Fritsch *Qumran Community* 19.
[3] Cross *Library* 47–8.
[4] In *War* IV viii 4 § 477.
[5] In *Lit. Suppl.* LVII 160.
[6] *E.g.* in *War* VII vi 1 § 163 (Herodium), 3 § 190–4 § 209 (Machaerus), and viii 5 § 304–1 § 409 (Masada); cp. vi 5 §§ 210–15 (battle of the Forest of Jardes, apparently a corruption of *Happardēs* near Herodium whence Nehemiah is said to have fetched timber, now called *Jäbäl älFärdês*; s. Jepsen in *ZDP-V* LXXIV 65–8.)

occupied the place at some time during these years because it is sur-
charged with the number of that legion; but this symbol is now thought
to have been misinterpreted.[1] An undated coin of this legion, however,
would in any case prove nothing, as it was continuously in the country
from A.D. 66 (except perhaps for a brief absence during the Parthian
campaign of A.D. 113–17) to A.D. 138.[2] Further, this same legion during
the relevant years, so far as the available information goes, was
stationed at Caesarea in A.D. 67 and was moved soon afterwards to
Scythopolis;[3] and nothing else is heard of it till A.D. 70, when Titus
ordered it 'to go up by way of Jericho' and join the army besieging
Jerusalem.[4]

Third, a small point, to which Dr. Roth draws attention,[5] against
supposing that Vespasian had conducted any sort of campaign against
Jericho and Qumrân in A.D. 68 is that Eusebius declares[6] that the
Romans only took and destroyed Jericho on account of its disloyalty
at the same time as Jerusalem, *i.e.* in A.D. 70; this piece of information
suggests that the Romans after Vespasian's visit had left the place
undisturbed, as they had no reason to doubt its loyalty, and even
withdrew their troops from it for use against Jerusalem.

The arguments here adduced, then, although *argumenta e silentio*, are
in favour of supposing that Qumrân too was left undisturbed in A.D. 68
and was not taken and destroyed till A.D. 70 or even A.D. 73, when
Lucilius Bassus and Flavius Silva reduced the region of the Dead Sea.[7]
This conclusion is further supported by the fact that Herodium (close
to Qumrân), Engaddi and Masada were occupied by the insurgents
early in the war and remained in their hands till the final collapse of
the Revolt in A.D. 73.[8]

The inferences, then, which have been drawn from the archaeological facts are in the highest degree precarious, even impossible;
accordingly, another reconstruction of the history may be attempted.

The site at Qumrân would be perhaps the earliest home of the
Covenanters in Palestine, and their predecessors probably developed it
as a refuge from persecution in the latter part of the 1st century
B.C.;[9] here the nucleus of a partly spiritual and partly political society
of refugees was formed and built up. When the work of the anti-
Roman factions increased the danger from Rome and the number of
political refugees grew, the society became ever less spiritual and ever
more political. When a clash with Rome became not only inevitable
but also imminent, the spiritually minded members who disapproved

[1] De Vaux *Archéologie* 32[1].   [2] Parker *Roman Legions* 138–63.
[3] Josephus *War* III vii 22 §§ 233–4 and 31 §§ 289–306, ix 1 §§ 412–13; IV ii 1 § 87.
[4] *Ibid.* V i 1 § 42; cp. ii 3 § 69.   [5] In *QS* XCI 127.
[6] Lagarde *Onomastica Sacra* 265 (131, 31); cp. 131–2.
[7] P. 210; cp. Schonfield *Secrets* 39–40, 160.
[8] P. 242, n. 3.   [9] P. 47.

of violence as well as the elderly and the sickly, in fact all unwilling to take or incapable of taking up arms, would be evacuated to some safe place of refuge (such as Damascus might then be); the militant members would have remained in the 'monastery' as an advanced post, while Masada served as their arsenal and base.[1] When however Vespasian and Titus invaded Palestine and even reached Jericho, prudence would dictate the withdrawal of the Covenanters' garrison to Herod's almost impregnable fortress of Masada; but on leaving the 'monastery' at Qumrân they would certainly have dismantled the buildings and set fire to them. Alternatively, if they had had no time to do so, the Roman commanders, who would hardly have left the neighbourhood without some sort of reconnaissance in force and would not be likely to leave an unreduced stronghold in their rear, would not improbably (for the suggestion is a mere conjecture, since Josephus says nothing of any such operations) have sent a small force forward to examine the ground and burn or demolish any positions likely to afford a refuge for the insurgents when they came back. When then the main body fell back from the region of the Dead Sea, a holding force could be sent to restore the damage and reconvert the 'monastery' into a fort to serve as an advanced post against their return and to harass the rear of the legions investing Jerusalem; this would explain why the repairs were 'crude' and carried out 'helter-skelter', since the conversion could only be a hasty improvization by Jews on Roman models. Such a force would have maintained a precarious existence at Qumrân for some years, supporting themselves by carrying out raids in the neighbouring country, probably almost till A.D. 73; then, when Bassus and Silva were eventually sent to wipe out the last pockets of resistance round the Dead Sea,[2] the little force would find the 'monastery' untenable and would naturally fall back on their last stronghold at Masada, where they met a heroic end in A.D. 73, when that place was totally destroyed.[3]

This reconstruction of the history of these years will explain also why the 'monastery' was found fit for occupation by the Jewish insurgents during the Second Revolt in A.D. 132–5, as coins issued by them and found *in situ* prove.[4] The Romans had not taken it by storm and dismantled or completely destroyed it in A.D. 68, since they had not then had to attack it in force, and they did not raze it to the ground in A.D. 73, because they had found it empty when they came to extinguish the last embers of revolt; for the rebels had fallen back on Masada, the strongest fortress in the neighbourhood, where the final resistance was offered.

---

[1] Cp. Josephus *War* II xvii 7 §§ 433–4 and IV vii 2 § 399.
[2] Josephus *War* VII vi 1 § 163–5, § 215 (Bassus) and viii 1 § 252–ix 2 § 406 (Silva).
[3] Cp. Schonfield *Secrets* 39–40.   [4] Cp. de Vaux in *RB*, NS LXVI 100–1.

III. Pliny[1] and Synesius[2] put the Essene centre respectively at Engada or Engaddi (Engedi in the Old Testament), which lies about midway between Qumrân and Masada, *i.e.* along the southern half of the western shore of the Dead Sea towards Sodom, whereas Qumrân lay near the northern end of this same shore; thus, if Masada also was held by Covenanters or Zealots, the area occupied by them and the Essenes overlapped.[3] The line of places from north to south was Qumrân, Engaddi, Masada, Sodom. The argument has then been put forward that, since no buildings of the Essenes have been found at Engaddi, none can ever have lived there and that the ancient authorities have made a mistake; the Essenes must then be supposed to have lived at Qumrân and to be identical with the Covenanters. Thus in the words of Fr. de Vaux[4] 'Pliny the elder, who had been in Palestine, says that the Essenes were living on the western shores of the Dead Sea, north of Engaddi, a little higher [than] and at some distance from the shore, in the sole company of palm-trees. Between Engaddi and the northern end of the Dead Sea Khirbet Qumrân is the only ruin which corresponds to Pliny's description, the Qumrân region is the only region where palm-trees could grow in number.' Pliny, who seems to have served on the Roman staff in Palestine in A.D. 69–70,[5] nowhere claims to have been down to Engaddi; and his brief account of the Essenes does not suggest a visit. He also does not say that the Essenes were living 'north of Engaddi'; what he does say[6] is that 'the Essenes live on the western side [*sc.* of the Dead Sea] away from the noxious exhalations of the coast . . . , having only palm-trees for company. . . . Lying below these (*infra hos*) was formerly the town called Engada, second only to Jerusalem in the fertility of its soil and its palm-groves but now just another ash-heap'. That 'below these' means that Engaddi lay further down the coast, *i.e.* to the south of the supposed Essene settlement at Qumrân (or in other words that the Essene settlement lay to the north of Engada)[7] is linguistically possible even though such a use of the preposition is rare; but it cannot at the same time mean also that the town lay lower (*sc.* in altitude) than the settlement (or, in other words, that the Essenes were living a 'little higher' than, *i.e.* above, the shore). The same phrase cannot bear a double translation; and, once again, invoking one of two alternative explanations of a word to prove a point is to commit the fallacy of equivocation. Also, the whole description does not suggest that the Essene settlement was nearly 20 miles distant from the town of Engada; rather, it implies that it was contiguous though out of reach of the noxious exhalations of the

---

[1] In *Natural History* V 17.
[2] In *Opera* (Petavius) 39.
[3] Cp. Cross *Library* 42–3.
[4] In *Listener* LIX 1008; cp. *Archéologie* 100–2.
[5] Ziegler in Pauly-Wissowa's *Real-Encyclopädie* XXI i [XLI] 277–8.
[6] In *Natural History* V xv 73.
[7] Dupont-Sommer *Nouveaux Aperçus* 18[3].

shore. The phrase must therefore be taken in its plain sense as meaning what it says, that the town lay 'below' (*i.e.* at a lower level than) the settlement, *i.e.* to the east of it and between it and the sea; the Essenes, then, were settled on the salubrious high land standing well back from and overlooking the coast, not down in the torrid and unhealthy coastal plain[1]. Further, several ancient writers disprove the assertion that Qumrân is the only locality in the neighbourhood where palms can grow; both Jesus ben Sirach (if a variant reading may be trusted)[2] and Josephus,[3] who knew Engaddai (as he calls the place), support Pliny on this point. Clearly, the present conditions there as at Jericho are no guide to its past fertility. The argument, too, that the Essenes could not have lived to the west of, *i.e.* on the high ground above, Engaddi because palms cannot grow on the heights whereas the members of the community are said to be *à la fois solitaires et entourés des palmiers*[4] will not hold water. Pliny's *socia palmarum* is as obviously a poetical exaggeration (for he had probably never seen the place) as his assertion that the Essenes *per saeculorum milia—incredibile dictu—gens aeterna est, in quae nemo nascitur*, which is certainly not intended to be literally taken, even though it is the only literary evidence for their presence by the Dead Sea before A.D. 70.[5] The palms could not have come to the Essenes, but the Essenes (albeit *solitaires*) could have gone to the palm-groves to collect the fruit, just as the Covenanters must have gone down to their farm at some distance from Qumrân for food; and exactly the same objection applies if the Essenes are confused with the Covenanters and transferred against all the evidence to Qumrân, where too palms can grow in the saline soil of the shore but not on the heights behind it. This argument, then, for identifying the Covenanters with the Essenes is as weak as any that has been put forward; and both Pliny and Synesius would have been capable of saying Qumrân if they had meant Qumrân, even though its ancient name is now not certainly known.[6]

Finally, this whole argument for identifying the Essenes and the Covenanters on this score is undermined by the archaeologists themselves; for Prof. Mazar (Maisler) reports[7] remains at Engaddi coinciding in style and period with those at Qumrân, *i.e.* the Roman period of Palestinian history. That these remains do not appear to have belonged to such substantial buildings[8] as those at Qumrân accords with the different outlooks of the Essenes and the Covenanters. The Essenes would not have required strongly fortified structures capable of resisting hostile attacks as well as the ravages of time; for a society

[1] Cp. Audet in *RB*. NS LXVIII 347–65.
[2] Ecclus. xxiv 13.
[3] In *Antiquities* IX i 2 § 7.
[4] De Vaux in *RB*, NS LXVI 105–6.
[5] Cp. Zeitlin in *Tradition* II 175–6.
[6] Pp. 36–7.
[7] In *BPES* XV 25–8.
[8] Cp. de Vaux *Archéologie* 101.

which, refusing any form of military training and possessing no weapons, abjured war would have no need of a fortress, and such a building would have constituted a negation of one of the fundamental principles of their order.[1] Contrariwise, opposition to foreign rule was the fundamental doctrine of Covenanters and Zealots; both must have long known that such a doctrine would inevitably bring them into conflict with Rome and would have prepared a stronghold or strongholds where in case of need they might take refuge.

IV. The connection of the Scrolls with the 'monastery', as distinct from the caves, at Qumrân is another assumption, which may be regarded with scepticism; for it is totally unproved, even although it is not therefore necessarily wrong.

The principal argument put forward to show that the Scrolls must derive from the 'monastery' is that the buildings and the caves attest the presence in these places of a group of human beings who lived and worked in them and buried their dead close at hand; the manuscripts can only have belonged to this group and so prove it to have been a religious community; its religious character is *confirmé par la destination collective de la plupart des constructions et par l'ordonnance regulière du grand cimetière*, and this presupposes *une société organisée selon un régime communautaire et soumise à une regle*; and examples of such a rule have been found in the Scrolls from the caves.[2] This is very nearly an *argumentum in circulo*; and individually, all the arguments connecting the Scrolls with the 'monastery' are weak. The appeal to the *destination collective* of the buildings simply begs the question, since no such institution as a Jewish monastery is known, and the buildings may have been intended collectively as much for a place of refuge or for a barracks as for a monastery. That the Scrolls are religious documents and that the 'monastery' may have been a religious establishment proves no necessary connection between the Scrolls and the buildings, just as the proximity of the caves to them proves nothing. Proximity would equally well prove that any scribe in Jerusalem who could write actually wrote, if he did not compose, all the documents in the *École Biblique et Archéologique* in the Old City!

The connection between the 'monastery' and the Scrolls is further thought to be supported by two other arguments, which are equally weak. First, jars have been found in it identical with those in which the Scrolls had been packed in the caves.[3] The coincidence, however, may be a pure matter of chance: for example, the Scrolls may have been brought at any time after their composition to the caves for concealment, and the persons charged with putting them there may have found the jars ready to hand, having been left by previous

[1] P. 117.   [2] De Vaux *op. cit.* LXVI 95.
[3] De Vaux in *RB*, NS LXIII 551–63; cp. *Archéologie* 44–6, 78–9.

occupants, and have at once put them to their own purposes; or similar jars may have been manufactured elsewhere, for the clay is said to be not local,[1] and other jars of the same type are reported from Egypt.[2] Pottery, too, goes as much by period as by place. Second, the hand-writing on the Scrolls is said to be identical with that on potsherds from the 'monastery';[3] but these are exceedingly few in number and certainly not enough to establish so important a point, and handwriting not *in pari materia* is a singularly fallible criterion and can by itself hardly be said to prove anything.[4]

Other difficulties, as Mr. del Medico also remarks,[5] not however all so serious as he claims,[6] beset the whole conception as built up by the archaeologists.

The idea of a 'monastery' cannot itself be rejected out of hand as non-Jewish and anachronistic, unless the Essenes are regarded as a myth; and this is improbable.[7] The *scriptorium*, too, cannot be dismissed as an anachronism; for Egyptian scribes wrote in a place called the 'house of life', as shown in pictures,[8] and Cicero's friend Atticus would have had some such place where the *librarii plurimi* and *anagnostae* employed by him in his publishing business did their work.[9] The small size of the chamber, the paucity of ink-wells and the absence of pens and parchment,[10] such as might be expected if it had been a *scriptorium*, would make it an unlikely place for the copying of many hundreds of manuscripts or for a 'college of scribes'[11]; it would have been adequate only as an office where letters and despatches might be drafted and copied as from the headquarters of a religious organiza-tion, a barracks or a garrison. The use, too, of jars instead of drawers or cases for the Scrolls (for jars are of little use except for storing documents which are not much wanted or are obsolete) would have been an anachronism in a library in Roman times, when *capsae* and *scrinia* were normally used; and the inkpots are actually Roman models.[12] The so-called 'writing tables' are anachronistic, since such things seem to be otherwise unknown before the 3rd–4th centuries A.D.[13] The only extant pictures of Assyrian scribes show them standing with the tablet or the leather on which they are writing held in the right hand;[14] Egyptian scribes squatted on the ground with a board carrying the 'paper' supported across their knees or propped against

---

[1] De Vaux *ibid.* LXVI 96–8.   [2] Pp. 40–1; cp. p. 391.
[3] De Vaux *ibid.* 94–5.   [4] P. 412.
[5] In *Énigme* 99–109; cp. *Sanctuaires et Pèlerinages* IX 1–12.
[6] De Vaux *ibid.* 108–10.   [7] Pp. 105–6.
[8] Erman & Ranke *Aegypten* 125–7.
[9] Cornelius Nepos *de viris illustribus* XV (*Atticus*) xiii 3.
[10] De Vaux in *Listener* LIX 1007; cp. *Archéologie* 79–80.
[11] Dhorme in *CRAIB-L* 1953, 319; 1955, 385.
[12] De Vaux *Archéologie* 23.   [13] *Ibid.* 23–4.
[14] Driver *Semitic Writing*[2] 34–6 (fig. 4 and pl. 24).

a piece of furniture.[1] Greeks wrote in the same position but with the writing tablet resting on the palm of the left hand[2] and Romans apparently wrote in the same way,[3] as also Arabs commonly did.[4] How the ancient Hebrews wrote is not known; but pupils sat at their masters' feet[5] and therefore probably wrote squatting on the ground like other ancient (including Oriental) writers. Jewish scribes presumably followed the same practice although they had a 'base' (*bāsîsyâ*), of which the nature is unknown,[6] at hand.[7] Further, the table has been thought unsuitable for writing, at any rate on a large scale; it has a slightly concave top, which must have made writing on it very difficult, and beneath it is so shaped that a scribe cannot have sat close enough to it for any such purpose. This concave top has been thought to suggest a seat (if its construction may have been strong enough to carry a man's weight), when the supposed benches may perhaps have been footstools.[8] These difficulties may however be exaggerated; the concavity of the surface of the table is very slight, and the scribe may have crouched with crossed legs on the bench and leant forward to write on the table.[9] Nothing, too, supports the suggestion that the shallow depressions in the table were intended for 'holy water' for the lustrations incumbent on scribes engaged in copying the Scriptures;[10] for this practice does not seem to be ancient, so far as the available evidence goes, and is in any case confined to copying the Law (*tôrāh*). The depressions, therefore, may equally well have been made to hold water for the purely secular purpose of washing ink off the fingers and cleaning the pens so as not to spoil the copy, if that is the purpose of the tables. An alternative suggestion, that the tables may have been *mensae* used in Christian funerary rites,[11] has nothing to commend it in default of archaeological or other evidence of Christian practices at Qumrân.[12] The habit of ascribing religious significance to every archaeological discovery is as insidious as it may be misleading!

Any connection of the Scrolls with the 'monastery' must then be held to be logically unproved, and it probably never will be proved; it is a working hypothesis and as such must not be allowed to stand in the way of a free examination of the whole problem of the Scrolls and the attempt to recover or reconstruct the history of the circle from

---

[1] Erman & Tizard *op. cit.* 100, 112–13; cp. Benzinger *Hebräische Archäologie* 185 [*Abb.* 182].
[2] Freeman *Schools of Hellas* 86–7.   [3] Wilkins *Roman Education* 44–5.
[4] Bauer *Volksleben*[2] 79.   [5] Cp. Acts xxii. 3 and Mishnah *Aboth* i 4.
[6] Levy *Wörterbuch* (T, M) I 245 and Jastrow *Dictionary* I 179; s. Krauss *Talmudische Archäologie* III 157–8.
[7] Mishnah *Kelim* xxiv 6.
[8] Bruce *Second Thoughts* 50 and Metzger in *RQ* I 509–15.
[9] De Vaux *op. cit.* 23–4.   [10] Fritsch *Community* 5.
[11] Teicher in *JJS* V 147; s. Del Medico & Garner *Riddle* 89.
[12] Cp. de Vaux in *RB*, NS LXVI 108–9 (who speaks of a *plate-forme aux deux alvéoles* and a *longue table de briques et de plâtre*, not of two tables).

which they emanate. At the same time, due consideration must be given to the accumulation of probabilities; so each of those which have just been discussed, though individually points of little if any weight, when taken together become significant as conveying hints of some kind of connection between the caves and their contents on the one side and the buildings and their occupants on the other side.

Here two notices in the Scrolls may be considered: the first describes the Covenanters as separating themselves from the world 'to go into the wilderness' (D viii 13) and the second designates their society 'the exiles of the wilderness' (W i 2). In these passages the 'wilderness' may be treated as a figure of speech,[1] as 'Damascus' is sometimes treated, though with as little reason; for a figure of speech must not be invoked if the fact can be established. Damascus has been shown to be a real place,[2] and the Wilderness of Judah where it is mentioned in the Scrolls can be similarly explained; for geographical necessity and the analogy of the Essenes compel the conclusion that this is the only part of the country where the Covenanters can have lived their solitary lives, as it is also the place where the Scrolls have been found. That the Covenanters and the Scrolls seem thus to be brought together suggests a real connection which, as hinted above, may be accepted as a working hypothesis if not as a logically established historical fact.

In conclusion, any Scrolls written before the destruction of the 'monastery' (whenever that is dated) may have been written elsewhere but may equally well have been written in it; any dated after that event cannot have been written there and must therefore have been written elsewhere. The Scrolls found in any one cave may and perhaps will have all been put there at the same time, whenever and wherever they may have been written. If therefore any of the Scrolls found in Cave I must be dated after the destruction of the 'monastery', all including any written before that date will have been put there after it; consequently even those written before it (even if written in the 'monastery') will probably not have been brought directly from the 'monastery' to the cave[3]. What may have happened to them in the meanwhile, then, becomes an important part of the problem of the Scrolls.

V. The archaeology of the caves is equally indecisive, partly because most of them had been seriously disturbed before their examination by competent archaeologists and partly because of the lack of comparable objects from other sites in Palestine.

The use of jars for the safe custody of the Scrolls *per se* affords no evidence of date; for it seems to have been a widespread custom in antiquity.[4] The Babylonians and Assyrians often stored their clay-

---

[1] Cp. Carmignac *Guerre* 5.   [2] Pp. 304–5.   [3] S. pp. 359–73.
[4] Conroyer in *RB*, NS LXII 76–81 and Milik in *Biblica* XXXI 504–8.

tablets in them;[1] the practice is mentioned in the Old Testament and
in a pseudapocryphal work[2] as also in the Talmud;[3] Origen speaks
of manuscripts found in a jar at or near Jericho;[4] Egyptian, Greek and
Arabic *papyri* have been found so preserved in places as far apart as
Egypt and Kurdistan, and one Arabic *papyrus* gives the price of
jars[5] for keeping documents.[6]

The jars in which the Scrolls from Cave I had been put away were
cylindrical in shape, on the average 2 feet high and 10 inches in diameter at the widest part; and they had lids to protect their contents.[7]
The fragments, apart from the two intact jars bought from the Arabs,
lying about the cave are estimated to be enough, if put together, to
reconstruct some fifty such jars.[8] Their shape is unique, at any rate in
Palestine (but two jars of a similar type, in which *papyri* of the 2nd
century B.C. are said to have been preserved, from Egypt are known),[9]
so that the period to which they belong cannot easily be calculated;
and the texture of the clay affords all too slight evidence for fixing an
exact date.[10] The pottery has been thought to be mostly Hellenistic
ware (or perhaps such a model carried on into Roman times), but
the now generally accepted view is that it is Roman.[11] The presence
of two lamps of the late Hellenistic age and of two others of Roman
work in the cave[12] and the series of coins scattered about the ruins of
the 'monastery' are held to support these opinions; but the lamps
may have had no connection with the jars, and the coins, even if they
were connected with them, cannot be used to support a date without
other evidence.[13] The original idea was that these jars, being unique,
had been specially made for the Scrolls;[14] but this suggestion, even
though it might be correct, could never have been proved[15] and was
afterwards withdrawn.[16] Also, not only have numerous fragments of
such jars now been recovered from other caves in the neighbourhood,
but one has been found in the 'monastery' itself where not a single
piece of parchment has come to light;[17] and this fact, coupled with the
presence of countless sherds of every size from other vessels mixed up
with animal bones[18] and a number of coins in the same buildings,[19]

---

[1] Driver *Semitic Writing*[2] 74–6.   [2] Jer. xxxii. 14 and Assumption of Moses i 17.
[3] B. Talmud *Megillah* 26b.   [4] P. 7.
[5] De Vaux in *RB*, NS LVI 591–2 and *ap.* Barthélemy & Milik *Discoveries* I 12.
[6] Grohmann in *Études de Papyrologie* I 36.   [7] Pp. 40–1.
[8] De Vaux in *RB*, NS LVI 593 and *ap.* Barthélemy & Milik *Discoveries* I 8–10,
14–17.
[9] De Vaux *ibid.* I 9.   [10] Lambert in *NRT* 1950, 507–8.
[11] Sellers *ap.* Wright in *BA* XII 32–3 and Albright *ap.* Burrows *op. cit.* 80; cp. de
Vaux in *RB*, NS LX 104–5.
[12] De Vaux *ap.* Barthélemy & Milik *op. cit.* I 11.
[13] Pp. 394–6.
[14] De Vaux in *RB*, NS LVI 593.   [15] Driver *Scrolls* 48–9.
[16] De Vaux in *RB*, NS LX 104–5.   [17] De Vaux *ibid.* LX 94.
[18] Pp. 84–5.   [19] Pp. 38, 47.

suggests that it may have been used for other purposes than the storage of Scrolls. If one jar could be so used, some of those in the caves might have served not only for books but also for a variety of other purposes; for the caves were clearly inhabited from time to time.[1]

Briefly, then, all this pottery, including that held to be contemporary with the 'monastery', is useless for determining the date of the Scrolls; the dates of the various pieces are themselves insufficiently established, and 'new scrolls could have been put in old jars and old manuscripts could have been put in new jars'.[2]

Archaeologically, therefore, not much can be made of the jars. They were evidently put to diverse uses besides the storage of the Scrolls; but the fact that the models are Egyptian, even though the ware is Roman, points to a connection of the Covenanters with Egypt.[3] If then the Scrolls, as here argued, were removed from Qumrân before the outbreak of the Revolt and were subsequently brought back and hidden in the caves at some distance of time after its collapse, the jars in which they were recently found then might well be those in which they had originally been kept, as in bookcases, whether in the 'monastery' at Qumrân or elsewhere. Then, when they were removed for safety in anticipation of the Revolt, they would have been transported presumably in the very jars in which they had always been kept (for several hundred Scrolls could not have been carried by hand and would have had to be conveyed in receptacles of some sort) by desert tracks to various Syrian and possibly other centres, where they would have been still preserved in them; for there would have been no need to make new jars, other than to replace any that might be broken, in these places. When the time eventually came to return the Scrolls to Qumrân, they would be taken back in these same jars and deposited in the neighbouring caves where they were found long afterwards, a few nearly intact but most of them broken into fragments.

VI. That the material on which the Scrolls are written is leather is equally unavailing for determining their date; its use from the remotest times till the present is well known both from literary sources and from the recovery of actual examples.[4] An Egyptian text of the IVth dynasty (c. 2900–2750 B.C.) contains the first known reference to skins for writing, Ctesias says that the ancient Persians used them for their historical records and Herodotus says that the Ionians and many barbarians used them for the same purpose. The 'writer on skins' perhaps appears on Assyrian monuments from the 8th century B.C. onwards and occurs in texts of the Seleucid age, while documents on leather are often mentioned in Neo-Babylonian texts. The oldest

[1] Cross *Library* 15–16.
[2] Burrows *ap.* Zeitlin in *JQR*, NS XL 57.
[3] Pp. 231–7.
[4] Driver *Aramaic Documents*[2] 1–2.

extant documents on leather are an Egyptian roll of the 17th century B.C. and another of the 12th century B.C., and a parchment of the 5th year of Rameses II (c. 1292–1225 B.C.) is known. A collection of a dozen or more Aramaic letters and other fragments of the fifth century B.C. from Egypt are also on leather. Dura-Europos has yielded a rich crop of parchments ranging from 195 B.C. to A.D. 243, and a few undated ones; and documents on parchment have come also from the Avromân Dâgh in Persian Kurdistan dated from 88 B.C. to 12/11 B.C. Further, a few literary Greek parchments belong to the early Christian period, probably to the 2nd century A.D.[1] Finally, leather or parchment is compulsory for copies of the Law intended for use in synagogues to this day.

Only the analysis of the leather (rather than parchment) of the Scrolls can be perhaps held to throw some slight light on their date: it apparently shows that they are much later than certain Aramaic documents from Egypt dated c. 411/10–408 B.C. and 'slightly older' than the documents from Murabba‘ât, which are dated from the time of the Second Revolt (A.D. 132–5). The methods of dating leather are yet in their infancy and cannot be trusted in detail; but they are sure enough to show that a medieval date, such as Dr. Zeitlin advocates,[2] is out of the question.[3] Here too caution is necessary: the date of a parchment is not necessarily the date of the text written on it.

An important test, which must be applied to a document when seeking to discover its date, is the chemical analysis of the ink: is it mineral or metallic? Metallic ink was used on the potsherds found at Lachish, dated c. 586 B.C.,[4] but the ink normally used by Jews was non-metallic, being made of soot mixed with oil and gum of balsam so that it was easily washed off with a sponge;[5] and, when R. Me'ir attempted some time after A.D. 100 to introduce a metallic ink, which was very durable, R. Ishmael forbade the practice, since the writing could only be erased with a penknife with the result that the surface of the scroll was injured.[6] A mineral ink, therefore, continued to be used, especially on scrolls of the Law, into the Middle Ages, although a metallic ink made of gall-apples and copperas (ferrous sulphate) had come into use for ordinary purposes by the time of the Babylonian Talmud, in the 5th century A.D. Consequently, although the ink on the Scrolls has been proved to be non-metallic, the discovery throws no light on their date.[7] Further, even though chemical analysis has shown the traces of ink in the inkpots found in the *scriptorium* to be identical

---

[1] Cp. p. 381.   [2] Pp. 346, 438.
[3] Burton & Poole & Reed in *Nature* CLXXXIV 533–4.
[4] Lewis *ap.* Torczyner *Lachish* I 188–93.   [5] B. Talmud *Shabbat* 23a.
[6] Blau *Studien zum althebräischen Buchwesen* I 151–7.
[7] Plenderleith *ap.* Barthelemy & Milik *Discoveries* I 39; cp. Rowley *Zadokite Fragments* 18–19.

with that used on the Scrolls taken from the caves,[1] it does not prove that these must have been written in the 'monastery'; for the ink was that commonly used by Jews in the early Christian centuries, as described above, and ancient scribes cannot have had the same wide choice of inks sold in the open market as modern writers have.

VII. The remnants of the linen in which the Scrolls found in Cave I were wrapped have been carefully examined. The Mishnah[2] speaks of wrapping Scrolls in linen for safe custody; but the allusion only proves the existence of such a practice in the 2nd century A.D. and throws no other light on the date of the Scrolls. So little, too, is known of ancient weaving techniques that they cannot be used for determining dates. All that Mrs. Crowfoot will say[3] is that a date for the deposit of the Scrolls in the cave towards the end of the 1st century A.D. is 'fully compatible with all the observations made on the linen'. This date, however, has little independent value; and the date of the linen would have no logical connection with that of the Scrolls themselves. Her other point,[4] that the yarn used in the cloths is spun as in ancient Egypt, is important in view of the probable connection of the Covenanters with Egypt, whence they may have brought the fashion with them.

One final witness remains to be called. The test of radio-active carbon, when applied to the linen wrapped round the Scrolls, yields a date between 168 B.C. and A.D. 233, which has been said to give c. A.D. 33 as the mean date when the flax of which they were made was pulled; for radio-activity runs down from that moment. Logically this test is valueless. First, any year within the period indicated by it is as likely as the middle year. Second, the test has been applied only to the wrapping of the Scrolls, not to the Scrolls themselves; but these might have been made many years before being wrapped round the Scrolls or they might have been wrapped round the Scrolls long after the time when they were copied.[5] The date yielded by it is the period of time within which the flax must have been pulled, not that within which the Scrolls may have been copied.[6] Even if such a test could be applied to the parchment (as it cannot be; for it requires the almost complete combustion of the matter subjected to it), it would reveal nothing but the approximate period within which the beasts whose skins were used had been slaughtered; it would only be their obituary notice and would give no other information except that the copy tested could not have been made before that period, whereas in fact the text written on it might have been composed at any time before or after.[7] Yet it has even been invoked to disprove the theory

[1] De Vaux in *Listener* LIX 1007.   [2] In *Kilaim* ix iii.
[3] In Barthélemy & Milik *op. cit.* I 26–7.   [4] *Ibid.* 19.
[5] Sellers in *BA* XIV 29; s. Rowley *Zadokite Fragments* 18.
[6] Del Medico *Énigme* 29–30.   [7] Driver *Scrolls* 46–7.

that the Scrolls are medieval documents planted in the cave as a hoax;[1] it is not the Scrolls but the test of radio-activity as thus misused that is the hoax!

All in all, while no use can be made of the archaeological evidence to prove that the Scrolls were composed in the 2nd or 1st century B.C., no valid archaeological objections to a date or dates in the 1st–2nd centuries A.D. can be produced. The facts which archaeology reveals may be correctly recorded, but they are susceptible of alternative interpretations or may even have been wrongly interpreted. Their evidence is therefore equivocal and the interpretation of them may be and often is misleading. Archaeology provides matter for the historian to use in supplementing and checking the written sources; its value apart from these is strictly limited and it must not be invoked to override them.

4. QUESTIONS OF PALAEOGRAPHY

The palaeographical arguments against any date in the 1st or 2nd century A.D. may now be examined; and they will be seen to have little value.

The starting point in these arguments is the *Nash Papyrus*; and this, though perhaps the strongest link in the chain, is extremely weak. It is a fragmentary *papyrus*, which was found in Egypt but might derive from Babylonian Jewry,[2] containing an imperfect copy of the Decalogue[3] and the old Hebrew confession of faith known from its opening words as 'Hear, O Israel' (the so-called *šema'* 'hear');[4] but both top and bottom of the text as well as the beginning and end of every one of its lines are missing, and one letter of the alphabet does not appear in it. Being in this state, its date has been much discussed and variously estimated between 200 B.C. and even the 6th or 7th century A.D.[5] This last date may be dismissed on general palaeographical grounds. The script contains ligatures which were forbidden in Biblical texts by Rab, the head of the Babylonian academy in the first half of the 3rd century A.D.[6] and which would probably have gone out of use about the same time in Palestine; and any so precise a date as 50 B.C. is something which palaeography *per se* cannot establish in any age or in any field of study.

Since 1903, when the *Nash Papyrus* was published, a certain number

---

[1] P. 22.
[2] Zeitlin *Dead Sea Scrolls and Modern Scholarship* 83–4.
[3] Exod. xx. 2–17 and Deut. v. 2–21.   [4] Deut. vi. 4–9.
[5] Birnbaum *Scrolls and Palaeography* [1952] 43 (*c.* 200 B.C.), Albright in *JBL* LVI [1937] 150–72 (150–50 B.C.), Trever in *BASOR* CXIII [1949] 19, 23 (*c.* 50 B.C. or *c.* 50–25 B.C.), Sukenik *Scrolls* [1955] 27–8 (not before 1st century A.D.), Burkitt in *JQR* XV [1903] 392–408 (middle of 1st century A.D.), Cook in *PSBA* XXV [1903] 34–56 (latter half of 2nd century A.D.), Zeitlin *op. cit.* 83–4 (3rd or 4th century A.D.), Margoliouth in *JE* VIII [1904] 304–5 (6th or 7th century A.D.).
[6] B. Talmud *Menahoth* 29a.

of new texts, mostly brief or incomplete, have come to light; and these, although none is exactly dated, suffice to determine its approximate period with a reasonable degree of assurance, as Prof. Albright has shown;[1] but palaeography must not be pressed too far. The comparative evidence which he assembles and by which the *terminus post quem* may be fixed is the following: Lidzbarski's Aramaic letter on a potsherd and a group of dockets on clay-tablets from Asshur, all written in ink and 'belonging to the seventh century B.C.'; Aramaic *papyri*, inscribed sherds and dockets, written by Jews in Egypt, some bearing dates between 515 B.C. and 408 B.C. and others which are undated or have lost their dates; similar texts published by Aimé-Giron, of which one may be dated 'somewhere about the second decade of the fourth century' and others 'about the middle of the fourth century B.C.'; two *papyri* and some eight *ostraca* written by Jewish colonists in Egypt and brought from Edfū, in which certain proper names are thought to reflect the 3rd rather than the 2nd century B.C.; and a *dipinto* in Alexandria, to which the most closely parallel text is that of Tobias from 'Arâq-al'Amîr 'dating from about the middle of the third century B.C.' The *Nash Papyrus* is thought to share many peculiarities with the fourth group, showing that it must be dated 'after the close of period IV but not necessarily long afterwards', so that the 'earliest reasonable date' for it will be 'in the first half of the second century B.C.' All these dates are vague enough in themselves to suggest caution; and neither the method of calculating what 'not necessarily long afterwards' imports nor its precise value is explained. The *terminus ante quem* is determined with equal vagueness by a number of Aramaic and Hebrew inscriptions of the period of the Second Temple from Jerusalem and its vicinity. One such is the slab recording the transfer of king Uzziah's bones to a new resting place which is dated 'somewhere in the period of Jewish autonomy, either under Herod the Great or under Agrippa; a relatively late date is probable' (although the inscription gives the impression of having been retouched and includes an Aramaic form not otherwise found at so early a date); another is the inscription over the tomb of the sons of Hēzîr, whose family may have included three high priests[2] in the last twenty-five years B.C., so that this is dated 'about the beginning of the Christian age' (although the text cannot have been composed before the passing of the next generation); and yet another is the brief inscription over the tomb of queen Helena of Adiabene, which is dated 'about 50–60 A.D.' on historical grounds. There are also a number of *dipinti* and *graffiti* scratched on ossuaries, the latter exhibiting a lapidary and the former a cursive style, which may be attributed 'all of them to the period

---

[1] In *JBL* LVI 150–72.
[2] Klein *Jüdisch-Palästinisches Corpus Inscriptionum* 14–15.

beginning with the reign of Herod the Great (37–4 B.C.) and most of them to the last fifty years of the Second Temple'[1] (which is obviously impossible; for if all belong to the former period, none can belong to the latter period); and one, the *graffito* from Bethphage, has a mixed script, so that 'it must belong to the first century B.C., presumably to the first half of the century' (why is not clear).

In all this collection the only texts which carry their own dates are the Aramaic *papyri* from Egypt, and these are too early to affect the problem. No absolute date can be determined for any of the rest, and the margin of error may easily be as much as a century; accordingly each can be only uncertainly dated by comparison with equally uncertainly dated documents. Further, texts from very various countries composed now in the Aramaic and now in the Hebrew language, written with diverse tools on diverse materials, are indiscriminately compared; and so Prof. Albright concludes[2] by saying that 'we cannot directly compare the "boundary of Gezer" with the list of workmen at Bethphage, since one is lapidary and the other cursive', thus admitting that nearly the whole argument which he has built up is illusory, since it rests almost exclusively on such comparisons. These texts, too, differ widely in their nature: some are letters and legal documents, others are formal inscriptions and others mere scratchings on wall. All are compared as though the authors in each group have been similarly trained and have equal skills, have mutually influenced one another and have developed their own peculiarities *pari passu* with the others. All experience, however, shows that, for example, professional scribes and monumental masons, educated private persons and semi-literate workmen, are very unlikely to have influenced each other and will probably have developed their varying styles at quite different rates; so in the last century in England the lettering of a mason engraving an inscription was very unlike that of a lawyer's clerk practising copyhand, and the same distinction would be expected elsewhere. Lastly, the *Nash Papyrus* stands out amongst all these texts as unique; it carries a religious text and is something in the nature of a phylactery or amulet on which an archaic script may be expected. These and similar considerations must at any rate be borne in mind in assessing the date of a religious text; for the Hebrew palaeographer must be as careful to keep the various types of hand distinct as the Greek papyrologist is to avoid dating a book-hand by a commercial hand.

If then the *Nash Papyrus* can be dated only very approximately and with no precision, its value for fixing the date of the Scrolls has been seriously over-estimated.

Dr. Birnbaum, carrying on the argument, tries to show[3] that the

---

[1] Albright *ibid*. 159–60.   [2] *Ibid*. 162–3.   [3] In *JBL* LXVIII 161–8.

4. QUESTIONS OF PALAEOGRAPHY 413

Scrolls range from *c.* 175 B.C. to A.D. 50[1], and he accordingly assigns the principal texts to the following approximate dates:[2]

Isaiah A	*c.* 175–150 or 125 B.C.
Discipline	*c.* 150–125 or 125–100 B.C.
Commentary on Habakkuk	*c.* 100–50 or 75–25 B.C.
Isaiah B	*c.* 75–50 B.C.
Thanksgiving Hymns	
War	A.D. 1–50
Genesis Apocryphon	

These dates are worked out on purely *a priori* principles without any regard to the contents of the documents; for their author begins by declaring[3] that 'it makes no difference to him [*sc.* the palaeographer] whether the Wicked Priest is king Jannaeus, Aristobulus II, Paul or a medieval allegory'. This assertion may be set against recent warnings[4] on 'the extent to which the palaeographer's art is governed by the recorded history of his manuscripts, the uncertainties that beset him when such evidence is lacking' and various other difficulties in establishing the date of an ancient document. Here then, where the history of the documents is quite unknown, especial caution is necessary; but the need of such knowledge, in default of it, is simply denied. The method is as unsound as the results are unconvincing; for *quand une telle méthode ne peut être recoupée par d'autres données, des erreurs énormes restent toujours possibles.*[5] It makes havoc of any attempt to interpret the Scrolls as historical documents, and no hesitation can be felt in calling it into question; but the real reason why it fails is that the basic rules of palaeography, laid down by the masters of the science, are simply disregarded.

Reasoning in palaeography must proceed from the dated to the undated, as argument can proceed only from the known to the unknown. When therefore no sure evidence from comparable dated documents is available, the palaeographer must rely on non-palaeographical evidence to give him a starting point.[6] Here he has scarcely one dated document between *c.* 200 B.C. and A.D. 100, so that his inferences can but be precarious; but the position is improving with the increasing number of documents, some dated, now becoming available.[7]

At the same time, too much reliance must certainly not be placed on single letters or isolated peculiarities; these depend to a very considerable extent on the whims of individual scribes and are generally a very fallacious means of fixing dates; older forms occur in later

[1] Cp. Bruce *Second Thoughts* 40 and Winter in *OLz.* LIV 160–1.
[2] Cp. Albright *op.* Wright in *BA* XI 22 and Albright *ap.* Davies & Daube *Background of the New Testament and its Eschatology* 164–7.
[3] In *Scrolls and Palaeography* 7. [4] In *Lit. Suppl.* LVII 740.
[5] Goussens in *Flambeau* XXXIV 33–4.
[6] Weinberger in Pauly & Wissowa's *Real-Encyclopädie* II 717.
[7] Cp. Cross in Wright *The Bible and the Ancient Near East* 133–202.

manuscripts, whether as mere survivors or as deliberate imitations, and apparently later forms may be detected in earlier periods. Further, the dates of book-hands are the most difficult to determine; they show a tendency to formalization, several styles may be in use together and different lines of development may run parallel to one another, so that as a rule 'periods may be only indicated'.[1] The dates of the Scrolls, however, have been fixed palaeographically almost exclusively by reference to the minutest details in the forms of the letters, to the almost complete neglect of the general style of the script, which is of prime importance. Another significant point is the professional conservatism of scribes; so the life of a style may be artificially prolonged by an archaizing scribe, especially in a religious community, cut off from external influences.[2] For example, according to Dr. Goitein, scribes working in the Jewish law-courts in the 11th and 12th centuries A.D. (e.g. Hillel ben 'Alî and his son-in-law Ḥalfon ben Manasseh) wrote almost indistinguishable scripts; and Yemenite scribes (notably those of the Manzilî family) continued to follow a common style from the 17th to the 18th century A.D. The writers, too, of the Scrolls will certainly have been subject to both these influences; yet no allowance has been made for them, and they do not seem to have been even considered. For example, the archaic script seems to be the sole reason why certain fragments of *Leviticus* have been dated *c.* 400 B.C.[3] or assigned to the 4th century B.C.;[4] but a date *c.* 100 B.C. has also been proposed for them![5] The argument is also weakened by the discovery of a fragment of *Job* in archaic script; this could not have been employed because *Job* was part of the Law and must therefore be due to regarding such a script as proper to the patriarchal period. Its use therefore is not natural but tendentious and so can have no value as evidence of date; and this conclusion is supported by its artificial appearance. The practice, too, of the Maccabaeans and of the insurgents of the First and Second Revolts in reviving the archaic script as propaganda on their coins[6] and that of writing the *tetragrammaton* in it, which persisted in some form or other till the time of Origen and even afterwards,[7] ought to be sufficient warning against taking this script at its face-value.[8]

The documents, too, with which the Scrolls are compared for this purpose are not all *in eadem* or even *in pari materia*; and this is a point of the greatest importance. Forms of letters vary enormously according

---

[1] Van Groningen *Short Manual of Palaeography* 29–30.
[2] Roberts in *Chambers's Encyclopaedia* [1950] X 355.
[3] Birnbaum in *BASOR* CXVIII 20–7.   [4] De Vaux in *RB*, NS LVI 597–602.
[5] Yeivin in *BASOR* CXVIII 28–30.   [6] Madden *Coins of the Jews* 32–3.
[7] Driver *Scrolls* 32–3; cp. Reider in *JQR*, NS XLI 69–70 and Del Medico *Énigme* 192.
[8] Cp. Teicher in *JJS* 11 80–7, Trevor *ibid.* 195–9, Teicher *ibid.* 200–2.

as they are carved with a chisel or written with a brush or a pen, whether that on which they are written is stone or an *ostracon* or *papyrus*, leather or parchment. Further, they are not all written in the same language, which is now Hebrew and now Aramaic; yet who would compare an English with a French script to establish the date of a document? What comparable matter is available is also extraordinarily scanty.[1] It does not all derive from the same country, which may be places as far apart as Syria and Palestine, Arabia and Egypt; it is spread over four or five centuries, and almost all that is cited for comparison is pre-Christian, since few documents which may be dated in the following century can be invoked, so that the palaeographer can but beg the question.[2]

Further, even if the development of the script can be traced with sufficient accuracy to fix the relative order, as distinct from the absolute dates, of the individual Scrolls, what criterion can be produced, in default of accurately dated contemporary documents, by which the time taken in the development of the various forms of a letter or symbol can be estimated? Palaeographers make the general assumption that a style lasts for a generation; but the rule is far from precise. The rate of development varies from country to country, from centre to centre and from school to school; it may vary even with the amount of writing done in this or that school or by a particular scribe, whose style may be gradually modified with advancing years. Some of those who copied the Scrolls might have been contemporaries sitting side by side as they wrote their texts each in his own distinctive style, rather than successors following one another with the passing generations. A sequence is not a chronology!

Finally, Fr. Martin in an exhaustive study of the habits of the scribes writing or copying the Scrolls points out[3] that thirteen different hands, including those of the correctors, can be traced in the six main Scrolls from Cave I, while only those of *Isaiah B* and *War* are each almost exclusively the work of a single hand; and the hands in each group, except the third hand in *Isaiah A*, would seem to have been separated by no very long interval of time. No unity of script can in his opinion be attributed to these thirteen scribes, although a certain community of practice, notably in the use of diacritical points, can be observed. He therefore argues[4] that 'the general picture could admit the existence of a school of scribes at Qumrân', but that no shred of evidence can be adduced to prove its existence and that most of the differences between the scripts can be explained 'as arising from the habits of scribes who transcribed the documents in different localities

---

[1] Cp. Vermès in *Cah. Sion.* IV 178.   [2] Teicher *ibid.* II 80-1.
[3] In *Scribal Character* I 403-8; cp. Segert in *RQ* I 518-26.
[4] *Ibid.* I 386-93.

but who by a natural process shared a technique that had points of resemblance and points of difference'. Briefly the Scrolls show 'no imposed handwriting' such as is likely to have been developed in a scribal school but a 'plurality of hands'; and this conclusion is supported by the orthographic practices of the scribes which show equal variations.[1] Fr. Martin therefore wisely disclaims[2] any attempt 'to classify these hands in a historical sequence against the general background of Hebrew palaeographical development and evolution'. Such a conclusion makes caution doubly advisable in trying to determine the dates, whether relative or absolute, of the Scrolls on palaeographical grounds.

The palaeographical argument then in all its forms is at the best inconclusive, at the worst inapplicable. If it is accepted, the warning that 'palaeographers are apt to differ widely in their opinions as to date and often can venture only on approximate dates, such as first–second century'[3] must always be borne in mind; and, if Greek palaeographers with thousands of documents at hand and a century of experience behind them will not go beyond such wide limits and English palaeographers, although they have a vast mass of dated documents to control their conclusions, find it 'impossible to fix precisely the date of any document within the range of a generation on the basis of palaeography alone',[4] if English palaeographers with dated documents for every successive decade (e.g. in the 14th or 15th centuries A.D.) as controls will not assign a document to any period less than a generation, how can the Hebrew palaeographer expect to fix a date for the six Scrolls within twenty-five years, even to a specific date such as 25 B.C.? The very idea is preposterous; for, if palaeography can fix a period, it cannot fix a date. All that can be said is that the palaeography of the Scrolls, if it does not demand, at any rate does not militate against a date in the 1st–2nd century A.D. Only when the date has been fixed by the historical evidence afforded by their contents will a sound basis have been established for the palaeography of the period; palaeography is the handmaid of history, not history of palaeography.

Certain scribal practices remain to be briefly considered; and they all tell the same tale.

One important point is the scribes' methods of cancellation or erasure. The commonest is the addition of dots above or below or round the word which he has wrongly written (e.g. Is. A vii 11 xvi 14 xlix 17; cp. D viii 14), just as the *Codex Sinaiticus* of the Bible has them in the 4th century A.D.[5] Elsewhere the scribe rubs out the incorrect word

[1] Pp. 412–13.   [2] *Ibid.* I 90–1.
[3] Kenyon *Books and Readers in Ancient Greece*[2] 36–7.
[4] Roth in *RQ* II 84 (citing Miss K. Major's agreement with this statement).
[5] Gardthausen *Schrift, Unterschriften und Chronologie*[2] 407–9.

(Is. A xl 20 xlii 26) or else strikes it out with a line (Is. A ii 12 xvi 14); this method was a very old device which a Jewish scribe of the Ptolemaic age had long ago employed,[1] and Greek *papyri*, both literary and non-literary, offer many other examples of the practice from the 2nd century B.C. onwards.[2] Once three letters, where the leather has been injured, are bracketed and have been recopied above the line by a second hand (W iii 11); and this too is a fairly early practice, which Greek papyri already show in the 2nd century A.D.[3] Obviously the writers or copyists of the Scrolls were well acquainted with ancient and modern (even Gentile) practice; these devices, then, have not yet been found on Hebrew manuscripts of the age of the Second Commonwealth only because none of that period have hitherto been known.[4] Occasionally compound or reduplicated words are wrongly written as distinct words (Is. A xxviii 30 xxix 2, 20 [!] xxx 4, 8, 13 xxvii 7 xxviii 30 xxix 2, 20 [!] xxx 4, 8, 13 xxxiv 19); all are unusual forms or foreign words, and their only significance is to suggest some unfamiliarity with the classical language. Lastly, omissions and corrections are inserted above the line or in the margin in accordance with a late Rabbinic rule.[5]

A subsidiary point, so far as evidence goes, supports the order here argued for the copying of the principal Scrolls.[6] Five letters of the Hebrew alphabet (*k, m, n, p, ṣ*) have different forms according to their position at the beginning or in the middle of a word or at its end. The final were the original forms of the letters, and the initial and medial were then created by bending the lower part of the vertical stroke leftwards into a horizontal stroke, so that it was turned towards the following sign, as though to join it. This curvature had long been the norm in the old Phoenician alphabet; but the old forms with the down-going stroke were retained in or reintroduced into the Aramaic script, from which the square Hebrew alphabet was derived, for use at the end of words to show that a ligature with the following letter or word was not intended, as the new forms might suggest. When these were adopted by the Jews cannot be precisely determined. Tradition, which being self-contradictory is obviously worthless, ascribes them now to the 'seers', *i.e.* the last prophets,[7] and now to the school of R. 'Aqîbâ early in the 2nd century A.D.[8] The only positive evidence is that they were not generally present in the manuscripts used by the

[1] Cowley in *PSBA* XXIX 267 k 10–11 (s. Cowley *Aramaic Papyri* 199).
[2] Roberts *Greek Literary Hands* 6 (pl. 6a col. ii l. i; 2nd century B.C.), 13 (pl. 13b . 21; *c.* A.D. 125).
[3] Schubart & von Wilhamowitz-Moellendorff *Berliner Klassikertexte* V ii no. 284 col. i l. 15 (2nd century A.D.) and Hunt *Oxyrhynchus Papyri* VII no. 1011 ll. 275a–278a (4th–5th century A.D.).
[4] Cp. Driver in *JTS*, NS VIII 141–2.   [5] Cp. *Masseket Soferim* V2.
[6] P. 373.   [7] B. Talmud *Megillah* 2b–3a.
[8] Midrash R. *Genesis* i § 11.

Septuagint[1] and that they appear only irregularly on coins of the Second Commonwealth; and coins, which are something in the nature of autographs and can often be dated to the very year, are the surest guide (although not all the letters of the alphabet appear on them, and the forms of those which appear are apt to be distorted by exigencies of space) in matters of epigraphy. Such inscriptions as survive, too, show these forms being gradually introduced during the same period.

In the Scrolls *Isaiah A* and *Discipline* have the final forms of two letters (*m, n*) with occasional lapses (*e.g.* D viii 1, 25 x 4 *bis*), while the other Scrolls have the final forms of all five letters everywhere except again for occasional lapses (*e.g.* ii 22 vii 9, *k*; iv 12, *m*; xii 4, 6, 8, 22 xii 26 xviii 11, *ṣ*). The incorrect form of *ṣ* in the *Thanksgiving Hymns* occurs only in the part written by the second hand and may be ascribed to the copyist's ignorance or carelessness; for none occurs in the first hand's work. Otherwise, the obvious conclusion is that the Scrolls found at Qumrân were copied in a period of transition when final forms were being but had not been fully introduced. This evidence further suggests that the copies of *Isaiah A* and of *Discipline* from Cave I, which have only two final forms, must be dated, as other evidence shows,[2] before the others which have them all.[3] This conclusion is confirmed by the evidence of the abecedaries: the only example from Qumrân has only one form of these letters (*m, n, p, ṣ*), while those from Murabbaʿât have all four final forms.[4] The Scrolls therefore also on this score fall within the period from the Septuagint to the 2nd century A.D.[5]

Since the use of hyphens had not yet been introduced to indicate the division of a word between two lines, the scribes wrote as many letters of a word as the line would carry at its end and repeated these letters at the beginning of the following line before continuing the word to its end, for example *wh* | *whwkyh* (Is. A ii 11–12) and *wms* | *wmslty* (Is. A xli 10–11);[6] by this means they avoided either dividing the word between two lines or leaving a blank space at the end of the first line. The earliest evidence of this practice, which seems to have survived in only one place in the Old Testament,[7] is in a text from Murabbaʿât of the 2nd century A.D. (II Q *42* 5–6). It was afterwards replaced by the elongation of the last letter to fill in the vacant space; such letters are known as 'dilatable letters', of which none are found in the Scrolls. Presumably this repetition of letters was given up as likely to be a cause of misunderstanding in reading the sacred text.

[1] Ginsberg *Introduction to the Hebrew Bible* 163–4.   [2] Pp. 359–60.
[3] Cp. Trever in *BASOR* CXIII 20–1 and Sukenik *Scrolls* 40.
[4] Benoit Milik & de Vaux *Discoveries* II 91.   [5] Pp. 359–73.
[6] Reider in *JQR*, NS XLI 70.
[7] Psa. xxxii 7 (*tṣrny* | *rny*), where it is confirmed by the LXX; s. Hitzig *Psalmen* 182.

Some of the Scrolls are ruled vertically to separate the columns and horizontally to keep the lines straight (Is.A, H, T, W, GA) while one is apparently not so ruled (Is.B); but the ruling does not seem always to have been consistently carried out and is often very difficult to see in the photographs. Possibly, then, the Scrolls were copied at a time when ruling was being introduced to improve the appearance of a text by ensuring a regular alinement of columns and lines, presumably about the 1st century A.D. This conclusion is surely supported by the almost complete absence of any ruled texts in the pre-Christian period. The only known example of this period is found in a copy of the Egyptian *Book of the Dead*, dated in the Ptolemaic age; otherwise ruled lines make their first appearance on some fragments of the 1st century A.D. found at Herculaneum, while others of the 2nd century A.D. are also known.[1] Clearly then the Scrolls may on this ground be assigned to the same period. That R. Johanan bar Nappachâ, who died *c.* A.D. 279, declared that Moses invented ruling proves nothing;[2] he was merely attempting to give a veneer of respectability to a new and convenient pagan practice by putting it under the sanction of a venerable name. Contrariwise, since the Talmud prescribes horizontal ruling for the scroll of *Esther* as for the Law,[3] it must have been well known by the 4th or 5th century A.D.

Chester Beatty's *papyri* of the Greek Old Testament show the beginning of the process of dividing the Biblical texts into paragraphs. The earliest texts of the 2nd and 3rd centuries A.D. exhibit a progressive increase in paragraphs and verses; the *papyrus* of *Deuteronomy* of the 2nd century A.D. indicates only a few such divisions with dots or points, and those of *Jeremiah* of the late 2nd or early 3rd century A.D. have nothing but arbitrarily placed dots, while that of *Ezekiel* of the 3rd century A.D. marks some paragraphs and all the surviving chapters, as in the Massoretic text, by means of capital letters and setting the beginning of the line back into the left margin. Finally, the great uncial manuscripts of the 4th and 5th centuries reveal the completed process, agreeing almost completely with the Massoretic text as printed (so far as a selective survey shows), although the variations in the paragraphing of many manuscripts of the prophets is so great as to make caution in using them necessary[4]; and the Scroll of *Isaiah* is practically in the same position as these three manuscripts.[5] This does not necessarily mean that it is as late as they are; the process must have been started in Hebrew manuscripts and copied from them in Greek manuscripts, so that the *papyri* will exhibit an earlier and less

[1] Driver *Hebrew Scrolls* 28–30; cp. Van Groningen *Short Manual of Palaeography* 21.
[2] B. Talmud *Megillah* 71d.
[3] P. Talmud *Megillah* 70a and B. Talmud *Megillah* 70a; cp. *Sopherim* xiii 2.
[4] Cp. Teicher in *JJS* II 74.
[5] Driver *op. cit.* 43–4.

developed, the uncial manuscripts a later and more developed form of the system. The Scrolls fall more or less between these two groups though nearer to rather than further from the manuscripts.

The Scrolls, then, display no general unity in the scribal presentation of the text in respect to ruling and paragraphing and the use of diacritical points; in fact 'no perfectly uniform and unbrokenly consistent scribal character' has been impressed on them. The non-Biblical texts, however, as a whole agree only in using one principle of diacritical points and two paragraphing systems; they belong therefore to more than one scribal tradition, even though a certain consistency of scribal habit be traced in them. In other words, all the scribes were 'tributary to some specific school of scribal activity'; but 'while working within objective frames of reference, they impressed personally different and specifically different characteristics on their work'. Consequently, the theory of local transcription and compilation at a single centre, *e.g.* Qumrân, is very difficult to accept; the caves therefore must be regarded not as a library but as a depository of ancient documents compiled or copied in geographically different places.[1] This instability, however, would be due not merely to a diversity of centres, which might all have represented the same tradition if one strong enough to hold the field had prevailed throughout the country; it might also be explained by the assumption that the Scrolls were written or copied in an age of transition, when experiments in orthography and the arrangement of the text were being made. Such a suggestion would have the advantage of being in harmony with the linguistic argument, which points to a similar period, namely that between *c.* 150 B.C. and A.D. 150 at the outside.[2]

5. LANGUAGE AND STYLE

The linguistic argument is by its very nature highly technical and therefore unsuitable for general discussion, and it cannot by itself prove anything very definite; at the same time it can be shown to have some, if only a permissive, value. For example, it contributes little to support those theories which assign the Scrolls to either a Ptolemaic or a medieval date. In the same way it may be applied as a test to other theories of their date: for example, does it require or permit them to be assigned to the 1st century B.C., or in the 1st or 2nd century A.D.?[3] Not a little has already been written on the language of the Scrolls, much of it prematurely before the publication of all the

[1] Martin *Scribal Character* I 403–8, II 696–715.
[2] Pp. 438–9.
[3] Cp. Gottstein in *Scr. Hieros.* IV 101–37, Rabin *ibid.* 144–61, Ben-Hayyim *ibid.* 200–14 and Gottstein in *RQ* I 103–12.

documents; but, since the main texts which have been recovered or are likely to be recovered have now all been published, methodical attempts have begun to be and are being made with some success to tabulate and analyze the facts and to assess their significance. Here only the most important can be briefly discussed.

Caution is necessary in such an enquiry. The writings of the Old Testament are spread over a period of a thousand years and they are restricted to a very narrow range of subjects; consequently the surviving vocabulary is very small, and the course of its development as it can be traced is very uneven. Unfortunately, too, the Old Testament has been known, till the discovery of the Scrolls, exclusively in Hebrew manuscripts of the 9th century A.D. and onwards, which present the Hebrew text not in its pristine purity but in an artificial form evolved by generations of scholars in school and synagogue intent on removing everything inconsistent with the linguistic norms established by themselves on no scientific principles. In other words, the language reproduced in these manuscripts is not Hebrew as it was spoken and written at any time in the classical period (c. 1250–165 B.C.) but as the Rabbis after c. A.D. 200 dressed it up for reading the Scriptures and reciting the ancient prayers.

The principal problem is that of pronunciation, which can hardly be recovered with any accuracy; for the value of some of the consonants shifted in the course of the centuries, and the old language had no method of indicating the vowels. The pronunciation, however, current in the 2nd–4th centuries A.D. can be partly recovered from Greek transliterations of Hebrew words in manuscripts of the Septuagint and in fragments of Origen's Hexaplaric Bible and in Latin transliterations of them in Jerome's works; but they are relatively few in number and not scientifically accurate. Further, no Hebrew literature (other than a handful of brief and often imperfectly preserved inscriptions) has survived for the whole period from *Daniel* (c. 165 B.C.) to the Mishnah (c. 200 A.D.), to which the Scrolls must be assigned. Linguistically, then, the Scrolls can be compared only with the Old Testament, which has a strictly limited range of subjects, and with the Mishnah, which is almost entirely confined to legal matters; and the subject of much of the Scrolls, notably of the *War*, is represented in neither of these collections. At the same time, the authors of the Scrolls felt themselves compelled to draw as much as possible on the language of the Old Testament, however much they might strain it; for they were forced either to adapt old words to new uses, to invent new Hebrew words or to import foreign words. Doing so, they have at times seriously embarrassed if they have not actually misled the modern student.

The picture generally is one of phonetic fluctuation or transition, if not decay, in which Aramaic influence (already traceable in the Old

EE

Testament) can often be detected. The laryngal and pharyngal phonemes (*'ālef, hê, ḥēṭ 'ayin*) are losing their distinctive force. They may be dropped, as in *hāreṣ* for *hā'āreṣ* 'the land' (H iii 1) and *hānāšîm* for *hā'ănāšîm* 'the men' (I Q 28A i 27), unless these and similar forms are not simply scribal errors; or *h* may be displaced by *y*, as in *pôtēy* for *pôṭeh* 'simple' (I Q 28A i 19), and the glottal stop and the glide may be interchanged, as in *ṣî'āh* for *ṣîyāh* 'dry land' (Is. A xli 18) and *hāyîš* for *hā'îš* 'the man' (A Fl. d 6); a few examples occur also in the Massoretic text of the Old Testament.[1] In the same way the *h*- prefixed to the causative theme of the verb has been weakened to '- in the late Aramaic fashion in a number of places (*e.g.* D x 2, Is. A xxxv 24).

One point which strikes even the most cursory reader of the Scrolls is the frequency with which the so-called *scriptio plena* (the insertion of the signs for weak phonemes, chiefly *w* and *y*, to indicate vowels) is employed; for, since the Hebrew script has signs only for consonants, the text can be easily misread or misunderstood. There is abundant evidence that the Septuagint translated from manuscripts into which this device had not yet or had only sparingly been introduced, but that it gradually increased as the knowledge of the classical language decreased or died out, until little room remained for misunderstanding the sacred text on this score. It is used only sparingly also on coins of the high-priests (141–37 B.C.) but abundantly on those of the two Revolts (A.D. 66–70 and A.D. 132–5); and Jerome makes few mistakes which can be imputed to the absence of these letters. These facts agree with the tradition which connects the *matres lectionis* (as they are commonly called after the name given to them by Jewish grammarians) with R. 'Aqîbâ, who may then have been responsible not for the invention of them but for standardizing their use (however uncertain the evidence of the Talmud may be; for no passage actually defines his work in this respect);[2] and the continuance of certain idiosyncrasies in the use of them in manuscripts of Yannai's poems in the 5th-6th centuries A.D. does not militate against it. Clearly they were introduced during the Second Commonwealth and their use was more or less standardized by the middle of the 2nd century A.D.; but no exact date can be given for the whole process, which must have been carried out gradually over a number of years. What had been permitted by the Maccabaeans on their coins could but be recognized as permissible also in Scripture. The Scrolls appear from this point of view to have been copied at a relatively late date within this period; if they had been contemporary with the Septuagint and the coins of the high priests,

---

[1] Kautzsch & Cowley *Hebrew Grammar* § 35d; cp. Jud. xx 38 (where *hrb* appears to stand for *h'rb*, to which *hā'ōrēb* 'the ambush' has been prefixed by way of correction).
[2] B. Talmud *Sanhedrin* 4b and *Sota* 20a.

their lavish use of these signs would be inexplicable. Their nearest points of contact are the coins of the other two Revolts and Jerome, but they are not necessarily so late as Jerome and can be safely put on this score between the Septuagint and him, close in all probability to the two Revolts.[1]

The symbols for the weak consonants used to indicate the vowels are written in the Scrolls before or after the consonant, especially when it is a weak phoneme (*'ālef, hê, ḥêṭ, 'ayin*); and this may even be dropped, as in *rw'š = rô'š* (Is. A i 7 xiv 10) beside *r'wš = r'ôš* (Is. A i 6 vii 8 *alq.*) and *rwš = rôš* (Is. A xxxv 4) for the classical *rō'š* 'head'. The suggestion is therefore attractive that this fluctuating spelling is intended to represent *ro'oš > rooš > rôš* in ordinary speech,[2] where the *'ālef* may have become quiescent, as it has in modern Arabic dialects; it is therefore significant that the contracted *rôš* occurs also in a letter of the Second Revolt (A.D. 132–5),[3] just as Jerome has *ros* in Latin transliteration.[4] The same principle will have operated with a hard guttural phoneme: so *šwḥwd = šôḥôd* (Is. A. xxxviii 19) beside the Massoretic *šôḥaḏ* (Is. A. i 26) and the Aramaizing *šᵉḥôḏ* (Is. A. v 9 xxvii 17) 'bribe', may all represent an attempt to write *šoḥod*, as the word may have been pronounced with two short vowels; and these may have become *šood > šôd* in common speech, as *tôḥ(a)ṭ* (D vii 13) and *tᵉḥôṭ* (Is. A iv 1) become *tôṭ* 'under' in the Aramaic[5] and Samaritan[6] dialects, and as *rōḥaḇ* is transliterated *rob* by Jerome.[7] This weakening of the guttural sounds in the Hebrew and Aramaic dialects of Palestine seems to have taken place between the time of the Septuagint and that of Origen,[8] thus too allowing a date in the 1st or 2nd century A.D.

In the same way the fluctuation between *nw'm = nû'm* (Is. A iii 20) and *n'wm = nᵉ'ûm* (Is. A i 24) for the Massoretic *nᵉ'ûm* 'utterance' points to an original **nu'um > * num > *nûm* with quiescent *'ālef*, just as *nw'm* once stands for *nûm* 'to sleep' (Is A xlvi 24), where no *'ālef* is possible; and Origen's *νουμ* may represent some such pronunciation,[9] which may be illustrated by Jerome's *busim* for the Massoretic *bᵉūšîm* 'sour grapes'.[10] Eventually such forms came to be discarded, presumably as colloquial, in favour of correct Aramaic or Hebrew forms; so the famous liturgical poet Yannai in the 5th-6th centuries A.D. has *nô'em*,[11] treating the word as a 'segholate' noun (*i.e.* one of the so-called second declension), whereas the Massoretes vocalized it *nᵉ'ūm* (as though

---

[1] Driver *Scrolls* 35–6.   [2] Ben-Hayyim *op. cit.* 82–7.
[3] De Vaux in *RB*, NS LX 270 iii 2 (*rwš*).   [4] Stade in *ZAtW* IV 56.
[5] Dalman *Aramäisch-neuhebräisches Handwörterbuch*[2] 440.
[6] Ben-Hayyim *op. cit.* 89–90.   [7] Stade *ibid.* 61.
[8] Cp. Kahle *Geniza* 165–6.
[9] Brønno *Studien über hebräische Morphologie und Vokalismus* 167–8.
[10] Stade *ibid.* 41.   [11] Cp. Reider in *JQR*, NS XLI 69.

meaning *dictum*) after the model of a passive participle. Thus the Scroll also of *Isaiah A* perhaps belongs to the period of transition.

A similar fluctuation in the position of the vowels occurs with strong phonemes, for example in *gᵉḏôl* for *gôḏel* 'greatness' (T x 16 xiv 23 xvi 12; W xiv 17). Only three examples of the former are found in the Old Testament,[1] where the latter form has been normally substituted for it by the Massoretes. In the same way the Scroll's *swdm* = *sôḏem* (Is. A i 11 iii 13) stands for *sᵉḏōm* 'Sodom', as the Massoretes always vocalize this word. It does not however reflect the Samaritan *sāḏem* 'Sodom'[2] but rather an original *sodom* with two short vowels, as the Greek *Σόδομα* and the Latin *Sodoma* show; for the Massoretic *sᵉḏôm* does not appear before the late Syriac and Aramaic versions. Similar fluctuations appear in the Samaritan dialect, for example *mâlek* beside *mlôk* 'king',[3] and in the Palestinian Aramaic dialect, for example *bōsam* beside *bᵉsām* 'sweet odour' and *ṣôrak* beside *ṣᵉrôk* 'need';[4] these too go back to an original *bosom and *sorak or the like, of which however no trace can be detected in old unvocalized texts. These 'reversed segholate forms', as they have been called, which were due to Aramaic influence,[5] belonged to a period when Aramaic and Hebrew forms still existed side by side[6], were common in the Christian Aramaic dialect[7] and lingered on until they were finally ousted by the true 'segholate' forms, which became the Hebrew norm in the Massoretic text as stabilized in the 2nd century A.D.[8]

Another form of some importance is *Pwrt* = *Pûrāṯ* or *Pôrāt* (W ii 11) for *Pᵉrāṯ*, as the river Euphrates is called in the Old Testament; for the unique Greek *Φόρας*, as Josephus spells[9] the name with a full *o* instead of the reduced *e* of the Massoretic form, exactly corresponds with it. As the Babylonian *Purattu* shows, however, the original vowel must have been *u*, so that *Φόρας* cannot be claimed as peculiar to the historian's time and be used to prove the Scroll in which it occurs contemporary with him, although his use of it shows that it is proper to the 1st century A.D. The Massoretic form therefore represents a late development, exemplifying their tendency to reduce *u* to *e* in an unaccented syllable.

This *w* (like the corresponding *y* for the *i*- and *e*-sounds), then, represents not the length of the vowel (*û* or *ô*), as it almost invariably does by Massoretic convention in the Old Testament, and hardly

---

[1] Exod. xv. 16 (*gᵉḏōl*) 1 Sam. xvi. 7 (*gᵉbōah*) Psa. xlvi. 5 (*qᵉḏōš*).
[2] Ben-Hayyim *op. cit.* 91.
[3] Diening *Das Hebräische bei den Samaritanen* 61 and Cowley *Samaritan Liturgies* I 643 (6).
[4] Dalman *Grammatik des jüdisch-palästinischen Aramäisch*[2] 143–4.
[5] Cp. Burrows in *JBL* LXVIII 203.
[6] Cp. Segal *Grammar of Mishnaic Hebrew* 15 § 21.   [7] Mansoor in *JSS* III 44–6.
[8] Cp. Jongeling in *RQ* I 483–94.   [9] In *Antiquities* I i 3 § 39.

even the accent, but rather the colour of the original vowel or half-vowel (*ō* or *ū*, *o* or *u*), whichever it may be.

A similar explanation will account for certain peculiar imperative forms found in the Scrolls. Such is *šmwrw* (Is. A xlvi 10), which is to be read not as an archaism (or as a pausal form, which is itself an archaism, here preserved though not in pause),[1] even though similar forms are known also from Babylonian tradition,[2] but as **šomorû*, a transitional form between the archaic pausal *šᵉmôrû* and the reduced Massoretic **šomrû* 'keep ye'. Thus the line of development will have been: *šmúrū > šᵉmôrû* (preserved only as an archaism in pause in the Massoretic text) > **šomorû* (found as a transitional form in which the pronunciation is facilitated by the insertion of a helping vowel in the Scrolls) > **šomrû*[3] or *šimrû* (the regular form in contact[4] in the Hebrew Bible). Such a transitional form still lingers according to Massoretic tradition in the Hebrew Bible in *qswmy*, which must be pronounced not *qᵉsômî* (as an archaic pausal form; for it is here in contact) but **qosomî* 'practise thou divination'[5] (as a transitional form which has accidentally escaped reduction to the modern form). Origen's λοομ for the Massoretic *lᵉham* 'fight thou'[6] shows that the original vowel of both syllables in imperative forms must have been still heard in his time.

The Old Testament has also two forms of the preterite and present-future tense, namely *yqṭwl* (*yiqṭôl*) and *yqṭl* (*yiqṭōl*) 'he killed, he will kill' and *yqṭwlw* (*yiqṭôlû*) and *yqṭlw* (*yiqṭᵉlû*) 'they killed, they will kill'.

The singular forms can hardly be distinguished in use or in meaning. In the Scrolls *yiqṭôl* serves as both a preterite (*e.g.* H viii 10, 11) or as a present-future (*e.g.* D viii 25 H vii 7 Z xiii 26) tense, while *yiqṭōl* similarly refers to future (D viii 22) or past (Z viii 3) time; the verbs in all these passages are not in pause. The absence of both forms from pausal positions in the Scrolls may be accidental, especially as *ô* or *ō* are most common in transitive verbs which are normally followed by the object, so that they can occur only exceptionally in pause. In the Hebrew Bible the two forms have been hopelessly confused by the Massoretes, and the proper distinction (if any) between them cannot now be made out.

The plural *yiqṭôlû* is an archaism which has been preserved in pause by the Massoretes, while *yiqṭᵉlû* is the form used in contact; and their preservation as distinct forms in the Old Testament is due rather to the practice of cantillation in school and synagogue than to the needs

---

[1] *I.e.* where the stress falls at the end of a sentence.
[2] Beer & Meyer *Hebräische Grammatik* II 24–5.
[3] Cp. Kautzsch & Cowley *op. cit.* § 46d.
[4] *I.e.* where followed by another word or words which will take the stress.
[5] 1 Sam. xxviii. 8; cp. Judges ix. 8, 10, 12.
[6] Psa. xxxv. 1 (s. Brønno *op. cit.* 50).

of ordinary speech. The heavy form may be found also here and there out of pause in the Scrolls if, for example, *yšmwrw* is rightly read *yišmôrû* (Is. A xlvi 15) for which the Massoretes have *yišm^{e}rû* 'they shall keep' in the very same passage;[1] and three such forms occur out of pause also in the Old Testament,[2] where the Massoretes have replaced *ô* by *û* under Aramaic influence. The preferable explanation of these forms in the Scrolls, however, is again that the inserted *w* is intended to indicate not the length of the vowel (*ô* or *û*)[3] but its colour (*o* or *u*, whether long or short). It will then show that *yšmwrw* is to be pronounced *yišmorû rather than *yišm^{e}rû*; and this has the advantage of agreeing with Greek and Latin transliterations, for example with Origen's ιεϱγού for the Massoretic *yaḥr^{e}gû* 'they shall limp'[4] and Jerome's *iezbuleni* for the Massoretic *yizb^{e}lēnî* 'he will exalt me'.[5] In other words, the primitive unaccented *u* of the final syllable was still heard as *u* or *o* in the time of the Scrolls, as it was by Origen in the 2nd and by Jerome in the 4th century A.D., and had not yet been reduced to the colourless half-vowel of the Massoretic tradition.

Beside *yqtwlw* the Scrolls have another form of this tense which is almost peculiar to themselves; this is *yqwtlw-*, which is never found in isolation but appears only with some other element of speech attached to it (although this may be merely a matter of chance; for analogous forms are found without suffixes in other dialects). This form, read *y^{e}qōṭ^{e}lû*, has been taken to represent a pausal form, which is out of the question, as it occurs both in and out of pause (H xii 5 T iv 6, 24). Alternatively, it has been regarded as a distinct tense-form importing futurity or obligation, corresponding to the Assyro-Babylonian *iqáṭilū* 'they will kill' (as distinct from *iqṭulū* 'they killed');[6] but, while a future sense is probable or certain in some passages (*e.g.* D vi 14, 17 H xii 5 T vi 21 W ii 9), in others the time intended may be past (*e.g.* T iv 24–5). Since too the ordinary *yiqṭ^{e}lû* is used throughout the Scrolls not only with preterite but also with present-future force, no need for such a new form can be urged to prove it. That the few analogous forms in the Hebrew Bible have a future sense[7] does not outweigh these objections; for they are too few to prove anything. Possibly therefore the inserted *w* once again indicates not a long vowel (*ō* or *u*) but a short vowel (*o* or *u*) inserted to indicate the colour of the half-vowel; and so Origen has ισουμοϰ[ου] and ισεμου for *yišm^{e}hû* 'they shall rejoice'.[8] Many analogous forms are found in the Palestinian tradition, for example in the Samaritan *vā'ômer*, *ya'úmer* for the Mas-

---

[1] Isa. lvi. 4.   [2] Exod. xviii. 26, Ru. ii. 8, Prov. xiv. 3.
[3] Cp. Kautzsch & Cowley *op. cit.* § 47g.
[4] Brønno *op. cit.* 35.   [5] Stade in *ZAtW* IV 48.
[6] Yalon in *KS* XXVI 241, Meyer in *VT* VII 140 and in Hempel & Rost *Von Ugarit nach Qumran* 118–28; cp. Gottstein in *JJS* IV 104–5.
[7] *E.g.* Isa. i. 20 and Jer. v. 6.   [8] Brønno *op. cit.* 35.

soretic *yō'mer* 'he spoke',[1] as well as in the Babylonian tradition, for example in *ysirṭû* for *yiśrᵉṭû* 'they shall incise';[2] the helping vowel, though always *o* or *u* in the Scrolls, may be *a* or *e* (very rarely *o* or *u*) in the Massoretic text and either these or *i* or *u* in the other dialects.[3] The forms in the Scrolls then may be intended to be read **yaquṭᵉlû* with the vowels (but not the accent) of the Samaritan *yaquṭelû* or perhaps rather **yiqᵒṭᵉlû*[4] after the fashion of Origen's transliteration. That analogous forms are found also in the late Neo-Babylonian and in certain modern Arabic dialects shows that they are a tardy linguistic development.[5]

The same procedure of retracting a vowel or inserting a helping vowel or half-vowel and dropping that of the following syllable can be seen at work in the Neo-Assyrian and Neo-Babylonian (written) and modern Arabic (spoken) dialects; but it has been maintained by the Massoretes only in verbs with a guttural sound in which any clash of consonants makes pronunciation difficult, for example in *yeḥerᵉdû* beside *yeḥrᵉdû* 'they shall tremble'[6] and perhaps also in *tᵉ'ukkᵉlû* for *tō'ḵᵉlû* 'ye shall eat' (cp. T iii 30).[7] The practice therefore is relatively late in the dialects or languages in which it occurs[8] and, once again, parallel examples which can be reasonably dated can be found only in Origen's transliterations.

If the arguments here put forward are accepted, the peculiar vocalization of certain classes of nouns and verbal forms receives a common explanation, which is always preferable to a multiple solution; and this is soundly based on contemporary linguistic evidence, so far as this is available. Unfortunately, the few Hebrew texts surviving in their original form from the preceding centuries are almost entirely devoid of vowel-letters; and, where these begin to occur, as on coins and tombs, verbal forms are very rare. The only known comparable forms are found in Origen's and Jerome's transliterations, which are not always trustworthy. Subsequent forms either diverge from them or, like the Samaritan, are known only from very late evidence and are therefore of doubtful value. The handful of analogous forms embedded in the Massoretic text may go back to the period of the Scrolls; but little can be said on this point, as the Massoretes have so often misunderstood, Aramaized or modernized them. Those in the Scrolls, however, may safely be said to be transitional forms; they therefore allow, if they do not require, a date in a period of transition

---

[1] Petermann *Brevis Linguae Samaritanae Grammatica* I 28–9, 37–8 and Diening *Das Hebräische bei den Samaritanen* 22–3.

[2] Ben-Hayyim *op. cit.* 87–8.   [3] Nöldeke *Mandäische Grammatik* § 25.

[4] Gottstein *loc. cit.* 126.   [5] Driver in *JJS* IX 96.

[6] Hos. xi. 10, 11; Ezek. xxvi. 18.

[7] Isa. i. 20 (s. Driver in *Von Ugarit nach Qumran* 42).

[8] Brockelmann *Grundriss der vergleichender Grammatik der semitischen Sprachen* I 212, 219.

such as the closing centuries of the Second Commonwealth seem to have been.

Another peculiarity is the redundant *'ālef* not infrequently appended to words ending in a (long) vowel. This has been thought to be an Arabism on the supposition that the Hebrew *pīy* (*pî*) 'my mouth' was written *py'* to ensure that it was pronounced **piya* (*pīyâ*) like the Arabic *fīya* 'my mouth' (since this was assumed to represent the primitive pronunciation of the suffix).[1] This *'ālef* however has now been found not only in words in which it may have carried a vowel requiring some such pronunciation as *-iya* (as in *kî'* for *kî* 'for') but also with others in *-ô*, whether particles (cp. T x 12 xv 21 with x 3 xii 31) or nouns (W iii 16), and in forms of verbs ending in *-û* (H ii 6 T vi 21), where it cannot have been so pronounced. A similar *'alif* indeed is regularly attached to Arabic verbal forms terminating in *-û* where its purpose is to prevent this final *-w* (*-û*), which is a mark of the plural form, being incorrectly detached from the verb and taken as *w[a]*-'and' and read with the following word;[2] but this explanation will not account for the *'ālef* occasionally appended to the corresponding Hebrew verbal forms with *-û* (T vi 21 [?]),[3] as it is found also with other parts of speech ending in *-î* and *-ô* in the Old Testament.[4] It cannot have been added to indicate the stress,[5] either in the Scrolls or in the Hebrew Bible; for it occurs most frequently where no stress falls, notably in *kî'* for *kî* 'for, because', which can never take it. That this *'ālef* is sometimes displaced by *h*, for example in *bôh* (Is. A 1 20) beside *bô'* (Is. A xxx 12 xxxvii 7, 8 lii 9) for *bô* 'in it', suggests that it is not a mere orthographic freak but an attempt to indicate something of value and so to help the reader. May its purpose be, as Dr. Bange has privately argued, to safeguard a long final vowel which, as no stress falls on it, is in danger of being slurred over or not fully sounded? If so, its orthographic variations and sporadic occurrences suggest that it may have been an experiment tried out but soon abandoned as unsatisfactory or needless. Such a conclusion once again points to a period of transition, even if it indicates no exact date for the Scrolls.

Mention must also be made of the unique *yktw* = *yikkāṭēv*, though corrected to *yktb* = *yikkāṭēb* 'he shall be enrolled' (D viii 19); for this use of *w* to represent aspirated *b* (*v*) recalls the equally unusual *Paav* for *Paωβ* = *Reḥôb* 'Rehob' in manuscript B (dated in the 4th century A.D.) of the Septuagint[6] and *ιεσκαν* for *yiškab* 'he will lie down' as reported by a Greek scholiast (dated somewhere between A.D. 90 and A.D. 340).[7] Aspiration indeed goes back to a time well before the

---

[1] Driver *Scrolls* 37; cp. Wright *Comparative Grammar of the Semitic Languages* 95–6.
[2] Wright *Arabic Grammar*[3] I 11a § 7.   [3] Josh. x. 24 and Isa. xxviii. 12.
[4] Kautzsch & Cowley *op. cit.* § 23 i.   [5] Gottstein *loc. cit.* 112.
[6] Josh. xix. 30.   [7] Gen. xxxiv. 2; s. Field *Origenis Hexapla* I 50.

Exile;[1] but this peculiarity, as hitherto recorded, is found only once in a Scroll and otherwise only in the early Christian age.

The independent pronouns also raise problems. The peculiar 'ănû for 'ănaḥnû 'we' (D i 25 W xiii 7, 12 xiv 5) is a pure Aramaism, which has made its way once into the Massoretic text of the Old Testament, where it can hardly be original;[2] it is, however, the regular form in the Mishnah, thus allowing a date in the 1st-2nd century A.D. for the Scrolls. The frequent hû'āh and hî'āh for hû' 'he' and hî' 'she' are not so easily explained. The original forms seem to have been *huwa and *hiya without 'ālef,[3] like the Arabic huwa and hiya, which have become hû and hî in modern dialects. The 'ālef, now otiose, may originally have been added to indicate and perhaps preserve the final short vowel; when this 'ālef itself became quiescent, the h may have in turn been added for the same purpose, to preserve the final vowel which, though dropped in speech, may have been preferred in elevated style.[4] This long form appears sporadically in Isaiah A; it is the only form used in Discipline, it occurs very rarely in the Commentary on Habakkuk (1–7) and the Thanksgiving Hymns (1–9) but predominates in War (10–3); it does not occur in Isaiah B, so far as the text is preserved. These figures support the view that hû'āh and hî'āh are neologisms formed on the analogy of hēm(m)āh (which has a quite different origin) beside hēm 'they';[5] they were an experiment which lasted but a short while, since the writers of the Scrolls are almost alone in using these forms. Such diversity of usage is a point which may throw light on the identity of the scribes, even of the authors, of the Scrolls.

The suffixed pronouns also show Aramaizing forms as well as others which cannot be ascribed, at any rate directly, to Aramaic influence. The occasional -ôhî or -êhû[6] (D v 5, 11 vi 13 viii 8) for -ôhî) 'his'[7] and -hâh for -āh[8] 'her' (W xviii 9) reflect the Aramaic dialect of Palestine,[9] while the rare -āw>-ô for -āyw 'his' with plural words (D i 17 iii 7) is found both in the Samaritan dialect and occasionally elsewhere;[10] and -kem(m)āh 'your' and -hem(m)āh 'their' recall the corresponding Samaritan -kimma 'you, your' and -himma, -hemma 'them, their'.[11] The peculiar -ôm (D l 21, v 20, ix 14) beside the pure Hebrew -ēm (D v 24) is unique; for the corresponding Aramaic forms are -hôm, -hôn or -ôn 'their', of which the last is found also in the Samaritan dialect. On this score, then, the Hebrew of the Scrolls shows the influence of various Palestinian Aramaic dialects,

[1] Driver Semitic Writing[2] 232.   [2] Jer. xlii. 6 (K.; corrected in Q.).
[3] Cp. Jer. xxix. 23 (Q.) and Jb. xxxii. 4, 6, xxxiv. 1, xxxv 1 ('ēlîthû' beside 'ēlîthû).
[4] Gottstein op. cit. 119.   [5] Ben-Hayyim op. cit. 149.
[6] Cp. Jb. xxiv. 23, xxv. 3 (where two similar suffixes appear in the Massoretic text, which however is in both places open to doubt).
[7] Cp. Cantineau Le Nabatéen I 54–5.   [8] Cp. M. T. at Ezek. xli 15.
[9] Dalman op. cit. 203–6.   [10] Ben-Hayyim op. cit. 79–82.
[11] Ben-Hayyim op. cit. 88–89; cp. Kahle in Festschrift für A. Bertholet 281–6.

now adapting its own form to theirs and now borrowing theirs outright; but none of these peculiar forms can be closely dated.

The forms of the pronominal affixes and suffixes with appended -($\bar{a}$)h are exceptionally important. The former, expressing the subject of the verb in the perfect tenses, appear as -t or -th 'thou' and -tm and -tmh 'you'; the latter, expressing the object of the verb and the possessor in the nouns, appear as -k or -kh 'thee, thy', and as -km or -kmh 'you, your' and -hm or -hmh 'them, their'. As Origen's Greek and Jerome's Latin transliterations of Biblical words show, these are to be read respectively, for example, as -t and -$t\bar{a}$(h) and as -$\bar{a}k$ and -$k\bar{a}$(h) and so on; and the question is whether they can be distinguished in time or use. Origen and Jerome show that both forms were current in the early Christian centuries in the proportions set out in the following table:[1]

	-$\theta\alpha$, -tha		-θ, -t		-$\chi\alpha$, -cha		-$\alpha\chi$ or -$\varepsilon\chi$, -ach	
Origen	20	—	3	—	2	—	40	—
Jerome	—	—	—	3	—	2	—	11

These frequencies suggest a period of uncertainty, possibly of transition.

After this period, in such more or less fragmentary pre-Massoretic Biblical texts as have survived two traditions are clearly defined. Forms with the overhanging vowel (-$t\bar{a}h$ and -$k\bar{a}h$) preponderate in Biblical and those without it (-t and -$\bar{a}k$) in non-Biblical texts in both Palestinian and Babylonian manuscripts; but Babylonian non-Biblical manuscripts have -$t\bar{a}h$ and -$k\bar{a}h$ not only in quotations from the Old Testament but also in ancient prayers, while all Samaritan texts have -ta with verbs but -ak with nouns,[2] as Origen mostly does. In liturgical poetry from the 5th century onwards -$t\bar{a}$(h) and -$k\bar{a}$(h) are usual while -$\bar{a}$(k) tends to be kept for use in pause, though actually only with certain words such as $l\bar{a}k$, pausal form of $l^e k\bar{a}$(h) 'for thee'; and this becomes the norm in the Massoretic text of the Old Testament.

The explanation of these divergencies cannot be attempted without examining the origin of the two forms; for the suggestion that the problem of the proto-Hebrew forms has no bearing on that of those in the Scrolls[3] is too facile and superficial to pass muster.

That these and similar forms must originally have terminated in short vowels, being read -ta and -ka and so on, is a now generally accepted theory, which is based on the analogy of the cognate languages. Hence, as a primitive $y\acute{a}duki$ '(fem.) thy hand' has become the classical $y\bar{a}d\bar{e}k$, so *$y\acute{a}duka$ '(masc.) thy hand' ought to have become $y\bar{a}d\bar{a}k$ (not $y\bar{a}d^e k\bar{a}$, as in the Massoretic text) by the customary shifting of the accent; and the Aramaic suffixes have actually followed this

[1] Ben-Hayyim op. cit. 22, 27, 43–6.   [2] Ibid. 27–38, 46–50.
[3] Gottstein op. cit. 118.

line of development.[1] Consequently *yāḏāḵ* must be assumed to have been the masculine form used in ordinary speech, and *yāḏᵉḵā* will have survived only as an archaism in poetry and elevated diction (while the corresponding feminine *yāḏᵉḵî* will have died out for lack of use, as special feminine forms often do). Clearly the Aramaic is the natural line of development while the Hebrew, an artificial creation of the Massoretes, is irrational; how can such a scheme have been evolved? The primitive final short vowel seems to have fallen away *c.* 1300 B.C.[2] before the emergence of the earliest Hebrew literature; but **yaduka* may be assumed to have survived as an archaism in poetry and elevated prose (in which archaisms tend to be preserved in all languages), rather than to have been introduced under Arabic influence;[3] while **yadak* will have become the form current in ordinary speech. Practically nothing direct is known of Hebrew pronunciation till the appearance of the Scrolls, in which *ydkh* (*yāḏᵉḵā*) is abnormal and *ydk* (*yāḏāḵ*) normal. The usage of the Scrolls, which belong to the age immediately preceding the Greek and Latin transliterations, reveals the purpose underlying this distinction between the two forms; for *Discipline* has -(*ā*)*ḵ* in prose and -*ḵ*(*ā*)*h* only in poetry, namely in the two liturgical chants (D ii 2–10) and the closing hymn (D xi 15–22). The other Scrolls agree with this practice; the long form of all these suffixes far outnumbers the short in the *Hymns*, while *War* has -*āh* only once in prose (W i 12) but regularly in solemn charges, chants and hymns (W x 1–xii 13 xiii 3–16 xiv 3–16 xvi 12–17 xviii 6–15); although one duplicate fragment seems to represent a different tradition (W xix 4, 5, 6). The original long form was still retained in elevated and poetic diction, while the shortened form was used, as it had been for over a thousand years, in ordinary speech.

The practice in the Biblical Scrolls, though apparently divergent, in fact conforms to that of the non-Biblical texts. The earliest is *Isaiah A*, in which -(*ā*)*ḵ* predominates and -*ḵ*(*ā*)*h* only rarely appears in the first part (i–xxxix), while the position is reversed in the second part (xl–lxvi), which must have been copied by a scribe following the new rule that the long form is proper to the Scriptures; the *Commentary on Habakkuk* (which has no instance of the second person in the comments) has -*t*(*ā*)*h* and -*ḵ*(*ā*)*h* in citations from the prophet, which are in verse (H ix 13 x 2 xi 8, 10, 11); and *Isaiah B*, the latest of the Biblical books, has only one instance of the long form (Is. B x 8). The bulk of the texts is too small to draw any secure or far-reaching conclusions; but the point may be made that the *Commentary on Habakkuk* is like *Discipline* the only Scroll (so far as the evidence goes) which follows an unbroken rule, and that both these documents are

---

[1] Cp. Driver *Scrolls* 37–8. [2] Harris *Development of the Canaanite Dialects* 51.
[3] Kahle *Geniza* 171–9.

the earliest Scrolls, being dated immediately before and after the First Revolt (A.D. 66–73).[1]

In the liturgical poetry of the 5th and 6th centuries A.D. as also in the Massoretic text of the Old Testament the same underlying principles can be clearly detected; for the full -$k\bar{a}(h)$ is the form regularly used in poetry and every kind of prose (so that it becomes the normal form throughout the Old Testament), while the short -$\bar{a}k$ is reserved for pause. In other words, this form has come to be regarded, quite incorrectly, as an archaism and therefore as suitable for use in pause; for pausal forms are normally archaic forms which have become stereotyped in certain positions.

Two lines of development were then followed in Biblical texts: the 'modern' -$(\bar{a})k$ was retained in copying and reading the Scriptures down to the time of the Scrolls and lingered on till that of Origen and even of Jerome in some circles; but the 'archaic' -$k(\bar{a})h$ took its place as proper to the ancient Scriptures and liturgical poetry at some time during that period and finally ousted the other form in the Massoretic text, where -$(\bar{a})k$ was retained only in pause.

No entirely consistent or definite answer, however, can be given on many or indeed on most of these orthographic and phonetic points. At the same time scribes inherited traditions, and a considerable time-lag might ensue between the introduction of a novelty in one centre or by one person and its introduction by someone else in another or even in the same centre. For example, even if the use of vowel-letters reached its peak c. 100 B.C., the tendency to introduce them would be unlikely to have proceeded everywhere at an equal pace or with equal intensity, and divergent customs might continue to run side by side; and in fact a period marked by a partial return to the old tradition of defective writing followed that of the peak.[3] So, even if *Isaiah B* in one respect exhibits peculiarities characteristic of orthography before the 2nd century B.C.,[4] in another it comes close to the Massoretic text,[5] now improbably thought to have reached its final form c. A.D. 65, shortly before the Revolt (A.D. 66–73);[6] but the test has little value in Biblical texts, since the orthography may be that of the archetype and not of the copy. Scribal traditions, too, were very sacred things,[7] especially in religious circles; and the Covenanters would have been tempted to go back to or to preserve many ancient usages out of antipathy to the prevailing Pharisaic activity in modernizing and standardizing the writing of the sacred language.

[1] P. 373.
[3] *Ibid.* I 8.
[5] *Ibid.* I 91–3.
[7] Martin *ibid.* I 8.

[2] Cp. Ecclus. xliv. 1–4, 6–8.
[4] *Ibid.* I 336–9, 361–2, 378–9.
[6] Segal in *JBL* LXXII 35–47.

Once again, no similar consistency can be detected in the Scrolls beyond a certain official and phonetic unity which is confined to the organizational texts, *i.e.* those dealing with the affairs of the community at Qumrân; and these, on the ground of their contents, must be assigned to a single school of thought and practice.[1] That all these must have been actually written then is no necessary conclusion; for, even though the society may have fostered a single scribal tradition, its scribes may have been trained at the main centre but have worked at local centres. All that can be said perhaps of the non-Biblical documents is that the linguistic test possibly puts *Discipline* before the *Commentary on Habakkuk* and, after them, *War* before the *Thanksgiving Hymns*,[2] thus more or less confirming the sequence which has already been established on other grounds.[3]

A few peculiar forms may here be noted. Such are *'ab-* for *bᵉ-* 'in' (H xi 6 W v 6), which has now been found in a letter from Murabba'ât (*c.* A.D. 132–5) and in the Tosefta[4], and *sôḏ* for *yᵉsôḏ* 'foundation, principle' (D iv 6 Ti 22, 27 iii 21 v 9, 26 vi 26 vii 8 xiii 15), which can be illustrated by analogous forms in the Mishnah[5] and is itself found in the Talmud.[6] A similarly late form, if it is not an error, is *qûl* for *qallû* 'they are swift' (H iii 6), which may be regarded as an Aramaism not found again before the Talmudic age.[7] Not one of these forms is found even in the latest parts of the Old Testament and none appears otherwise before the 2nd century A.D.

Words, whether old or new, which have not been found in other Hebrew literature and of which the sense is quite unknown or can only be guessed from the context are very few (*e.g.* D iv 20 T v 28 xvii 26 and fr. xlviii 5, *tkm*; D xi 1, *rkn*; T viii 11 ix 1, xvi 9, *ḥyš*; W v 5 and 8, *mwzz*; W v 12, *sp* or *sph*). Many neologisms are formed from well-known roots so that they are readily intelligible; such are those denoting the 'bending, curving' of a line of troops (W ix 11), 'ploughing' metaphorically for 'scheming' (D iii 2)[8], a 'crucible' in the sense of a fiery trial or persecution (D viii 4 W xvii 1, 9), 'foot-shaped' for 'tapering' (W v 13),[9] 'advance' (W viii 7), 'pursuit' (W ix 6; cp. iii 9) and 'turning back, return, retreat; repentance' (W i 13 iii 6, 10, 11 D iii 1). Others are nothing but variant forms of words found in the Old Testament, such as those for 'deed' (D viii 3 ix 1) and 'thanksgiving' (D x 16).

Biblical words are used also for something different from and analo-

---

[1] Martin *Scribal Character* I 407 and II 711, 714.   [2] Gottstein *loc. cit.* 131–4.
[3] P. 373.   [4] Cp. de Vaux in *RB*, NS LX 271–2.
[5] Segal *Mishnaic Hebrew Grammar* 37 § 62 and 104 § 228; s. Nötscher *Terminologie* 76–7.
[6] B. Talmud *Sanhedrin* 92b.
[7] Levias *Grammar of the Aramaic Idiom of the Babylonian Talmud* 119 § 450.
[8] Cp. Hos. x. 13.   [9] P. 185.

gous to the concept which they denote in the Old Testament, *e.g.* '(miserable) wretches' in the sense of 'wretches, knaves' (T iii 25, 26; iv 25, 35),[1] 'end' for 'period of time' (*passim*), 'hand' for 'signal' (W viii 5, 7), 'belly' for 'bulge, curve' (W v 13), 'pericardium' for 'socket' (W v 7, 9), 'order' for military 'array' (W iii 1, 6 v 3, 4 vi 8 viii 6 ix 10 xvi 5), 'standard' for 'cohort' (W i 14 iii 6 iv 10 v 3 vi 1, 4 viii 4, 14 ix 4, 10 xvii 10), 'tower' for a military formation protected by a wall of shields (W ix 10–14), 'gate' for an *intervallum* in the ranks of a legion (W iii 1, 7 vii 9, 16, 17 viii 4 xvi 4), 'band' for 'collecting point (for troops), headquarters' (W iii 3, 13), and 'supported' for a 'sustained' note on a trumpet (W viii 7, 14). Several of these words are demonstrably reflections of Roman, whether late Republican or early Augustan, military terms.[2]

A favourite device of the authors of the Scrolls is to take a well-known Biblical expression and slightly to modify its form, sometimes with a bizzare effect: for example 'book of life'[3] is changed into 'pen of life' (W xii 3, where a Greek word is wrongly postulated[4]) and 'book of remembrance'[5] into 'engraving' or 'stele of remembrance' (T i 24).[6] That this is deliberate is shown by a curious instance in which the classical 'man of Belial' is altered into the un-Hebrew 'one of Belial' by correcting 'man' into 'one', which is written over it (A Fl d. 23).

Rabbinic forms and terms become not uncommon. Forms common in this literature, though found occasionally also in the Old Testament, are represented by the common word for 'norm, standard, rank' and the like (D v 3, 7 vi 4, 8–10, 22 vii 21 viii 4, 13, 19 ix 3, 4, 7, 12, 18, 21 x 5, 7, 9, *tikkûn*), and for 'ordered fate, destiny' (D xi 21, *siddûr*), if these are rightly so read.[7] Words not found before the Rabbinic period in the form or sense which they have in the Scrolls are those for the 'wing' of a door or gate (T iii 29)[8] and for the 'order, rule' of a community (D i 16 ii 20, 21 v 1, 23 vi 8, 22) as well as a military 'file, line, rank' (W vi 11, 14 vii 1 xv 4), for 'low, quiet' as describing the note of a trumpet (W viii 7, 14) and for 'brightly polished' (W v 11); others have acquired quite different meanings, such as 'spit' for the 'point, tip' of a weapon (W v 10). Rabbinic conceits may perhaps be seen in the use of 'other' as an euphemism for 'heretical' (T ii 16–19)[9] and in the word which has been translated 'two lights' as meaning 'double, exceedingly bright light' (T iv 23 xviii 29),[10] if it may be compared with that for 'two lazinesses' (*i.e.*

---

[1] Psa. x. 8, 10, 14 (*ḥelqā'îm*); s. Driver in *JTS*, NS XIII 373.
[2] Pp. 180–97.   [3] Psa. lxix. 29.   [4] P. 198.
[5] Mal. iii. 16.   [6] Driver in *JTS*, NS XIII 372.
[7] Cp. Jongeling in *RQ* I 483–94 and Wernberg-Møller *ibid.* 148–50 (where forms like *tekôn* and *sedôr* are preferred).
[8] P. 300.   [9] Cp. Isa. xxviii. 1.
[10] Dupont-Sommer *Hymnes* 42.

'double, excessive laziness' in the Old Testament;[1] but the word in the Scrolls has also been read 'light of perfection' *i.e.* 'perfect light',[2] and the interpretation of the Biblical word here mentioned is not recognized in the Greek and Latin versions.

A very few words can be explained only from other languages, especially the post-Mishnaic cognate (Aramaic or Syriac and Arabic) languages.

Two Assyrian words or phrases occur, namely those for 'vehemence' (*dnt*) of pain' (T v 13) and for 'advocates (*'ōḥăzê 'āḇûṭ* . . .)' (D ii 9); the former is an old Assyrian word (*dannatu* 'force') and the latter an Assyrian idiom (*abût . . . aḥāzu* 'to be advocate for . . .'), which passed eventually into the Syriac language. Their long hibernation is a useful warning against over-facile linguistic arguments. Aramaic or Syriac roots explain the word for 'engraved text (*ḥereṭ*)'[3] (T i 24); and Arabic words[4] explain those for 'purpose' (D iii 2: *sā'ôn*; cp. *sa'ā* 'purposed'), an 'ornamental band' (W v 6, 9, *bāḏān*; cp. *badan* 'ornamental girdle') and a 'company, group' (D iii 3, *'ayin*; cp. *'ayn* 'throng, troop')[5] and 'disaster' (D x 15, *bûqāh* or *bôqāh*; cp. *bauqat* 'disaster'),[6] for a 'dart' (W vi 3; *zereq*, cp. *zurq* 'javelins'), for 'prolonged' (W viii 9 xvi 7 *ṭārûḏ*; cp. *ṭarrada* 'prolonged' a note) and 'resonant' (W iv 6–8, 11 *mᵉruddāḏ*; cp. *raddada* 'threw back, echoed' a sound) as describing trumpet-notes, as also for 'announced' (Is. A xxxv 7, *nāmāh*; cp. *nāmā* 'reported').[7] Two words are Persian, the common word for 'secret' (*rāz*, found already in the Old Testament) and that for 'pursuit' (W i 9, *naḥšîr* which appears long afterwards in Syriac literature). One word is possibly Greek, namely that for 'boy, lad' too young for military service (W vii 3, *za'ṭûṭ*); it is otherwise found nowhere before the period of Targum and Talmud.[8]

A few newly coined compound expressions may also be noted, for example those for 'every one of' (D i 13–14), which has the appearance of a colloquialism, 'legion' (W ix 4), 'combatant soldiers' (W vi 11 vii 1, xv 4), 'commandants of camps' (W vii 1), 'latrines' (W vi i7), 'helmets' and 'greaves' (W vi 15). These last two expressions replace classical terms found in the Bible, which have become obsolete or been forgotten[9] but actually occur in medieval literature;[10] but, since analogously formed terms are found in early Rabbinic literature,[11]

---

[1] Eccles. x. 18.   [2] Sukenik *Scrolls* 38, 52.
[3] Dupont-Sommer *op. cit.* 28; cp. Exod. xxxii. 16.
[4] Cp. Mansoor in *JSS* III 50.   [5] Driver *ibid.* 368.
[6] Cp. Nah. ii. 11 (*buqāh* 'emptiness').   [7] P. 444.
[8] Cp. Levy *Chaldäisches Wörterbuch* I 226 and *Neuhebräisches und Chaldäisches Wörterbuch* I 507–9.
[9] Cp. 1 Sam. xvii. 5, 38 *alq.* (helmet) and xvii. 6 (greaves).
[10] Ben Yehuda *Thesaurus totius Hebraitatis* I 536b.
[11] Cp. Mishnah *Kelim* xxvi 3 (finger-stalls), viii 1 (sleeve), xx 3 (handle).

they cannot be used to prove a medieval date for the Scrolls, since their failure to appear in literature may be due to the chances or mischances of transmission.

The copyist of *Isaiah A* has different words from those in the Massoretic texts in some thirty-five places. Some may simply represent a different recension of the text and none make any material difference to the sense;[1] others, however, are historically interesting as showing that words must have in the course of centuries become obsolete or been forgotten. So on the one hand the archaic and equivocal *mî* 'who, what?' in the sense of 'what?' has been replaced by the classical and unambiguous *māh* 'what?' (Is. A xliii 19), which is preferred also in a Massoretic note on the Hebrew text; and on the other hand the Hebrew words for 'straggler' and 'plucker' have been replaced respectively by a late Syriac word for 'deserter' (Is. A xiii 4, *môdēd* for *bôdēd*) and by an Arabic word for 'beater' (Is. A xlii 7, *môṭēl* for *môrēṭ*),[2] Neither however can be used to prove a late date for the copy of *Isaiah* in which they are found; for the roots of both occur in the Old Testament and both therefore may have existed long before their appearance in the Scrolls.

The syntax shows some deviations from the strictest classical standards, especially in the development of Biblical idioms in the direction of Mishnaic usage. So, for example, the peculiar 'and what' for 'moreover', which may perhaps be found once in the Old Testament,[3] occurs in several places of the Scrolls (D v 10, 14–16 ix 26); and in some documents the Biblical *'ăšer* has given place to the Mishnaic *še-* 'which'.[4] New compound prepositions are developed, such as 'which (is) not with' for 'without' before nouns (D v 17 vi 1, 12 vii 8, 11, 18)[5] in close conformity with Mishnaic usage,[6] and new conjunctions are formed such as 'by not' for 'without (having done so and so, so and so having been done)' with the perfect tense (T x 6, 7, 19 xii 34 xviii 19; i 23 viii 10, 11, 14, 35)[7] and 'for not' for 'such as cannot be . . .' with the imperfect tense (T v 37 vi 27, 28 vii 9);[8] both are extensions of Biblical idioms. The article, which ought to be prefixed to a noun qualified by an attribute which itself takes the article, may be omitted (Z ix 29, 37) and the independent personal pronoun, which strictly serves only as the subject of a verbal or nominal clause, is loosely used in other positions (Dvii 16 Zx 1) as also rarely in the Old Testament when special emphasis falls on it;[9] both divergencies from the classical norm are found in the Mishnaic

---

[1] Cp. Driver in *JTS*, NS II 26–7.
[2] Isa. xiv. 31 and l. 16.
[3] Neh. x. 31.
[4] Bardtke *Handschriftenfunde* II 154.
[5] Psa. x. 6 (Septuagint).
[6] Cp. Strack & Siegfried *Lehrbuch der neuhebräischen Sprache* § 76ε.
[7] Cp. Lam. iv. 14.
[8] Cp. Isa. lxv. 1.
[9] Isa. xviii. 2 and Nah. ii. 9.

dialect.[1] Other peculiarities[2] are the tendency to abandon the so-called consecutive constructions with the strong form of the conjunction for simple continuation with its weak form; this tendency, already clearly marked in the latest books of the Old Testament, reaches its fulfilment in the Mishnah, where the construction hardly survives except in Biblical quotations. So it is most common in the *Hymns*, where it lingers as an archaism inherited from the *Psalter* on which they are modelled. Yet others are the abandonment of co-ordinating for subordinating conjunctions and of passive for impersonal active idioms, the extensive use of infinitive gerundial constructions, and considerable indulgence in variations of person, number and gender.

If then the language of the Scrolls is strictly not Mishnaic Hebrew, Dr. Rabin may well be right[3] in seeing a protest against this idiom rather than against the growing use of the Aramaic language in several passages of the Scrolls. Thus the author of the *Thanksgiving Hymns* says of his or his party's opponents that 'they have exchanged it (*sc.* the author's wisdom) for an uncircumcised language and a foreign tongue for a people of no understanding that they may be tripped up in their confusion' (T ii 18–19) and 'they speak to Thy (*sc.* God's) people in a barbarous language and in a foreign tongue so as to make all their works mad through deceit' (T iv 16–17); and the author of the *Zadokite Documents* complains that they have 'defiled the spirit of their holy things and with a blasphemous tongue have opened their mouths against the law of God's covenant' (Z vii 12). Also, as Dr. Rabin tentatively suggests, in the first extract 'their confusion' (*mišgāṭām*) may be an intentional play, albeit a derisory play, on 'their Mishnah' or 'their teaching' (*mišnāṭām*); for the Scrolls contain other such plays on words. If the suggestion is right, the authors were hitting at the Rabbis who were largely responsible for the introduction of Aramaisms and the development of the Mishnaic idiom and so afford one of the hints which can be detected in the Scrolls that the Covenanters held the Pharisees to be insufficiently strict in maintaining the purity of the language as they were in observing the Law itself.[4] Unfortunately, nothing is known of the early development of Mishnaic Hebrew; but it is not likely to have diverged so markedly from the Biblical standard as to have become a cause of abuse long before the time of the published Mishnah. Rabbis have taken up a similar position as regards the use of the 'sacred language' of the Scriptures in daily life and its adaptation to the needs of the present time during the last half century or thereabouts in Palestine.

---

[1] Segal *op. cit.* § 352 (pronoun) and § 376 (article).
[2] Cp. Reider in *JQR*, NS XLI 59–70.   [3] In *Scr. Jud.* II 67–9.
[4] Pp. 91–5.

The presence of late, even medieval, forms and words, phrases and idioms, in the Scrolls does not militate against this conclusion so as necessarily to prove them to have been late or medieval works, as Dr. Zeitlin has argued.[1] These may have been current in the language long before their first appearance in literature or they may have appeared in works which have perished; for no Hebrew literature has been preserved for a period of some 350 years, from the composition of *Daniel* about 165 B.C. till the final codification of the Mishnah about A.D. 200; no one knows how much literature of this period has been lost, nothing therefore is known of its language, and much that now seems strange may already have occurred in it. Again, many unique or rare Hebrew words in the Old Testament can be explained only by comparing them with cognate Aramaic or even Arabic words not found before Muḥammad; but the Nabataean (Aramaic) dialect, although it is contemporary with the Scrolls, already shows strong Arabic influence, and indeed the Arabic language is known to have existed in one form or another for many centuries before the classical period. Arabisms therefore are no proof of a late date; they may merely represent long lost Semitic roots which have not survived in any Hebrew literature or have only recently come to light in the Scrolls. Even Arabisms in the *Zadokite Documents*, which are preserved on very late manuscripts from Egypt, may have been substituted for genuine Hebrew words by scribes familiar rather with the Arabic than with the Hebrew language; for ancient copyists had little feeling for preserving the *ipsissima verba* of an author and freely modernized what they were copying. Finally, as Dr. Teicher has remarked,[2] the Scrolls represent an entirely new category of Hebrew literature in which terms not found elsewhere will naturally be expected; that these can often be explained only from the cognate languages proves nothing. Such details, then, as the appearance of apparently late forms and terms in the Scrolls only acquire force when their evidence converges in mass on a single point; isolated instances have little weight.

In conclusion, then, the language and style of the Scrolls is that neither of the Old Testament, of which the latest work may be dated *c.* 165 B.C., nor that of the Mishnah, published in the 2nd century A.D. The orthography has here all marks of a period of transition, when the pronunciation was in a state of flux and the principles of vocalization were ill-defined; the vocabulary contains a number of non-classical words, the sentences are ill formed and rambling. In these respects the prose goes beyond even the ill-written closing chapters of *Daniel* but does not reach the clarity of the Midrashic style. Both vocabulary and style suggest a time when the local Aramaic dialects would strongly influence the Hebrew language. The poetry is largely

---

[1] Pp. 346, 408.   [2] Cp. Rowley *Zadokite Fragments* 59.

a patch-work from Biblical poetry, and what is new is apt to be bizarre or based on misunderstanding the Old Testament; the verse is shapeless, having largely lost the rhythmical control and balanced parallelism of the classical poetry, but it has not acquired the strictly metrical form of the liturgical poems of the 5th century A.D. and onwards. All these features are indicative of a date round the end of the Second Commonwealth, when the old Biblical forms were dying but the new language of the schools had hardly established itself.

6. PSYCHOLOGICAL DIFFICULTIES

The problems of reconciling on the one hand the teaching and practice of the Essenes, at any rate on some points, with those of the Covenanters and on the other hand the internal contradictions which the writings of the Covenanters betray have attracted some attention.

The first question arises only if the Essenes and the Covenanters are identified; but, even if they are dissociated as in the present work, it is worth while considering it inasmuch as the answer to it is also to some extent the answer to the second question.

Prof. Klausner[1] asks how, if the group which produced the Scrolls were Essenes, they could have become violent revolutionaries despite the spiritual and ascetic rules of the order, which forbade military training and the carrying of arms except for self-defence on a journey; or, as the question may now be put, how could a religious and other-worldly group like the 'Sons of Light' have become at the same time violent revolutionaries, whether Zealots or *sicarii*, assassins and brigands? Mr. Goodman[2] similarly asks whether it would not be too great a coincidence to conclude that there were living not very far apart during the 1st century A.D. two distinct sects, formerly bearing some close relation to one another but subsequently taking different paths, the one Essene and completely pacifist and the other Zealot, formally linked to the Essenes, *i.e.* Covenanters but fanatic and extremist?

Such questions, which betray a surprising ignorance of human nature, are easily answered: the most pious are often the most savage. The Hasidaeans or 'pietists' (Heb. *ḥāsîd* 'loyal, pious'), whose origins went back into the Old Testament, were an ultra-strict party of the Pharisees; beginning as a *societas ecclesiastica*, they became a *factio politica* in the Maccabaean wars[3] when, though ready to make peace even at the risk of their lives,[4] they constituted a *corps d'élite* as 'mighty men' and 'not suffering the kingdom to find tranquillity' in their

[1] In *Sēfer Bîram* 163.　　　[2] In *Jewish Chronicle* 20 ix 1957, 20–1.
[3] Scaliger *ap.* Wellhausen *Pharisäer und Sadducäer* 86.
[4] 1 Macc. vii. 13–17.

zeal for the Law.[1] Again, as some Essenes identified themselves with
the active methods of the Zealots,[2] so the 'Sons of Light' became
militant Zealots;[3] for *tout mouvement commence en mystique et finit en
politique* (Péguy); for all things are possible where fanaticism, whether
political or religious, is rife. Indeed, the origin of the Covenanters, as
it has here been traced, makes such a clash of interests almost inevitable.
The movement was at once religious and political, as it could not but
be in so desperate a struggle as that with Rome,[4] having taken shape
as a protest against political interference, supported by foreign
interests, with spiritual supremacy in religious affairs; it would then
include two classes of members,[5] those chiefly interested in the spiritual
aspect of the Zadokite priesthood and traditions and those moved
principally by antipathy to Seleucid or Roman intrusion into Jewish
affairs, whether religious or political. The differences in such a
composite party, though normally quiescent, would flare up from
time to time, *e.g.* over the question whether the twofold threat to
religious and national autonomy should be met by pacific or by
military methods. All such groups, however, would naturally have
included many sober members who would not go all the way with the
extremists; at the same time, the party's intolerance of any other lord
or master but God, which was their fundamental doctrine and the
charter of their existence, was bound inevitably sooner or later to lead
them into open insurrection against Rome, from which they would
be unable to turn back.

In the same way the Knights Hospitaller began their career as an
offshoot of the Benedictine order, but their aims and conduct soon
came to differ widely, even while the two still lived side by side in
Palestine. The latter continued to live the lives of peaceful monks
while the former, beginning with the task of guiding and entertaining
pilgrims to the holy sites, ended by fighting to keep open the routes to
them and so became a purely militant order recruited for war against
the heathen; but it still contained members whose duties were purely
pacific. Or again, the Knights Templar began by following the same
rule; but they almost immediately became an independent order
whose avowed aim was to keep the road from the coast to Jerusalem
free from bandits who came to take part in any campaign in which the
kingdom of Jerusalem was engaged. All these were *rudes guerriers en
campagne, moines et ermites à l'Eglise*, as Jacques de Vitry described them,[6]
and these words *mutatis mutandis* would equally describe the Covenanters of Qumrân.

Mr. Goodman goes on to ask[7] how such sentiments, which he finds

---

[1] 1 Macc. ii. 42–4 and 2 Macc. xiv. 6.   [2] Pp. 116–17.
[3] Pp. 237–51.   [4] Cp. Hengel *Zeloten* 85.
[5] Pp. 234–5, 250–1.   [6] Abel *Livres des Maccabées* 43–4.   [7] *Ibid.* 21.

in the Scrolls, as 'I will not repay evil to any man, I will pursue all men only with good; for the judgement of all living lies only with God . . . ; I will cherish neither anger nor hatred for those who turn from rebellion' can be reconciled with the conduct of the Zealots; he has not noticed that the same person can say 'neither will I show any compassion for those who turn from the way' (D x 17–21). Could not the ancestors of Covenanters and Zealots alike declare 'how good and pleasant it is for brethren to dwell together in unity' and yet pray 'remember, O Lord, against the sons of Edom the day of Jerusalem'?[1] Psalmists and Covenanters alike observed different standards in their dealings with their fellow Jews and with the enemies of the nation[2] (cp. D i 9–10). Here too history illustrates the obvious answer. The profession even of the Christian faith has not deterred the ministers of the Gospel from the torture of those with whom they have differed in doctrine, from the murder and massacre of their enemies; and Islam presents an equally sorry spectacle of crimes against humanity committed in the name of religion.

The psychological arguments, then, which may be brought against the picture of the Covenanters as here drawn contradict human nature as it is depicted in the history of the human race; and so *tantum religio potuit suadere malorum* will be the true answer, as concise as it is sufficient to all such doubts and questions.

[1] Psa. cxxxiii. 1 and cxxxvii. 7.　　　　　[2] Cp. Matt. v. 24.

IX

JEWISH SCRIPTURES, DOCTRINES AND CUSTOMS

1. OLD TESTAMENT

Naturally the value of the Scrolls for the study of the Old Testament has been eagerly canvassed; but unfortunately all the Biblical texts so far recovered, except Scroll A and Scroll B (so far as it goes) of *Isaiah*, are fragments, often minute fragments; but they are not necessarily for that reason valueless. Yet, when everything has been said, few readings differing from the Massoretic text have real critical value and even so the improvement in the sense is rarely striking.[1] The real importance of the Scrolls is that they establish the general trustworthiness of the text, which otherwise rests on the evidence of very late manuscripts; of these the earliest are those of the Former and Latter Prophets dated A.D. 895, of the Latter Prophets dated A.D. 916, and of the whole Old Testament dated A.D. 1008.

The object of the present study, however, is not the value of the Scrolls for establishing the true or earliest text of the Old Testament but the unravelling of their history; and the use of the Biblical texts is here restricted, except for purposes of illustration, to that purpose.

The readings of the Scrolls which diverge from the Massoretic text are occasionally independent, *i.e.* not supported by any ancient Version;[2] but commonly they are found in one or other or in several of them, and they have even not infrequently been conjectured by modern scholars,[3] rightly as the Scrolls now sometimes prove.

Those which agree with the Greek translation of the Septuagint are the most important for the present purpose because they are witnesses to the influence of the Egyptian tradition.

The following examples illustrate this divergent tradition, which is often superior to that of the Massoretes:

---

[1] Cp. Elliger *Habakuk-Kommentar* 58.
[2] *E.g.* Isa. xxi. 8 (Lowth), xxxiii. 3, xl. 12, lxiv. 6 (Grotius).
[3] *E.g.* Isa. xiv. 4 (Michaelis with Septuagint, Peshitta) xiv. 30 (Bredenkamp with Vulgate), xlix 17 (Houbigant with Vulgate, Targum), xlix. 24 (Houbigant with Vulgate, Peshitta), li. 19 (Lowth with Septuagint, Vulgate, Peshitta, Targum), lxiv 6 (Grotius with Septuagint, Peshitta, Targum, Hebrew manuscripts), Hab. ii. 16 (Cappellus and Houbigant with Septuagint, Vulgate, Peshitta; Budde with Septuagint, Targum).

Isaiah xlv 2: 'I will ... make the swelling hills plain', where the unique word for 'swelling places (*hădurîm*)' is replaced by the ordinary word for 'mountains (*hărārîm*).[1]

Isaiah liii 11: 'he shall see the travail of his soul, he shall be satisfied; by his knowledge shall my righteous servant justify many, and he himself shall bear their iniquities', where the verb translated 'satisfied' lacks an object and 'my righteous servant' is ungrammatical, while the half-line is hypermetrical; the Scroll supplies the required object in the second clause, and the metre of the previous line is restored if the word rendered 'righteous (*ṣaddîq*)' is transferred to it and read as meaning 'righteousness' or 'justification (*ṣedeq*)', so that the verses may now be translated

'through the travail of his soul he shall be flooded <with light>[2]
(and) through his humiliation[3] win full† justification;[4]
(so) shall my servant justify many
and himself bear the punishment of their iniquities',
whereby sense, metre and grammar, are alike recovered;[5]

Isaiah lx 19: 'the sun shall no more be thy light by day, neither for brightness shall the moon give light unto thee', where the Scrolls have 'neither for brightness <by night> shall the moon give light unto thee', once again making sense by restoring a missing word.[6]

Habakkuk i 17: 'therefore he shall lay bare, *i.e.* empty his net (*ḥermô*)', where the object is unsuitable to the verb, which is forced to yield a dubious sense, and the Scroll's 'he shall lay bare (*i.e.* draw) his sword (*ḥarbô*)' is surely preferable;[7]

Habakkuk ii 5: 'wine (*hayyayin*) is treacherous', where the Scroll's 'the scorner (*hawwān*) is treacherous' makes good sense and agrees well with the parallel term.[8]

Another deviation from the traditional text has a different interest, as it occurs in a famous passage. The traditional 'she shall' or 'thou shalt call his name Immanuel'[9] appears as 'one shall call his name Immanuel', in agreement with the New Testament's 'they shall call his name Immanuel',[10] which means the same thing; for impersonal or

---

[1] Cp. Marti *Jesaia* 308 (s. Wernberg-Moller in *RQ* II 448–9).
[2] Cp. Houbigant *Biblia Hebraica* 150; s. Driver in *JTS* XXXVI 151–3.
[3] Thomas *ibid.* XXXVIII 404–5; s. Driver *ibid.* 48–9.
[4] Cp. Torrey *Second Isaiah* 421–2.
[5] S. pp. 256–7; cp. Seligman in *BO* VI 7.   [6] Cp. Lowth *Isaiah* 259.
[7] Cp. Giesebrecht *Jesaiakritik* 197.
[8] Cp. Houtsma in *Th. Tijdskr*, XIX 181–2.
[9] Isa. vii. 14.   [10] Matt. i. 23.

indefinite constructions are but a Hebrew way of indicating a passive sense, which the Vulgate's *vocabitur* supports. This reading seems to reflect a tradition of the 1st century A.D.

Two other variant readings may be noticed not so much because they give or restore good sense as because they introduce late words. In the first 'like a weaver I have rolled up (*qippadtî*) my life'[1] becomes 'like a weaver I have cut short (*sippartî*) my life'; the new verb, not found elsewhere before the Mishnah, makes sense as good as, if not actually preferable to, that of the Massoretic text[2]. In the second the obviously unintelligible '(I) first (will say) to Zion: Behold, behold them!'[3] (where the bracketed words, missing from the Massoretic texts, have been added in the translation in the hope of making sense) is replaced by 'behold! one who will first bring a charge on Zion's behalf', whereby sense is won by the restoration of a Hebrew verb which, though long forgotten and therefore garbled by the Massoretes, can be identified from the corresponding Arabic verb (Hebr. *nāmāh* 'brought a charge' = Arab. *namā* 'reported').[4]

One other very interesting divergent reading which the Septuagint confirms occurs in the well-known verse which says that

> He (*sc.* God) sets the bounds of the peoples
> according to the number of the children of Israel',[5]

which has long puzzled commentators.[6] Here the Septuagint has 'according to the number of the angels of God' or 'of the gods'; and this conjecture has now been proved right by a fragment which has this very reading.[7] The substitution of 'according to the number of the children of Israel' is now seen to have been a tendentious alteration, of which there are not a few examples in the Massoretic text, introduced with a view to eliminating anything derogatory to Jehovah (for, if the Most High God had allotted the nations to the 'sons of God' *i.e.* subordinate gods or guardian angels, as He had appointed the gods to the nations,[8] Jehovah as one of these deities must at one time have been himself an inferior deity)[9] and at the same time glorifying the Jewish race. This fragment therefore must be dated before the introduction of this alteration[10] into the Massoretic text. That may be before *c.* A.D. 125, since Aquila as well as Theodotion and Symmachus have got it; but how long before cannot be said, unless the reaction to the disaster of A.D. 70 may be thought to have caused its introduction as an encouragement to national pride.

[1] Isa. xxxviii. 12.
[2] Cp. de Boer in *Oudt. St.* IX 172.
[3] Isa. xli. 27.
[4] Guillaume in *JBL* LXXVI 40.
[5] Deut. xxxii. 8.
[6] *E.g.* Cappellus *Critica Sacra* [1650] 271.
[7] Skehan in *BASOR* CXXXVI 12.
[8] Cp. Deut. iv. 9, xxix. 26 and Ecclus. xvii. 17.
[9] Emerton in *JTS*, NS IX 241.
[10] Cp. Driver in *OBL* I 144, 145, 153.

The influence of the Septuagint on the Hebrew text as represented by the Scrolls is further illustrated by two portions of *I* and *II Samuel* found in Cave IV, which are as considerable (though fragmentary) as they are important; for their text not only differs frequently from the Massoretic text but also for the most part agrees, where it so differs, with that underlying the translation of the Septuagint. This text, whose superiority to the Massoretic text in this book has long been recognized, seems to have originated in Palestine so that it must go back to a time before the Jewish migrations to Egypt out of which the need for a Greek translation of the Scriptures must have arisen; for *Chronicles* shows traces of its influence here and there.[1] These however are hardly strong enough to justify the assumption that this pre-Septuagintal Hebrew text can have persisted in Palestine with such effect that the Hebrew fragments from Qumrân which reflect it can be said necessarily to have come from that country; nothing in their text suggests that it may not have originated in Egypt.

Other divergencies from the Massoretic text in the Scrolls have been found only in very late writings, for example two in Justin Martyr (*c*. A.D. 100), of which one appears in the same form in Cyprian (*c*. A.D. 200–58), one in the Jewish poet Yannai (5th-6th century A.D.) and another in the Jewish prayer-book.[2]

The suggestion has been made[3] that in a few places, where *Isaiah A* is supported by all the ancient versions against the Massoretic text, the Scroll preserves an early text and that the Massoretic form of the passage may be due to deliberate alteration in the interests of a theory or a sect; some of these are claimed to be ancient readings which have been intentionally eliminated from the official Massoretic text as expressing the *ex hypothesi* unorthodox Messianic beliefs of the Covenanters. Even if there were such manipulations of the text,[4] and they are well known even in the orthodox text,[5] the question posed by Professor Burrows[6] would still remain: did the official scribes alter the text to get rid of implications which they considered objectionable or did the Covenanters alter it to introduce their own theories into it?

The possibility that the authors of the Scrolls have interpreted or even adapted the text of the Old Testament to suit their own purpose cannot be excluded. For example, the prophet's 'wherefore . . . holdest Thou (*sc.* God) Thy peace when the wicked swalloweth up the man that is more righteous than he?'[7] is explained as referring to those 'who were put to silence (*i.e.* destroyed) at (the time of) the chastisement of the Rightful Teacher' (H v 8–10) by the Wicked Priest, having been

---

[1] Cross in *BASOR* CXXXII 23–4; cp. *Library* 140–5.
[2] Burrows *Scrolls* I 11–12.
[3] Barthélemy in *RB*, NS LVII 530–49.   [4] *E.g.* Deut. xxxii 8.
[5] Geiger *Urschrift und Uebersetzungen der Bibel* 259–433.
[6] In *Scrolls* I 313.   [7] Hab. i. 13.

adapted to the murder of Menahem by Eleazar son of Hananiah;[1] and 'that thou (*i.e.* the person addressed by the prophet) mayest look on their naked orgies (*ma'ărêhem* for *mᵉ'ôrêhem*)'[2] is quoted as 'that thou mayest look on their fixed feasts (*mô'ăḏêhem*)' (H xi 3) in contemptuous allusion to their opponents' divergent calendar, *i.e.* the orthodox calendar of the Pharisees.[3] The suggestion therefore that 'the Commentary represents a tradition quite different from any attested in the Massoretic text' or in the versions[4] cannot be accepted out of hand.

What must in any case not be overlooked is that the authors of the Scrolls may even have misunderstood the text of the Old Testament; and this, which seems to be the only possible explanation of occasional deviations from the Massoretic text (*e.g.* T iv 34),[5] is an additional reason for caution in drawing far-reaching conclusions from their readings.

What light these divergencies from the Massoretic text throw on the date of the Scrolls is not clear; certainly they do not allow anything precise. On the one hand, the *terminus a quo* can only be very roughly inferred. In theory, since a (possibly Palestinian) pre-Septuagintal (*i.e.* pre-Egyptian) text must have been the basis of that used by the Septuagint in making their Greek translation of the Old Testament, the Biblical Scrolls representing such a text may go back to this period. Although however they show Septuagintal peculiarities, they betray none of the serious divergencies or gross corruptions (so far as the mostly fragmentary samples permit generalization) represented by the Septuagint, so that they must derive from a Hebrew archetype of an age when something was being done to establish a pure text, *i.e.* late in or soon after that of the Septuagint; that the Covenanters seem to have been resident in Egypt *c.* 175–50 B.C. agrees with such a conclusion. Yet the lowest date cannot be put arbitrarily on this score *c.* 50 B.C.; for the Egyptian tradition may have influenced the Covenanters even after their return to Palestine about that time. The *terminus ante quem* is clearly the standardization of the Massoretic text by the Rabbis *c.* A.D. 70–150, after which no divergent readings (other than permitted orthodox variations, few as they are, and mere copyists' errors) will have made their way into it, while deliberate manipulations of it in the interests of this or that party will have been rigidly excluded. That the text which the non-Septuagintal pieces represent is only approaching this ideal condition in matters of orthography, while the replacement of an obsolete by a modern term is occasionally permitted, shows that they must be dated well before this standardization. Briefly, then, the Biblical Scrolls represent a text

---

[1] Pp. 267–9.   [2] Hab. ii. 15 (s. Wellhausen *Die kleinen Propheten* 169).
[3] Pp. 317–18.   [4] Van der Ploeg *ap.* Burrows *Scrolls* I 318.
[5] Driver in *JTS*, NS XIII 370–1.

in a relative state of fluidity, when some control over it is beginning to be introduced but absolute uniformity has not yet been reached, since it is neither so erratic as that of the Septuagint nor as unvarying as that of Jerome; it may then be dated between *c.* 150 or even 100 B.C. and A.D. 70, if earlier rather than later in this period.[1]

That two different types of text are found at Qumrân, of which the smaller group is 'Septuagintal' and the large 'Massoretic', raises interesting questions: for example, do both lots come from the same source or do the former derive from Egypt and the latter from Palestine; and are the Scrolls a unified collection belonging to a single group of people, *e.g.* the Zadokites or Covenanters of Qumrân, or are they a miscellaneous collection brought together in the caves at Qumrân more or less by chance? This Zadokite acquaintance with a Septuagintal text is significant; for no Palestinian Jews but only those from Egypt will have had any use for the Septuagint.

However important the Scrolls may be for textual work, they are too late to throw any light on problems of literary composition. That the text of the first thirty-nine chapters of *Isaiah A* is by a different hand from that of the remaining sixty-seven chapters proves nothing; the *Thanksgiving Hymns* come from the hands of two different copyists, and the change from the first to the second occurs in the middle of a sentence (T xi 22). That the *Commentary on Habakkuk* is based on the first two chapters alone and that the third is not used does not necessarily mean that, as scholars generally hold, the last chapter is not an original part of the book; this would indeed be a possible reason for its absence from the Scroll, but the commentator might equally well not have used it because it was not suitable to his purpose.[2] Not even the discovery of fragments of *Daniel*, containing portions of both the Hebrew and Aramaic sections, in Cave I affects the critical date of that book *c.* 165 B.C.; for the dates assigned to the Scrolls on purely palaeographical grounds are largely fanciful.[3] Pentateuchal manuscripts written in the archaic script are not necessarily archaic[4] since the old script may have lingered long in copies of the Law and indeed of other books of Scripture, for example *Job*[5] (just as breviaries and prayer-books are still sometimes printed in an archaic or pseudo-archaic founts), as it was revived as propaganda at various periods of Jewish history;[6] Dussaud is therefore not necessarily right in arguing[7] that a *Leviticus* in archaic (*i.e.* pre-exilic) script proves that the Priestly Code must be dated before Ezekiel. If *Leviticus* is proved pre-exilic, so also is *Job*, of which fragments have been found in the archaic script,

---

[1] Cp. Burrows *Scrolls* I 319–20.
[2] Cp. Burrows *op. cit.* I 321–2.
[3] Pp. 410–20.
[4] Pp. 413–14.
[5] P. 19.
[6] Cross *Library* 33–4.
[7] In the *CRAIB-L* 8 iv 1949, 96–7.

by the self-same argument! As *Genesis* and *Exodus* as well as *Leviticus* continued to be copied in the archaic or pre-exilic script because they were thought to be pre-exilic as Mosaic compositions, so *Job* was copied in that script because *Job* was thought to belong to the patriarchal age. Allowance must be made for the pre-critical opinions of the ancient copyists and the conservatism characteristic of religious communities.

2. INTER-TESTAMENTAL AND POST-BIBLICAL LITERATURE

The Scrolls have thrown some light also on Jewish apocryphal and pseudepigraphical writings. Unfortunately all that has been recovered of this class of literature is fragmentary; but it has in spite of its defective condition considerable importance. First, the scraps of this literature, being written in the Hebrew or Aramaic language, have proved what has long been suspected, that many works of this class (for example *Tobit, Jubilees, I Enoch, Testaments of the Twelve Patriarchs*), which have till now been known only in translations, are Hebrew or Aramaic in origin. Second, they enable a certain number of points, which these translations leave obscure, to be cleared up. By no means all the apocryphal works are represented in the collections recovered from the caves round Qumrân; those of which most pieces have been recovered are naturally works which have had a direct bearing on the doctrine of the Covenanters (notably *Jubilees* and *I Enoch* and the *Testaments*); and the most conspicuous book of which no fragment has been found is that of *Judith*, possibly because the Covenanters may have disapproved of its contents.[1] Third, a substantial portion of an entirely new work of descriptive interpretation has been discovered, which belongs to Targumic or Midrashic literature.

The Scrolls afford many proofs that their authors were very well acquainted not only with the earliest but also with the latest of the apocryphal or intertestamental writings.

A notable echo of the *Wisdom of Ben Sirach*, which appeared *c.* 190 B.C., occurs in two Scrolls; for, as the former says that 'Shem, Seth and Enosh, were honoured (*nikbᵉdû* for *nifqᵉdû*) and were above all that lives the pride (*tifʾeret*) of Adam' or 'of mankind',[2] so the latter declare that the 'glory (*kābôd*) of Adam' or 'of mankind' shall belong to those 'whom God has chosen for an eternal covenant' and 'who hold fast to it (*sc.* the sure house)[3] unto everlasting life' (D iv 22–3 Z

---

[1] Pp. 384–6.
[2] Ecclus. xlix. 16; s. Lévi *L'Ecclésiastique* II 205–6 (who rightly follows the Gr. 'εδοξασθησαν and takes 'ādām against the Gr. ἐν κτίσει Αδαμ not as a proper name but as a common noun).
[3] P. 368.

v 6), *i.e.* any joining the society of the Covenanters. As too Ben Sirach says that 'they that fear the Lord will seek His good favour',[1] so one of the Scrolls speaks of 'the sons of Zadok, the priests, those who keep the covenant and who seek His (*sc.* God's) good favour' (D v 9). Also, as 'He (*sc.* God) gave Aaron authority over law and justice',[2] so 'the sons of Aaron shall have authority over justice and wealth' (D ix 7) in the society of the Covenanters; thus the high position of the priests in the society of the Covenanters is justified by quoting the very words of the ancient sage. This work is the source, too, of the title of the 'Interpreter of the Law' which, though only a common term here,[3] acquires particular importance in the Scrolls, where the person who bears it has become a Messianic figure;[4] and other quite ordinary words and phrases, not found before it, such as 'mammon' (D vi 2, Z xviii 9)[5] and 'the face of the dry land' (Z ii 9)[6] have been traced to it.

The most noticeable point in this work in connection with the Scrolls is its apparent Zadokite interest. Both Hebrew and Greek versions have a poem reciting the praises of 'Simon the priest' or 'high-priest',[7] presumably Simon II[8] the *ṣaddîq*, who may have been so called as representing the true Zadokite line of high-priests;[9] and the Hebrew version in an intruded collection of benedictions (which are not in the Greek version and are clearly out of place where they stand) includes special thanks to God 'who has chosen the sons of Zadok for priests'.[10] The author himself might well be responsible for the praises of Simon, who lived not long before him; but the thanksgiving for the Sons of Zadok would seem to have been an interpolation made in the Zadokite interest[11] in Egypt, where the Zadokites lived for the next hundred years and where the only known manuscripts of the Hebrew version were found. It would then be additional evidence for the Egyptian connections of the Zadokites.

The books of *I Enoch* and *Jubilees* and the *Testaments of the Twelve Patriarchs*, a product of the school which must have done much to prepare the way for the New Testament, seem to have been the chief pseudepigraphical sources from which matter in the Scrolls has been drawn. All three works are generally thought to have come from Pharisaic circles; but their dates are still debated.[12] The whole of *I Enoch* has recently been assigned to the last decades of the 3rd century B.C. or the first quarter of the 2nd century B.C.;[13] but the prevailing opinion has been that, while the earliest parts may be pre-

[1] Ecclus. ii. 16.   [2] *Ibid.* xlv. 17.   [3] *Ibid.* xxxii. 12.
[4] Pp. 228–9.   [5] Ecclus. xxxi. 8.   [6] *Ibid.* xxxvii. 3.
[7] *Ibid.* l 1–21.   [8] Lévi *op. cit.* II 206.   [9] Pp. 228–9.
[10] Ecclus li. 12 (i).   [11] Cp. Rabin *Scr. Jud.* II 75–6.
[12] Cp. Charles *Pseudepigrapha* 282, 291–3.
[13] Bickermann in *JBL* LXIX 245–60.

Maccabaean, the latest ought to be dated before the Roman conquest of Palestine in 63 B.C.[1] The work is quoted in *Jubilees*, which may be put between 135 B.C., when John Hyrcanus became high-priest, and his breach with the Pharisees not long before his death in 105–104 B.C.[2] The *Testaments*, although sometimes put as far back as 200 B.C.,[3] seem to contain matter reflecting the decline of the Hasmonaean or Maccabaean dynasty and may perhaps be dated *c.* 109–107 B.C.; possibly its anti-Maccabaeanism may be put as late as *c.* 70–40 B.C.[4] Other writers of the period have left sporadic traces of their influence on the Scrolls, but they are negligible.

The echoes of *I Enoch* and *Jubilees* in the Scrolls, apart from the calendar which seems to have been derived directly from them,[5] are numerous, showing their authors to have been well acquainted with these works.

In *I Enoch* such are the notions that God has given 'insight into the knowledge of the Most High to the upright and into the wisdom of the Sons of Heaven to the perfect' (D iv 22),[6] of the angels as 'sons of heaven' here and elsewhere (D xi 8 T iii 22 W xii 5),[7] of the 'fountain of righteousness' (D xi 5),[8] of the members of the society of the Covenanters as 'children' or 'sons of righteousness' (D iii 20, 22)[9] and 'elect of righteousness' like the Messiah of the Scrolls (T ii 13),[10] of the council of the righteous depicted under the figure of an 'eternal plantation' (D viii 1 xi 8; cp. T viii 6),[11] of the 'garments of glory' and the 'garments of life'[12] like the 'raiment of glory' in which they, like the Mandaean saints,[13] will hereafter be clothed (D iv 8), when they will be with the 'sons of heaven' (D iv 22, viii 12),[14] of denouncing the commandments of God as false (D viii 12),[15] of the 'angels of destruction (*mal'ăkê ḥabbāl*)', which reappear in Rabbinic literature,[16] waiting to punish the wicked (D iv 12 Z ii 4),[17] of men becoming in the words of the Old Testament[18] 'as though they had not been' (Z iii 6),[19] and of Sheol as 'hollow places, deep and dark to view',[20] which recalls the description of the place of punishment in the underworld as 'dark chasms' (D iv 13). Lastly, one form of this book contains the first hint of a final eschatological war.[21] In *Jubilees*, too, a number of coincidences have been noted: for example, 'the sons of the righteous

---

[1] Charles *Religious Development between the Old and New Testaments* 224.
[2] Charles *op. cit.* 230.
[3] Eppel *ap.* Eissfeldt *Einleitung in das Alte Testament*[2] 784.
[4] Charles *op. cit.* 232–2.   [5] Pp. 319–26.   [6] Cp. I Enoch xiv 3.
[7] *Ibid.* vi 2 xiii 8 xiv. 3.   [8] *Ibid.* xlviii 1.   [9] *Ibid.* xci 3, xcii 2.
[10] *Ibid.* xxxix 6.   [11] Cp. *ibid.* lxxxiv 6 xciii 5, 10; also Ascension of Isaiah iv 3.
[12] *Ibid.* lxii 16; cp. II Enoch xxii 8.   [13] P. 567.
[14] I Enoch vi 2 xiii 8 xiv 3; cp. ci 1, where the expression designates pious Jews.
[15] Cp. *ibid.* civ 9.   [16] Pp. 456–7.
[17] I Enoch liii 3 lvi 1 lxii 11 lxiii 1 lxvi 1.   [18] Obad. 16.
[19] I Enoch cii 11.   [20] *Ibid.* xxii 2.   [21] II Enoch xc. 19.

one' (D ix 14)[1] and the 'spirit of truth' (D iv 21),[2] the 'angel (of) Mastema' and the 'prince (of) Mastena' as the name of the angel of temptation or Satan (Z xvi 5 xx 2),[3] which is derived from the Old Testament,[4] the prohibition of striking anyone on the Sabbath (Z xiii 15),[5] the idea that God with men's increasing corruption 'commanded that their understanding should depart before the completion of their lives' (Z xi 4)[6] and the punishment of the wicked with a multitude of plagues after death (D iv 12).[7] Occasionally the rules show slight divergencies: for example, the command to wear clean clothes on the day of the new moon in the apocalypse[8] but on the Sabbath in accordance with Rabbinic practice in the Scroll (Z xiii 12).

Coincidences have been detected also between the Scrolls and the *Testaments*: for example, the 'unique teacher' (Z ix 29, if the Hebrew expression is rightly thus translated)[9], as compared with the 'only' or 'only-begotten prophet',[10] the 'eternal peace' promised to the righteous hereafter (D ii 4) recalling the 'great peace' and 'joy for ever and ever' promised them in these works,[11] the 'spirit of truth' (D iv 21; cp. D iii 19 iv 23 W xiii 10)[12] and the 'period of wickedness' though in a different application (Z viii 9 112 xix 7)[13], and the doctrine of the 'two ways' (D iv 2–26),[14] which appears also in Christian literature.[15] In the *Testaments*, too, as in *War* the enemy are the Kittians while Judah, Levi and Benjamin come to the help of their descendants in the final conflict (W i 1–4).[16]

A few points in the Scrolls are common to several of these apocryphal works, such as the notion that the wicked are 'eternally accursed' (D ii 17)[17] and destroyed by fire (D ii 8),[18] and the addiction to a solar instead of the orthodox lunar calendar.[19] The former is an idea not confined to these works but widespread.[20] The latter, which has considerable importance, may reflect a practice antecedent to the time when these works were composed; but *Jubilees* must have been written before the *Zadokite Documents*, since these quote it under the title of the *Book of the Divisions of Times into their Jubilees and Weeks* (Z xx 1), which is almost identical with the description of it as 'the history of the division of the days . . . of their weeks (and) of their

---

[1] Jubilees x 6 (s. Nötscher *Qumran-texte* 185, Wernberg-Møller in *VT* III 310–13 and *Discipline* 91).
[2] *Ibid.* xxv 14.   [3] *Ibid.* xi 5, 11 xvii 16 xviii 9 xlviii 9.
[4] Hos. ix. 7.   [5] Jubilees l 12.   [6] Cp. *ibid.* xxiii 11.
[7] *Ibid.* xxxvi 10.   [8] *Ibid.* xxxi 1.   [9] P. 258.
[10] Testaments *Benjamin* ix 2; s. Charles *Testaments of the Twelve Patriarchs* 212.
[11] Testaments *Dan* v 11–12 and *Jubilees* xxiii 30.
[12] Testaments *Judah* xx. 1.   [13] Testaments *Dan* vi 6.
[14] Testaments *Asher* i 3–v 2.   [15] Pp. 552–8.
[16] Pp. 197, 216.   [17] I Enoch v 5 xxvii 2 and *Jubilees* xxxvi 10.
[18] I Enoch ciii 5–8 and Testaments *Levi* iii 1–2.   [19] Pp. 317–26.
[20] *E.g.* Judith xvi. 17, 4 Macc. ix. 8–9, Matt. xvi. 19, xviii. 18 and Jn. xx. 23; cp. Moore *Judaism* II 388–9.

years' in the prologue to the Ethiopic version.[1] Similarly, several
sources may be cited for the story of the downfall of the 'watchers of
heaven' (Z iii 4)[2] and for the curious notion that a man's (here David's)
sin would be forgiven 'because he had not read in the sealed book of
the law which was inside the ark' (Z vii 5).[3]

The *Psalms of Solomon*, which are regarded as Pharisaic in origin
and dated *c.* 70–40 B.C., also have several phrases which appear in
the Scrolls.[4] These are 'the heave-offering of the lips', which is a
somewhat bizarre expression for the praises of God (D x 6; cp. x 14)
and 'the fruit of the lips' (T i 18),[5] which means the same thing and
appears also in both Testaments.[6] One passage in this work has
especial interest, partly as being perhaps echoed in the description of
the Wicked Priest and partly as introducing two expressions found in
some of the Scrolls; it says that 'the alien, the adversary wrought
insolence . . .; and the sons of the covenant in the midst of the mingled
people (*sc.* the Gentiles) surpassed them, none amongst them in the
midst of Jerusalem did mercy and truth. They that loved the assemblies
of the saints fled from them'.[7] This is perhaps echoed in 'Jerusalem
wherein the Wicked Priest wrought deeds of abomination' (H xii 7–8);
and it may be the source of the two expressions which the Covenanters
occasionally apply to themselves, namely 'the sons of His (*sc.* God's)
covenant' (W xvii 8); cp. T fr. iv 8), which is employed also by the
Septuagint in one or two passages of the Old Testament,[8] and 'the
assembly of the saints' (cp. T iv 25 and fr. v 3, W xii 7), which recalls
'the churches of the saints' in the New Testament.[9]

The brief apocryphal book of *I Baruch*, which is probably dated
c. A.D. 50–90, has only a few points of contact with the Scrolls.[10]
Its author and the compiler of the *Zadokite Documents* seem to use the
same pseudonym to conceal a foreign conqueror's name;[11] and he
describes the enemy, who too are in all probability the Romans, as
'a shameless nation . . . who neither reverenced old men nor pitied
children',[12] using almost the same words as those in the *Commentary
on Habakkuk*, where they are called a people 'who destroy many by
the word—youths, men and old men, women and little children;
and they have no mercy on the fruit of the womb' (H vi 10–12). The
author also refers to the burning of Jerusalem by fire,[13] to which one

---

[1] Charles *Apocrypha and Pseudepigrapha II* 11.
[2] 1 Enoch i 5 xii 4–5 xiii 10 xiv 3 xv 2–7 xvi 1–4 and Testaments *Naphtali* iii 5.
[3] Jubilees xxxiii 15–16 (Reuben) and Midrash R. *Ruth* vii 7 (Ruth).
[4] Cp. Schoeps in *ZRGG* III 328–31 and *ZAtW* LXIII 256–8.
[5] Psalms of Solomon xv 5.   [6] Hos. xiv. 3 (Septuagint) and Heb. xiii. 15.
[7] Psalms of Solomon xvii 15–18.
[8] Ezek. xxx. 5 (LXX) and Ps. cli *ad finem* (Sandars in *ZAtW* LXXV 75–6 and
Rabinowitz *ibid.* LXXVI 195–6); cp. Jubilees xv. 26 and Acts iii. 25.
[9] 1 Cor. xiv. 33.   [10] 1 Baruch i 11–12.   [11] Pp. 313–14.
[12] *Ibid.* iv. 15.   [13] *Ibid.* i. 2.

of the *Hymns* almost certainly alludes (T iii 29–31).[1] The *Assumption of Moses*, which reflects the events leading up to A.D. 70, has one or two interesting contacts with the Scrolls. It depicts the end of the final conflict as a 'day of vengeance',[2] as also the Covenanters do (W vii 5; cp. D ix 23 x 19). It has also a mysterious reference to the leaders of a party *qui magistri sunt doctores eorum* and to its members who are *homines pestilentiosi, qui se iustos esse docent*[3]; these two passages can hardly be explained otherwise than as indirect denunciations of the Zadokites[4] and the Rightful Teacher or succession of such Teachers.[5] The *Ascension of Isaiah*, dated *c.* 1st-2nd century A.D., has two expressions which inevitably recall the language of the Scrolls, namely 'true (Hebr. *ṣeḏeq* = Eth. *ṣedq*) faith' (D iv 2; cp. xx 30) and the 'lot of the Lord'[6] which is none other than the 'lot of God' in the Scrolls (D ii 2 W x iii 5 xvii 7). The corresponding Gr. μοῖρα 'lot', which Josephus[7] uses in connection with the Essenes, also becomes almost a military term in *War* (W iv 2 xiii 2, 4, 5, 9, 12); and this is one of its regular meanings in the 1st and 2nd centuries A.D., when both Josephus[8] and Herodianus[9] so employ it. Lastly, the apocalyptic work called *II Esdras*, plausibly dated *c.* A.D. 100–120, shares the prohibition, which is already found in the New Testament,[10] to keep secret the teaching which it imparts[11] with the Scrolls (D ix 17); this, then, like so much else in them, seems to be characteristic of the 1st-2nd centuries A.D., when the expression of political opinions and the formation of secret societies was too dangerous.[12] Consequently, it uses the figure of an eagle to allude indirectly to the Roman empire,[13] as the author of the *Commentary on Habakkuk* describes the Romans under the figure of the Kittians coming 'like an eagle' (H iii 9–12).[14]

These pseudepigraphical works also contain references, of which not a few are echoed in the New Testament, to the 'spirits of truth and perversion' (D iii 18–19),[15] the 'time of visitation' (D iii 18 iv 19)[16], and the 'gloom of eternal fire' (D ii 8) or 'the fire of the dark regions' (D iv 12–13)[17] to which sinners are condemned and which Mr. Del Medico has improbably connected[18] with the late story of a column of black smoke continually going up from two palm-trees marking the entrance to the Valley of Hinnom.[19] At the same time they describe

---

[1] Pp. 299–303.
[2] Assumption of Moses ix 7.
[3] *Ibid.* v 5 vii 3.
[4] Pp. 258–60.
[5] Pp. 253–8.
[6] Ascension of Isaiah i 13 viii 12.
[7] In *War* II viii 10 § 150.
[8] *Ibid.* IV ix 1 § 486.
[9] Lentz *Herodiani Technici Reliquiae* VI vi 3.
[10] Pp. 567, 578.
[11] 2 Esdras [4 Ezra] xiv 6, 45–6.
[12] Pp. 348–9.
[13] Pp. 199, 211–13.
[14] *Ibid.* xi 1–4 (where the three heads are Vespasian, Titus and Domitian); cp. Deut. xxviii. 49 and Hab. i. 8 (to which the commentary refers).
[15] Testaments *Judah* xx 1 (cp. 1 Enoch xli 8); 1 Jn. iv. 6.
[16] Wisdom of Solomon iii 7; Lk. xix. 44.
[17] Cp. 1 Enoch cii 8 ciii 8; Jude 6–7.
[18] In *Énigme* 279.
[19] B. Talmud *Erubin* 19a.

what happens in man's physical body as 'in the body of his flesh' (H ix 2), though in very different connections.[1] Another interesting coincidence is the Covenanters' description of themselves as the 'sons of His (*sc.* God's) covenant' (W xvii 8) and of their opponents as the 'sons of perdition' (Z xiii 12 xvi 7). The former, which is applied by several writers to those who shared in the covenant with Abraham,[2] became the normal appellation of Christian monks in the Syriac-speaking church;[3] the latter, which goes back to the Septuagint's inexact rendering of the exilic prophet's 'children of transgression',[4] is applied by the same writer to the sinners who perished at the flood and those who rejected the covenant of Abraham[5] and by others to the Antichrist[6] and to Judas.[7] The eastern church may have borrowed 'sons of the covenant' from one of the apocryphal writers (if their works were accessible to them) but cannot have got it from the Covenanters, and the authors of the Scrolls, unlike the writers of the New Testament, are not likely to have borrowed 'sons of perdition' from the Septuagint; the only possible conclusion therefore is that both expressions were religious commonplaces of these centuries. So too the authors of the Scrolls call their society a 'plant' or 'plantation' (D viii 5, ix 10 Z i 5), playing on a word or figure of speech which has occurred in previous centuries[8] but becomes almost a commonplace of the literature, apocalyptic[9] and other,[10] of the 1st century A.D.

Allusions to seeking refuge in the wilderness, which are found here and there in the Scrolls (*e.g.* D viii 13–14 ix 19–20 W i 2–3; APs. a ii 1), appear also in apocalyptic literature of the 1st–2nd century A.D.[11]; they occur however in every period of Hebrew and Jewish history, including the Maccabaean,[12] so that those in Jewish apocalyptic, Christian and Rabbinic, literature, though frequent, have only negative value in the present connection.[13] They serve only to show that this is a period to which the Scrolls may be assigned without fear of contradiction on this score.

Incidentally the apocryphal writings and the Scrolls sometimes explain each other's obscurities. For example, when Enoch mysteriously says 'Then I asked about all the hollow places: why is one separated from another?',[14] as the Ethiopic version renders the (lost original)

---

[1] Ecclus. xxiii. 23 and Col. i. 22; s. pp. 535–6.   [2] S. p. 452.
[3] Payne-Smith *Thesaurus Syriacus* 595–6, 3534.   [4] Isa. lvii. 4.
[5] Jubilees x 3 xv 26 (where different words for 'perdition' are used).
[6] Jn xvii. 12.   [7] 2 Thess. ii. 3.
[8] Isa. lxi. 3 and 1 Enoch lxxxiv 6.
[9] 1 Enoch lxxxiv 6 xciii 5, 10; also Ascension of Isaiah iv 3.   [10] Pp. 567–8.
[11] *E.g.* Psalms of Solomon xvii 19, Assumption of Moses ix 6, Ascension of Isaiah ii 8–12.
[12] P. 550 n. 6.   [13] Cp. Hengel *Zeloten* 255–61.   [14] 1 Enoch xxii 8.

text, he puts a question which is very difficult to understand. This is the form of the question also in all the Greek manuscripts except one, which has 'I asked about the judgements of all men: why is one different from another?', which makes good sense;[1] and it is supported by a *Discipline's* statement 'that under His (*sc.* God's) control are the judgements of all' (D iii 17), which seems to show that 'judgements of all (men)' must have been a recognized expression, though not found elsewhere. Here a Scroll explains an apocryphal passage; elsewhere, an apocryphal expression removes an obscurity in a Scroll. For example, the awkward and, as it stands, almost unintelligible expression in *Discipline* that 'he (*sc.* one who refuses to enter the covenant) is not strong for a return of his life' is now seen to mean that 'he is not able to make repentance unto life' (D iii 1);[2] for it clearly corresponds to God's declaration to Ezra regarding those who scorn His law that *non possunt reversionem bonam facere ut vivant*,[3] which too has been doubted but is now confirmed.[4] The New Testament's 'repentance unto life'[5] shows what is meant in both texts, which must surely belong to the same age.

So far, then, the trend of the argument has been not to show merely that the Scrolls are so closely connected with the inter-testamental period that they must belong to it but even that they must be brought down to its very end; for they cannot be dated before the latest works quoted in them, even if quotation is indirect, based not on the written word but on contemporary thought lying behind it.

Similarly the ancient versions, or the traditions behind them, are reflected in the Scrolls. So the classical 'spirit of holiness' (D iv 21 ix 3 and elsewhere) is once replaced by the un-Hebraic 'holy spirit' (D iii 7); this is yet another instance of the influence of the Egyptian tradition on the Scrolls, reflecting the Greek πνεῦμα ἅγιον which appears only in the Septuagint's translation of the latest book of the Old Testament (where the Aramaic text has 'excellent spirit')[6], occasionally in the inter-testamental literature[7] and regularly in the New Testament. So again the description of the novice's examination 'according to his understanding and his works' (D v 21 vi 18; cp. vi 14) is echoed in the Vulgate's *secundum meritum operum suorum et secundum intellectum peregrinationis ipsius*, which corresponds to nothing that Jesus ben Sirach seems to have written; it is found neither in the Hebrew text nor in the Greek or Syriac translations of it.[8] The former then is a Graecism which will not have come into common use in

---

[1] Charles *Book of Enoch* 48–9, 299.
[2] Cp. Wernberg-Møller *Discipline* 58, 69–70.　　[3] 4 Ezra [2 Esdras] vii 81.
[4] Bensly *ap.* Box *Ezra-Apocalypse* 145.　　[5] Acts xi 18.
[6] Dan. v. 12, vi. 3 [4].
[7] *E.g.* Psalms of Solomon xvii 42; cp. Wisd. of Sol. i 5.
[8] Ecclus. xvi 4 (s. Wernberg-Møller *Discipline* 99).

the Hebrew language before the 1st century B.C. or even the 1st century A.D.; the latter is a divergent reading not found in the Greek rendering of the author's grandson, made presumably after his coming to Egypt in 132 B.C., nor anywhere else before the 4th century A.D. Both points then are evidence, if only slight evidence, pointing away from the 2nd or 1st century B.C. and towards the 1st century A.D. as the period of the Scrolls.

Echoes of the Aramaic translations of the Bible called *Targûmîm*, too, can be detected here and there in the Scrolls. These versions obviously contain much early matter but cannot have come into existence before the time when Hebrew is giving way to Aramaic as the language generally understood by the Jews of Palestine, approximately the end of the pre-Christian or the beginning of the Christian epoch. For example, the Messianic application of the prophecy concerning the 'star out of Jacob' and the 'comet out of Israel',[1] which occurs on several occasions in the Scrolls[2] and has influenced the story of the birth of Jesus,[3] is first explicitly enunciated in the Palestinian Targum; and this, though probably based on pre-Christian matter, in its present form may be assigned to the 1st-2nd century A.D.[4] Another echo can be found in the translation of 'thou shalt love the Lord thy God with all thy strength,[5] which is interpreted in the Targum of Pseudo-Jonathan (*c.* 7th century A.D.) as meaning 'with all thy wealth'; for the Covenanters are told to bring 'all their knowledge and their strength and their property into the community of God' (D i 11–12).[6] Other small points may also be mentioned: for example, the Biblical *ma'ărākāh* 'line, rank' gives place in a military sense to the Targumic *s^edōr* 'rank' (W *passim*),[7] the elaboration of the priests' robes as worn in battle follows the Targumic model[8], and the names of the military commanders of the various units, which are only mentioned in the Old Testament, are worked on their banners in *War*[9] as they are engraved on their breastplates in the Targum's embellishment of the account in the Old Testament.[10] Another echo of a Targum is the quotation of God's promise that 'he that trusteth shall not tremble'[11] as 'its (*sc.* Zion's) foundations shall not tremble or be shaken (*yizda'z^{e'}û*) from their place' (D viii 7–8); and this is translated in the Targum as 'the righteous who trust in these things shall not be shaken (*yizda'z^{e'}ôn*) when distress cometh'. The choice of this verb in these two passages can hardly be unconnected; and even a straw will show in which direction the wind blows. It is, too, perhaps no accident that, although angels both good and bad are variously

[1] Num. xxiv. 17.   [2] Pp. 151, 478.   [3] Matt. ii. 1–12.
[4] Macho in VT, *Suppl.* VII 236.   [5] Deut. vi. 5.   [6] Black *Scrolls* 122–3.
[7] Yadin & Rabin *Scroll of the War* 143–4.   [8] *Ibid.* 219.
[9] P. 434 ('order' for 'array').
[10] Targum Pseudo-Jonathan on Num. ii. 3, 10, 18, 25.   [11] Isa. xxviii. 16.

described in Jewish literature, the actual appellation of the 'angels of destruction (*ḥabbāl*)' in three Scrolls (D iv 12 W xiii 12 Z ii 4), although the notion is ancient,[1] occurs otherwise only in one Targum[2] and in the Talmud.[3]

An interesting point of contact within this period is the names given to the two brothers who are said to have resisted Moses in the presence of Pharaoh.[4] Neither the Old Testament nor Josephus[5] names them, but they are called 'Johanah and his brother' in one of the Scrolls (Z vii 19); Pliny the elder[6] (*c.* A.D. 23–79) and Apuleius[7] (born *c.* A.D. 125) agree on the first name but give quite a different second name. They are called 'Jannes and Jambres' in the New Testament[8] and similarly in the Rabbinic literature of the following centuries.[9] This Scroll then would belong to the period when speculation was rife about these two names but the tradition had not been formulated or at any rate crystallized, *i.e.* approximately the end of the 1st or beginning of the 2nd century A.D.

The doctrine of the origin of man in the Scrolls is purely Rabbinic. Man is said in Scripture to come from dust or earth[10] or from 'water', *i.e.* seed;[11] the Scrolls go further and say that he is 'earth' (T x 3; cp. D xi 21–2)[12], and they also introduce a new notion when they describe him as issuing from a combination of both, as 'formed of clay and kneaded with water' (T i 21; cp. iii 23–4) or 'built of dust and kneaded with water' (T xiii 15). Here clay or dust is the source of primeval man, the first father,[13] and water is the father's seed[14]; and this combination of clay and 'water' as constituting man is not apparently found until it appears as a Moslem idea in the 7th century A.D.[15] Another Rabbinic notion is that of the future world to which man may hope to be raised as the 'height of the world (*rûm ʿôlām*)', as it may be literally translated (T iii 19–20); for this descriptive expression, which has not been found before the Scrolls, reappears again, so far as current dictionaries show, only in the Jewish morning service, where it occurs twice.[16] The date of the liturgy, however, is uncertain, so that

---

[1] P. 450.
[2] Targum Pseudo-Jonathan at Exod. iv 26.
[3] B. Talmud *Shabbath* 55a.
[4] Exod. vii. 8–13; s. Schürer *Geschichte*[3] III 292–4.
[5] In *Antiquities* II ix 2 § 1.
[6] In *Natural History* XXX i 2 § 11.
[7] In *Apology* § 90.
[8] 2 Tim. iii. 8.
[9] Targum Pseudo-Jonathan on Exod. i. 15, vii. 11 and Num. xxii. 22; B. Talmud *Menahoth* 85a.
[10] *E.g.* Gen. ii. 7 (dust from earth), iii. 19 (dust); Isa. xlv. 9 (earth, clay); Job x. 9. xxxiii. 6 (clay); Ecclus. xvii. 1 (earth); cp. Qur'ân xv 26 (mud, clay).
[11] Isa. xlviii. 1; cp. Mekilta viii (Exod. xv. 11) and Qur'ân xxi. 31 and also II Enoch xxx 8 (where man's flesh is made from earth and his blood from dew).
[12] Ecclus. xxxiii. 10; Josephus *Antiquities* I i 2 § 34.
[13] Wisd. of Sol. vii. 1.   [14] *E.g.* B. Talmud *Sanhedrin* 91a.
[15] *E.g.* Qur'ân xxxii 6–7 (clay and water); cp. xxii 5 xxiii 12–13 xxxv 12 (dust or mud and seed).
[16] Cp. Van der Ploeg in *VT* III 191–2.

the coincidence cannot be used to throw light on that of the Scrolls in which it occurs.

Another Rabbinic figure of speech occurs in the passage in which the author of the *Thanksgiving Hymns* describes how he was 'like a man who has entered a fortified city and sought refuge in a steep wall awaiting deliverance' and then goes on to praise God 'who sets the foundation on a stout rock (cp. T vii 8–9)[1] . . . in order to build a stout building that will not be shaken' and into which 'no stranger shall enter [and] whose [gates] are doors of a shield that cannot be be entered' (T vi 24–8); here the 'shield' is none other than the society of the Covenanters or perhaps, as Mr. Snaith suggests, the Law on which righteous Israel is built in Rabbinic tradition.[2]

A curious Rabbinic conceit is seen in the references to the community of the Covenanters under the figures of the 'sanctuary' and of 'Lebanon', which Dr. Vermès has recently explained,[3] although he has missed its full significance. The community of the Covenanters is described as 'an eternal plantation and a house of holiness (*i.e.* sanctuary) for Israel' (D viii 5) and its members as 'a house of holiness for Aaron' (D ix 5–6), and the Wicked Priest will be treated 'as he has treated the poor; for Lebanon is the council of the community and the beasts are the simple ones of Judah who fulfil the Law' (H xii 2–5). The 'simple ones of Judah' are the descendants of Judah and the members of his party who in simplicity of heart fulfil the Law in accordance with the party's interpretation of it; and the 'beasts' are the same people depicted as pasturing on 'Lebanon', here representing the hill of the Temple on which their aspirations are centred. At the same time, Lebanon represents the community of the Covenanters, just as it comes not long afterwards to be used by Christians[4]; for example, Origen (*c.* A.D. 185–254) applies[5] it to the church of his own times. Contrariwise, the author of a fragmentary *Commentary on Isaiah* uses 'Lebanon' as a figure for the nations,[6] *i.e.* the last enemies; for he seems to understand the prophet's words as referring to the eschatological war against the Kittians.[7]

This symbolical use of Lebanon is a figure of speech of Palestinian origin used for the nations arrayed against Israel, for the rich, for the Davidic king, for the Temple and for Jerusalem.[8] Passages in early literature by which such ideas may have been suggested are not hard to find;[9] but what is important is that the first application of the

[1] Pp. 365, 519.
[2] Cp. Midrash R. *Canticles* IV iv 9 (s. Jastrow *Dictionary* II 729).
[3] In *TICP*, IV (*Mélanges Bibliques*) 316–25 and *JTS*, NS IX 1–12.
[4] Cp. Sparks in *JTS*, NS X 264–79.
[5] Migne *PL.* XIII (*Hom. xi in Ezech.* xvii. 1–10) 751–2 [397–8].
[6] Allegro in *JBL* LXXV 177–80.   [7] Isa. x. 33–4; s. p. 205, 215–6.
[8] Cp. Hahn in *AOASH* XIV 131–5.
[9] *E.g.* Deut. iii. 25, 1 Kings vii. 2, Isa. lx. 13, Psa. xcii. 12–13; Ecclus. xxiv. 10–13.

symbolic use of the name is attributed by tradition to Johanan ben
Zakkai, a Tannaite teacher of the last half of the 1st century A.D.
Smuggled out of Jerusalem during the siege, according to an apocryphal
legend he told Vespasian that he would become a 'king' because the
prophecy that 'Lebanon shall fall by a mighty one'[1] meant that
Jerusalem would never be destroyed except by a king;[2] and he also
explained 'open thy doors, O Lebanon, that the fire may destroy thy
cedars'[3] as foretelling the destruction of Jerusalem by the Romans.[4]
So too Jerome says *per metaphoram Libani et Basan, regionum et montium
trans Jordanem, ad Jerusalem sermo dirigitur;*[5] and the same figure of
Lebanon for the Temple occurs often in the Targums and other
Rabbinic literature.[6] The authors of the Scrolls, however, nowhere
equate Lebanon directly with the Temple; but the equation of the
community now with the 'house of holiness', *i.e.* the Temple,[7] and now
with 'Lebanon' implies that of Lebanon with the Temple. The underlying idea may be, as the Talmud suggests,[8] that 'Lebanon' (being
derived from a root which denotes 'white') symbolizes Jerusalem as
'whitening', *i.e.* cleansing, Israel's sins; but it cannot be proved. That
its point lies in the fact that the Covenanters may have worn white
clothes, like the Samaritans and Mandaeans,[9] is a fancy which equally
cannot be proved; and the practice of the Essenes of always wearing
white garments[10] is not evidence for that of the Covenanters.

This figure of speech, although foreshadowed in the Scriptures, the
apocalyptic and pseudepigraphical literature, where Lebanon and the
comparable term are juxtaposed but not equated, is there only a
vague concept. It does not seem to have been expressly defined and
applied to any historical situation till the First Revolt; for, although
the Targums contain much ancient matter going far back into the
period of the Second Commonwealth, no individual statement can be
dated except by external evidence, of which there is here none. The
conclusion, therefore, can hardly be resisted that this symbolical use
of Lebanon was a figure deduced from Scripture at a time when men
were anxiously scanning the ancient oracles to see what the issue of
the struggle in which they were engaged might be; for many of the
passages from which it might be derived were concerned with the
threat or the promise of coming disaster or the promise of vengeance
and restoration.[11] If then Johanan indeed originated such an application of the figure to the situation of his own times, the Covenanters

[1] Isa. x. 34.   [2] Midrash R. *Lamentations* I v § 31.
[3] Zech. xi. 1.   [4] B. Talmud *Yoma* 39b.
[5] Migne *PL.* XXIV 922 D (*Commentarius in Jeremiam Prophetam* xxii 20).
[6] *E.g.* Targum Pseudo-Jonathan on Deut. 1. 7; Midrash R. *Genesis* xv § 1 and
xvi § 2; B. Talmud *Gittin* 56b.   [7] Cp. Isa. lxiv. 10 and 1 Chron. xxix. 3.
[8] Midrash R. *Leviticus* i § 2 and B. Talmud *Yoma* 39b.
[9] Gaster *Scriptures* 253.   [10] Josephus *War* II viii 3 § 123.
[11] *E.g.* Isa. x. 34, xxxvii. 24; Ezek. xxxi. 16; Hos. xiv. 7; Zech. x. 10, xi. 1.

might have learnt from him to adapt it to their own circumstances, which too would be those of the first Revolt (A.D. 66–70).

Passing mention has already been made of the so-called *Genesis Apocryphon*, dated by the script and the language at the end of the 1st century B.C. or the beginning of the 1st century A.D.;[1] this, whether it is classified as a Targum or a Midrash,[2] may be grouped with the apocryphal and pseudepigraphical writings, although nothing quite like it is known. Midrashic writers indeed often refer to such themes as Sarah's beauty,[3] but this new work goes beyond anything found in them in the way in which it elaborates the subjects with which it deals. It contains a descriptive paraphrase, highly embellished, of the stories of the patriarchs at the beginning of the Old Testament, written in a Palestinian Aramaic dialect; but unfortunately the text has been very badly preserved, and the editors have so far succeeded in making only a few columns available for study.

The parts of the text so far issued deal only with three or four of the patriarchal stories (Methuselah and Lamech, Abraham and Sarah at the court of the king of Egypt, Abraham's parting from Lot, and the campaign of the four against the five kings), treated in a highly imaginative style. For example, when Abram tries to pass off Sarai as his sister at the court of the king of Egypt, who is called by the hybrid name of 'Pharaoh-Zoan', *i.e.* Pharaoh (king) of Zoan, one of the princes at his court named Hyrcanus, for whom the model is evidently Hyrcanus son of Joseph the tax-collector at the court of Ptolemy V Epiphanes (203–180/181 B.C.),[4] speaking of Sarah says: '[how] beautiful is the look of her face . . . and how . . . fine is the hair of her head, how fair indeed are her eyes and how pleasing her nose and all the radiance of her face . . .; how beautiful is her breast and how lovely is all her whiteness! Her arms are goodly to see, and her hands how perfect . . .! How fair are her palms and how long and fine all the fingers of her hands! How beautiful are her legs and how unblemished her thighs! Yea, no maiden and no bride passing beneath the wedding canopy is fairer than she; and she is lovely beyond all women, and her beauty excels that of them all, and with her beauty is much wisdom in her. Even the tips of her hands are comely' (GA xx 2–8). All this is quite unhistorical and has little interest beyond affording a glimpse of a type of literature hitherto unknown.

This elaboration of the story of Sarai, however, contains one very interesting detail, which cannot go unnoticed. When the Egyptian king took her, Abram prayed to God to punish him, and He afflicted

---

[1] Kutscher *ap.* Avigad & Yadin *Genesis Apocryphon* 38; s. Kutscher in *Scr. Hieros.* IV 1–35 and de Langhe in *RTHP* IV xxiv (*Scrinium Lovaniense*) 128–9.
[2] Cp. Sparks in *Hibbert Journal* LX 343–3.
[3] Cp. Ginzberg *Legends of the Jews* I 221–2, 258 (s. V 84, 220 and VI 273).
[4] Josephus *Antiquities* XII iv 7 § 196–9 § 222.

the king and his household with plagues for two years. When none of the physicians could heal him, the king sent and begged him, as Abram recounted, to come and 'to lay my hands upon him that he might live'. Lot however sent back word that the king could be healed only if he returned Sarai to Abram; and, when he did so, Abram related how 'I laid my hand upon his head, and the evil spirit was driven by rebukes (*'itgᵉᶜaraṯ*)[1] from him . . . and he lived' (GA xx 21–2, 29). The important point is that no other instance of healing by the imposition of hands[2] and rebuking evil spirits[3] is reported outside the New Testament, where both practices are of fairly common occurrence.[4] That Jesus and His followers took them over from the Covenanters, who made so much of keeping their customs and doctrines to themselves, is in the highest degree improbable; the possibility must therefore be borne in mind that its appearance in a solitary passage in the Scrolls may be an echo of a Christian practice which must have become well known during the 1st century A.D. Also, the Covenanters certainly did not make much success of these practices; for, if they had, some record of it would surely have survived. Contrariwise, Jesus used them with conspicuous success; He would however be unlikely to have adopted them from unsuccessful practitioners, so that the Covenanters would seem to have been attempting to imitate His methods of healing, having learnt them either by seeing them in operation or by having heard of them by repute.

Naturally this work, although belonging to a new type of Jewish literature, shows contacts with known types. On the one hand it has affinities with the book of *Jubilees*, which is otherwise called the *Little Genesis*, in which the Covenanters had considerable interest, on the other hand it offers glimpses of Rabbinic lore: for example, the chronology of Abraham's journey from Haran to Canaan agrees with that of *Jubilees*,[5] and the patriarch crosses a river called 'Kermôn', clearly the Rabbinic Qirmēyôn, of which the exact position is not given in the Talmud,[6] between Canaan and Egypt (GA xix 11). Such facts as these suggest a date not far from the end of the Second Commonwealth; and, while the general circumstances of the discovery of this text seem to require a date in this period, the evidence of the language has been thought to indicate a date about the same time, *sc.* the 1st century B.C. or the 1st century A.D.[7]

---

[1] Cp. Zech. iii. 1 (where the corresponding Hebrew verb is used).
[2] Cp. Matt. ix. 18, xix. 13; Mk. v. 23, vi. 5, vii. 32, viii. 23–5; Lk. iv. 40, xiii. 13 (Jesus); Mk. xvi. 18; Acts ix. 12, 17, xxviii. 8. (followers).
[3] Cp. Mk. i. 25, ix. 25; Lk. iv. 39, 41 (Jesus) and Jude 9 (the Lord).
[4] Cp. Flusser *ap.* Schubert *Community* 140 and Dupont-Sommer in VT, *Suppl.* VII 247–52.
[5] Avigad & Yadin *Genesis Apocryphon* 24–5; s. Van der Ploeg in *Rech. Bibl.* IV 105.
[6] Mishnah *Parah* viii 10; cp. B. Talmud *Baba Bathra* 74b.
[7] Cp. Kutscher in *Scr. Hieros.* IV 1-35, Kahle in *ZNtW* XLIX 100–16 and Altheim & Stiehl *Aramäische Sprache* 214–22.

In conclusion, however much the Scrolls may owe to the apocryphal writings, they owe almost as much to Rabbinic literature in the strict sense, whether this is borrowed directly in the form of verbal quotation or is but an echo of a common background. The dates, indeed, of most Rabbinic works are quite uncertain; but what can be traced to them is such as to confirm the general impression that the Scrolls belong not to the earlier but to the later years of the inter-testamental period. This impression will perhaps be strengthened when the Messianic doctrine latent in them and their contacts with the New Testament come to be closely examined.[1]

3. MESSIAH OR MESSIAHS

One of the most important doctrines which the Covenanters shared with Jews on the one side and with Christians on the other is that of the Messiah, which must now be examined in some detail, especially for the light which it may throw on the date of the Scrolls.

I. The Hebrew term denoting the Messiah meant literally 'anointed' and as such was applicable to both king and priest, especially the high-priest; for both were anointed, as also one prophet (Elisha) was.[2] The Jews, convinced that they were God's chosen people, looked back in times of national distress to the promises conveyed by the prophets that, after the chastisement of the righteous and the punishment of the wicked, God would restore the national life to a state of unsurpassed prosperity; and they cherished such hopes even when the expectation of a unique person who was to come was still unformulated. The prophets, recalling the days of David and Solomon, saw this hope, based on God's covenant with His people, as a pledge of the restoration of the house of David in renewed glory or of a succession of kings sprung from it, or they even focused it on a single descendant of the royal line. This Davidic figure was called the 'Messiah' in the Hebrew Old Testament and the 'Christ' in a pseudepigraphic work transmitted in the Greek language.[3]

This Messianic figure was elaborately developed in post-Biblical literature, all of it written while the Jews were under a foreign yoke, now that of the Seleucid kings and now that of Rome, from both of which in turn they looked for deliverance.

The author of *Jubilees*, a supporter of the Maccabaean dynasty, still clung to the hope of a Messiah from the tribe of Judah, albeit only once referring to him and ascribing no function to him. He thought apparently that the Messianic era had begun, that it would be achieved by a progressive spiritual development of man and a corresponding transformation of nature, that the members of the kingdom

---

[1] Pp. 484–6.   [2] I Ki. xix. 16.   [3] Psalms of Solomon xvii 23–6.

would enjoy a thousand years of peace and bliss, during which the evil powers would be held in check, and that the final judgement would take place at its termination, when the righteous would enter into everlasting joy.[1] The picture in *I Enoch* is confused, inasmuch as it is a composite work. In the first part (*c.* 200–170 B.C.) a final judgement precedes the establishment of the Messianic kingdom on earth, and both body and soul rise to enjoy a state of temporary bliss; in the second part, the so-called 'Parables' (*c.* 95–79 B.C.), the final judgement precedes the kingdom which embraces heaven and earth, and the resurrection is to a spiritual kingdom; in the fourth part (*c.* 165–164 B.C.) the judgement again precedes the kingdom, which is eternal, and both righteous and wicked rise to a Messianic kingdom on earth; in the fifth part (*c.* 104–95 B.C.) this kingdom is temporary and the judgement comes at its end, and only the spirits of the righteous rise after the final judgement to a state of eternal bliss in the new heaven.[2] The Messiah appears only in the second and fourth parts of the book. In the second he pre-exists, sits on the throne of God, possesses universal dominion, exercises all judgement and slays the wicked by the word of his mouth; in the fourth he is a human figure, although he appears in the form of a white bull, his throne is in Palestine and his kingdom is the new Jerusalem, where life is transfigured by his presence.

The Jewish *Sibylline Oracles* in one passage, which belongs very probably to the 2nd century B.C., contain hints of a king from the east who would establish universal peace and bring prosperity to the Jews sufficient to arouse the jealousy of the Gentiles; they would assemble against the Jews, seeking to destroy them and to desecrate the Temple, but would themselves be destroyed by God, whereupon all would hasten to the Temple and be converted.[3] In another they prophesy that 'a blessed one, holding a sceptre in his hand,' would win a great victory, punish the wicked and restore the righteous 'at the last time of the saints when God . . . brings these things to pass'.[4] The *Psalms of Solomon*, which may be assigned to the middle of the 1st century B.C., contain two pieces showing an expectation of a Davidic Messiah, who is described in terms drawn largely from the Old Testament. This Messiah will destroy all wicked rulers and deliver Jerusalem from Gentile hands, he will rule over Israel and admit no aliens into the land; he will hold the nations under his yoke, judging all men with the wisdom of his righteousness; Gentiles will come from every land to behold his glory and will bring the exiled Jews back to him as their gifts.[5] Whatever the particular application of these passages may have

---

[1] Charles *Book of Jubilees* lxxxvii–lxxxviii, 9–10, 150.
[2] Charles *Book of Enoch* li–lii, xic–cx, 66, 179–80.
[3] Geffchen *Oracula Sibyllina* iii 652–713, 767–784.   [4] *Ibid.* v 414–33.
[5] Psalms of Solomon xvii 23–38, xviii 6–10.

been, they only reflect a general Jewish expectation of a kingly lay Messiah, such as is already known from other sources.

That the Jews would become or expected to become masters of the whole world became a commonplace also of Roman historians in the 1st century A.D.,[1] when the Jewish theory was that this conquest of the world would be the work of an individual Jewish leader.[2] This conqueror and ruler is the Messiah, who is commonly described as the 'son of David' in the New Testament[3] as also in Rabbinic writings.[4] In these, too, he is not dissimilarly described; but especial emphasis is laid on his function of personally defeating the nations of the world and their rulers as the enemies of the Jewish race in the apocalypses of *Baruch* (dated *c.* A.D. 50–100) and of *Ezra* (dated soon after the reign of Domitian, A.D. 81–96). In the former God says that 'my Messiah will convict him (*sc.* the last leader of the enemy, when these have been destroyed) of all his impieties and will gather and set all the works of his hosts before him, and afterwards he will put him to death and protect the rest of My people';[5] and the latter speaks of 'the Messiah, whom the Most High has kept till the end of the days, who will spring from the race of David . . . , and will annihilate them (*sc.* the rulers of the earth) but will mercifully deliver the remnant of my people, those who have been preserved in my land, and will make them joyful till the day of the final judgement'.[6] Here, the Messianic age is not final; the Messiah, after leading God's people (as David and Judas Maccabaeus had done) to victory over their enemies (*i.e.* the Romans, who had destroyed the holy city of Jerusalem), would die, and his death would be followed by the last judgement and its issues.[7]

This doctrine of a single Messiah was only one side of the picture; for on the other side a doctrine of two Messiahs, a lay and a priestly Messiah, was evolved. This went back to the high-priest[8] Joshua and the Davidic Zerubbabel[9] who however, although they were described as 'two sons of oil'[10] (*i.e.* anointed persons, 'Messiahs' or 'Christs'), never became Messianic figures in Rabbinic literature;[11] and it was subsequently developed by the Targumists in their interpretation of Balaam's prophecy of the 'star out of Jacob' and the 'comet out of Israel'.[12]

[1] Tacitus *Histories* v 13 and Suetonius *Vespasian* 4.

[2] Josephus *Jewish War* VI v 4 § 312.

[3] Cp. Matt. xxii. 41–2 w. xxvi. 63–4 and Mk. xii. 35–7 w. xiv. 61–2.

[4] *E.g.* B. Talmud *Sanhedrin* 97–8 and Targum on Jer. xxx. 9 and Hos. iii. 5; cp. Targum on 1 Ki. v. 13.

[5] 2 Baruch xl. 1–2.   [6] Cp. Mowinckel & Anderson *He that Cometh* 314–15.

[7] 4 Ezra [2 Esdras] xii 32–4.   [8] Cp. Hagg. i. 1.

[9] Grandson of Jehoiachin king of Judah and therefore descended from David (1 hron. iii. 1–19).

[10] Zech. iv. 14; cp. Midrash R. *Lamentations* I 16 § 51.

[11] Cp. Zeitlin in *JQR*, NS XLV 102–13.

[12] Onqelos and Pseudo-Jonathan on Num. xxiv. 17.

While *Jubilees* promises the descendants of Levi both ecclesiastical and civil power,[1] the *Testaments* suggest a high-priestly Messiah of the tribe of Levi beside a king (or royal and lay Messiah) from Judah. If these passages are correctly interpreted,[2] they indicate a belief now in two Messiahs, a priestly and a lay or Davidic Messiah, of whom the latter is to be subordinate to the former[3], and now in one combining both offices in his own person;[4] and these two would in due course appear and save Israel.[5] The division of civil and ecclesiastical power, which had lapsed for a brief while, when the lay Zerubbabel disappeared and the priestly Joshua alone was left,[6] continued until Hyrcanus I (135–105 B.C.), who was of a priestly though not of the high-priestly line, combined the two offices of high-priest and king. The position thus attained by the Hasmonaean priest-kings is commonly thought to constitute the background of the *Testaments*, even though the functions assigned to the Messiah from Levi exceed anything that the Hasmonaeans may have achieved; the author of the *Testaments*, however, is not writing history but idealizing a conception based on the achievements of the Hasmonaean family and thinking of a coming priestly Messiah who would overthrow the forces of evil. So intense however was the dislike of the royal title[7] that only Alexander Jannaeus (105–78 B.C.) and John Hyrcanus II (63–57 B.C. and 47–40 B.C.) and his successors put the title of 'king' on any (and only a few) of their coins; they mostly styled themselves 'high priest' and added 'and the community of the Jews' after their names and titles,[8] showing thereby that the civil power was held in popular opinion to be vested in the people but to be inferior to ecclesiastical authority.[9] After the Hasmonaean age this pretence of a dual authority lapsed for a considerable period of time. It reappeared, according to the literature hitherto available, only for a short time when the high-priest Eleazar stood beside Simon bar Cochba, the political Messianic leader, during the Second Revolt.[10]

This doctrine of the two Messiahs was greatly elaborated in Rabbinic literature.[11] The Rabbis, however, derived their doctrine not from the 'two sons of oil', but from the 'four smiths' whom the Lord had shown to the prophet;[12] and R. Simeon the Pious had already in the

[1] Jubilees xxx 18 xxi 13–17.
[2] Cp. Charles *Testaments of the Twelve Patriarchs* xcvii–xcviii § 27 and Ginzberg *Sekte* I 326–9, 353–5 (who accepts the passages from *Simeon* and *Naphtali* but rejects those from *Reuben* and *Levi* as Christian interpolations).
[3] Testaments *Reuben* vi 7–12, *Levi* viii 13–14, *Naphtali* viii 2–3, *Joseph* xix 11.
[4] Testaments *Simeon* vii 2.   [5] Testaments *Gad* viii 1.
[6] Zech. iii. 1–iv. 14.
[7] Josephus *Antiquities* XIV iii 2 § 41; cp. *War* II vi 1 § 80.
[8] Madden *Coins of the Jews* 71–103 and Reifenberg *Ancient Jewish Coins*[2] 39–42.
[9] Kuhn in *NTS* I 174–5.
[10] Reifenberg *op. cit.* 61/169 (s. Milik in *RB*, NS IX 169).
[11] Cp. Ginzberg *Sekte* I 299–63.   [12] Zech. i. 20 [ii. 3].

Tannaitic period (*c.* A.D. 10–220) declared that these were 'the Messiah of David and the Messiah of Joseph, Elijah and the Priest of Righteousness' or 'Rightful Priest'.[1] As too God had given Moses and Aaron the priest to His people to redeem them from Egypt, so He was held to have promised that they should never lack a king for guide and ruler and a priest to deliver them;[2] these would be the 'Messiah son of David' and 'Elijah the prophet of the house of Aaron'.[3] At the same time Phinehas, the priest whom Moses had sent with the host 'to the war' against Midian,[4] became the prototype of the 'priest anointed (*māšûaḥ*) for war' (cp. W ix 81),[5] as he indeed soon came to be called;[6] and this 'anointed for war' became a Messianic figure, being as such set beside 'the Messiah appointed to rule over Israel, the Messiah of Israel'.[7] Here was a Messianic title ready to hand; and Elijah, who was presumably thought to have been anointed to the prophetic office as he had anointed Elisha to it[8] and whom R. Simeon had already named beside the two Messiahs and the Rightful Priest, succeeded in Rabbinic imagination to the title and function of Phinehas, becoming the 'great priest' and as such being mentioned beside 'the anointed (*mᵉšîḥâ*)[9] king'; and finally the two redeemers corresponding to Moses and Aaron came to be identified as the 'Messiah of David', who would come as a teacher,[10] and 'Elijah the prophet of the house of Aaron', who would in the fulness of time save Israel.[11] Thus Elijah became in effect the priestly Messiah beside the lay Davidic Messiah. Alternatively, the two Messiahs were called respectively the 'Messiah (son) of David' or 'of Judah' and the 'Messiah (son) of Joseph' or 'of Ephraim' (*sc.* Joseph's son). The former would be king, enjoy all the glories foretold in the Old Testament for the Messiah and live for ever; the latter would suffer all the afflictions foretold for him and, having successfully waged the final Messianic war, would die.[12]

The development of the doctrine of the two Messiahs, as the present outline shows, is confused and inconsistent, but it has been briefly summarized for the light which it may throw on the speculations of the Covenanters, who come midway between the apocalyptists and the Rabbis as their views are represented in literature compiled for the most part long afterwards. Further, R. Simeon's identification of the

---

[1] B. Talmud *Sukkah* 52b; cp. Midrash R. *Song of Songs* II § 4.
[2] Buber *Midrash Tanhuma* I 188.
[3] Midrash *Tehillin* xliii 2 in reference to Psa. cv. 26.
[4] Num. xxxi. 6.   [5] Mishnah *Sotah* viii 1.
[6] Tosefta *Sotah* vii 17.   [7] Friedmann *Pesikta Rabbati* viii 13c.
[8] 1 Ki. xix. 16.
[9] Targum Pseudo-Jonathan on Deut. xxx. 4.
[10] Midrash R. *Genesis* xcviii § 9.   [11] Friedmann *op. cit.* iv 13a.
[12] Buxtorf & Fischer *Lexicon Chaldaicum Talmudicum et Rabbinicum* 644 and Moore *Judaism* II 370; cp. B. Talmud *Sukkah* 52a, Friedmann *op. cit.* viii 13c, and Targum Pseudo-Jonathan on Exod. xl. 11.

'four smiths' and its subsequent elaboration show how easily such figures may coalesce. Incidentally, that Elijah is eventually identified with the priestly Messiah helps to explain why this Messiah has precedence over the lay Messiah; the reason is not so much the dignity ascribed to the priesthood as that Elijah, though inferior in rank to the true Messiah, is his predecessor in time.[1] Lastly, it explains also why Elijah as well as Moses is said to be present at the Transfiguration of Jesus; both are in some sense Messianic figures.[2]

In the same way the Samaritans, who knew no Messiah son of Joseph, recognized two Messiahs: the Messiah proper (*tā'eb*), who as Moses or Joshua *redivivus*[3] would appear for the liberation of his people and the restoration of the Temple, and the high-priest who would renew the sacrificial service. The *tā'eb*'s functions were performed only once and he would then die, while those of the high-priest would continue; further, the *tā'eb*, though of priestly descent, might not be regarded as a real priest, and even as king he was inferior to the high-priest.[4] The date of the documents in which the Samaritan functions of the Messiah are expounded is uncertain, and they are probably in their present form relatively late; but the ideas enshrined in them almost certainly go back to the period of the Second Commonwealth.

Accordingly the conception of a dual authority, of a civil and a priestly ruler, and that of two Messiahs were familiar enough to the Jews of the period of Roman domination; and two Messiahs recurred long afterwards in Qara'ite doctrine, in which they came to be identified under the common title of the 'Messiah of Righteousness' or 'Rightful Messiah'.[5]

The great deliverance of the Jewish nation from foreign oppression was connected with the appearance of a descendant of David; he might bring it about himself as God's agent or he might appear after its completion. In the apocalypses the role of the Messiah was shifted from the historical to the supernatural plane; but, except in some extravagant flights of apocalyptic fancy, the Messiah remained essentially a man of human kind, however miraculous his coming might be.[6]

II. The Scrolls contain no elaborate imagery in their picture of the Messiah. Their authors have no definite doctrine of a resurrection or of a future life,[7] and the ideas expressed in them on the subject of the Messiah approximate closely, except perhaps on one point, to those of orthodox Pharisaism. Accordingly in them the expected Messiah was not a supernatural figure who would miraculously rise from the grave to judge mankind and possess an everlasting kingdom but a

---

[1] Ginzberg *op. cit.* 353–5.   [2] Matt. xvii. 3–4, Mk. ix 4–5, Lk. ix. 30–3.
[3] Merx *Messias oder Ta'eb* 43 (Joshua) and Gaster *Samaritans* 90–1 (Moses).
[4] Cp. Bammel in *VT* VII 381–4.
[5] Wieder in *JJS* VI 14–23 and Bammel in *VT* VII 384–5.
[6] Cp. Moore *Judaism* II 349.   [7] Pp. 74–6.

human deliverer who was confidently expected to appear within the lifetime of many still living and to reverse the disasters which they had experienced; this is expressed by saying that 'when he appears, he will then smite all the sons of Seth' (Z ix 9–10), *i.e.* all mankind, as a Targum interprets this expression.[1] This is almost the sole function which is certainly ascribed to the Messiah in the Scrolls. Their Messiah therefore is the Messiah of the 1st century A.D. coming to make their nation the rulers of the world.

This conclusion is confirmed by a Messianic fragment from Cave IV in which the writer, taking his cue from God's promise conveyed by Nathan to David,[2] says: 'He (*sc.* God) has told thee that He will build for thee a house and [has promised, saying]: I will set up thy seed after thee and I will establish his royal throne … (?). I will be to him a father, and he shall be to me a son; this is the shoot of David who will appear with the Interpreter of the Law, who . . . (?) in the last days in Zion' (AFl. b 1–3). Here the writer infers that the lay Messiah is the 'son of God'. This same notion is found again in one of the contemporary apocalypses, dated not so long after the destruction of Jerusalem in A.D. 70, which implies that the 'son of God' and the 'son of David' are one and the same person; for here God is made to say: 'For my son the Messiah shall be revealed together with those who are with him and shall gladden those who survive for four hundred years; and it shall be after these years that my son the Messiah and all in whom there is human breath shall die.'[3] These two passages can hardly be dissociated in time; if then one belongs to the closing half of the 1st century A.D., the other is likely to belong also to this period, when the same idea appears in the New Testament.[4]

The question whether one or two Messiahs are contemplated in the Scrolls is to a large extent a matter of grammar. First, no one can doubt that 'Messiahs of Aaron and Israel' (D ix 11) designates two Messiahs; but 'Messiah of Aaron and Israel' (Z ix 10, xv 4) equally clearly designates only one Messiah; the former can be made to refer to one Messiah only by mistranslating or altering the text,[5] while the latter can be taken as meaning 'a Messiah of Aaron and (another Messiah) of Israel' (*i.e.* two distinct Messiahs)[6] only by violating normal Hebrew usage[7] (although constructions approaching this interpreta-

---

[1] Targum Onqelos at Num. xxiv. 17.
[2] 2 Sam. vii. 11–14; cp. Schubert *Community* 119–20.
[3] 4 Ezra [2 Esdras] vii 28–9.
[4] Matt. xxvi. 3, Lk. iv. 41, Jn. xx. 31 (Acts viii. 37).
[5] Cp. Del Medico *Deux Manuscrits* [1951] 33 (where the plural form is tacitly treated as singular) w. *Énigme* [1957] 311 (where it is accepted).
[6] Van der Woude in *Rech. Bibl.* IV 122–5.
[7] Cp. Le Sor in *VT* VI 425–9.

tion occur in late or debased style).[1] If these translations are correct, the only possible conclusion is that the earlier *Discipline* contemplates two Messiahs, the later *Zadokite Documents* one Messiah. Second, the point has been made that 'Aaron and Israel' are not intended as separate entities connoting respectively the priestly and lay elements in the community and that consequently one of the two Messiahs will be a priestly and the other a lay Messiah,[2] but that it is rather a composite designation of the whole community as consisting of priests and laymen.[3] The latter view is thought to be supported by the description of the community as 'a house of holiness for Israel . . . and a house of unity for Aaron' (D ix 6);[4] but this may equally well be taken to describe the community as consisting of Aaron (*i.e.* priests) and Israel (*i.e.* laymen),[5] as indeed it must obviously have done. This explanation of the expression is not supported by another passage which speaks of a 'Messiah from Aaron and from Israel' (Z ix 29; cp. i 5–8), even if it does not indicate a Messiah from each, one of priestly and the other of lay descent, since 'Aaron-and-Israel' as a single entity can hardly be intended here if the phrase is strictly interpreted; for the repetition of the preposition, while it allows one Messiah, forbids the merging of Aaron and Israel into a single concept. Here then there is one Messiah; and, where two Messiahs are admitted (as the grammar of one passage in any case requires), the history of the doctrine shows that one must be a priest and the other a layman.

In *Discipline*, then, two Messiahs must be accepted. This lays down what the 'sons of Aaron' *i.e.* the priestly members of the community, shall do and how 'they shall be ruled by the first laws by which the men of the Community began to be disciplined till the coming of a prophet and the Messiahs of Aaron and Israel' (D ix 10–11). Two Messiahs perhaps appear also at the so-called 'Messianic banquet'[6] (if the text of the fragment of a Scroll describing it is rightly restored) on the assumption that the priest present at it is the high-priest and priestly Messiah.[7] At this meal the priest (apparently high-priest) takes his place at the head of the whole congregation, including the chiefs of the Aaronic priesthood; after these the Messiah of Israel takes his place at the head of the chiefs of the clans, of the whole congregation and of the leading men. Here the lay Messiah takes precedence, as commander-in-chief, over the chiefs of the clans who are the leaders of the nation (I Q *28* A ii 11–17); and so the name of Israel precedes

---

[1] *E.g.* 2 Ki. xii. 14 = 2 Chron. xxiv. 14 (s. Kropat *Syntax des Autors der Chronik* 55); cp. Psa. lxxii. 10, Esth. x. 2, Dan. viii. 20, and Cowley *Aramaic Papyri* v 9 (*bcl dgl wqryh*) = xiii 10 ([*bc*]*l dgl wbcl qryh*).

[2] Ginzberg *Sekte* I 351–3.
[3] Lagrange in *RB*, NS XI 135.
[4] Rowley *Fragments* 40–4.
[5] Wernberg-Møller *op. cit.* 133–4.
[6] Pp. 507–14.
[7] Kuhn in Stendhal *Scrolls* 55–6.

HH

those of Aaron and Levi on the shield or baton[1] of 'the prince of the whole community' (W v 1–2), as Israel precedes Aaron with 'the great standard at the head of the whole people' (W iii 13–14).[2] Contrariwise, the title of the high-priest always precedes that of the bearers of civil power, *e.g.* on Hasmonaean coins.[3] Further, at this meal no one may touch bread and wine[4] until the priest has blessed them and the Messiah of Israel has blessed the whole company of those present (I Q *28* A ii 12–21); thus the priest (*i.e.* the priestly Messiah) takes precedence in ritual, the lay Messiah in secular matters. The text describing this meal is fragmentary and belongs with (if not to) *Discipline*, so that the same circle of ideas may be expected in both documents; this connection is confirmed if the priestly Messiah is rightly recognized in this fragment beside the Messiah of Israel.

Contrariwise, the *Zadokite Documents* seem to recognize only one Messiah. These indeed in one passage speak of 'anointed ones' or 'Messiahs' in the plural number, when they say that the Israelites in old times rebelled against God's commandments given 'through Moses and His holy anointed ones' or 'Messiahs' (Z viii 2); but the reference here is to the prophets, as other passages show (D i 3 W xi 7–8; cp. Z ii 10).[5] Elsewhere they speak only of one Messiah in the singular number. They say that those who give heed to God's commandments will escape in the time of visitation but that 'those who are left shall be delivered to the sword when a Messiah from Aaron and from Israel comes' (Z ix 10) and that 'those who, having entered the new covenant (*sc.* in Damascus), have shown themselves traitors shall not be counted in the assembly of the people from the day when the Unique Teacher is gathered (*sc.* to his fathers) until a Messiah shall arise from Aaron and Israel' (Z ix 28–9); and they add that such and such are the rules of the camps 'during the period of wickedness, until the Messiah of Aaron and Israel shall arise' (Z xv 4).

The co-existence of these two conceptions, the first of two Messiahs, the one priestly and the other lay, and the second of one Messiah who is both priestly and lay Messiah, has caused some perplexity, although the general history of the doctrine shows it to be feasible; and an attempt must now be made to see if such an assumption is practically justified by the events of contemporary Jewish history as reflected in the Scrolls.

The view here maintained is that the Messiahs in the Scrolls are human figures, leaders of the Covenanters who are expected to

---

[1] Cp. Dupont-Sommer *Écrits* 193[1].
[2] Schubert *Community* 118–19.
[3] Kuhn in *NTS* I 177–8.
[4] Pp. 507–8.
[5] Rabin *Zadokite Documents*[2] 21; cp. Gen. xx. 7 (where the patriarch Abraham is called a 'prophet') and Psa. cv. 15 = 1 Chron. xvi. 22 (where 'my Messiahs' is a designation of the patriarchs, who are there mentioned beside the prophets).

appear 'at the end of the days' in order to lead party and nation to victory in the final Messianic war.

This argument, however, cannot be followed to its conclusion until one objection has been met; this is that the Rightful Teacher is not one of the two Messiahs. Ginzberg tries to prove[1] that the founder of the party, being called only 'a teacher of righteousness' (Z i 7 ix 53), is so described simply as 'the interpreter of the law'[2] and 'the teacher of the community' (Z ix 29), sc. of the Covenanters, so that 'teacher of righteousness' is nothing but a title of honour amongst these people as also it becomes long afterwards amongst the Qara'ites;[3] such a title as 'the Teacher of Righteousness' would be applicable only to Elijah as the priestly Messiah. The argument, however, will not hold water. First, the Messiah whose function is to teach the nation is not the priestly but the Davidic Messiah.[4] Second, a distinction between 'a teacher' and 'the teacher' must be drawn, as the *Commentary on Habakkuk* (not known at the time to Ginzberg) shows. On the one hand the Teacher is called 'a Rightful Teacher' when his coming is described as still future (Z i 7) and when the party are warned to listen to him as one who is still expected rather than present (Z ix 53); and the same vagueness appears in the reference to 'the appearance of one who shall teach righteousness at the end of the days' (Z viii 10), inasmuch as his identity at the time of writing is unknown.[5] On the other hand, the actual historic leader of the party who is or has been fighting the Kittians, *i.e.* the Romans, is regularly called 'the Rightful Teacher' (H i 13 v 10 vii 4 viii 3 ix 9 xi 5). Both expressions, then, may and even do refer to the same person: the Teacher is called 'the Teacher' as an actual person in his human capacity but 'a Teacher' in his as yet unrealized function of Messiah.

The history of Joshua and Zerubbabel, whom the Covenanters must have had in mind when they called their Messiah the 'shoot (*ṣemaḥ*) of David',[6] would seem to indicate that the reference to the two Messiahs in *Discipline* must in the first instance be similarly based on two human figures known to the author from the history of the society or the nation; that they were expected to appear or reappear some time afterwards would then be a secondary development due to the contemporary historical situation. The suggestion might then be hazarded that the co-founders of the party, Judah and Sadduk or Saddok (Zadok),[7] revived or inspired this dream of two Messiahs. Judah's name would associate him with the historic Messiah, who would spring from the tribe of Judah;[8] and Judah, like his son

---

[1] In *Sekte* I 303–17.   [2] Pp. 477–8.   [3] Pp. 258, 473.
[4] Pp. 465–6.   [5] Cp. Black *Scrolls* 160.   [6] Pp. 357–8.
[7] Pp. 252–9.
[8] Targum Pseudo-Jonathan on Gen. xlix. 11 and Exod. xl. 9.

Menahem, as his conduct in A.D. 66 showed, had royal pretensions which would cast him for the part of the Davidic Messiah. Nothing is known of Sadduk's lineage; but his name on the one hand recalls the title of the 'Messiah of Righteousness' or 'Rightful Messiah' ($m^e\check{s}iah$ $\c{s}edeq$) given to the lay Messiah (AFl. a 3) and that of the 'Righteous' or Rightful ($\c{s}addiq$) Messiah' named in a fragmentary Scroll and in the Targum on the Prophets,[1] while on the other hand it would readily suggest that he had a priestly connection with Zadok the priest of David's court, which might fit him for the part of the Aaronite or priestly Messiah. Both Judah and Sadduk were dead by this time. Judah had been executed or, as his followers would think, martyred by the Romans in A.D. 6–7 and his colleague, who had been old enough to join in forming a new party before those years, would hardly be alive half a century afterwards; they might therefore be expected to reappear and deliver their people from foreign oppression in the middle years of the 1st century A.D.

In the course of time the picture changed. When forty years had already passed since Judah and Sadduk had disappeared from the scene and neither had reappeared to lead the nation to victory, Judah's two sons, Jacob and Simon, who had presumably succeeded to the leadership of the party, might then come in their turn to be regarded as the destined Messiahs; for Sadduk had apparently left no son to succeed him. On their execution c. A.D. 46–8 the leadership of the party would have devolved on Menahem;[2] thus, as Zerubbabel had disappeared from the scene and Joshua alone had been left to represent both ecclesiastical and civil authority and as Hyrcanus I had combined the offices of priest and king, so Menahem would come alone to combine both forms of authority in his own person. The author of *Discipline*, however, which was the earliest of the non-Biblical Scrolls, writing between A.D. 46–8 and A.D. 66[3], still thought of 'a prophet and the Messiahs of Aaron and Israel' (D ix 11); the Messiahs would at that time still be Judah and Sadduk or perhaps Simon and Jacob, while Menahem might be regarded as a future leader destined to lead the party to victory although he had not yet taken the decisive step of putting himself forward to be the leader of the Revolt; for that would still be before their expected reappearance 'at the end of the days' (cp. Z viii 10). This would be the stage reached when *Discipline* was composed.

When the Revolt broke out in A.D. 66, Menahem, who was very probably of priestly descent[4] and was already leader of the party as the Teacher, claimed also the leadership by hereditary right and appeared

---

[1] Targum Jonathan on Jer. xxiii 5 and xxxiii 15.
[2] Pp. 241,267–9.   [3] Pp. 360–1.
[4] Pp. 275–7.

in the Temple to do worship 'clad in royal attire',[1] thus perhaps claiming the two offices of king and priest in conjunction on the Hasmonaean model. This bold stroke might have led his followers to combine the offices of the priestly and lay or Davidic Messiahs in him as a single Messiah, in one who had claims of some sort to the office on both scores. Menahem, who had thus claimed the leadership of the Revolt by virtue of his descent, could obviously be identified with the Davidic Messiah, while as σοφιστής or teacher of wisdom, in which capacity he was also 'the priest [the Rightful] Teacher' (APs. a ii 15), he could equally well be identified with the Aaronic Messiah. Thus the two offices would be combined in one and the same person. This suggestion does no violence to the traditions preserved in Jewish literature; for the Mishnah could still describe the high-priest as an 'anointed (māšîaḥ) priest',[2] while the Midrash and the Babylonian Talmud knew something of a Menahem who was thought to be the Davidic Messiah;[3] and the idea of a Messiah who was also a 'teacher (môreh)'[4] and the partial identification of the two Messiahs in respect of title, if not of function, inasmuch as both were styled 'Rightful Messiah',[5] reappeared long afterwards among the Qara'ites, who were connected with and possibly derived from the Covenanters.[6]

The murder of Menahem in A.D. 66 would make no difference to his position as presumptive Messiah; for the Messiah's death accorded with contemporary doctrine.[7] When he died, his reappearance would be presently expected or the office would devolve on a successor; so the Messianic age would again be delayed for forty years, i.e. another generation. Thus Menahem's attempt, albeit unsuccessful, to play the part of a Hasmonaean priest-king left its mark on the Covenanters' conception of the Messiah, who ceased to be two figures after the manner of Zerubbabel and Joshua and became a single figure on the Hasmonaean model, one consonant with the orthodox teaching of the Rabbis. In any case he might be only a hidden Messiah or a Messiah designate during much of this period.[8] How long after his death he continued to be regarded as the coming Messiah and how soon another figure would take his place must also be left an open question. Possibly, when he failed to reappear and to deliver his people from oppression at any moment when he might be expected, e.g. in A.D. 70 (when he might especially be expected to reveal himself; for according to one story the Messiah would be born on the day on which Jerusalem fell),[9] his

---

[1] Pp. 268–9.
[2] Mishnah *Sotah* vii 1 and *Horayoth* ii 1; cp. Lev. iv. 3, 5, 16.
[3] Pp. 356–8.
[4] Nemoy *Qara'itic Anthology* 34; cp. Hvidberg *Menigheden af den Nye Pagt* 262.
[5] Wieder in *JJS* VI 21.   [6] Pp. 9–15, 264–6.
[7] Cp. 4 Ezra [2 Esdras] vii. 29 (s. Oesterley *II Esdras* 71–2).
[8] Cp. Mowinckel & Anderson *op. cit.* 302–8.
[9] Midrash R. *Lamentations* I 16 § 51 and P. Talmud *Berakoth* 5a.

temporal successor in the leadership of the party, Eleazar ben Jair, would probably succeed also to his spiritual title and functions and take his place as the expected Messiah. The picture must remain vague; for the Covenanters may never have formulated such questions or the answers even to themselves. Each successive crisis would compel them to postpone the moment of his coming, whoever he was. Whatever the answer may be, however, the *Zadokite Documents* demonstrably belong to the period in which only one Messiah was expected, and they put his appearance or reappearance in the 'period of wickedness' (Z xv 4) *i.e.* the period of Roman rule after the destruction of Jerusalem (for the 'kingdom of wickedness' denotes the Roman empire after the destruction of Jerusalem),[1] within which the forty years from the 'gathering' of the Rightful Teacher would fall. The references in these documents are thus capable of a strictly historical interpretation in conformity with the orthodox view, which looked to one rather than to two Messiahs; was this one of the points on which the party split in Damascus?

Thus the expected Messiah is not necessarily or everywhere the Rightful Teacher murdered on the Day of Atonement but may be any Teacher preceding or succeeding him; for, as the designation of both Judah and Menahem, father and son, as 'teacher of wisdom $(\sigma o \varphi \iota \sigma \tau \dot{\eta} \varsigma)$' implies a succession or line of teachers, presumably of the same family, so that of 'Messiah' as used in the Scrolls may have been hereditary, being applied to a succession of such teachers. When one died or was killed, another member of the family would take his place; and as 'the end of the days' obviously did not come but was necessarily postponed to a future period, so the attributes of the Messiah were transferred from one Teacher, when he obviously had failed to fulfil the expectations of his followers, to a successor who might be expected to arise after forty years, *i.e.* in the course or at the end of another generation. This identification of the Messiah with a historical person, whether before or after death, though otherwise unknown before the 1st century A.D., would be in keeping with Rabbinic thought and practice at that time. Judah's father Hezekiah (for the king of Judah of that name cannot be meant, whatever the compiler of the Talmud may have thought), who had been executed *c.* 46–48 B.C.,[2] had already been recognized as Messiah by Hillel the elder,[3] who flourished at the end of the 1st century B.C.; and Simon bar Cochba, who was executed in A.D. 135, was similarly acknowledged by R. 'Aqîbâ.[4] That Judah and Sadduk and Judah's son Menahem and perhaps his nephew Eleazar ben Jair should have been regarded as

---

[1] Pp. 202–3.   [2] P. 357.
[3] B. Talmud *Sanhedrin* 94a; s. Roth *Background* 25.
[4] P. Talmud *Taanith* iv 5/6 (21a).

presumptive Messiahs by their followers would then be no cause for surprise. It is also consonant with the fact that the Covenanters do not seem to have thought of a resurrection from the dead, such as appears in Jewish literature of the 1st and 2nd centuries A.D.;[1] they expected rather an after-life in which the righteous would enjoy eternal bliss and the wicked suffer a multitude of plagues in eternal ruin.[2] Accordingly, the allusions to a period of waiting till the appearance of a Messiah from or the Messiah of Aaron and Israel (Z ix 29, xv 4) must not be taken as implying a resurrection; they imply only his appearance as a human saviour to deliver his people from the Roman yoke.

The ultimate identity of the Rightful Teacher and the Messiah, as here argued, may be supported by yet other arguments.

The Scrolls on the one hand in the first stage speak of 'the coming of a prophet and the Messiahs of Aaron and Israel' (D ix 10) and in the last stage now of 'the appearance of the Messiah of Aaron and Israel' (Z ix 10 xv 4) and now of 'the appearance of a Messiah from Aaron and from Israel' (Z ix 29); on the other hand the Rightful Teacher is described as a 'root of planting' sprung 'from Aaron and from Israel' and sent by God 'to possess His land and to enrich His soil with good things' (Z i 5–8). Thus both Teacher and Messiah are said to be derived from the same source.[3] Israel is then described as having walked in darkness 'during the whole period of wickedness'[4] and as not receiving instruction 'till the appearance of one who shall teach righteousness at the end of the days' (Z viii 9–10). Further, those who entered the 'new covenant' at Damascus[5] and afterwards defaulted would not be reckoned 'in the company of the people' nor entered in the register of them 'from the day when the Unique Teacher was gathered in (sc. to his forefathers in the grave) till the appearance of a Messiah from Aaron and from Israel' (Z ix 29), and this period is described as being 'from the day when the Unique Teacher was gathered in until all the men of war who defaulted with the Man of Falsehood come to an end, about forty years' (Z ix 39); then 'at the end of the forty years, when they are completed, no wicked will be found in the land' or 'on earth' (APs. a i 6–8). The connection of thought between 'the end of the days', after which 'one [who] shall teach righteousness' will appear and the forty years within which the Messiah will do so is obvious; for contemporary thought put the appearance of the apocalyptic Messiah 'at the end of the days'.[6] Consequently, the Teacher who is expected to come 'at the end of the times', i.e. after forty years, may

---

[1] E.g. Dan. xii. 2–3 and Psalms of Solomon iii 16 xv 6, 8, 15.
[2] Pp. 74–6. [3] Cp. Teicher in *JJS* II 134–5.
[4] Pp. 202–3. [5] Pp. 305–10.
[6] E.g. 4 Ezra [2 Esdras] xii. 32.

be identified with the Messiah who will appear within forty years, *i.e.* 'at the end of the days', in apocalyptic speculation. Teacher and Messiah are expected to appear or reappear at the same moment of time; they can therefore again hardly be dissociated.

The two last links connecting the Rightful Teacher with the Messiah have already been mentioned: they are the tradition of a Messiah named Menahem who observed a solar year, as the Covenanters under the Rightful Teacher did, and the *gîmāṭr^eyâ* of the name of Menahem and the Teacher's Messianic title of the 'shoot' (*ṣemaḥ*), which both have the same numerical value.[1]

This Messianic period of 40 years, the time expected to elapse before the Messiah's appearance (APs. b i 6), is important for two reasons in connection with the Scrolls.

First, the date of the rising of Hezekiah, the father of Judah the co-founder of the so-called 'fourth philosophy',[2] *c.* 47 B.C. was perhaps expected to inaugurate a new epoch, even though in fact it ended in disaster. Another 40 years coincide with Judah's first rising in 4 B.C., and yet another 40 years reckoned from his second rising in A.D. 6 coincide almost exactly with that of his sons Jacob and Simeon *c.* A.D. 46–8. So again, after a lapse of 7 years till the final suppression of the Revolt in A.D. 73, another period of 40 years culminates approximately in the next rising in the reign of Trajan (A.D. 115–17). No one knows with what high hopes each of these movements may have begun, how the *mystique* of numbers and Messianic dreams may have stimulated them, disastrous as all are known to have been in the issue; not impossibly their impetus may in each case have come from such calculations combined with the circumstances, now unknown, of the moment which may have seemed to be an augury of success. In any case, the history of the Covenanters was bound up with 40 years as a round number indicating the approximate period after which the coming of the Messiah might be expected, even though the actual date had to be continually postponed, as the expectation of the Lord's coming was postponed by each successive generation of Christians.[3]

Second, R. Eliezer ben Hyrcanus (*c.* A.D. 50–120) is credited by tradition with the official promulgation of 40 years, which R. 'Aqîbâ also recognized,[4] as the oldest statement of the time of the appearance of the Messiah,[5] having traditionally derived it from the number of the years spent by Israel in the wilderness;[6] but neither this event nor the fact that 40 years is approximately the length of a generation will have sufficed alone to determine the Messianic period, and the

---

[1] Pp. 356–8.
[2] Pp. 240–1.
[3] Cp. 2 Peter iii. 1–13.
[4] B. Talmud *Sanhedrin* 99a.
[5] Cp. Midrash *Tehillim* § 393 (xc 15).
[6] Deut. ii. 7, viii. 2; Josh. v. 6; Psa. xcv. 10.

actual impulse must have come from the observation of the events of the age in which he lived.[1] No document, therefore, which cites it *totidem verbis* (Z ix 39 Pb i 6–8) can be safely dated before his lifetime.

III. Two other figures mentioned in connection with the Messiah are the 'Interpreter of the Law' and the 'Prophet'; and their identity must now be examined.

The title of the 'Interpreter (*dôrēš*) of the Law'[2], though old as a term of general application,[3] seems to have acquired a technical sense in the Scrolls (cp. D viii 15 Z x 33), notably when it appears in two fragments on the promises to David. The author of the first of these texts says: 'A ruler shall [not] cease from the tribe of Judah.[4] When there shall be dominion for Israel, [there will not] be cut off one sitting (*sc.* on the throne) for David,[5] because the staff (*meḥôqēq*) is the covenant of kingship [and] the clans of Israel are the feet, until the Rightful Messiah (*mešîaḥ haṣṣedeq*), the shoot (*ṣemaḥ*) of David, shall come; for to him and to his seed the covenant of kingship over this people has been given for endless generations, (the covenant) for which the [Interpreter] of the Law has waited with the men of the community (*yaḥad*); for it is the assembly (*kenēset*) of the men of . . .' (AFl. a i 2–4); and somewhat similarly the second says: 'Moreover, the Lord hath told thee that He will build thee a house, and (has promised, saying): I will set up thy seed after thee, and I will establish his royal throne for ever. I [will be] his father, and he shall be my son.[6] He is the shoot (*ṣemaḥ*) of David, who will stand with the Interpreter of the Law who will arise in Zion (?) [at] the end of the days, as it is written: I will raise up the tabernacle of David that is fallen:[7] that is the tabernacle of David that is fallen, and afterwards he (!) will arise to save Israel'; and he goes on to speak of 'a midrash from Blessed is the man that hath not walked in the counsel of the wicked:[8] the interpretation of this saying is [those who] have turned aside from the way of the people', and 'these are the Sons of Zadok and the men of his counsel . . . at the end of [the days when they are gathered into] the community (*yaḥad*)' (AFl. c 10–17 = YFl. i 10–17). Here the Interpreter of the Law is expressly distinguished from the Davidic, *i.e.* lay, Messiah; he has waited with the men of the community for the covenant when this Messiah will appear and accompanies him when he shows himself 'at the end of the days' to the faithful members of the community.

This conclusion is confirmed by the *Zadokite Documents*, whose author,

---

[1] S. p. 60.
[3] Ecclus. xxxii. 15.
[5] Cp. Jer. xxxiii. 17.
[7] Am. ix. 11.

[2] Cp. Gertner in *BSOAS* XXV 9–10.
[4] Cp. Gen. xlix. 10.
[6] 1 Sam. vii. 11–14 (which is not exactly quoted).
[8] Psa. i. 1.

expounding the Song of the Well,[1] says that 'the staff is the Interpreter of the Law, as Isaiah says: Who bringeth forth an instrument for his work;[2] and the nobles of the people are they who have come to dig the Well (*i.e.* for the study of the Law; cp. Z viii 6) with the staffs which the Staff has instituted, that they may walk with them during the whole period of the Wicked One (*sc.* the Roman emperor for the time being),[3] without which they will not attain [perfection] till the appearance of one who shall teach righteousness at the end of the days' (Z viii 8–10). This last expression cannot refer to the Rightful Teacher of these documents, if he has already come (Z i 7) and is still there (Z ix 53); the person meant may then be not the actual Teacher but some future Teacher expected in the Messianic age (D ix 11). The same author goes on shortly afterwards similarly to explain Balaam's oracle of the star and the comet, which (like other Messianic concepts in the Scrolls) was current in the 1st century A.D. in an eschatological or Messianic application,[4] saying 'the Star is the Interpreter of the Law who shall come to Damascus, as it is written: A star shall come forth out of Jacob and a comet shall rise out of Israel.[5] The comet is the prince of all the congregation and, when he appears, he will smite all the sons of Seth'[6] (Z ix 8–10). Here the 'comet out of Israel' must be the Messiah of Israel, *i.e.* the lay Davidic Messiah; at the same time the Interpreter of the Law as the 'star out of Jacob' seems to be distinguished from him, although in the original poem the 'star' and the 'comet' designate the same person, *i.e.* David. This identification is required by the fact that Jacob and Israel are but different names of the same person and is permitted by the parallelism of the thought in the poem. The Zadokite author of the 'midrash', however, is free to accept or reject the identification of the 'star' and the 'comet' as his argument requires.

If however the Interpreter of the Law is not the lay Messiah, the question whether he may have been the priestly Messiah arises. On the one hand, the title of the 'star' is given to the 'new priest' as 'lighting up the light of knowledge' in the inter-testamental literature;[7] on the other hand, the Scrolls give not the slightest hint that he is a priest. This question, then, cannot hardly be answered on the available evidence.

The title of the Interpreter of the Laws has been thought to have had a Maccabaean origin,[8] like much else in the Scrolls,[9] because

[1] Num. xxi. 18.   [2] Isa. liv. 16.
[3] Pp. 202–3.   [4] Cp. Josephus *War* V v 3 § 289.
[5] Num. xxiv 17, where 'sceptre' is a mistranslation for 'comet' (Michaelis *ap.* Lowth & Gregory *Lectures on the Sacred Poetry of the Hebrews* 62; s. Ehrlich *Randglossen zum Alten Testament* II 205–6).
[6] Pp. 467–8.   [7] Testaments *Levi* xviii 2–4.
[8] Cp. Heinemann in *Leshonenu* XIV 184.   [9] Pp. 353–6.

Mattathias the father of the famous rebels is described as one of the 'most celebrated expounders of ancestral (*sc.* Jewish) laws'.[1] This may be so; but the title can at the same time be brought into close connection with Zadokite history in the light of contemporary evidence. The Hellenistic Jewish historian Artabanus, as Alexander Polyhistor writing in the 1st century B.C. relates[2], is said to have declared that Moses was called Hermes by the Egyptian priests 'for his interpretation of the sacred writings (διὰ τὴν τῶν ἱερῶν γραμμάτων ἑρμηνείαν)'; and Philo in the 1st century A.D. speaks of him as 'according to some a lawgiver (νομοθέτου) of the Jews but according to others an interpreter of sacred laws (ἑρμήνεως νόμων ἱερῶν)'.[3] Accordingly Egyptian tradition, with which the Covenanters are shown elsewhere to have been acquainted,[4] suggests that the Interpreter may well have been Moses; and this identification is supported, as Dr. Wieder has shown,[5] by Rabbinic reasoning. Already in the Old Testament Moses is said 'to declare' or 'to expound this law (*tôrāh*)',[6] while long afterwards in the *Zadokite Documents* the Interpreter of the Law is the 'staff' with which the 'penitents of Israel', *i.e.* the Covenanters who have gone into exile in defence of their principles as based on their own interpretation of the Mosaic law, dig the 'well' of the ancient song;[7] and 'the well is (a figure for) the Law' not only here (Z viii 3–9) but also in Rabbinic literature.[8] Moreover, as the Interpreter is the 'weapon' or 'instrument' or 'vessel' (for the Hebrew word has all these senses) of which Isaiah speaks in the passage quoted above[9] (Z viii 8), so Moses is bidden to be a 'vessel full of words' as the mediator of the divine revelation.[10] Further, when the Interpreter is equated with the 'star out of Jacob' of Balaam's prophecy (Z ix 8),[11] here again Moses may be meant, if 'star' may be taken not in the general sense of any star (as it must be taken in the prophecy) but in its special sense as the planet Hermes or Mercury.[12] Thus Hermes or Mercury god of wisdom, learning and literature, and the λόγος ἑρμηνευτικὸς of Gnosticism[13] and Moses as the supposed inventor of various arts and sciences are again brought together. The Interpreter of the Law is then a figure based on ancient history but regarded as a Moses *redivivus*, even though he is nowhere actually said to be Moses; but Moses was only a forerunner of the Messiah and not the Messiah.

[1] Josephus *Antiquities* XVII vi 2 § 149.
[2] Müller *Fragmenta Historicorum Graecorum* III 221.
[3] In *Life of Moses* I i 1.   [4] Pp. 226–37.
[5] In *JJS* IV 158–75.   [6] Deut. i. 5.
[7] Num. xxi. 18.   [8] *E.g.* Friedmann *Sifré debé Rab* 84 § 48.
[9] Isa. liv. 16.
[10] Lauterbach *Mekilta* II (*Amalek* 4) p. 182 ll. 45–47.
[11] Num. xxiv. 17.
[12] Cp. Levy *Neuhtlräisches und Chaldäisches Wörterbuch* II 304.
[13] Justin Martyr *Apology* i 21.

Apparently only one reference to a second Moses can be found in orthodox Rabbinic literature;[1] he perhaps was purposely dropped when Jesus came to be depicted as the 'second lawgiver' in the 2nd century A.D.[2] So a midrash, itself of unknown date, declares explicitly: 'Moses said to them (sc. Israel): You must not say that another Moses will arise and bring us another Law (tôrāh) from heaven. I therefore tell you: It is not in heaven; that is to say, no part of it has remained in heaven'.[3] This fact has some bearing on the date of the non-Biblical Scrolls; for any in which the Interpreter is mentioned must be dated before the time when as Moses redivivus he disappeared from the scene.[4]

The rule of the society of the Covenanters requiring them to have 'one studying' or 'interpreting the law (dôrēš battôrāh)' in every gathering of ten members engaged in prayer and study (D vi 6–7)[5] does not mean that 'the Interpreter of the Law (dôrēš hattôrāh)' was this very person; for the terms are different, the former being indefinite and the latter definite. That he was a distinct person, living with the Covenanters in exile at Damascus, as Dr. Wieder argues,[6] is also not implied in the description of him as one 'who had come' there; for the participle is equivocal, and the words may equally well be translated 'who is coming' as 'who will come (habbā')' there (Z ix 8). Somewhere there the last battle would be fought and the final Messianic victory would be won 'against the kings of the north' (W i 4–5). The only passage which seems to describe the Interpreter of the Law as having already come is expressed in terms of ancient history (Z viii 3–9) and proves nothing factual about him.

Another mysterious figure is the 'Prophet', who is mentioned twice in the documents so far recovered. First, the author of Discipline declares that the Covenanters will be ruled by the original laws laid down by the society 'till the appearance of a prophet and of the Messiahs of Aaron and Israel' (D ix 11). Second, the compiler of a fragment, which is classed as a testimonium, describes the Lord as saying to Moses: 'Thou hast heard the words which this people has addressed to thee. If only they could have a heart such as this, to fear me and to keep my commandments always, that they and their children might be happy for ever, I would raise up a prophet like thee from among their brethren for them; I would put my words in his mouth, and he would tell thee all that I should command him. If there is anyone who does not listen to my words which this prophet shall pronounce in my name, I shall require it of him' (AFl. d 1–8); and he goes on to quote the passages from Balaam's oracle[7] and the

---

[1] Midrash R. Deuteronomy III § 17.
[2] E.g. Justin Martyr Dialogue xiv 3, xviii 3.
[3] Midrash R. ibid. VIII § 6.
[4] Pp. 373–4.
[5] P. 60.
[6] In. JSS IV 158, 175.
[7] Num. xxiv. 15–17.

blessing on Levi[1] and to expound the curse uttered by Joshua on any one who shall rebuild Jericho.[2]

The doctrine of a returning prophet is nothing new; and its chief importance here is that it affords evidence that the idea also of a prophet coming as a forerunner of the Messiah must have been current amongst the Covenanters as amongst other Jews and in the early church.[3] A secondary question is his identity, whether he is supposed to be someone unknown or Moses or Elijah, who are all mentioned in various places as expected forerunners of the Messiah,[4] or another known prophet. He is neither Messiah, as he appears with them. He cannot be Jeremiah, who (although he appears in a similar context in one of the Gospels) is not mentioned as a forerunner of the Messiah in the Old Testament and has no such part in Rabbinic speculation. He can hardly be Elijah, as Dr. Schonfield has suggested;[5] for, although Elijah's reappearance as a forerunner is anticipated in the Old Testament and an Elijah *redivivus* is found in the New Testament and in Rabbinic literature, he is nowhere mentioned in the Scrolls, so that he seems to have had no place in the theology of the Covenanters. Is he then another Moses *redivivus*, especially as he is said to be 'like Moses'?

That the Prophet appears only in the earliest scroll (D ix 10), while the Interpreter of the Law is introduced only in the latest document in the collection (Z viii 8 ix 10), has been thought to show that the Prophet must have preceded the Interpreter but may subsequently have become one with him; this argument, however, ought perhaps to be discounted, as both are found also in fragments of Scrolls, even though the position of these in the chronology of the main Scrolls cannot be determined as they are undated. That the Interpreter might actually be living while the Prophet was expected to appear only at the coming of the Messiahs would also seem superficially to distinguish them; but this argument is undermined by the statement that the Interpreter will appear with the Messiah 'at the end of the days', when the Prophet too is expected. The Interpreter, then, if he was present with the society, was also expected (whatever might happen to him in the meanwhile, *e.g.* if he died) to reappear at the same time as the Prophet in the Messianic age; no objection to their identification, therefore, can be raised on this score. The suspicion that they are one and the same figure is strengthened, as Fr. Sutcliffe observes,[6] by the similarity of their functions. Already in the Old Testament the Lord

---

[1] Deut. xxxiii. 8–11.   [2] Josh. vi. 26 (s. pp. 294–5).
[3] Cp. Mowinckel & Anderson *op. cit.* 298–302.
[4] Deut. xvii. 15–19, 1 Macc. iv. 46, xiv. 41 and Philo *Special Laws* i 64–5; Jn. vii. 40 (unnamed prophet); Mal. iv. 5–6 (Elijah); Matt. xvii. 3 and Mk. ix. 4 (Moses, Elijah); Matt. xvi. 14 (Elijah, Jeremiah); Mk. viii. 28 and Lk. ix. 19 (Elijah); Midrash R.
[5] In *Secrets* 64, 129; cp. Milik & Strugnell *Discovery* 126 and Burrows *Scrolls* II 70.
[6] In *Monks* 87–8.

had promised Moses that He would send 'a prophet from the midst of thee, of thy brethren, like unto thee' to teach Israel what they should do, *i.e.* the law, when they had entered the Promised Land;[1] and again Judas Maccabaeus in 165 B.C., when he had cleansed the Temple, scrupled to rebuild the altar of the stones which had been defiled 'until a prophet should appear to give an answer concerning them'.[2] In both cases a prophet is concerned with the law; the Prophet could therefore properly be described as 'like Moses' and might have been regarded as in some sense a Moses *redivivus*, as the Interpreter in all probability was. That he too might be so regarded would not be impossible; for any combination, however fanciful, was possible in Rabbinic speculation (as, for example, the 'zealot' Phinehas came to be identified with the prophet Elijah, who in turn became one of the forerunners of the Messiah and eventually also the priestly Messiah!).

Thus both the Interpreter of the Law and the Prophet came very close to the Rightful Teacher, so close indeed that they might both easily have come to be identified with him. The Teacher was concerned with the Law; for the society at Damascus consisted of those 'who have clung to these ordinances, going and coming in accordance with the Law, and have listened to the voice of the Teacher . . . and who have let themselves be instructed in the first ordinances by which the men of the community were judged and have given ear to the voice of a Rightful Teacher and have not disputed the statutes of righteousness when hearing them' (Z ix 50–53). At the same time the Teacher was almost certainly 'the priest[3] whom God placed in the [congregation] (*sc.* the society of the Covenanters) to expound all the words of His servants the prophets, [by] means of whom God has recited all that will befall His people and [the nations]' (H ii 8–10), as he certainly was 'the Rightful Teacher to whom He made known all the mysteries of the words of His servants the prophets' (H vii 4–5) and the Teacher whom He raised up 'to make known to the last generations what He would do to the last generation, a congregation of traitors' (Z i 8). Briefly, the Teacher had two functions, a prophetic as expounding the ancient prophecies and a legal as interpreting the Law, both in the Zadokite interest. The two offices of the Interpreter of the Law and that of the Prophet seem then to reflect two aspects of the Rightful Teacher's functions, the one as teacher and the other as preacher. The Teacher, however, would not always be the same Teacher; for, as argued above, a series of teachers probably succeeded one another in the leadership of the community.

A corollary of the identification of these figures would seem to be that, if the Rightful Teacher was a Messianic character, they too were such. Two arguments, however, have been urged to prove that the

[1] Deut. xviii. 15.   [2] 1 Macc. iv. 46.   [3] P. 129.

Prophet, though an integral part of the Messianic age, cannot be either of the two Messiahs. The first is that no Messiah can have been both priest and prophet,[1] the second that the Prophet cannot be either of the two Messiahs with whom he is expected to appear,[2] in the same way as the Interpreter of the Law cannot be identified outright with the Davidic Messiah with whom he too is expected to reappear.[3] The first objection has little force, inasmuch as the fusion of the two functions of priest and prophet had already found its way into Messianic doctrine long before the time when the Scrolls were composed.[4] The second is within limits valid; the three figures in 'till the appearance of a prophet and the Messiahs of Aaron and Israel' (D ix 11) are explicitly distinguished. The distinction, however, had only a temporary validity; and the story of Phinehas and Elijah shows to what lengths confusion of persons can go in these speculations.[5] A third objection, that Moses and Elijah and the Christ (Messiah) are kept distinct in the interrogation of John the Baptist,[6] has no force; for the distinction lies in the form of the question rather than in the identity or otherwise of the persons named, and in any case the Gospels are not the Scrolls, whose content and doctrine are not necessarily the same. The fusion of the two offices may or may not have been *ab initio* implicit in Messianic doctrine; when it may have become explicit can hardly be exactly determined although, if the present argument is correct, it must have been current in some circles by the 1st century A.D., even if the story in the Gospel is held to contradict it.

Briefly, then, the figures of the Interpreter of the Law and the Prophet represented attempts based on ancient history to depict the Rightful Teacher's dual function of expounding Biblical prophecy and interpreting the ancestral law in a Zadokite sense; certainly the passages in which they occur do little to suggest that they were distinct or separate persons. The lines, too, of the picture were either never clearly drawn, if only because the Biblical allusions from which they were derived were themselves imprecise and uncertain in import, or had become blurred by subsequent embellishment at once uncontrolled and totally divorced from reality. Not improbably the Covenanters themselves had formed no clear picture of the two figures either in themselves or in relation to the Rightful Teacher, while it was complicated by the Messianic framework into which it was fitted; and this vagueness was in keeping with the habits of the Rabbis, who had little and often no regard for clarity, consistency or probability, in their speculations.

---

[1] Schubert *Community* 115–6; cp. Burrows *Scrolls* II 313–39.
[2] Yadin in *Scr. Hieros.* IV 53–4.   [3] Pp. 477–8.
[4] Testaments *Levi* viii 2–15; cp. xviii 2–12.
[5] P. 482; cp. Wieder in *JJS* IV 14–25.
[6] Jn. i. 21–2; s. Le Sor in *Studies and Essays in Honor of A. A. Neuman* 352–4.

Accordingly, the Interpreter of the Law and the Prophet seem originally and historically to have been distinct figures; but, in so far as they come to represent the Rightful Teacher, they tend to merge insensibly with him in the Messiah. Most important of all, they are characteristic of Jewish thought in the 1st century A.D., when Moses and Elijah and possibly also other figures from the Old Testament seem to have been expected as forerunners of the Messiah or as his companions at his appearance; as such they are found in the New Testament, e.g. at the interrogation of John the Baptist[1] and at the Transfiguration of Jesus.[2]

As then the Rightful Teacher was regarded as a prophet by his followers at the same time as he set himself up as a Messiah and was accepted as such, so Jesus was hailed by his disciples as a prophet[3] and as the Messiah,[4] while He himself also claimed to be both.[5] Yet, as the Scrolls do not identify the Teacher explicitly with the three figures of the prophet and the two Messiahs in any single passage, although their general trend implies such an identification, so no passage in the New Testament declares that these three 'saving figures' will find their fulfilment in Christ, although diverse passages speak of Him now as the expected prophet, now as the Messiah and now as a 'merciful and faithful high priest' having an 'unchangeable priesthood'[6], i.e. as the priestly Messiah. The idea of such a threefold function was evidently current in the 1st century A.D., since Josephus[7] said that John Hyrcanus I was worthy of three things, namely the rule of the nation and the office of high-priest and the gift of prophecy inasmuch as τὸ θεῖον was in him; but Eusebius was the first explicitly to ascribe[8] the three functions of prophet and of priestly and Davidic Messiah in so many words to one person, namely Christ.

The ultimate identification of prophet and teacher and Messiah seems, then, to have been a product of the religious ideology of the 1st century A.D., when it is found both in Jewish circles and in the church;[9] and the Scrolls, which reflect it, must belong to this period.

IV. One point remains to be noticed. The Messiah of the Scrolls has been brought into connection with Christ as a redeeming Messiah on the strength of a single passage, which says '. . . the Messiah of Aaron and Israel; and he will make atonement for our iniquity . . .' (Z xviii 8–9). This passage, if it could be so used, would be of the

[1] Jn. i. 21; cp. Mk. vi. 15 and Lk. vii. 8.
[2] Matt. xvii. 3–4, 10–12, Mk. ix. 4–5, Lk. ix. 30, 33.
[3] Matt. xxi. 11, 46; Mark xi. 32; Luke vii. 16, xxiv. 19; John iv. 4, vi 14, vii. 40, ix. 17.
[4] John i. 41.
[5] Matt. xi. 9, Mk. viii. 28, Lk. vii. 26, Jn. i. 21, vii. 40 (prophet); Mk. viii. 29, Jn. iv. 25–6 (Messiah).
[6] Heb. ii. 17, vii. 24.
[7] In *Antiquities* XIII x 7 §§ 299–300.
[8] In *Ecclesiastical History* I iii 2–20.
[9] Cp. Kuhn in *NTS* I 178–9.

highest value for understanding the Covenanters' doctrine of the Messiah and its relation to Christian doctrine; but unfortunately both beginning and end of the phrase are lost, only the last letter of 'Messiah' is certain, and the subject of the verb may not have been the Messiah. If it is the Messiah, as it may well be, the reference is not necessarily Christian but may even be Jewish, although a redemptive Messiah in the strict sense is unknown in Judaism.[1] The meaning may then be that, as 'God in His wonderful mysteries made atonement' or 'covered over their iniquity and forgave their transgression and built a sure house for them' (Z v 5; cp. ix 54), namely as He had forgiven the sins of His people and sent them the 'house of Judah' (sc. Judah the Galilaean and his successors) to teach them the true interpretation and practice of the law, so the Messiah when he came as His agent would make atonement for all the sins of the Covenanters and teach them anew to understand the Law and to carry out its precepts;[2] possibly then God, as He may be the implied, is also the actual, the missing subject of the verb.

However this may be, the conceptions of the Messiah in the Scrolls and in the New Testament, although they have come very close, can still be distinguished. On the one hand, the meaning of the term in both has been considerably narrowed down from that reflected in the normal usage of the Old Testament: in the Scrolls, except in so far as it may refer to the heroes of a past age, it is related exclusively to 'the end of the days', but it is scarcely a title as it is in the New Testament, where it has become a technical term limited almost always to the Davidic king of the last times.[3] On the other hand, while the Christian Messiah was regarded as both king and priest, i.e. as the Davidic Messiah of the tribe of Judah and the priestly Messiah of the tribe of Levi[4], and the Covenanters' Messiah was originally both Davidic or lay and priestly Messiah,[5] the 'eschatological realities' were held by Christians to have been fulfilled in Jesus,[6] the Messiah who had already come, whereas the Covenanters were still looking for the coming of their Messiah and therewith for the fulfilment of these or similar expectations.[7]

In conclusion, the picture of the Messiah or Messiahs in the Scrolls, so far as it can be drawn (for many texts giving other details must have been lost), seems to reveal contradictory features; but consistency

---

[1] Ginzberg *Sekte* I 357–9.　　[2] Rabin in *Scr. Jud.* II 100–1.
[3] Cp. Freedman in *JBL* LXXVIII 328–9.
[4] Hippolytus *Commentary on the Benedictions* (Diobouniotis & Beïs in *Texte und Untersuchungen* XXXVIII i 25–6 and 30–1) 136a–b § 12 and 141b–143a § 15; s. Mariès in *RSR* XXXIX 381–96.
[5] Pp. 472–5; cp. Milik & Barthélemy *Discoveries* I 122.
[6] Jn. iii. 15 (eternal life), iii. 18 (judgement), vii. 38 (outpouring of living water) xi. 25 (resurrection), xvii 13 (knowledge of God).
[7] Daniélou in *Strasbourg* 124.

is by no means characteristic of Rabbinic thought, so that even the orthodox doctrine of the Messiah is in some respects as unclear as that of the Covenanters. Further, the two Scrolls from which most of the details are gleaned are separated by many years of the most troubled centuries in all Jewish history; these years cannot have been conducive to a lucid development or exposition of theological speculation. The doctrine, however, so far as it is revealed in the Scrolls, is certainly not that of the 2nd or 1st century B.C. (so far as it is known) but bears all the marks of the form or forms current in the 1st century A.D.

4. ANTI-MESSIAH OR ANTI-CHRIST

Echoes of an anti-Messiah or anti-Christ have been detected in the Scrolls, notably in the account which the author of the *Hymns* gives of the births of two figures who, though not so called, seem to be the Messiah and the anti-Messiah.

In describing the sufferings and dangers from which he has been delivered, the poet says:

'Thou [didst save my] soul [from destruction when] men were counting me [a worthless wreck] and treating [my] soul (as that of a man) in a ship on the deep [seas] or as a fortified city before [its besiegers].

'I was in distress like a woman in child-birth, bearing her first-born child, when [her] intestines are turned over and a sharp pang at the breach of her womb (is a signal) for the painful birth of the first-born son of a pregnant woman. When sons come to the deadly breach of the womb, then she that is pregnant with a man-child feels anguish in her pangs; when she brings a man-child to the birth at the deadly breach of the womb, then with pain of hell a wonderful counsellor with his power bursts forth from the pregnant woman's hot womb, and a man-child is delivered from the breach of the womb by reason of her pregnancy. All the breaches of the womb suffer, and bitter pangs (come) at the time when they give birth, convulsions for those who are pregnant; and at the hour of his birth all (her) intestines are turned over in the hot womb of her that is pregnant; and she that is pregnant with a viper (is doomed) to bitter pangs, and the breakers of the pit (are stored up) for all acts of convulsion. And the walls' foundations are shattered like a ship on the surface of the sea, and the skies thunder with a thunderous sound, and those who dwell on earth are like those who go down to the seas, dismayed at the thunder of the waters; and all its wise men are like sailors on the deep seas, since all their wisdom is confounded by the thunder of the seas when the deep oceans boil over the sources of the waters; and the waves tossed on high and the watery breakers at the thunder of their noise are in turmoil; and in their turmoil Sheol and Abaddon are thrown open, [and all] the arrows of destruction (fly) in pursuit of them. They make their noise reverberate to the deep ocean, and the gates of Sheol are opened to all the works of corruption (*'ef'eh*); and the doors of the pit are closed over her that is pregnant with iniquity, and the everlasting bars over all the spirits of the viper (*'ef'eh*)' (T iii 6–18).

This bizarre medley of mixed figures is primarily a twofold *double entente*, a play on the homonymous Hebrew words for 'viper (*'ef'eh*)' and 'corruption (*'ef'eh*)'[1] and the almost homonymous Hebrew words for the 'breach' or 'mouth (of the womb)' (*mašbēr*) and a 'breaker' or 'wave' (*mišbār*). Secondarily, it is an elaboration of the well-known figures, used elsewhere, of the storm-tossed mariner (T vi 22–4 vii 4–5) and the woman seized by birth-pangs (T v 30–1); these are designed primarily to describe and emphasize the extreme and deadly perils from which the author has escaped and are secondarily worked up into an account of the births of the Messiah and the anti-Messiah, the former under the figure of the 'Wonderful Counsellor' and the latter under that of a viper, both derived from the Old Testament.[2] The New Testament similarly describes the coming of the end as the 'beginning of birth-pangs'[3] and the approaching day of the Lord as 'travail upon a woman with child',[4] and the 'serpent' is a figure for the devil;[5] and similar ideas appear in Rabbinic literature.[6]

The historical occasion to which the writer is referring cannot be certainly determined for lack of precision in the allusions, and its identification will in any case be bound up with the date of the Scrolls, especially of the particular Scroll which speaks of it. It is as likely to be the destruction of Jerusalem in A.D. 70 as the earthquake at Antioch in A.D. 115 which is said to have nearly caused the death of Trajan.[7] The events of A.D. 70 were a portent of the utmost moment to the whole Jewish nation, of which the Scrolls would seem to contain hints here and there, whereas the latter was of but passing significance to it, whatever it was to Jews living there at that time. Also, one of the Scrolls may conceivably show acquaintance with the Neronic myth which was widely current *c*. A.D. 70–100,[8] whereas certain allusions to events after that date are few.

Belial is in origin an abstract term denoting worthlessness or wickedness; and it has this sense everywhere in the Old Testament[9] as often also in the inter-testamental literature and in the Scrolls (*e.g.* D x 21

---

[1] Cp. Isa. lix. 5; s. Driver in *JTS*, NS XIII 374–5 (Arab. *'af'ā* 'viper' and *'afģā* 'became corrupt; was disobedient').
[2] Gen. iii. 1–19 (the tempter a serpent) and Isa. ix. 5 (the 'wonderful counsellor' a Messianic figure).
[3] Matt. xxiv. 7–8 and Mk. xiii. 8.   [4] 1 Thess. v. 2–3.
[5] Rev. xii 1–17.
[6] Cp. B. Talmud *Shabbath* 118a and *Sanhedrin* 98b.
[7] Del Medico *Énigme* 438–9.   [8] Pp. 489–91.
[9] So even at Nah. ii. 1 (which is hardly an exception).

T ii 16 22 iv 10, 13 vi 21). Already in the earlier apocalypses, however, it begins in the form of Beliar to be personalized: he dwells in darkness,[1] he is the accuser[2] (*i.e.* the Satan or the devil)[3] and the enemy of God who rules the light;[4] he is one of a number of evil spirits and even sends them to do his bidding;[5] he is also destined to be opposed by one who shall arise from the tribes of Judah and Levi (*i.e.* the Messiah) and is thus the anti-Messiah whom the Messiah will bind and deliver up to punishment.[6] In the later literature he becomes the chief of the evil spirits,[7] as he is in the Scrolls; for, though not so called in so many words, he there has an army of followers described as the Sons of Darkness (W i 13; cp. iv 1–2 xi 8 xv 3) who are the adversaries of the Sons of Light (W i 1), and as their leader he is matched against the Prince of Light(s) who commands the Spirits of Truth (W xiii 10–12 Z vii 19). As too Beliar rules the souls of men[8] and is 'the ruler of this world'[9] and 'the prince of this world',[10] so Belial exercises dominion over the children of Israel (D i 22–4) and indeed over all men so long as his dominion lasts (D ii 19; cp. iii 20–3); he is the cause of avarice and fornication[11] and of the profanation of the sanctuary (Z vi 9); any man over whom the spirits of Belial gain dominion falls into apostasy (Zx iv 5; cp. W xiii 10–11 Z vi 10, vii 19)[12] and those who forsake the covenant are punished with extinction at his hands (Z ix 12),[13] as the incestuous man is delivered to Satan 'for the destruction of the flesh'.[14] At the same time, as there had been a number of Satans[15] and as the name of Beliar belonged to many spirits,[16] so there might still be 'spirits of Belial' (Z xiv 5) and any number of Satans (T fr. xlv 3, which speaks of 'every Satan'); and, as Belial had been created 'to destroy' (W xiii 11), so Satan could be called a 'destroyer' (T fr. iv 6). Consequently, Belial or Beliar were eventually identified with Satan, and the two names could be used interchangeably in a late apocalypse;[17] hence Beliar came to be nothing but a synonym of Satan in the New Testament.[18]

Parallel to these two figures is that of the anti-Messiah or anti-Christ. He can be traced, though not under these names, from the Old Testament, where as a human figure 'he shall exalt himself and magnify

---

[1] Testaments *Joseph* xx 2.   [2] Jubilees i 20.
[3] Cp. 1 Enoch xl 7 and Rev. xii. 10.   [4] Testaments *Levi* xix 1.
[5] Testaments *Levi* iii 3, *Issachar* vii 7, *Dan* i 7, *Benjamin* ii 3, iii 8.
[6] Testaments *Levi* xviii 12, *Dan* v 10, *Judah* xxv 3; cp. Matt. xxv. 41.
[7] Ascension of Isaiah iv 14, 16.   [8] Testaments *Asher* i 8.
[9] Ascension of Isaiah ii 4; cp. i 3, iv 2.   [10] Jn. xii. 31, xiv. 30, xvi. 11.
[11] Testaments *Reuben* iv 7, 11 vi 2–3, *Simeon* v 3.
[12] Cp. Testaments *Issachar* vi 1–2.   [13] Cp. Testaments *Benjamin* iii 3–4.
[14] 1 Cor. v. 5.   [15] 1 Enoch xl 7.
[16] Testaments *Levi* iii 3.
[17] Ascension of Isaiah i 9 (Beliar in the Ethiopic and Satan in the Greek version); cp. ii 4 w. ii 7.
[18] 2 Cor. vi. 15.

himself above every god and shall speak marvellous things against the God of gods',[1] through the inter-testamental literature where he appears as the overweening 'dragon'[2] and the adversary of the Messiah who will eventually destroy him,[3] and thence into the New Testament, where he becomes the arch-deceiver (though one emerging from the bosom of the church) against whom Christians are warned, as the Covenanters are warned not to be led by Belial in rejecting the Covenant which has been offered to them (D i 17–18; cp. T vi 21–2 W xiii 10–11 Z vi 10 vii 19).[4] Finally, as the 'great dragon, the old serpent (ὄφις)' is identified with Satan at the end of the New Testament, where the birth of 'a man child who is to rule the nations with a rod of iron' is announced,[5] so the Scrolls speak not only of the 'spirits of Belial', as already said, but also of 'the spirits of the viper ('ef'eh)' in the passage describing the births of the Messiah and of the anti-Messiah.

When Nero committed suicide in A.D. 69, many people refused to believe that he was dead, and the notion became current that he would come back to destroy his enemies; and three impostors claiming to be the dead emperor appeared between A.D. 70 and A.D. 88. All these stories agreed on one point, that Nero had fled to the east and would come back thence to regain his empire; and one declared that he would make Jerusalem the seat of this new empire.[6] In the earlier stages of the myth he remained a more or less human figure 'raising a huge spear aloft' and coming 'with many myriads' of followers;[7] but he soon acquired superhuman attributes. He was the 'dragon' having 'the form of a beast'[8] and the 'terrible serpent (ὄφις)' who would be borne through the air by the fates;[9] he was identified as 'Beliar the great king, the king of this world' and 'he will descend from his firmament in the likeness of a man';[10] and as 'Beliar of the Augustan house he will come . . . and raise up the dead and perform many wonders for men'.[11] Finally, the New Testament declares that 'the beast that thou sawest was and is not and is about to come up out of the abyss and to go into perdition'.[12] Thus Nero *redivivus* has been assimilated to Beliar and the serpent, as described above; and the question whether any trace of this last myth can be detected in the Scrolls must now be asked and, if possible, answered.

Only one passage in the *Hymns* appears to require consideration,

---

[1] Dan. xi. 36 (where Antiochus IV is meant); cp. 2 Thess. ii. 3–4.
[2] Psalms of Solomon ii 29 (where Pompey is meant); cp. Apocalypse of Moses xvii 4.
[3] 2 Baruch xl. 1–2.
[4] 1 Jn. ii. 18, 22, iv. 3 and 2 Jn. 7; cp. Ascension of Isaiah iv 4–11.
[5] Rev. xii. 9.   [6] Suetonius *Nero* 40.
[7] Geffchen *Oracula Sibyllina* iv 137–8.   [8] *Ibid.* viii 88, 157.
[9] *Ibid.* v 29, 215–19.   [10] Ascension of Isaiah iv 2–3.
[11] Geffchen *op. cit.* iii 63–7; cp. ii 167–8.   [12] Rev. xvii. 8.

that in which the author, describing the last great struggle, says: 'Then God's sword will hasten at the time of judgement, and all His Sons of Truth will rouse themselves to [overthrow the hosts of] wickedness (*sc.* the Romans),[1] and the Sons of Guilt will live no more; and the Warrior (*sc.* God; cp. W xii 10)[2] will be stringing His bow and will raise the siege and [bring] infinite relief to [the besieged]; and [His purpose will be] to send forth weapons of war through the everlasting gates, and they will prevail (?) from end to [end of the world . . . , so that there will be no] escape for men with guilty impulses; and they (*sc.* the hosts of God) will trample them (*sc.* the sons of guilt) to destruction so that none will survive. [There shall be no] hope in a multitude [of warriors . . .] and no place to which armed warriors may flee; for the [victory] shall be to God Most High . . .; and they who sleep in the dust of earth[3] will have raised a standard and dead men's worms will have hoisted an ensign to [wage war against the Sons of Truth; but they will be] cut off . . . in battles provoked by presumptuous men, and one transporting a torrential flood shall come to no safe haven' (T vi 29–35). The author is depicting the perils from which he has been delivered. He connects these with the 'wars of wickedness' (T vi 29; cp. vii 7), *i.e.* the war with Rome; and the picture in which 'the Warrior . . . will raise the siege [and bring] infinite relief to [the besieged]' links this in turn with the siege of Jerusalem in A.D. 68–70, as Mr. Patterson privately suggests. This war however is now projected into the 'final time of judgement' or 'period of doom' (T vi 29); and this will see a titanic struggle in which the enemy leader appears *sub specie Neronis* but of which the issue will be very different. Only a Nero *redivivus* fits the two descriptions of this future event, that in the *Hymns* and that in the *Sibylline Oracles*: in the former a leader who is bringing back an army recruited from the grave and proclaiming its presence with proudly waving banners and who is thus 'transporting a torrential flood' across the world, and in the latter one who advances 'having raised a huge spear aloft' and 'having crossed the Euphrates with many myriads (of followers)'. This identification cannot be proved, but the coincidences are remarkable and call for explanation. Meanwhile the dates agree; for, while the *Hymns* were probably composed *c.* A.D. 73–81, as argued above on quite different grounds,[4] the Neronic myth came into circulation soon after A.D. 70 and reached its peak *c.* A.D. 100, dying out *c.* A.D. 200

The first two of these myths, those of Belial or Beliar and of the anti-Messiah or anti-Christ seem to have been merged in one another by *c.* A.D. 30–60 and both to have been independently fused with the

---

[1] Pp. 202–3.
[3] Cp. Dan. xii 2.
[4] Pp. 365–7.

[2] Cp. Isa. xlii. 10 and Zeph. iii. 17.

third, the Neronic myth, at some time during the last quarter of the 1st century A.D.[1] The development of ideas in these myths appears then to have proceeded *pari passu* in the inter-testamental literature and the New Testament and in the Scrolls. All three indeed reflect the same stage when Belial has become the chief of the evil spirits, is identified with Satan and depicted under the figure of a dragon or serpent and when he is entrusted with the punishment of sinners, and when Belial and the anti-Christ are similarly depicted as dragons or serpents and as the arch-deceivers. None of these ideas can be traced anywhere before the middle of the 1st century A.D., which must be the earliest moment to which any Scroll can be assigned; and, if echoes of the Neronic myth are rightly caught in the *Hymns*, they cannot be dated before Nero's suicide in A.D. 69 or even some years afterwards, when acquaintance with this myth had become widespread.

5. JOHN THE BAPTIST AND JESUS

Two important questions which have been raised and have received affirmative answers are whether John the Baptist and Jesus can be held to have had personal contact with the Covenanters or to have ever been at Qumrân. Can these answers be accepted?

John the Baptist and Judah the founder of the 'fourth philosophy' and *ex hypothesi* the re-founder of the Zadokite Covenanters overlapped one another and have been compared;[2] the latter must have been born before the execution of his father Hezekiah in 47 B.C. and was himself executed in A.D. 6, while John was born *c.* 7–6 B.C., shortly before the birth of Jesus, and was beheaded by order of Herod Archelaus at some time *c.* A.D. 28–30. Further, according to tradition John's birthplace was in Judah, either Hebron or the village now called 'Ain Kârim to the north-west of Bethlehem; neither is above 20 miles distant from Qumrân.

Nothing is known of John's early life and training beyond the statements[3] that 'he shall drink no wine nor strong drink and he shall be filled with the Holy Ghost even from his mother's womb' and that 'the hand of the Lord was with him' and 'the child grew and waxed strong in spirit and was in the deserts till the day of his showing unto Israel'. There he proclaimed himself to be the messenger 'which shall prepare the way before Thee' and as 'the voice of one crying in the wilderness', conveying the prophet's message 'Prepare ye the way of the Lord, make his paths straight':[4] and he 'did baptize in the wilderness and preach the baptism of repentance for the remission of

---

[1] Cp. Charles *Ascension of Isaiah* li–lxxiii (§ 17).
[2] Cp. Brownlee in *BA* XIII 69–72.   [3] Lk. i. 15, 66, 80.
[4] Isa. xl. 3.

sins', and 'many came out from Jerusalem and all the land of Judaea and were baptized of him in the river Jordan, confessing their sins'. Further, he taught[1] that 'there cometh one mightier than I after me', adding 'I indeed have baptized you with water: but he shall baptize you with the Holy Ghost' or, as in one account, 'with the Holy Ghost and with fire'.

Certain superficial resemblances between John and the Covenanters have been noted.[2] For example, John is said to have been 'born of a woman'[3] as the author of the *Thanksgiving Hymns* refers to himself as one 'born of a woman' (T xiii 14, xviii 12–13, 16): but all men are so born, and the expression is but a commonplace of literature.[4] John was in opposition to the Pharisees,[5] as the Covenanters were;[6] so also were Jesus and many others before and after Him. John, like the Covenanters,[7] expected the coming of the Messiah;[8] so again did Jesus and many other Jews.[9] Such arguments prove nothing; they do but emphasize the straits to which those who seek to connect John the Baptist with the Covenanters are reduced.

The brief accounts of John in the New Testament, while they give the essential points, leave obvious gaps which have given only too easy opportunities for the undue exercise of the imagination; and once the Essenes and the Covenanters have been identified,[10] these gaps can be filled out at will. For example, the inference has been drawn that John must have been familiar with Essene thought regarding the coming of the Messianic age and may even have been reared as an Essene, since he went out into the desert as a mere boy; for how otherwise could he have lived out there and how otherwise could he have received proper training for his prophetic mission?[11] The answers given to these questions are that the Essenes adopted him, as they normally adopted children to maintain their numbers, or that he lived with them and so learned their manner of life and their doctrines.[12]

Such phantasies are pure fiction. The Greek word translated 'child' in the Gospel, though denoting a child up to seven years of age in classical or strict usage, can be used in the Hellenistic dialect for any adult, since Tobit's son Tobias is so called throughout the story in the Greek text (possibly because his parents are alive to the end); similarly, the Hebrew word for 'child' can be applied to persons of ripe age, even up to fifty years or thereabout.[13] The force, too, of the Greek

---

[1] Matt. iii. 1–3, Mk. i. 4–8, Lk. iii. 2–17.
[2] Del Medico *Énigme* 145.   [3] Matt. xi. 11, Lk. vii. 28.
[4] *E.g.* Jb. xiv 1, xv. 14, xxv. 4; Pseudo-Clement *Homilies* II xvii 2, III xxii 2.
[5] Lk. vii. 30.   [6] Pp. 84–95.   [7] Pp. 466–77.
[8] Matt. xi. 3.   [9] Pp. 462–7, 502–3, 542–3, 527   [10] Pp. 106–9.
[11] Fritsch *Community* 112.
[12] Brownlee in Stendahl *Scrolls* 35 and in *BA* XIII 69–72; cp. Geyser in *Nov. Test.* I 70–75.
[13] Cp. 1 Ki. xii. 8 w. xiv. 21.

idiom in 'and he was in the deserts' does not necessarily imply that John went or was there while he was still a child; for the corresponding Hebrew idiom often allows a considerable lapse of time. In any case, boys in the East matured then as now at a very early age, as many stories show; for example, Josephus[1] says that he went to live with an anchorite in the wilderness when he was only sixteen years old and stayed with him for three years. Josephus, too, knew of John the Baptist by repute and thought well of him, as he said,[2] just as he knew and thought of the Essenes;[3] accordingly, his failure to bring him into connection with them in his remarkably full account of that group, whom he knew at first hand, would be surprising and even inexplicable if John had been an Essene, even for a short while.[4] Moreover the prophetic calling required no formal training, so far as the evidence of the Old Testament goes; for, although there were schools of the prophets, few if any of the canonical prophets had anything to do with them. In other words, 'the spirit bloweth where it listeth' and has no need of professional training, which may be a hindrance rather than an advantage. That the author or compiler of *Discipline* (D viii 14) and John the Baptist both used the prophecy about preparing the Way of the Lord as a proof-text proves nothing; it was an obvious *testimonium* which both, being steeped in the Old Testament, would know well.[5] Further, John's whole manner of life was quite different from that of the Essenes: he was an anchorite, they were coenobites; he was a Nazarite who drank no wine, they drank liquor[6] regularly at their common meals, as the Covenanters perhaps did (D vi 4–6);[7] he was a popular preacher, they were forbidden to divulge their doctrines to persons not of their order; he had nothing to say of the Law, they set themselves to prepare the way of the Lord by the study and observance of the Law. Others beside him retired to the wilderness in flight from the world or to prepare themselves for a mission;[8] Jesus spent forty days and nights there[9] and Bannus, with whom Josephus spent his three years, lived there.[10] No one has tried to prove that Bannus was an Essene or a Covenanter, and there is no reason for supposing that John was either in default of positive evidence, which has not been adduced.

These arguments, while they seem to prove that John like Bannus was neither an Essene nor a Covenanter, are not intended to suggest that he did not know either group. Spending his whole life within a few miles of their settlements and inspired to a certain extent with the same ideals,

[1] In *Life* ii §§ 11–12.   [2] In *Antiquities* XVIII v 2 §§ 116–9.
[3] P. 120.   [4] Cp. Schubert *Community* 127–8.
[5] S. pp. 527–31.   [6] P. 510.   [7] Pp. 507–8.
[8] *E.g.* 1 Ki. xix. 4 (Elijah), Matt. xiv. 13, Mk. i. 45, Lk. v. 16 (Jesus); cp. Psalms of Solomon xvii 18–19.
[9] Matt. iv. 1, Lk. v. 16.   [10] Cp. Sutcliffe *Monks* 123–4.

he could hardly have failed to know of them and might even have been personally acquainted with individual members, he might have imbibed some of their teaching, whether directly or indirectly, and he might in return have influenced them, while both he and they might have drawn something, little or much, from a common reservoir of language and ideas; but such contacts would not necessarily make him an Essene or a Covenanter.

Whether Jesus was ever at Qumrân is a question which Dr. Hjerl-Hansen has raised and has sought, somewhat tentatively, to settle with an affirmative answer.[1]

Not a few passages in the Gospels in his opinion connect Jesus with the wilderness, whether merely reflecting a desert environment or even attesting His familiarity with desert life. So, for example, He is depicted as knowing the habits of the eagle or vulture,[2] characteristically desert birds.[3] So, too, He went 'into a country near the wilderness, into a city called Ephraim';[4] and, if this place is rightly identified with the modern atṬaiyibäh, a village set on a conical hill overlooking the valley of the Jordan and the northern end of the Dead Sea,[5] He must have been within range of Qumrân itself. Or again, as most travellers were said to go down to the wilderness,[6] Jesus was 'led up' into it to be tempted[7] and 'went up' into it in search of solitude,[8] and this use of verbs importing journeys uphill points perhaps to Qumrân, which lies some 200 feet above the level of the Dead Sea, as His goal on both occasions.

One or two other passages are also thought to reflect the immediate background and even the actual circumstances of Qumrân. First, when Jesus asks 'If therefore they say unto you: Behold! he is in the wilderness, go not forth. Behold he is in the inner chambers, believe it or not',[9] the caves round Qumrân where the Scrolls were stored and fugitives lived and possibly also the chambers in the 'monastery' there immediately spring to mind; for the choice of a word properly meaning 'store-chamber' for 'closet' ($\tau\alpha\mu\varepsilon\tilde{\iota}o\nu$) both here and elsewhere[10] seems definitely intended to indicate something of the sort. In the same passage Jesus goes on to say 'as the lightning cometh forth from the east and is seen even unto the west, so shall be the coming of the Son of man',[11] reflecting a peculiarity of the western side of the Dead Sea; for lightning is thus visible only at Qumrân and Engedi owing to the wall of rock behind them. An opening in this wall behind Engedi, however, allows the lightning to be seen from there in the western sky and so puts it out of consideration; contrariwise, at Qumrân

---

[1] In *RQ* I 495–508
[2] Matt. xxiv. 28.
[3] Rev. xii. 14.
[4] Jn. xi. 54.
[5] Alt in *P-Jb.* XXI 31.
[6] *E.g.* 1 Macc. ii. 29.
[7] Matt. iv. 1.
[8] *E.g.* Mk. i. 35, Lk. v. 16.
[9] Matt. xxiv. 25–6.
[10] Matt. vi. 6.
[11] *Ibid.* xxiv. 27.

the rocks rise sheer and, having no opening, completely hide the lightning from the west, while it is visible eastwards for some six miles across the Dead Sea towards the hills of Moab on its eastern side. If Jesus was thinking of Qumrân, this would be the original form of the saying which Matthew, addressing Jews, would preserve; for they, especially any that had local knowledge, would seize the point. Luke, however, simplifies the saying, giving 'as the lightning, when it lighteneth out of one part of the heaven, shineth unto the other part under heaven, so shall the Son of man be in that day';[1] he thus eliminates the peculiarity, which would be unintelligible to Gentile readers not familiar with conditions at Qumrân.

Other possible allusions to the society of the Covenanters at Qumrân have been detected here and there in the Gospels. So, for example, Jesus answered all three temptations with quotations from *Deuteronomy*,[2] which is the book of the Old Testament of which the greatest number of copies (or rather fragments of copies) have been found in the caves.[3] Again, Jesus had sought out John the Baptist at the beginning of His ministry[4] and showed Himself eager, wherever He went, for theological discussions with local religious leaders and even with ordinary strangers;[5] and He would be likely also to have pursued the same course if or when He found Himself in the neighbourhood of Qumrân, especially as this was the only religious centre suitably situated between the Jordan and the mountains bounding the wilderness at this time. Further, the question put by the Pharisees to John, asking him 'Why baptizest thou, then, if thou be not Christ nor Elias nor a prophet?'[6] and that put by Jesus to the multitude when He asked them 'What went ye out into the wilderness to see! . . . to see a prophet?'[7] as well as the notice telling how Theudas 'boasting himself to be somebody' led many into the wilderness on a futile errand,[8] show how general was the expectation that religious teachers and reformers, including 'false Christs and false prophets', would emerge from the wilderness.[9] The leaders of the Zadokites, too, who had Messianic pretension, came and went in the wilderness of Judah, and long afterwards one of them, Menahem son of Judah, emerged from the vicinity of the Dead Sea 'like a veritable king' to claim the leadership of the nation in revolt.[10] Jesus then might have recognized the devil himself as his chief adversary in some such false prophet and have been preaching against a desert Messianism, in which the Covenanters might have been involved, as a serious threat to His claims and His mission.

All this evidence is quite insubstantial. Bethlehem and Bethany lie

---

[1] Lk. xvii. 24.   [2] Matt. iv. 1-11 and Lk. iv. 1-13; Deut. vi. 13, 16, viii. 3.
[3] Pp. 17-19.   [4] Matt. iii. 13.
[5] *E.g.* Lk. ii. 46-7 (religious leaders), Jn. iv. 7-26 (Samaritan woman).
[6] Jn. i. 24-5.   [7] Matt. xi. 7-9.   [8] Acts v. 36, xxi. 38.
[9] Cp. Matt. xxiv. 24-6.   [10] Pp. 268-9.

scarcely 15 miles from Qumrân, and their inhabitants must have been as familiar with the neighbouring desert conditions as with the natural peculiarities of the locality. Jesus therefore could have learnt everything about them as easily from others as from personal acquaintance with the locality. Whether a journey is called an ascent or a descent depends on the direction in which the traveller is said to be going; and in any case the ascent from the Jordan to Qumrân is not the only ascent in the district. Only 15 miles to the north the journey from the same river to the traditional site of the Temptation on a hill is an ascent of some 300 feet. The use, too, of 'store-chambers' for 'closets' is not unusual; for the Septuagint, following Hellenistic usage, has the same Greek word for the chamber which Joseph is said to enter in order to conceal his emotion from his brothers.[1] Lastly, no direct evidence has been adduced to show that Jesus ever met or talked with any Covenanters, who (like the Essenes) are nowhere mentioned in the Gospels, none too that He visited the wilderness at the time of the Temptation not for solitude but in order that He might make contact with these people and so meet it in an historical environment; and not a single hint supports the suggestion that He was definitely separating Himself from some desert Messiah, claiming Himself to be the only Messiah and realizing that the true Messianic expectation would be fulfilled in Himself.

These objections do not mean that Jesus knew nothing of the settlement at Qumrân or never came into contact with any of its members; that would be as difficult to maintain as the reverse would be to prove on the available evidence. One possible piece of evidence in its favour has been missed. If the Covenanters have been rightly identified with the Zealots,[2] Jesus must have heard of them and may have learnt something of their manner of life and their doctrines from Simon the 'Cananaean', who seems to have left the Zealots to become one of His disciples.[3] This may not unfairly be claimed as the only piece of positive evidence on the subject.

6. LUSTRATIONS AND BAPTISM

That the Covenanters ought to be regarded as a baptizing sect may be disputed. The numerous cisterns found at Qumrân, as said above,[4] prove little or nothing. Probably however these people, who rivalled the Essenes and outdid the Pharisees in the strict observance of the Law, did in fact observe ritual or ceremonial lustrations, possibly by total immersion; but the Scrolls nowhere enforce or even imply such an obligation as a condition of admission to the community of the Covenanters.

[1] Gen. xliii. 30.   [2] Pp. 237–51.   [3] P. 245.   [4] Pp. 41–4.

Lustrations are prescribed in the Pentateuch as a means of getting rid of ceremonial uncleanness, *e.g.* that acquired by the sexual act or by contact with a corpse; they are mentioned also in the apocryphal writings and in the New Testament.[1] By the 1st century A.D., however, the general maxims regarding baths of purification for persons, the washing of hands and domestic vessels, and the gradations of water allowed for such purposes, had been developed into an elaborate system of casuistry which had already lost itself in endless detail.[2] These were the burdensome regulations which Jesus denounced[3] as having no value except in so far as the heart is 'sprinkled from an evil conscience'.[4]

The Essenes, as Josephus[5] describes their practice, following the requirements of the Law in their attempt to escape or rid themselves of ritual defilement by contact with persons or things ceremonially unclean, bathed themselves in cold water before every meal and after relieving nature; and a member of a higher grade within the order even required a purifying bath after coming into contact with one of a lower grade. Josephus[6] explains their practice by saying that the Essenes 'have their own purer lustrations,' *i.e.* lustrations so pure that animal sacrifices have become unnecessary, and that the novice on admission is 'made a partaker of the water of purity'. The novice is not subjected to such lustration as a condition of entering the society; but by or after joining it he is allowed to partake of these ceremonial lustrations which absolve him from the necessity of offering the sacrifices required of ordinary Jews. In other words, the rules of the Essenes were but an extension in form and efficacy of those in the Pentateuch; they were in no sense a baptismal rite to which the postulant submitted as a condition of entering the order. The historian is careful, therefore, in describing them not to use the technical term for baptism, with which he was perfectly well acquainted.[7]

The rules on the subject of lustration or baptism (if that is meant) in *Discipline* are purely negative; but the *Zadokite Documents* contain one positive enactment.

The concern of *Discipline* is with those who obstinately remain outside the society of the Covenanters, in which alone they can find salvation. It lays down that, so long as a man persists in this attitude, 'he will not (be able to) purify himself with water for (the removal of) impurity nor sanctify himself in seas or rivers nor cleanse himself with water for ablution' (D iii 4–5). It then goes on to deal with 'men of perversity' who are not 'reckoned in the covenant', saying that 'these

---

[1] Lev. xiv. 8–9, xv. 2–30; Ecclus. xxxiv. 25; Matt. xv. 2 and Jn. xiii. 10.
[2] Cp. Schürer *Geschichte*³ II 481–3.
[3] Matt. xxiii. 25, Mk. vii. 2–8, Lk. xi. 38–9. [4] Heb. x. 22.
[5] In *Jewish War* II viii 5 § 129, 9 § 149, 10 § 150. [6] In *War* II viii 7 § 138.
[7] In *Antiquities* XVIII v 2 §§ 116–7.

shall not enter into water to touch the purity of the saints (*i.e.* to render themselves fit to handle the food and drink of the society); for they will not be (able to be) cleansed unless they have turned away from their wickedness' (D v 13–14); and, if a man does enter the covenant, 'he may not eat or drink anything belonging to them (*sc.* men of perversity) nor accept anything from them except for payment' (D v 16–17). The last rule makes the purpose of these ablutions clear: they are intended to wash away the ceremonial defilement which a man may incur by contact with persons in the world outside and may bring with him into it, so to defile its members by contaminating what they eat and drink, whether in the handling of it or in the sharing in their meals.[1] At the same time these rules only say that such ablutions will not avail to cleanse a man who rejects the principles of the society and so make him fit to enter it unless he repents; they do not say that he must submit to them before being admitted to it. In other words, they cannot be construed in a positive sense as requiring such a rite as a condition of admission, just as the prohibition of infanticide cannot be construed as a command enjoining the procreation of children. Such expressions as those here used, then, must rather be read as warning against attaching undue value to mere rites and ceremonies, especially to lustration as practised in contemporary Jewish society. This rite is not prohibited nor is it enjoined, it is not enforced by a positive injunction because it is regarded with a large measure of indifference; it is permitted and used as an additional safeguard against defilement by impurity incurred by contact with the world. If then members underwent such a rite, they would do so not so much because it was an obligation imposed by the society as because it was backed by the authority of the Mosaic law.

A small point in the Covenanters' rules which calls for a passing comment is the assertion regarding one who refuses to enter the society of the Covenanters that 'he cannot sanctify himself in rivers or seas' (D iii 4–5). The exaggeration is startling, and parallel passages have been sought to account for it:[2] for example, how the Septuagint translators of the Law, working in a house by the sea-shore, 'after washing themselves in the sea and purifying themselves would betake themselves in this state to the work of translation',[3] how Halicarnassus allowed the Jews resident there to build their synagogues 'near the sea in accordance with their native custom'[4] and how Paul and his companions found a synagogue at Philippi 'by a riverside', where Lydia and her household were baptized.[5] Yet these instances are hardly parallel, and an apocryphal story about the

---

[1] Pp. 55–6.
[3] Josephus *Antiquities* XII ii 13 § 106.
[5] Acts xvi. 13–15.

[2] Brownlee *Discipline* 13.
[4] *Ibid.* XIV x 23 § 258.

Septuagint translators and a reference to a by-chance of established Jewish practice have no point in the present connection. The question may therefore be asked, whether the author is not aiming a blow at the baptism of John (or of his self-styled successors the Mandaeans),[1] the only person who is known to have practised the rite on a large scale in such a situation; for he administered it in the largest river in the country, not far from one of two points (for the tradition fluctuates) either that at which the Sea of Galilee discharges its waters into the Jordan or that at which the Jordan flows into the Dead Sea.[2] The memory of his mission and of the crowds who flocked out of the cities to see him might provide the yardstick by which successive generations of Covenanters would condemn all such rites as the antics of a revivalist, which they would not wish to see introduced into their own solemn ceremonies.

The author of the *Zadokite Documents* adds a positive regulation prescribing immersion when the rite is carried out; he says that 'no man (*sc.* no member of the society) may bathe in water that is dirty or less than enough to cover a man; let him not purify a vessel in it' (Z xii 1–2). The verb here used for 'bathed (*rāḥaṣ*)' serves in the Old Testament as also elsewhere for both ordinary physical ablution (Z xiii 10) and for ceremonial or ritual lustration (D iii 5) and is therefore equivocal; that for 'purified (*ṭihēr*)' usually has this last meaning. The passage in question, however, being headed 'purification (*hiṭṭahēr*) with water', must be taken as referring not to ablution but to lustration. The reason for this regulation is clear: rules are being prescribed for members living in the world, where ceremonial or ritual pollution must have been easily incurred and where therefore careful rules for purification will be necessary. Such rules, which would be of little use to members of the society living in seclusion at Qumrân, would become a necessity under the ordinary Jewish law, so soon as they went out into the world. The purpose of the Covenanters was not to abrogate but to strengthen the Law, which was in constant danger of being weakened. Here too, then, the reference is not to baptism as a rite of initiation, as the inclusion of purifying vessels shows, but to lustration; and the technical term (since it may also be used in its ordinary non-theological sense)[3] for 'baptized (*ṭābal*)' by immersion, as by the Pharisees for the admission of proselytes by baptism to their society, is avoided. If baptism had been intended, it would surely have been unequivocally described as baptism. In keeping with this fact the Covenanters never spoke of themselves as 'immersed' or 'baptized' but only as 'those who repent of transgression' or as 'penitents of

[1] Pp. 567–9.
[2] Jn. i. 28 (where the reading is obscure); s. Smith *Historical Geography of the Holy Land*[25] 496.   [3] *E.g.* Mishnah *Yebamoth* xvi 4.

Israel' (D x 20, Z ii 3 ix 42; cp. Z viii 6 ix 24); as such they could dispense with such rites as a society, however desirable they might be for some people, even for members of their own society. The important point was not lustration but penitence for the Covenanters; for the Essenes it was not penitence but lustration.

The ceremony of initiation and presumably any rite of lustration which had accompanied it were annually repeated in a service of re-dedication (D ii 19 iii 9 v 24–5); this rule is laid down only for ordinary members but would presumably have been applicable also to lapsed members on readmission, since they might otherwise have contaminated the society with defilement contracted in the world. The original rite might indeed have had a special significance for the person undergoing it for the first time, but otherwise it did not differ in kind from all other subsequent lustrations; it was therefore, as Prof. Rowley says, 'not an administered rite but a bath'.[1] This kind of bathing was apparently a feature of the 1st century A.D.; so the Essenes washed themselves daily before meals in cold water,[2] and Bannus bathed daily in cold water.[3] The probability therefore is that the Covenanters followed the same practice, but that the annual ceremony was attended by a certain solemnity which was naturally absent from the daily rite. Such daily or annual ceremonies were in no way baptisms in the ordinary sense of the term, although they had a certain religious as well as a purely physical purpose.

In so far as the Covenanters permitted these practices, they then, while taking precautions against counting too much on their efficacy, were but following approximately contemporary Jewish practice. As Judaism came to win recruits from the Gentile world and the Jewish community ran a constant risk of contamination by the admission of such persons, the practice of ceremonial ablution as prescribed in the Old Testament received a fresh application in the immersion of proselytes. The Rabbis based the need for such a ceremony on the command given to the ancient Hebrews to wash their garments before the delivery of the Law at Sinai;[4] and, as they regarded bathing after the sexual act both as a purification and as a form of consecration for intercourse with the sacred words of the Law, so they considered bathing of proselytes necessary as a purification from contact with heathenism in preparation for admission to the society of God's people. The convert who wished to become a Jew was conducted to the bath and there immersed himself in the presence of the Rabbis, who recited passages from the Law over him.[5] When this practice

---

[1] Rowley *ap.* Higgins *New Testament Essays* 222.
[2] Josephus *War* II viii 5 § 129.   [3] Josephus *Life* ii 11.
[4] Exod. xix. 10–14; cp. B. Talmud *Yebamoth* 46a–b and *Kerithoth* 9a.
[5] Brandt in Hastings' *ERE* II 408–9.

began cannot be determined with certainty; no evidence of its existence before A.D. 65 has been found, but Epictetus speaks of it (if he is not confusing Jews with Christians) as well known in his time, *i.e.* at the end of the 1st and the beginning of the 2nd century A.D.,[1] and it is mentioned in the Mishnah,[2] so that it must already have been established at the time when most of the Scrolls were being composed.[3]

The Prophets had naturally been familiar with the principle of ritual lustration, even though the rules in the Pentateuch prescribing and regulating it were written down long after their times; and they had used the metaphor of washing the heart clean from wickedness and cleansing the sinner by sprinkling him with clean water.[4] Such figures of speech lie behind the notion of a spiritual lustration, of which *Discipline* speaks when it says that 'it is through the spirit of God's true counsel [in regard to] a man's way that all his iniquities will be wiped out . . . , and through a holy spirit he will be cleansed of all his iniquities . . . and through the submission of his soul to all God's ordinances his flesh will be cleansed, purifying himself with water for (the removal of) impurity and sanctifying himself with the water for impurity' (D iii 6–9)[5] and again that 'God will purge by His truth all the deeds of man . . . to cleanse him through a spirit of holiness from all wicked practices, sprinkling upon him a spirit of truth like water for (the removal of) impurity, to cleanse (him) from all untrue abominations and from being defiled by the spirit of impurity' (D iv 20–2). Here physical lustration cannot be meant. Neither of these passages too, then, imposes ceremonial lustration as a condition of entry into the society of the Covenanters; for the expressions used are figures of speech based on contemporary Jewish practice.

John's baptism differed in several respects from the lustrations of the Covenanters.[6] Both were apparently rites of total immersion; but John's baptism, like that of the Rabbis admitting a proselyte to Judaism, was an administered rite, whereas the Scrolls give no hint of any minister required to perform the lustrations of the Covenanters. John performed the rite in running water, thereby apparently introducing something new into it;[7] for the Rabbis certainly did not insist on this,[8] and the rules of the Covenanters allowed standing water for personal lustrations, if certain precautions were taken (Z xi 1–2).[9] John's baptism was carried out publicly, in the presence of the crowd, whereas the lustrations of the Covenanters were a private ceremony. John summoned those who accepted baptism to forsake the world, and

[1] Arrian *Epicteti Dissertationes* II ix 19–21.
[2] Mishnah *Pesachim* viii 8.   [3] Cp. Zeitlin in *RÉJ* XCVIII 50–57.
[4] *E.g.* Isa. i. 16, Jer. iv. 14, Ezek. xvi. 9 and xxxvi 25–7, 33.   [5] S. p. 72.
[6] Cp. Rowley in Higgins *op. cit.* 218–28.   [7] Cp. Bammel in *HTR* LI 105–6.
[8] Mishnah *Mikwaoth* i 7–8; cp. Schürer *Geschichte*[3] II 481–3.
[9] P. 68.

the Rabbis at a Jewish baptism warned the proselyte what would be expected of him and recited extracts from the Law over him; the Scrolls contain no mention of such charges. John imposed no period of probation on those who accepted his baptism and did not call on them to join a highly organized society; the Covenanters who might undergo a ceremonial lustration followed it up by a prescribed period of probation and then entered a semi-monastic society. John's baptism was a ceremony which might not be repeated, inasmuch as it had conferred an indelible mark on the person baptized; contrariwise the Covenanters' ceremony of initiation, accompanied apparently by lustration, which was immediate and temporary in its application, was annually repeated.

John adapted the familiar Jewish ceremony of washing the whole body to get rid of the ceremonial or ritual contagion to a moral purpose, that of a baptism of repentance for the remission of sins: the cleansing of the participant of the stain due to his previous state of sin admitted him to a new religious state in the spirit of repentance symbolized by a cleansing with water in view of the speedy coming of the Kingdom of God. Such a baptism was not merely a rite 'for the purification of the body', as Josephus described it,[1] looking at it from a purely Jewish point of view. The conception was primarily corporate, relative to a salvation as of a holy people; consequently Jesus could accept it without any feeling of sin except in a corporate sense. John, however, claimed no saving virtue for his baptism, only a certain preparedness, when it was the outward sign of an inward penitence, nor did he make it a condition of entry into a new society; the real gift of a new experience would come with the baptism not with water but with the Holy Spirit, which the Messiah or Christ would impart.

Jesus himself baptized no one, and only His disciples performed the rite of baptism;[2] and, like John, He never made it a condition of discipleship. As yet, then, Christian baptism had not been instituted; but, when it came, it added a spiritual element which that of John lacked. Meanwhile, Jesus showed plainly that Pharisaic ceremonial washings had no permanent claims on the conscience, and His words were even explained as altogether repealing the ceremonial distinction of clean and unclean.[3] Only when these were abolished was the way prepared for Christian baptism, of which the essence was that it should be performed only once, with no possibility of repetition, unlike the repeated lustrations of other Jewish parties; and in the final interview with the disciples Jesus spoke of a baptism not with water but with the Holy Spirit.[4] Baptism thus became the door of admission to the Church for Jew and Gentile alike; so even certain of John's disciples

[1] In *Antiquities* XVIII v 2 § 117.   [2] Jn. iv. 2.
[3] Mk. vii. 4, 18–20.   [4] Acts i. 4–5.

were baptized afresh 'in the name of the Lord Jesus'.[1] Further, baptism by water did not enter into Messianic baptism, which is brought rather into connection with the purely spiritual baptism of suffering.[2] The apostolic rite of baptism in its conjunction of baptism by water with baptism with the Spirit sensibly outpoured was initiated by the Apostles themselves, like other primitive Christian rites whose forms were instinctively inspired by their Jewish training. Immediately on the Day of Pentecost they recognized the connection between the rite of baptism as a means of admission to the church and the solemn invocation of the Lord as protector;[3] and this invocation came to be embodied in the rite.[4] The conception of baptism as requiring the confession of sins and the renunciation of the old false allegiance and at the same time the acknowledgement of Jesus as Messiah or Lord and loyalty to a new true allegiance was fundamental. Christian baptism implied identification with Him as Messiah or Lord, and after it a man was regarded as 'in Christ' or 'in the Lord'.[5] It was also regarded as effecting a union with the death of Christ, a kind of burial of the man's former self with a view to a resurrection and a new life;[6] for a new birth was a condition of entry into the kingdom of God.[7] Again, Christian baptism was not a symbol of something already complete but a sacrament, i.e. a symbol conditioning a present and decisive experience of divine grace already embraced by faith; it was 'not a putting away of filth in the sphere of the flesh, but the interrogation of a good conscience through God'[8] as pledged to give part and lot in Christ's resurrection to those who yield 'obedience of faith' to Him.[9]

The same varying ideas reappear in other sects of this and the following century, so far as their practices are known.

The Mandaeans, whose origins perhaps went back to the 1st century A.D., practised baptism by immersion. This had to take place in running water, in which the member clothed in white robes was totally immersed, and certain divine beings were invoked by name; the ceremony was performed by the individual member himself or, as on feast-days, with the co-operation of a priest, or it was administered by some other person to a child. The underlying idea was that the water of the river, with which the participant was required to set a mark on his brow and of which he had to drink, streamed from the world of eternal life and infused life into all who bathed and shared in it. The immersion was originally performed by any ordinary Mandaean as time and opportunity permitted, morning and evening every day or only on

---

[1] Ibid. xix. 5.
[3] Acts ii. 38. [4] Ibid. xxii. 16.
[6] Rom. vi. 1–12. [7] Jn. iii. 3–6.
[2] Mk. x. 38–9.
[5] Gal. iii. 27.
[8] 1 Pet. iii. 21.
[9] Bartlet in Hastings' ERE II 357–9 and Armitage Robinson in EB I 471–6.

Sundays and feast-days, and could be regularly performed without the assistance of a priest; but subsequently an annual ceremony was introduced, at which all the members of the community were assembled on a river-bank, and a priest included all the ceremonies required to be performed in the river or with the water of the river at their celebration.[1]

In the third year of the emperor Trajan (A.D. 96–117) a Jew named Elkasai, whom the Essenes and the Ebionites accepted as a prophet, announced a new means of obtaining remission of sins. He required his followers to undergo total immersion, fully clothed, in the water of a spring or a river, to accept circumcision and the observance of the Sabbath and generally to live in accordance with the Jewish law; he permitted marriage but prohibited the eating of flesh or perhaps rather participation in animal sacrifices. The candidate was required immediately before the immersion to declare that he would abstain from improper conduct and sin, and the rite was then carried out 'in the name of the Most High God'. The same ceremony was employed also for the cure of disease and similar troubles; for the sacramental bath was supposed to expel the evil demons which were the cause of them. This baptism, with its preliminary pledge of a changed heart and the remission of sins which was its object, recalls that of John the Baptist; but there was little that was otherwise common to both rites. Elkasai did not deliberately set himself to preach repentance of sins to his own people and to rouse their consciences; he was rather an ecstatic who had received revelations, though also a man of practical judgement who counted on the convincing power of his arguments with those who were ready to listen to him with a serious mind and who looked for the approbation and adherence of those who believed in a divine retribution for sin. He was an idealist and a religious leader who promised an indulgence, which would bring no personal advantage to himself, to those who adhered to his doctrine.

Elkasai's baptism was not a mere ceremonial ablution but a total immersion of the candidate in his clothes as a necessary condition of bodily healing or remission of sins. Judaism never required such a procedure, although the Essenes bathed in loin-clothes.[2] The Mandaeans, however, did require something of the sort: they bathed in river-water, clothed in white robes for the occasion, in order to obtain remission of sins. The resemblance is striking; but the Mandaeans, unlike the Elkasaites, required no vow at the immersion. Their religious rite of immersion was associated with the notion of a new birth which entered into the mysteries, and it was therefore probably derived from the priests of the mystery-cults; and Elkasai, too, probably obtained it from

[1] Brandt in Hastings' *op. cit.* VIII 386–7, 389.
[2] Josephus *Jewish War* II viii 2 § 161; cp. 4 § 129.

some such source, even though other influences cannot be entirely excluded.[1]

The development of the theory of lustration and baptism may now be summarized. In the Old Testament the ablutions prescribed in the Pentateuch were ritual lustrations carried out for the purpose of removing ceremonial uncleanness caused by contact with unclean persons or things, which were regarded as contagious; and the idea was extended by the prophets to that of metaphorically cleansing Israel from its sins, chiefly the sin of apostasy. Lustration thus began as a magical or religious ceremony to which a person submitted himself as a safeguard against or a purification from various forms of uncleanness; it became a ritual proceeding undertaken before embarking on any sacred function such as initiation or consecration, and it passed into a social ceremony which became an occasion of hospitality; and finally it acquired a symbolic aspect, for example when Jesus washed the feet of the Disciples at the Last Supper. It was never itself a rite of initiation. The Essenes practised a like lustration to rid themselves of ceremonial uncleanness, and the baptism of proselytes by the Rabbis was similarly a lustration washing away any contagion with which the convert from the Gentile world might infect the people of God. Neither involved a changed heart, confession of past faults or remission of sins. Accordingly neither Essenes nor Rabbis had advanced beyond the ritual requirements of the Pentateuch and their mechanical application. The Covenanters, who cherished the teaching of the Prophets, rejected such a view and also lustration itself as a necessary rite but insisted on a changed heart, *i.e.* repentance of sins; otherwise it had no value for them. Thus the Covenanters, by connecting lustration with repentance, introduced something new into the doctrine.[2] Herein one of the main reasons for abandoning the identification of the Covenanters with the Essenes may be found.

John's baptism was something quite different. It was neither a lustration nor rite of purification but a baptism; it too required a changed heart and at the same time admitted the postulant not to the 'purity' of a society which might without it be defiled by contact with him but to a new religious state through repentance symbolized by a washing with water and holding out the promise of a remission of sins. John, the first to make baptism a rite of initiation,[3] had already carried the doctrine beyond the point to which the Covenanters had perhaps brought it, although he was *ex hypothesi* approximately contemporary with them; and on this ground alone he must be completely dissociated from them. Jesus went yet further; He profoundly altered the whole conception by virtually repealing the old ceremonial dis-

---

[1] Brandt *ibid.* V 263–4.   [2] Black *Scrolls* 97–8.
[3] Cp. Rowley *Scrolls* 15–16.

tinction of clean and unclean and replacing baptism with water by baptism with the Holy Spirit, but He too did not make baptism a condition of entering His society. In the Church, however, baptism became a door of admission to the new society; it was therefore carried out once and could not be repeated. In it, too, Messianic baptism was connected with the spiritual baptism of suffering, the identification of the baptized person with Jesus as Messiah and Lord and a union in the death of Christ; and lastly it was not a mere symbol but became a sacrament.

No such ideas, however, were developed by the Covenanters: their lustrations were not a rite of initiation nor a baptism into the name of the Teacher.[1] The baptism of the Elchasaites, in its requirement of a changed heart and its promise of the remission of sins, was not unlike that of John the Baptist; but it was an indulgence, and it contained no appeal to the conscience nor summons to repentance. Unlike that of the Covenanters, it was in no sense a lustration. Mandaean baptism was quite different; for it was a ceremony that might be repeated many times, it required no special minister and made no demand for repentance of past sin, but it was regarded as infusing a new life into the person baptized or effecting a new birth like that offered to the devotees of the mystery-cults. It resembled the lustration of the Covenanters on the first two but differed from theirs on the last two points.

In the development of the doctrine of lustration or baptism, then, the Covenanters came between the Essenes and John the Baptist. On the one hand they rejected the mechanical rite of purification as practised by the Essenes; on the other, while sharing John's view that such rites without repentance of sins had no value, they did not reach his use of the ceremony as a rite unto remission of sins. The simplest explanation of this approximation of the practice and theory of the Covenanters on the one side to that of the Essenes and on the other to that of John the Baptist is to regard them as contemporary; he may be put shortly before them in time, but his religious insight puts him doctrinally in advance of them.

7. COMMUNAL MEALS

The communal meals of the Covenanters and of other Jewish groups of the same period raise important questions.

Josephus,[2] describing the communal meals of the Essenes, says that after working strenuously at their various tasks till the fifth hour 'they again assemble in one place and, after girding their loins with a white cloth, bathe their bodies in cold water; and, after this purification,

---

[1] Rowley *op. cit.* 12–13, 19.   [2] In *War* II viii 5 §§ 129–31.

they assemble in a private apartment which none of the uninitiated is permitted to enter; and, pure themselves, they repair to the refectory as to some sacred shrine. When they have taken their seats in silence, the baker serves out the loaves to them in order and the cook sets one plate with a single course before each person. The priest says a grace before meat, and none may partake till after the prayer; when breakfast is ended, he pronounces another grace. Thus at the beginning and at the close the Essenes do homage to God as the bountiful giver of life. Then, laying aside their white raiment as holy vestments, they again betake themselves to their labours till the evening. On their return they sup in like manner, and any guest who may have arrived sits down with them.' This is all that is known of the common meals of the Essenes.

The daily meals at Qumrân were similarly communal. The rule in *Discipline* prescribing the behaviour of the members 'in all their settlements', says that 'they shall eat communally and bless communally and take counsel communally; and in every place where there are ten men of the council of the community, there shall not fail from among them one who is a priest; and let each one sit according to his assigned rank in his (*sc.* the priest's) presence. . . . And it shall be, when they arrange the table to eat or the liquor (*tîrôš*)[1] to drink, the priest shall first stretch out his hand that they may be blessed in the first' or 'best of the bread (*leḥem*) or the liquor to drink' (D vi 2–6). The meagre information thus gleaned can be supplemented from a fragment, also derived from Cave I, which has commonly (though wrongly) been supposed to be prescribing the rules for the Messianic banquet.[2] This text says '[This is the order of] sitting of notable persons, summoned to a meeting for the consultation of the Community, if God should bring the Messiah with them: [the priest] shall enter at the head of all the community of Israel; and all the priests, fathers [of the house of] Aaron, (who are) summoned to a meeting, (being) notable persons, shall take their seats in [his presence, each] according to his dignity; and afterwards the Messiah of Israel shall [take] his [seat], and the heads of the clans of Israel shall take their seats in his presence, each according to his dignity and according to [his position] in their camps and according to their stages; and all the chiefs of the fathers[3] [of the] community shall take their seats in their presence, each according to his dignity; and, [when they] meet [at] table [or to drink] liquor and the table for the community is arranged [and the] liquor [mixed] for drinking, no one may put forth his hand on to the first' or 'best of the food and [liquor] before the priest; for [he will be] blessing the first' or 'best of the food and the liquor and will put forth his hand to the food first, and afterwards the Messiah of Israel [shall] put forth his hands to the food; [and afterwards] the whole congregation of the community shall pronounce a blessing, each according to his dignity. And they shall do according to this rule in all the arrangement, when as many as ten men are assembled' (I Q *28* A ii 11–22). Here the striking point is the absence of all reference to the Rightful Teacher; but this is easily explained. In the first account the text says nothing of the persons who will partake of the communal meals. In the second it makes clear in the opening line that it is concerned with 'the arrangements for all the congregation of Israel at the end of the days' (I Q *28* A i 1), *i.e.* at the time of the final victory of Israel, as represented by the society, over the world, when the office of the Rightful Teacher will have been merged in that of the 'Messiah of Israel', *i.e.* the lay Messiah;[1] and he as a layman takes rank below the priest, whether this is the high-priest or the priestly Messiah.[2] The Teacher therefore is expected to be present, though in a different guise, that of the Messiah; his presence as such, however, does not necessarily imply that the meal here intended is the Messianic banquet.

The Messianic banquet, which is distinguished from the meal just described on several points, as argued below, in spite of superficial resemblances, can be traced back to hints extracted from the Old Testament[3] and developed by Rabbinic methods. It is ultimately derived from the passage describing how Ezekiel's Messianic 'prince (*nāśî'*)' shall enter the Temple by a special gate 'to eat bread before the Lord';[4] and this bread has been thought to be the shew-bread.[5] So, too, 'the prince (*nāśî'*) of (all) the congregation' (Z ix 10, I Q *28* B v 20) of the Covenanters will be present at their 'banquet', and again the 'bread' eaten at it appears to be the shew-bread according to an Aramaic text found in Cave II (if it does in fact refer to this meal; but the text is badly damaged, and this point cannot be certainly established).[6] These appear to be the only points common to the Messianic banquet and the Covenanters' meal; and both derive from the Old Testament. As the notion behind Ezekiel's conception was developed, speculation became rife about the banquet which would be held when the Messiah came and had conquered the world,[7] attended by 'all that were left', *i.e.* the remnant left to have a share in the Messianic kingdom. Jesus refers on several occasions to such a banquet, *e.g.* when He says that 'many shall come from the east and the west and shall sit down with Abraham and Isaac and Jacob in the kingdom of heaven'[8] and 'blessed is he that shall eat bread in the

---

[1] P. 60.   [2] Pp. 475–6.
[3] *E.g.* Exod. xviii. 12; Deut. xii. 7, 18, xxvii. 7.   [4] Ezek. xliv. 3.
[5] Black *Scrolls* 109.   [6] Baillet in *RB*, NS LXII 222–45.
[7] Cp. Targum of Jerusalem on Exod. xii. 42 and Num. xi. 26.
[8] Matt. viii. 11; cp. Lk. xiii. 29.

kingdom of God',[1] and most notably when He declares 'I say unto you, I will not drink henceforth of this fruit of the vine, until that day when I drink it now with you in My Father's kingdom'.[2] In specifically Jewish accounts of the Messianic banquet now the flesh of Leviathan and Behemoth, now a vegetable diet and a heavenly food, *i.e.* manna, was expected to be eaten,[3] and apparently wine preserved in the grape since the six days of creation would be drunk.[4] This banquet, then, was a part of popular Messianic expectations in the 1st century A.D. Nothing of this sort, however, can be found in this fragmentary Scroll, which merely lays down rules for the conduct of the communal meals when 'at the end of the days' the lay Messiah may be expected to be present. It is not envisaged as taking place in heaven; the plain fare, even if it was the shew-bread, does not suggest a banquet; many of those present are in no sense cultic persons; and the requirement of ten persons, as urged below, leaves no doubt that the rule is aimed at a regular meal of the society at which the Messiah is expected to be present.[5]

The meals of the Essenes and the Covenanters, as Josephus and the authors or compilers of the Scrolls respectively described them, were the ordinary meals as eaten by every Jew *mutatis mutandis* according to circumstances, though invested with a certain degree of solemnity and sacredness such as might be expected of religious bodies living in community. Thus Josephus in describing the ordinary daily meals of the Essenes could say[6] 'now pure themselves, they present themselves in the refectory as in some sacred shrine' and that strangers regarded their silent meal 'as some awful mystery', though perhaps with some exaggeration. They went in fact so far as to entrust the preparation of their common food to priests, just as ordinary pious Jews were wont to invite priests for the processing of oil and other foodstuffs likely to convey ceremonial uncleanness. In the same way, the Covenanters would seem to have taken similar precautions by forbidding the employment of novices in the preparation of their meals;[7] they would thus be 'eaters of unclean things in purity'.[8] Their communal meals were cultic only in the sense that religious people naturally tend to be as strict as lay people are negligent on such points, and every meal was therefore in some sense a ritual meal for ordinary pious Jews. The common elements in these meals are purely Jewish: for example, the Pharisees had religious meals in their 'associations';[9] the washing of

---

[1] Lk. xiv. 15.   [2] Matt. xxvi. 29; cp. Mk. xiv 25 and Lk. xxii. 18.
[3] 2 Baruch xxix. 4–8.
[4] Targum on *Song of Songs* viii 2, B. Talmud *Baba Bathra* 74b–75b, *Sanhedrin* 99a, *Abodah Zarah* 3b.
[5] Sutcliffe *Monks* 111.   [6] In *War* II viii 5 §§ 130–3.
[7] Pp. 55–6.   [8] Rabin *Scr. Jud.* II 7–8.
[9] *Ibid.* 19.

the hands was a regular custom at all meals,[1] as also the blessing of the food was,[2] amongst Jews following the custom of the Old Testament;[3] and the blessing was usually pronounced by the father of the family or a priest, if one was present,[4] at the beginning of the meal but by some other person, e.g. a guest of honour, at its end.[5] There was therefore nothing peculiar in these meals except the washing of the whole body by the Essenes and the regular blessing of the food by a priest in both communities; the washings were partly physical and partly ceremonial, and the customary precedence of the priest would explain why he, if one was present, and not a layman would pronounce the blessings.

At the same time there are obvious differences between the Essenes and the Covenanters in respect to the common meals as in other matters.[6] The Essenes bathe themselves before meals, while the Covenanters are not required to do so; grace is said among the Essenes before and after, amongst the Covenanters only before the meal (although the omission may be accidental, since both bread and wine are blessed before and after the meals of the Covenanters). No uninitiated person may enter the Essene refectory, although guests are admitted; nothing is said of guests or uninitiated persons at the Covenanters' meal in this passage. The Covenanters require only that members shall be addressed in the order of their rank (D vi 4), while the Essenes further enjoin silence at their meals, just as Christians 'who are invited to the agape must partake of it in silence, without argumentation, speaking only when addressed by the bishop'.[7] The Essenes ate not only bread but also cooked food and apparently drank only water (for nothing is said of liquor or wine), while the Covenanters ate only bread (if the text is interpreted literally) and drank 'liquor' (tîrôš) of some sort;[8] but the accounts leave so much unsaid that such details cannot be pressed.

Although then the communal meals of the Essenes and the Covenanters were very similar, clear differences can be detected between them; the similarities can be traced back to their common Jewish origin while the differences may be explained as due to the different habits of the two groups. Similarity does not mean identity; and, even if their communal meals were not essentially different from those of the laity, this approximation does not mean that Essenes and Covenanters were identical groups. Nothing here compels the identification of

[1] Mishnah *Berakoth* viii 2–4; cp. Matt. xv. 2, Mk. vii. 3–4, Lk. xi. 38–9.
[2] Mishnah *ibid.* vi 1–vii 5; cp. Matt. xiv. 19, Lk. ix. 16, Jn. vi. 11.
[3] 1 Sam. ix. 13.   [4] Letter of Aristeas vii § 184.
[5] Strack & Billerbeck *Kommentar* IV 72, 627–8.
[6] Pp. 110–20.
[7] Funk *Didascalia et Constitutiones Apostolorum* II 113–14.
[8] Pp. 507–8, 512–14.

these two groups with one another, and nothing here can be regarded as necessarily the source of any Christian practice.

The Pentecostal feast of the Therapeuts,[1] who ate only bread seasoned with salt or hyssop and no flesh and abstained from wine,[2] has also been cited in this connection; but it bears little real comparison with the meals of the Essenes and the Covenanters, and the resemblances, as the description of these meals given above shows, are superficial and partial. Their feast may agree in this or that detail with the meal now of the Essenes and now of the Covenanters; and, while the former was an annual feast, both the latter were daily meals.

Whether the so-called 'Messianic banquet' of the Covenanters, though in no sense that of Rabbinic fancy, has any connection with the Paschal meal or with that celebrated on the eve of the Sabbath, as of other feasts, for their 'sanctification (qiddûš)' or even with the Last Supper, as some writers have suggested,[3] must now be considered.

The Jewish Paschal meal followed a special order which included the following requirements amongst others: the lamb, the unleavened bread and bitter herbs, the 'festal offering (ḥăgîgāh)' and 'mixed dish (ḥărōšeṭ)' and the four cups of wine; and ten persons were required to make up a company.[4] The head of the company blessed the first cup, which was then drunk; he then washed his hands and recited a prayer; then the bitter herbs, dipped in the ḥărōšeṭ, were passed round; after the pouring of the second cup, the youngest member was asked what was the significance of the feast, and the father explained it, whereupon the first part of the hallēl[5] was sung; after the third cup a grace was said and after the completion of the hallēl[6] the fourth cup was drunk; all then washed their hands, and the meal was eaten. At the qiddûš[7] two specially prepared loaves were baked and one cup of wine was drunk. The father of the family, having recited the praises of the virtuous wife,[8] blessed the cup of wine and drank from it and then handed it to his wife; and she, after drinking from it, passed it in turn to the children and to any other persons who might be there. Both these occasions were gatherings of the family, neighbours and friends; and persons of both sexes, old and young alike, might be present.

Contrariwise, the rules of the 'Messianic banquet' of the Covenanters, brief as they are, clearly distinguish it from either of these meals; the only common point, which it shares with the Paschal meal, is the requirement of ten persons (I Q 28 A ii 21–2). This rule would not necessarily imply that the 'banquet' was a cultic meal[9] like the Paschal

---

[1] Pp. 122–3. [2] Philo Contemplative Life ix 73–4, 82.
[3] E.g. Davies Scrolls 127–30; cp. Kuhn in ET 1950–1, 508–27.
[4] Josephus War VI ix 3 § 423 and Targum Pseudo-Jonathan on Exod. xii 4.
[5] Psa. cxiii. 1–cxiv. 8. [6] Psa. cxv. 1–cxviii. 29.
[7] Cp. Box in JTS III 360–2. [8] Prov. xxxi. 10–31.
[9] Black Scrolls 104.

meal, which was subject to a similar rule; and it would not prove
that any number above ten persons would not starve but would partake
of a separate non-cultic meal, so that that of which the ten would
partake would be cultic. No text gives any hint that the ten are to be
regarded as in any way different from the other members of the society
or as taking their meals elsewhere;[1] and ten was the minimal number
for many institutions not only among the Covenanters but also in
various Jewish organizations.[2] Every meal is a cultic meal to a theo-
logian unless it can be proved not to be such; rather, every meal must
be assumed to be an ordinary meal unless it can be proved cultic.
Clearly the 'banquet' cannot be connected with the Paschal meal; for
that its regulations should include only this relatively unimportant
provision and no others would be surprising in a document intended
for the guidance of so strictly orthodox a Jewish group as the Covenanters were.[3] Equally clearly the rules of the qiddûš cannot be harmonized with those of the 'banquet'. Only men were expected to
be present at this, so far as the present evidence would suggest, a priest
would preside in accordance with the normal practice of the Covenanters,[4] no special food or drink would be served except that 'liquor
(tîrôš)' and not 'wine (yayin)' would be drunk, the priest would bless
both and, when he had helped himself, the others would do likewise;
and no explanation of the ceremony, no reading of set passages from
the Scriptures and no singing of Psalms is prescribed.

Equally the Last Supper must be dissociated from the 'Messianic
banquet', with which it agrees only on a few small points: that men
only were present (possibly only an exceptional arrangement because
Jesus, expecting to be arrested at any moment, wished to have only
the innermost circle of his followers with him on so solemn an occasion
and perhaps because for the same reason he thought it one unsuitable
for women), that according to the majority of the witnesses the bread
was blessed and handed round before the wine (I Q 28A ii 17–20;
cp. D vi 4–5),[5] and that those present helped themselves to the food.[6]
That Peter beckoned to John at the Last Supper to ask Jesus who
would betray him[7] was not the consequence of rules of seniority
similar to those enforced among the Covenanters in addressing fellow-
members (D vi 4–5)[8] but was simply that he preferred to put an
embarrassing question to him not openly but through the disciple
sitting nearest to him. Otherwise, the differences between the two

[1] Sutcliffe in HJ I 49–56; cp. Rowley in BJRL XLIV 144–5.
[2] P. 60; cp. Brownlee Discipline 23.
[3] Jeremias Die Abendmahlsworte Jesu 30.   [4] P. 61.
[5] Matt. xxvi. 26–8, Mk. xiv. 22–4 and 1 Cor. xi 23–7 (bread before wine); Lk.
xxii. 17–20 and 1 Cor. x. 16, 21 (wine before bread).
[6] Matt. xxvi. 23 and Mk. xiv. 20.   [7] Jn. xiii. 23-4.
[8] Kuhn in Stendahl Scrolls 69.

meals are marked. The 'Messianic banquet' was not expected to take place at any named time of day, as the Last Supper was eaten in the evening; Jesus, though not a priest, presided and after washing the feet of His disciples spoke the words of institution over the bread and the wine[1] and then passed them round the company, whereupon the meal proceeded; and at its end they sang a hymn. On the one hand, no ceremony comparable to the washing of the feet, not even of the hands, although the Covenanters practised frequent ablutions or lustrations,[2] no ceremony in the least degree resembling the solemn blessing of the elements and the handing of them to the company, was prescribed at the 'Messianic banquet'; and no hymn was sung at the end of any of the Covenanters' meals. On the other hand, nothing in the Christian meal resembled the Covenanters' strict observance of precedence or the provision whereby, after the priestly blessing of the bread and wine, the Messiah laid his hand on the food and each member of the company pronounced a blessing according to his rank (I Q 28A ii 20–1).

Reference has already been made to the fact that the Covenanters drank 'liquor (tîrôš)'; this, whatever the term meant to the ancient Hebrews,[3] was clearly distinguished from yayin by the Rabbis.[4] Its choice, therefore, looks deliberate and suggests that, as the Essenes practised 'invariable sobriety' and the limitation of their allotted food (τροφή) and drink (ποτόν) to the requirements of nature,[5] so the Covenanters avoided fully fermented wine in favour of must or the lightly fermented juice of the grape. Contrariwise, what was drunk at the Last Supper, though called only 'the fruit of the vine',[6] was soon identified as 'wine (οἶνος)',[7] i.e. the fully fermented juice of the vine (which οἶνος always means). At the same time, although the food of the Covenanters at their ordinary meals (D vi 5, 6) as also at the 'Messianic' banquet, is called 'bread (leḥem)', this word, though commonly so translated,[8] does not necessarily mean this; it is used also for 'food, meal' in a general sense,[9] even for that of animals e.g. worms (W xi 21),[10] and it can include honey[11] and meat.[12] The Covenanters would hardly have lived on bread alone; consequently leḥem in the passages under discussion must have had the same connotation as τροφή

---

[1] Cp. Edersheim Jesus the Messiah II 497.   [2] P. 68; cp. p. 43.
[3] Cp. Driver & Lanchester Joel and Amos 81–2.
[4] P. Talmud Nedarim vii 40b; cp. Tosefta Nedarim iv 3.
[5] Josephus War II viii 5 § 133.
[6] Matt. xxvi. 29, Mk. xiv. 25, Lk. xxii. 18.   [7] Clement Ad Paedagogum ii 32.
[8] Brownlee Discipline 23 and Gaster Scriptures 59.
[9] E.g. Gen. xliii. 25, 32 and Exod. xvi. 22, 29.
[10] Cp. Isa. lxv 25 (food of serpents) and Prov. vi 8 (food of ants).
[11] 1 Sam. xiv. 24, 28.
[12] Judg. xiii. 15–16 (kid), Ezek. xliv. 7 (fat and blood of sacrifices), Ecclus. vii. 31 (bulls).

when applied to the food of the Essenes and must be taken to include whatever they ate.[1] The *leḥem* of the Covenanters therefore is hardly on the same plane as the 'bread' (ἄρτος, which has no other sense) of the Last Supper and the Eucharist;[2] and the attempt to identify them involves the fallacy of identifying a general with a particular term.

Strong as these arguments may appear against connecting the Last Supper with and so deriving the Christian sacrament, however indirectly, from the supposed 'Messianic banquet' of the Covenanters, two others may be added, as they seem as nearly conclusive as possible against any such identification. First, the 'words of institution', showing the purpose of the Last Supper, clearly marked it off as something quite different from this 'banquet', which lacked any explanatory words or phrases, and from the other two meals which were accompanied by different explanations showing what their respective purposes were. Second, the purposes of all these meals were distinct: the Paschal meal was a memorial feast recalling a long-past historical event, the *qiddûš* was celebrated to sanctify the following day, whether Sabbath or other feast, the Last Supper was made the occasion of the Lord's final charge to his disciples, and the 'Messianic banquet' was intended as the celebration of the Messianic victory 'at the end of the days'.

What has hitherto also been overlooked in the desire to connect the communal meals of the Essenes and the Covenanters with the Last Supper or the Eucharist and even to derive the latter from one or both of the former is the primitive practice of the church immediately after the Resurrection (as Dr. L. Bange privately suggests), when 'all that believed were together and had all things common. . . . And day by day, continuing steadfastly with one accord in the temple and breaking bread at home, they did take their food with gladness and singleness of heart, praising God and having favour with all the people'.[3] Here is a daily communal meal; and, as these early Christians will almost certainly still have observed the ordinary Jewish ablutions before meals (although the text says nothing of them), this meal, and this alone, held by groups of Christians in their own homes, can be compared or identified with those of the Essenes and the Covenanters in their refectories (or in their homes in the case of members living in the world). This Christian meal is obviously not the Last Supper, and the account of it attaches no Eucharistic significance to it; it can therefore have been, like the communal meals of the Essenes and the Covenanters, nothing but the customary Jewish evening meal, adapted

---

[1] Sutcliffe *Heythr. Journ.* I 49–51.
[2] Matt. xxvi. 26, Mk. xiv. 22, Lk. xxii. 19; cp. 1 Cor. xi. 23–4, 26–7.
[3] Acts ii. 44–6.

to the circumstances of the moment and the needs of the society holding it.

The Lord's Supper or Eucharist, in so far as it came to be celebrated in the earliest Palestinian tradition and as a complete meal, only superficially resembles the common meal of the Essenes and the Covenanters. Their meals were taken twice daily, while the Lord's Supper was celebrated only once a week; both were eaten together after a grace, but this was how many, if not most, Jewish meals were taken. Also, only men were present at their meals, whereas persons of both sexes partook of the Eucharist. The meals of the Essenes and the Covenanters derived their peculiar nature, incidentally cultic rather than sacramental, from the unavoidable circumstances in which they took place and remained always the ordinary meals of the day, like those of members of religious orders in their refectories; the Lord's Supper was in essence a cult-meal and eventually grew into the Eucharist. Whatever the model of this Supper was, Jesus changed its nature by his explanatory words and so turned it into such a meal celebrated in memory of his death;[1] but not the slightest evidence has been found to show that the Covenanters' meal was in any sense a commemoration of the Rightful Teacher or of his death.[2] The apostle Paul then interpreted partaking of the bread and the wine of the Eucharist as enabling the believer to share in the body and blood of Christ and to become incorporated thereby in His mystical body; no such doctrine appears in the Scrolls.

A somewhat similar idea is developed in the story of *Joseph and Asenath*, in which the God-fearing man or woman 'eats the bread of life and drinks the cup of immortality'.[3] This is a Jewish story and the meal described in it has been compared with those of the Essenes and the Covenanters on the ground that it, like theirs, was a cult-meal.[4] The story however has been Christianized and in its present form can hardly be dated before the 4th or 5th century A.D.[5] while it recalls the 'bread of life' of the Gospel[6] and the Eucharist as the 'medicine of immortality'[7] rather than anything in the meals of the above-mentioned groups.

In conclusion, all these meals, whether of Essenes or of Covenanters or of Pharisaic 'association', whether Paschal meal or *qiddûš*, whether Last Supper or Eucharist, were or arose out of the ordinary evening meal of any pious Jewish group; but a special character was given to them when any event was brought into connection with them. Fundamentally, therefore, the same general procedure was followed

---

[1] 1 Cor. xi. 26.
[2] Rowley *Scrolls* 19.
[3] Batiffol *Stud. Patr.* I 64.
[4] Kuhn in Stendahl *Scrolls* 83–4.
[5] Cp. Black *Scrolls* 105–6.
[6] Jn. vi. 35.
[7] Ignatius *Ephesians* xx 2.

in all of them, so that the details would be similar if not identical; but the particular rites appropriate to each occasion naturally varied with the event, past or present or future, with which any individual meal was associated. Consequently such statements as these, that 'the early Christian sacrament was the Essenic [*i.e.* Covenanters'] sacrament with, perhaps, some Christian adaptations'[1] or that the 'Messianic banquet' of the Covenanters is now to be seen as 'the framework of the Last Supper'[2] are nothing but travesties of the facts. The Covenanters had no sacrament, and the only resemblance of the Christian sacrament to the Covenanters' 'Messianic banquet' was that both were adaptations of regular Jewish meals; and several other Jewish ceremonial meals were derived from the same source.

[1] Davies *Scrolls* 130.
[2] Allegro *People of the Dead Sea Scrolls* 190.

X

COVENANT AND TESTAMENT

1. Common Words and Phrases

Coincidences between[1] the Scrolls and the New Testament are numerous, some trivial but others significant. Here too enthusiasm has tended to outrun caution and rash claims, based on mistranslation or misinterpretation or unproved assumptions, have been put forward. For example, the title of the Rightful Teacher, even if it is translated Teacher of Righteousness,[2] and the description of Noah as a 'preacher of righteousness'[3] cannot properly be compared;[4] the two are not identical in form and the underlying conceptions are quite different. Recourse has even been had to inventing a fictitious Hebrew expression, namely *rûaḥ ṭā'ût* 'spirit of error',[5] to illustrate the Greek πνεῦμα πλάνης of the New Testament[6]; but the noun is otherwise spelt (*ṭā'ût*, not *ṭā'ût*) in the Scrolls (D iii 21 T ii 14 iv 12, 16, 20), and the phrase itself is not found in them. It is also unknown in Hebrew literature, if the dictionaries may be trusted; but the Greek form of it occurs once in a work commonly supposed to have been translated from an original Hebrew text,[7] and the corresponding Aramaic phrase is used in the Targum to render two quite different Hebrew expressions.[8]

Both Testaments and the Scrolls describe life as a 'refining' (D i 17–18 viii 4; cp. Z ix 49) or a 'time of refining' (APs.b i 3 ii 4),[9] which may perhaps be identified with 'the end of the days' (AFl.e i 19–ii 1);[10] and similarly religion is called a 'way' (D ix 18 x 21; cp. Z i 8 ii 4).[11] Both, too, use similar terms to describe false teaching: for example, the apostolic charge 'that they teach no other doctrine'[12] is parallel to the denunciation of 'the preaching of false prophets . . .; for they speak with barbarous lips and another tongue to Thy people' in one of the Scrolls (T iv 16; cp. ii 19); for 'other' connotes not 'foreign',

---

[1] Cp. Grossouw in *Stud. Cath.* XXVII 1–8, Winter in *St. Th.* XII 103–5, Flusser in *Scr. Hieros.* IV 263–4.

[2] Pp. 253–6.   [3] 2 Pet. ii. 5.

[4] Vermès in *Cah. Sion.* IV 194.

[5] Albright in Davies & Daube *Background of the New Testament* 168.

[6] Jn. xiv. 17, xv. 26, xvi. 13 and 1 Jn. iv. 6; cp. Jer. iv. 11 (LXX) and Psalms of Solomon viii 15.

[7] Testaments *Judah* xx. 1.   [8] Targum on Isa. xix. 14 and Hos. iv. 12, v. 4.

[9] Dan. xi. 35; 1 Pet. iv. 12 (cp. i. 7) and Rev. iii. 10.

[10] Cp. 1 Cor. x. 11.   [11] Prov. xxiii. 19; Acts ii. 28.

[12] 1 Tim. i. 3.

as in the original use of the expression,[1] but 'unorthodox' in both passages.[2] Other expressions, some coming very close (so far as the difference of language allows a comparison) to the corresponding expressions in the New Testament, are 'dominion of darkness' (T xii 6), 'wealth of wickedness' (Z ix 15; cp. D x 19), 'eyes of adultery' (D i 6, Z iii 12), and 'to cleave to all good works' (D xi 7–8).[3]

Far the most important common terms are those for the 'covenant' and the 'new covenant', which the Covenanters took directly from the Hebrew Bible and which the Church adopted in the Greek form from the Septuagint; for the whole conception was fundamental to the two societies and runs through all their writings. So the former called themselves 'the men of the covenant' (T fr. iv 8) and 'the sons of His (*sc.* God's) covenant' (W xvii 8),[4] while the latter were 'the children of the prophet and of the covenant which God made with our fathers'.[5] This conception of the covenant as a pact or agreement between God and the society at Qumrân or the church, as the case might be, was more or less the same in the Scrolls and the New Testament; but those of the 'new covenant' in the Scrolls (H ii 3 [?], Z viii 15) and the New Testament[6] were very different, as shown above,[7] and the language was almost the only link between them.

Other expressions identical in form but different in import can be found in the Scrolls and the New Testament. For example, both the Scrolls and the New Testament use the figure of a fountain of living water, derived from the Old Testament, where it is now a figure for God Himself[8] and now for the teaching of the sages;[9] in the Scrolls the 'spring' or 'well of living waters' is now the words put into the poet's mouth by God (T viii 16) and now the Law (Z ix 28; cp. v 3),[10] but in the New Testament it is now Christ himself,[11] now a gift bestowed by God on the believer[12] or the source to which He leads him,[13] and now a power within him 'springing up to everlasting life'.[14] The figure is the same but its application is different. In all such cases the differences are especially important, as they tell against any theory of direct or immediate borrowing on the part either of Covenanters or of Christians; both, if they have not independently developed these and such like figures of speech, have derived them from the common religious vocabulary of the age.

---

[1] Isa. xxviii. 11.   [2] Gertner in *BSOAS*. XXV 1–2.
[3] Cp. Lk. xxii. 53 and Col. i. 13 ('power of darkness'); Lk. xvi. 9 ('mammon of unrighteousness'); 2 Pet. ii. 14 ('eyes full of adultery'); Rom. xii. 9 ('cleave to that which is good').
[4] Cp. Ps. cli *ad finem* (Sandars in *ZAtW* LXXV 75–6 and Tosefta *Berakoth* iii 7 (s. pp. 452, 454).   [5] Acts iii. 25.
[6] Matt. xxvi. 28, Mk. xiv. 24; 1 Cor. xi. 25, 2 Cor. iii. 6; Hebr. ix. 15, xii. 24.
[7] Pp. 73–4, 305–10.   [8] Jer. ii. 13; cp. Psa. xxxvi. 9.
[9] Prov. xiii. 14.   [10] P. 52.   [11] Rev. vii. 17.
[12] *Ibid.* xxi. 6.   [13] *Ibid.* vii. 17.   [14] Jn. iv. 14; cp. vii. 38.

The attitudes of the two societies to the Law differed fundamentally, although they used identical expressions in reference to it. Jesus and perhaps also the Rightful Teacher (if he is the speaker) claimed to have come 'to fulfil the Law' (T vi 10, if the text is then rightly restored);[1] but the aim of the former was to spiritualize it, that of the latter to ensure its literal fulfilment in every petty detail.[2] Both spoke of 'the works of the Law' (AFl. c i 7 = YFl. c i 7)[3] but while in the one they were contrasted with works of faith, in the latter they meant the ritual requirements of the Mosaic law as carried out in the Temple. In fact, this expression had almost opposite meanings for the two societies; and the divergence suggests not that the one borrowed it from the other but that each took it from contemporary speech and then put its own meaning on it. So, too, as the Covenanter must cultivate 'zeal for righteous ordinances' (D iv 4) and show himself 'zealous for the precept and its season . . . so as to do the acceptable thing in every occupation of his hands' (D ix 23), the Apostle claimed to be 'exceedingly zealous of the traditions of my fathers'[4]; but they meant differing things, the former thinking of the law as interpreted by his society and its aspirations and the latter referring to the law as understood by the ordinary Jew.[5] The language was the same but its import was different.

Not unnaturally Covenanters and Christians, having so much common to them both, described membership of their respective societies, their position in the world and manner of life, their hopes and fears, their organization and their hierarchy, in comparable terms. Some of these were shared with other bodies, others were peculiar to themselves.

Both societies are said to be founded 'on a rock' (T vi 26; cp. vii 8–9)[6] in a world in which 'men of holiness' and 'men of wickedness' (D v 10–14 and similarly elsewhere), the 'unrighteous' and the 'saints',[7] are for ever set against one another; and the Covenanters are held 'by the bonds of the spirit' (T fr. ix 6, if the phrase is rightly taken as referring to them; for it preserved on a minute fragment, so that the context is lost), just as Paul is 'bound in the spirit' to the fulfilment of his mission.[8] Further, as the Apostle declares that 'we are made as the filth of the world, the offscourings of all things,'[9] so the Rightful Teacher describes himself in similar terms as having been placed by God 'with the muck in the sweepings beneath the feet' (T v 21). Thus the Covenanters are 'meek in spirit' (W xiv 7) as Christians are

---

[1] Matt. v. 17; cp. Dupont-Sommer *Écrits Esséniens* 233[1] and Licht *Thanksgiving Hymns* 112 (who reads 'to magnify the Law', which is perhaps preferable).
[2] Cp. pp. 83–94.   [3] Rom. iii. 28 and Gal. ii. 16, iii. 2, 10; cp. Rom. ii. 15.
[4] Gal. i. 4.   [5] Cp. 2 Macc. iv. 2.   [6] Matt. xvi. 18.
[7] 1 Cor. vi. 1.   [8] Acts xx. 22.   [9] 1 Cor. iv. 13.

'poor in spirit';[1] and the description of them as 'sons of favour' or 'good will' (T iv 32–3 xi 9) and as 'elect of favour' or 'good will' (D vii 6) recalls both the Evangelist's 'men of goodwill'[2] and the Apostle's 'election of grace' or 'favour'.[3] Further, the members of both societies are urged 'to do truth' (D i 5)[4] and to be engaged in all the 'works of God' (D iv 3–4);[5] they are God-fearing (Z x 15)[6] and 'elect of God' (D ix 14 H x 3),[7] they are 'perfect' (D iii 3)[8] and 'saints' (D v 13 viii 17, 23 ix 8; cp. v 18);[9] they walk 'by' or 'in the spirit' (D iv 6)[10] and sing 'with understanding' (D x 9);[11] they look for 'the end of the days' (H ii 56 Z vi 2) or 'the last time' (D iv 17),[12] expecting the Messianic age to be ushered in by a world-wide war (W i 10–12 and *passim*)[13] and hoping for the 'crown of glory' awarded to the righteous hereafter (D iv 7 T ix 24);[14] and, while the one is warned that the faithless steward's master 'will appoint his portion with hypocrites and sinners',[15] the other is taught that God 'will put his (*sc.* the apostate's) lot in the midst of the eternally damned' (D ii 17).

A common terminology, some of it derived ultimately from the Old Testament, serves also to a considerable extent to describe the organization of the two communities; for both were essentially sacerdotal or hierarchical societies.[16]

Already in the Old Testament men had been chosen by lot for special duties,[17] and so election to the society of the Covenanters was by lot (D v 2–3 vi 15–23), as it was to office among the Essenes[18] and in the Church;[19] and new members were said to be 'added' both to it and to the Covenanters (D vi 4).[20] Already, too, in the Old Testament the Lord had been called the 'lot' (κλῆρος according to the Septuagint) of the Levites;[21] but long afterwards, by an inversion in the use of the term, the Covenanters called themselves the 'lot of God' (D ii 2 W xiii 5) and their adversaries the 'lot of Belial' (D ii 5 W i 5) or the 'lot of darkness' (W xiii 5), just as the ministers of the church came to be called 'clergy', *i.e.* the 'lot' of God, early in the 2nd century A.D.[22] This use of 'lot', therefore, for a group or body of men seems to be characteristic of the early Christian centuries; for it has not been

---

[1] Matt. v. 3.   [2] Lk. ii 14 (s. Hunzinger *ap.* Kuhn in *ZNtW* XLIV 85–90).
[3] Rom. xi. 5.   [4] Jn. iii. 21; cp. Neh. ix. 33.   [5] Jn. vi. 28.
[6] Acts xiii. 16.   [7] Rom. viii. 22, Col. iii. 12, Tit. i. 1.
[8] Phil. iii. 15 and Col. iv. 12; Jas. i. 4.
[9] Acts ix. 13, 32, 41, xxvi. 10 (and elsewhere).   [10] Gal. v. 16.
[11] 1 Cor. xiv. 15; cp. Targum on Psa. xlvii. 8 (where the Hebrew and Aramaic nouns are different from that in the Scroll).
[12] Heb. i. 2, 1 Pet. i. 20.   [13] Cp. Matt. xxiv. 6–8 and Lk. xxii. 36–8.
[14] 1 Pet. v. 4   [15] Matt. xxiv. 51; cp. Lk. xii 46.
[16] Cp. Black *Scrolls* 80–1.   [17] 1 Chron. xxiv. 7, xxv. 8.
[18] Josephus *War* II viii 3 § 123.   [19] Acts i. 23–6.
[20] Deut. xviii. 1–2.   [21] Deut. x. 9, xviii. 2.
[22] Moulton & Milligan *Vocabulary of the Greek Testament* 347 and Sophocles *Greek Lexicon of the Roman and Byzantine Periods* 668.

found otherwise before the age of the Church. Other terms which may be compared are those for 'mass, multitude (*rōḇ* or *rôḇ*; πλῆθος)'; for the uses to which they are put are strangely parallel.[1] As the Hebrew term designates both the 'mass (*rōḇ*)' of Israelite converts to the society of the Covenanters and apparently also the 'group (*rôḇ*)' of senior members who have certain responsibilities shared with the priests, so the Greek term designates both the 'mass' of early believers in the Church[2] and also the 'group' of Disciples who present seven members to the Apostles for appointment 'to serve tables';[3] for the supposition that the whole mass of believers or disciples, already exceeding 3000 and even 5000 persons,[4] can have been engaged in this business is highly improbable. Indeed, the *rôḇ* and the πλῆθος as plenary committees perform similar functions, the *rôḇ* being concerned especially with the admission of novices to full membership (D vi 18–20) and the πλῆθος presenting persons for appointment to office. So too the πλῆθος is the supreme council of Apostles and Elders who decide questions of policy at Jerusalem[5] but the general mass of believers at Antioch.[6] In the same way 'the Many (*hā-rabbîm*)' among the Covenanters and 'the More (οἱ πλείονες)' in the Church may be equated; for they have at any rate one common function, that of trying disputes between the members of their respective societies (D vi 1).[7] That the Essenes and the Pharisaic 'associations (*ḥaḇūrôt*)' used corresponding or identical terms, as the case might be,[8] for their fully professed members argues contemporary social custom and religious jargon.

Briefly, then, if the society of the Covenanters is rightly regarded as composed not of four orders (priests, elders, lay members, novices) corresponding to the four orders of the Essenes[9] (which however are generally thought to be quite different, namely, those of full membership and of the three stages of the novitiate),[10] but of three orders (priests with Levites, lay members and novices in *Discipline*; or priests with Levites, Israelites and proselytes in the *Zadokite Documents*),[11] its organization can properly be compared with that of the Church with its three orders (clergy, baptized laymen, catechumens).

Each society had its own hierarchy with parallel grades (so far as these can be determined) and functions. Thus, as the Christian 'deacon (διάκονος)' cared for the material needs of his fellow Christians,[12] so the

---

[1] Pp. 58–60.
[2] Acts iv. 32.
[3] *Ibid*. vi. 2–6.
[4] *Ibid*. ii. 41, iv. 4.
[5] Acts xv. 12; cp. i. 15 (where ὄχλος describes an informal or unofficial number of Christians assembled more or less by chance).
[6] *Ibid*. 30.
[7] 2 Cor. ii. 6; cp. iv. 15 (where οἱ πλείονες seems to have the same connotation).
[8] Pp. 95–8.
[9] Josephus *War* II viii 10 § 158.
[10] Lightfoot *Colossians* 128–9.
[11] P. 63.
[12] Phil. i. 1 and 1 Tim. iii. 8–10; cp. Acts vi. 1–6.

Covenanters' 'censor' or 'inspector $(m^e\underline{b}aqq\bar{e}r)$' (D vi 20) was responsible for the management of their property; in the same way 'stewards
($\dot{\epsilon}\pi\dot{\iota}\tau\varrho o\pi o\iota$)' and 'overseers of property ($\tau\tilde{\omega}\nu$ $\varkappa o\iota\nu\tilde{\omega}\nu$ $\dot{\epsilon}\pi\iota\mu\epsilon\lambda\eta\tau a\dot{\iota}$)'
performed similar duties for the Essenes.[1] The Covenanters' 'censor'
or 'inspector who is over the Many', as he is once further described
(D vi 11–12 Z ix 18), is probably identical with the 'officer $(p\bar{a}q\hat{\iota}\underline{d})$
at the head of the Many' (D vi 14);[2] and so he seems to have been,
as his title implies, the principal officer of the society. As such, he
has not unnaturally been regarded as holding the same sort of
position as the 'bishop $(\dot{\epsilon}\pi\dot{\iota}\sigma\varkappa o\pi o\varsigma)$',[3] who is always named at the
head of the officers of the Church in the New Testament;[4] and this
identification has been illustrated by a passage in the Old Testa-
ment in which the Hebrew word for 'officer $(p\bar{a}q\hat{\iota}\underline{d})$' is translated
'overseer $(\dot{\epsilon}\pi\dot{\iota}\sigma\varkappa o\pi o\varsigma)$' by the Septuagint.[5] Such a rendering, however,
has no value as evidence for the identification of the officers in question.
What is worth notice is that 'inspector $(m^e\underline{b}aqq\bar{e}r)$' was a known Jewish
title in the Talmudic age, being borne by the official 'inspector'
who examined beasts and birds offered for sacrifice to ensure that they
had no defects which might disqualify them as offerings in the Temple;[6]
and it may also perhaps be recognized as a personal name (although
its meaning here is disputed) in Nabataean inscriptions from the
1st century A.D. onwards.[7] Lastly, both societies granted a certain
precedence to the 'elders' (D vi 8–9; cp. Z x 2),[8] as also the Essenes
did;[9] but, although both derived the title from the Old Testament[10] and
were well acquainted with it from contemporary Jewish usage,[11]
Christians seem to have gone beyond the other societies in making the
elder a specially appointed or ordained officer.[12]

The comparison of the hierarchy at Qumrân, however, with that of
the Christian church is largely superficial; for the resemblances are for
the most part purely external.

The 'censor' or 'inspector' of the Covenanters was not (at any rate
necessarily) a priest; for, even though described as being 'at the head
of' or 'over' the community, he had beside him 'the priest appointed
for the Many' (Z xvii 5), who was senior in age to himself and would
have been capable of performing all the required priestly offices.
Further, although some of the censor's duties, e.g. giving religious
instruction, might suitably have fallen to a priest, others were purely

[1] Josephus War II viii 3 § 123 (overseers) and 6 § 134 (stewards).
[2] P. 62; cp. Rowley Zadokite Fragments 37¹.
[3] Eiss in Welt des Orients II 514–19; cp. Hölscher in ZNt W XXVIII 39.
[4] Acts xx. 28, Phil. i. 1, 1 Tim. iii. 1–7.   [5] Neh. (2 Esdras) xi 9, 14, 22.
[6] B. Talmud Ketuboth 106a.   [7] Euting Sinäitische Inschriften 2–3.
[8] E.g. Acts xv. 6.
[9] Josephus Antiquities XVIII i 5 § 22 and War II viii 9 § 146.
[10] E.g. Lev. iv. 15.   [11] Cp. Acts iv. 5, 23.
[12] Ibid. xiv. 23.

secular, *e.g.* the management of property; in this respect the Essenes' 'steward (ἐπιμελητής or ἐπίτροπος)' rather than the Christian 'bishop (ἐπίσκοπος)' resembled the 'inspector' of the Covenanters, even if the titles of 'inspector' and 'overseer' (*i.e.* 'bishop') would seem to argue similarity if not identity of functions. The priests and Levites, who played an important part in the community of the Covenanters, performed the duties reserved for their class, as the clergy of the church did for theirs; but, while the church rejected the Jewish priesthood, the Covenanters sought to replace the old and, as they thought, corrupt priesthood serving the Temple at Jerusalem by a purer priesthood of the Zadokite line.[1] The 'elders' of the Covenanters had no official duties but merely enjoyed a modest precedence after the priests (D vi 8–9, Z x 2), such as the older enjoyed over the younger Essenes;[2] they were in no sense a body of ordained ministers with definite spiritual obligations corresponding to the 'presbyters' or 'elders of the church'.[3] The 'twelve men' and the three priests 'perfect in all that is revealed of the Law' at Qumrân (D viii 1), who were responsible for the spiritual welfare of the Covenanters,[4] cannot be identified with the twelve Apostles, of whom three were held in especial honour as 'reputed to be pillars' of the Church[5] (James, Cephas, John); for the form of the Hebrew expression indicates that the 'three priests' were additional to, not included in, the 'twelve men' and indeed that these twelve were laymen. This conclusion is confirmed by a recently discovered fragment of a Scroll which gives their number as fifteen.[6] Further, as Prof. Rowley has pointed out,[7] the disciples cannot have been in any way connected with these officers at Qumrân; for, whether the ministry of Jesus lasted for one or for three years, they would not have had time to pass through the three years' novitiate prescribed for those who wished to join the society and then to attain sufficient seniority to qualify them for such posts. In any case, none of the officers of the Covenanters, however they may or may not resemble those of the church in external respects, bears any resemblance to the apostles and prophets as a ministry of special gifts or any real resemblance to the bishops, presbyters and deacons, appointed by the Apostles as an ordinary local ministry of officers 'who are over' or 'which bear rule over' the several churches.[8] Lastly, the Covenanters set up ten judges to try disputes between members living in outlying communities away from Qumrân;[9] but the early church apparently

---

[1] Cp. Freedman in *JBL* LXXVIII 329.
[2] Josephus *Antiquities* XVIII i 5 § 22 and *War* II viii 8 § 146 and 10 § 150.
[3] Acts xi. 29–30, xv. 22–9, xx. 17; 1 Tim. iv. 14, Jas. v. 4, 1 Pet. v. 1–3.
[4] Pp. 61–2.
[5] Gaster *Scriptures* 107 and Reicke *ap.* Van der Ploeg in *Rech. Bibl.* IV 63.
[6] Milik in *RB*, NS LXIV 588–9.   [7] In *BJRL* XLIV 140.
[8] 1 Thess. v. 12 and Heb. xiii. 7, 17.   [9] Pp. 64–5.

had no such officers. Both societies otherwise left such disputes to be settled in ordinary sessions of their members, thus preventing them from being taken 'before the unjust' or 'before unbelievers' and keeping them 'before the saints', *i.e.* before their fellow-believers; in this way the whole body, the *rabbîm* of the Covenanters[1] and the πλείονες of the Church[2], tried its own members. The Essenes, too, took similar precautions to save their society from grave public scandal.[3]

A practice of the Christian community which has been cited as proof of an organic connection between it and the Covenanters is the supposed communism of the two groups. Reasons, however, have been given for believing that, while the Essenes observed a strictly common ownership of property, the Covenanters were content with the common administration of the property of individual members and each member retained the power, under certain restrictions, to dispose of his as he liked.[4] The early church does seem for a brief while to have practised some form of common ownership;[5] but the offence for which Ananias and Sapphira were punished was withholding something which they had devoted, *i.e.* solemnly promised to contribute, to a capital fund for poor relief, not for failing to surrender their possessions to a common pool, since Peter said 'while it remained, was it not thine own? And after it was sold, was it not in thine own power?'[6] The property had been declared 'corban', as it were, and might not be diverted to other purposes. The practices of these groups were in no sense identical: the Essenes practised communism, the Covenanters observed a common administration of members' property, and the Christians normally retained possession and control of their own property while making generous contributions to the needs of other members or churches.[7] The Covenanters' contributions for the relief of widows and orphans and such like persons are of course comparable to those made by Christians to similar purposes, of which writers in the New Testament and the fathers of the church often speak; but other Jewish and even pagan societies did likewise. Yet, although the rules of these societies in the matter of property do not seem in actual practice to have been identical, the significant point is that the idea of a common ownership or administration (or whatever it may have been) of members' possessions is apparently quite unknown before the 1st century A.D., when three or four different communities are suddenly found practising it in some form or other (Essenes and Therapeuts,[8] Covenanters and Christians). This can be no accident; and, although nothing is known of Essene practice before this period, the assumption is possible that the full development of the practice as

[1] Pp. 57–8.   [2] 1 Cor. vi. 1–6.   [3] Josephus *War* II viii 9 § 145.
[4] Pp. 114–5.   [5] Acts ii. 44–5, iv. 32.   [6] *Ibid.* v. 1–10.
[7] Cp. Teicher in *JJS* IV 6–7.   [8] P. 122.

Josephus and other writers describe it cannot have been reached much before then. Once again, on this as on other scores, the Covenanters fall into place in the 1st century A.D.

Two different points of contact between the practice of the Covenanters and the church have here been examined; these are those of language and organization. Comparison however of the terminology of the Scrolls with that of the New Testament is made imprecise by difference of language; and their organizations can be studied only through the language which, being imperfectly understood, often leaves the precise equivalence of Hebrew and Greek terms hard to define.

Linguistic similarities raise three difficult questions. First, are the common terms derived from a common source or not; and, if so, is the source a work composed long ago and very possibly now lost or is it the current and usually very imperfectly known jargon of the time, whether of the market-place or of synagogue or church? Second, if the common matter in a written work is borrowed, which writer is the borrower? Third, do the echoes of the Gospels in the Scrolls reflect the *ipsissima verba* of the speaker or the words of the Evangelist who is reporting them? Every case must be examined on its merits; but one rule can safely be laid down, that a work is as late as the latest contact which it makes or the latest allusion which it contains. For example, Josephus is otherwise the earliest writer to make the distinction between touching food and drink on the one hand and eating and drinking them on the other hand;[1] but, as the Essenes may have drawn the same distinction both in practice and in speech before his time, it cannot be pressed to prove the date of the Scroll in which it too is found. Contrariwise, other expressions in the Scrolls have some evidential value. One such phrase is the 'household of truth' (D v 6), which immediately recalls 'them that are of the household of faith';[2] but Strabo speaks of 'them that are of the household of wisdom'[3] and Iamblichus of 'them that are of the household of innovation'.[4] Or again, the Scrolls talk of the 'mystery of iniquity' (Q I 27 A i 2, T v 36; cp. fr. 50, 6) which has naturally been compared with Paul's 'mystery of lawlessness';[5] but Josephus[6] similarly describes Antipater's career as a 'mystery of wickedness'. Both expressions may then be accepted as *clichés* of the 1st century A.D., as many others in the Scrolls may be, and so suggest that the three works are approximately contemporaneous.

Something of the same sort can be inferred from the organization and administration and the hierarchies of these societies. The all too scanty notices regarding the Essenes before the Christian age contain no hint of any peculiar arrangements or manner of life, and the only plausible inference is that these must have been gradually developed;

---

[1] Pp. 55-6.   [2] Gal. vi. 10.   [3] In *Geographica* XVII i 5.
[4] In *Vita Pythagorica* xxx 176.   [5] 2 Thess. ii. 7.   [6] In *War* I xxiv 1 § 470.

in fact, the conjecture may be hazarded that some (certainly not most or all) Essenes only left the towns and villages, where the rest remained, when the growing hellenization of Jewish life, their persecution at the hands of their fellow Jews for their resistance to these tendencies and their increasing opposition to Roman rule, drove the most zealous members to seek a refuge where they could freely develop their own manner of life, unmolested by native or foreign enemies; such a movement would not be likely to have gathered much force before the complete occupation and administration of Palestine by the Romans after the death of Herod the Great (who befriended the Essenes)[1] in 4 B.C., namely before the 1st century A.D. This was the time when the movement inspired by Judah and Saddok was taking shape[2] and when the Christian church would soon be following suit. It was also the time when the Roman religious and social and other *collegia* were rapidly increasing not only in Italy but also over all the provinces of the empire, when religious persecution by the Romans began and when various Jewish religious 'sodalities' were springing up in Palestine. Such movements in society are catching and the various groups which come into existence commonly exert considerable influence, direct or indirect, on one another; and this must especially be so when two or three such societies, speaking the same language and sprung from the same religion, come into existence within fifty miles of one another. These factors will explain why the three groups, Essenes and Covenanters and Christians, not only formed similar societies but also organized them on parallel lines and even used analogous if not identical terms to describe their customs and practices.

If the Covenanters are thrown back into the 2nd or even the 1st century B.C., these resemblances cannot be explained; for they were forbidden to reveal the secrets of their order to outsiders and their literature disappeared without leaving a trace of itself, lost and unknown till the chance of an accidental discovery at the end of the 8th century A.D. All this does not mean that the Essenes were the Covenanters (for they seem to have grown up in different countries and the differences are too great to permit their identification)[3] or that the Covenanters borrowed their organization and their terminology from the Essenes or from the Church or that the Church borrowed it from either of these groups (for the differences are again such as to exclude any possibility of direct borrowing by either group);[4] what it means is that the societies of the Essenes and the Covenanters reached maturity and the Church grew up in an age when societies and *collegia* proliferated and were a matter of common knowledge and conversation throughout the Roman world; and the various groups or parties in Palestine would be no exception to the general rule.

[1] P. 46.   [2] Pp. 240–1.   [3] Pp. 109–21, 226–37.   [4] Pp. 570–84.

2. PROOF-TEXTS

A practice of the Covenanters, that of the use of proof-texts taken from the Old Testament and their methods of interpreting it to prove this or that doctrine, calls for examination at this point; for, while traces of it can be detected in writings of the Maccabaean age,[1] it appears nowhere in so highly developed a form before the emergence of the strikingly similar methods of proof found in the New Testament.[2]

First, the framework of history is the same and is used for the same purpose, to prove that what has gone before is the preparation for that which is to come. So the apostle Paul and the author of the *Zadokite Documents* both divide the history of the world into three periods: the former into that till Abraham, that from Abraham to Christ and that of faith in Christ,[3] the latter into those from the creation to the days of Noah (Z iii 1–iv 1), from Noah to Abraham (Z iv 2–v 4) and from the covenant with Abraham to that with the Covenanters (Z v 1–vi 8). These three epochs are particularly striking, since they are quite different from the 'ten weeks' or 'twelve weeks' into which history is divided in various apocalyptic works of the 2nd to 1st centuries B.C. and even of the 1st century A.D.[4]

Then both Christians and Covenanters sought proof-texts or *testimonia* in the Scriptures to establish their doctrines; and the three methods which they used are all exemplified in the Scrolls.

First, Epiphanius (*c.* A.D. 315–403) gave a list[5] of signs put against passages in the Scriptures regarded by Christians as theologically important, including a cross for those of christological significance; and in the same way the Scroll of *Isaiah A* has some ten or twelve different symbols inserted against passages which the Covenanters must have regarded as important. As Dr. Schonfield[6] and Fr. Martin[7] have shown, the passages so marked fall into classes dealing with (i) the functions of the Teacher of Righteousness, and (ii) the treachery of the Wicked Priest and the external enemy, exile and restoration.

Those in the first group, marked with a sign resembling a cross (Greek χ), include the following passages:[8]

'behold, a king shall reign in righteousness[9] and princes shall rule in justice';

'behold, my servant whom I uphold, my elect one[10] . . . ; and he shall dispense judgement to the nations';

---

[1] *E.g.* Dan. ix. 2 and 1 Macc. vii. 16–7.
[2] Cp. Dodd *According to the Scriptures* 28–110.
[3] Rom. iii. 1–31, iv. 1–22 and 23–5.
[4] Cp. Daniélou in *Colloque de Strasbourg* 112. [5] In *de Mensuris et Ponderibus* § 1
[6] In *Secrets* 48–51. [7] In *Scribal Character* I 185–7.
[8] Isa. xxxii. 1, xlii. 1, 6, 21, xliv. 28, xlix. 7 (liii. 7), liv. 14, lv. 4, lvi. 1.
[9] Pp. 254–8. [10] Pp. 74–5.

528 COVENANT AND TESTAMENT

'I have called thee in righteousness . . . and will give thee for a covenant[1] of the people, for a light[2] to the Gentiles';

'the Lord is well pleased for his righteousness' sake; He will magnify the Law[3] and make it honourable';

'that saith of Cyrus: He is my shepherd who shall perform all my pleasure; even saying of Jerusalem: She shall be rebuilt, and thou, O temple, shalt be refounded';

'thus saith the Lord God, thy redeemer, O Israel . . .: kings shall see and arise, princes also shall worship';

'in righteousness shalt thou be established: thou shalt be far from oppression . . . ; for it shall not come near thee';

'behold, I have given him for a witness of the peoples, a leader and commander of the peoples';

'thus saith the Lord: Keep ye judgement and do righteousness; for . . . my righteousness is to be revealed'.

All these passages can be applied to Christ as Messiah; but they are equally Messianic in the Jewish sense and as such clearly recall characteristic beliefs of the Covenanters, notably the covenant offered to all who aspire to enter their society (D i 16–18), the position of the Rightful Teacher as 'His (sc. God's) elect' (H v 4 ix 12) and his office as one who is to teach righteousness (Z viii 10), the importance of the study of the Law (D vi 6–7) and of doing justice and righteousness (D i 5–6 v 3–4 viii 1–2 T i 5–6 xiii 19), and God's revelation of His righteousness and salvation to those who fear Him (Z ix 43).

That these passages are selected as Messianic in the Jewish sense is proved by the remaining passages marked by the same symbol,[4] which have little if any specifically Christian relevance.

Those in the second class, which are marked with various other symbols, refer to the actual history and circumstances of the Covenanters and include the following passages:[5]

'for the head of Syria is Damascus';

'and they (sc. Egyptians and Assyrians) shall come and shall rest all of them in the desolate valleys and in the holes of the rocks and upon all thorns and upon all pastures';

'bind up the testimony, seal the law among my disciples; and I will wait for the Lord that hideth his face from the house of Jacob';

[1] Pp. 52–3. [2] Pp. 532, 539–40, 545–6, 558–9. [3] Pp. 94–5.
[4] Isa. xxx. 26, xli. 8–11, 25, xliii. 25, xlviii. 1, liv. 11, 14, lv. 5, lvii. 10, lxv. 12 (s. Mowinckel & Anderson He that cometh 137, 147–8, 214, 243, 269–70, 365–6).
[5] Isa. vii. 8, 19, viii. 16–17, ix. 2, xi. 11, 15, xxviii. 8–9, 15, xxxiii. 1, xl. 2, xliii. 14, xlviii. 20, xlix. 5, 8, li. 7, lii. 7.

'the people that walked in darkness have seen a great light';

'in that day the Lord shall set His hand the second time to recover the remnant of His people';

'and the Lord shall utterly destroy the tongue of the Egyptian Sea and with his scorching wind shall he shake his hand over the River';

'therefore he that made them will not have compassion upon them and he that formed them will show them no favour. And it shall come to pass in that day that the Lord shall beat off his fruit from the flood of the River unto the brook of Egypt';

'all tables are full of vomit and filthiness, so that there is no place clean. Whom will he teach knowledge and whom will he make to understand the message?'

'because ye have said . . .: we have made lies[1] our refuge and under falsehood have we hid ourselves';

'and when thou shalt make an end to deal treacherously, they shall deal treacherously with thee';

'speak ye comfortably to Jerusalem . . . : that her warfare is accomplished, that her iniquity is pardoned';

' . . . and the Chaldaeans in the ships of their triumph';

'go ye forth of Babylon, flee ye from the Chaldaeans';

'though Israel be not gathered, yet shall I be glorious';

'in an acceptable time I have heard thee . . . and will give thee for a covenant of the nations';

'hearken unto me, ye that know righteousness, the people in whose heart is my law . . . ' ;

'how beautiful upon the mountains are the feet of him that bringeth good tidings'.

Here, as there is no single symbol, there is no single theme; yet all the passages are equally applicable to the history and position of the Covenanters. They are the profligacy of the official rulers of the nation and the impossibility of teaching them, and the apostasy of the nation; the summons to the Assyrians and the Egyptians (*i.e.* the Kittians of Asshur and Egypt)[2] to come and punish Israel and their swarming over the land; the vision of the 'great light', *i.e.* the new teacher, and the injunction to his followers to keep his teaching secret; the order to the righteous who are left, *i.e.* the Covenanters, to flee before the enemy; Damascus, the headquarters of the exiles; the ultimate destruction of the enemy without pity, the ingathering of Israel to be a 'covenant of the nations'.

[1] Pp. 53-4.   [2] Pp. 197-216.

The device of using such signs may be due to the influence of Alexandrian scholars; but the exact implication of each remains to be worked out; and the difficulty of the task is increased because some are not clearly placed on the Scroll and the import of the passages, of which there are many others, is not always obvious.[1]

Incidentally the authors of the Scrolls and the writers of the New Testament may use the same or similar *testimonia* from the Old Testament in their respective writings to prove a point and bring out its application to their own circumstances.

For example, both Jesus and the author or compiler of one Scroll applies the statement that 'male and female created He them'[2] to their teaching about divorce (Z vii 1–2);[3] and the promise that 'I will raise them up a prophet from their brethren like unto me',[4] which Peter applies to Jesus,[5] is quoted also in a fragment of a Scroll, of which the context is not clear (for the full text has not yet been published).[6] Or again, the well-known passage describing Zion as 'a stone, a tried stone, a precious corner-stone, a sure foundation'[7] is applied to both the Christian church[8] and the community of the Covenanters (D viii 7–8) and 'prepare ye the way of the Lord in the wilderness, make straight a high way in the desert for our God'[9] is applied to the mission of John the Baptist in the Gospels[10] as to the study of the Law by the Covenanters (D viii 12–16; cp. ix 20–21). Similarly 'a star shall come out of Jacob and a comet shall come out of Israel',[11] which an early apocalyptist referred to the Messiah[12], Christians of the sub-Apostolic age to Christ[13] and Jews to Dositheus and Simon Bar Cochba,[14] are both taken as referring to the 'new covenant' at Damascus by the Covenanters (Z ix 8); and 'smite the shepherd and the sheep shall be scattered',[15] which Christ adapts to Himself,[16] is quoted *verbatim* as applicable to the punishment which the Covenanters will inflict on their enemies (Z ix 2–3).

A final point arising out of the use of proof-texts may here be noticed, namely the three or four set phrases which the authors of the Scrolls employ when introducing formal quotations from the Old Testament. These (literally translated) are generally 'like what is written' (D v 17 viii 14 Z ix 8; All. 9 i 2, 12), occasionally 'for so it is written' (D v 15 Z xiii 27), once 'for it is written' (Z xiv 1) and also

---

[1] Cp. Isa. iii. 1, v. 3, vii. 20, viii. 8, xi. 16, xxi. 12 or 13, xxix. 13, 14, 21, xxx. 1, xli. 1, 4, 16, 21, xlii. 12, xliv. 1, xlv. 1, 11, xlix. 1, liii. 1, lviii. 13, lix. 1, lxi. 9, lxiii. 5, lxiv. 11 or lxv. 1, lxvi. 4, 5.

[2] Gen. i. 27.   [3] Mk. x. 2–9.   [4] Deut. xviii. 18.
[5] Acts xiii. 22.   [6] Barthélemy & Milik *Discoveries* I 121–2.
[7] Isa. xxviii. 16.   [8] Pet. ii. 6.   [9] Isa. xl. 3.
[10] Matt. iii. 3, Mk. i. 3, Lk. iii. 4, Jn. i. 23.   [11] Num. xxiv. 17.
[12] Testaments *Judah* xxiv 1.   [13] Justin Martyr *Dialogue* cvi 4.
[14] Rabin *Zadokite Documents* 30.   [15] Zech. xiii. 7.
[16] Matt. xxvi. 31 and Mk. xiv. 27; cp. Daniélou *op. cit.* 121–2.

perhaps 'as written' (AFl. c i 16; cp. i 15). The first, which is derived
from the Old Testament (where however it is somewhat differently
used),[1] and the second appear in Greek form in the New Testament[2]
and in Aramaic form in Jewish literature of the Amoraic period
(c. A.D. 220–500); the third seems to be confined to the New Testament[3] and the fourth, though not found there, is also not uncommon
in Amoraic literature.[4] No such set phrases are used to introduce
quotations in Maccabaean literature.

Further, as Dr. Schonfield has also pointed out,[5] the allegorical
method of interpreting the Old Testament, which Philo (born c.
20 B.C.) seems to have introduced into Judaism,[6] is used both by the
authors of the Scrolls and by the writers of the New Testament in
precisely the same manner. For example, the author of one of the
Scrolls takes 'the well which the princes have digged (and) the nobles
of the people have delved with the sceptre'[7] and makes the 'well' a
figure for the Law (cp. D vii 20) and the 'staff' for one who interprets
it, the 'princes' for those in Israel who repent and the 'nobles' for those
who walk by it 'in all the epoch of wickedness' (Z viii 3–10),[8] i.e. figures
for the Covenanters under Roman rule.[9] Elsewhere the same author
could say that 'they (sc. the original members of the Covenant) dug a
well for much water, and he that rejects it shall not live' (Z v 3). This
figure of a 'well' for instruction goes back to the apocryphal period,[10]
and 'water' is often similarly used for instruction, especially sacred
instruction, in the Talmud;[11] but Jesus meant something quite different
when He said to the Samaritan woman: 'whosoever shall drink of the
water that I shall give him shall never thirst; but the water that I
shall give him shall be a well of water springing up to eternal life'. The
figure is the same but its interpretation is different.[12] Two prophetical
passages are similarly treated, namely 'ye have borne the tabernacle
of your king and the pedestal of your image . . . ; therefore will I take
you into captivity beyond Damascus' and 'in that day I will raise up
the fallen tabernacle of David . . . , and I will raise up its ruins and
rebuild it as in olden days';[13] the same writer explains that 'the tabernacle of the king' is the Law and the 'king' the head (?) of the congregation (sc. of the Covenanters), while the 'pedestal' is 'the books of the
prophets whose word Israel has despised' (Z ix 5–7), just as James the
brother of Jesus uses 'the tabernacle of David which is fallen down' in
reference to the conversion of the Gentiles.[14] The most striking example

[1] Dan. ix. 13.   [2] E.g. Rom. iii. 4, ix. 13; 2 Cor. iv. 13 (1); Matt. ii. 5 (2).
[3] Matt. xxvi. 31 and Gal. iv. 27.
[4] Bacher Exegetische Terminologie der jüdischen Traditionsliteratur II 91–3.
[5] In Secrets 46–8.   [6] Cp. Preliminary Studies § 44.
[7] Num. xxi. 19.   [8] S. pp. 478–9.   [9] Pp. 202–3.
[10] Cp. Jubilees xxiv 1.
[11] E.g. B. Talmud Chagigah 3a, Baba Metzia 84a, Horayoth 14a; cp. Mishnah Aboth i 11.
[12] Jn. iv. 13–15.   [13] Am. v. 26–7 and ix. 11.   [14] Acts xv. 15–18.

of this method in the present connection is the apostle Paul's comparison of Hagar to mount Sinai 'which gendereth bondage' and of Sarah to Jerusalem which is above and free and 'which is the mother of us all';[1] for in precisely the same way the author of another Scroll, also speaking of the violence done to 'Lebanon' and the 'beasts' by the Wicked Priest, explains that 'Lebanon is the council of the community and the beasts are the simple ones of Judah who fulfil the Law' (H xii 2–4), *i.e.* those of the Covenanters who have remained loyal to the original covenant after the schism.[2] That nothing is known of this method of expounding the Scriptures before the 1st century A.D. is of some moment for fixing the date of the Scrolls; and the use of it in them and in the New Testament suggests that they must be regarded as approximately contemporary.

Philo the Alexandrian early in the 1st century A.D. had set the fashion of the allegorical interpretation of the Hebrew scriptures, for which *testimonia* or proof-texts were necessary;[3] and that both Covenanters and Christians adopted the practice of using such texts as suited to their methods of religious controversy would suggest that the two groups were approximately contemporary. Three facts confirm this impression; that the practice is almost unknown in the religious literature of the preceding centuries; that the two groups tend to employ the same texts, although they adapt them each to their own ends; that both marked such passages in the margins of their copies of the Scriptures; and, lastly, that they both use the same introductory phrases in citing Scripture. Once again, then, the Covenanters are seen to be children of the 1st century A.D. or thereabouts, employing both the language and the tools of that age.

3. PAULINE AND OTHER EPISTLES

In the Scrolls as in the New Testament man appears as flesh, frail and weak, constantly subject to temptation or engaged in ceaseless warfare with the powers of darkness; victory can be gained by the Covenanter only in joining the society of the Sons of Light, by Christians in becoming 'children of light'. For the former 'the way of the Spirit of truth' brings the 'victorious life of eternity' (D iv 2, 7); for the latter faith is 'the victory that overcometh the world.'[4]

During his life on earth man, according to the Scrolls, walks through 'the anguish of a refining furnace' (D viii 4) and those who enter the society of the Covenanters are bidden 'not to turn aside from following Him (*sc.* God) out of fear or anguish or the testing crucible when they are tried in the dominion of Belial' (D i 17–18) or, in other words, are

---

[1] Gal. iv. 22–6.
[3] Cp. Heinemann *Methods of Aggadah* 158.

[2] Pp. 305–10.
[4] 1 Jn. v. 4.

'tested in the refining furnace' (W xvii 1). This testing is going on all the time, throughout a man's whole life, although there is also an ultimate testing which is that of the apocalyptic war at the end of time; this is called 'God's furnace', for which 'the sons of His covenant' are bidden to gird themselves and in which the 'dominion of wickedness'[1] will be finally overthrown (W xvii 4–9). So in the New Testament the world is depicted as a place of trial or testing, in which man lives in constant danger from and ever on guard against the tempter, like a soldier against the enemy. Man is thus constantly 'tempted' or 'tried';[2] and in a similar idiom Jesus speaks of those who 'in the time of temptation' or 'trial' fall away.[3] Here, too, the period of trial is something continuous, lasting throughout the believer's life; and here too there is a final trial, 'an hour of temptation which will come upon all the world, to try them that dwell upon the earth',[4] from which the believer will emerge triumphant. The originator of this trial or temptation besetting man in his earthly life is the devil[5] or Satan,[6] and the idea that it can have been God is expressly repudiated;[7] contrariwise, in the Scrolls God is the creator of both good and evil spirits (D iii 25).[8] The figure of the refining furnace comes, of course, from the Old Testament, and the same Hebrew root is used to describe it there as in the Scrolls, and the writers of the New Testament are as likely to have derived it directly from the Scriptures as from some other religious group; at the same time, while the idea that God can be responsible for tempting man, which comes from the story of Abraham,[9] is retained in the Scrolls, it disappears from the New Testament; and this difference is as significant as the resemblances are in determining the relationship between the Scrolls and the New Testament.

The final test comes in the war against the party of Belial, the angel of darkness and his followers; so 'the going astray of the sons of righteousness is (caused) by the angel of darkness; all their sins and their iniquities and their guilt and their rebellious deeds are (caused) by his dominion in accordance with God's secret purposes till His appointed term; and all their afflictions and their appointed periods of distress are (caused) by the dominion of his hostility, and all the spirits of his party seek to throw down the Sons of Light. The God of Israel and His true angel, however, help all the Sons of Light' (D iii 21–5). Thus God helps His own followers in this spiritual warfare, but He does not extend help to those who have not entered into His covenant and are not therefore members of His party; the destiny of these is fixed, and there is no escaping it. God has also helped His followers by setting a limit to the dominion of wickedness. All men walk in one or other of

[1] Pp. 202–3.	[2] Heb. ii. 18; cp. iv. 15.	[3] Lk. viii. 13.
[4] Rev. iii. 10.	[5] Matt. iv. 3, 5, 8, 11.	[6] 1 Cor. vii. 5.
[7] Jas. i. 13.	[8] Pp. 558–9.	[9] Gen. xxii. 1–19.

MM

the two paths, the path of Good or the path of Evil, according as He has allotted their fate equally to both groups, and He has put eternal enmity between them; but 'by the mysteries of His insight and His glorious wisdom He has set a term for the existence of iniquity and at the appointed time of His visitation He will destroy it for ever; and then the truth of the universe will appear for ever' (D iv 18–19). The Covenanter, like the Christian, in the world was a soldier at war with Belial or Satan and his hosts above and on earth, constantly attacked by temptation and affliction; his weapons are prayer and watching, which is entirely devoted to the study of the Scriptures (D vi 6–8).

This struggle appears most clearly in Paul's epistles, which were being written more or less in the same years as *Discipline* was being compiled.[1] If these were *c.* A.D. 46–66, the link between the Apostle and the Covenanters cannot have been 'the great company of the priests' who were won over to the new faith in Jerusalem *c.* A.D. 33;[2] and it equally cannot have been Damascus, where he was received into the Christian community *c.* A.D. 36–8,[3] even though that city was a haven of refuge for the Covenanters. The two groups of writings, however, reflect much the same background and similar controversies which may have been going on for a number of years; and the similarities are often so striking that discussion of them becomes imperative, whether the contacts between the two groups are direct or indirect. These resemblances are to a certain extent purely verbal; but some are fundamental, notably those in the sphere of the doctrine of the flesh and the spirit. Here much that has been sought, often without success, in Hellenism is now shown by the Scrolls to have been endemic in Judaism.

In the Scrolls as in the Epistles 'flesh' often enough has its natural sense of man's physical body. For example, as in an apocryphal work the body in life suffered undeserved pains[4] and as the Apostle 'was sorely tried by a thorn in the flesh'[5] and 'such (*sc.* those who are married) shall have trouble in the flesh';[6] so the Wicked Priest is threatened with punishment and torture 'in the body of his flesh' (H ix 12);[7] but, although the wording is similar, the circumstances are totally different. Also, in both groups of writings the same term is employed by a natural extension of meaning for 'kith and kin' (Z viii 17, ix 17)[8] and even for all mankind; so the 'community of flesh' in parallelism with 'sons of Adam' or 'sons of mankind' (D xi 6–7)

[1] Pp. 360–1, 373.   [2] Acts vi. 7; s. Braun in *RB*, NS LXXII 34–5.
[3] Acts ix. 10–25 and Gal. i 17; s. Grossouw in *Stud. Cath.* XXVII 5 and Cullmann in Stendhal *op. cit.* 25.
[4] I Enoch cii 5.   [5] 2 Cor. xii. 7; cp. Gal. iv. 13.
[6] I Cor. vii 28.   [7] Cp. Col. i. 22.   [8] Rom. ix. 3, xi. 14.

designates human society as 'all flesh' designates all mankind (Z i 2 iii 6).[1] Here words and sense coincide.

In places the sense of 'flesh', whether it is meant literally or meta-phorically, is equivocal. For example, when the author of *Discipline* says that 'God will purge by His truth all the deeds of man, refining some of mankind for Himself by removing every evil spirit from the midst of his flesh' (D iv 21–2), the meaning of the term is very nearly literal; but, when he says of a man that 'through the submission of his soul to all God's ordinances his flesh will be cleansed by purifying himself with water (for the removal) of impurity and purging water' (D iii 8–9), the sense may well be metaphorical. This ambiguity is as natural as it is frequent, and it rarely seriously affects the interpretation of a passage.

At the same time the weakness and corruption of the flesh is a common-place of both New Testament and Scrolls, as also of other literatures. Its weakness is emphasized by the Apostle speaking of men as 'earthen vessels'[2] and in passages where the author of the *Thanks-giving Hymns* asks 'who is such flesh or such vessel of clay as to (be able to) glorify (God's) marvels?' (T iv 29; cp. i 21 iii 24 xi 3 xii 26, 32 xviii 13) and where the author of *Discipline* exclaims 'what indeed is he, a son of man, amongst Thy marvels and what is one born of a woman in Thine estimation? For he is kneaded from the dust and his last dwelling place is to be food for worms; for he is something shaped, fashioned only of potter's clay, whose impulse is toward the dust. What can clay and that which is shaped by hand answer and what sort of counsel can he understand?' (D xi 20–2; cp. T iv 29–30). The corruptibility, if not corruption, of the flesh, where the word imports the morally lower nature of a man, appears in Paul's 'I am fleshly (carnal), sold under sin',[3] and in the author of *Discipline*'s 'I belong to wicked humanity and to the society of the flesh of iniquity' and 'I stumble in the guilt of flesh' (D xi 9, 12); and such expressions as 'bodies of guilt' (W xiv 3) and 'flesh of guilt' (W xii 12) and 'flesh of iniquity' (D xi 9 W iv 3) or 'flesh of iniquities' (D ix 4) in the Scrolls when compared with Paul's 'flesh of sin'[4] and 'body of sin'[5] do but emphasize the community of thought. As, too, the author of *Discipline* says that 'the spirits of truth and perversion strive within a man's heart' (D iv 23), so Paul acknowledges 'another law in my members, warring against the law of my mind'[6] and that 'the flesh lusteth against the spirit and the spirit against the flesh'.[7] Thus the 'body of flesh'[8] describes man's corrupt bodily state, of which Paul asks 'who

---

[1] Cp. Rom. iii. 20, 1 Cor. i. 29, Gal. ii. 16.   [2] 2 Cor. iv. 7.
[3] Rom. vii. 14.   [4] *Ibid.* viii. 3.   [5] Rom. vi. 6, Col. ii. 1.
[6] Rom. vii. 23.   [7] Gal. v. 17.
[8] Col. i. 22; cp. Ecclus. xxiii. 16.

will deliver me from this body of death?';[1] it is something which must be purified at the end of the period of wickedness, as *Discipline* insists in saying that 'God will purge all the deeds of men by His truth, refining a man for Himself by abolishing every evil spirit from his fleshly members' (D iv 20–21), or which in Pauline thought must be put off.[2] The import is the same in such an expression as 'society of flesh' as designating all mankind; for, although it is immediately parallel with 'sons of men', the rest of the passage shows that it is synonymous with 'wicked humanity' and the 'society of perverse flesh' (D xi 6–10). So in *War* the 'sons of darkness', *i.e.* the opponents of the Covenanters, are called also 'all erring flesh' (W iv 3) and 'guilty flesh' (W xii 12). In these last the reference is to humanity without the Covenant; but the point has been made and is worth consideration, that passages in the Scrolls, especially in the *Thanksgiving Hymns*, where 'flesh' has a moral connotation are chiefly those in which the writer is dealing with his own personal experience of sin; they are almost entirely absent from those which set out a system of belief.[3] The same principle can be detected, though not exclusively followed, in Paul's use of the corresponding term.[4]

This use of 'flesh' as something frail and erring, though found sporadically in the Old Testament,[5] is not a feature of Rabbinic teaching, so far as this is known, in the last centuries B.C., even if passages in which it may be perhaps detected can be cited; it is also un-Hellenistic, although some impetus may have been given to the notion by Hellenistic influences.[6] Consequently, its appearance in the Scrolls as well as in the New Testament is striking and calls for explanation. May it be regarded as an outcome of the struggle against the Greek cult of the human body? The Covenanters, like Christians and many Jews who did not belong to either party, would have been strongly opposed to this cult.[7]

The Covenanters called man simply 'flesh', thereby indicating his unworthiness over against God; yet, even if their ideas were based on the thought of the Old Testament contrasting man as frail flesh with the spirit of the Lord, which alone is worthy of trust,[8] a great difference can be detected. In the Scrolls flesh is set in contrast not only to the spirit of God but also to the spirit of truth, which he who was admitted to the covenant possessed by virtue of his predestination. Man as flesh was regarded as unworthy of God and naturally inclined to succumb to Belial, *i.e.* to sin, while the spirit of truth possessed by the

---

[1] Rom. vii. 24. [2] Col. ii. 11.
[3] Kuhn in Stendahl *Scrolls* 102–3 and Davies *ibid.* 164.
[4] *E.g.* Rom. vii. 14, 23–4. [5] *E.g.* Gen. vi. 3, Psa. lvi. 4.
[6] Kuhn *ibid.* 164 and Davies *ibid.* 162.
[7] *E.g.* 1 Macc. i. 13–15 and 2 Macc. iv. 9–17; also Mishnah *Abodah Zarah* i 7.
[8] Isa. xxxi. 3, Psa. lxxvii. 39.

pious Covenanter enabled him to resist and overcome the powers of darkness. Thus flesh as weak and as the seat of the evil impulse in man is contrasted with the spirit, *i.e.* the spirit of truth, which determines the pious man's actions and enables him to prevail in the struggle;[1] but this contrast is not so strongly emphasized as is that between the 'two ways'[2] in the Scrolls.

In the Scrolls the Covenanter may recognize that 'I belong to wicked humanity and to the society of the flesh of iniquity' (D xi 9; cp. W iv 3), *i.e.* that he is erring man; but by God's predetermination he is also heir to 'the lot of the saints' and one of the 'elect of mankind' destined to stand before God for ever (D xi 7, 16–17), and the society to which he belongs are 'the men of God's lot' or 'party' (D ii 2). Thus he can say 'mine eye has beheld the wisdom which is hidden from men, knowledge and prudent purpose [concealed] from the sons of man, a source of righteousness and a reservoir of strength as well as a well-spring of glory [concealed] from the society of flesh' (D xi 6–7). The Covenanter belongs to both groups: as sinful man he is 'flesh of sin' but as 'elect of God' by virtue of the indwelling spirit of truth determining his actions he is one of 'the sons of the eternal society' (D ii 25). The New Testament depicts a similar picture of a warfare in which the believer, strengthened by the indwelling spirit and clad in the 'armour of light', wars with the 'works of darkness';[3] he is not however, predestined to take this or that side in the struggle but is called by the preaching of the Gospel to leave his former state of darkness and become a new man as one of the sons of light. This spirit is not a predestined *habitus* but the divine gift of grace of an existence which is grasped in faith and conferred at baptism.[4]

In the Scrolls, again, all men have a share in the 'spirit of truth' and the 'spirit of error', whereby they can be called respectively 'sons of truth' and 'sons of error', and these two spirits are at enmity; but God has set a limit for the spirit of error, after which 'the truth of the world' will emerge, man will be cleansed of the evil spirit and sprinkled with the spirit of truth (D iii 13–iv 26). Both these spirits were held to have been created by God and were regarded as a permanent element in all men. At the same time references to a 'prince of light' and an 'angel of darkness' show that they were not inherent or immanent properties of man; they were forces other than, if not external to, man.[5] So Belial was said to be 'let loose' on Israel (Z vi 9); and, if a man repeated and returned to the law of Moses, 'the angel of hostility would depart from him if he carried out his words' (Z xx 2). These two spirits were constantly opposed to one another, appearing

---

[1] Cp. Kuhn in Stendahl *op. cit.* 101 and Avni in *Tarbiz* XXVII 158–65.
[2] Pp. 552–8.
[3] Rom. viii. 9–11, xiii. 12.
[4] Kuhn in Stendahl *op. cit.* 105–6.
[5] Davies in Stendahl *op. cit.* 172–3.

even in certain historical persons, as 'in ancient times Moses and Aaron arose by the hand of the Prince of Light (*i.e.* the spirit of truth), and Belial by his evil device raised up Jannes and his brother'[1] (Z vii 19);[2] and 'the truth of the world' *i.e.* the spirit of truth, was expected to appear as a sign of the end, when 'God through the mysteries of His understanding and through His glorious wisdom has appointed a term for the existence of iniquity and at the appointed season of visitation will destroy it for ever . . . ; and then by His truth God will purify all a man's actions . . . and will sprinkle a spirit of truth upon him like water (for the removal) of impurity, so as to make the upright understand the knowledge of the Most High and the wisdom of the sons of heaven for the instruction of those whose conduct is blameless' (D iv 18–22). Here the spirit performs not merely the negative function of purifying a man but also the positive function of instructing him in the knowledge of God; but an eschatological significance is assigned to the spirit only here in the Scrolls, and even here it somehow lacks that connotation of empowering energy associated with the eschatological gift of the Spirit in both the Old and the New Testaments.[3]

The conceptions of 'spirit', then, in the Scrolls are not unlike those in the Pauline Epistles; but differences can be detected. For example, on the one hand, in both 'spirit' may denote a person's disposition or temperament, whether a 'spirit of humility' or 'meekness' (D iv 3; cp. iii 8)[4] a 'spirit of knowledge' or 'understanding' (D iv 4 xi 1 T xiv 25; cp. T iii 22–3), or a 'spirit of wisdom',[5] or a 'spirit of holiness' (D iii, 6, 8, ix 3; cp. T viii 12)[6] and in both God's holy spirit inspired prophecy (D viii 16).[7] On the other hand, while Paul for the most part uses 'spirit' for the spirit of God and only once or twice for an evil spirit,[8] the authors of the Scrolls employ it as often of the good as of the evil spirit and but once directly of the Spirit of God (D viii 16); they never speak of 'the spirit which is of God', unless this may be identified with 'the spirit of God's true counsel' (D iii 6), nor of 'the spirit of the world', whatever this exactly means.[9] Again, while Paul defines the Spirit of God as 'the spirit which is of God', the author of *Discipline*, while making God the creator of both the spirit of truth and the spirit of perversion, puts the source of the former in a 'spring of light' and that of the latter in a 'fountain of darkness' (D iii 17–19, 25); thus these, though created by God, are not from God. Accordingly, the parallelism between the two spirits in the Scrolls and in the Pauline Epistles is not complete. Further, in the Scrolls these spirits are under

---

[1] P. 457.
[2] Cp. Apocalypse of Moses 36 and 2 Tim. iii. 8.
[3] Davies *ibid.* 173–4.   [4] 1 Cor. iv. 21; Gal. vi. 1.
[5] Eph. i. 17; cp. Deut. xxxiv. 9.   [6] Rom. i. 4.
[7] 1 Cor. xii. 8.   [8] 1 Cor. ii. 12; cp. Eph. ii. 2.
[9] 1 Cor. ii. 12.

their respective chiefs, the 'prince of lights' (D iii 20) and the 'angel of His (sc. God's) truth' (D iii 24) and the 'angel of darkness' (D iii 20, 21). Lastly, nothing corresponding to the contrast between the spirit and the law, which is so marked a feature of Pauline thought, can be found in the Scrolls. The Covenanters are 'a community in respect to the Law' (D v 2), the novice is examined before admission 'in regard to his understanding and his conduct in the Law' (D v 21 vi 18) and full members 'shall not depart from the whole counsel of the Law' (D ix 9), which is 'an institution of a spirit of holiness' (D ix 3). Here there is no tension between law and spirit; and the total absence of it is one of the principal and most striking differences between the Scrolls and the Pauline Epistles. Once again, the words are often similar but the thought may be quite different.

The language and even the thought of the *Epistle to the Ephesians* shows the closest contacts of all the Epistles with the Scrolls. Some contacts are purely verbal: for example, God's 'eternal counsel' or 'purpose' (D ii 23)[1] and 'the purpose of His good will' (Z v 15)[1] and 'the mysteries of His will' (T fr. iii 7),[3] or again 'the spirit of His mighty power' (T iv 32) as compared with 'the working of His mighty power'.[4] So too both Covenanter and Christian describe God's purposes, the former as 'the mystery of that which happens and is happening for ever' or briefly as 'His marvellous mysteries' (D xi 3, 5) and the latter as 'the dispensation of the mystery which from all ages hath been hid in God'.[5] The resemblances are superficially linguistic, but the repeated emphasis on the mystery of God's purpose and work shows how close these writers may occasionally come to one another in thought.

Other contacts come near to the substance of the matter. As the Covenanters are 'sons of light' (D i 9 ii 16 iii 13, 24, 25), so Christians are 'children of light';[6] as the opponents of the former in the world are 'sons of darkness' (D i 10) engaged in 'ways of darkness' (D iii 11, iv 11; cp. ii 7), so those of the latter are occupied in 'works of darkness'.[7] The community of the Covenanters is to be 'an institution of spiritual holiness' (D ix 3) as the church 'shall grow into a holy temple',[8] the members of the former society 'cleansed with water for (the removal of) impurity' (D iii 8–9) and the latter a body 'cleansed . . . by the washing of water'.[9] Other closely parallel ideas are those of 'the spirit that now worketh in the children of disobedience'[10] and of the 'spirit of perversion' and all its works (D iv 9, 20), which is constantly contrasted with the 'spirit of truth' (D iii 18–19 iv 23; cp. iv 18); and lastly 'the

[1] Cp. Eph. iii. 11.   [2] *Ibid*. i. 11.   [3] *Ibid*. i. 9.
[4] *Ibid*. i. 19.   [5] *Ibid*. iii. 9.   [6] Eph. v. 8.
[7] *Ibid*. v. 11.   [8] *Ibid*. ii. 21.   [9] *Ibid*. v. 26–7.
[10] *Ibid*. ii. 2.

principalities and powers in heavenly places',[1] like the 'angel of light',[2] similarly recall the 'prince of lights' (D iii 20 Z vii 19), whether Uriel[3] or Michael[4] (cp. W xv 6–8), and analogous conceptions in the Scrolls. Too much importance, however, must not be attached to these and such-like coincidences which, even when identical in form, are not always so in sense. Many in fact are not peculiar to the Scrolls and the New Testament and, like the language, are often nothing but the current coin of the period. The *Epistle*, even if it is a non-Pauline composition of the sub-Pauline age, must have been very close to the Scrolls themselves in various respects.

The general opinion of those who have studied the Scrolls seems to have been that the *Epistle to the Hebrews* (tentatively dated *c*. A.D. 70–90) has the fewest contacts of all the writings of the New Testament with the Scrolls.[5]

Yet points, perhaps largely superficial, at which *Hebrews* recalls the Scrolls can be detected.[6] For example, great importance is attached to the Law (*sc*. the Mosaic law) and to the 'covenant' (though very different covenants), to living 'in these last days',[7] to purification in 'pure water'[8] (cp. D iii 9 Z xii 2) and the danger of the fire which consumes rebels against God (D ii 7–8 iv 12–13).[9] The writers of the Scrolls and the author of this Epistle also employ the same or similar figures of speech: for example, they speak of the community as a 'camp' (Z ix 49 xvi 6, 8),[10] of the 'sacrifice of praise . . . that is the fruit of our lips'[11] (T i 28; cp. D x 6, 14)[12] and of well doing and 'fellowship' (D i 1–2; but here too the connotation of the word is not exactly the same).[13] These are slight points, each in itself of little importance, but they are witnesses to a common linguistic and ideological background; at the same time the very differences have their significance, since they preclude the possibility that either party has borrowed words or expressions directly from the other.

Prof. Yadin, however, has recently drawn[14] attention to certain lines of argument in *Hebrews* which suggest to him that it may perhaps be directed against the opinions or doctrines of the Covenanters.

The theme of the *Epistle*, as he argues, is the superiority of Jesus over various heavenly and historical persons of a Messianic or eschatological type whom its readers are in danger of regarding as superior to Him, since He is only a lay Messiah, and as appointed at the end of

[1] *Ibid*. iii. 10.   [2] 2 Cor. xi. 14.
[3] Charles *Apocrypha and Pseudepigrapha* II 811 and Ginzberg *Sekte* I 35–7.
[4] Yadin *War* 214–15.   [5] Cp. Schmitt in *Colloque de Strasbourg* 108.
[6] Cp. Braun in *RB*, NS LXII 35–7.   [7] Heb. i. 2.
[8] *Ibid*. x. 22.   [9] *Ibid*. x. 26–7; cp. xii. 29.
[10] *Ibid*. xiii. 13.
[11] Cp. Hos. xiv. 3 (where the Septuagint have 'the fruit of our lips').
[12] *Ibid*. xiii. 15.   [13] *Ibid*. xiii. 16.
[14] In *Scr. Hieros*. IV 36–55.

the period to perform certain functions usually reserved for the Messiah. The subjects discussed are treated under three or four heads: these are Jesus and the angels, Jesus and Moses and the prophets, and Jesus and Aaron. The beliefs which the readers of the *Epistle* are apparently supposed by its writer to hold and against which he may be thought to be arguing can be inferred from these arguments and may then be compared with the opinions of the Covenanters, as expressed in the Scrolls, on the same subjects.

First, the writer adduces arguments against the view that the part played by angels in the eschatological period was of supreme importance inasmuch as they would be operating not as the servants of any Messianic agent but under the direct orders of God. Contrariwise, according to the Scrolls 'Thou, [O God,] . . . didst appoint from aforetime the Prince of Light to be our helper, and [all the sons of righteousness are] in [his lot (*i.e.* party)] and all spirits of truth are under his dominion' (W xiii 9–10), and 'the rule over all the sons of righteousness is in the hand of the Prince of Light' and 'the God of Israel and His angel of truth have helped all the Sons of Light' (D iii 20, 24–5), and lastly 'He will send eternal help to all the lot of those whom He will redeem (?) by the might of an angel; He has magnified [the authority of Michael] through eternal light to enlighten the [house] of Israel with joy in peace and blessing for the lot of God to exalt the authority of Michael over the gods (*sc.* angels) and the dominion of Israel over all flesh' (W xvii 6–8). Here Michael, who presumably is the 'prince of light' and 'angel of truth',[1] is under God's direct command and controls His army of angels, called 'gods', in the struggle against the prince of the realm of wickedness (*i.e.* Rome personified as the evil power *par excellence* on earth). Elsewhere, too, God is described as the 'captain of gods (*i.e.* angels) and king of the honoured ones and lord of every spirit' (T x 8), and the angels are called also 'sons of gods' (T fr. ii 3) and 'sons of heaven' (T iii 22). These passages, then, show that the angels are regarded as taking the next place in the heavenly hierarchy after God, and neither Messiah nor anointed chief, whether lay or priestly, is mentioned; but the *Epistle* runs directly counter to these views. Its author argues that, although God had spoken in times past by the prophets, He now did so 'at the end of these days' by a son to whom alone His revelation had been made[2] and that this Son, Jesus, was superior to the angels inasmuch as he had inherited a 'more excellent name than they', namely that of a son, and though 'made a little lower than the angels' by submitting himself to death he had become 'the captain of their (*sc.* his readers') salvation', while they were but 'ministering spirits'.[3]

Second, the Jews of the Second Commonwealth looked for the

<hr>

[1] Yadin *War* 213–15.   [2] Heb. i. 1–2.   [3] *Ibid.* i. 3– ii. 18.

coming of an eschatological prophet,[1] who should be a representative of Moses or a Moses *redivivus*, as they argued from Scripture;[2] and so the Covenanters dreamed of 'the coming of a prophet and of the Messiahs of Aaron and Israel' (D ix 11).[3] So Moses is made to say in an apocalypse dated *c.* A.D. 7–30 that 'He (*sc.* God) prepared me before the foundation of the world, that I should be the mediator of His covenant';[4] but the writer of the *Epistle* argues that Moses was but the mediator of the old law and had nothing to do with any 'new covenant', whereas Jesus had obtained 'a more excellent ministry' and become 'the mediator of a better covenant', which had superseded the old law.[5] Thus he is apparently tilting at the expectation of these other Jews, including the Covenanters, that Moses would reappear in the Messianic age to mediate a new covenant.

Third, the Covenanters believed at one period of their history in two Messiahs, a priestly and a lay, and at another in one Messiah combining both offices in his own person; the priestly Messiah was of the line of Aaron and superior to the lay, kingly or Davidic, Messiah.[6] Contrariwise, the writer of the *Epistle* is at pains to prove that, although Jesus was a priestly Messiah, he was so not 'after the law of a carnal commandment', *i.e.* not by virtue of descent from Aaron, but as 'a great high-priest' of an order above that of Aaron, namely 'after the order of Melchizedek'; and, as Melchizedek was both priest and king, so Jesus by inference was both in his own person.[7] Further, the two anointed priests, the 'chief priest' and 'the prince of the whole congregation', who take part in the apocalyptic war 'at the end of the days' are conducting an earthly war, while the archangel Michael is in charge of the whole war both in heaven and on earth (W vii 8–xviii 15). Here then Michael is superior to both Messiahs, while the priestly is superior to the lay Messiah. In the *Epistle*, however, Jesus as Christ or Messiah is superior to the heavenly powers *i.e.* the angels, who are but 'all ministering spirits, sent forth to do service for the sake of them that shall inherit salvation',[8] *i.e.* for all who become Christ's followers.

Fourth, the Covenanters tolerate if they do not enforce lustrations,[9] whereas the author of the *Epistle* will have nothing of the 'teaching of washings.'[10] The Covenanters, as the *Hymns* show, also look for the restoration of the ancient sacrifices in an ideal future age with 'twelve priests serving regularly with the burnt offering before God', when 'the heads of the courses . . . shall assist at the burnt offerings and the sacrifices, to set forth the offering of incense as a soothing odour for God's pleasure, to make atonement for all His congregation and to

---

[1] *E.g.* 1 Macc. iv. 46, xiv. 41 and Matt. xvi. 14; Jn. i. 21, vi. 14; Philo *On the special Laws* i 65 and Josephus *Antiquities* XX v 1.
[2] Deut. xviii. 18.   [3] Pp. 468–71, 480–2.   [4] Assumption of Moses i 14.
[5] Heb. iii. 1–7, viii. 1–13.   [6] Pp. 466–7.   [7] Heb. iv. 14–x. 18.
[8] *Ibid.* i. 14.   [9] Pp. 68, 72–3.   [10] Heb. vi. 2.

remove the ashes on the glorious table regularly from His presence' (W ii 1–6). Contrariwise, the writer of the *Epistle* argues that the need for such sacrifices has passed away since 'now once at the end of the ages hath He (*sc.* Jesus) been manifested to put away sin by the sacrifice of Himself'.[1]

These apparent contacts between the Scrolls and the *Epistle to the Hebrews*, if admitted, will have some importance for the light which they may throw on the date of the Scrolls. Whatever the writer of the *Epistle* was countering, it would not be doctrines two centuries old. They would be live issues of his own times, more or less contemporary with the *Epistle* itself. If then its author was directly attacking beliefs of the Covenanters, which had been committed to writing in the Scrolls and which his readers were in danger of adopting, the Scrolls could not have been written long before his time. Two or three reasons, however, may be given for doubting whether the *Epistle* is to be understood as referring directly to the Scrolls. First, the Covenanters were forbidden to reveal their doctrines to outsiders (D ix 17), and the languages of the Scrolls and the *Epistle* were different;[2] further, that one of the doctrines (namely, that Moses was expected to reappear in the Messianic age) attacked by the writer of the *Epistle* is found in the *Assumption of Moses* shows it to have been a belief shared also by Jews outside the circles of the Covenanters and the Church in the 1st century A.D. The other points common to the Scrolls and the *Epistle* may similarly be derived from other Jewish groups of the same age. The probability then is that he is combating opinions not confined to the Covenanters but widely held in Jewish circles in the 1st century A.D.; but the point that the Covenanters are thus shown to have shared opinions widely current at this time does not thereby lose its significance.

The *Epistle of James*, too, shows contacts with the Scrolls which have not yet been fully worked out, especially in its structure; and a few somewhat superficial points, some dubious but others possible, may here be mentioned. One suggestion, that some connection perhaps exists between the title of the author as the 'Just' or 'Righteous'[3] and those of the Covenanters as 'Sons of Zadok' and also as 'sons of righteousness' (D iii 20, 22),[4] may at once be ruled out of court as fanciful; for he can hardly have been James the Just. The Apostle's '(perfect) law of liberty'[5] has also been detected in the author of *Discipline*'s assertion that 'as long as I exist, an ordinance is engraved upon my tongue' (D x 8) and 'His (*sc.* God's) justice will I declare . . . as an engraved ordinance' (D x 11);[6] for the word here translated

---

[1] *Ibid.* ix. 26.   [2] S. pp. 570–1.
[3] Hegesippus *ap.* Eusebius *Ecclesiastical History* II xxiii 3.
[4] Gaster *Scriptures* 26–7.   [5] Jas. i. 25, ii. 12.   [6] Brownlee *Discipline* 40.

'engraved (*ḥārût*)[1] ordinance' may be read with one different vowel as 'an ordinance of liberty (*ḥērût*)'.[2] The first rather than the second reading seems to suit the thought of the author; but the possibility of a *double entente* cannot be absolutely excluded,[3] especially as this very play on these words appears long afterwards in a medieval Rabbinic work.[4] If however this possibility is admitted, it has a certain importance; for *ḥērût* 'freedom' is perhaps a neologism of the period of the First Revolt against Rome.[5] Several other clear points of contact can be cited and compared: for example 'every good gift is from above, coming down from the Father of lights'[6] with the statement that 'the rule of all the sons of righteousness is in the hands of the Prince of lights' (D iii 20) who, as the Spirit of Truth, is the source of all the virtues found in man (cp. D iv 2–6); and 'blessed is the man that endureth testing; for, when he hath been approved, he shall receive the crown of life'[7] with the picture of the perfect man who 'through the anguish of testing' (D viii 4) shall win 'the victorious life of eternity and a crown of glory' (D iv 7). The passage, too, in which the questions are raised: 'think ye that the Scripture speaketh in vain? doth the spirit, which He (*sc.* God) made to dwell in us, long unto envying?'[8] recalls the teaching that 'to the spirit of perversion belongs greed' (D iv 9), since God is said to have planted His spirit in man (D iii 17–18). Since no such question can be found in the Scriptures, Dr. Gaster has suggested[9] that the 'scripture' mentioned in the *Epistle* may be *Discipline*, in which so closely similar a thought may be found. Taken literally, the suggestion is improbable,[10] since the Covenanters made a point of keeping their scriptures secret (D ix 17); but the authors, if roughly contemporary, would have been alert to problems which were being mooted in their time.

4. JOHANNINE WRITINGS

The relation of the Johannine writings (*c.* A.D. 90–100 or 110) to the Scrolls is not dissimilar to that of the Epistles; for many expressions and notions, some simple and others profound, are common to both.[11]

Comparisons must of course be made with caution; but verbally similar expressions, even though they have different connotations, have some value as evidence of the period in which they are current. An example will be found in the use of 'light' in the saying that one

---

[1] Cp. Exod. xxxii. 16 and Ecclus. xlv. 11 (where *ḥārût* is applied to the inscription on Aaron's breastplate).
[2] Burrows *ibid.* 41; s. Van der Ploeg in *Rech. Bibl.* IV 48–9.
[3] Cp. p. 198.
[4] Schechter *Aboth de Rabbi Nathan* 10 § 2 = Goldin *Fathers according to Rabbi Nathan* 20.
[5] Hengel *Zeloten* 123–7; cp. Mishnah *Aboth* vi 2.   [6] Jas. i. 17.
[7] *Ibid.* i. 12.   [8] *Ibid.* iv. 5.   [9] *Ibid.* 25.   [10] Cp. Burrows *Scrolls* II 131.
[11] Cp. Braun in *RB*, NS LXXII 12–26 and Brown in Stendahl *Scrolls* 183–207.

who, cleansed of his sins, joins the society of the Covenanters will be cleansed of his sins 'that he may[1] look upon the light of life' (D iii 7) as compared with 'he that followeth me [*sc.* Christ] . . . shall have the light of life'.[2] Another example may be seen in the description of the council of the community of the Covenanters as 'witnesses to truth' (D viii 6) in comparison with the statement regarding John the Baptist that 'he has borne witness to the truth'[3] and with that in which Christ proclaims that he has come 'to bear witness to the truth';[4] for 'light' and 'truth' respectively have different meanings in these passages.

In both the Scrolls and the Johannine literature good and evil are constantly contrasted under the figures now of light and darkness, now of truth and perversity or iniquity. Thus in the Scrolls the 'spirits of light and darkness' are identical respectively with the 'spirits of truth and iniquity' (D iii 18–19, 25) and the 'spirit of truth' is contrasted with the 'spirit of iniquity' (D iv 2, 9); in the Johannine literature the 'spirit of truth' is opposed to the 'spirit of error'.[5] Men are said also in both, in the style of the Old Testament, to walk in the ways of light or of darkness (D iii 20),[6] as their lives are good or evil, and so too the spirit of the novice must be examined (D v 20–2, 24–5 vi 17) just as the spirits of those claiming to be prophets must be tested.[7] Further, the Covenanter is bidden 'to do truth' (D i 5 v 3 viii 2) just as the Christian is described as 'he that doeth truth';[8] and Covenanters called themselves 'sons of light' (D i 9 ii 16 iii 13, 24, 25) even as Christians were called 'children of light'.[9]

According to the Scrolls a man became a 'son of darkness' by refusing to do God's will, especially by his rejection of the covenant which God offered to men (D iii 6); and he became a 'son of light' by dedicating himself 'to do God's ordinances so as to be brought into the covenant of friendship, to be united in God's counsel, and to walk before Him perfectly in all things that are revealed according to their appointed seasons and to love all the sons of light' (D i 7–9). Thus the Covenanters were required to submit themselves to instruction in all the observances of the society (D iii 13) and especially to devote themselves to the study of the Law (D vi 6–8); for this purpose God 'raised up a Rightful Teacher to lead them in the way of His heart' (Z i 7), and for their loyalty to him some 'doers of the Law' were saved when he was murdered (H viii 1–3). In this way they might hope to attain 'insight of life' and 'knowledge of eternity' (D ii 3); and so eternal life for Christians is to know God in the Gospel.[10] At the same time, a Covenan-

---

[1] Cp. Psa. lvi. 13.
[2] Jn. viii. 12; cp. Matt. v. 14.
[3] Jn. v. 33.
[4] *Ibid.* xviii. 37.
[5] 1 Jn. iv. 6.
[6] Jn. viii. 12, xii. 35; 1 Jn. i 6–7 ii, 11.
[7] 1 Jn. iv 1.
[8] Jn. iii. 21; cp. 1 Jn. i. 6.
[9] Jn. xii. 36.
[10] Jn. xvii. 3.

ter was required to cultivate practical virtues by following 'the way of the spirit of truth . . . according to the truth of the mysteries of knowledge' (D iv 2–6), which may perhaps be compared to the advice given to a deacon to be grave and truthful 'holding the mystery of the faith in a pure conscience'.[1] Quite differently Christians became 'children of light' not through the study and fulfilment of the old Law but because they believed in the light, *i.e.* had faith in Christ;[2] and 'he who does the truth comes to the light that his deeds may be manifest';[3] but the obligation to do good deeds was not ended by the acceptance of faith in Christ. Finally, those who walk in darkness will be judged, while the 'children of light' who keep His commandments will be saved. Briefly, a Covenanter became a 'son of light' by joining the society and accepting its interpretation of the Jewish law, while the Christian became a 'child of light' through faith in Christ; but both were required to be sincere in their professions and faithful in fulfilling their requirements.

This dualism,[4] which runs through the Scrolls and the Johannine literature, raises serious problems. The bare doctrinal similarity, which goes back to the very beginning of the Old Testament, proves nothing; but one definite difference must be kept in mind, that in the Gospel, while God makes all things, it is actually the Word that performs the creative act,[5] whereas in the Scrolls it is God's knowledge that brings everything into existence (D iii 15 xi 11), including the spirits both of light and of darkness (D iii 25). They are, however, not both explicitly said to be created by God in the Gospel as they are in the Scrolls (D iii 25);[6] for 'God is the light, and in Him is no darkness',[7] and with God light has come into the world, so that Christ can call Himself 'the light of the world'.[8] Consequently, there is in the Gospel no 'prince of lights' (D iii 20 Z vii 19), no 'angel of truth' nor 'spirit of truth' nor 'spirit of holiness' (D ix 3; cp. Z ii 10) distinct from God Himself as the Holy Spirit; nor are there many 'spirits of truth' forming the army of the 'prince of light' (W xiii 10) in it. Contrariwise, the Covenanters speak of a 'spirit of truth' and a 'spirit of holiness', which are more or less undistinguished, as the means whereby God cleanses a man from his uncleanness on admission to their society (D iv 21; cp. iii 6–8).[9] So too the evil spirit, the devil or Satan, though often mentioned in the Gospel, is nowhere depicted as the leader of the forces of darkness; contrariwise, in the Scrolls the evil spirit is described as the 'spirit of iniquity' (D iv 9, 20), the 'angel of darkness' (D iii 20–1) and the 'angel (of) Mastemah' (W xiii 11 Z xx 2), a name based on the Old Testament[10]

---

[1] 1 Tim. iii. 9; cp. Eph. vi. 19. [2] Jn. xii. 36. [3] *Ibid.* iii. 21.
[4] S. pp. 550–62. [5] Jn. i. 3. [6] Cp. Isa. liv 16.
[7] 1 Jn. i. 5. [8] Jn. ix. 5.
[9] Cp. Flusser in *Scr. Hieros.* IV 245–56. [10] Hos. ix. 7–8.

and found also in apocalyptic literature;[1] and he is also called Belial,[2] which is a name of similar origin.[3] Belial like the 'prince of light' has subordinate spirits, called 'angels of destruction' (D iv 12, W xiii 12, Z ii 4). These spirits, as the spirits respectively of light and darkness, contend for the possession of man's soul (D iv 23; cp. iii 17–25); and the 'angels of destruction' are even employed to fulfil God's purposes (Z ii 4). Such functions as these, ascribed in the Scrolls to the spirits, are quite unlike anything in the Gospel. There Christ himself is the light and life of men and as such is the object of Satan's enmity, but 'the darkness overcame it not';[4] or in other words 'the prince of this world cometh but hath nothing in me'[5] and 'shall be cast out'.[6]

The determinism implied in the dualism of the Scrolls, however, is not fully worked out;[7] for the Covenanters never resolved the dilemma which confronted them when they grafted Persian dualism on to Hebrew monotheism. In the Gospel the dilemma hardly exists. There, although the Evangelist says 'you have not chosen me, but I have chosen you',[8] there is no hint that anyone's fate is predetermined without choice on his part; and, although 'the light has come into the world, yet men have loved the darkness rather than the light; for their works were evil'.[9] In other words, they were free to choose which they would.

Another marked difference between the Scrolls and the Gospel may be seen in the views of their respective authors regarding the great struggle between good and evil. The former, in speaking of the spirits of good and evil, says that 'God has set them in equal parts till the last period and has put eternal enmity between their divisions' (D iv 16–17; cp. 25–6) but that 'He has appointed a term for the existence of wrong-doing and at the season of visitation He will destroy it forever; and then the truth of the world will appear forever' (D iv 18–19). Thus the conflict will be waged on equal terms, except in so far as God and 'his angel of truth' help the 'sons of light' (D iii 24–5), until at the end 'wickedness will disappear before justice as darkness before light' (I Q 27, i 4–5). Here therefore the writer is living in the testing period, the battle is sometimes engaged but is usually regarded, notably in the *War*, as still future; in the New Testament the 'darkness has not overcome the light'[10] but 'the darkness is passing, and the true light is already appearing'[11] and Christ can therefore exclaim 'I have overcome the world',[12] although the victory will not be complete until the ultimate battle described in the *Apocalypse* has been won and Christ's second coming has taken place.

---

[1] Jubilees x 8 xi 5, 11 xvii 16 xviii 9, 12 xix 28 xlviii 2, 9, 12, 15 xlix 2.
[2] 2 Cor. vi. 15.   [3] Pp. 487–8.   [4] Jn. i. 4–5.
[5] *Ibid.* xiv. 30.   [6] *Ibid.* xii. 31; cp. xvi. 11.   [7] Pp. 559–61.
[8] Jn. xv. 16.   [9] *Ibid.* iii. 19.   [10] John i. 5.
[11] 1 Jn. i. 8.   [12] *Ibid.* xvi. 33.

Yet another difference between the Scrolls and the Johannine literature, as Fr. Braun shows,[1] lies in the attitude of their respective authors to sin. John declared it wrong to deny and necessary to confess sins but that God would assuredly purify the sinner (cp. D ii 6–11); man must commit himself entirely to God, trusting in Jesus who is the propitiation for our sins.[2] All this naturally flows from faith. The Covenanters had no such faith. They recognized that they were culpable (Z iv 9), and candidates for admission to their society were required to confess as much and to acknowledge the abundance of God's grace which had been conferred on them (D i 24–ii 1), of that God who offered pardon to all who repented of their sins and entered the covenant (Z ii 3 iv 6); but their hope was always precarious, since they belonged to 'wicked humanity and the company of perverse flesh' and their conduct and destiny depended on God's decision (D xi 9–11; cp. iv 14–26). Thus man's path in life was unsure, he had no absolute claims to justice and no complete confidence in God's mercy (D xi 20–2 T iv 31–3). The Covenanter therefore was uneasily poised between the knowledge of his own frailty and the feeling of guilt on the one side and the assurance of pardon on the other side; for 'righteousness lies not with man nor perfect conduct with the sons of men' and to cleanse a man from his sin rests solely with God who has made good and evil alike (T iv 29–38; cp. D iii 25 Z ii 10).

Briefly, both the authors of the Scrolls and the writer of the Gospel believe in the creation of everything by God and both separate the world into two divisions, those of light and darkness; for the Covenanters the leaders of these divisions are the two created spirits of good and evil, in the Gospel the one is the uncreated Word and the other 'the prince of this world'. In both determinism and freewill are strangely mixed; but, while the deterministic view is prevalent with the Covenanters, in the Gospel man's choice of light or darkness is the predominant thought. For the Covenanters victory is not yet assured and is still future; for Christians the climax is past and victory is certain. Finally, the person and position of Christ make the ultimate difference between the Gospel and the Scrolls, in which there is no remotely corresponding person, spirit or power.[3]

The Evangelist further distinguishes the spirit of truth as contrasted with the spirit of error, operative in man, from 'the Spirit of Truth whom the world cannot receive, because it neither sees him nor knows him' and 'who proceeds from the Father'[4] and 'who will teach you all truth';[5] for in this sense the Spirit of Truth is a designation of the Third Person of the Trinity, the true witness of Christ. Contrari-

---

[1] In *RB*, NS LXII 21–2.   [2] 1 Jn. i. 8–10, ii. 2 = iv. 10, iii. 20–22, v. 1–20.
[3] Brown in Stendahl *op. cit.* 194–5.
[4] Jn. xiv. 17, xv. 26.   [5] *Ibid.* xvi. 13.

wise the authors of the Scrolls refer only vaguely to the spirit of God working in or through the prophets (W viii 16); the two conceptions are totally different.

Lastly, the truth is regarded both by the author of *Discipline* and by the same Evangelist as a means of purification; so the former says that 'God will purge all the deeds of men by His truth . . . to cleanse him through a holy spirit of truth like water (for the removal) of impurity upon him' (D iv 20–1), as in the Gospel Jesus said 'sanctify them in the truth; Thy word is truth. Thou didst send me into the world, so I sent them into the world; and for their sakes I sanctify myself that they themselves also may be sanctified in truth'.[1]

All these resemblances between the Scrolls and the Johannine literature, whether matters of language or matters of substance, argue some connection between the authors of these very different collections of writings.[2] At the same time, the differences between them cannot be disregarded; they seem to preclude direct borrowing on either side. The relationship then will rather be one of using a common source or common sources.[3] In other words, the Scrolls are not 'the native soil of the Gospel of St. John'[4] but another plant growing from the same soil.

The contacts between the Scrolls and the *Apocalypse* are few and mostly insignificant but perhaps add something to the argument;[5] attention may therefore be drawn to several points which are worthy of notice in the present connection.

The first are linguistic peculiarities: for example, the description of the respective authors' societies as 'the camp of the saints' (W iii 5),[6] which seems to be a unique expression; the curious preposition used in 'all the world wondered after (*i.e.* at) the beast',[7] which resembles the similar idiom in 'may He (*sc.* God) ordain total destruction after (*i.e.* for) thee!' (D ii 6);[8] the employment of 'amen' as a cryptogram (D x 1–4),[9] which occurs for the first time in these two works;[10] and the violation of normal grammar in 'peace from He-who-is and who was and He-who-is-to-come',[11] which can be illustrated by corresponding idioms in the Scrolls.[12] The peculiar indeclinable use of the participial 'He-who-is (*hôweh*)' for God[13] is illustrated by the statement of the author of the *Thanksgiving Hymns* that time is controlled 'by the mouth of God and the charge of Who-is' (T xii 9). As the author of the

---

[1] Jn. xvii. 17–19.   [2] Cp. Kuhn in *ZTK* XLVII 209.
[3] Cp. Albright *ap.* Davies & Daube *Background of the New Testament and its Eschatology* 167–9.
[4] Dupont-Sommer *Manuscrits* 212–13.   [5] Cp. Braun in *RB*, NS LXII 27–31.
[6] Rev. xx. 9.   [7] *Ibid.* xiii. 3.
[8] Cp. Burkitt in *JTS* XXIII 24 on Eccles. vii. 14.
[9] Rev. i. 18, iii. 14.   [10] Pp. 337–53.
[11] Rev. i. 4.   [12] Pp. 436–7.
[13] Rev. i. 8, iv. 8, xi. 17, xvi. 5.

NN

Apocalypse must have taken the idiom from the Greek Old Testament,[1] his misuse of it otherwise than as the subject[2] will be an imitation of this late Hebrew usage, in which the participle is correctly employed;[3] alternatively, the Jewish author is imitating a Greek expression which has become stereotyped in contemporary religious jargon.

Second, a possibly important contact may be seen in the treatment of the figures of the Messiah and the anti-Messiah or anti-Christ, whose births have already been described.[4] In addition to presenting the anti-Christ as a serpent in the same way as the author of the *Thanksgiving Hymns* depicts him as a viper, the author of the *Apocalypse* tells how the woman 'which brought forth the man-child', *i.e.* the Messiah, to bear rule over all the nations 'fled into the wilderness where she hath a place prepared by God' to escape from the serpent anti-Christ;[5] and the compiler of *Discipline*, speaking of the relation of the council of the community to its members, says 'they shall separate themselves from the midst of the habitation of men of iniquity to go into the wilderness . . .; that is studying the Law [which] He (*sc.* God) commanded through Moses' (D viii 12–16). In the first passage the retreat into the wilderness signifies the church's breach with the world of unbelievers and in the second that of the Covenanters from the society of those who refuse to join them by accepting the covenant of God. This use of the wilderness was not new; others before as again in the 1st century A.D. had fled into it to escape persecution,[6] so that the idea may have occurred independently to both Covenanters and Christians.

Third, although *double entente* may be implied here and there in the Old Testament,[7] it occurs perhaps nowhere explicitly before this book, where the seven heads of the beast receive a twofold explanation,[8] after which it rapidly reaches its full development in the Midrashic literature; that it is also well developed in the Scrolls strongly supports a date within this period for their composition.

Such points of contact, though in themselves slight, agree with the conclusions drawn from a comparison of the Scrolls with other books of the New Testament, that all have a common background in the same period of history.

5. DUALISM AND DETERMINATION

The important question of dualism, the theory of the choice between 'two ways' or 'two spirits', symbolizing that between good and evil or virtue and vice with their respective consequences, must now be examined;[9] for it plays an important part not only in contemporary

[1] Septuagint at Exod. iii. 14.   [2] Rev. i. 4.
[3] Cp. Driver in *JTS* NS XIII 373.   [4] Pp. 486–7.   [5] Rev. xii. 5–6, 13–17.
[6] *E.g.* 1 Ki. xix. 4; 1 Macc. ii. 29–30, ix. 33, 62 and 2 Macc. v. 27.
[7] *E.g.* Gen. xlix. 16, Is. lxiii. 11, Ps. lx. 8–10 = cviii. 8–10, and perhaps Dan. v. 25–8 (s. Kraeling in *JBL* LXIII 11–18).   [8] Rev. xvii. 9–10.
[9] Cp. Nötscher *Zur theologischen Terminologie der Qumran-Texte* 79–148, Wernberg-Møller in *RQ* XI 413–41 and Seitz in *NTS* VI 82–95.

Jewish literature and the New Testament but also in the Scrolls. Whether dualism in the strict sense can be ascribed to an Iranian origin is largely an academic problem, which cannot be discussed here; for little or nothing is known of Zoroastrianism before the Sassanian age *c*. A.D. 250, when its written records begin. Certainly this may be held to have been a dualistic religion, inasmuch as it opposes good and evil, truth and falsehood, life and death, Ahuramazda and Ahriman, as antithetic forces or powers. The underlying conceptions, however, differ from those implied in the Scrolls.[1] Here light and darkness are contrasted not as spirit and matter, as in Hellenistic and gnostic theories, but rather as belief and unbelief, life and death in the spiritual sense; these terms are thus used in the Scrolls not in the literal but in a figurative or metaphorical sense. Light, too, in the Scrolls is not a quasi-material substance nor darkness the present world of evil; for the words have not a cosmical sense as in Mandaeism, but one that is eschatological as in Judaism. Further, the antitheses are so obvious that they may have occurred more or less simultaneously in different centres. For example, good and evil, truth and falsehood, life and death, God and Satan, are contrasted in the Old Testament at times long before any to which the Scrolls can be assigned; such ideas therefore are as likely to have reached the Covenanters from their own Hebrew scriptures as from some remote Iranian source.

The simplest form of dualism may be seen in the doctrine of the 'good imagination' (*yēṣer haṭṭôḇ*) and the 'evil imagination' (*yēṣer hārā‘*), which is parallel to that of the 'spirit of good' and the 'spirit of evil' warring for the control of a man's soul;[2] and it is at the same time the counterpart of that of the 'two ways', so that the account of the 'good way' and the 'evil way' in the Mishnah is immediately followed by that of the 'evil imagination.[3] The Rabbis have derived[4] this doctrine, as so many others, from the Old Testament, in which traces of it may be found;[5] a single allusion to it may be found also in the *Testaments of the Twelve Patriarchs*[6] and another may be recognized in one of the Scrolls, which declares 'man's imaginations (*sic*)' to be ever prone to evil practices (T xi 20–1).[7] The references to this doctrine, however, in the Old Testament are very slight, that in the Scrolls almost equally so, and it does not reach its fullest development before a relatively late date in the Rabbinic period.[8]

The doctrine of the two spirits can be traced somewhat uncertainly from the Old Testament, through the intertestamental literature, into the Scrolls and the New Testament. Its origin may perhaps be found in the story of Saul, of whom the historian says that 'the spirit of the Lord had departed from Saul, and an evil spirit from the Lord troubled

---

[1] Cp. Nötscher *op. cit.* 131–33.
[2] Pp. 537–9, 545–7.
[3] Mishnah *Aboth* ii 11.
[4] B. Talmud *Berakhoth* 61a.
[5] Gen. ii. 7; cp. Hos. x. 2.
[6] Testaments *Asher* i 3.
[7] Cp. Deut. xxxi. 21.
[8] Cp. Moore *Judaism* I 479–93.

him'.[1] The writers of the period between the Old and New Testaments speak often enough of various good and evil spirits, but only one definitely sets them against each other as two opposing spirits warring for the soul of man; he says 'Know, therefore, my children, that two spirits, the spirit of truth and the spirit of deceit, wait upon man . . .; and the works of truth and the works of deceit are written upon the hearts of men, and each one of them the Lord knoweth.'[2] This doctrine reaches its culmination in the New Testament and the Scrolls: in the former the spirit of truth stands over against the spirit of error or of this world, each warring to conquer the world, while in the latter the spirits of truth and perversity or iniquity, the spirits of light and darkness, are similarly warring for the possession of men's souls.[3] The sources of the doctrine are the same, and the point of development which it reaches in the New Testament and the Scrolls is the same; the conclusion therefore can hardly be resisted that these two collections of documents are roughly contemporary.

The doctrine of the 'two ways', which may for the moment be kept distinct from that of the 'two spirits', passes through almost exactly the same stages of development.

The earliest traces of this doctrine can be found before the Exile in the Old Testament; for Moses according to the Deuteronomist in the course of his final charge,[4] says to the Israelites: 'See, I have set before thee this day life and good, and death and evil' and Jeremiah similarly warned his contemporaries that God had said: 'Behold, I set before you the way of life and the way of death', referring to the choice of staying in the city to die by sword, famine or pestilence, and going out to the Chaldaeans and enduring the miseries of captivity.[5] An echo of it has been found also in the proverb that 'he that is perverse in (his) ways shall fall at once', which the Rabbis (but not the ancient translators) read as 'he that is perverse in two ways shall fall at once';[6] but the reference, as Jesus ben Sirach's allusion to 'the sinner that embarks on two ways'[7] shows, is rather to double-dealing than to the choice between two opposite ways. A variation on this theme is seen in the contrast between light and darkness; this can similarly be traced to the Old Testament, which teaches that 'the path of the righteous is as a shining light' and that 'the way of the wicked is as darkness.'[8] The doctrine is formally developed towards the end of the 2nd century B.C., when the 'way of light' comes to be contrasted *tout simple* with the 'way of darkness'. Thus the author of the *Testaments of the Patriarchs*, which is dated *c.* 109–7 B.C., declares that 'God has given two ways and two inclinations and two kinds of actions and

[1] I Sam. xvi. 14.
[2] Testaments *Judah* xx 1–3.
[3] Pp. 537–9, 545–7.
[4] Deut. xxx. 15.
[5] Jer. xxi. 8–9.
[6] Prov. xxviii. 6.
[7] Ecclus. ii. 12.
[8] Prov. iv. 18–19.

two modes of life and two issues to the sons of men' and, after developing the theme at some length, concludes that 'there are two kinds in all things, the one against the other and the one hidden by the other';[1] and the author of the Slavonic *Enoch*, writing *c.* A.D. 1–50, sets the 'way of light' against the 'way of darkness', when he makes God say 'I gave him (*sc.* Adam) his will and I showed him two ways, the light and the darkness'.[2] The Mishnah similarly speaks[3] of 'the good way to which a man must cling' and 'the evil way which a man must shun'; and it defines the former as a good eye, friend or neighbour, or one who regards the consequences of his actions or a good heart, and the latter as an evil eye, companion or neighbour, or one who borrows and does not repay or an evil heart. Jesus in the same vein sets the choice between the 'narrow way' and the 'broad way' before His followers;[4] and the New Testament contains several references to the 'way of righteousness',[5] which recall the 'way of true righteousness' in one of the Scrolls (D iv 2), as also to the 'way of salvation'[6] and the 'ways of life'.[7] One Gospel and two Epistles speak also of walking in the light or in the darkness;[8] and the Scrolls similarly talk of the 'ways of light' (D iii 3) and of the 'ways of darkness' in which men may walk (D iii 20 iv 11), of the 'ways of truth' (D iv 17) and the 'ways of wickedness' (D iv 19; cp. v 11) or the 'way of perversion' (T xiv 26). They go however beyond the New Testament and lay the foundations of a schematized doctrine of 'two ways', in which each aspect of the one is balanced by the corresponding aspect of the other.

The author of *Discipline* develops the doctrine of the 'two ways' in a long passage devoted to it (D iii 17–iv 16); and in doing so he fuses that of the 'two spirits' with it. He says that God has designed two spirits for men by which they shall walk, according to the one in the 'ways of light' and according to the other in the 'ways of darkness' (D iii 17–18, 20–21); and he then describes 'their ways (*i.e.* those of the two spirits) in the world' and how men walk 'in their ways' (D iv 2, 15). Such a fusion would only be possible when the two doctrines were so far developed that the details of each were clear enough to be individually picked out, set down side by side and then worked up into a composite theory. This author, in his schematic treatment of these two doctrines, comes close to the point reached in certain other works of the last quarter of the 1st and the first half of the 2nd century A.D.: these are the *Epistle of Barnabas* (approximately A.D. 70–80), the Latin *Duae Viae* or 'Two Ways' (of which the date is unknown), the Greek *Teaching of the Twelve Apostles* (approximately A.D. 80–100), and the *Shepherd of Hermas* (A.D. 140–55). The various

---

[1] Testaments *Asher* i 3–v 2.   [2] II Enoch xxx 15.   [3] In *Aboth* ii 9.
[4] Matt. vii. 13–14.   [5] *Ibid.* xxi. 32.   [6] Acts xvi. 17.
[7] *Ibid.* ii. 28.   [8] Jn. viii. 12, xii. 35; 1 Jn. i. 6–7, ii. 11; 2 Pet. ii. 2.

expositions of the two doctrines in these works must now be compared with their treatment in *Discipline* with a view to seeing how they are related and what, if any, light they throw on the date of this work.

The doctrine is set out in *Discipline* in a section instructing the 'Sons of Light' about man's moral nature and how he comes under the control of one or other of two spirits. It describes how everything that is and that will be exists from God's knowledge and how He has created man for dominion over the world and how 'He has assigned him two spirits by which he shall walk till the season of his visitation; they are the spirits of truth and perversion. From a well of light are the generations of truth but from a fountain of darkness the generations of perverseness. In the hand of the prince of lights is dominion over all the sons of righteousness; in the ways of light do they walk. But in the hand of the angel of darkness is dominion over the sons of perversion; and they walk in the ways of darkness. And it is because of the angel of darkness that all the sons of righteousness go astray'; for he and the spirits allotted to his service strive to bring down the sons of light but God comes to their help, although 'He has created the spirits of light and darkness', and will love the one and hate the other through all eternity (D iii 17–iv 1).

The text then goes on to say: 'Now these are their ways in the world. [The way of the spirit of truth is] to illumine the heart of a man and to make all the ways of true righteousness straight before him' that he may practise various virtues, of which a list follows with the rewards which will follow such conduct. It then says: 'But to the spirit of perversion belong' such and such vices, of which a detailed list is given together with their appropriate punishments (D iv 2–14).

The section is brought to a conclusion with a general statement, to the effect that all the families of mankind come under the dominion of these spirits which are equally balanced 'till the last period'; and 'He (*sc.* God) has put eternal enmity between their divisions: an abomination to truth are acts of wrong-doing, an abomination to wrong-doing are all ways of truth. God however 'through the mysteries of His comprehension' and through His 'glorious wisdom' has appointed a limit of time for the existence of wrong-doing, and He will destroy it 'at the time of the visitation', when 'the truth of the world will appear for ever' (D iv 15–26).

The author of the *Epistle of Barnabas* deals somewhat differently with the 'two ways'.[1] He says:

'There are two ways of teaching and of power, the one of light and the other of darkness; and there is a great difference between the two ways. For light-bearing angels of God are stationed on the one and the angels of Satan on the other; and the one is Lord from all eternity

[1] Lightfoot & Harmer *Apostolic Fathers: Revised Texts* 262–4 (285–7).

and unto all eternity, whereas the other is lord of the season of iniquity that now is.

'This then is the way of light, if any one wishing to travel on the way to his appointed place would be zealous in his works; the knowledge then which is given to us that we may walk therein is such as follows';

and this 'knowledge' is set out at length, starting from the rule that 'thou shalt love Him who made thee, thou shalt fear Him who has created thee' and that 'thou shalt not walk in the way of death' and continuing with a list of works which may or may not be done; and this list ends with the warning that

'thou shalt confess thy sins; thou shalt not betake thyself to prayer with an evil conscience.

'This is the way of life.'

The author then briefly describes the opposite way, saying:

'But the way of darkness' (or 'the dark one') is crooked and full of cursing; for it is a way of eternal death with punishment, wherein are things that destroy men's souls'; and these are tabulated in a similar list of vices and offences.

The texts of the Latin *Two Ways* and the Greek *Teaching* are so alike[1] that they can be set out in parallel columns:

Viae sunt duae in saeculo, vitae et mortis, lucis et tenebrarum; in his constituti sunt angeli duo, unus aequitatis alter iniquitatis.	'There are two ways, one of life and one of death;
Distantia autem magna est duarum viarum.	and there is a great distance between them.
Via ergo vitae haec est: primo diliges deum aeternum qui te fecit, secundum proximum tuum et te ipsum.	The way of life is this: first thou shalt love God who has made thee, second thy neighbour as thyself.'

An 'interpretation of these words' is then given. The Greek text contains some general precepts from the Gospels, which the Latin text omits; then a 'second commandment', common to both texts, is added containing mostly specific prohibitions from the Scriptures and also some positive counsels. The last of these counsels is

non accedas ad orationem cum conscientia mala.	'in church thou shalt confess thy transgressions and thou shalt not betake thyself to prayer with an evil conscience.
Haec est via vitae.	This is the way of life.'

[1] Schlecht *Doctrina XII Apostolorum* 105–12.

The 'way of death' is then set out shortly in the following words:

mortis autem via est illi contraria,	'but the way of death is this.
primum nequam et maledictis plena	First of all it is evil and full of curses';

and these 'curses' are then set out in a long list of specific sins or vices, ending with the general wish:

abstine te, fili, ab istis omnibus.	'may ye be delivered, my children, from all these things.'

Lastly, the author of the *Shepherd of Hermas*, who speaks of the 'two ways' in one of the 'Mandates',[1] says that 'the way of righteousness is straight but the way of unrighteousness crooked; but walk thou in the straight [and level] path and leave the crooked alone'. Then, after briefly expanding this theme, he says: 'there are two angels with a man, one of righteousness and one of wickedness', and describes their works, ending with 'here then thou hast the workings of both the angels. Understand then and trust the angel of righteousness, but stand aloof from the angel of wickedness inasmuch as his teaching is evil in every matter . . . ; it is good to follow the angel of righteousness and to take leave of the angel of wickedness. This commandment declareth what concerneth the faith, that thou mayest trust the works of the angel of righteousness and doing them mayest live unto God; but believe that the works of the angel of wickedness are difficult, and by not doing them thou shalt live unto God.'

The resemblances and the differences between these various descriptions of the 'two ways' are clear enough; but in order that the proper conclusions may be drawn from a comparison of them, they are here briefly summarized in parallel columns:[2]

The accounts in the *Epistle* and the *Two Ways* are the shortest, inasmuch as the lists of corresponding virtues and vices are not so long; the *Two Ways* omits a number of virtues and vices which the *Teaching* seems to have derived from Christian sources, especially the Gospels. Inasmuch therefore as it is Judaic in outlook, it comes closest of all three to the account in *Discipline*, which is purely Jewish. This difference alone is enough to throw doubt on the supposition that the Latin *Two Ways* is an abridged translation of the Greek *Teaching*; and the improbability of such a supposition is increased by the fact that the two angels are absent from the *Teaching*, though present in some form or other in all the other accounts.[3] The *Epistle* has the two angels though in a different form, and it has the same summary of the 'way of light' as these two. Contrariwise, the accounts in *Discipline* and the

[1] Lightfoot & Harmer *op. cit.* 325–7 (428–9).
[2] Cp. Audet in *RB*, NS LIX 219–98 and LX 47–82.   [3] Cp. 2 Cor. xi. 14.

Two Ways	Discipline	Barnabas	Teaching
two ways	two ways	two ways:	two ways:
in the world:	in the world:		
life and death			life and death;
or			
light and darkness;	light and darkness	light and dark-	
	or	ness;	
	truth and wickedness;		
duo angeli:	two spirits:		
	prince of light and	light-bringing	
unus aequitatis	spirit of light or truth	angels of God	
	over sons of righteous-		
	ness or generation of		
	truth;		
and		and	
	angel of darkness and		
	spirit of darkness	angels of Satan;	
alter iniquitatis;	and perversion		
	over		
	sons of perversion or		
	generation of perversion;		
	[confession (D i 24–5)];	confession of sins;	
way of life			way of life
	ways of light	way of light	
	those of the sons of		
	righteousness;		
to love Creator[1]	complete loyalty	to love Creator[1]	to love Creator[2]
and neighbour,	to all sons of truth[2]	and neighbour;	and neighbour
not to pray with			not to pray with
evil conscience;			evil conscience;
	eternal life;		
	ways of darkness	way of darkness	
	those of the sons of		
	perversity,		
way of death evil			way of death evil
and full of curses	eternal ruin	eternal death	and full of curses

Two Ways, which agree with the *Epistle* in calling the 'two ways' those of light and darkness, stand alone in describing them as 'in the world' (D iv 2); and the 'two spirits', the 'spirit of truth' and the 'spirit of perversion', in the former and the *duo angeli aequitatis* and *iniquitatis* in the latter, almost exactly correspond. The *Shepherd* stands outside the main stream; its 'two angels . . . , one of righteousness and one of wickedness' are clearly the *angeli aequitatis* and *iniquitatis* of the *Two Ways* and may be compared with the 'angels of holiness' (W vii 6 x 11; I Q 28 B ii 6) and the 'angels of destruction' (D iv 12 W xiii 12 Z ii 4) in other Scrolls. Otherwise the fact of the 'two ways' is its only direct point of contact with the other four documents.

[1] Cp. Ecclus. vii. 30.   [2] Cp. Rom. xii. 10 and 1 Pet. iii. 8.

The close parallelism in matter and form (although this last must not be over-emphasized; for it is to some extent conditioned by the matter) of the accounts in the *Two Ways* and *Discipline* reveal a related type of composition, suggesting either a common source or mutual influence, if not both; but the simplicity of the *Two Ways* seems to indicate that this is the earlier and the highly elaborated and indeed literary account in *Discipline* is the later. Further, the rare and sporadic references to the doctrine of the 'two ways' before the 2nd century A.D. is significant; the crop of references in the New Testament, though unsystematized, shows that the doctrine was very much in the air and ripe for systematization, of which the *Two Ways* and *Discipline* offer the earliest examples. Once again, then, a comparative study of its contents proves that at any rate *Discipline* cannot be assigned to any pre-Christian date; it can only be approximately contemporary with the New Testament and other more or less contemporary writings.

The doctrine of the 'two ways' is by implication dualistic; and the Scrolls show definite dualistic tendencies.

God has appointed two spirits, the spirit of holiness or truth and the spirit of perversity, which struggle continually for the mastery of man's soul. In fact, a man is virtually predestined to be numbered with the 'sons of light' or the 'sons of darkness', with the 'men of truth' or the 'people of perversion', to belong to the 'lot (*i.e.* party) of God' or to the 'lot of Belial'; for, as the author of *Discipline* says: 'from the God of knowledge everything that is and everything that will be comes; before their coming into existence He has established the whole design of them and, when their appointed roles are realized, they fulfil their functions according to His glorious design, and nothing can be changed. Every kind of law is under His control, and He sustains them in all their pursuits. So He created man for the dominion of the world and assigned two spirits to him, whereby he should walk till the appointed time of His visitation. These are the spirits of truth and iniquity; in the source of light are the origins of truth and in the well-spring of darkness are the origins of error. In the hand of the prince of light is dominion over all the sons of righteousness, and they walk in the ways of light; and in the hand of the angel of darkness is all dominion over the sons of error, and they walk in the ways of error', but 'the God of Israel and his angel of truth help all the sons of light' (D iii 15–25). This is clearly dualism, but it is subject to the Biblical doctrine of the God 'who formed light and created darkness, who makes peace and creates evil',[1] for 'He has created the spirits of light and darkness and has established all his works in them . . . God has loved one of them for all the duration of the ages and delights for ever in all its works; but He has rejected the counsel of the other and hates all its ways for

---

[1] Cp. Isa. xlv. 7 (s. pp. 532–3).

ever' (D iii 25–iv 1). Thus the world becomes the scene of a Titanic struggle between these two spirits, God's spirit of truth and holiness and the spirit of perversity, called Belial. This struggle is at the bottom of the work which has been called the *War of the Sons of Light and the Sons of Darkness*, in which the former, *i.e.*, the Covenanters, are engaged in an apocalyptic struggle with the latter, depicted under the figure of the Kittians, *i.e.* the Romans, and in which the party is promised final victory over the powers of this world. Here the good and the wicked are separated, and the good must take every care not to be defiled by contact with the wicked. Men could achieve this end only by forsaking the world and joining the holy community; for 'they shall separate themselves from the midst of the habitation of perverse men by going into the wilderness to clear a way for Him there', by studying the Law and acting in accordance with 'all that has been revealed from time to time and in accordance with that which the Prophets have revealed through His holy Spirit' (D viii 13–16). At the same time 'man is not master of his ways and the sons of 'man cannot direct their steps; for justification belongs to God and perfect conduct comes from His hand' (D xi 10–11); for the Covenanters believed in a doctrine of divine election whereby every man was predestined to the 'lot of God' or the 'lot of Belial', while they only were the chosen Israel.

Accordingly, the doctrine of the Scrolls has been called a deterministic theology. This description of it is further supported by the apparent division of men into four groups according to their allotted destinies (Z ix 2–54), which is totally unlike the old Hebrew conception of the whole nation as elect of God;[1] it is supported also by that of the history of the human race, as exemplified in the Hebrew people, into five periods, in each of which God set apart a remnant destined for salvation under the leadership of his chosen servants (Z iii 3–viii 2).[2] Marked, however, as the deterministic elements in the Scrolls are, their teaching is not through and through deterministic; as just said, man could escape his destiny by joining the holy community, *i.e.* that of the Covenanters, and putting himself under the leadership of the Rightful Teacher and his disciples who had been initiated into the mystery of the time when God would fulfil what the prophets had foretold; for, since the Teacher came, the Law could be kept only under his guidance. In this way, Prof. Burrows says, 'the idea of the chosen people has become in effect the idea of a church'.[3]

The determinism of the Scrolls, then, is incomplete; it is not pushed to its logical conclusion. The ancient Hebrews had already been puzzled by the problem: for example, the doctrine of the Old Testament, allowing that God might put a lying spirit into a man for His

[1] Rost *ap.* Burrows *Scrolls* I 263.   [2] Vermès *ibid.* 263.
[3] *Ibid.* 263.

own purposes,[1] might superficially be taken to mean that God could be the author of evil; but the inspiration of false prophets was already denied by the canonical prophets,[2] and Jesus ben Sirach taught explicitly that God could in no way be the cause of a man's sin.[3] The same uncertainty is found in the Scrolls, where the certainty of the Apostle is not reached.[4] On the one hand they contain such an extreme statement as 'Thou hast created the righteous man (*ṣaddîq*) and destined him to be preserved in thy covenant for a time of acceptance . . . and Thou hast created wicked men for [the time of] Thy wrath and hast dedicated them to a day of slaughter, because they have walked in a way that is not good and have rejected [Thy] covenant' (T xv 14–18), that 'Thou hast chosen them (*sc.* the members of the society) for an eternal covenant' (D iv 22) and that 'he makes those whom He hates to err' (Z ii 10). Or again 'according as man's inheritance is in truth and righteousness, so he hates evil; but, in so far as his heritage is in the lot of iniquity and wickedness in him, so he abominates truth' (D iv 24–5); and in the same spirit the Covenanter must love the Sons of Light and hate the Sons of Darkness, of whom the former are such 'each according to his lot in the purpose of God' and the latter are such 'each according to his guilt by the vengeance of God' (D i 9–11). Here there is little if any room for the exercise of the will. On the other hand those who reject the covenant are punished not because they are foredoomed to sin and punishment but 'because they hearkened not to the voice of their Maker' (Z iv 7); and one passage (if rightly translated) speaks of 'the secret (unconscious) sins into which they have strayed, incurring guilt; and they have wilfully committed open (conscious) sins . . . , bringing great judgements upon themselves unto eternal damnation without survivor' (D v 11–13). The references, too, to God as 'patient in judgement . . . [and] Thy righteousness (appears) in all Thine acts' (T i 6) and the clear assertion that 'patience is with Him and plenteous forgiveness to make atonement for those who repent of transgression' (Z ii 3) and that He has 'plenteous mercy on those whom He accepts' as well as 'abundance of mercy' to 'forgive sin' (T iv 32–3, 37 vii 37) are incompatible with the notion that a man may be punished for the commission of offences beyond his control. Allowance must also be made, in estimating the doctrine of the Covenanters on the subject of determinism, for the Hebrew habit of speaking of the result of an action as its purpose. When therefore the poet says to God 'Thou hast appointed them (*sc.* the wicked who reject the covenant) to execute great judgements on them in the sight of all Thy creatures and that they be a sign . . . for ever that [all] may

---

[1] Judg. ix. 23; 1 Sam. xvi. 14, xviii. 10, xix. 9; 1 Ki. xxii. 21–2 = 2 Chron. xviii. 20–1.

[2] *E.g.* Jer. xxiii. 16–28 and Ezek. xiii. 6–7, xiv. 9.

[3] Ecclus. xv 20.   [4] Rom. ix. 14.

know Thy glory and Thy great might' (T xv 19–20), he may only be describing as a purpose what a modern thinker or writer will treat as a result.[1] The emphasis also on repentance and the readmission of lapsed members mitigates the harshness of the doctrine and to this extent leaves open the possibility of free will.

Determinism or predestination, of which some few traces have been detected in the Old Testament,[2] is a foreign doctrine derived from Iranian theology to which the origin of the dualism of the two spirits, the good and the evil, has been traced; according to this mankind is divided into two contrasted groups, namely 'the people of truth' and the 'people of falsehood'. These two primeval spirits themselves made the original choice of their own destinies, and in the same way each individual man was thought to make his own choice between truth and falsehood, good and evil, and each must act according to his choice throughout his life, thus at the same time determining his ultimate destiny, whether happiness and glory or damnation and annihilation. The choice before the Covenanters was somewhat different; for this Iranian dualism had come under the influence of Jewish monotheism and the doctrine of creation, by which it was saved from indulging in the absurd and extravagant speculations of true gnosticism. For these people 'He (sc. God) created spirits of light and darkness' (D iii 25), and He decided to which spirit each man should owe allegiance before his creation, thus irrevocably fixing his ultimate fate. This doctrine of its very nature[3] inevitably raised for a Jew the problem: how could God create good and evil and predetermine every man to the one or the other and then judge him worthy of eternal bliss or eternal punishment according to his predestined actions? This problem did not arise under the purely dualistic Iranian system; under that every individual man, like the two original spirits, was free to choose good or evil. It only arose when, like the Christian Church, the Covenanters did away with the determination of man's fate by his own free choice or the limitation of God's power by refusing to regard Him as the cause not only of good but also of evil and accepted the divine determination arising out of the divine creation without reservation. Their conclusion was something like that reached by the Rabbis, who held that everything has been created by God,[4] as set out in a conversation between Acher and his pupil R. Me'ir, who flourished c. A.D. 90–130, in the following words: 'The Holy One (praised be He) made a counterpart for all that He created . . . : He created godly and ungodly, He created paradise and hell. Every one has two portions, one in paradise and one in hell: the godly man who has shown himself worthy receives his and his neigh-

---

[1] Cp. Sutcliffe *Monks* 72–3.
[2] *E.g.* Prov. xxi. 1.
[3] Kuhn in Stendahl *Scrolls* 97–101.
[4] Cp. Grintz in *Sinai* XXXII 35–6.

bour's portion in paradise; the ungodly man who has proved himself guilty receives his and his neighbour's portion in hell.'[1] All three groups, Christians and Covenanters and Rabbis, have reached the same point; and all three leave the dilemma unresolved.

Such problems would be inconceivable in the 1st or 2nd centuries B.C. when the principal if not the only questions perplexing the loyal Jew were political; they were characteristic of the 1st century A.D., when their philosophical and especially their theological implications were coming to the fore.

6. GNOSTICISM

Gnosticism can already be detected in Jewish apocalyptic writings, while some very uncertain allusions to it have been noted also in the New Testament.[2] Essene doctrine, too, was not free from its influence, and Mandaeism was a gnostic system. That the Scrolls reveal some traces of its influence is therefore no cause for surprise; but that the teaching both of the Essenes and of the Covenanters can be shown to have been affected by it does not compel their identification. Scarcely any philosophy and no religion of the time was entirely free from it.

Gnosticism[3] was neither the doctrine of any particular party, group or sect, nor a definite scheme of thought in Judaism but a many-sided and ever-changing movement generally pervading the educated classes in the East; it came into prominence in Egypt and Palestine in the 2nd and 1st centuries B.C. and reached its apogee in the 2nd century A.D., when its leading teachers flourished under the Antonines.

The origin of gnosticism, an amalgam of Hellenic philosophy and Oriental theosophy, lay in the syncretism resulting from the break-up of the old pagan religions and the lingering belief that a deep wisdom was enshrined in the Oriental mythologies. Its basic principle was the doctrine of a knowledge supernaturally attained, an immediate vision of truth, whereby the nature of the deity, the interaction of the spiritual and the material, the origin of good and evil, could be explained; this knowledge was not knowledge in the scientific sense but something acquired by immediate revelation. The adept on the one hand underwent a mystical experience whereby he apprehended the true nature of God and entered into communion with Him; on the other he was instructed in magical passwords and secret names, participated in mystic rites and learned an occult lore. In gnostic doctrine the divine and the material worlds, the worlds of light and darkness, the worlds of good and evil, stood over against each other; and all the wickedness and misery in the world were due to the forbidden intermixture of

---

[1] B. Talmud *Hagigah* 15a. [2] Cp. Headlam in Hastings' *DB* II 187–9.
[3] Scott in Hastings' *ERE* VI 231–42.

light and darkness regarded as spirit and matter and irreconcilably opposed to each other in a metaphysical, not a physical, dualism. The world of evil was regarded as full of energy and hostile powers; it was the seat of all that is evil in this material and corporeal world, in which the powers of good and evil are continually at war. The gnostic adept must strive for a life that had no part in this lower world, ruled by the demons and spirits of darkness, and must raise himself by virtue of his knowledge above them to the good of the higher realm of life. At the same time an absolute indifference towards the material world made him look upon marriage and the propagation of the race as worthless, if not as absolutely evil; and the resulting asceticism sometimes passed into libertinism. Gnosticism however, did not leave its adherents without hope. It taught, first, a redemption that was a deliverance from this material world, which was regarded as intrinsically evil; second, this idea of deliverance from a material world was blended with that of an escape into a world of freedom. Fate had come to be regarded as a veritable tyranny, especially since it had been connected with astrological beliefs of Babylonian origin. Gnosticism sought for deliverance from this tyranny along the lines of astral mythology. The soul, held captive by astral powers, in order to win its freedom had to ascend through the spheres over which they ruled, subduing their guardian demons by passwords and charms; and the adept was prepared for this journey by lustrations and sacraments and by instruction in the mysteries. This escape was conceived as a rising from the material to the spiritual world; a bodily resurrection or even personal immortality was precluded by the fundamental conception of matter as evil. A characteristic mark of gnosticism was that redemption was expected for only a limited number of chosen spirits, who were destined to return to their original place in the kingdom of light; the rest were doomed to the misery of everlasting degradation in the realm of darkness. As there were two worlds, so there were two classes of men, who were absolutely distinct, the good and the wicked; God was responsible for the former but not for the latter. The redeeming *gnōsis* or knowledge could deliver only the spiritual, and to impart it to the unspiritual was profanation. Every sect had its own lustrations and anointings, sacramental meals and magical forms, and the secret names of angels[1] and demons were carefully committed to memory; but certain notions, notably that souls were native to the higher world and could be redeemed only by divine intervention and that matter was intrinsically bad, were common to all gnostic systems. In conclusion, gnosticism represented the final effort of paganism to maintain its hold on the world by allying itself with current systems of belief, for example with Judaism and above all with Christianity as a new and vital faith; but, as Scott says,[2]

[1] S. pp. 108–9. [2] Scott *ibid.* 241.

associated with a profound search for truth as well as genuine and enthusiastic religion, it belonged to past history and, abandoning itself to wild and delirious speculations, it clashed with the Church, which after a long struggle threw it off as a heresy, and it died out in the 3rd or 4th century A.D.

As Dr. Reicke argues,[1] what is meant by 'knowledge (da'aṯ)' in the Scrolls is neither the abstract γνῶσις of gnosticism nor modern intellectual knowledge; and the God of the Covenanters is not a philosophical idea but a living person. For these people da'aṯ embraced various senses corresponding to those found in it in the Old Testament, especially voluntary and practical knowledge. Speculation however in the Scrolls has advanced beyond anything found in the Old Testament and so shows some progress towards Jewish gnosticism, but it hardly exceeds anything found in apocalyptic literature or such a work as *Wisdom*, which may be dated *c.* A.D. 30–45.

The Covenanters were interested not in the immediate spiritual development of a man's soul but in God's realization of His will through the Scriptures and the 'covenant'; and this, which was the covenant into which they had entered on becoming members of the society, was for them the framework of the divine knowledge.

In the Scrolls da'aṯ is used primarily in its ordinary senses *e.g.* of mind (D i 12) and 'consideration' (D iv 4) and practical 'understanding',[2] especially of 'righteous laws' (D iii 1), even while its content is described as 'mysteries of knowledge' (D iv 6). That the required knowledge is of God's realization of His purposes is the reason why such emphasis is laid on obedience to His commands, and the insight expected of members is the knowledge and practice of the Law (D v 20–2 vi 18). This insistence on the knowledge of the Law explains the repeated prescriptions for instruction in and study of the Law (D vi 6–7 viii 1–2, 15); and, even if members were vouchsafed special 'insight (śēḵel)' and illumined by the spirit of truth on entering the covenant, instruction was still necessary to ensure their correct behaviour in every situation (D ix 12–16), as also Christians became as 'full of goodness, filled with all knowledge, able also to admonish one another'.[3] This ideal of 'eternal knowledge' (D ii 3) as the study of the Law and obedience to the covenant (D iv 2–6 xi 3–7) is a genuine Jewish ideal devoid of any gnostic tendency. God's knowledge is the divine providence (D iii 15), which belongs to the 'mysteries of God' (D iii 23). For example, no real gnostic ideas can be traced in 'all that is and will be comes from the God of knowledge; before their coming into existence He had established all their design' (D iii 15–16), which simply says that God has planned and created everything, or 'by His knowledge everything has been brought into being, and He has established

---

[1] In *NTS* I 137–41.   [2] Cp. Isa. xi. 2.   [3] Cp. Rom. xv. 14.

everything by His purpose and apart from Him nothing is done' (D xi 11), where 'His knowledge' exercises the same function as the Word by whom 'all things were made' and without whom 'not anything was made which was made';[1] even 'from the fountain of His knowledge He has opened my sight,[2] and my eye has beheld the wonders that He has wrought and my heart is illumined with the mystery of that which comes into being' (D xi 3–4) betrays no gnostic influence, since the 'fountain' can be taken to be the Law and the Prophets (cp. Z viii 5) as easily as gnostic baptism in spiritual water. The writer even who says 'Thou hast taught all knowledge, and everything that has come to pass [has been] by Thy will' (D xi 17–18) is not thinking of any metaphysical secrets known to God but means only that there is no knowledge available to man in himself; for God possesses all knowledge and communicates it to men as He thinks fit. This knowledge is the knowledge of God's deeds and acts, not of metaphysical secrets, even though 'there is none beside Thee to respond to Thy counsel and to understand all Thy holy purpose and to gaze into the depths of Thy mysteries and to comprehend all Thy marvels' (D xi 18–19); but even this is no gnostic doxology of man's splendid epistemological resources. These and many similar passages can all be interpreted in a non-gnostic sense even while they may be pointing the way to Jewish gnostic speculations; but they betray no traces of genuine mystic gnosticism.

Contrariwise, the emphasis on knowledge as divinely imparted is clear in the psalm at the end of *Discipline*, from which several of the passages just quoted are derived. Thus its author says 'blessed art Thou, O my God, who hast opened the heart of thy servant to knowledge. . . . Thou hast taught all knowledge, and all that has come to pass exists by Thy will; and there is none other beside Thee to gainsay Thy decision and to understand all Thy holy purpose and to ponder the depth of Thy mysteries and to apprehend all Thy marvellous deeds together with Thy mighty power' (D xi 15–20); and again 'the light in my heart comes from His marvellous mysteries; in the eternal Being mine eye has seen wisdom, because knowledge is hidden from men and prudent counsels from the sons of men' (D xi 5–6). This is secret knowledge which may not be revealed; for 'no one shall admonish or dispute with the sons of perdition; but the purpose of the Law shall be hidden in the midst of perverse men' (D ix 16–17). A part of this secret knowledge, revealed only to the initiated, was the special calendar which the Covenanters shared with the group from whom the books of *Jubilees* and *I Enoch* emanated; for, as said in the *Zadokite Documents*, He revealed to them 'hidden things in which all Israel had gone astray: His holy sabbaths and glorious fixed seasons' (Z v 1–2) and

[1] Jn i. 3.   [2] Cp. Psa. xxxvi. 9.

required them 'to observe the sabbath according to its exact reckoning and the feasts and the fast-day' (Z viii 15). This too is a divinely imparted esoteric knowledge into which an echo of astral elements has been imported[1] and to that extent may be regarded as approaching gnosticism; but the knowledge required to calculate the times of the holy days and feasts is Jewish lore imbedded in the Law, whence it can be extracted by any Jew trained in the methods considered correct by the Covenanters.

This 'knowledge' approaches that of gnosticism only in the insistence on knowledge as divinely imparted to certain initiated believers. Thus the Scrolls insist that only the 'sons of truth', *i.e.* those 'who enter the covenant', will win the 'victorious light of eternity . . . in eternal light' (D iv 6–8), while those who walk by the spirit of perversion will perish 'in eternal ruin . . . amid the calamities of darkness' (D iv 11–14; cp. ii 8); but this doctrine can be traced back to the Old Testament[2] and has left its mark in other Jewish writings[3] as well as in the New Testament.[4] In so far as it is *gnōsis*, it is *gnōsis* properly controlled, not wild and untrammelled.

A concept of frequent occurrence in the Scrolls is that of 'mystery (*rāz*)'.[5] The word itself is of Iranian origin, but that does not mean that it necessarily implies Iranian influence, whether direct or even indirect; for *Ecclesiasticus* already uses it to denote anything that is secret.[6] In *Daniel* it describes what is known only to God as secret;[7] so in the Scrolls it may describe what is known only to Him as still future, *e.g.* His extirpation of 'wickedness (*riš'āh*)'[8] in the world (W iii 9), or anything inexplicable to man, *e.g.* the enmity of Belial (W xiv 9) and 'sin (*peša'*)' itself (T v 26, I Q 27 i 2).[9] Most often it is used in speaking of the 'mysteries of God' (D iii 23 H vii 8 W iii 9 xvi 11, 16); these include His insight or understanding (D iv 18 T ix 23 xiii 13) and truth (D ix 18), His purpose (T fr. iii 7), His marvellous power (D ix 18 xi 5 H i 21 ii 13 iv 27 vii 27 xi 10 xiii 2 Z v 5) and works (W xiv 14); and the way of the spirit of truth is to enlighten a man's heart that he may walk circumspectly 'according to the truth of the mysteries of knowledge', *sc.* of God's government of the universe (D iv 6). Thus the 'mysteries' of the Scrolls are theological and eschatological, whether the attributes of God or His present and future dealings with men; they are not the cosmological, metaphysical or theosophical, *i.e.* the doctrines of any gnostic system.

---

[1] Cp. Scott *ibid.* 235.
[2] Dan. xii. 2–3; cp. Isa. lx. 19 (light) and Ezek. xv. 6 (fire).
[3] *E.g.* I Enoch xlv 4, lviii 2–6, cviii 8–13 (light); ciii 7–8 cviii 6 (fire).
[4] *E.g.* Matt. xviii. 8, xxv. 41 (fire) and Col. i. 12 (light).
[5] Cp. Reicke *ibid.* 138.   [6] Ecclus. viii. 18, xii. 11.
[7] Dan. ii. 29, iv. 8.   [8] Cp. pp. 202–3.

The idea that 'knowledge' or *gnōsis* was something secret which must be jealously guarded and not revealed to anyone outside the member's own society, which was strictly prescribed for the Covenanters (D iv 6, v 15–16 ix 16–19 x 24–5), became current in the 1st and 2nd centuries A.D.; the reason was that the ever-present risk of persecution at the hands of fellow Jews[1] or of the Roman authorities[2] forced members of secret societies, driven in on themselves, to withhold potentially dangerous knowledge, *e.g.* that the member of a society was in some way superior to ordinary man and specially chosen by God for a spiritual or political purpose, and not to reveal it to others who might betray them. So Jesus on several occasions gave orders that what He had done or said would not be told to any man;[3] and similar secrecy was imposed on the Essenes[4] and perhaps also on the Ebionites[5] and was prescribed also in the apocalyptic *II Esdras* (*c.* A.D. 90–130).[6] The Mandaeans also enjoined secrecy on all who were admitted to the mysteries of their religion,[7] following the practice of the age.

In connection with the Scrolls the literature of these Mandaeans, one of the gnostic sects, acquires fresh significance. These were a group claiming spiritual descent from John the Baptist, who was said to have left a number of disciples.[8] They lived on the eastern banks of the Jordan until they migrated (possibly between *c.* A.D. 30 and A.D. 37)[9] to Mesopotamia, where again they settled beside rivers; a dwindling community still survives in the same and neighbouring districts. They were so called as claiming a mysterious 'knowledge' (Aram. *mandâ*) of divine origin, and they described themselves as a 'plantation of the pious',[10] as the 'elect of righteousness' (*bahîraiyâ dziḏqâ*)[11] and as 'elect' and 'perfect'.[12] So Christians called themselves 'elect'[13] and 'perfect'[14] and the Church considered itself the 'planting of God's vineyard',[15] while the Covenanters claimed to be 'perfect' and 'elect of righteousness' (T ii 13) and also an 'eternal plantation' (D viii 5, ix 10; Z i 7);[16] here all three echoed a well-known expression, which recurs in other

---

[1] *E.g.* Jn. ix. 5 and 1 Cor. xv. 9.   [2] Pp. 348–9.
[3] S. p. 578 n. 4.   [4] Josephus *War* II viii 7 §§ 141–2.
[5] Rehm *Pseudoklementinen* I ii (Epistle of Peter to James) § 3.
[6] 2 Esdras xii. 37–8, xiv. 26, 45–6.
[7] *E.g.* Drower *Naṣoraean Commentaries* 1–2 i 11–12, 65 iii 132–8, 66 iii 150–60.
[8] Matt. xiv. 12 and Acts xviii. 25, xix. 2.
[9] Macuch in *TLz.* LXXXII 401–8; cp. Albright in *Studies in honour of C. H. Dodd* 154 (where the Mandaeans are said not to be traceable as a sect before the 5th century A.D., although its sources are allowed to go much further back).
[10] Lidzbarski *Johannisbuch* 219–20; cp. *Ginzā* II 61–2, *Mandäische Liturgien* 149–50.
[11] Lidzbarski *Johannisbuch* 50.
[12] Lidzbarski *Ginzā* II 35–45; cp. *Mandäische Liturgien* 75, 106–7.
[13] Cp. Odes of Solomon xxxiii 13.   [14] Pp. 520.
[15] Connolly *Apostolic Constitutions* 2–3 § 1.
[16] P. 61.

Jewish literature of this century.[1] The members of the Mandaean sect, who were destined to eternal light as well as the angels, were called 'sons of light';[2] they believed not only in angels of light but also in a 'king of light',[3] who recalls the Covenanters' 'prince of light' (D iii 20, Z vii 19); they applied the title of 'lord of greatness' (*mârâ drâḇûṭâ*) to the mystic Adam, who in their theology preceded the physical and human Adam, as the divine and priestly teacher,[4] just as the author of one of the Scrolls calls God the 'lord of greatness' (GA ii 4; *mārēh r'ḇûṭâ*); and they held that they would win a 'robe of state' or a 'garment of splendour' with a 'great crown' or a 'splendid crown',[5] corresponding respectively to the 'crown of glory' and the 'garments of majesty' expected by the Covenanters (D iv 7–8; cp. T ix 24)[6] and to the 'white raiment' or 'white robes' and the 'crown of glory' to which Christians looked forward in a future life.[7] Their opponents were called the 'men of lies',[8] as a leading opponent of the Covenanters was called by them the 'Man of Falsehood' (H ii 2 v 11 Z ix 39)[9], and the angels of light were opposed by the 'spirits of lies' (cp. D iv 9);[10] thus they believed in a dualism of light and darkness.[11] Admission to their society was by baptism in running water, which might be repeated as often as purification was required and to which they submitted fully clothed in white garments (which the laity wore only on special occasions, while their priests regularly wore them); and they repudiated animal sacrifices. They rejected celibacy and enjoined monogamy, though allowing a succession of wives, and they made procreation a religious duty. They held that man was created by the demiurge or perhaps by the evil spirits but was incomplete until 'knowledge of life' (cp. D ii 3) or true *gnōsis* breathed a soul into him; that the world is peopled by good and evil people and that good and evil spirits are at war with one another; that the Messiah, whom they called the 'prophet of the Jews', was a leader of evil spirits who led men to abandon the true religion; that the soul at death passes to an after-life in which it is rewarded or punished in accordance with its life on earth. Thus they peopled the universe with strange theological phantasies and demonic creatures. Basically, therefore, Mandaeism was a gnostic dualistic religion, but neither dualism nor gnosticism was original in Mandaeism; each was derived from earlier sources and might thus equally easily have found its way into other contemporary or later religions, since both were widespread at this time. Contrari-

---

[1] Pp. 61, 454.
[2] Lidzbarski *Ginzâ* II 13, 246 and *Mandäische Liturgien* 17–18, 24–5, 36–7, 41–2, 71.
[3] Lidzbarski *Ginzâ* II 31. [4] Drower *Secret Adam* 26, 63–4.
[5] Lidzbarski *Mandäische Liturgien* 27, 57; 103, 158, 160.
[6] Pp. 72, 75. [7] Rev. iii. 5, vi. 11; 1 Pet. v. 4.
[8] Lidzbarski *Ginzâ* 43–4. [9] Pp. 285–8.
[10] *Ibid.* 449. [11] *Ibid.* 67.

wise, the combination of fundamental dualism with asceticism, so characteristic of Manichaeism, is not found in Mandaean doctrine or practice.

Essenes[1] and Therapeuts[2] as well as Covenanters and to some extent Mandaeans, breathed the same spiritual atmosphere. They found a vast stock of common ideas derived from various sources, *e.g.* the Old Testament and Jewish apocryphal literature, Persian dualism and Egyptian gnosticism, Oriental religions and Greek philosophies. Each group took what it wanted from this common stock, adapted it to its own purposes and in so doing transmuted it; but the transmutation was not always the same. Many of the coincidences here listed are striking, especially when the scantiness of the sources is taken into consideration; and, if more information were available, more such resemblances might be found. Once again, however, resemblances few or many do not by any means prove identity. Movement to and fro between parties must have been not uncommon (for example, two of John the Baptist's disciples left him and Simon left the Zealots for Christ);[3] but such movement only emphasizes the differences. That the similarities between parties which cannot possibly be identified are so numerous ought to be a warning against premature identification of other parties where the similarities are not counterbalanced by differences so far as present knowledge goes. On the one hand, therefore, when the differences far outweigh the resemblances between groups or parties, the greatest possible caution ought to be observed in identifying them, *e.g.* Essenes and Covenanters or Covenanters and Christians; on the other hand, the resemblances are enough to suggest that these various groups must be regarded as closely if not exactly contemporary in time.

At the same time the Covenanters shared with Mandaeans and Christians certain peculiarities, many of them apparently first found in the 1st century A.D. All three assigned a great place to priests in their respective communities and regarded baptism as exceptionally important; all three also recognized some form of dualism and cultivated their own particular kind of 'knowledge' and also believed in the rewards and punishments of the after-life. Other Jewish bodies, however, accepted some of these notions. What therefore is most important is the use of a number of common technical expressions, many of them not found before this century and not shared with orthodox Jews. That the Covenanters invented a number of such expressions in the 2nd or even the 1st century B.C., often using the very same Hebrew and Aramaic words as the Mandaeans, that they

---

[1] Pp. 100–21.   [2] Pp. 121–4.
[3] Matt. x. 5, Mk. iii. 18, Lk. vi. 15 and Acts i. 13 (Simon); Jn. i. 35–7 (disciples of John).

kept them secret and in the end buried all the records in which they were mentioned so successfully that all memory of them was otherwise forgotten and that the Mandaeans independently invented them in the following century is beyond belief. If however they derived them from contact with the Covenanters, the two groups must be regarded as contemporary; for the Covenanters had disappeared as a recognizable body by the end of the century. The same point emerges from a consideration of various expressions shared with the Christian Church, in so far as these can be equated in view of the differences in language and cannot be referred to the climate of contemporary opinion. Since then neither Christians nor Mandaeans can be put back before the 1st century A.D., the Covenanters must be brought down to that period.

7. COVENANTERS AND CHRISTIANS

The question may now be asked: what conclusions can be drawn from the presence of so much common matter, both of language and of ideas, in the Scrolls and the New Testament?

Any date for the Scrolls in the 2nd or 1st century B.C. presents a dilemma which its advocates cannot avoid. On the one hand, how can the Covenanters have left no mark on these centuries and yet display contacts as numerous as they are remarkable with the late 1st and perhaps even early 2nd century A.D.? On the other hand, how can the writers of the latter period have become acquainted with the contents of the Scrolls which are supposed *ex hypothesi* to have been secreted long before their time in the caves round Qumrân and to have been so utterly forgotten or lost that they have left no mark in subsequent literature? Even if the Scrolls could be held to have been composed in the 2nd or 1st century B.C. and not to have been put away till *c.* A.D. 70, how did Christian writers obtain access to them in the chaotic conditions during and after the Revolt?[1] Indeed, any theory of direct borrowing from the Scrolls as written sources is confronted by insoluble difficulties of which that of the different languages, Hebrew (and Aramaic) on the one side and Greek on the other, is the least. On the one hand, too, Christians would be very unlikely to have wanted or to have obtained access to the writings of the Covenanters; for, even if they could be supposed to have gone to Qumrân or to have visited any other community of the Covenanters, they would hardly have been allowed to consult their esoteric writings, especially as these were forbidden to reveal their doctrines to anyone (D v 15–16 ix 16–18; cp. x 24). On the other hand, the Covenanters would have found few Christian works to consult before A.D. 70, and

[1] Cp. Matt. xxiv 15–21, Mk. xiii. 14–19, Lk. xxi. 20–26.

the study of such as were written thereafter impossibly difficult in the general dispersion following the destruction of Jerusalem.

If then borrowing from written sources is excluded, other forms of borrowing call for consideration; and these may have been of several kinds.

First, individual Covenanters and Christians may have been in contact with one another and so have become acquainted with each other's societies. That Simon the 'Cananaean' or Zealot left the Zealots, whose connection (such as it may have been) with the Covenanters has already been argued,[1] is decisive on this point; movement to and fro between the various Jewish groups took place, and members of the two groups here discussed could well have known and influenced each other. Informal contacts, too, would be probable on many occasions; for Palestine is a small country, and the whole body of the Covenanters must not be pictured as permanently isolated at Qumrân. The two parties also had many common points which might bring them together: for example, the Covenanters looked for the establishment of the Messianic kingdom on earth,[2] while some Christians similarly dreamt of a kingdom in this world;[3] and a fundamental doctrine of both was the sovereignty of God, however differently they interpreted it. Further, Jesus taught and preached openly in many places; and this habit, if Covenanters were on occasion amongst his hearers, might have provoked replies and discussions, as the Pharisees attempted at times to argue with him. Lastly, the injunction laid on the Covenanters not to divulge their doctrines must not be interpreted too narrowly or pressed too far; the esoteric teaching and practice of a secret society is rarely perfectly kept. So, for example, Josephus has revealed much about the Essenes, and what Freemasons hold and practise has long been known. Many contemporary Jews, including Jesus and the disciples, therefore, would be likely to have known something, possibly much, of the Covenanters.

Second, both parties were using common matter, derived in part from Jewish tradition and Scripture and in part from contemporary speculation and thought. Both parties were the children of their own times and circumstances, they were Jewish by race and religion, and they would instinctively reproduce what their fellow Jews thought and said; and much that appears in the Scrolls and in the New Testament is found also in discussions preserved in Rabbinic literature. This will explain why so many ideas and arguments are common to the Scrolls and the New Testament, even if the interpretation put on them and the conclusions drawn from them are often widely different.[4]

[1] Pp. 237–51.   [2] Pp. 470–1.
[3] Matt. xx. 20–8 and Mk x. 35, 45; cp. Jn vi. 15.
[4] Cp. Albright in *Essays in honour of C. H. Dodd* 169.

If then Jesus, his disciples and the early Church had ample opportunity of knowing something of the Covenanters, the question naturally arises whether he anywhere shows direct acquaintance with them. Certainly, they are nowhere mentioned by name in the Gospels; but equally certainly passages can be cited in which they seem to have been in his mind as reflected in sayings attributed to him.

Sometimes this allusion is perhaps merely verbal, as when Jesus declares that 'one jot or tittle shall in no wise pass away from the law'[1] as compared with the Covenanters' expulsion of 'anyone of the men of the community . . . who wilfully removes a word from all that He (*sc.* God through Moses) has commanded' (D viii 16–18); the similarity of the words proves nothing because the sentiment is one common to all Jews. When he warns his followers not to squabble over precedence amongst themselves[2] or denounces those who seek the first places for themselves,[3] he may be thinking of the Covenanters' insistence on the observance of precedence amongst themselves (D v 23 vi 2, 4, 8–9); but the Essenes are recorded as having been equally strict in this respect,[4] and eagerness for such recognition is a common failure in all societies. When Jesus answered those Pharisees who asked him whether 'it was lawful to pay tribute unto Caesar or not' by advising them 'render unto Caesar the things that are Caesar's and unto God the things that are God's',[5] he was in fact addressing himself to the Zealots and similar groups; for it was not the Pharisees but these people who objected to the payment of taxes to a foreign government as infringing the sovereignty of God.[6] In the same way, when he forbade a disciple to resist the secular power, saying 'put up again thy sword into its place; for all they that take the sword shall perish by the sword',[7] he was perhaps thinking not of the Pharisees, who were appeasers in their dealings with Rome, but of such fanatical groups as the Covenanters, who believed that 'God had called down a sword on all the proud and will achieve victory through the saints of His people' (W xvi 1). Yet again, although in his insistence that 'the Sabbath was made for man, not man for the Sabbath'[8] he was combating that exaggeration of the sanctity of the Sabbath which was common to all Jews but was pushed beyond the prevalent norm by the Covenanters,[9] in due point he was possibly aiming at their excesses. The Rabbis forbade only the actual delivery of the young of cattle, while allowing the dam to be helped, on a feast-day;[10] they permitted the young to be

---

[1] Matt. v. 18; cp. Lk. xvi. 17.   [2] Mk. ix. 34–5.
[3] Matt. xxiii. 6 and Lk. xi. 43, xiv. 8.
[4] Josephus *War* II viii 6 § 134 and 10 § 150.
[5] Matt. xxii. 15–21, Mk. xii. 13–17, Lk. xx. 20–5.   [6] Pp. 232, 240–1.
[7] Matt. xxvi. 51–3; cp. Jn. xviii. 10–11 and Rom. xiii. 1–2.
[8] Mk. xvi. 15; cp. Matt. xxviii. 19.   [9] Pp. 88–91.
[10] Mishnah *Shabbath* xviii 3.

held during the birth so that it might not fall on the Sabbath[1] and
they even came to allow food and a means of escape to be provided for
a beast which had fallen into a pit on that day.[2] The Covenanters,
however, laid down the rule that 'no man shall assist a beast in birth
on the Sabbath; even if she drops (her young) into a cistern or pit, he
shall not keep (it) alive' (Z xiii 22–3). Directly contradicting this rule
and indeed tacitly implying that ordinary practice was not so harsh as
even the Rabbinic rule, Jesus asked who of his hearers would not save
a sheep which had fallen into a pit or an ox or an ass fallen into a well
on the Sabbath by immediately drawing it out on that very day.[3] The
clearest case is that in which Jesus says 'Ye have heard that it was said:
Thou shalt love thy neighbour and hate thine enemy; but I say unto
you: Love your enemies and pray for them that persecute you';[4] for
the command to hate one's enemies has been found neither in the Old
Testament nor in Jewish literature and is indeed repugnant to the
Jewish spirit, although the Rabbis do at times go so far as to permit
and even to enjoin hatred of sinners.[5] That it has now been found in a
Scroll, where the Covenanters are bidden 'to hate all sons of darkness'
(D i 10) and to cherish 'eternal hatred for the men of perdition'
(D ix 22–2), *i.e.* those who reject their teaching and whom therefore
they regard as sinners, is significant; for it is the only known source of
the sentiment *tout simple* which Jesus here ascribes to his opponents.

Possibly only the last two of these instances can be held to show that
Jesus may have been acquainted with the teaching of the Covenanters;
and, even if such acquaintance is granted (for the argument must be
to some extent only *e silentio*, being dependent solely on such documents
as happen to have been preserved), it does not prove personal contact,
since the knowledge shown in them may be nothing but common
knowledge. In either case, however, it inevitably suggests that Jesus
and the Covenanters must have been contemporary; for he would
not be contradicting doctrines which had had but a brief currency
and had then passed out of men's minds, buried in the decent obscurity
of the caves round Qumrân.

The moral sentiments expressed in the Scrolls are often almost
verbally identical with those found in the New Testament; but, when
closely examined, they are seen to be derived from a common source or
to have at bottom a very different import. The resemblances are superficial, the differences fundamental.

Precepts from the Old Testament and the apocryphal literature,
which may also appear in Rabbinic literature, are found in both New
Testament and Scrolls: for example, not to render evil to any man

---

[1] B. Talmud *Shabbath* 128b.   [2] Rabin *Zadokite Documents* 57 (14).
[3] Matt. xii. 11, Luke xiv. 5.   [4] Matt. v. 43–4.
[5] Strack & Billerbeck *Kommentar zum Neuen Testament* I 353, 364–8.

(D x 17–18)[1] but to love one's neighbour as oneself (Z viii 17),[2] and not to take away a single word from the Law (D viii 18).[3] Other moral precepts in the Scrolls are not so closely identifiable with but are still reminiscent of similar precepts in both the Old and the New Testaments. Thus *Discipline* requires the Covenanter to be humble, slow to anger and compassionate, filled with the spirit of knowledge and holy intentions, zealous for righteous laws, pure and full of loathing for idolatry;[4] the inferior must defer to the superior;[5] a member must not interrupt another speaker (D vi 10);[6] he must not speak in anger to or bring false charges against a fellow-member or bear a grudge against him;[7] he must not indulge in blasphemy or obscene talk[8] but must behave himself with decency in the community;[9] and he must not speak ill of or be false to the community or do it any harm in matters of money or property[10] (D iv 2–8 v 23–6 vi 2, 25–7 vii 1–19). The *Zadokite Documents* condemn the 'three snares of Belial', *i.e.* whoredom and covetousness and defiling the sanctuary (Z vi 10–12).[11] Further, the compiler of *Discipline* and Paul both give lists of some twenty or so vices: in the former they are arranged in such a way that the offender sinks ever deeper in sin (D iv 9–11), while the latter makes them rise to a peak with murder and then sink to less serious offences.[12]

The authors of the Scrolls, however, while proclaiming high moral principles, generally fall short of those inculcated in the Gospels. The author of *Discipline* urges those who seek God 'to love everything that He has chosen and to hate everything that He has rejected, to keep far from evil and to cling to every good deed' (D i 4–5), just as Peter bids his fellow Christians eschew evil and do good.[13] Even the positive command, however, to everyone who joins the community of the Covenanters 'to love all the sons of light, each according to his lot in the counsel of God' (D i 9–10) and the negative command that 'he shall not speak to his brother in anger ... and shall not hate him' (D v 25–6) do not approach Christ's universal command to love one another enshrined in numerous passages of the Gospels;[14] and the command to hate any who do not belong to the society as sinners (D i 10, ix 22–3) directly conflicts with it. In the same spirit the 'sons of light' are

---

[1] Prov. xx. 22; 1 Thess. v. 15.   [2] Lev. xix. 18; Matt. v. 43.
[3] Deut. iv. 2, xiii. 1; Rev. xxii. 19
[4] Cp. Lk. xiv. 11 and Jas. iv. 10 (humility); Eph. iv. 31–2 and Col. iii. 8, 12–14 (long-suffering); 2 Pet. i. 5–7 (zeal for knowledge); Matt. v. 6 (longing for righteousness); 1 Cor. x. 7 (rejection of idolatry).
[5] Cp. Col. iii. 20, 22; 1 Pet. v. 5.
[6] Ecclus. xi. 8; 1 Cor. xiv. 30–1; Mishnah *Aboth* v 7.
[7] Cp. Eph. iv. 31 and Col. iii. 12–13; Jas. iv. 11, v. 9.
[8] Cp. Col. iii. 8; Eph. v. 4.   [9] Cp. 1 Cor. xiv. 40.
[10] Cp. 1 Cor. vi. 8, vii. 5, x. 32.   [11] Cp. Eph. v. 5 and Col. iii. 5.
[12] Rom. i. 29–31.   [13] 1 Pet. iii. 11.
[14] Matt. v. 43–4, Lk vi. 27, 35, Jn xiii. 34–5, xv. 12; cp. 1 Jn iv. 7.

blessed while the 'sons of darkness' are cursed respectively by priests and Levites at the inaugural ceremony in the style of the Old Testament (D ii 2–10).[1] The fact is that the rules of the Covenanters are aimed at ensuring harmony between the members of the society itself, to whom those without the covenant are enemies, whereas the purpose of those in the New Testament is to regulate the behaviour of all who call themselves Christians not only towards one another but also towards all men, whether members of their immediate circle or not. Briefly, the former are particular, the latter universal in their aims. Yet this narrow view of their duty is not entirely characteristic of the society's rules for its members; for the author of the hymn at the end of *Discipline* exclaims 'I will repay evil to no man, (but) I will pursue a man (only) with good; for the judgement of every living creature is with God, and He will pay his due recompense to a man' (D x 17–18).[2] Here the two trends, the official and the personal, are strongly contrasted; but the reason is not so much that the former belong to the ceremonies of initiation and the formalized teaching of the society and the latter to the standards of personal piety[3] as that corporate morality always falls short of that of individual members of a community.

The author of the *Zadokite Documents* lays down the rule that a member shall swear neither by God nor by the Lord but only with an oath of agreement corroborated by adjuration by the covenant (Z xix 1, Rabin), and in the same spirit Jesus says to His followers 'swear not at all, neither by heaven (for it is His footstool) . . . ; but let your communication be yea, yea; nay, nay';[4] but neither of these rules are new, being only amplifications of the old law forbidding a man to take the name of the Lord in vain.[5] The author of *Discipline* says that 'a man (*sc.* member of the community) shall not accuse his fellow in the presence of the Many if he has not been subject to (previous) rebuke before witnesses' (D v 24–vi 1), somewhat as Jesus says 'if thy brother shall trespass against thee, go and tell him his fault between thee and him alone; if he shall hear thee, thou has gained thy brother. But, if he will not hear, take with thee one or two more, that in the mouth of two or three witnesses every word may be established. And, if he shall neglect to hear them, tell the church; but if he neglect to tell the church, let him be unto thee as a heathen man and a tax-collector'.[6] The thought is the same; but Jesus takes it further and amplifies it.

Here two strikingly parallel lines of thought in the Scrolls and in Paul's Epistles may be cited. In both the claim to do what one wills is made: in the Scrolls the sinner excuses his impure or impious conduct by saying 'for it is ours (to choose)', just as Paul claims freedom of

---

[1] Cp. Deut. xxvii. 9–26.
[3] Brown in Stendahl *Scrolls* 198.
[5] Exod. xx. 7 and Deut. v. 11.

[2] Cp. Prov. xx. 22.
[4] Matt. v. 33–7.
[6] Matt. xviii. 15–17.

action, though with a very different purpose, on the ground that 'all things are lawful unto me'.[1] Yet again, as the Scrolls say of those who spurn the Law and give themselves up to idolatry that 'they have no share in the house of the Law' (Z xx 38), Paul goes further and says that 'no . . . covetous man who is an idolater hath any inheritance in the kingdom of Christ and of God.[2]

The teaching of the Covenanters on the subject of the Law was sharply distinguished from that of the Gospels. The prophet's 'prepare you the way of the Lord',[3] with which John the Baptist had called men to repentance,[4] is very differently taken by the author or compiler of *Discipline* as 'studying the Law which He (*sc.* God) commanded through Moses, so as to act in accordance with all that was revealed time after time and with that which the prophets revealed through His holy spirit'; and he expands this to mean that 'anyone of the men of the community, [in] the covenant of the community, who wilfully removes a word from all that He has commanded,[5] shall not touch the purity of the holy men', which he explains as meaning that such an offender shall be expelled from the community and not be readmitted 'until his deeds are purified from every kind of perversion' (D viii 12–19). The *tôrāh* was as essential to the Covenanters as to all other Jewish parties and was to be interpreted in every detail in all its rigour; each member had to act 'according to all that had been revealed from time to time' (D viii 15), namely to attain a legalistic perfection based on the progressive revelation of the Law.[6] What this involved in practice can hardly be imagined; for, great as was the burden of the Law as denounced in the Gospels, the Covenanters did not hesitate to increase them; so, for example, the 23 rules of the Rabbis regulating the conduct of the strict Jew on the Sabbath were raised to 28 or 29 by them (Z xiii 1–xiv 3, 6).[7]

In due course the Covenanters came to believe themselves to be the sole 'doers of the Law' (H vii 6 viii 1), meaning only those who did so 'according to the interpretation of the Law whereby former generations shewed themselves right' (Z vi 5), *i.e.* according to the supposed original interpretation of it as handed down in the traditions of their society. So they could boast that those 'who give ear to the Rightful Teacher and do not reject the rightful ordinances when they hear them shall rejoice and be glad and their heart shall be strong and they shall overcome all the inhabitants of the world; and God shall make propitiation for them and they shall be witnesses of His salvation' (Z ix 53–4). Consequently they could denounce any who sought 'to change the Law' (T iv 10); but this attitude is far from the uncom-

---

[1] I Cor. vi. 12.
[2] Eph. v. 5.
[3] Isa. xl. 3.
[4] Matt. iii. 1–3, Mk. i. 2–4, Lk. iii. 2–8, Jn. i. 23.
[5] Cp. Josh. xi. 15.
[6] Cp. Black *Scrolls* 119–22.
[7] Pp. 88–90.

promising denunciations of the whole Jewish race which John the Baptist and Jesus pronounced.[1] So too Jesus declared that he had not come to destroy the Law or the prophets but 'to fulfil' them.[2] He recognized the Law as a divine institution and had come to identify himself with that revelation and to consummate it; he therefore often counselled those who came to him to keep the commandments[3] and to respect its sanctity, even as interpreted by the scribes and Pharisees, while unsparingly denouncing the burdens that these laid on men in the way of countless petty observances and the hypocrisy which they inevitably involved.[4] He spoke of the old revelation as a whole and looked to its spirit, which he expressed in summaries comprehending and transcending it.[5] At the same time he criticized the old Law, whether the letter of the Old Testament or the Rabbinic interpretation of it, and in doing so raised it to a new power, even going so far as tacitly to withdraw a permission conceded by the Mosaic law;[6] thus he came into conflict with the ecclesiastical authorities, especially on the subject of the observance of the Sabbath.[7] In this spirit, too, he set aside the laws governing ritual cleanness and uncleanness, so 'making all meats clean'.[8] Eventually he came to denounce the doctors of the law as 'blind leaders of the blind'[9] and so brought about a definite breach with legalism.

The extreme legalism of the Covenanters showed itself also in their rigorous exclusiveness, which went far beyond that of the Pharisees. Jewish exclusiveness was largely religious and national: the preservation of the purity of the national religion hindered contact with Gentiles and necessitated the prohibition of intermarriage with them. The Pharisees adopted a similar attitude to 'the people of the land', on the ground that these were less scrupulous in the fulfilment of their religious duties, in their observance of the law, and in their neglect of precautions regarding what was clean and unclean. Such persons might bring the disfavour of God on the land, and those who came into contact with them would run the risk of being ritually defiled. At the same time, the religious leaders tried to instruct the peasantry in the complications of the law and to induce them to fulfil its requirements. The attitude of the Covenanters was far different. They alone were the 'saints', the 'sons of light' and the 'men of God's lot', and all outside the covenant were 'sons of darkness' or 'men of perdition' and so on and as such worthy only to be cursed (D ii 5–10); those who

---

[1] E.g. Matt. iii. 7–12 (John); Matt xi. 20–4, xii. 34–42, xxiii. 1–33 and Lk. x. 13–16 (Jesus)
[2] Matt. v. 17–19.   [3] Matt. xix. 17 and Lk. x. 26–8, xvi. 29.
[4] Matt. xxiii. 2–33.   [5] Ibid. vii. 12, xxii. 36–40.   [6] Ibid. xix. 8–11.
[7] Matt. xii. 1–8; Mk. iii. 1–6; Lk. vi. 1–5, xiii. 10–17, xiv. 1–6; Jn. v. 1–16, ix 1–38.
[8] Mk. vii. 18–20.   [9] Matt. xv. 14.

refused to enter the covenant were unclean (D ii 25–iii 6). Accordingly, newly elected members bound themselves by a covenant 'to separate themselves from all perverse men' (D v 1–2); there was *nulla salus extra ecclesiam*, only 'eternal destruction' (D ii 8). So all the community's rules against hatred and anger were binding on members only in their relations with their fellow-members (D vi 25–6 vii 4–9), unlike those of the Sermon on the Mount.[1]

Again, the legalism of the Covenanters was based on an esoteric study of the Law. The society was 'a community in Law and in property', in which a man was enrolled 'among his brethren for Law and for judgement and for (ceremonial) purity' and in which the Law was studied by the members in relays continually day and night (D v 2–3 vi 6–7). Every novice was examined 'with respect to his understanding and his conduct in regard to the Law' (D v 20–1 vi 18); and the member was ordered 'to conceal the counsel of the Law among perverse men' and to teach it only to those 'who choose the way' (D v 15–16 ix 16–19). Thus the society's peculiar interpretation of the Law was a secret *gnōsis* or knowledge, which might be imparted only to initiated members.[2] This notion of an esoteric knowledge which might not be divulged became current in the 1st century A.D. So Jesus, while on occasion he forbade what he had said or done to be revealed to avoid undue or dangerous publicity,[3] also early in his ministry told his disciples that it was given only to them to know the mystery of the kingdom of God but that everything was done in parables 'unto them that are without . . . lest at any time they should be converted and (their) sins should be forgiven them';[4] and the idea reappears at the end of the century in the *Odes of Solomon*, in which Christ in the words of the poet says 'Keep my secret, ye who are kept by it; keep my faith, ye who are kept by it'.[5] At the same time, while the duty of the Covenanters not to divulge their doctrines was absolute, the chance was always open to Christ's disciples of understanding what He taught, and the Gospel was essentially something to be preached to the whole world.[6]

God's purposes as expressed in the Law were a mystery to the Covenanters. The 'sons of perdition' had been put 'under the dominion of the angel of darkness according to God's mysteries' (D iii 20–3) and a period for wrong-doing was fixed 'through the mysteries of His understanding and His glorious wisdom' (D iii 20–3 iv 18), and 'the way of the spirit of truth' was to illumine the hearts of men 'according

---

[1] Matt. v. 43–7.   [2] Cp. Black *Scrolls* 121.

[3] Matt. viii. 4 = Lk. v. 14; Matt. ix. 30, xii. 16; Matt. xvi. 20 = Mk. viii. 30 = Lk. ix. 20–1; Matt. xvii. 19 = Mk. ix. 9 (cp. Lk. ix. 26); Mk. iii. 12; Mk. v. 43 = Lk. viii. 56; Mk. vii. 36.

[4] Mk. iv. 11–12 (cp. Matt. xiii. 11 and Lk. viii. 10); cp. Matt. xvii. 9.

[5] Odes of Solomon viii 10–11.   [6] Matt. xxviii. 19–20; Mk. xvi. 15.

to the truth of the mysteries of God' (D iv 2–6). The Covenanter's heart was further illumined 'by a mystery fulfilled' and his justification was 'one of His (*sc.* God's) wonderful mysteries' (D xi 3 5); God opened His servant's heart to knowledge, none without God was able 'to gaze into the depth of Thy mysteries', and only 'those who choose the way' might be instructed 'in the wonderful mysteries and in the truth in the midst of the community, that they may walk perfectly each with his fellow in all that is revealed to them' (D xi 16, 18–20). Thus the Covenanters, while they failed to solve the problem of determinism,[1] accepted divine revelation as a mystery, in the same way as Paul declared 'we speak the wisdom of God in a mystery (cp. T ix 23), even the hidden wisdom' and that 'the things of God knoweth no man, but the Spirit of God'.[2] The Covenanters however regarded these mysteries as a revelation reserved for their own society, whereas the 'hidden mystery' of God after 'being made manifest to His saints' was preached by the church to all men, even to Gentiles.[3] Therein lies a world of difference between the covenant of Qumrân and the New Testament.

The Covenanters, like the writers of the New Testament, accepted divine revelation through the unfolding of the prophets (D i 2–3 ii 7–9 viii 15–16).[4] They held the prophetic tradition in high esteem, notably the books of the three great prophets, and also that of *Daniel*; and portions of all these have been found in the caves round Qumrân.[5] In this connection attention may be drawn to their use of the figure of the Suffering Servant of the Lord; it strikes a very different note from that heard in the predominantly legal part of the Scrolls. This difference appears most clearly in the passage describing the twelve laymen and three priests constituting the Council of the community.[6] These were required to be 'perfect in all that is revealed of the whole Law through practising truth and righteousness and justice and unfailing devotion and walking circumspectly[7] each with his fellow in order to maintain faithfulness in the land with steadfast purpose and a broken spirit, to expiate iniquity through deeds of justice and the anguish of the refining furnace and to walk with all in the measure of truth' (D viii 1–4); when all this has come to pass in Israel, the Council of the community will have been established in truth 'to be an eternal plantation, a holy house for Israel, a most holy foundation (*sôḏ*) for Aaron, true witnesses to justice and the elect of goodwill[8] to atone for the land and to render their deserts to the wicked. That is the tried wall, the costly cornerstone, whose foundations shall not be convulsed nor shaken out of

---

[1] Pp. 559–62.
[3] Col. i. 26–8; cp. Matt. x. 5–6 and xxviii. 19.
[5] Pp. 19–21.
[7] Cp. Thomas in *JJS* I 182–6.

[2] I Cor. ii. 7–8.
[4] Cp. Am. iii. 7.
[6] Pp. 61–2.
[8] P. 520.

their place' (D viii 5–8). These will be fit 'with eternal knowledge to enact laws and to offer up a soothing odour' and 'to establish a covenant with eternal ordinances'; and again 'these will serve the purpose of grace to make atonement for the land and to decree the condemnation of wickedness, that there may be no wrong-doing' (D viii 9–10). These men, the 'chosen of grace to atone for the land', are the 'precious corner-stone' on which the future living community, the new Israel,[1] composed of the remnant who will turn back and be saved, will be built, and the 'living stones' which are 'built up a spiritual house, a holy priesthood to offer up spiritual sacrifices';[2] and they will fulfil the mission of the Suffering Servant by expiating wrong-doing in the furnace of affliction. Thus a redemptive value is attributed to their sufferings. At the same time they are 'to render their deserts to the wicked'; thus they fill the part of the Servant who 'by his humiliation shall justify many'[3] as also of the Son of Man to whom authority is given in *Daniel* to execute judgement.[4] That, however, the Rightful Teacher is to be identified with the Suffering Servant, as Dr. Brownlee[5] suggests, is extremely doubtful; the texts have nothing explicit to say on such an identification.

Another passage, to which Professor Burrows has drawn attention,[6] showing great spiritual depth is the poem at the end of *Discipline*, in which the author declares his gratitude to God for all His gifts and confesses his own unworthiness, saying: 'As for me, my justification is of God and in His hand is the perfection of my way, a light in my heart from His marvellous mysteries in Eternal Being. Mine eye has beheld that wisdom which was hidden from men of knowledge and that prudent purpose (hidden) from the sons of men. . . . But I belong to wicked humanity and to the society of perverse flesh. My iniquities, my transgressions, my sin together with the perversions of my heart, belong to the dark company of worms and of creatures that walk in darkness' (D xi 2–10). He then goes on: 'For a man's way is (not) his own; a man does not direct his steps, but the decision is God's and His counsel is a perfect way, and by His knowledge everything has been brought into being, and He has established everything that is by His purpose, and apart from Him nothing is done. As for me, if I slip, God's acts of unfailing love (*ḥăsāḏîm*) are my salvation for ever; and, if I stumble through the guilt of the flesh, my justification through God's righteousness will endure everlastingly; and, if He began my affliction, He will draw out my soul from the pit to direct my steps in the way. In His compassion He has brought me near and by His acts of unfailing love (*ḥăsāḏîm*) he will bring about my justification. In His steadfast

---

[1] Isa. xxviii. 16.
[3] Isa. liii. 11.
[5] In Stendahl *op. cit.* 50–1.

[2] I Pet. ii. 5.
[4] Dan. vii. 13–14; cp. I Enoch xlvi 3–6.
[6] In *Scrolls* I 334–5.

righteousness He has justified me and in His great goodness He will atone for all my iniquities, and in His righteousness He will cleanse me from man's impurity and from the sin of the sons of men' (D xi 10–15). He concludes: 'For what indeed is he, a son of man, among Thy miraculous works and (what is) one born of a woman in Thine estimation? As for him, his formation is from dust and his ordered destiny is (to be) food for worms; he is fashioned only of potter's clay (*mᵉṣaw-war raq ḥōmer qôṣēr*) and his impulse is toward the dust. What will clay and something shaped by hand reply and what sort of counsel will it devise?' (D xi 20–2). The sentiments expressed in these passages are echoed in the Gospels but combine much that can be found also in the Prophets and elements from the piety expressed in many of the Psalms. They approach a doctrine of justification and sanctification: man has no righteousness but what God confers. So the Apostle says that 'all have sinned and come short of the glory of God, being justified freely by His grace through the redemption that is in Christ Jesus, whom God hath sent forth (to be) a propitiation through faith in his blood, to declare His righteousness for the remission of sins that are past through the forbearance of God'.[1] That he borrowed these ideas from the Covenanters is no necessary inference, just as there is no need to suppose that they have borrowed anything from him; the doctrines here adumbrated can already be traced in pre-Christian Judaism, and both may be drawing on common sources or taking up contemporary speculation. The Covenanters' means of grace, however, are not those of Paul, who looks to faith in Christ; the Rightful Teacher had done no redemptive work such as Christ had done.

In these passages of *Discipline* there is 'a real glimpse of spiritual insight', as Dr. Black has remarked in a lecture, although it is far below the level of that shown in the New Testament; but both might well have been composed at a time when the ideas sketched in them were all in the air.

In conclusion, much suggests and nothing forbids the belief that the Scrolls and the New Testament belong to the same period of history; they both use terminology and reflect beliefs current in the 1st century A.D., even though some (but not all) of these go back to the inter-testamental literature or even to the Old Testament. There are many contacts of language, too many perhaps to be accidental but readily explicable as reflections of contemporary idiom and current concepts. Common ideas are those of the new society as based on a 'covenant', the need for repentance on admission to it, the snare of wealth; the reproof of the brethren in the first instance privately[2] and only secondly before the community, the avoidance of oaths, of sacrifice and of worship in the Temple; healing by the imposition of

---

[1] Rom. iii. 23–5   [2] Cp. p. 58.

hands and rebuking evil spirits; the antithesis of flesh and spirit, the two spirits and the two ways and of light and darkness, the value of redemptive suffering, justification and sanctification, rewards and punishments in a future life; the use of proof-texts and the practice of marking significant passages in the Scriptures as well as the form of the commentaries; the appeal to Moses and the prophets, the emphasis on knowledge and the revelation of the mysteries of God, the Messianic expectation and the ideas associated with it. Yet the connotation acquired by comparable terms and the emphasis laid on common or similar doctrines for the most part vary greatly between the Scrolls and the New Testament; traces of most, if not of all, can be found in other literatures than the Scrolls and the New Testament, and the fact that any single concept can or may with a high degree of probability be referred to a particular source does not exclude the use of other sources or even the possibility of independent thought.[1]

At the same time there is an infinite difference between the doctrines sketched in the Scrolls and those in the New Testament on both the legalistic and the ritualistic sides, even though similar moral sentiments may be found in the teachings of Covenanters and of Christians. The rigorous and esoteric legalism, the recruiting of new members and the organized life of the community at Qumrân are far removed from the freedom of the Gospel; the closed religious order, living only for itself, is totally unlike the world-wide Church with its missionary enthusiasm in preaching the Gospel to all men, Jew and Gentile alike. Both appeal to Scripture and even use the same proof-texts; but the spiritual insight of the Covenanters rarely goes beyond that of the Old Testament, whereas the New Testament starts where that leaves off, even though the two groups overlap in time and occasionally in outlook. The Rightful Teacher, whoever he was, was a learned doctor of the law and the practitioner of an esoteric doctrine which he and his followers cultivated principally in a lonely 'monastery' by the Dead Sea; Jesus was a popular preacher teaching a simple morality in homely language and picturesque imagery to the common people by the shores of the Sea of Galilee, whence he sent out followers to carry the good news of the Gospel to the world.[2] Jesus made no effort to conceal his name, which everyone knew; that of the Rightful Teacher was kept secret or revealed only in cryptograms intelligible to a narrow circle of devotees. Jesus ate with publicans and sinners,[3] whereas the Covenanter was bound by the rule of his order that 'he may not eat or drink anything belonging to them (*sc.* persons outside the society)' (D v 16); Jesus taught his disciples not 'to hate' their opponents as the

---

[1] Cp. Cervaux in *Rech. Bibl.* IV 237–41.
[2] Cp. Dupont-Sommer *Nouveaux Aperçus* 207–8 and in *Diogène* XXII 27–8.
[3] Lk. vii. 34, xv. 2.

Covenanters were bidden 'to hate all sons of darkness' (D i 10; cp. ix 21–2) but to love their enemies.[1] He rejected an earthly kingdom, preferring to come 'preaching the Gospel of the kingdom (of God) and healing all manner of disease and all manner of sickness'.[2] The Covenanters represented the spiritual side of a revolutionary movement while believing that the Messianic kingdom could be established by the sword (W xvi 1); Christians were warned that 'the weapons of our warfare are not carnal'.[3] No clear trace of a doctrine of atonement through suffering or of a resurrection appears in the Scrolls. The resurrection of Jesus and the manifestation of the Holy Spirit produced a spiritual explosion to which nothing can be compared amongst the Covenanters; the work of Jesus was continued on earth with unabated vigour by disciples and apostles, whereas the Teacher's party maintained only a very tenuous existence after his death.[4] The Teacher may have been regarded as a martyr and even as a Messiah; but nothing in the Scrolls suggests that he was thought, as Jesus was thought, to possess any redemptive power.[5] The eschatology of the Covenanters like that of the Church was grounded in Judaism; but, while the former remained firmly rooted in Jewish beliefs in which a Messiah of Israel was identified with the Davidic Messiah of popular conception in a secular sense, the material trappings of Messianic doctrine were laid aside or fell away in Christian thought. Jesus believed that the Messianic kingdom would be established by dying, the Covenanters thought that it could be brought about by slaughter.[6]

If the Scrolls are regarded as approximately contemporary with the New Testament, the probability that the authors of these two collections of Jewish works influenced one another is necessarily great; in fact, that two religious groups should live for a considerable time within a few miles of each other without affecting one another would be a cause for surprise; but that two groups, whose doctrines diverged so widely as did those of the Covenanters and Christians, should have had a common origin or should have borrowed anything essential from one another would be equally surprising. Essenes and Covenanters influenced each other both in practice and in doctrine, but neither was derived from the other; and the same thing may be said of the other known groups, including Christians, that they certainly arose independently, however much they influenced each other in petty details. They were but two of the numerous religious and political groups which grew up in the small state of Palestine in the 1st century A.D., the most important period in human history, and the discovery of a collection of contemporary documents has suddenly thrown a

---

[1] Matt. v. 43–4 and Lk. vi. 27–8.   [2] Matt. iv. 23, ix. 35.
[3] 2 Cor. x. 4.   [4] Cp. Cervaux *ibid.* 234–5.
[5] Cp. Rowley *Scrolls from Qumran* 18–19.   [6] *Ibid.* 20.

flood of light on one such group whose very existence had not even been suspected. This collection incidentally lights up the background of the New Testament, showing clearly that its secular this-worldly and nationalistic aspects must not be neglected over against its other-worldly apocalyptic and eschatological elements, on which most emphasis has usually been laid,[1] and it has also shown that the New Testament reflects the speech, the thought and the life, of the age in which its various books were written; but the originality of the Gospel is not impaired by the use of current expressions and ideas or its significance changed because it shares a common background with contemporary Jewish literature.

EPILOGUE

The picture presented in the Scrolls as here interpreted is consistent and harmonious.

Nothing in the Scrolls demands a date in the 2nd or even in the 1st century B.C. They contain no hint of any of the pressing problems which confronted the loyal Jew in those centuries; they never so much as refer to any single aspect of Hellenism, for example the difficulties raised by circumcision and public appearances at the games, to the propriety or legality of combining the office of king with that of high-priest or to the misconduct and rivalries of the priest-kings which disgraced the Holy City. If, however, the Zadokites were in Egypt during these centuries, they would not be likely to show much interest in events occurring at that time in Palestine; and in fact the Scrolls contain no allusions which can only and indisputably be referred to them. At the same time, such residence in Egypt accounts for their familiarity with the Egyptian tradition of the text of the Old Testament as seen in passages quoted in the Scrolls and in fragmentary copies of Biblical books (*e.g.* Samuel) found at Qumrân, as also with the solar calendar which, though sporadically employed in ancient Israel, was in regular use in Egypt; it accounts too for the use of signs of Alexandrian origin in manuscripts of the Scriptures and of Egyptian models in making jars and weaving linen. Further, it explains why no references to the Zadokites or Covenanters *eo nomine* can be found in any works composed before the 1st century A.D., while intermittent allusions to them begin to appear from that century onwards.

As a corollary to this conclusion, nothing in the Scrolls precludes a date in the 1st or 2nd century A.D., while certain points in the Scrolls and some of the facts mentioned in them or to which they allude permit or suggest but do not necessarily require a date in these centuries. The

---

[1] Farmer, *Maccabees, Zealots and Josephus* 193–6.

most noteworthy are a number of grammatical forms and peculiar words not known before this period (in so far as purely linguistic evidence is valid) and the use of acrostic and cryptographic devices (for which this was a golden age); the compilation of commentaries (of which the Mishnah has the earliest fragmentary examples) on books of Scripture and its application to contemporary events; the use of the solar calendar, as in the New Testament; the attitude of the Covenanters to marriage with a niece, divorce and remarriage; the resemblance of certain customs of the Covenanters to those of the Pharisaic associations (*ḥăḇūrôṯ*); the injunction to observe secrecy; the figures of an earthly Messiah and the Messianic forty years; the military equipment and dispositions of the Covenanters which, while retaining some Republican practices, are essentially those of the Roman Imperial army; the general description of the 'Kittians' as the enemy whose characteristic marks are again Roman, and the resort to Damascus as a place of refuge, which was possible for fanatically anti-Roman Jews only when the city and surrounding country were under non-Roman rule.

Other factors require a date and permit no other than one in the middle or late 1st century A.D. or very early in the 2nd century A.D. Such are the loss of the *ius gladii* implied in the Covenanters' inability to inflict the extreme penalty; the adoption of the curved dagger (introduced *c.* A.D. 50–60 into Palestine) and military signalling with trumpets (introduced in A.D. 66–7) by the Covenanters; the identification of the central episode in the Scrolls, namely the attack of the Wicked Priest on the Rightful Teacher, with an outrage recorded under A.D. 66 and with no other event of the whole period, so far as historical records show; the description of the enemy as divided between Syria and Egypt (as in A.D. 66–7) and as sacrificing to their standards (obviously in reference to A.D. 70); various details in the Messianic doctrine of the Covenanters; the hint that Nero *redivivus* was a not unknown figure and the disappearance of the doctrine that a Moses *redivivus* may be expected to show himself 'at the end of the days' early in the 2nd century A.D.; the prohibition of marital intercourse in Jerusalem which was conceivable only at the end of the 1st or early in the 2nd century A.D., when the city lay waste and desolate and was forbidden to Jews; the numerous contacts with the New Testament, which can be most easily explained if they are contemporary with it, the use of proof-texts and the contacts in the Rabbinic practice and literature. Finally, the only two Rabbis to whom ideas mentioned in the Scrolls are traditionally ascribed (Johanan ben Zakkai and Hyrcanus ben Eliezer) both lived in the last half of the 1st century A.D.

The period, then, to which the Scrolls, taken as a unified collection of writings, must be assigned is clear. Alternatively, if the individual

Scrolls are examined, each will be found to contain one or some of the elements by which this period has been determined; and this fact in turn confirms the suspicion that they must in fact be considered together and not in isolation.

The origin of the movement, of which the Scrolls are the only literary monument, must be sought in the period when the Zadokite line of high-priests was interrupted. As the title of Simon II (?) the *ṣaddîq* implied, he and his sons Onias III and Jesus (Jason) were Zado-kites, being the last of their immediate line to hold the office of high-priest, which Menelaus and Alcimus (who were not Zadokites) in time usurped with Seleucid support. Meanwhile Onias (IV), son of Onias III, and his followers fled, *c.* 162 B.C., to Alexandria in Egypt where they established a rival temple at On the 'city of righteousness (*ṣedeq*)' with a Zadokite priesthood *c.* 154 B.C. Some Zadokites would be likely to have stayed behind in Jerusalem or elsewhere in Palestine; and these or their successors, either soon afterwards or perhaps rather when John Hyrcanus I (135–104 B.C.) broke with the Pharisees, might have fled to Qumrân and established the 'monastery' there as a retreat from secular activities and a refuge from persecution. When the Seleucid power was overthrown and Jerusalem fell to Pompey in 63 B.C., an 'Alexandrian priest' of the Zadokite line in Egypt named Boethus came back to Palestine and, when the Hasmonaean line of high-priests was suppressed by Herod in 37 B.C., saw his son Simon nominated by him to the sacred office and his grand-daughter married to Herod *c.* 24 B.C. All that is known of their party, the Boethusians, connects them with that of the 'fourth philosophy', which was being formed about that time by Judah son of Hezekiah and Saddok or Sadduk, and with the Covenanters of Qumrân; and the conjecture would not be improbable that the Boethusians, whose ancestors had left Jerusalem in disgust at Seleucid interference in spiritual matters as seen especially in their support of a non-Zadokite high-priesthood, now in disgust at their leaders' subservience to the half-Edomite Herod and his Roman patrons, left them and joined the new party. Hence they could claim to be 'Sons of Zadok' in a double sense, as priests after the historic Zadok and as layman after this Saddok or Sadduk; and Hezekiah's son Judah the 'sophist' became their first Teacher and the father of another 'sophist' or Teacher, whose sup-porters could thus properly be called the 'house of Judah'. Meanwhile another Zadokite group, less spiritual and more worldly, had stayed in Jerusalem, and, when Hyrcanus I forsook the Pharisees and joined them, became the leading party in the state; these were the historic Sadducees of the New Testament.

Thus at the beginning of the Christian age not two but three parties were opposed to each other. The first two were the worldly, aristocratic and high-priestly Sadducees and the Pharisees who were the party of the rabbis, lawyers and scribes, and whom the people followed, both in their different ways 'appeasers', *i.e.* content to accept foreign rule. The third was the Zadokite or 'Sadducaean' party sprung from Onias (IV), which became the successor party of the Boethusians in combination with the adherents of the 'fourth philosophy'; it was Zadokite in outlook so far as the high-priestly office was concerned but Pharisaic or rather ultra-Pharisaic in doctrine, disliking the Pharisees' laxity in matters of law but like the Pharisaic extremists opposed to foreign rule. This party's composite origin thus made it at once spiritual and political, pacifist and militant; but, as the situation *vis-à-vis* the Roman authorities worsened, the spiritual and pacifist elements were pushed into the background until the political and militant extremists gained the upper hand; these, pressing the policy of intolerance of foreign rule to the farthest limits, dragged the whole nation into active rebellion against Rome. The elderly, the spiritual and the pacifist, members of the party presumably sought refuge where they could, *e.g.* in the wilderness or at Qumrân, until the militarists drove them from the place to make it their base and stronghold, or perhaps left them for other non-militant groups such as the Essenes or the Christians; the extremists, the so-called Zealots and the *sicarii* who flocked to their banner, partly intransigent and fanatically anti-Roman members of the Zadokite society and partly political malcontents or penniless outcasts owing allegiance to any party which promised revolution or to no party, became inextricably confused in bitter internecine feuds and the desperate struggle with Rome.

The current identification of the Essenes and the Covenanters cannot be sustained. If the Zadokites, who were the nucleus of the party of the Covenanters, were in Egypt *c.* 160–60 B.C., they could not have been the Essenes who were in Palestine throughout these years. If the manner of life and the doctrines of the two groups were in many respects alike, the resemblances arose out of their similar circumstances or were entirely trivial. Contrariwise, they differed completely in everything essential, most notably in their attitude to war; the Essenes were convinced and devoted pacifists, while the Covenanters came to regard war as the only means of ridding their country of foreign rule.

Already in 46 B.C. Hezekiah had rebelled against the Romans and had been caught and executed by the youthful Herod. His son Judah had staged an abortive revolt on Herod's death in 4 B.C.; and again in A.D. 6 he rebelled but was caught and executed. Those of his followers who escaped might well have fled to Qumrân, where the buildings were then reconstructed, and lain hidden to await the chance of striking another blow at Rome. Two other sons, Simeon and Jacob, followed his example c. A.D. 46–8 and met the same fate.

Judah's third son, Menahem, now became leader of the party and presumably lingered quietly by the Dead Sea, building it up and organizing it. When the Revolt broke out in the late summer of A.D. 66, he and his followers raided the fort of Masada further down the Dead Sea to provide themselves with arms; they then went up to Jerusalem, where Menahem intended to take command of the Revolt as the hereditary privilege of his family, which had given so many of its sons to the cause of freedom in the service of God. Eleazar, the high-priest's son whose boldness had precipitated the revolt, saw his own position as leader threatened. He organized opposition and, when Menahem entered the Temple decked in royal attire and claiming priestly privilege, he instigated the populace against him; they hunted him and his followers out of the city down on to Mt. Ophel, where they murdered him, while his lieutenant Absalom and a party fleeing with him were similarly murdered close at hand on the same hill; meanwhile, Menahem's nephew Eleazar with others escaped to Masada. There he apparently remained as leader of the party until he perished with the whole garrison in A.D. 73, having perhaps succeeded Menahem as the Messiah whom the party expected to reappear within forty years and liberate Israel from Roman oppression.

This Menahem, who was regarded as a 'teacher of wisdom' and was murdered on the Day of Atonement or very near to that day by the high-priest's son Eleazar, a priest by birth and at the time captain of the Temple, was *ex hypothesi* the 'Rightful Teacher' or 'Teacher of Righteousness (ṣedeq)', who according to the Scrolls was attacked and apparently murdered (for blood was shed) on the Day of Atonement by the Wicked Priest; this Eleazar was then the Wicked Priest. The 'house of Absalom', which fled but was 'silenced' *i.e.* destroyed, at the same time and so could not help the leader, was the Absalom and his party murdered at the same time as Menahem; and the 'house of Judah' which escaped by God's help was Eleazar ben Jair, nephew of Menahem and grandson of Judah, and his followers who escaped to Masada on the same occasion. Other characters mentioned in the Scrolls, *e.g.* the 'Man of Falsehood' as John of Gischala and the 'Young Lion of Wrath' as Simon bar Giora, can also perhaps be fitted into the picture.

These identifications are supported by a number of coincidences which have not otherwise been satisfactorily explained and some of which only the present hypothesis will explain. Such are the abbreviations and cryptograms of which the Scrolls contain several and which are already well known in the 1st and 2nd centuries A.D., and the double interpretation of the three hundred and ninety *plus* twenty years from Nebuchadnezzar to the appearance of the Rightful Teacher, which is nothing absurd; for it is but an example of the Rabbinic method of interpretation known as the 'double meaning (*tartê mišmā*'), which can only be unravelled by the application of like methods. The unorthodox solar calendar of the Covenanters, as contrasted in the orthodox lunar (or rather lunisolar) calendar, and other contradictions of current Pharisaic practice and doctrine also fit the period and agree with contemporary, Talmudic and medieval evidence.

At the end of the Revolt the survivors fled in two directions; those who saw the futility of resistance and hoped to rebuild the party on spiritual lines made their way to Syrian villages and towns where they might find safety, while the extremists, the *sicarii*, fled to Egypt. The Romans, who were not likely to be mistaken about the identity of these two groups, thereupon destroyed the Zadokite temple at On, evidently regarding it as a centre of Zealot anti-Roman fanaticism, thus confirming the opinion here maintained that the Zealots and *sicarii* were nothing but the extreme wing of the Zadokite party.

Thus a continuous history of the Zadokites can be reconstructed, beginning with the old Zadokites in Egypt who are linked by the Boethusians to the new Zadokites in Palestine and ending with the party who are called *Ṣaddûqîm* or *Ṣadduqîn* in Jewish and Aramaic and *Ṣadduqîyatu* in Arabic writings of the Rabbinic age; the history of these people, as distinct from the Sadducees of the New Testament, urgently calls for investigation in the light of the new knowledge shed on Jewish history by the Scrolls.

Literary contacts confirm the assignment of the independent non-Biblical Scrolls to the period of the inter-testamental apocryphal and apocalyptic writings, especially of the latest of them, and of the New Testament if not almost of the Mishnah, from *c.* 200 B.C. to *c.* A.D. 200 or not long afterwards. On the one hand, the important echoes of the earlier literature, notably of *I Enoch* and *Jubilees*, superficially suggest a date in the 2nd-1st centuries B.C. On the other hand, some of the coincidences with the later literature, especially with parts of the New Testament, require a date late in the 1st or even early in the 2nd century A.D.; but, as borrowing on either side is improbable, the common matter must be regarded not as borrowed but as the common stock in trade of the writers of these two centuries. At the same time it is not the earliest but the latest allusions which determine the date of any document in which they occur.

The earliest Scroll was *Discipline*, which may be dated *c.* A.D. 46–66, while Menahem was leader of the party; the *Commentary on Habakkuk* may be assigned to A.D. 70–3 after the destruction of Jerusalem but when the Romans were still in the country and memories of the Revolt were still fresh and bitter; the *Thanksgiving Hymns*, reflecting its author's deliverance from a great disaster, may be put soon after A.D. 73, when the Revolt finally collapsed with the utter ruin of all Jewish hopes and the survivors escaped to Damascus; the *War* and the *Zadokite Documents* may be put late in this period, the former probably before the Revolt of A.D. 115–17 and the latter certainly before that of A.D. 132–5. Consequently, the Scrolls may be regarded as a collection of documents approximately contemporary with the writings of the New Testament; their authors breathed the same atmosphere, as they spoke a common language and had in some respects similar aims.

The Scrolls were probably hidden in the caves in consequence of the increasing orthodoxy of the Rabbis after the failure of the Revolt, when the text of the Scriptures was finally standardized and all imperfect or damaged copies of them as well as all works which violated Rabbinic standards of propriety were put away; for after the Revolt the Covenanters gradually ceased to be a body strong enough to defend themselves, and their deviations came to be regarded as heterodox if not as actually unorthodox or heretical, as shown by their treatment in the Talmud. Accordingly, the Zadokite 'city of righteousness (*ṣeḏeq*)' was condemned in it as heretical and worthy only of destruction, while the anti-Pharisaism of the Zadokites of the Scrolls lived on in the obscure quarrels of the so-called 'heretics', chiefly the Zadokites or 'Sadducaeans (*Ṣaddûqîm*)', with the 'Rabbanites', *i.e.* the Rabbis who succeeded the Pharisees as the religious leaders of the people, until the party received a fresh lease of life by the discovery of Hebrew manuscripts in a cave at the end of the 8th century A.D.; then, when the connection between the heresy of the Zadokites of the 'city of righteousness' and the deviations of the Zadokites or Covenanters of Qumrân were overlooked or forgotten, their doctrines once again became respectable, in a different form, in Qara'ism.

Those who refuse to accept the solution of the problem of the Scrolls here maintained must find a second Zadokite or Sadducaean party which is at war with a ruthless foreign enemy, which has the same peculiar calendar and the same views on matrimony, as well as a second episode in which a teacher is 'swallowed up' by a wicked priest, in which a 'house of Absalom' is silenced and from which a 'house of Judah' escapes, all on a second Day of Atonement; they must also find another party armed with a curved dagger and signalling with trumpets, doublets of the Young Lion of Wrath and of the Man of Falsehood, and another enemy who offer sacrifice to their standards, all in the same period of history. The dilemma is inescapable. No such doublets can be found in the recorded history within which archaeology firmly sets the Scrolls; consequently, any alternative solution of the problem must be based (if only in the present state of knowledge) on arguments from silence or on the assumption that the authors of the Scrolls were describing practices and foretelling events unknown during their lives; the former has no logical force, the latter is from the human point of view beyond belief.

The hypothesis here presented is based on the principle that, although no historical theory is ever proved in the strict sense, that is useful which covers a larger body of facts than any of those that have preceded it and has recourse to fewer assumptions and which supports those that are made with adequate evidence. In the present study baseless assumptions are avoided, and such as are made are buttressed with facts well attested by ancient and, where feasible, contemporary authorities; and a mass of coincidences is brought together which imperatively call for explanation. The hypothesis here put forward is offered as being as nearly valid as possible for establishing the date, circumstances and purpose of the Scrolls. It cannot of course be absolutely proved, since the historical knowledge of the period is and always will be inadequate for the purpose; and indeed, until the missing link connecting the Covenanters of Qumrân with the Zealots of Masada is found, it cannot be checked. Meanwhile, the argument is based, as it can only be, on a consideration of all the historical facts which can be detected in the Scrolls, set beside those which other external sources provide. It is therefore cumulative: the greater the number of correspondences, the stronger the argument. This argument can only be met by outnumbering these correspondences by others drawn from some other period of history within that allowed by archaeology; for a cumulative argument is ultimately valid only if and when the accumulation of evidence is complete.

The possibility always remains that any solution of a problem may be disproved by subsequent discovery and research and that the true explanation may then be found to take its place. The present work, however, will have served its purpose if it compels those who have committed themselves to a date in the 2nd or 1st century B.C. for the Scrolls to take account also of the possibility of one of the 1st-2nd centuries A.D. on the evidence here set forth; for this has hitherto gone largely by default.

BIBLIOGRAPHY

Editions of texts with abbreviations.

S. Schechter	*Documents of Jewish Sectaries:* I (Oxford, 1910)[1]	Z
M. Burrows	*The Dead Sea Scrolls of St. Mark's Monastery:* I 1–54 The Isaiah Manuscript; I 55–61 The Habakkuk Commentary (New Haven, 1950) . Is. A, H	
„	*op. cit.* II ii The Manual of Discipline (New Haven, 1951)[2] . . . . D	
E. L. Sukenik	*The Dead Sea Scrolls of the Hebrew University.* Pl. 1–15 Isaiah; pl. 16–34 The War of the Sons of Light with the Sons of Darkness; pl. 35–58 Thanksgiving Scroll (Jerusalem, 1954). . . Is. B, W, T.	
J. M. Allegro	*The Treasure of the Copper Scroll*[3] (London, 1960) SC	
N. Avigad & Y. Yadin	*A Genesis Apocryphon: a Scroll from the Wilderness of Judaea* (Jerusalem, 1956) . . . GA	
J. M. Allegro	in the *Palestine Exploration Fund, Quarterly Statement* LXXXVI [1954–5] 29–75 (commentary on Ps. xxxvii 8–26) . . . . . . APs.a	
„	in the *Journal of Biblical Literature* LXXV [1956] 89–95 (commentaries on Nahum ii 12–14, Hosea v 14, Psalm xxxvii 14–15, 32–33) ANa1, AHo., APs.b	
„	*ibid.* LXXV [1956] 174–87 (*florilegia*) AFl.a-d	
„	*ibid.* LXXVII [1958] 215–21 (commentary on Is. v 5–vi 9, xxx 14–21 liv 11–12) . AIs.a-c	
„	*ibid.* LXXVII [1958] 350–4 (*florilegium*) . AFl.e	
Y. Yadin	in *IEJ.* IX [1959] 95–8 (*florilegium*) . . YFl.f	
J. M. Allegro	in the *Journal of Semitic Studies* VI [1961] 71–3 (ordinances) . . . . . AOrd.	
„	*ibid.* VII [1962] 304–8 (commentary on Nahum) ANa 2	

---

[1] Also L. Rost *Damaskusschrift* (Berlin, 1933), whose numbering of the sections of the text is here followed, and C. Rabin *Zadokite Documents*[2] (Oxford, 1958), whose divergent readings are noted where necessary.
[2] All published.
[3] Republished by R. de Vaux and F. Milik in III Q 211–99 (1962).

D. Barthélemy   *Discoveries in the Judaean Desert* I. *Qumran Cave I*
& J. T. Milik   (1955) . . . .   I Q

P. Benoit, J. T.   *Discoveries in the Judaean Desert* II. *Qumran—Les*
Milik & R.   *Grottes de Murabba'ât* [1961] . . .   II Q
de Vaux

M. Baillet, J. T.   *Discoveries in the Judaean Desert of Jordan.* III *Les*
Milik & R.   *'Petites Grottes' de Qumrân* [1962] . .   III Q
de Vaux

ABBREVIATIONS

AOASH.	*Acta Orientalia Academiae Scientiarum Hungaricae* (Budapest)
Arch. Or.	*Archiv Orientální* (Prague)
BA.	*Biblical Archaeologist* (New Haven)
BASOR.	*Bulletin of the American Schools of Oriental Research Library* (New Haven)
BJRL.	*Bulletin of the John Rylands Library* (Manchester)
BO.	*Bibliotheca Orientalis* (Leiden)
BPES.	*Bulletin of the Palestine Exploration Society* (Jerusalem)
BSOAS.	*Bulletin of the School of Oriental and African Studies* (London)
BZ.	*Biblische Zeitschrift* (Paderborn)
BZAtW.	*Beihefte zur Zeitschrift für die alttestamentliche Wissenschaft* (Giessen)
Cah. Sion.	*Cahiers Sioniens* (Paris)
CBQ.	*Catholic Biblical Quarterly* (Washington)
CRAIB-L.	*Comptes Rendus de l'Académie des Inscriptions et Belles-Lettres* (Paris)
DB.	*Dictionary of the Bible* (Edinburgh)
EB.	*Encyclopaedia Biblica* (London)
ERE.	*Encyclopaedia of Religion and Ethics* (Edinburgh)
Heythr. Journ.	*Heythrop Journal* (Chipping Norton)
Hibb. Journ.	*Hibbert Journal* (London)
HTR.	*Harvard Theological Review* (Cambridge, U.S.A.)
HUCA.	*Hebrew Union College, Annual* (Cincinnati)
ILN.	*Illustrated London News* (London)
JA.	*Journal Asiatique* (Paris)
JAOS.	*Journal of the American Oriental Society* (New Haven)
JBL.	*Journal of Biblical Literature* (Philadelphia)
JDU.	*Journal of Durham University* (Durham)
JE.	*Jewish Encyclopedia* (New York)
Jew. Chron.	*Jewish Chronicle* (London)
JNES.	*Journal of Near Eastern Studies* (Chicago)
JQR.	*Jewish Quarterly Review* (Philadelphia)
JS.	*Journal des Savants* (Paris).
JJS.	*Journal of Jewish Studies* (Manchester)
JTS.	*Journal of Theological Studies* (Oxford)
KS.	*Kiriath Sefer* (Jerusalem)

Lit. Suppl.	*The Times Literary Supplement* (London)
NRT.	*Nouvelle Revue Théologique* (Paris)
NTS.	*New Testament Studies* (Cambridge)
Num. Chron.	*Numismatic Chronicle* (London)
OBL.	*Orientalia et Biblica Lovaniensia* (Louvain)
OLz.	*Orientalistische Literaturzeitung* (Berlin)
Or. Chr.	*Oriens Christianus* (Leipzig)
Oudt. St.	*Oudtestamentische Studiën* (Leiden)
PAAJR	*Proceedings of the American Academy for Jewish Research* (Philadelphia)
Pal.-Jb.	*Palästina-Jahrbuch* (Berlin)
Patrol. Gr.	*Patrologia Graeca* (Paris)
Patrol. Lat.	*Patrologia Latina* (Paris)
PQS.	*Palestine Exploration Fund: Quarterly Statement* (London)
PSBA.	*Proceedings of the Society of Biblical Archaeology* (London)
RB.	*Revue Biblique* (Paris)
Rech. Bibl.	*Recherches Bibliques* (Louvain)
RÉJ.	*Revue des Études Juives* (Paris)
RQ.	*Revue de Qumran* (Paris)
RSR.	*Revue des Sciences Religieuses* (Paris)
RThPh.	*Revue de Théologie et de Philosophie* (Lausanne)
Scr. Hierosol.	*Scripta Hierosolymitana* (Jerusalem)
Scr. Jud.	*Scripta Judaica* (Oxford)
St. Ev.	*Studia Evangelica* (Berlin)
St. Th.	*Studia Theologica* (Lund)
Stud. Cath.	*Studia Catholica* (Nijmegen)
Stud. Patr.	*Studia Patristica* in *Texte und Untersuchungen LXIII–LXIV* (Leipzig)
Th. Zeitschr.	*Theologische Zeitschrift* (Basel)
TICP.	*Travaux de l'Institut Catholique de Paris* (Paris)
TLz.	*Theologische Literaturzeitung* (Halle; Berlin)
VT.	*Vetus Testamentum* (Leiden)
ZDP-V.	*Zeitschrift des Deutschen Palästina-Vereins* (Wiesbaden)
ZNtW.	*Zeitschrift für die neutestamentlichte Literatur* (Giessen)
ZR-Gg.	*Zeitschrift für Religions-und Geistesgeschichte* (Köln)
Z.T.K.	*Zeitschrift für Theologie und Kirche* (Tübingen)

TABLE OF DATES

B.C.

145–139	Demetrius II Nicator king
142	Jonathan murdered;
	Simon son of Judas high-priest
142–138	Tryphon usurper
c. 135–105	*Jubilees*
139–129	Antigonus VII Euergetes (Sidetes) king
138	Syrian invasion of Palestine
c. 135	Murder of Simon, high-priest and civil governor
135–104	John Hyrcanus I high-priest and king;
	buildings at Qumrân constructed.
c 132–117	*Ecclesiasticus* (Greek translation)
109–107	*Testaments of the Twelve Patriarchs*
104– 95	I *Enoch* xci–civ (5)
103	Aristobulus I high-priest and king
103–76	Alexander Jannaeus high-priest and king
c. 100	I *Maccabees*
95–86	Rising against Alexander Jannaeus
c. 95–79	I *Enoch* xxxvii–lxxi (2)
c. 88	Demetrius III Eucaerus invited into Jerusalem
c. 80	Simeon ben Shetah
76–67	Salome Alexandra
75–66	Hyrcanus II high-priest and king
70–40	Greek *Psalms of Solomon*
67–63	Aristobulus II high-priest and king
65	Onias the 'circle-maker' or 'rain-maker' murdered
63	Capture of Jerusalem by Pompey
63–40	Hyrcanus II high-priest, restored
61	Aristobulus II taken captive to Rome
c. 60	II *Maccabees*
57–55	Jewish operations against Romans
49	Aristobulus II poisoned in Rome
46	Rising and execution of Hezekiah the 'arch-brigand'
40	Hyrcanus II taken prisoner by the Parthians
40–37	Antigonus, last Hasmonaean king
37	Herod the Great king
31	Buildings at Qumrân destroyed by an earthquake and abandoned
c. 30	Hillel and Shammai, leading teachers
30	Hyrcanus II poisoned by Herod's order
c. 24	Simon, son of Boethus, named high-priest and his daughter (?) Mariamme married to Herod
20	Philo born
10	Birth of Agrippa I

B.C.

9–6	Saturninus legate for the first time
7	John the Baptist born
7–6	Census in Palestine;
	Jesus Christ born (?)
4	Death of Herod the Great and Archelaus king;
	first abortive rising of Judah son of Hezekiah

A.D.

c. 1–50	Slavonic II *Enoch*
4	Popular disturbances led by R. Judas and R. Matthias
4–5	Saturninus legate for the second time.
4–6	Buildings at Qumrân restored and re-occupied
6	Archelaus deposed
6 (?)	Quirinius legate; census in Palestine
6–7	Second abortive rising, capture and execution of Judah
6–9 (?)	Coponius procurator,
	and *jus gladii* withdrawn from Jewish authorities
c. 7–30	*Assumption of Moses*
c. 25–26	Preaching of John the Baptist
25–36	Pontius Pilate procurator
30 or 33	Jesus Christ crucified
c. 30–40	*Wisdom of Solomon*
37–38	Josephus born
37–40	Gaius (Caligula) emperor
40	Philo's embassy to Rome
44	Death of Agrippa I
44 (?)	Cuspius Fadius procurator
48 (?)	Tiberius Alexander procurator
46–48	Rising, capture and crucifixion of Jacob and Simon,
	sons of Judah son of Hezekiah the 'arch-brigand'
c. 46/8–66	DISCIPLINE
c. 48	*Epistle to the Galatians*
48–52	Ventidius Cumanus procurator
c. 50	*Epistles to the Thessalonians*
c. 50–70	*Ascension of Moses*
c. 50–90	*II Baruch*
c. 50–100	Agrippa king
c. 50–120	R. Eliezer ben Hyrcanus
52–60	Porcius Felix procurator;
	the *sicarii* active in Jerusalem

A.D.

c. 75–125	Syriac *Odes of Solomon*
79–81	Titus emperor
c. 80–100	*Teaching of the Twelve Apostles*
81–96	Domitian emperor
c. 85	WAR OF THE SONS OF LIGHT AND THE SONS OF DARKNESS
	Gospel according to St Luke
c. 90	First council of Jabneh (Jamnia)
c. 90–100	*Gospel according to St John*
c. 90–130	Joshua ben Hananiah
91–117	Trajan emperor
93–94	*Josephus: Antiquities* completed
c. 95	*Acts of the Apostles*
c. 96–110	I–III *Epistles of St John*
c. 100	II *Esdras* (IV *Ezra*)
c. 106–115	ZADOKITE DOCUMENTS
115–117	Jewish risings in various countries
117–138	Hadrian emperor
c. 118	Second council of Jabneh (Jamnia)
128–129	Aquila, Greek translator of the *Old Testament*
132–135	Second Revolt against the Romans under Bar Cochba and execution of R. 'Aqiba
135	Jerusalem razed to the ground and Aelia Capitolina built on its site; R. Judah the patriarch born
c. 140	II *Epistle of St Peter* *Epistle of St James* (commentary)
c. 140–155	*Shepherd of Hermas*
c. 150	R. *Jose ben Halafta* (chronographer)
150–180	Hegesippus, Jewish Christian writer
c. 160–200	*Mishnah* edited by R. Judah
c. 165	R. Judah appointed patriarch
180–192	Lucius Aurelius Commodus emperor
193–211	Septimus Severus emperor
c. 200–300	*Tosefta*
202	Septimus Severus in Palestine
c. 210	Hippolytus
217	Origen in Palestine
256–286	Arius, heresiarch
299–362	Raba, Babylonian Jewish teacher

A.D.

c. 300	R. 'Ammi
303	Persecution of Diocletian
c. 320–370	*Palestinian Talmud*
c. 324	Eusebius: *Ecclesiastical History*
c. 346	Birth of Jerome
373	Death of Ephraem the Syrian
c. 380–500	*Babylonian Talmud*
386–420	Jerome in Palestine
c. 500–1040	*Midrashim* and connected works
611–629	Persian occupation of Palestine
638	Capture of Jerusalem by the Arabs
684–705	'Abd-alMalik ibn Marwan caliph
c. 695	'Abu 'Isâ
726–819	Timotheus, patriarch of Seleucia
c. 770	Emergence of Qara'ism　　'Anan: *Book of the Laws*
c. 805	Sergius metropolitan of Elam
896	Foundation of Qara'ite synagogue at Old Cairo
900–950	Sahal ben Mazliach
909	Death of 'Abu 'Isa-'lWarraq
915	Hasdai ibn Shafruth
930	Hasan ben Mashiach
c. 930	End of 'Isawite sect
937	Jacob alQirqisani: *Books of Lights and Beacons*
950–990	Yafet ben 'Ali, Qara'ite writer
973–1048	'Abu Rayhan alBiruni
1071–1153	Muhammad alShafrastani
1975–1160	Judah Hadassi, Qara'ite writer
1099	Jerusalem captured by the Crusaders
c. 1200	Zadokites in Egypt
1364–1442	Taqiyyu-'lDin alMaqrizi

N.B. Hellenistic period from 323 B.C. to 63 B.C. and Roman period from 63 B.C. to A.D. 330 in Palestinian archaeology.

49589

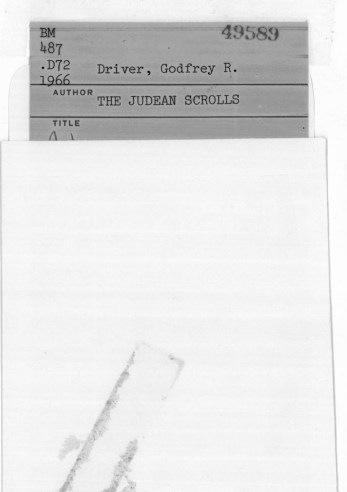

INDEX

[Abbreviations: br. = brother, f. = father, id. = identified, k. = king, mt. = mount, r. = rabbi, st. = saint, s. = son, u. = uncle, w. = wife]

Aaron 52–3, 74, 130, 144, 147, 170, 227–8, 276, 302, 356, 449, 458, 466, 468–70, 472, 475, 507, 537–8, 541–2, 579
Aaronite priesthood, priests 115, 158, 227, 276, 469
abbreviations: s. *nôṭārîqôn*
ablutions, 79, 102, 107, 111, 497–8, 504–6, 514
Abraham ibn Ezra 265, 329
Absalom s. of David 136, 272
— Maccabaean leader 142–3, 279
— u. of Aristobulus II 152
— follower of Rightful Teacher 127, 130, 135–6, 142–4, 147, 150, 167, 307
— lieutenant of Menahem 267–8, 291–2, 277–81, 336–7
— Qara'ite 167
'Abû 'Isâ, sectarian 167
'Abŭ-'lfath, historian 79–80
Acco (Ptolemais) 203–4, 206, 313
acies duplex, triplex 176–7, 193
Acra, fort 355
Adam, first man 448–9, 534–5, 553, 568
'additions of the Sabbath' 88
adoption 112
'advancing their times' 323–4
after-life: s. life, future
'after the manner of the kingdoms' 290–1
age 64, 69, 168–9, 175
Agrippa I 139, 195–6, 350, 411
— II 139, 208–9, 217, 219, 286, 309, 351
Aiath 204
'Ain Fäšhah 42–5, 304, 394
Albinus, procurator 201–2
Alcimus, high-priest 143, 147, 158, 226–8
Alexander Balas 137
— Jannaeus: s. Jannaeus

Alexander the Great 167, 190, 221, 303, 313–16, 367–8
—, Tiberius 201–2, 241
Alexander Salome 144–5
Alexandria 203, 206, 227, 411
Alexandrian scholars 530
allegorical interpretation 108, 122, 531–2
alpha 347
Amalekites 222
amen 339, 342, 344, 347, 549
'Ammî, R. 264
Ammon(ites) 216–17, 222, 242
Amos, prophet 304
'Anan, 'Ananites 11, 13, 167, 230, 324, 334–5
Ananias: s. Hananiah
Ananias and Sapphira 115, 524
Ananias, Sadducaean 242–3, 245, 307
Ananus 287, 298, 352, 355
Angelic Liturgy 19, 76
angelology, angels 10–11, 29, 70–2, 76, 101, 108–9, 176, 216, 262, 272, 347, 450, 456–7, 538–42, 544, 547, 556–7, 578–9
animal bones 84–5, 406
'anointed ones' 470
Antigonus, br. of Aristobulus I 148
— s. of Aristobulus II 200
— of Socho 228–9
Anti-Christ 162, 458, 486–91, 550
anti-Messiah 308, 366, 486–91, 550
Antioch 31, 203–4, 206, 219–201, 487, 521
Antiochus IV Epiphanes 32, 133–4, 163, 210, 220–1, 303, 319, 346–7, 352, 354–5, 384
— V Eupator 312
— VII Euergetes (Sidetes) 33, 141
— (?) 199, 289
— k. of Comagene 220
Antipater, f. of Herod 139, 294, 525
Antipatris 375

603